Emerging Perspectives on Anti-Oppressive Practice

Emerging Perspectives on Anti-Oppressive Practice

Wes Shera, Editor

Canadian Scholars' Press Inc.   Toronto

Emerging Perspectives on Anti-Oppressive Practice
Edited by Wes Shera

First published in 2003 by
Canadian Scholars' Press Inc.
180 Bloor Street West, Suite 801
Toronto, Ontario
M5S 2V6

www.cspi.org

"Race, Class, and Gender in the Everyday Talk of Social Workers" by Donna Baines was originally published as "Radical Social Work, Race, Class, and Gender" in *Race, Gender & Class Journal*, Vol. 9, No. 1, 2002, pp. 145–167. Copyright © *Race, Gender & Class Journal*. Reprinted with permission.

Every reasonable effort has been made to identify copyright holders. CSPI would be pleased to have any errors or omissions brought to its attention.

CSPI gratefully acknowledges financial support for our publishing activities from the Government of Canada through the Book Publishing Industry Development Program (BPIDP) and the Government of Ontario through the Ontario Book Initiative.

National Library of Canada Cataloguing in Publication

Canadian Association of Schools of Social Work. Annual Meeting (2002 : Toronto)
    Emerging perspectives on anti-oppressive practice / Wes Shera, editor.

Papers originally delivered at the annual meeting of the Canadian Association of Schools of Social Work in Toronto, May 25-27, 2002.
Includes bibliographical references.
ISBN 1-55130-225-X

    1. Oppression (Psychology) 2. Equality. 3. Social work with minorities. I. Shera, Wes, 1946-

HM821.C65 2003   305   C2003-902714-7

Cover design by Zack Taylor
Cover art by Steve McVeigh, Presidential Environment Inc.
Page design and layout by Brad Horning

03   04   05   06   07 08   7   6   5   4   3   2   1

Printed and bound in Canada by AGMV Marquis Imprimeur Inc.

DEDICATION

This book is dedicated to my two wonderful children, Emily and Matthew. It was completed during a sabbatical leave spent in Ireland and I cherish the many days we spent together there walking the hills and beaches, making blackberry pie, and listening to traditional Irish music. Our children teach us much about unconditional love and their joyous, curious, energetic natures ignite our spirits. I trust, as Emily and Matthew grow into adults, that they will also work towards making the world a less oppressive, better place to live.

With love,
Dad.

Table of Contents

vii

SECTION 2: FIELDS OF PRACTICE

SECTION 3: CRITICAL ISSUES

Anti-Oppressive Practice: Emerging Perspectives and Future Challenges

Wes Shera
Faculty of Social Work
University of Toronto

This book represents the outcome of the thinking and hard work of many individuals. The chapters contained in this book were originally presented at the Annual Meeting of the Canadian Association of Schools of Social Work in Toronto, May 25–27, 2002. The theme of the conference was "Anti-Oppressive Practice and Global Transformation: Challenges for Social Work and Social Welfare." The theme evolved from a significant process of dialogue among the Toronto, Ryerson, and York schools of social work. Many of the thematic topics incorporated within the conference reflected: the recommendations coming out of the sector study report, *In Critical Demand: Social Work in Canada: Strategic Human Resources Analysis of the Social Work Sector* (Thornton & CS/RESORS, 2000); the subsequent national round tables process; and, the deliberations of the Social Work Forum. Many of the recommendations coming out of these reports and processes highlighted the importance of addressing issues of social justice and developing a better understanding of the knowledge, skills, and values needed to promote anti-oppressive practice.

In framing this challenge to improve our understanding, we raised a series of critical questions for both presenters and those attending the conference. Some of these questions included:

- How do social work practitioners experience and define their professional identity in the changing context of services?
- What are the new narratives of practice and of practitioners?

- What has happened to social work's commitment to political activism and social justice?
- How can service users be more effectively involved in the design, delivery, and evaluation of services and resources?
- How have the recent series of terrorist activities challenged social work practice and education?
- How can social work develop effective alliances to address issues of social justice?
- What is the knowledge base of international social work and is it relevant to the present global context?
- What are the mutual benefits and difficulties experienced in community-university partnerships?
- What is the role of research in promoting effective practice?
- What strategies can be implemented to counter the erosion of workplace conditions?
- How can social work as a professional discipline improve its ability to advocate in the political arena?
- How can we, in social work education, respond to the increasing pressure to provide greater depth of content in an ever-increasing range of "isms"?
- How can we help resistant faculty, field educators, and students to develop their pedagogical and practice expertise in working with issues of oppression?
- How can we teach and model anti-oppressive practice in the delivery of social work education?

Over 330 people attended the conference and almost one-third of those attending presented a paper, participated in a panel, or conducted a workshop. We also organized four major special sessions to highlight central issues in social justice and anti-oppressive practice. Our keynote speaker, Linda McQuaig, who recently published *All You Can Eat: Greed, Lust and the New Capitalism* (2001), addressed the implications of globalization for social work and social welfare and discussed the linkages between economic and social justice. Other special sessions focused on competency-based practice, a student-driven model of an anti-oppressive coalition, and the voices of service users in child welfare, children's mental health, and psychotherapy.

The dialogue that ensued at the conference was excellent and, I believe, resulted in a better grasp of the theoretical issues involved and a more in-depth understanding of how to teach anti-oppressive practice in the social work curriculum. All peer-reviewed presenters were invited to submit their papers for consideration for the book. We received over fifty submissions and, due to length restrictions, were able to accommodate only twenty-seven of the papers. The chapters in the book have been divided into four major sections: Theoretical Perspectives; Fields of Practice; Critical Issues; and Social Work Education. This chapter provides a brief overview of each of the sections and identifies some of the central challenges in the future development of anti-oppressive practice.

THEORETICAL PERSPECTIVES

While the literature on anti-oppressive practice is now quite extensive, its theoretical development continues. As we see from the five chapters in this section on theory, there are many perspectives that can be brought to bear under the broad umbrella of anti-oppressive practice. Luann Gingrich maintains that many have not prospered from global restructuring and that our understanding of poverty is inadequate in its simplicity and inertia. She suggests that the concept of social exclusion as developed in the European context may have some utility in furthering our understanding in this area. In carrying out her in-depth theoretical review of social exclusion, she points out that many non-exclusionary practices that aim only at integration into mainstream social and economic structures obfuscate the practices of power that are integral to intersecting relations of race, class, and gender. She raises several important theoretical issues and identifies specific questions for future investigation.

Rick Sin and Mui Chung Yan critically examine the concept of social inclusion in the multicultural Canadian context, particularly in relation to social work practice. To improve the utility of the concept, they claim that it is critical to examine how and what constitutes difference, and how issues of power influence how differences are perceived and defined. In their view, positioning difference becomes a strategy, a way of constructing oneself, a source of radical social action, and a site of resistance. Their analysis concludes with a call for an integrative anti-racist model of practice that consistently examines how race, gender, disability, sexuality, and class relations manifest themselves in society and for social work practitioners who do not replicate, in their practice, the inequalities found in society.

Donna Baines continues on this theme of race, class, and gender and presents the results of an ethnographic study that examined the everyday practices of front-line left-of-center social workers in Toronto. Her study found that social workers employed in politically engaged, community-based settings tended to formulate the race, class, gender triumvirate in its dynamic wholeness, whereas workers employed in bureaucratic, depoliticized settings used more limited and segmented formulations. This chapter examines the underpinnings of these differences and calls for the development of an anti-racist, anti-sexist, and class-conscious social work to respond to the current conditions of social services today.

Cyndy Baskin's chapter provides a comparative review of the structural social work perspective, as articulated by Robert Mullaly (2002), and an Aboriginal approach to helping. A critical framework is used to compare and contrast these approaches in terms of historical analysis, internalized oppression, cultural values and practices, resistance, and the role of social work education. While she concludes that the structural social work model is useful, she claims that it cannot be used alone when working with First Nations peoples. She provides a detailed rationale for this conclusion and identifies areas for further research.

The final chapter in this section, by Connie H. Nelson and Dennis H. McPherson, challenges social work practice to look at its own role in the management of diversity through codification and definitions of what are acceptable behaviors against the invisible norms of White and European-based cultures. Through a critical content analysis of recently published textbooks, they demonstrate how competency-based practice primarily views cultural difference as problematic and objective fact, based on innate ethnocultural traits. They believe that this approach to practice is hierarchical and hegemonic, and that it solidifies rather than eradicates conditions of injustice and oppression. They conclude by proposing a model of contextual fluidity, which they believe has the potential to embrace the real richness of cultural diversity.

FIELDS OF PRACTICE

The second section on fields of practice contains six chapters and identifies both the common and unique aspects of anti-oppressive practice across a range of practice settings and client groups. Several of the chapters speak to the role that human service agencies play in perpetuating oppressive conditions for service users. Gary Dumbrill believes that anti-oppressive practice meets its most poignant challenge in the field of child welfare. He poses a critical question—can child welfare social work transform itself into an activity that not only protects children but also challenges and changes the dominant discourses that gave it birth? In other words, he challenges us to look at the oppressive nature of the child welfare system itself and maintains that we can begin to work our way out of this dilemma only by listening more closely to service users. Findings from his research on parents' experiences with child welfare services are used to develop ideas regarding more appropriate interventions.

Charis Romilly discusses current practices in working with street youth and her research examines their experience of oppression in helping agencies. She argues that street youth are one of the most oppressed groups in the community and that helping agencies, often inadvertently, play a role in reproducing, contributing to, and/or perpetuating their oppression. She also points out that several oppressed groups— such as First Nations youth, gay, lesbian, bisexual, and transgendered youth—are overrepresented in the street youth population. Her chapter deconstructs current practices, theories, and beliefs, and identifies various oppressive conditions embedded within systems and the dominant society. She hopes that this increased awareness of the dynamics of oppression will lead to the development of more empowering and anti-oppressive practices.

Evelyn Ferguson focuses on the issue of meaningful governance and consumer participation in the field of child care. She describes the historical development of this tradition and then pursues the issue of how users define "meaningful participation." Her research asked mothers involved in daycare centres to discuss participation and found that it can be either oppressive and/or empowering, and that this experience varies by gender, class, and cultural background. This chapter alerts us to the complexity, challenges, benefits, and dangers of empowering human service consumers.

Donald R. Leslie, Kaye Leslie, and Michelle Murphy's chapter focuses upon the need for the profession of social work, and particularly social work education, to reassess their commitment to and involvement in the workplace accommodation process for people with disabilities. The authors compare social work generalist practice theory with major approaches to workplace accommodation and find a very close fit. A number of hypotheses to explain social work's lack of involvement are put forward, and a range of possible actions, to be taken by social work educators and practitioners to improve this situation, are explored. The chapter concludes with a discussion of how social work can play a leadership role in this important area.

Alain Beaulieu examines the new mental health deinstitutionalization policies of Quebec and Ontario, and cautions that we should not institutionalize the community by focusing on controlling those who are experiencing mental illnesses. He discusses these dangers and presents a new model of "community" based on diverse lifestyles that includes sporadic positive withdrawal and an authentically inclusive community that is free of oppression and the will to control.

Deborah O'Connor argues that the ideas of post-structuralism, while exciting, do not transcend the intellectual in order to inform the day-to-day practice of professionals. She feels that this is particularly true in the area of gerontological social work, which is often significantly grounded in the medical model. The purpose of this chapter is to begin to explicate the practical relevance of ideas associated with feminist post-structuralism for gerontological practice. Potential strengths and limitations of this perspective for social work practice in this area are also discussed.

CRITICAL ISSUES

The third section on critical issues contains eight chapters that cover a wide range of issues, including professional identity, narrative therapy, cultural competence, the voices of service participants, community-based intervention, and the war against terrorism. In Chapter 12, Ken Barter identifies the policy initiatives in Canada that are reforming and restructuring health, education, and social welfare programs and services. He describes the impact these reforms are having on social work, including a predominant feeling that they are being "left out in the cold" and losing ground to other human service professionals. He believes that social work's identity, purpose, ethical obligations, and distinctive features are being challenged. He raises a number of key questions and lays out some critical choices for the future of the profession of social work.

We then move to a group of four chapters that deal with various aspects of direct practice. Catrina Brown observes that narrative therapy has emerged in recent years as an alluring and popular method of intervention for social workers. Situated within a constructionist frame and shaped by postmodernism, it offers practical techniques toward deconstructing and reconstructing clients' stories. There are, however, within this method a variety of approaches that result in significantly different practices. By comparing Harlene Anderson's and Michael White's approaches to experience, knowledge, and power in narrative therapy, she investigates differences in their treatment of clients' stories. She concludes by arguing that White's approach to client narratives is more likely to successfully challenge oppressive stories.

Janet Clark identifies the increasing interest in, and commitment to, cross-cultural practice as an opportunity to understand how the frame of reference or world view of others can be comprehended and negotiated in the actual conduct of practice. Her chapter reports the findings of a qualitative study that examined both theoretical knowledge and the "theories in use" of front-line cross-cultural practitioners. A critical finding from this study is the need to create space for a reciprocal exploration of meanings and the co-creation of shared understandings. Critical issues in this process include: epistemological humility, a learner's stance, inductive interpretation, dialogical understanding, and the need for rigorous reflection on power, location, and context.

Charmaine Williams complements the previous chapter by evaluating an educational program designed to increase the cultural competence of practising social workers. The program was based on the latest theoretical and empirical literature and notes that there are very few studies of educational interventions in this area. The study employed both standardized measures and qualitative follow-up data. Learning for cultural competence was shown to be highly affected by the contributions that learner group composition and facilitator style made to the creation of a safe environment. The implications for social work education are also discussed.

Marshall Fine, Sally Palmer, and Nick Coady bring a very important perspective to this section by highlighting the importance of listening to the voices of service users. They argue that service users' ability to relate to social workers and obtain the help they need depends greatly on their social locations. Many of them are poor, are from visible minority groups, and experience racism from not only the larger society but frequently from social service agencies. Their extensive literature review of service user voices in child welfare, children's mental health, and psychotherapy identified a number of themes related to the experiences with, and attitudes toward, professional helpers, including: caring attitudes and behaviours; uncaring and critical attitudes and behaviours; organization friendly and unfriendly features; respectful and validating/invalidating actions; and practices reflecting professional competence or incompetence.

Roopchand Seebaran moves us to the community level of practice. He argues that the elimination of racism is primarily the responsibility of government and our various societal institutions and focuses on how this can effectively be carried out using a community-based approach. His chapter includes a rationale for initiatives to combat racism; the components of a community-based model of intervention; identification of some barriers and obstacles in implementing the model; some suggested outcome measures for determining the impact of anti-racism programs; and implications for the education and training of social work students.

Steven Hick proposes that the Internet and information and communications technology more generally have important ramifications for social work advocacy and activism. While this technology is facilitating the acceleration of economic globalization and the concentration of power, it is also becoming a new tool for global social activism. His chapter maps out the present state of Internet use for social work advocacy and activism and explores possible future scenarios in Internet use in activism by drawing on an interview with Noam Chomsky, follow-up e-mail discussion, and a review of his recent writing.

The final chapter of this section by William H. Whitaker delves into the very difficult area of terrorism and argues that the recent war on terrorism falls short of what is needed to successfully respond to this current crisis. He documents the worldwide nature of poverty, malnourishment, and the lack of basic health care, which provide the conditions under which terrorism flourishes. He argues that the most critical step in meeting the social and economic needs of humankind is to promote international food security. His chapter traces the development of food security as a basic human right and argues in support of the thesis that an internationally guaranteed right to food must be affirmed by the United Nations and implemented globally as an essential element in a successful war against terrorism.

SOCIAL WORK EDUCATION

This final section of eight chapters addresses the challenges to be faced by social work education if it intends to educate future professionals for anti-oppressive practice. The authors discuss some of the teaching techniques, curriculum and field development work and the institutional changes that are needed to achieve this mission. Judy Hughes, Shirley Chau, Pamela James, and Steven Sherman set the stage for these discussions by examining the challenges of providing content about oppression, domination, exploitation, and anti-oppressive practice in the social work curriculum. They highlight the difficulty of determining the most effective methods of developing course content and discussing this content in the classroom. Their chapter provides an excellent review of the social work literature on how social work educators are engaging with these pedagogical issues and the challenges involved in teaching and learning about oppression, domination, and exploitation.

Samantha Wehbi shares her struggles, insights, and growth in teaching a course on anti-oppressive practice. Starting with a more structured approach in teaching her class of seventy students, she takes us through the development process of using more flexible alternative teaching methods over time. She stresses participation in the learning enterprise and developed strategies such as the use of puzzles, the inductive development of anti-oppression practice principles, poster exercises, role plays, reflection papers, workshops, games, skits, and other small group exercises. The results of this experimentation, as documented by course evaluations, was positive but did underline that the process of relinquishing the role of expert in the classroom can potentially be disempowering. The challenge in using alternative teaching methods, she concludes, is to find the balance between sharing power in the classroom and not abdicating your responsibility as a teacher.

Gilles Tremblay describes a postmodern adaptation of an exercise originally developed by Maurice Moreau. This exercise is intended to raise the awareness of students beginning their social work studies by allowing them to experience the complexity of the process involved when marginalized people ask for help and to understand the counter-transference reactions that affect such requests for assistance. The exercise allows the re-examination of various assumptions that interfere with the assistance process from both the perspective of the person being helped as well as the social worker. It is a highly participative process and helps students to understand multiple oppressions from the perspective of gender, ethnic origin, sexual orientation, health condition, age, spiritual/religious affiliation, social class, political orientation, etc. It is a relatively simple but powerful consciousness-raising exercise that can be used in a variety of anti-oppressive practice education courses.

Carolyn Campbell begins to move us in the direction of promoting anti-oppressive educational institutions by addressing the issue of the congruence between what we teach and how we teach and organize ourselves in schools of social work. She asks a very pointed and critical question—how do educators strive for congruency between the content and process of education for anti-oppressive social work education? An analytic technique known as "the ideal type" is used to represent the findings of her research with a selected group of social work educators who have had responsibility for teaching anti-oppressive practice. The ideal type used for the discussion is Dr. Terry Swice (social work ideal congruent educator), hypothetically an individual applying for a position within a school of social work. The methodology, while intended to portray the consensus among respondents, also identifies the diversity among participants.

Mike Woodford and Leslie Bella present an innovative approach to educating social work students about homophobia and heterosexism. Their pedagogical approach moves beyond the simple provision of facts and emphasizes both personal stories and critical reflection to facilitate the increased self-awareness and empathy needed for anti-oppressive practice with lesbians, gays, bisexuals, and transgendered (LGBT) individuals. A central component of their approach is an invitation to students, regardless of their sexual orientation, to publicly "come out" and join with others to advocate against oppression and discrimination. This process challenges students' comfort levels and facilitates advanced insight regarding the dilemmas and challenges faced by LGBT individuals.

Field instruction is a very critical component of any social work program and provides students with experience in applying the theory, learned in the classroom, to the real world of practice. Jeanne Bertrand Finch, Jean Bacon, Donna Klassen, and Betty-Jean Wrase, all experienced field educators, argue that the supervisory relationship is critical in terms of the manner in which power differentials are recognized and minimized to promote empowering experiences for the student. They believe this will, in turn, result in practitioners who are more capable of working in an empowering manner with client systems. They provide several examples of how a framework of empowerment can be used in the supervisory process and discuss the implications for improving service delivery to disenfranchised client systems.

The final two chapters of this section move into how we can change organizations to be more responsive and less oppressive institutions. This is often very difficult in higher education, given the bureaucratic, hierarchical nature of our institutions, but some schools of social work are taking up the challenge and implementing innovative approaches that demonstrate that we can practise what we preach by engaging in major organizational change. Chapter 26, by Michael Kim Zapf and his colleagues at the University of Calgary, describes a learning circle approach to BSW curriculum design and delivery, which arose from a collaborative effort to reach students in rural, remote, and Aboriginal communities across Alberta with a BSW opportunity that would have geographic and cultural relevance. Implementation of this model involved a dynamic partnership involving the faculty's new BSW Access Division, the larger university, community stakeholders, students, employers, and host colleges in the regions. The authors discuss the implementation of this model, the specifics of curriculum content, and university-community collaboration to encourage anti-oppressive practice.

The last chapter provides an overview of the journey taken by the Maritime School of Social Work in Halifax to institutionalize diversity. This journey began in the 1970s and employed a variety of strategies—some were successful and others were not. During this process, a number of critical issues were faced in various areas of the life of the school, including: school governance, the recruitment and retention of faculty and students, admissions policies and practices, program models, curricular development, community partnerships, scholarly activities, classroom pedagogical practices, institutional privilege, and links to the gay, lesbian, bisexual, and transgender caucus of the School of Social Work. A selected number of initiatives in these areas are discussed and help us to understand both the rewards and challenges in promoting institutional change to support diversity.

CONCLUSION AND FUTURE CHALLENGES

This collection of chapters, in my view, demonstrates the high level of commitment that social work educators both in Canada and abroad have toward seriously addressing the call to engage in social work education that speaks to social work's fundamental mandate to promote social justice through anti-oppressive practice. I have thoroughly enjoyed working with the chapter authors to produce a volume that should be a helpful resource to students, faculty, and field educators. In reviewing these chapters, a series of major themes emerged that provide a framework for the future development of anti-oppressive practice.

In terms of theoretical development, it is clear that we are at a very exciting time of using a wide diversity of theoretical frameworks. We are also witnessing the integration of many of these frameworks, and in the future I believe will we see a much more sophisticated blending of these approaches. A continuing area for future work is in the translation of these approaches for direct practice. Narrative therapy (White, 2001) and constructivist/ empowerment practice (Franklin & Nurius, 1998; Shera & Wells, 1999) are significant examples of how we are moving in this direction. A continuing challenge will be the need to be open to a diversity of theoretical approaches and to avoid the tendency to cling dogmatically to a favourite framework (Williams, 1999). These authors have also helped us to understand the necessity of recognizing multiple oppressions and intersecting identities and to appreciate the need to look across the world for concepts and ideas such as social exclusion/inclusion that can further our understanding.

In appreciating how anti-oppressive practice plays out in different fields of practice, we observe the difficulty of working in settings with a high social control agenda. Many of the authors, in fact, argue that human service agencies perpetuate rather than alleviate oppression. Even when agencies or practitioners engage in anti-oppressive practice, they often do it from an expert-led perspective rather than joining collaboratively with users of service (Wilson & Beresford, 2000). User involvement in the design, delivery, and evaluation of both human services and social work education should be a high priority for future development (Shera, 1996). A fundamental value emerging from the chapters on practice in different fields is the need to work in partnership with users of service, not imposing our professional definitions and responses. Being a critically reflective learner is pivotal in effective anti-oppressive practice.

Some of these same themes are played out in the chapters on critical issues in anti-oppressive practice. Clarifying and redefining our identity as social workers is a critical step in renewing our confidence and guiding our actions. What is exciting is that many of the emerging frameworks allow for inclusiveness and breadth in our practice. Another major challenge is the need to engage in community-based work—many of the initiatives discussed in these papers—such as working with youth, integrating persons with mental illnesses, combating racism, etc., often require a community- rather than an agency-based approach. The community can act as a very effective crucible for anti-oppressive efforts. We would also be remiss if we do not identify the importance of anti-oppressive practice at the global level (Dominelli, 1999). The issue of poverty and hunger and its relationship to terrorism is a profound one. A future challenge will be to ensure adequate coverage of these issues in our social work curricula.

Social work educators in recent years have been challenged to rethink what and how they teach and even how they run schools of social work. Our students are quick to pick up incongruities in what we say and what we do. The chapters in the section on social work education, I believe, offer some excellent first steps in moving us to pedagogical practices, curriculum development, and institutional change (George, Shera, & Tsang, 1998) that are more congruent with anti-oppressive practice. We must appreciate that this is a life-long learning process, but with humility and partnership with students, faculty colleagues, and the community we can make very significant gains. I have benefited greatly from reading this collection of chapters and dialoguing with the authors. I hope you will also find this book an enriching experience.

REFERENCES

Dominelli, L. (1999). Neo-liberalism, social exclusion and welfare client in a global economy. *International Journal of Social Welfare 8*, 14–22.

Franklin, C., & Nurius, P. (1998). *Constructivism in practice: Methods and challenges*. Milwaukee: Families International Inc.

George, U., Shera, W., & Tsang, K.A. (1998). Responding to diversity in organizational life: The case of a Faculty of Social Work. *International Journal of Inclusive Education 2*(1), 184–197.

McQuaig, L. (2001). *All you can eat: Greed, lust and the new capitalism*. Toronto: Viking.

Mullaly, R. (2002). *Challenging oppression: A critical social work approach*. Toronto: Oxford University Press.

Shera W. (1996). Market mechanisms and consumer involvement in the delivery of mental health services. *Journal of Sociology & Social Welfare 23*, 13–22.

Shera, W., & Wells, L. (1999). *Empowerment practice in social work: Developing richer conceptual foundations*. Toronto: Canadian Scholars' Press.

Thornton, G., & CS/RESORS Consulting. (2000). *In critical demand: Social work in Canada: Strategic human resource analysis of the social work sector* (Vols. I & II). (Unpublished research report).

White, M. (2001). Narrative practice and the unpacking of identity conclusions. *Gecko: A Journal of Deconstruction and Narrative Ideas in Therapeutic Practice 1*, 28–55.

Williams, C. (1999). Connecting anti-racist and anti-oppressive theory and practice: Retrenchment or reappraisal? *British Journal of Social Work 29*, 211–230.

Wilson, A., & Beresford, P. (2000). Anti-oppressive practice: Emancipation or Appropriation? *British Journal of Social Work 30*, 553–573.

Chapter 1

Theorizing Social Exclusion: Determinants, Mechanisms, Dimensions, Forms, and Acts of Resistance

Luann Good Gingrich
Ph.D. Candidate
Faculty of Social Work
University of Toronto

AN INTRODUCTION TO SOCIAL EXCLUSION

Relations among people are rapidly shifting and reorganizing as the evolving economic system of capitalism penetrates the social world with unprecedented intensity and ubiquity. Even in the most technologically advanced and prosperous regions of the world, social ailments of generations past remain tenacious, manifesting themselves in both old and new ways. Theoretical and research literature reflects a growing perception that our understanding of poverty is inadequate in its simplicity and inertia. The notion of *social exclusion* has been used in a systematic way to inform social policy analysis and planning, particularly in the European context, since the 1970s (Atkinson, 2000). While the term is too often used as a synonym for poverty and deprivation, the concept of social exclusion is distinguished by its comprehensive and dynamic character. As such, however, it has defied succinct definition, is diversely applied, and remains strikingly reminiscent of the tired concepts it seeks to replace.

Sources of exclusion most often referenced are poverty and unemployment, yet European discourse acknowledges deeper sources of exclusion from central elements of society. These include factors such as health, education, income, access to services, housing, debt, quality of life, dignity, and autonomy, which interact to result in various forms and degrees of social exclusion. Klasen (1998) distinguishes two mechanisms of social exclusion, stemming either directly or indirectly from existing disadvantage.

The related sources of exclusion he identifies are economic, social, birth or background, and societal/political. Evans (1998, p. 43) presents four dimensions: exclusion from civic integration, the labour market, welfare state provision, and family and community. The "solution" to social exclusion—social inclusion—is often understood to be synonymous with terms and concepts such as "social integration," redistribution, and full participation in society, and in North America it is frequently applied to the inclusion of children with disabilities in the public education system. The concept of social cohesion is also used to reference an alternative, or a response to social exclusion. Social cohesion most often refers to notions of social participation, health (in a broad sense), community integration, and social and physical well-being.

A review of the literature on social exclusion/inclusion reveals significant theoretical deficiencies and inconsistencies. Indeed, criticisms of this literature claim that a vague and inadequate conceptual framework remains a hindrance to the study of social exclusion and the formulation of appropriate policy responses (Bhalla & Lapeyre, 1997; Garonna & Triacca, 1999). More significantly, common formulations of social exclusion have been charged with neglecting, obscuring, and depoliticizing economic inequality, relations of power, and social suffering (Levitas, 1996; Room, 1999; Veit-Wilson, 1998). Exclusion understood to be the result of disadvantage does not address the social processes that must first be exercised to constitute disadvantage from some kind of difference. Non-exclusionary practices that aim only at integration into mainstream social and economic structures obfuscate the practices of power that are integral to intersecting relations of race, class, and gender. Much of the literature focuses exclusively on society as a unified entity, ignoring the various and imminent "everyday/everynight local actualities" (Smith, 1999) of individuals and groups that comprise this society. Consistent with the broad range of views and definitions of the problem, the solution of social inclusion is variously understood, ranging from simplistic, situation-specific interventions to broader, multidimensional shifts in societal structures (Barry & Hallett, 1998). These inconsistencies and weaknesses in the literature evidence the insufficient theoretical development of these concepts. Notions of social exclusion, social inclusion, and social cohesion have been applied in social policy without clear understandings or articulation of the concepts, the mechanisms that accomplish such processes, the conditions (political, economic, social) that impel such practices of power, or the full impact of such operations on the lives of people. The goal of my current work is to theorize these terms in more depth, in an effort to refine, expand, and enrich their meanings.

This chapter provides an inchoate articulation of my own theorization of social exclusion, as advanced from a focused review and synthesis of selected texts. In an effort to avoid ending up trapped in a recursive conceptual loop, I did not look to the social exclusion literature for this project. Instead, I selected a few representative pieces of work that relate in some way to post-colonial literature. The primary texts that inform this study include the following: Adams (1999), Brah (1996), Church, Fontan, Ng, & Shragge (2000), McClintock (1994), Murphy (1999, 2000), Ng (1998a, 1998b), and Sassen (1998). Reflecting my research interest in migrant groups, the particular pieces were chosen for their emphasis on the forces compelling the global movement of people.[1] My reading of these works was approached through the lens circumscribed by the following questions:

- What makes social exclusion happen? What are the activating *conditions*, *determinants*, and *mechanisms* that set its operation into motion?
- What does it look like? What are the *procedures* through which social exclusion is accomplished, and what are its lived *characteristics*, *dimensions*, and *forms*?
- What are the responses to the experience of social exclusion? What assertions and acts of *resistance* and *contestation* are envisioned and practised?

Recognizing that these sets of questions do not reference distinct and independent categories, I will use them only as conceptual guides and organizing tools. I will summarize and integrate the understandings gleaned through my inquiry in a theoretical model of social exclusion (Figure 1.1).

The authors of these literatures most often do not identify the social processes and patterns described as social exclusion per se. Therefore, the appropriation of this material for the theorizing of social exclusion demands some preconceived criteria for its recognition, identification, and differentiation. It is not my intention to claim definitive accuracy, or even steadfast certainty, in the decisions required to sort and synthesize these rich and complex texts. It is my hope, rather, to promote the expansion and permeability of the conceptual boundaries that restrict and obscure our view of social exclusion.

CULTIVATING SOCIAL EXCLUSION

The context out of which processes of social exclusion emerge is described at length and with various words in the works studied. A common thread

Figure 1.1: CONCEPTUAL MAP OF SOCIAL EXCLUSION

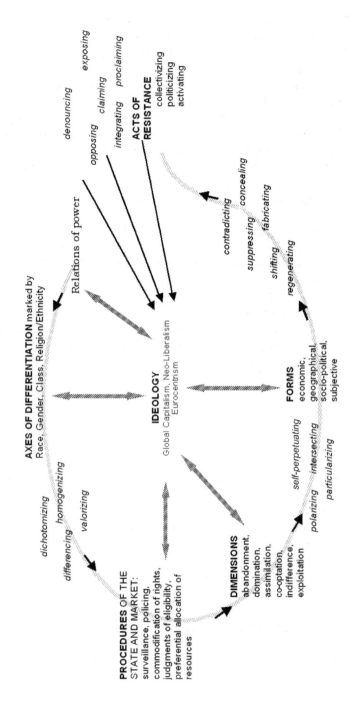

woven through these texts is the crucial role of *ideology*. Described as a force that concerts behaviour and modes of operation, ideology is conceived as much more than a benign set of "ideas." It provides a schema for naming, categorizing, evaluating, and interpreting that is replicated across multiple and various sites (Ng, 1998a, p. 15). Ideology defines the conditions, determines the mechanisms, conducts the procedures, situates the boundaries, and constitutes the consequence of social exclusion. It provides impetus and breath for each aspect of exclusionary practices. Systems of oppression and inequality, and processes of exclusion, are shown to be spontaneous and necessary products of the ideology of the superior, as its preservation presumes the rejection and marginalization of all who are unable or unwilling to conform—and therefore do not belong—to the dominant group. Ng (1998a) and Adams (1999) uncover and examine the power and self-sustaining nature of ideological codes, which rely on their taken-for-granted acceptance by whole groups of people, thus rendering them invisible as "common sense" and "part of the natural order of things" (Adams, 1999, p. 37). Brah (1996, p. 218) similarly notes that "Gramsci's concept of ideology as everyday processes and practices of 'making sense of the world'" permits the analysis of these concrete social relations that secure the hegemony of a dominant group over a series of subordinate ones. Murphy (1999) defines ideology as the "established rationality," and its arrogation of "common sense" as the widespread and uncritical adoption of a number of assumptions that ordinarily remain obscured by their familiarity. Hence, the imposition of ideology and its related practices of power are masked and hidden from view. To remain so, part of the work of ideology must be to keep "the colonized masses politically ignorant and illiterate" (Adams, 1999, p. 86). This is accomplished through enforcing ideological codes in discourse, or the writing of texts and the production of talk. Murphy (2000) notes that discourse has to do with that which is consciously known, and therefore real. Among the many parallel and competing realities in the world, the one that prevails or rules "is the one that reflects and serves the interests of those who control how reality is described, what is seen to be 'true', and what is allowed to be talked about" (Murphy, 2000, p. 339). Acknowledging the subjectivity of his work, Adams's (1999) gaze remains firmly fixed on the colonization of his people. From this vantage point, the exploits of ideology are pervasive and penetrating: "Ideological domination is the primary means by which the state maintains control over its citizens … . Ideological authority is thought control, the manipulation of one's entire belief system and thus of one's consciousness" (Adams, 1999, p. 37). In this way, ideology functions to manipulate and manufacture identity as it is taken up and taken in by both the dominant and the subordinate, resulting in a recursive self-perpetuation. "By accepting the ideology of the dominant class as their own, the subordinate masses not only submit to it, they also legitimize the rule of the establishment" (Adams, 1999, p. 37). Murphy (1999) also considers the self-sustaining nature of ideology, but diminishes relations of power in his reflections. He describes the recursive characteristic of ideology as a deliberate and essential end in and of itself, as ideology seeks to accomplish the primary goal of all societies: to impede basic change and preserve the status quo (Murphy, 1999, p. 13).

Strands of the prevailing ideology are differently emphasized and variously named in these works, yet all authors converge on some notion of the *global market* as a primary ideological force. Identified as neo-liberalism, capitalism, globalization, "male economic self-interest" (McClintock, 1994, p. 298), Western imperialism, and colonialism, the social and economic systems of the global market are recognized as ideology in motion. Adams (1999, p. 40) summarizes the essence of this ideology: "the glorification of competition, individualism, greed and the pursuit of power and wealth." Conflating social systems and ideology, Adams (1999, p. 111) asserts: "In Canada, capitalism structures society and thus shapes its ethics, customs and culture as well as the economy." He equates the culture of imperialism with capitalist ideology. Murphy (2000, p. 334) states that neo-liberal economic ideology "declares the logic of the market—and in particular, the global market—as the motor of society, rather than the logic of society itself determining the mechanisms of the market and the economy." Similarly, the reorganization and ideological abduction of the state *and* the community—the public *and* the private—by a revised, global capitalism is evidenced by several authors (i.e., Church et al., 2000; McClintock, 1994; Murphy, 2000; Sassen, 1998). The globalization of the economy is the focal point through which Sassen (1998) examines the movement of people and money, but her propositions begin and end outside of the ideology that concerts these systems of global capitalism, preserving its invisibility and assumed inevitability. This omission introduces a hint of implausibility and absurdity to her prescriptions for change when considered alongside the poignant and impassioned analyses of global capitalism as ideology offered by other authors.

The values and guiding principles of the globalized economy reproduce and reinforce intersecting and dynamic patterns of social relations that mark difference according to *race*, *gender*, *class*, and *religion and ethnicity*. McClintock (1994), with the support of global economic and political data, argues that the term "post-colonialism" obscures the intersecting power relations and boundaries of difference that operate with fresh enthusiasm in this "post-colonial" age. Brah (1996) struggles to see and explicate these

> distinctive fields of power as they are played out in the constitution and transformation of social relations, subjectivity and identity. Each of these constructs—class, gender, racism, [ethnicity, nationalism generations and sexuality]—signifies a specific type of power relation produced and exercised in and through a myriad of economic, political and cultural practices. (Brah, 1996, p. 211)

Economic restructuring, essential to the project of globalization and corporatism, was promoted with promises of unprecedented prosperity the world over. However, as Murphy (2000, p. 341) articulates, the real issue in the competition of the global market is "who benefits and loses today, and who decides? ... The choice of who pays, and who is left out, at the table of globalised progress, is not haphazard. We know who they are, and their characteristics—race, gender, class—and we know where they live." Maintaining that "Racism is a deeply entrenched characteristic of capitalism" (p. 67), Adams (1999, p. 143) observes that with the change from industrial capitalism to financial capitalism, there is a "growing emphasis on class formation based on culture and ideology." Ng (1998b, p. 23) conceptualizes capitalism as both an economic system and a dynamic mode of production and reproduction, in which gender, race, and class are essential ingredients for particular transformations and reorganizations of people's livelihoods according to the requirement of capital accumulation. Locating herself in the changing conditions for workers in the garment industry, she shows that the "progress" of globalization "has differential and differentiating effects on groups of people by virtue of their gender, race, and class locations in society" (Ng, 1998b, p. 21). Growing inequality, polarization in the service industries, and the production of urban marginality are the primary impacts of economic globalization as identified by Sassen (1998). The expansion in the supply of low-wage and casual jobs, accompanied by the ascendance and overvalorization of the new finance and services complex, are central to Sassen's (1998) argument for revised government regulation of economic practices that resist such polarization. Although she describes the recruitment of immigrants, women, and people of colour into devalorized and low-wage jobs, nurturing the proclivity toward polarization, she avoids articulating these organizing relations of race, gender, and class as fundamentally essential and axiomatic to the global capitalist project. These texts clearly delineate that processes of *differencing*—manufacturing "otherness"—are practised with new vigour and scope, as the demands of the increasingly polarized and fragmented labour market must be met.

The racialized, gendered, and classist axes of differentiation perform the consequential functions of *dichotomizing, homogenizing,* and *valorizing,* manifesting themselves as dynamic social relations of power. Social exclusion presupposes mechanisms that simultaneously polarize and synthesize across boundaries of difference. Adams (1999, p. 110) uses cogent words to describe the construction of the dichotomy: "The first thing which the Native learns is to stay in his place and not to go beyond certain limits." This is the boundary circumscribing exclusion. "It is a divided world of the Native and the colonizer, of darkness and light, of vice and virtue. It is a world divided between the well-fed and the hungry, the rich and poor, the haves and have-nots" (Adams, 1999, p. 110). These literatures interrogate numerous binary production sites: the savage Indian, signalling the civilized European (Adams, 1999, p. 21); the urban war zone contrasting the urban glamour zone (Sassen, 1998, p. xxxiii); the severed and disavowed left hand of the state conflicting with the overvalorized right, accomplished through "the ascendance of agencies linked to furthering globalization and the decline of those linked to domestic equity questions" (Sassen, 1998, p. 21); the mythical antipodes of the First and Third Worlds, or "the West and the rest" (Brah, 1996, p. 221; Ng, 1998b, p. 24); the branding of women as "emblematic figures of contemporary regimes of accumulation" by the men who rule those regimes (Brah, 1996, p. 179); the positioning of "minorities" in relation to the "majorities" (Brah, 1996, p. 189); the polarized class divisions of the labour market, represented by the core, professional centre, oppositional to the peripheral, unskilled margin (Brah, 1996; Sassen, 1998); the rupture of linear time into the uncivilized, colonial past and the progressive, "post-colonial" present (McClintock, 1994); and dichotomous notions of I and "thou" (Murphy, 1999), the source of all differencing criteria and processes.

Difference is marked beyond the border that separates presumed homogeneity on either side. Homogenization processes are essential in the constitution of the collective "we," and for the recognition of "them." Homogenization across racialized borders is broad in its scope. "If it is known that a person has a 'drop of Indian blood' then he or she is automatically deemed an Aboriginal person, and treated accordingly regardless of appearance" (Adams, 1999, p. 111). The lines embracing superiorized homogeneity are drawn closely, with careful discrimination. It is generally assumed that there is a single dominant identity "whose overarching omnipresence circumscribes constructions of the 'we'" (Brah, 1996, p. 184).

Marked by a uniform "otherness," the excluded are differentially positioned in relation to one another, cultivating dissension, conflict, and factionalization among the marginalized. Brah (1996, p. 215) notes that the creation of "European Man" as the universal subject in Western social and political thought "constructed these various 'Others' in complex hierarchical relations *vis-à-vis* one another." Paradoxically, processes of homogenization incorporate complex power dynamics that propagate endless fragmentation and particularization in social exclusion (Brah, 1996; Murphy, 2000).

It is important to note that difference in and of itself does not constitute exclusion, and not all difference counts. It is the *meaning* that is attributed to difference, "and how this meaning is played out in the economic, cultural and political domains, that marks whether or not specificity emerges as a basis of social division" (Brah, 1996, p. 235). In this way, "the problematic of 'difference' is inseparable from the production, representation and contestation of meaning" (Brah, 1996, p. 245). The devalorization and complementary overvalorization of activities, positions, and identities along lines of gender, race, and class organize people according to the desires and goals of the global finance and corporate services (Ng, 1998b; Sassen, 1998). The fundamental mechanism, then, is the transformation of difference into *opposite*—in every way—from and to the classifying group, erecting a steeply hierarchical binary relationship. Difference and its meaning, are manufactured and ascribed by the "difference which makes the difference" (Corrigan, 1991, p. 320). As those barred from social involvement and advancement, constituting an objective lower class position, confront imposed limitations, generalizations are made and the exclusionary practices are deemed justified (Adams, 1999, p. 10). Such vindication is necessary as valorization processes are often not founded on reason or objective reality. "The willingness and capacity to lie, to lie big, is perhaps the most powerful weapon in the arsenal of oppression and injustice. All those with wealth and power gained their advantage, and sustain this advantage, by lying to those without wealth and power, who they will not allow to lie" (Murphy, 1999, p. 138). One of the most pernicious lies is the dichotomous categorization of people and the world, beginning with those who are permitted to lie and those who are not, those who inscribe boundaries, and those who do not. This is the crude work of identity assemblage, arrogation, and ascription. Brah (1996, p. 237) states: "Identity, then, is invariably established through difference, posing a continual challenge to moves of self-enclosure through metaphoric substitution and metonymic displacement." The ultimate function of *differencing* and meaning-making is not to inferiorize and vilify the excluded, but to superiorize and sanctify the excluders.

Spontaneously and necessarily, exclusionary practices are set in motion and directed by the mechanisms and ideology in which these operations are embedded. Once the boundaries of inclusion and exclusion are cultivated and harvested, they merely fall into place.

UNDERSTANDING SOCIAL EXCLUSION

By investigating the procedures and channels through which social exclusion is accomplished, its dimensions, characteristics, and forms are exposed. Described in these texts as emanating from the ruptured state or the polarized labour market, social exclusion is implemented through policies and practices that assign value, determine entitlement, and judge legitimacy in shifting social relations. Several authors illustrate the destabilized, precarious personality and authority of the nation-state within global corporate rule (Church et al., 2000; Murphy, 2000; Sassen, 1998). Facing unprecedented constraints in its authority and legitimacy, the state is portrayed as divided and conflicted, yet uniformly guided by the values and requirements of the global market (Murphy, 2000; Sassen, 1998). The prominence of neo-liberal ideology is manifested in pervasive government withdrawal of financial and symbolic support for domestic social concerns, necessitating the proliferation and intensification of disentitling and delegitimizing policies and procedures. As the conductors of these procedures, social services are increasingly directed toward social control, endorsed by new partnerships with law enforcers and the judicial system (Adams, 1999; Murphy, 2000). The withdrawing state is tenaciously erecting new barriers to solidify the walls of social exclusion. Church et al. (2000, p. 6) state: "Rather than attacking the issues of poverty and unemployment, governments have used cutbacks and workfare programs to attack the unemployed and the poor." Exclusion as *abandonment* provokes practices of exclusion as *domination*.

In this contrived climate of scarcity and uncertainty, the allocation of government resources materializes as a particularly impressive exclusionary procedure. The preferential and conditional dispersal of money and services to certain individuals, groups, and nations is conventional practice for wealthy government regimes. Drawing parallels between the local co-optation of Native leaders through government grants, and the distribution of U.S. military aid and arms credits to certain leaders in the Third World, Adams (1999) defines this system of exclusion and domination as "neo-colonialism." He states: "In short [neo-colonialism] involves giving some benefits of the dominant society to a small, privileged minority of Aboriginals in return for their help in pacifying the majority" (Adams, 1999, p. 54). Veiled by its familiarity and ubiquity, exclusion as *co-optation* has infiltrated social services and civil society. Murphy (2000, p. 343) articulates the way in which individuals and agencies seeking social justice and equity have become "deliverers of (charitable) services, partners of (downsized) government, and handmaidens to the (corporate) philanthropic sector which sponsors charitable activity, often as advertising." In exchange for obedience, social service workers and volunteers are provided with inferior, dependent, and disentitled clients who define them as opposite. Similarly, Adams (1999, p. 57) describes the way in which compliance from the Native elite is secured, for "if they do not behave themselves then the state can remove the privileges."

Exclusion as *assimilation* is intrinsic to—but not peculiar to—exclusion as co-optation. Masquerading as inclusion, assimilation procedures permit participation, even status, in exchange for the total and unwavering transformation of self. Adams (1999, p. 147) states: "In order to maintain legitimization, subjugated workers need to be trained for certain positions in the job market and conduct themselves properly in the performance of their functions." The objects of assimilation projects—those who are somehow different from the hermetically sealed homogeneous whole into which they are expected to integrate—are assisted in discarding all aspects of their lifestyle, culture, and identity deemed undesirable or inferior (Brah, 1996. p. 229). The difficulty, of course, is that the target identity, the presumed uniform "we," is continually moving and redefining itself, so that the annihilating process is never finished. Exclusion as assimilation works in tandem with exclusion as co-optation. The *polarizing, self-perpetuating* character of social exclusion is displayed as the contest for resources incites social fragmentation and strife, and promises of inclusion and power motivate co-opted leaders and service providers to execute exclusionary procedures against their own.

Concomitant with local "hyper-regulation" is the "deregulation of key operations and markets in the financial industry [which] can be seen as a negotiation between nation-based legal regimes and the formation of a consensus among a growing number of states about furthering the world economy" (Sassen, 1998, p. 199). This "deregulation" is accomplished through very deliberate and precise manoeuvring in and through the international economy as "the global mobility of capital requires not only state rule, but a conglomerate or complex network of institutions and apparatuses ... to ensure its smooth movement within and across national boundaries" (Ng, 1998b, p. 24). The nation-state has transformed itself through new intersections and fusions with the global market. The conflation of corporate economic growth with the well-being and interests of the nation's citizens has wrought a perversion of "good governance" that remains cogent and unyielding, and exclusion as *indifference* is standard practice. Consequently, people must increasingly rely on wage labour and the market to meet their material and social needs (Church et al., 2000; Murphy, 2000). Producing compounding effects, global economic practices have polarized and internationalized the labour market, creating a dramatic increase in temporary, part-time, unregulated, and low-wage jobs (Church et al., 2000; Murphy, 2000; Ng, 1998b; Sassen, 1998). Immigration policies perform in concert with this fragmented labour market, and exclusion as *exploitation* is accomplished. For example, Ng (1998a, p. 17) describes how the points system of Canada's immigration policy is constantly revised to reflect the demands of the Canadian labour market, so that class bias and reinforcement is deliberate and explicit. At the same time, growing anti-immigrant sentiment has led to a considerable shrinking in immigrant eligibility for social services (Sassen, 1998, p. 23). Brah (1996, p. 203) notes that with global flows of money and people, new border zones are erupting, "not only at the port of entry but also internally." The excluded are *both* "diasporized" and displaced, *and* situated and positioned (Brah, 1996, p. 242). The boundaries that mark social exclusion are perpetually *shifting* and *regenerating*, while striving toward stability and maintenance.

The co-ordering of activities by the state and global market has rendered the individual the primary site for regulation and accountability (Brah, 1996; Sassen, 1998). Disintegrating national borders on the one hand, and their contradictory fortification on the other, have destabilized the meanings and claims of "citizenship" and "entitlement." Murphy (2000, p. 334) notes that the "basic rights of citizens are privatised and commodified, available for purchase, but only for those with the means." This is exclusion as abandonment and indifference at work. For those unable to trade money for citizenship entitlements, social programs will accept one's identity, as diagnosis and assessed risk are currency in these systems. They are attached to individuals, and the personified label becomes a commodity, exchanged for agency funding. Social services and welfare programs utilize procedures of surveillance, policing, the commodification of rights, judgments of eligibility and legitimacy, and preferential allocation of resources to implement exclusion as domination and co-optation. The global market effects racialized, gendered, and classist power relations to promote trade and increase profits, while the state performs these ideological practices to exact judgments of individual entitlement and legitimacy. Once excluded, it is extremely difficult to re-enter, and exclusion as exploitation or assimilation may become the only hope for survival.

FORMS OF SOCIAL EXCLUSION

Various interdependent and entangled forms of social exclusion are articulated in the selected literatures. Occupying centre stage in most of these texts, the rapidly shifting and complex dynamics of *economic social exclusion* within global and local labour markets are described in depth. The interplay between increasingly pronounced income disparities, the fragmented and polarized labour market, and the demise of the welfare state inscribe deep, thick boundaries of economic exclusion. While Adams (1999) maintains that economic exclusion, particularly through exploitation, is intrinsic to capitalism, others explore possibilities and strategies and instances of resistance within current economic structures (Church et al., 2000; Murphy, 2000; Sassen, 1998).

Global and local apartheid, and the dislocation and mobilization of people provoked by the global economy can be understood, at least on the surface, as a second form—*geographical* or *spatial social exclusion*. The placement and confinement of Natives onto reserves, as passionately denounced by Adams (1999), is a shamelessly blatant example of exclusion through geographical segregation. Sassen (1998, p. 167) observes that "income polarization is also expressed spatially," so that the organization of urban businesses and services, policing practices, and physical concentration of technological infrastructures widen the divide between new high-income neighbourhoods and enterprise zones, and low-income communities and "war" zones. Brah's (1996) concept of diasporic trajectories, incited by intersecting power relations and global economic patterns, is profound and complex. Fundamental to the lived actuality of diaspora is territorial dislocation and geographical dispersion, intensifying the particularizing and isolating characteristics of social exclusion through physical, objective processes. Various forms of "cyber-segmentation," as described by Sassen (1998), marks a geography both on the ground and in the emergent electronic space itself. A new "unequal geography of access" (Sassen, 1998, p. 182), constituting a technological form of geographical exclusion, presents new opportunities for exclusionary practices.

Pointing toward a third form, Adams (1999, p. 59) argues that constitutional society is exclusionary in and of itself, as it is organized by a system of *political social exclusion* through systematically barring the masses from decision-making processes and preserving their political illiteracy. He perceives the very essence of the constitutional process to be rooted in a "liberal-capitalist definition of rights and citizenship ... in which people are separate entities who come together in competitive economic markets which are regulated according to laws of the corporate class" (Adams,

1999, p. 47). Political exclusion is portrayed as operating primarily through regulating and administering claims of "citizenship" and "entitlement." Concerted by power relations of gender, class, and race, citizenship is mediated for women by their relationship to a man (McClintock, 1994, p. 298), jeopardized for the poor by the market (Murphy, 2000), and revoked for the "home"-less and displaced by transnational regimes of accumulation and geopolitics (Brah, 1996, p. 192; Sassen, 1998, p. xx). Setting into motion the *concealing* and *suppressing* characteristics of social exclusion, geographical and political exclusion collaborate to make those on the other side of the border invisible and silent (Adams, 1999, p. 141; Sassen, 1998, p. 87).

A fourth form of social exclusion penetrates culture and psyche, inscribing internal boundaries that divide an individual from others and within one's self. *Subjective social exclusion*, comprising cultural and psychological processes, is revealed in these texts to be a potently productive force, *intersecting* with all other forms of exclusion to nourish, fortify, justify, and regenerate material and relational barriers. Subjective exclusion operates on the collective and the individual, through processes that are at once social and psychic (Brah, 1996, p. 235), producing a false consciousness and a particular cultural ideology (Adams, 1999). It defines and situates individuals "within multi-axial fields of power relations" (Brah, 1996, p. 247). Subjective exclusion functions to imbue the totality of one's internal spaces—one's psyche, experience, identity, knowledge, and consciousness—with the objective, material reality wrought by economic, geographical, and political exclusion. Its experience is fierce, as articulated by Adams (1999):

> Halfbreed gave me an identity—it signified who I was. It categorized me and it marked boundaries and limits for me. It spelled out my character as sneaky, lazy, filthy and as a drunk. Halfbreed is in my head—deeply rooted in the crevices of my brain, and just as deep in my heart and soul, but most of all it's in my guts. (Adams, 1999, Introduction)

The excluded identity is inferiorized, criminalized, and ossified (Adams, 1999; Brah, 1996; Murphy, 2000). And, as declared by the writers in each of these texts, it is a *lie*. Within the lie, the spaces of contestation and resistance come into view.

RESISTING SOCIAL EXCLUSION

To engage in human relationships is to respond to social exclusion as "there can be no neutral act" (Murphy, 2000, p. 342). The only options available are compliance or contestation. These authors choose resistance in various forms, and the preferred strategies and desired outcomes appear to depend on underlying suppositions about the relationship between the state, the market, and society; the nature of capitalism as an economic system and ideology; and the selected target of transformative efforts (including the perception of one's position in or relationship to that target).

The sharply contrasting visions of Adams (1999) and Sassen (1998) reveal opposing perspectives, and perhaps disparate standpoints. In her formulations of resistance, Sassen (1998) portrays the state as autonomous, with the ability to detach itself from the market, and therefore the capacity and the will to act in ways that contradict the norms, values, and requirements of global capitalism. Following careful and thorough analysis of the consequences of economic globalization, the relations of power that organize the market are minimized in her proposals for change as she situates policy production outside of economic structures and systems. Sassen (1998) directs her vision for resistance to the modification of the state and its policies, particularly in the regulation of immigration. With the "de facto transnationalization of immigration policies"—policies marked by informality and fragmentation—she identifies several emerging trends requiring change for sound immigration policy making. These include: (1) obsolete and inadequate frameworks for immigration policy within the formation of transnational economic spaces; (2) the displacement of government functions onto non-governmental or quasi-governmental transnational institutions; (3) the enforcement of human rights codes, sometimes against decisions made by national legislatures; and (4) the restraints faced by the state in its role to make and implement immigration policy. "These constraints signal that international migrations are partly embedded in conditions produced by economic internationalization both in sending and in receiving areas" (Sassen, 1998, p. 13). Clearly, Sassen (1998) perceives that even within capitalist society, alternative and adequately just social arrangements are possible. Asserting a legitimate voice in societal and government structures, and fixing her gaze on the state, she articulates a point of departure for acts of resistance.

For Adams (1999, p. 37), the abolition of current structures and systems through revolution is the only credible resistance vision as he characterizes the state, the market, and dominant society as fused and saturated at every level by the ideology of capitalism. Located in a prevailing history of exclusion, in its most extreme forms and through the most violent means, he sees no room for fruitful resistance within capitalist society and rejects inclusion of any kind in "a decaying white society. Why enter a house that is burning down?" (Adams, 1999, p. 74). He remembers that capitalism "robbed us of our lands, resources, and rights" (Adams, 1999, p. 86). Denoting the focal points of his decolonized vision, Adams (1999, p. 118) states: "A genuine, liberating nationalism must promote revolutionary and socialist ideologies; these are essential and perhaps the greatest weapons Natives need to win self-determination." Through the cultivation of a counter-consciousness, pride in a shared history of struggle, and class solidarity, revolution is born. Adams's work calls into question the relevance of the concept of social exclusion, and the potential of its application in Canadian policy for meaningful change in the lives of society's excluded.

Perhaps from a more privileged location, Murphy (1999) cautions against Adams's revolutionary dreams. Identifying this form of resistance as "ideological radicalism," he argues that "in politics, as in physics, one revolution usually brings you back to your starting point; movement through 360 degrees leaves you standing still. Trading places with the slaver does not do away with slavery" (Murphy, 1999, p. 30). Murphy (1999) notes that the more prevalent response to social exclusion is non-resistance, or conformity, which he identifies as "the psychology of inertia." Manifested as despair and defeat, it is the internalization of a belief system—the taking in of external barriers to change and their justification—so that the behaviour and attitudes adopted come to be defined as normal and natural, inevitable. This is subjective social exclusion at work, as individual human potential and the intricacies of social relations are negated. Like ideological radicalism, conformity is rooted in the assumption of boundaries that exclude and include. When the psychology of inertia loses its grip, the seduction of the revolution, according to Murphy (1999, p. 31), is "ego-gratification, in that harmony is established between belief and action; identity is provided through doctrinaire solidarity; sense of significance is strengthened by the role of the protagonist against the evil society." Murphy (1999, p. 33) boldly asserts: "The ideological response, once codified and set in motion is a socio-political cul-de-sac, containing in itself all of the root social evils of the prevailing order." At the end of the revolution—a struggle with force seeking power and control—the simple trading of places between the excluders and the excluded can be avoided only through ideological reversal, and the absolute equalization of power across the dividing line. Revolutionary reorganization may not be palatable for many, but for some it may constitute the only conceivable hope for liberation.

Both conformity and radicalism preserve the dichotomy—the division of the world into absolutes—so that "all contradiction, all ambiguity, all doubt, is removed" (Murphy, 1999, p. 31). Without the binaries of "all or nothing" (Murphy, 1999, p. 14), good and bad, the collective versus the individual, and without the assumption that exclusion and inclusion are absolutes, despair cannot find a home. Resisting social exclusion from within this oppositional space—made vast and sovereign in Western ideology—is futile, for "When we reject one truth, we feel the need to replace it with another" (Murphy, 1999, p. 31), and new boundaries of exclusion are inscribed. Central to Brah's (1996) articulation of resistance is the *contestation of the binary*. She contends that the oppositions assembled by the dichotomizing work of the dominant ideology must be rendered unviable. "The binary is a socially constructed category whose trajectory warrants investigation in terms of how it was constituted, regulated, embodied and contested, rather than taken as always already present" (Brah, 1996, p. 184). The rejection of oppositional identity and role constructions was observed to be important for people joining in the existing resistance efforts described by Church et al. (2000). Work that is meaningful to the communities in which people participate provides a "means of personal redefinition" (Church et al., 2000, p. 6), as well as a contrary response to economic exclusion. The longer-term goal of one particular resistance effort "is to demonstrate that the marginalized people of the district can be other than clients of the services of community organizations, they can also be workers and effective managers" (Church et al., 2000, p. 19). In the contestation of the binary, the lie of subjective social exclusion is exposed and the "client" is redefined so as to supplant the identity of passive and dependent recipient or object with that of active, speaking, interdependent subject. Similarly, Murphy (1999, p. 63) attempts to integrate the I/thou dichotomy in mutual relationships and shared action. He states that harmony is not found in balancing the dichotomy, "but in doing away with the dichotomy in a situation in which our expression of self, and our expression of self-in-group, are a unity intrinsic in all acts." While Murphy (1999) denounces the oppositional foundations of the psychology of inertia and ideological radicalism, he unwittingly exhibits the tenacious, insidious nature of dichotomizing forces. With notable incongruity, he promotes a "profound distrust of absolutes and ideology" (Murphy, 1999, p. 34), rejects the prevailing ideology and the "central assumptions on which this established rationality is built" (Murphy, 1999, p. 66), and proceeds to assemble a counter-ideology with their antitheses.

Remaining primarily in the theoretical realm, Murphy's (1999) step-by-step change process begins with the individual and culminates in a particular paradigm shift as he understands the discrete structures of the state and the market to be embedded in the relationships among individuals that comprise society. His vision for society transformed mingles civil and social justice, equality, and interdependence on the one hand, with individual freedom, health, growth, and creativity on the other (Murphy, 1999, p. 127). His approach to change, which incorporates key concepts of his resistance strategy, focuses on the "development of people" through: the personal affirmation of sanity and action; the formation of reference/action groups; the continuous expanding cycle of acquiring "action-knowledge"; and the formation of alliances. These paired notions of *politicization* and *collectivization—counter-consciousness within solidarity*—are shared themes in the resistance visions of these texts, although the constitution of the politicized and active collective varies. Conceding to the lines of exclusion inscribed by relations of power, Adams (1999) promotes solidarity of consciousness and action among those inferiorized by racial and class difference. Among Aboriginal peoples, solidarity in anger, frustration, distress, and deep hostility is "germane for developing a counter-culture and an opposition movement to the racist culture" (Adams, 1999, p. 144). Ng (1998b) makes an appeal for the formation of alliances across geographical, racial, gender, and class divides—transgressing the boundaries of exclusion and working across differences—to challenge globalization. Ignoring the divisive and dynamic axes of differentiation, Murphy (2000, p. 338) calls for the collectivization of *all* citizens, and the advancement of the role of civil society, defined as: "The sum of citizens organized into formal and informal associations to contribute to their collective lives and communities and to propose and contest social and economic policies with their fellow citizens, their governments, and the state." In his disregard for the contentious and unstable identity of "citizen," Murphy (1999, 2000) displays his consistent tendency to overlook the ideological practices of power that work to keep people in their place. Alternatively, Brah (1996, p. 230) carries politicization to the foreground, and attempts to make "'othering' processes around race, class, and so on" visible and conscious. She notes that the boundaries of exclusion, or the markers of difference representing "articulating and performative facets of power" (Brah, 1996, p. 189), are patently ignored in the model of multiculturalism. She seeks to refigure and revalorize the "multi" of multiculturalism, as "this can be made to work in the service of effecting politics which fosters solidarity without erasing difference" (Brah, 1996, p. 227), and *undermine the forces of homogenization* that must precede polarization across lines of exclusion.

Brah's (1996) comprehensive analysis of power relations extends through to her vision of resistance. She states: "Power is not always already constituted but is produced, and reiterated or challenged, through its exercise in multiple sites. Its effects may be oppressive, repressive, or suppressive, serving to control, discipline, inferiorise and install hierarchies of domination" (Brah, 1996, p. 243). Murphy's (1999) momentary glance toward practices of power lands on the injuries inflicted by the abuse of power. He denounces all power as ultimately destructive, stating: "When we fight violence with violence, violence wins; and when we replace power with power, power wins" (Murphy, 1999, p. 124). He fails to articulate how the "psychology of inertia" can be overcome from a powerless place. Brah (1996, p. 243), on the other hand, contends that "power is also at the heart of cultural creativity, of pleasure and desire, of subversion and resistance. Power is the very means for challenging, contesting and dismantling the structures of injustice." In summary, this genre of literature points toward a vision of resistance *activism*, founded on the direct participation of *individuals* as a *collective*, motivated by personal *experience* and a *politicized consciousness*, that *exposes and opposes the homogenizing and dichotomizing* work of social exclusion through claims and acts of *power*.

CONCLUSION

These diverse literatures offer meaningful insight into the complex and penetrating processes of social exclusion. They reveal that the work of constructing identity and drawing lines is never done, as decisions about where to draw the line—which differences to claim in and which ones to name out—must be made over and over again. And these texts denounce the "common sense" myths of the inevitable global and intractable social, and proclaim that change *is* possible as the dynamic relations of power that work to inscribe boundaries marking difference and exclusion are interrupted and contested with tenacious acts of collective resistance.

NOTE

1. More specifically, my current work for my Ph.D. dissertation is an exploration of social exclusion among people who comprise various ethnic-religious communities of immigrant, Low German-speaking migrant workers in Ontario. These people, numbering over 25,000 in southern Ontario, are most commonly and erroneously referred to as Mexican Mennonites. A tenacious commitment to their distinct way of life—a culture that is intensely traditional, religious, agrarian, and patriarchal—has contributed to a diasporic history that is over 400 years old, and has taken them from northern Germany to Russia, Canada, and Central and South America. Since the 1960s, migration has become a way of life for many, moving from Mexico and Bolivia to various regions of Ontario and Alberta, and back south again.

REFERENCES

Adams, H. (1999). *Tortured people: The politics of colonization* (rev. ed.). Penticton: Theytus Books Ltd.

Atkinson, R. (2000). Combating social exclusion in Europe: The new urban policy challenge. *Urban Studies 37*(5–6), 1037–1055.

Barry, M., & Hallett, C. (1998). *Social exclusion and social work: Issues of theory, policy and practice.* Lyme Regis: Russell House Publishing Ltd.

Bhalla, A., & Lapeyre, F. (1997). Social exclusion: Towards an analytical and operational framework. *Development and Change 28*(3), 413–433.

Brah, A. (1996). *Cartographies of Diaspora: Contesting Identities.* London & New York: Routledge.

Church, K., Fontan, J.M., Ng, R., & Shragge, E. (2000). *Social learning among people who are excluded from the labour market. Part One: Context and case studies.* Network for New Approaches to Life-Long Learning (NALL).

Corrigan, P. (1991). Viewpoint: Power/difference. *The Sociological Review 39*(2), 309–334.

Evans, M. (1998). Behind the rhetoric: The institutional basis of social exclusion and poverty. *IDS Bulletin 29*(1), 42–49.

Freiler, C. (2000). *Social inclusion as a focus of well being for children and families.* Draft. Advisory Committee for the Children's Agenda Programme, Laidlaw Foundation.

Garonna, P., & Triacca, U. (1999). Social change: Measurement and theory. *International Statistical Review 67*(1), 49–62.

Klasen, S. (1998). *Social exclusion and children in OECD countries: Some conceptual issues.* OECD: Centre for Educational Research and Innovation. Retrieved from: <www.oecd.org/els/edu/ceri/conf220299.htm>.

Levitas, R. (1996). The concept of social exclusion and the new Durkheimian hegemony. *Critical Social Policy 16*, 5–20.

McClintock, A. (1994). The angel of progress: Pitfalls of the term "post-colonialism." In P. Williams & L. Chrismas (Eds.), *Colonial discourse and post-colonial theory—A reader* (pp. 330–347). New York: Columbia University Press.

Murphy, B.K. (1999). *Transforming ourselves, transforming the world: An open conspiracy for social change.* London: Zed Books.

Murphy, B.K. (2000). International NGO's and the challenge of modernity. *Development in Practice 10*(3–4), 330–347.

Ng, R. (1998a). Conceptual considerations in gendering policy analysis on immigration. In Status of Women Canada (Ed.), *In Gender, Immigration/Integration: Policy Research Workshop and Selective Review of Policy Research Literature, 1986–1996* (pp 13–21). Ottawa: Status of Women Canada.

_____. (1998b). Work restructuring and recolonizing Third World women: An example from the garment industry in Toronto. *Canadian Woman Studies 18*(1), 21–25.

Room, G. (1999). Social exclusion, solidarity, and the challenge of globalization. *International Journal of Social Welfare 8*(3), 166–174.

Sassen, S. (1998). *Globalization and its discontents: Essays on the new mobility of people and money.* New York: The New Press.

Smith, D.E. (1999). *Writing the social: Critique, theory, and investigations.* Toronto: University of Toronto Press.

Veit-Wilson, J. (1998). *Setting adequacy standards: How governments define minimum incomes.* Bristol: Policy Press.

Chapter 2

Margins as Centres:
A Theory of Social Inclusion
in Anti-Oppressive Social Work

Rick Sin
Doctoral Student
Ontario Institute for Studies in Education
University of Toronto
Miu Chung Yan
School of Social Work
San Francisco State University

In spite of the promises of economic development and technological innovation, the division between the dominant groups and marginalized bodies has deepened. Racism, sexism, disability, and other forms of social division either persist or change their faces in our societies. In response to these challenges, social inclusion has recently been widely explored and adopted as a conceptual and policy focus in the West (Commission of the European Communities, 2000; Haan, 1999). In 1997, the Social Exclusion Unit[1] was established in Britain by Blair's New Labour government to coordinate policy-making on specified crosscutting topics such as school exclusion and truancy, homelessness, teenage pregnancy, youth at risk, and deprived neighbourhoods (Social Exclusion Unit, 1999, 2001). Three years later, the European Union took a major initiative by making the fight against social exclusion one of the central elements in the modernization of the European social model (European Union, 2000).

In Canada, the federal government has declared its commitment to making our society the most inclusive country in the world (Canadian Heritage, 2001). Promoting greater inclusion and equality of opportunity is listed as one of the four social policy goals of Human Resources Development Canada. Among the local non-governmental organizations, the Canadian Association for Community Living has moved toward adopting social inclusion as its strategic direction (Freiler, 2001), while the Maytree Foundation has called for replacing settlement policies with inclusion policies and programs (Omidvar, 2001). In the past few years, the Laidlaw Foundation has also been actively making the concept of social inclusion front and centre in its program and funding framework. Not only has the foundation made "Building Inclusive Cities and Communities" the new focus of its Children's Agenda Program, it also strives to promote understanding of the concept and cross-sector dialogues by commissioning a series of working papers and organizing a national conference and focus group round tables across the country (Laidlaw Foundation, 2002). The foundation has also developed a "concept paper" and arrived at a definition and the key components of social inclusion after a massive public consultation that involved over 120 policy analysts, academics, and practitioners from within and outside of government.

As professionals dedicated to serving all citizens with a special concern for the poor and the oppressed (Rondeau, 2001), shall we as social workers also jump on the bandwagon and make social inclusion a central focus for social work education, research, and practice? In this chapter, we will argue that social inclusion is a hybrid concept prone to theoretical and political slippage, particularly with reference to the tension between its totalizing tendency and transformative claims. To make social inclusion a "transformative agenda" for the oppressed, we must question what constitutes social difference and domination in our society by critically examining their theoretical precursors—i.e., the notions of difference, positionality, and power. We will apply Avtar Brah's insightful idea of a multiaxial conception of performative power to highlight the multiple, fluid, and intersecting nature of social difference, and the importance of making space for marginalized individuals and communities to assert their own human agency in social change. In other words, instead of endorsing a totalizing vision of "*social and economic mainstream of common life*" with "*eliminating boundaries*" (Freiler, 2001), the issue of concern shall be recognizing the coexistence of social differences and, more important, positioning marginalized people at the centre of the social inclusion discourse. The chapter will end with exploring implications for anti-oppressive social work practice and calling for social workers to be border-crossing intellectuals.

Two contextual issues are important in the following discussion. First, coming from working-class, immigrant, and racially marginalized backgrounds, we choose to focus our research on developing theories about the politics of difference and race. Discussion in this chapter privileges such subject locations. However, as will be seen, this is not separate from other positionings, especially those of disability, gender, and sexual orientation. Second, there are many narratives on social inclusion. Recognizing the Laidlaw Foundation's pioneering efforts in initiating the current dialogue and its focus on the application of the concept of social inclusion in the Canadian context, we would like to start our discussion by reviewing the definition, major components, and dimensions of social inclusion introduced in the concept paper (Freiler, 2001) and a related essay entitled "The Laidlaw Foundation's Perspective on Social Inclusion," posted on the foundation's Web site (Laidlaw Foundation, 2002).

CONCEPTION OF SOCIAL INCLUSION: A CANADIAN PROPOSAL

In her book *The Inclusive Society? Social Exclusion and New Labour*, Levitas (1998) summarizes the debates on social inclusion and exclusion and the related policies in Europe into three discourses of social exclusion that lead to different policy prescriptions. The first is a *redistributive discourse* developed in British critical social policy, whose prime concern is about poverty. It broadens out from its concern about poverty to a critique of inequality, and contrasts exclusion with a version of citizenship that calls for substantial redistribution of power and wealth. The second discourse is a *moral underclass discourse*, which centres on moral and behavioural delinquency—i.e., *the culture of dependency*[2]—of the "criminally inclined," unemployable young men, and "sexually and socially irresponsible single mothers" for whom paid work is a necessary means of social discipline, but whose exclusion is moral and cultural. The third is the *social integrationist discourse*, which focuses more narrowly on unemployment and economic inactivity, pursuing social integration or social cohesion primarily through inclusion in paid work. Levitas (1998) rightly points out that social exclusion is a contested concept with a multiplicity of meanings and it operates as "a shifter between different discourses." All of these approaches take employment as a major factor in social integration; however, they differ in how they characterize the boundary, and thus what defines people as insiders and outsiders and how inclusion can be brought about.

Drawing on the European experience in making social exclusion into policy frameworks that focus on the social dimension of poverty and participation in the labour market, the local discourse capitalizes on the broader appeal of social inclusion. In the concept paper, Christa Freiler (2001), the program coordinator of Children's Agenda, illustrates that social inclusion and social exclusion are the two ends of a continuum. While social exclusion refers to "what has been done to those who are vulnerable, considered 'disposable' or, less than human" (Freiler, 2001, p. 11), social inclusion is a positive concept that "links the notions of life chances and social cohesion," and "reinforces the move away from the traditional 'deficit' measures" of social marginality (Freiler, 2001, p. 9). Hence, the public policy focus should be on social inclusion. To facilitate the discussion, the foundation put forward the following working definition of social inclusion:

> Social inclusion is the capacity and willingness of *our* society to keep all groups within reach of what *we* expect as a society— the social commitment and investments necessary to ensure that socially and economically vulnerable people are within reach of *our common* aspirations, *common* life and its *common* wealth. (Emphases added) (Freiler, 2001, p. 5)

It needs to be emphasized that social inclusion is a normative concept that "guides the development of forward-looking indicators and strategies, rather than simply measuring 'what's wrong'" (Freiler, 2001, p. 12) Social inclusion is used as a metaphor for the way in which "we are alike as human beings, for what binds us together as persons" (Freiler, 2001, p. 11). It is also a transformative agenda that requires investment and action at structural, civic, and community levels to bring about the condition for inclusion (Freiler, 2001, p. 16). Unlike its European counterparts, the foundation is concerned with social proximity rather than elimination of particular social problems like poverty. Social inclusion/exclusion is more about social distance and social proximity than it is about "in" and "out." They see boundaries between people as permeable and fluid, rather than rigid or solid. The goal of social inclusion is "closing the distance, rather than crossing the line" (Freiler, 2001, p. 13).

Through the consultation process, the Laidlaw Foundation (2002) has identified five critical dimensions in its conceptual framework of social inclusion: (1) valued recognition of social difference and common worth; (2) human development; (3) involvement and engagement in decision-making processes; (4) proximity in terms of social and physical space; and (5) material resources for active participation (as shown in Box 2.1).

As a result of a two-year consultation process, the foundation has officially adopted social inclusion as a tool for evaluating and advancing social policy in support of children and families, and made "Building Inclusive Cities and Communities" the new focus of the Children's Agenda Program (Laidlaw Foundation, 2002).

INHERENT PROBLEMATIC OF THE PROPOSAL: FOUR CHALLENGES TO THE CONCEPT OF SOCIAL INCLUSION

A brief overview of the concept paper reveals some problematic underlying narratives in the current discourse that require further clarification of at least four major issues of the concept of social inclusion.

Box 2.1: Five Critical Dimensions/Cornerstones of Social Inclusion

1. *Valued recognition:* Conferring recognition and respect on individuals and groups. This includes recognizing the differences in children's development and, therefore, not equating disability with pathology; supporting community schools that are sensitive to cultural and gender differences; and extending the notion to recognizing *common worth* through universal programs such as health care.
2. *Human development:* Nurturing the talents, skills, capacities, and choices of children and adults to live a life they value and to make a contribution both they and others find worthwhile. Examples include: learning and developmental opportunities for all children and adults; community child care and recreation programs for children that are growth-promoting and challenging rather than merely custodial.
3. *Involvement and engagement:* Having the right and the necessary support to make/be involved in decisions affecting oneself, one's family, and community, and to be engaged in community life. Examples include: youth engagement and control of services for youth; parental input into school curriculum or placement decisions affecting their child; citizen engagement in municipal policy decisions; and political participation.
4. *Proximity:* Sharing physical and social spaces to provide opportunities for interactions, if desired, and to reduce social distances between people. This includes shared public spaces such as parks and libraries; mixed-income neighbourhoods and housing; and integrated schools and classrooms.
5. *Material well-being:* Having the material resources to allow children and their parents to participate fully in community life. This includes being safely and securely housed and having an adequate income.

Source: Adapted from the Web site of the Laidlaw Foundation as of June 18, 2002 <www.laidlawfdn.org/>.

First, social inclusion is a forward-looking transformative agenda that moves away from the "*deficiency model*" toward a "*positive, proactive human developmental mode.*" Social inclusion is also seen as a "*process for achieving other concepts such as equality, citizenship or social rights as well as a goal in its own right.*" As a public policy, it emphasizes investments and intervention more than removing barriers, and it acknowledges the importance of all actors' human agency. In this framework, individuals are members of society participating in decision-making processes of decisions affecting their lives, rather than clients on the receiving end of services.

The concept paper also recognizes structural and historical oppression (Freiler, 2001). Yet, when it comes to prescribing solutions, the framework adopts a "capability-based approach" that centres on nurturing individuals' skills and capabilities, but the structural inequalities of material resources remain largely uninterrogated. It strongly implies that the current problems of social exclusion are merely results of inadequate resources for nurturing required skills and capabilities to become active civic participants. One of Levitas's (1998) major critiques of the social exclusion model prevalent in Europe is that the current political discourses within which social inclusion is deployed are primarily based on a Durkheimian organic framework. It conjures up a vision of the good society, which represses conflict. It distracts attention from the structural and historic barriers dividing members of society by race, gender, sexual orientation, class, and disability. From this position, the reality of offering equal membership without equal power is totally sidelined.

In this situation, social inclusion is assumed to lead to two possible scenarios: (a) all of the dominant groups suddenly become altruistic civic participants and are willing to share privileges and resources, or (b) the marginalized/excluded are able to assert their human agency to gain equitable access to opportunities and resources. The concept paper fails to account for how their prescription can make these two scenarios come true. Without a convincing explanation, the notion of inclusion becomes problematic, particularly if the transformative agenda only focuses on enhancing the individual's own capacity instead of tackling the structural barriers that confine individuals. For instance, as we all know, it is not that foreign-trained physicians do not possess the skills and capabilities to ameliorate the acute shortage of family doctors in Ontario. As widely reported in the media, many of them have practised in other countries, including England (Muti, 2002). Despite their acquired proficiency, they have hardly any opportunity to utilize their skills and knowledge in serving the host country they now call home. Many foreign-trained professionals, particularly those coming from non-European countries, are excluded not because of a lack of capabilities or skills, but because of the short-sighted and utterly discriminatory policies of licensing bodies and the government (Basran & Zong, 1998).

Second, as shown in Box 2.1, social inclusion is constructed as a framework "conferring recognition and respect on individuals and groups" and is "sensitive to cultural and gender differences" (Freiler, 2001). This framework takes the diversity of an individual actor's own cultural and social characteristics into consideration; however, the issue of power difference disappears when it comes to proposing change. West (1993) notes that in the current neo-liberal discourses on social difference, the issue of power relations is always absent. The issue of diversity is framed in a way that avoids the centrality and salience of racialization and racism that cut across social exclusion and poverty in Canada. For instance, in Toronto, racial minorities are more likely to be unemployed and living in poverty (Ornstein, 2000). While the child poverty rate in Ontario is 22.1 per cent, 45.3 per cent of Aboriginal children and 42.3 per cent of racial minority children are living in poverty (Campaign 2000, 2000). Again, in Canada, the youth unemployment rate was 14.5 per cent in 1998, almost double that of adults. However, for racial minority youth, the unemployment rate was 23.1 per cent and for Aboriginal and black youth, it was about 32 per cent (Galabuzi, 2001).

The neo-liberal discourse also assumes that the specificity of social difference is only the matter of the excluded. In this case, social inclusion becomes merely a mainstreaming strategy for the dominant group reaching out to and recruiting the marginalized Others, while the latter remain passive actors. This tendency is apparently contradictory to its original theoretical claims—the human agency of all actors and the absence of a centre-periphery relationship in social inclusion.

Third, it is suggested that social inclusion "extends beyond bringing the '*outsiders*' in, or notions of the *periphery* versus the *centre*. It is about closing physical, social and economic distances separating people, rather than primarily about eliminating *boundaries* or *barriers* between *us* and *them*" (Freiler, 2001, p. 6). This vision of social inclusion effects changes that can bring everybody toward "*common aspiration*," "*common life*," and "*common wealth*." We have to point out that such a desire of transcultural and transcendental togetherness disregarding the notion of essentialization of core and periphery will only turn social inclusion into a totalizing narrative. Not only does it ignore the mutually contradictory and multiple character of domination and struggle, but also assumes that sameness and universality are necessary and achievable. By doing so it conceals the power and privileges of the dominant, as well as the inequalities and differences in society. We tend to agree with Giroux's (1994, p. 145) proposition that all these totalizing narratives—"we," "all," and "common"—are merely another way for the dominant groups "to refuse to address their own politics by appealing to the imperatives of politeness, objectivity, and neutrality," thereby constraining the excluded groups from producing new spaces of resistance, and imagining new ends and opportunities to reach them.

Lastly, current thinking recognizes that social inclusion is a normative concept—"it is about values, a 'high mark' that points to where we want to be, rather than a descriptive term for where we are now" (Freiler, 2001, p. 5). The claims of "our society," "we expect as a society," "our common aspirations," "common life," and "common wealth" all imply a monolithic and integrative reality. How is this "high mark" set? How can an indisputable common ground be arrived at among diverse interests in society? Who would have the final say as to our "common aspiration" and "common goal"? These questions are left unanswered in the discourse. Using a Habermarian (Habermas, 1984) analysis, no society can assume "our/we/common" normative values without a proper negotiation/dialogue among the diverse interest groups and individuals. Typical of human subjectivity, these values are complex, multiple, shifting, and never static. Very often, due to the asymmetry of power, the voices of the minority are silenced and involuntary inclusion is justified, or self-exclusion is naturalized and assumed by the imposition of the superimposing common goal(s). These dynamics of common goodness and involuntary inclusion can be elucidated by Ontario's Learning and Employment Assessment Profile (LEAP) program. This program assumes that being a "good" parent is a common aspiration. Because of this assumed aspiration, the policy forces unmarried mothers on social assistance to attend parenting courses and to stay in school.

SOCIAL DIFFERENCES, DOMINATION, AND INCLUSION: A DIALECTIC OF MARGIN AND CENTRE

The intent of this chapter is not to refute the importance of the concept of social inclusion. Nor do we question the positive intention of any organization proposing it as a public policy focus. Given its hybrid character and flexibility, and the desire to endorse the concept of social inclusion for the purpose of anti-oppression and social justice work, the social work profession needs to examine how power, difference, and human agency all come into play in shaping the questions of "who," "from where," "who is," "how," and "for what purpose." Is social inclusion necessarily good for the excluded? Is it done by choice or by power? Is it really a solution for social exclusion or is it reproducing the very problems it is attacking? It is our contention that between the notion of commonality and diversity, individuals and groups must negotiate how to position their differences and identities in complex and shifting social, cultural, and political conjunctures. Since differences are relational and multidimensional, it is impossible and inappropriate to assume any static and monolithic common goal(s) for all members of a society. Instead, common good exists only as an outcome of negotiation through coexisting struggles of individuals (and groups) in striving for a diversity of goals, which may, at times, be in conflict.

To participate in civil society, what matters most is not the common aspirations but the universal rights that provide all members with equal access to opportunities, resources, and space to assert their human agency. In short, inclusion cannot be totalizing—"all," "we," and "common"—nor can it ignore the existence of boundaries, core, and peripheries. The challenge to society is how to share power, relegate privileges, and give space for people at the margins to define and locate the centre as a strategy of anti-oppressive struggles. This alternative notion of social inclusion envisions multiple and intersecting struggles in different sites that keep shifting the power landscape of our society. Instead of the capability-based approach proposed by the Laidlaw Foundation, we should advocate for a rights-based framework of social inclusion.

RECOGNIZING DIFFERENCES VERSUS POSITIONING DIFFERENCES

Social inclusion is always about how to seek a common base among different social interests. Social difference is always political. As Hall (1992, p. 257) forcefully asserts, "difference, like representation, is also a slippery, and therefore, contested concept." Social differences are clearly and irretrievably embedded in different forms of our material existence. Our bodies, ages, and genders often play significant parts in defining ourselves. Yet, to a great extent, differences are also "positional, conditional and conjunctural." Arber (2000, p. 26) points out that "positioning is both nothing, an everything, an invention, and everything, our everyday lives." Thus, our Chineseness and Canadianness are subject to negotiation in daily social situations. In the racialized environment, the male identity of Asian men is always compromised by the imposed feminization of the dominant cultural industry (Eng, 2001). In her article "Radical Black Subjectivity," bell hooks (1990) persuasively demonstrates how the marginal aspect of Blackness can be centralized and used for counter-hegemonic cultural practice.

One way or another, by nature, positioning differences is relational depending on the particularity of the social, cultural, and political context. We are multi-positioned, implicated in unequally empowered ways of understanding and doing. Our social positions are entangled and cannot simply be defined by a set of binaries: Black/White, working class/middle class, female/male. Positioning can also be strategic. It can be a form of coalition, a way of resistance, a precursor of agency. It is something relational and contingent, mediated by and mediating, and always a criss-crossing of understanding and ways of doing (Arber, 2000).

The interplay of difference and positioning refutes any essentialist notion of any form of differences. Instead, it leaves room for individuals to be active agents to interpret contextual demands and then to identify themselves strategically. The notion of positional difference, in turn, justifies Bhabha's (1994) claims of identity as strategy, which "enable us to begin to deconstruct the regimes of power which operate to differentiate one group from another; to present them as similar or different" (Brah, 1996, p. 183). It also enables us to include or exclude diverse groups from constructions of the common ground. Only then is difference no longer a site of exclusion and repression. Positioning ourselves differently becomes a strategy, a way of constructing oneself, a source of radical social action, and a site of resistance.

MULTIPLE AND INTERSECTING IDENTITIES

Since positions vary and the purpose of positioning oneself is strategic, we always have multiple identities that are fluid and historically contingent (Hall, 1996). Being Chinese, male, immigrants, and social workers, just to name a few, we position and are positioned in different social locations. Brah (1996) suggests that the major reference we use to position ourselves is always in relation to the main dominant group. However, due to the multiple nature of identity, "a group constituted as a 'minority' along one dimension of differentiation may be constructed as a 'majority' along another" (Brah, 1996, p. 189). The notions of minority and majority are socially situated and contested. "Minorities" are positioned in relation not only to "majorities" but also with respect to one another, and vice versa. In other words, the centre and margin are not fixed but contingent. Individual subjects may occupy "minority" and "majority" positions simultaneously, which has important implications for the formation of subjectivity. Therefore, a multiaxial perspective of social relations is more tenable in understanding our own identity and our social positions.

REDISTRIBUTIVE VERSUS PERFORMATIVE CONCEPTION OF POWER

Social positions differentiate power, but power is not necessarily distributive in a zero-sum mode. Instead, power can also be performative by nature, which is "understood as relational, coming into play within multiple sites across micro and macro fields" (Brah, 1996, p. 197). In Foucault's (1980) perspective, power must be analyzed in a circular manner, in which people are the vehicles of power circulating between the threads of a net-like interpersonal organization. In this sense, like differences, power is relational, positional, and discursive. Resistance by the marginalized group can be an important form of power, particularly when marginality is a chosen position.

hooks (1990) argues that the chosen marginality can be a site of resistance that is also a location of radical openness and possibility. The determination of inclusion and exclusion is, therefore, largely subject to how a particular individual or group exercises the power within a particular position, be it self-identified or imposed. If power is not a fixed but positional base, the margin and centre are fluid depending on the interplay of power, identity, and position.

Brah's idea of multi-axial performative power is particularly important in examining how common aspirations and common goals can be attained by social inclusion. Instead of understanding social inclusion as a totalizing narrative gearing toward a monolithic and exclusive set of universal goals and imposed solidarity, the relational, contingent, and multiaxial perspective interprets social inclusion as coexisting, voluntary, and strategic groupings among individuals and communities in particular social and historical conjunctures. It also helps resolve the major paradox of competing marginality—i.e., the challenge of according equal weight to all forms of oppressions. Once power is not set beyond a zero-sum game, one group's resistance against oppression does not necessarily lead to the loss of power for other groups.

HUMAN AGENCY: MARGINS AS CENTRES IN SOCIAL INCLUSION

Unlike the dominant discourse of social inclusion, marginality is not a site of deprivation but a space of resistance. Giving human agency is not about enhancing capabilities, skills, and talents of individuals but politically providing resources and space for marginalized people to assume "the central location for the production of a counter-hegemonic discourse that is not just found in words but in habits of being and the way one lives" (hooks, 1990, p. 149). Instead of concealing cores and peripheries in a monolithic social and political reality, we need to reframe our vision of centres and margins, which are vividly described by bell hooks in her book *Yearning—Race, Gender, and Cultural Politics*:

> To be in the margin is to be part of the whole but outside the main body ... . We could enter the world but we could not live there. We had always to return to the margin ... Living as we did—on the edge—we developed a particular way of seeing reality. We looked both from the outside in and from the inside out. We focused our attention on the center as well as on the margin. We understood both ... I was not speaking of a

marginality ONE wishes to lose—to give up or surrender as part of moving into the center—but rather of a site one stays in, clings to even, because it nourishes one's capacity to resist. It offers to one the possibility of radical perspective from which to see and create, to imagine alternatives, new worlds. (hooks, 1990, pp. 149–150)

IMPLICATIONS FOR ANTI-OPPRESSIVE SOCIAL WORK PRACTICE

Social inclusion is an important dimension of anti-oppressive social work practice that "aims to end oppressive hierarchical relations and replace them with egalitarian ones facilitating individual and group fulfillment" (Dominelli, 1997, p. 247). The oppressive hierarchical relationship always manifests itself as the centre/margin in social relations. Social inclusion can, therefore, be understood as a strategy to equalize the centred and marginalized groups. However, as we have contested, the concept of social inclusion must be reframed to prevent a totalizing effect that replaces one type of hierarchical relations with another by imposing dominant groups' normative values on and forcing involuntary participation from the marginal groups. This is particularly important in anti-oppressive social work practice, which has already been criticized as silencing the client's voice (Wilson & Beresford, 2000), subjugating clients' expertise (Pease, 2002), and imposing workers' interpretations of the truthfulness on clients' experiences (Payne, 1997). To be an anti-oppressive practitioner, one needs to consider the following issues:

First, there seems to be a tension in being a professional and being committed to anti-oppressive practice. An essential part of the definition of a profession is the possession of a specific knowledge base. Professionals are supposed to be experts, but the power in their expertise can disempower clients and thus subvert the goals of the profession. Professionals are placed in positions of power over others through their institutional position, which also undermines the activity of empowerment (Pease, 2002). Thus, the professional knowledge claims of social work can become a means of ideological domination. In spite of the good intentions of those who seek to empower others, the relations of empowerment are themselves relations of power. In these relations of power there is a constant tension between compliance and resistance. Actions considered empowering by a worker may be experienced by a client as stifling.

Anti-oppressive practice requires social workers to not only reflect but also reposition their own social locations. Our social location is often a double-edged sword—it is up to us to authorize the voices of our clients, or to silence them. Instead of denying the privilege attached to this position, we must recognize it and strategically use it together with clients for a mutually agreed-upon purpose. For instance, "What if I think a woman is oppressed and she does not? What does empowerment mean here—the imposition of my set of values over hers?" (Wise as quoted in Pease, 2002, p. 136). As Arber reminds us, "People have a choice, that choosing difference can become strategy, that people can decide who they want to be and how they want to be placed" (Arber, 2000, p. 51); positioning is strategic and contingent to the presenting issue of concern. Clients can therefore choose to collaborate with workers on different issues for different purposes. For instance, a straight man of racially marginalized background can be mobilized to work along with gay and lesbian members of the community to promote an inclusive and equitable social service system.

Second, we must also recognize the centre/margin position between workers and their clients. Being employees of social agencies funded by the government, and educated professionals with decent incomes, social workers cannot deny their own power and the fact that their clients are very often in marginalized positions. However, this centre/margin analogy is not sufficient in an anti-oppressive practice within a multidimensional reality. People have multiple identities, which are the results of the multiple positions that people choose or are imposed in. In other words, anti-oppressive practice must take into consideration these multiaxial dimensions. The multidimensional nature of social differences makes it possible to identify allies and build coalitions. While people may share some common dimensions, they cannot simply be defined by any one set of binaries: Black/White, working class/middle class, female/male, heterosexual/homosexual, just to name a few. Each of these binaries signifies a border that must be criss-crossed by the parties involved.

Third, social workers are also border crossers. Border crossing, as defined by Henry Giroux (1994, p. 142), means that intellectuals are able to "problematize and take leave of the cultural, theoretical, and ideological borders that enclose them within the safety of those places and spaces we inherit and occupy" and to "reinvent traditions as transformation and critique." As border crossers, social worker must constantly re-examine and raise questions about what kinds of positional borders are being crossed and revisited. We must question what kinds of identities are being remade and refigured within new historical, social, and political borderlands, and what effects such crossings have for redefining anti-oppressive practice (Giroux, 1994). For instance, to reform the existing adoption policies, social workers have to reflect on whether their conception of family and family relationship are constrained by their own sexual orientation and socio-economic status. By the same token, the review of child welfare policies also requires that workers re-examine their own education and gender privileges, in order to understand the challenges faced by working-class families and single mothers.

Social workers who promote anti-oppressive practice must recognize the borders in which they themselves are bounded and the new border that they create. We would like to call for an integrative anti-racist model of practice that consistently examines how race, gender, disability, sexuality, and class relations are reconfigured in contemporary societies to produce new forms of inequality and difference in Canada. It is a new kind of social work relationship in which professional practitioners will not reproduce the class, gender, and racial hierarchies of the dominant social order (Leonard, 1993).

Fourth, as one of the major concepts of social inclusion, people have their own will or human agency. Positioning of differences and identities is a result of choice or imposition subjected to the interplay of human agencies in any social engagement. It is relational and contingent, mediated by and mediating, criss-crossing of understanding and ways of doing (Giroux, 1994). How should social workers relate to services users in anti-oppressive practice? It involves not only the courage but also the openness of workers and clients to engage in dialogue (Irving & Young, 2001). Dialogue is the means to generate the agreeable purpose(s) for the anti-oppressive engagement. In an effective dialogue, workers must position themselves as participants along with their clients. Embedded in Foucault's power notion, Falzon (1998) suggests, is a social dialogue that is also a process in which various social forces compete among different interests in interpreting the social agenda. Anti-oppressive social workers and their clients may not always see things eye to eye. They are at least two forces positioned in different social locales in any social work encounter. Therefore, a dialogue is not necessarily started from a position of consensus. The normatively defined good will of social workers may not always be what clients want or even agree with.

Instead of taking the assigned marginal position of clients for granted, workers must give their clients the opportunity to define their own identity and position. In a dialogic process, a critical anti-oppressive social worker "must give more thought to how the experience of marginality at the level of everyday life lends itself productively to forms of oppositional and transformative consciousness. Similarly, those designated as Others must both reclaim and remake their histories, voices, and visions as part of a wider struggle to change those material and social relations that deny radical pluralism as the basis of democratic political community" (Giroux, 1992, p.

33). It is the responsibility of social workers to nurture the environment for this form of dialogue.

CONCLUSION

Arguing through the theoretical and strategic issues revealed by the Laidlaw Foundation's concept paper, this chapter contends that social inclusion is a powerful concept, not because of its analytical clarity (which is conspicuously lacking), but because of its flexibility. At individual levels, it mobilizes personal fears of being excluded or left out. At a political level, it has a broad appeal, both to those who value increased participation and those who seek greater social control. It allows shifting between the different discourses in which it is embedded (Levitas, 1998). This also explains why it lies at the heart of our current political debates.

Apparently, social inclusion constitutes a normative notion of positive and proactive meaning with a transformative agenda for the common good. It addresses the multidimensional nature of social change and emphasizes the human agency of all actors. Nevertheless, as long as it fails to address how diverse sectors and communities can come to terms with *shared aspirations,* we have to cast doubt on making it a focus or guiding principle for social policy and social work practice. The tension within its totalizing transformative agenda provokes skepticism regarding its positive valuing of diversity, human development, involvement and engagement, and material well-being.

We have mobilized the idea of a multiaxial performative concept of power to explain that difference is hybrid, fluid, and intersecting. To recognize the human agency of all actors requires us to understand the strategic nature of how difference is positioned in particular social locations. The total development of a society is an outcome relying on whether individuals and communities have equitable access to space and resources for the realization of their own aspirations. The notions of "mainstream," "all," "common goals," and "common aspirations" should be replaced with a vision of the multicentric civil society in which margins become centres of multiple struggles for diverse but intersecting and shifting goals and aspirations. To realize the latter vision, anti-oppressive social workers are required to consistently examine how race, gender, disability, sexuality, and class relations are being reconfigured in contemporary societies to produce new forms of inequality and difference in Canada. This also implies a new kind of social work relationship in which professional practitioners will not reproduce the class, gender, and racial hierarchies of the dominant social order.

NOTES

1. As illustrated in the article, while "social exclusion" is more often used in official policy documents, "social inclusion" and "social exclusion" are interchangeably used in political and academic debates as the two ends of a continuum. We want to note that the two can also be viewed as a dialectic of social relations in which inclusion and exclusion are simultaneously situated in a particular social and political conjuncture.
2. It refers to the assertion that the welfare spending gave rise to a culture of dependency that promotes a downward spiral of idleness, crime, and erosion of the work ethic. It shifts the focus of social policy debates from the structural basis of poverty to the moral and cultural character of the poor themselves.

REFERENCES

Arber, R. (2000). Defining positioning within politics of difference: Negotiating spaces "in between." *Race, Ethnicity and Education 3*(1), 45–63.

Basran, G., and Zong, L. (1998). Devaluation of foreign credentials as perceived by visible minority professional immigrants. *Canadian Ethnic Studies XXX*(3), 7–23.

Bhabha, H.K. (1994). *The location of culture*. London: Routledge.

Brah, A. (1996). *Cartographies of diaspora: Contesting identities*. New York: Routledge.

Campaign 2000. (2000). *Child poverty in Ontario—Report card 2000*. Toronto: Campaign 2000.

Canadian Heritage. (2001). *Annual report on the operation of the Canadian Multiculturalism Act, 1999–2000*. Ottawa: Minister of Public Works and Government Services Canada.

Commission of the European Communities. (2000). *Communication from the Commission—Building an inclusive* Europe. Brussels: Commission of the European Communities.

Dominelli, L. (1997). *Sociology for social work*. London: MacMillan.

Eng, D.L. (2001). *Racial castration—Managing masculinity in Asian America*. Durham: Duke University Press.

European Union. (2000, October 17). *Fight against poverty and social exclusion—Definition of appropriate objectives, employment and social policy*. Brussels: Commission of the European Communities.

Falzon, C. (1998). *Foucault and social dialogue*. New York: Routledge.

Foucault, Michel (1980). *Power/knowledge: Selected interviews and other writings 1972–77*. New York: Pantheon Books.

Freiler, C. (2001, August 13). *What needs to change? Social inclusion as a focus of well being for children, families and communities*. Paper presented at Community Roundtable on Social Inclusion organized by the City of Toronto.

Galabuzi, G. (2001). *Canada's creeping economic apartheid*. Toronto: The Centre for Social Justice & Foundation for Research and Education.

Giroux, H. (1992). *Border crossing—Cultural worker and the politics of education*. New York: Routledge.

_____. (1994). *Disturbing pleasures*. New York: Routledge.

Haan, A. (1999). Social exclusion: Towards a holistic understanding of deprivation. In Villa Borsig Workshop Series—Inclusion, Justice, and Poverty Reduction. Deutsche Stifting fur internationale Entwicklung's Web site: <www.dse.de/ef/poverty/dehaan.htm>.

Habermas, J. (1984). *The theory of communicative action* (Vol. One). Translated by Thomas McCarthy. Boston: Beacon Press.

Hall, S. (1992). New ethnicities. In James Donald & Ali Rattansi (Eds.), *"Race," culture and difference* (pp. 252-259). London: Sage.

_____. (1996). Cultural identity and diaspora. In P. Mongia (Ed.), *Contemporary postcolonial theory: A reader* (pp. 84–109). New York: St. Martin's Press.

hooks, bell. (1984). *Feminist theory: From margin to center*. Boston: South End Press.

_____. (1990). *Yearning—Race, gender, and cultural politics.* Toronto: Between the Lines.

Irving, A., & Young, T. (2001). Paradigm for pluralism: Mikhail Bakhtin and social work practice. *Social Work 47*(1), 19–29.

Laidlaw Foundation. (2002). Web site

Leonard, P. (1993). Critical pedagogy and state welfare: Intellectual encounters with Freire and Gramsci, 1974–86. In Peter McLaren & Peter Leonard (Eds.), *Paulo Freire—A critical encounter* (pp. 155–167). London: Routledge.

Levitas, R. (1998). *The inclusive society? Social exclusion and New Labour.* Hampshire: Macmillan Press.

Muti, F. (2002, June 22). Not wanted at home—A familiar medical tale: Employed in Britain, out of luck in Toronto. *Toronto Star*, H7.

Omidvar, R. (2001, September). Social inclusion: A new vision of immigrant settlement in Canada. *Caledon Commentary*. Ottawa: Caledon Institute of Social Policy.

Ornstein, M. (2000). *Ethno-racial inequality in the City of Toronto: An analysis of the 1996 census*. Toronto: Access and Equity Unit, Strategic and Corporate Policy Division, City of Toronto.

Payne, M. (1997). *Modern social work theory* (2nd ed.). Chicago: Lyceum.

Pease, B. (2002). Rethinking empowerment: A postmodern reappraisal for emancipatory practice. *British Journal of Social Work 32*, 135–147.

Rondeau, G. (2001, October 12). Challenges that confront social work education in Canada. Unpublished paper presented at the National Social Work Forum in Montreal.

Social Exclusion Unit. (1999). *Review of the Social Exclusion Unit*. London: Cabinet Office, United Kingdom.

_____. (2001). *Preventing social exclusion—Report by the Social Exclusion Unit, March 2001*. London: Cabinet Office, United Kingdom.

West, C. (1993). *Keeping faith: Philosophy and race in America*. New York: Routledge.

Wilson, A., & Beresford, P. (2000). "Anti-oppressive practice": Emancipation or appropriation? *British Journal of Social Work 30*, 553–573.

Chapter 3

Race, Class, and Gender in the Everyday Talk of Social Workers: The Ways We Limit the Possibilities for Radical Practice

Donna Baines
McMaster University
Labour Studies and Social Work

Jim Thomas (1993) asserts that critical ethnography asks what could be, while conventional ethnography describes what is. In the late 1990s I undertook a study of how race, class, and gender were part of the practices of front-line, left-of-centre social workers in Toronto, Canada. Rather than merely describe the life worlds of this small population of left-of-centre professionals, the study targeted the self-reported conceptual and concrete practices of these workers as the object of study. By making conceptual and concrete practices the focus of this study, I sought to reveal the ways that these practices may have been liberatory, oppressive, or both, and to make recommendations that could increase the likelihood of emancipatory ways of thinking about and acting upon the political, cultural, and economic struggles that form the ground for social work interventions. If one were to use Thomas's distinction as outlined above, the study described what was (conventional ethnography), as well as explored what could be (critical ethnography).

Social work operates within a distinctly gendered terrain in which the majority of clients, workers, volunteers, and activists are female and the social problems in which we are collectively engaged are highly gendered (Baines, Evans, & Neysmith, 1998). Despite this feminized terrain, feminist and pro-women services are seen as specialized rather than mainstream services. Even where feminist services have managed to gain a foothold, they are often absorbed by state processes and remade as gender-neutral problems that are amenable to existing mainstream social work solutions

(Maguire, 1987; Morgan, 1981; Walker, 1990; Weeks, 1994). As a feminist practitioner I have grown somewhat accustomed to the lack of feminist analyses within social work. The depoliticized and quasi-therapeutic way that most of the research participants framed gender came as little surprise to me, while the way they talked about class proved to be startling and perplexing. Indeed, within this study, the way the research participants talked about class proved alarming to me and to many of my more radical colleagues who had not anticipated this theoretical/practice limitation. Hence, I am using class as an entry point to this discussion in which I promote a model for theorizing the race/class/gender triad that unsettles the depoliticized and descriptive formulations of class and gender that were very present in my study and, instead, opens discussion of greater complexity. I could have just as easily used gender as my entry point to this discussion. In a moment I will explain why I could not have used race as my entry point to this discussion.

In a chapter that promotes the notion of race, class, and gender as a contentious but continuous amalgam, it is risky to single out one of the three aspects for closer examination and critique. However, I need to do this in order to tease out the limitations that I discerned in the conceptual practices of front-line practitioners who were struggling to put theory into practice. My goal is to strengthen the theory-practice relationship within radical social work, as well as to expand our theoretical understanding of the interrelationship of race, class, and gender and to understand how it is that class—even among this group of left-of-centre practitioners—is articulated in a very narrow fashion. So, while I am arguing that class is indivisible from gender, I am doing so by conceptualizing class as the relationship between groups of people and systems of production and reproduction (Ng, 1993), rather than simply a relationship to production as orthodox, male-centric Marxists might argue. Twinning reproduction with production recognizes the continuities of these two processes in women's lives and necessarily ties gender to class in any analysis of either process. Although I am using class as my entry point to this discussion, clearly I am not arguing that all forms of injustice emanate from the central contradiction of class. Rather, I am asserting that the flat, undynamic understanding of class was part of a snowball effect that quashed the interplay of dynamic understandings of class and gender, as well as the unbroken, interlocking of these social relations with each other, and with race.

As noted earlier, one might question why race is not part of the discussion above. A lively public discourse existed at the time of my study concerning how to address systemic and interpersonal inequalities experienced by ethno-racial and other marginalized groups in the province of Ontario. In public, official accounts, Toronto, Ontario, Canada, the site of my study, is described as the most multicultural city in the world, with 54 per cent of its citizens identifying themselves as members of visible minority or ethno-racial communities and 48 per cent using a language other than English or French as their primary mode of communication (Doyle & Visano, 1991; EA Update, 1999). Equity-enhancing legislation such as employment equity had been introduced some years prior to my study and significant levels of funding existed for multicultural and anti-racism projects. This created a social context in which ethno-racial issues were hotly debated in the legislature, media, workplaces, schools, social service agencies, community groups, and activist circles. This context of heightened social debate created a politicized space in which many Torontonians, including the research participants, talked about and enacted anti-racism in dynamic, fluid, and politicized ways. In contrast, most of the participants' talk about class and gender was flat, service oriented, and detached from the larger social context that generated and profited from unjust class and gender relations.

I speculate that had the politicized context surrounding race not been in existence during the time of my study, race would have been similarly understood and mobilized in everyday talk as a bland label for various groups of people rather than as an interactive and contested set of relationships. Since 1995, cuts in funding, widespread backlash, and the repeal of equity-enhancing legislation have severely constricted the public spaces in which anti-racist debate and action could and can flourish. Indeed, I speculate that should I repeat this study today, the results would be very different and race would be also mobilized in the talk of many of the participants as a flat, limited descriptor. Finally, I will argue later in this chapter that the rapidly changing working conditions of the research participants made it hard to think about class and gender (and today probably about race) in other than "a day-to-day kind of survival way." Most of the research participants excelled at actions that resisted class, race, and gender oppression in the work site. However, there was very little evidence that their actions of resistance produced the far-reaching, social justice-directed economic, political, and social restructuring that is the goal of left-of-centre social work practice. The failure to produce fundamental change does not rest solely or even primarily in the conceptual limitations of practitioners. Rather it lies in the capacity of dominating forces to contain resistance, no matter how sophisticated (Carniol, 2000; Mullaly, 1999; Swift, 1990; Ng, 1989).

Despite this I remain concerned that when practitioners talk about and understand oppression as flat—labels for groups of people, rather than as dynamic relationships of power and contestation (or in descriptive rather than in analytic ways)—they reduce their capacity to produce anything more substantial or long lasting than minor sabotage, and microresistance to the larger neo-liberal agenda. The challenge for left-of-centre social workers and others concerned with justice-directed social work practice is to develop, teach, and practice social work in a way that reflects race, class, and gender as a dynamic, contestatory but seamless whole that simultaneously resonates with the actual, depoliticizing, backlash conditions in which social workers and their clients work and struggle.

METHODOLOGY

I am an insider to this community and built a purposive, snowball sample (Lincoln & Guba, 1985) from the membership lists of two grassroots, activist, left-of-centre social work organizations I was involved with in Toronto. One of the groups was composed of social service workers with and without degrees whose main goal is the development of radical consciousness, critique, and activism within the broader social services sector. While the majority of its members are White, it has a strong commitment to anti-racism and struggles with a broad cross-section of socio-politico-economic issues.

The second group, from whom I drew only one or two participants, was comprised of doctoral students committed to creating a left-of-centre space inside and outside of social work academia, although admittedly the focus of most of its efforts was the academy. While some members of these groups did participate in the study, the sample snowballed from these initial contacts to include more people of colour, lesbians, and gay men than are found in the field. The sample was also more likely to have a university degree than the sum total of all workers in the social services sector. All the participants in this study were self-defined left-of-centre practitioners (feminist, anti-racist, structural, anti-oppressive, Marxist, post-structuralist, or some combination of the above), and as they were willing to assume the risk inherent in this identity, I undertook no further screening of their political values or knowledge. This recruitment technique provided sufficiently vibrant data while avoiding the imposition of screening processes that might offend or alienate potential research participants and their communities.

The participants worked in all the usual spots for social workers—hospitals, child welfare, welfare, vocational rehabilitation, schools, community service centres, seniors' programs, grassroots groups, feminist services, private practice, lobby groups, policy analysis, and research—for an average of 7.2 years, although a few participants had less than two years of paid social work experience (social workers earlier in their careers seemed to have less demands on their time and more often responded affirmatively to requests for participation than did workers further along in their lives and careers). As noted earlier, the study took place in a city that claims to be the most multicultural in North America at a time of transition from a social democratic government to a neo-liberal government. While the findings may have greater resonance for those working in metropolitan areas with social democratic or left liberal traditions, the substance of my argument concerning the difficulty social workers have in talking about and acting on race, class, and gender as a three-part whole is important to workers in any setting as race, class, and gender are part of every social work encounter.

The study involved a total of five tape-recorded, two-hour focus groups and nine tape-recorded in-depth interviews (one-and-a-half to two hours long) with twenty-one self-defined, left-of-centre social workers seen either in groups or individually. Two of the focus groups met twice (one of five and one of six people), and they were amalgamated for a final feedback loop (for a total of five meetings). The interview guide used for the focus groups and the interviews asked a few basic questions and developed from the interaction of the interview. Hence, the order of the questions was different in each interview as well as the number and type of follow-up questions, probes, adjunct issues, and so forth. The focus group and the interview participants were asked to provide a story from their work life about each of race, class, and gender, as well as the three categories as a conglomerate. Discussion flowed easily from this starting point and produced a cornucopia of data.

Tapes were transcribed verbatim. Data analysis involved fracturing the data into concepts, and subsequently labelling, sorting, and resorting (Strauss & Corbin, 1990). The emerging themes were also iterated back to the literature, through a final focus group, and through subsequent themes until a mapping of the interconnections between concepts, surface realities, hidden realities, and existing knowledge was possible. As this was a critical or openly ideological study (Andersen, 1989; Lather, 1991; Thomas, 1993), throughout the analysis I sought to be aware of contradictions and tensions between and within the belief systems and the practices of left-of-centre social workers. The analysis also explored how these practices were internally inconsistent and sometimes at odds with the values and knowledge base of the research participants (Schwandt, 1997). Finally, I connected the themes in the data to broader structures of social power and control (Thomas, 1993, p. 6).

LEFT-OF-CENTRE SOCIAL WORK LITERATURE ON RACE, CLASS, AND GENDER

Critical social work is part of a cluster of theories that intertwine theory and practice in order to produce knowledge aimed at interpreting the world and changing it. While left-of-centre social work theory and values draw on broader social science theory on race, class, and gender, interconnection theorists such as Anthias and Yuval Davis (1992); Collins (2000); Anderson and Collins (2001); Albert, Cagan, Chomsky, Hahnel, King, Sargent, and Sklar (1986); and Ng (1993, 1990), distinct and significant body of social work literature exists on the same topic. For example, the parallel oppressions model developed by Moreau (1979, 1989a, 1989b, 1993, n.d.), the "father" of structural social work in Canada, envisions multiple oppressors lining up alongside each other with none more central or important than the next. Wineman's (1984) intersectionist model asserts that oppressions criss-cross each other in an intricate and complicated mass of hierarchies. Postmodern social work theorists such as Brown (1994) focus on understanding race, class, and gender in ways that avoid silencing marginalized voices while maintaining the liberatory potential of single analytic and political categories such as gender. In a similar project, Leonard (1997) melds Marxism and postmodernism in an attempt to reconstruct an emancipatory project through the development of "confederacies of difference" in which multiple differences are represented and affirmed, and common interests are collectively advanced.

In the tradition of the interlocking social relations model (Ng, 1993), I argue that race, class, and gender should be regarded as continuous, dynamic, and constantly changing in relation to each other and to how subordination and domination are played out in this society. When race, class, and gender are understood as continuous, contentious, and mutually reinforcing social processes, it is possible to see how fixed descriptions of one piece of the conglomerate obstruct the development of strategies that might liberate us from the oppressive aspects of all these social relations. In the stories below, I show how oversimplified formulations of class, in particular, truncated ways that race, class, and gender were understood, and how a continuous, contentious model would have better served the goals of left-of-centre social work.

MORE RELATIONAL FORMULATIONS OF RACE, CLASS, AND GENDER

As I emphasized earlier in this chapter, not all of the research participants formulated class and gender in simplified, unidimensional ways. Interestingly, the participants who invoked more analytic constructions of race, class, and gender tended to be those who worked in research and policy development, or in grassroots, activist agencies. Thinking analytically was part of the requirement of the jobs of these particular participants, and while not all employees comply with the requirements of their jobs, these workers did so admirably. Similarly, those employed in grassroots, activist agencies worked in a more politicized and fluid context in which critical thinking was a recognized and rewarded asset to the job. While it is not inevitable that those who work in more bureaucratic settings will have little or no encouragement to think critically or analytically, it is far more likely that they work in a context in which it is more difficult to step out from behind the fast pace and standardized form of everyday social work in order to formulate work concepts and practices in more critical ways. Below are some examples of more relational thinking.

When telling a story about how gender was part of her everyday work, one participant simultaneously critiqued feminists who fail to recognize class and race and the world of gender injustice beyond the social service agency:

> Some women who are really good feminists will talk like there's nothing that happens except at the agency. Like, there isn't a whole world of inequality beyond that. As if women's access to good jobs and being able to keep good jobs has nothing to do with the world outside of the agency. Like, the fact they may have children, … so that they don't have as much time to get as many credentials, especially Canadian credentials if they are new to the country, or as much experience as men. As if they don't have to take more time off to care for sick kids, and then they don't get the promotion or raise. It all seems to have been erased somehow.

In this quote the speaker analyzes some of the ways that unpaid work (in the form of family responsibilities) and race (in the form of difficulty immigrant women experience in establishing Canadian credentials) are all part of women's unequal experience in the world of paid social services work as well as in the larger society. She is also concerned about how these issues become depoliticized and difficult to act on even among feminist social workers.

This next worker understands gender as an aspect of herself that is present and part of the many overlapping aspects of paid and unpaid work life she experiences on a day-to-day basis:

> It [gender] is everything I do all the time, everywhere—at work, at home, with the board, with my staff, with my supervisor, with my landlord, my bank, the crummy services we get in our rundown neighbourhood, with my computer, my vacuum, my garden hose, my lover (if I had one, but that's another story),

with homeless people on the street, and the fact that I am one paycheque from being homeless myself, and it's in with the programs for new immigrants that I volunteer with. Basically, there's nowhere it isn't.

Another research participant commented on the difficulties of negotiating paid and unpaid work within a newly formed, grassroots, ethno-specific, womanist, non-hierarchical collective that provides a wide range of services to women:

> Social justice and race, class, and gender are all clearly laid out in our mandate. Our big challenge is how to really operate as a non-hierarchical collective with two paid staff and a bunch of volunteers. It's not easy and we don't always get support from the community, but we all believe that it is the best way that we can work together.

The preceding quotes, as well as a number of the narratives in my discussion of race, show that some of the research participants sometimes formulated race, class, and gender as aspects of each other or in more relational, analytic ways. They alluded to aspects of class within services aimed at addressing gendered racial issues and racialized gender issues, they wove productive and reproductive issues through their discussion of gender's presence in their lives, and they decried their fellow feminists who failed to recognized that the gendered social organization of home life was indivisible from the gendered, classed, and racialized organization of promotion, credentialing, and security within the social services labour market.

CLASS

When I asked research participants working in more bureaucratic settings to tell me a story about a time when class was part of their social work practice, most of them told stories about poverty, and about how there is little or nothing that can be done about poverty: "most of our clients are poor and there is not too much that can be done for them"; "the poverty among our community members is very clear to see, they are poor, so, so poor, especially the women, and there are no programs for most of them and nothing we can offer"; "there are so many really poor people out there who call in, and there is so little that I can do for them."

I became disturbed not just that poverty was the central way that class was present in the talk of many of the participants in this study, but that the formulation of poverty emphasized a resigned acceptance of a largely unchangeable condition—"there's nothing we can do about it [poverty] anyways." Further probing confirmed that when the research participants talked about poverty, they usually meant a lack of formal attachment to the paid labour market. The corollary to this conclusion was an assumption that entry into the world of paid work would end poverty for most, if not all, individuals. (I discuss the contradiction of paid employment producing poverty for an increasing number of working people in greater detail below.) When referring to clients, most of the research participants said things such as: "My clients want admittance to the workforce and can't get it." Without this admittance, they "have no choices and will remain poor." "If only I could find jobs for my clients, ... then maybe we'd see a lot less poverty around here." "Many of the people I work with hate being poor and hate living near other poor people even though they are poor themselves. They just want to get a job and get away from it." These storylines do not dovetail with left-of-centre social work theory. They are more compatible with neo-liberal storylines promoting the private labour market as the solution to all social needs and malaise and welfare reform as necessary to end dependency on the public purse (see Lightman, 1995, or Shragge, 1997, for a critique of workfare, or Fraser & Gordon, 1994, for a discussion of dependency and welfare in the United States).

When referring to themselves, the research participants repeated the same theme that paid work equals a move to middle-class comfort: "All the staff are middle class. Obviously, we all get middle-class paycheques." "We have one poor person on staff, well, she was working class and now she is a professional, so she is middle class." "I come from a working-class background and although now I'm middle class, I remember what it was like and use that in my work." It is interesting to note that in the research participants' talk, class took the form of something that other people—in this case, clients—experience in a negative way, whereas the social workers themselves experience a pleasant, almost "classless" state when they gained professional employment. This is consistent with Ehrenreich's (1989) observation that "in our culture, the professional, and largely white, middle class is taken as the social norm—a bland and neutral mainstream—from which every other group or class is a kind of deviation."[1]

Racialized, gendered, and classed problems weave in and out of each other in the quotes above and are very difficult to separate analytically. The discussion below arbitrarily divides some of these continuities in order to clarify how weaknesses in one area actually limit how the other components of the triumvirate can be thought about and acted upon. The formulations above are arguably raced and gendered, and I will explore them below. However, in addition to the raced and gendered problems, there are two classed problems.

Generally speaking, the classed problems coalesce around the myth that paid work equals an end to poverty and admittance to the neutral and safe mainstream of middle-classness. Recent research by Burke and Shields (1999) shows that 60.7 per cent of Canadians are employed in vulnerable employment, or employment that does not generate sufficient income and benefits to meet the cost of living. Canadians employed in jobs that generate sufficient income and benefits to sustain them and their families comprise only 39.3 per cent of the total stock of jobs. For prime-age workers this trend has remained constant despite the much-touted recovery in the economy, while for youth, single mothers, and older workers the gap has increased. In other words, there are a growing number of working people in our society for whom paid work equals poverty rather than middle-class comfort.

The parameters, size, working conditions, median income, and relative security of the so-called middle class are in the process of profound and ongoing change. As Burke and Shields's data shows, the middle class is an increasingly less secure place for women, people of colour, people with disabilities, and all other oppressed groups who are the targets of anti-oppressive social work practice. Despite this grim picture, my quotes show that the most of the participants believed that gaining paid employment could solve or, at least reduce, their clients' poverty.

However, within the restructured North American economy, most social service clients will never gain sustainable employment. They will remain a reserve supply of low-wage workers who can be drawn into the labour market during labour shortages and pushed out when the labour supply exceeds demands. While the quotes from the participants confirm that they saw themselves as secure, middle-class professionals, in actuality, they share much in common with their clients' precarious positioning. Social workers are an increasingly temporary, casual, involuntarily part-time and low-waged workforce (Baines, 2000; Ontario Public Service Employees Union, 1999a) in a highly gendered and racialized, rapidly downsizing sector of the labour market. While part-time, low-wage, insecure, or temporary work has long been the reality for those working in community and grassroots social work endeavours, part-time and contract workers now make up the majority of employees in the government-run or government-mandated settings such as child welfare, developmental services, and social assistance (Baines, 2000; Ontario Public Service Employees Union, 1999b). These previously secure, full-time jobs with a comprehensive complement of benefits are being cut back and remade as precarious work. In short, social workers' strategic positioning vis-à-vis economic structures and relative power to resist economic exploitation is increasingly similar to that of their clients.

The second classed problem in the data is a gendered one. This problem is also necessarily highly racialized and I will explore it in a moment. Gendered portions of this formulation rotate mainly on the notion that people who live in poverty are not part of the paid labour market, hence they are not workers, do not perform any socially valuable work, and do not merit a paycheque. However, as many would argue, the majority of women in receipt of welfare benefits are responsible for the care of their children and therefore perform important, endless, socially valuable work (Fraser, 1997; Swift, 1990). Many of these women also perform significant amounts of formal and informal volunteer work in their communities (Neysmith & Reitsma-Street, 2000) which is similarly devalued and erased within masculinist formulations of work defined as only paid work outside the home.

Failure to accord social and economic value to women's unpaid (or low-paid) work means that it is hard to explain why women raising children are working and do not deserve cuts to their welfare cheques or punitive measures to push them into the low-wage labour market.

As noted above, the "work equals paid work" storyline is also highly racialized. A disproportionate number of people of colour and First Nations peoples are among those who lack formal attachment to the paid labour market. Many participate instead in social assistance-supported but unpaid child, elder, or home care, and/or participate sporadically in the paid labour market, and/or frequently in the informal, black market, or "under the table" labour market. Historically, women of colour and Aboriginal women have found it exceedingly difficult to move out of job ghettos or labour market segments such as that of low-waged domestic work (for a discussion of the race and gender aspects of labour market segmentation, see Gordon, Edwards, & Reich, 1982; Humphries & Rubery, 1984). These women simultaneously undertake most of the unpaid labour in their own homes and communities (Baines, 2000).

Strategically speaking, their highly exploited and segmented labour market positioning, as well as their unpaid caring labour, amplifies the intensity of their ongoing struggles to resist cultural/racial denigration and economic exploitation. Regrettably, my research participants' common-sense solutions to poverty ignored who is already working and who stands to benefit or to lose from their clients' participation in the segmented labour markets of Toronto. In the following sections I will look at how the weak formulation of class contributed not only to inadequate understandings of class as part of a continuous race/gender/class triad, but also contributed to truncated formulations of gender and race within this three-part social relation.

GENDER

As mentioned earlier, the social work milieu is a highly gendered terrain with women making up the majority of the paid practitioners, unpaid caregivers, clients, activists, and volunteers. Hence, one might expect left-of-centre social work analyses to have a heightened gender analysis. However, as mentioned earlier, when asked to tell a story in which gender was part of their everyday work, most workers responded with a story about violence in the lives of women: "the violence that my clients experienced makes you feel sick to your stomach"; "all of the females and most of the males have been sexually assaulted at some point"; "women are violated a gazillion times more than men"; "the kind of sexual abuse that goes on within programs and within families is horrendous. It is absolutely shocking what women and girls have to put up with."

Given that violence is such a disturbing and pervasive occurrence, it is not surprising that the research participants mentioned it with great frequency. Unfortunately, the way it was discussed narrowed the possibilities for analysis and action. Some of the respondents in this study seemed to believe that violence was the only gender issue worth discussing, in fact, it was the only issue they raised. Also, as shown in the quote below, many participants told stories in which male violence was constructed as an individual psychological problem requiring professional, clinical attention: "these women grew up with violence, hook up with a violent boyfriend, get the crap beat out of them, and then we get to fix them up with some basic support and counselling." This quote unintentionally emphasizes two things. First, that people can have problems such as violence "fixed" with some counselling and support. This ignores the pervasiveness of violence and the need for larger solutions such as an interlocking series of immediate supports as well as longer-term pro-equity policy initiatives (women's relationship to and positioning within reproduction and production). Second, counselling focuses on individual rather than society-wide change, thus subtly remaking the problem and the solution as the responsibility of the victim/survivor. This remake of the problem, not coincidentally, means that the gendered violence issue can be addressed by existing clinical social work services rather than requiring workers and agencies to develop new, holistic, politicized strategies.

Women's vulnerability to violence and poverty, and the lack of meaningful cultural, economic, and social alternatives are inseparable from the gendered meanings and practices that constitute the everyday experience of working within the paid and unpaid spheres of life. In other words, how a woman feels about housework, caring for her frail elderly parents, volunteering at a free lunch program at her local church (or mosque or temple), working part-time at Wal-Mart, and remaining with her abusive male partner are inextricably connected to the organization of production and reproduction or the organization of class in any given society.

As the discussion in the previous section on class showed, most of the research participants discussed class as if it were gender neutral. However, since class is actually any group of people's relationship to reproduction and production (Ng, 1993), as well as reproduction's relationship to production, class is entirely saturated with gender. Class issues can be more effectively contained or depoliticized when they are understood to be gender neutral. Conversely, class becomes more difficult to depoliticize when it is understood as a system that sorts out men and women in terms of their life chances based on their social and economic relationships to paid and unpaid work, as well as the identities, cultural practices, power, and privileges that spring from this division and organization of work. Similarly, when gender is understood as saturated with class, it becomes very difficult to think about it as only a problem of violence that requires therapeutic interventions. Gender and the solutions to gender injustice are thereby moved out of the realm of the therapeutic and into the realm of a complex set of social, economic, and political relations. As the formulations of the research participants showed, failure to understand gender as part of a larger system of production and reproduction results in single-issue, quasi-therapeutic understandings of gender that were denuded of their capacities to oppose gendered systems of domination and subordination.

RACE

As noted earlier, within the time frame of my study anti-racism was a hotly debated social issue with widespread social participation (see the earlier discussion of employment equity and similar initiatives). Indeed, the heightened social awareness of racism and anti-racism in Toronto, coupled with a disappointing lack of public discourse on gender or class, compelled a number of the participants to assert that "race is in, whereas class and gender are out." Reflecting the possibilities that abound when any issue is hotly debated across publics and policies, one participant asserted that "an 'in' issue, even an impossible one, is always easier to develop some action around than [is] an 'out' issue." In this case, the participant felt that race had long been an issue that politicians and the public failed to act on with sufficient fervour. While that era was not entirely over, the public contestation of race issues seemed pregnant with possibility. The narratives of the research participants reflected this larger politicized social context, hence they talked about race in terms of its historical and ongoing connections to colonialism and imperialism, as well as the need for change at the agency level, society-wide, and globally—"wars overseas and cutbacks in service provision in Canada are all part of the legacy of colonialism and the impacts of the third world debt crisis, and the globalization of capitalism."

Highlighting the breadth and depth of the anti-racism strategies, many of the research participants argued that the anti-racist struggle was not only addressing racism, it was also integrating other types of oppression in its analysis and program. For example, more than one participant told a story about an agency-based anti-racism committee that won same-sex spousal benefits for staff. Anti-heterosexism and homophobia strategies are not often demands found on the agenda of anti-racism, although many activists and academics have seen their inclusion as essential to emancipatory politics (hooks, 1988; Lourde, 1990). However, in this case, the campaign for same-sex spousal benefits was initiated and won through the efforts of the anti-racism committee. Multi-demand, multi-oppression, anti-racist work was viewed by most of the participants as powerful and hopeful, although not at all easy: "the reality is that it's one hell of a nasty, messy process ... , but I think we could actually eventually see multi-level and sustainable anti-racist, multi [oppression] change."

Unlike the stories they told about class and gender in which singular, common-sense solutions were dominant ("get a job"; "we fix them up with ... counselling"), when asked to tell a story about race, responses from the participants varied greatly reflecting the existence of a more complex and politicized analysis of race than of class or gender. Rather than identifying a single aspect of racism as the most important or the sole solution, the participants viewed racism and anti-racism as a multi-level struggle over resources, affirming identities, and power.

For example, many participants reveal a sophisticated analysis of how to actually shift power and resources within agencies and the larger society beginning with anti-racist organizational change projects in individual agencies. The participants displayed a keen sense that change needed to take place at all levels of the agencies and in the image that agencies project into the larger community: "hiring, promotion, retention, remuneration, cultural climate, as well as what messages we are giving out to clients about racism and equality long before they ever come through our door." Participants also revealed a sophisticated critique of inclusion practices that failed to redistribute resources or control. For example, one worker was critical of her management for "inviting everyone to sit at the table while giving no one any power." The study participants believed it was necessary for anti-racist initiatives to work in tandem with far-reaching changes in wider society: "change in one agency or one part of society is never going to be enough; we gotta go for the whole enchilada." Many study participants were frustrated about the slowness of anti-racist organizational change projects, but maintained optimism and talked about the lengthy processes required to realize anti-racist goals: "we keep pushing, but people on top want to move slowly and avoid open conflict. Still, at least we're still moving."

Although it is not explicit within the quotes above, the anti-racist formulations of most of the participants included a sense that the organization of work, power, and privilege within agencies and the wider society were constantly shifting relationships that had to be contested in an ongoing way at every level. Interestingly, although not mentioned by most of the participants, this contestation over work, power, and privilege also defines many of the central aspects of class and gender, although it was not present in my participants' narratives on those topics.

Also of central importance, and as I have described elsewhere (Baines, 2002), many of the participants told stories that underscored the importance of understanding racism as multiple racisms that must be dismantled as a multiple rather than as singular phenomena. The changes required in society to disrupt and remove anti-Aboriginal racism will not be identical to those required to address the racism faced by Chinese, African, or Jewish Canadians. All these groups experience distinct forms of racism that rely on unique storylines and denial of particular kinds of resources, affirmation, participation, and justice in Canadian society.

The research participants also spoke of their awareness that, while class and gender struggles had been bureaucratized and depoliticized, "our institutions and systems haven't really had time to figure out how to steal the anti-racist struggle from us" and neutralize it into apolitical, administrative aspects of everyday social work practice. As one social worker put it:

> I'm disturbed by the notion that we can wrap racism up in the next little while and move on. Women certainly do not feel that sexism has been all wrapped up and resolved, although it is difficult to have anyone see it as an issue any more. We can't let this happen to race.

As this quote shows, the participants strategized about how they could expand and exploit the opportunity presented by the slowness in which some institutions adapt to and absorb changes wrought by struggles for social justice.

Finally, reflecting on their more sophisticated, multi-faceted, and analytic understandings of race, more of the informants tied race to gender and class than was seen in discussions of gender or class:

> Somebody who is poor is likely to be a person of colour, and disproportionately the sole supporter of her children. They say that racism doesn't exist, and sexism doesn't exist. A poor Black woman who receives welfare benefits and has two kids is just seen as just natural. It is a way that class issues are both acknowledged and at the same time glossed over and ignored.

Responding to the question "How is or isn't race a part of your work?" the participant above notes that poor people are more likely to be people of colour. Using the female pronoun, the speaker notes that this poor person of colour is likely to be a single parent with complete responsibility for the support of her children. The speaker noted that sexism and racism are central forces organizing the world of the woman in this example, despite the fact that larger society tends to deny the existence of these forces. The participant simultaneously emphasized how class issues are present but made invisible or natural. This same participant noted later in the same discussion that race operates as "kind of a proxy for gender and class, ... letting society off the hook by blaming poor people of colour for their situation" rather than acknowledging how race is wholly embedded in the organization of gender and class. This speaker's analysis revealed that how race issues were often an entry point for the participants to develop more complex understandings of and solutions to multiple oppressions.

WORK INTENSIFICATION AND ALIENATION: STIFLING DYNAMIC UNDERSTANDINGS

I am an insider to the community that I studied and as such I could see my own frustrations and failings in the stories of their struggles to find emancipatory solutions in an environment in which there is never enough time, energy, or resources. I felt compelled to peel back the layers of concepts and practices in order to find a comprehensive explanation for the non-relational descriptors used by my friends, colleagues, and, at times, by myself. Through a back-and-forth comparison between the narratives of workers employed in bureaucratic versus non-bureaucratic settings, I uncovered the following pattern: workers employed in politically engaged social service agencies were much more likely to talk about race, gender, and class in interconnected, relational ways while the more simplified, undynamic formulations of race, gender, and class were more often part of the talk of those employed in bureaucratic, depoliticized settings.

Looking more closely at what the employees of bureaucracies were likely to discuss when questioned about how class was or was not part of their everyday work, I noticed that they described a rapidly changing set of working conditions, such as enormous increases in the intensity (severity of cases and increased requirements for service), pace (much less turnaround time per case), and volume of work including massive increases in caseloads and the rapid expansion of the documentation required for each case. These study participants argued that standardization of assessments, intake, and case notes displaced worker discretion and control over individual cases and larger caseload issues. Standardization of work or breaking work down into ever smaller, repetitive and routine tasks dovetailed with work speed-ups, unpaid overtime, record levels of burnout, and huge increases in workplace stress (see also Baines, 2000).

Standardization also meant that the work itself involved less creative thinking and problem solving on the part of the social workers, while simultaneously being more boring, highly supervised, and easier to speed up. Full-time, skilled, secure employees were consistently being replaced with part-time, casual, contract, and temporary workers who often had lower credentials, pay, and benefits. Finally, and probably most important, standardization, increased workload, and decreased worker control created an environment in which social workers were increasingly restricted in their opportunities to think about or act upon social and political issues in more than an immediate, service-oriented, routine-like way. Workers in the larger, government-run and government-mandated agencies felt these changes more intensely than did their counterparts in the community.

To borrow an insight from one of my participants, being poor (read being part of the class system in the social services) meant that it's hard for clients to think about class in other than a day-to-day survival kind of way, such as "where will I get food to feed the kids tonight, will the landlord kick us out, how will I ever save enough money to buy winter boots?"

Similarly, the increasingly restrictive, overworked, and alienated conditions under which the research participants worked made it difficult for them to think about class, gender, and race in other than a day-to-day survival way. Not coincidentally, their resistance strategies focused on the day-to-day rather than larger-scale actions and analyses of the structures and systems that perpetuate and benefit from injustice and inequality.

The research participants may not have expressed liberatory constructions of race, class, and gender in their talk about their everyday work, but they actively and admirably resisted raced, classed, and gendered forms of oppression at the agency level and in larger society. For example, they bent and stretched rules to get clients everything to which they were entitled, and more. They coached clients on how to appeal and agitate for better services even when it meant that the clients had to lodge complaints against the workers themselves; they refused to document things that might jeopardize clients; they grieved increased workloads; they leaked documents to the media regarding agency cuts to service; they built new services from the ground up; and they organized and attended innumerable actions against cuts to human service funding.

Microresistance, like most of the tactics detailed above, only slows down or temporarily sidetracks right-wing agendas rather than fundamentally reorganizing the systems that generate oppression and exploitation. The conceptual practices of the participants, coupled with narrowing, depoliticizing work content and processes, limited their capacity to take resistance beyond the immediate to more comprehensive and complex solutions. Hence, their way of talking about and understanding oppressions needed to be challenged and further developed. The resistance practices of the research participants may not have fundamentally restructured systems of power, but they continued a left-of-centre tradition of agency-level activism, solidarity with clients, a critique of the system in which they were employed, and space for opposition to larger oppressive relations. As one worker observed, "we may not be building a Brave New World, but we are not unreflectively complicit."

CONCLUSION

The data in this study showed that when class or gender are discussed as separate from each other, it makes it difficult to understand them either on their own or as the continuously contesting and overlapping relations that they are in actuality. At the time of my study, race was a hotly contested topic in struggles for resources, power, and affirming identities, hence my participants formulated this part of the race/class/gender triad in more dynamic and politicized ways. I will refer to this again in a moment.

In contrast to the more sophisticated analyses of race, most of my research participants discussed class as if it were gender and racially neutral. However, since class is actually any group of people's relationship to reproduction and production (Ng, 1993), as well as reproduction's relationship to production and the racial segmentation of production and reproduction, class is entirely saturated with gender and race. The separation of class from race and gender resulted in understandings of both class and gender and, for the reasons noted above to a lesser extent, of race that were stripped of political and analytic content. The de-classed and de-raced understanding of gender also meant that some of the research participants viewed the individual as the target of change efforts through interventions such as counselling rather than change efforts targeting the individual and the larger system simultaneously. Examples of these strategies include the reorganization of paid and unpaid work, aggressive income distribution, the provision of social housing, universal child care, and equitable job training, hiring, and retention, as well as comprehensive political/social campaigns for the eradication of all forms of violence.

Single-strand formulations of gender and class simultaneously limited the ways that they could be understood on their own as well as how they could be seen to interlock with race in uninterrupted but volatile ways. However, reflecting the excitement and possibilities that saturated the widespread social debate on racism and anti-racism that was underway during my study, my participants demonstrated a much more nuanced, multi-level and complex understanding of race as a contested social relationship involving the distribution of power, affirming identities, and resources in society. This meant that it was easier for the participants to analyze race in more sophisticated ways and to combine race with gender and class in many of their narratives. These findings demonstrate the importance of participatory democracy in the form of public policy debates about social injustice, not only because of the progressive policy gains they present but also because these debates expand social and political spaces for critical and innovative thought and action on issues of inequality and oppression.

The non-relational or non-continuous use of gender, class, and sometimes race was not universal among the research participants. Using the stories told by some of the research participants, I showed that it is possible to formulate race, class, and gender in more explicitly dynamic and political ways. The participants' more politicized formulations of class demonstrate the importance of models of race, class, and gender in which each component is conceived of as in perpetual interaction with each other, thus removing the likelihood that any component will be talked about, acted on, or conceptualized in ways that are denuded of power or dynamism. As proposed earlier in this chapter, each component of the race/class/gender triumvirate must be viewed as part of a continuous, interconnected whole that is active in processes of domination and subordination in any given society.

Finally, this chapter argued that the rapidly changing working conditions in the restructured bureaucratic workplaces of many of the research participants made it hard to think about class and gender (and today probably about race) in other than "a day-to-day kind of survival way," which in turn limited the kinds of actions they could undertake to better the lives of their clients and themselves. This chapter does not have sufficient space to permit a discussion of how to redress these challenges. As a beginning offering to this important debate, I suggest that we need to develop, teach, and practise anti-racist, anti-sexist, and class-conscious social work in a way that reflects race, class, and gender as a dynamic, contestatory but seamless whole, and that resonates with the actual, depoliticizing, backlash conditions within which social workers and their clients work and struggle.

REFERENCES

Albert, M., Cagan, L., Chomsky, N., Hahnel, R., King, M., Sargent, L., & Sklar, H. (1986). *Liberating theory.* Boston: South End Press.

Andersen, G.L. (1989). Critical ethnography in education: Origins, current status and new directions. *Review of Educational Research 59*(3), 249–270.

Anderson, M.L. and Collins, P.H. (2001). *Race, class and gender: An anthology.* Belmont, CA: Wadsworth Publishing Company.

Anthias, F., & Yuval Davis, N. (1992). *Racialized boundaries, race, nation, colour, class and the anti-racist struggle.* London: Routledge.

Baines, C., Evans, P.M., & Neysmith, S.M. (1998). *Women's caring: Feminist perspectives on social welfare.* Toronto: Oxford University Press.

Baines, D. (2000). *Resisting restructuring: Deskilling, gender and race in the social services sector.* Research report, McMaster University, Hamilton, Ontario, Canada.

_____. (2002). Story lines in racialized times: Racism and anti-racism in Toronto's social services. *British Journal of Social Work 32*,185–199.

_____. *Losing relationship and expertise in the era of restructuring: Social workers, resistance, race and gender.*

Brown, C. (1994). Feminist postmodernism and the challenge of diversity. In A. Chambon & A. Irving (Eds.), *Essays on postmodernism and social work* (pp. 35–48). Toronto: Canadian Scholars' Press.

Burke, M., & Shields, J. (1999). *The deficit of sustaining employment: Exclusion, polarization and vulnerability in the new Canadian labour market.* Toronto: Ryerson Polytechnic University.

Carniol, B. (1990). Structural social work: Maurice Moreau's challenge to social work practice. *Journal of progressive human services 1* (4), 1–25.

Collins, P.H. (2000). *Black feminist thought: Knowledge, consciousness, and the politics of empowerment*. New York: Routledge.

Dominelli, L. (1988). *Anti-racist social work*. London: Macmillan.

Doyle, R., & Visano, L. (1987). *A time for action! Access to health and social services for members of diverse cultural and racial groups in metropolitan Toronto* (Report 1). Toronto: Social Planning Council of Metropolitan Toronto.

EA Update. (1999). *EA Update 10*(1), 1.

Ehrenreich, B. (1989). *Fear of falling: The inner life of the middle class*. New York: Pantheon Books.

Fraser, N. (1989). *Unruly practice: Power, discourse and gender in contemporary social theory*. Minneapolis: University of Minneapolis Press.

Fraser, N. (1997) *Justice interruptus: Critical reflections on the "postsocialist" condition*. New York and London: Routledge.

Fraser, N., & Gordon, L. (1994). A genealogy of dependency: Tracing a keyword of the U.S. welfare state. *Signs: Journal of Women in Culture and Society 19*(2), 309–336.

Gordon, D.M., Edwards, R., & Reich, M. (1982). *Segmented work, divided workers: The historical transformation of labour in the United States*. New York: Cambridge University Press.

hooks, b. (1988). *Talking back. Thinking feminist. Thinking black*. Toronto: Between the Lines.

Humphries, J., & Rubery, J. (1984). The reconstitution of the supply side of the labour market: The relative autonomy of social reproduction. *Cambridge Journal of Economics 8*, 331–346.

Lather, P. (1986). Issues of validity in openly ideological research: Between a rock and a soft place. *Interchange 17*(4), 63–79.

_____. (1991). *Getting smart: Feminist research and pedagogy with/in the postmodern*. New York: Routledge.

Leonard, P. (1997). *Postmodern welfare: Reconstructing an emancipatory project*. London: Sage.

Lightman, E. (1995). You can lead a horse to water: The case against workfare in Canada. In J. Richards (Ed.), *Helping the poor: A qualified case for "workfare"* (pp. 151–183). Toronto: C.D. Howe Institute.

Lincoln, Y.S., and E.G. Guba (1985). *Naturalis sic inquiry*. London: Sage Publications.

Lorde, A. (1990). Age, race, class, and sex: Women redefining difference. In R. Ferguson, M. Gever, T.T. Minh-ha, & C. West (Eds.), *Out there: Marginalization and contemporary cultures* (pp. 281–288). Cambridge: The MIT Press.

Maguire, P. (1987). *Doing participatory research: A feminist approach*. Amherst, MA: Center for International Education.

Miles, R. (1989). *Racism*. London: Routledge.

Moreau, M.J. (1979). A structural approach to social work practice. *Canadian Journal of Social Work Education 5*(1), 78–94.

Moreau, M.J. (1981). *A comparative study of the preferred helping networks of women and men*. Unpublished doctoral thesis, Columbia University, New York City, New York.

_____. (1989b). *The politics of social work practice: From a clinical to a structural approach*. Montreal: University of Montreal, unpublished manuscript.

_____. (undated). *The politics of social work practice: From a clinical to a structural approach*. Draft paper, Faculty of Social Work, University of Montreal.

Moreau, M J., & Leonard, L. (1989a). *Empowerment through a structural approach to social work*. Ottawa: Carleton University Press.

Moreau, M.J., Frosst, S., Hilywa, M., Leonard, L., & Rowell, M. (1993). *Empowerment II*. Ottawa: Carleton University Press.

Morgan, P. (1981). From battered wife to program client: The state's shaping of social problems. *Kapitalistate 9*, 17–39.

Mullaly, R. (1997). Structural social work: Ideology, theory and practice. Toronto: Oxford University Press.

Neysmith, S.M., & Reitsma-Street, M. (2000). Restructuring and Community Work: The Case of Community Resource Centres for Families in Poor Urban Neighbourhoods. In S.M. Neysmith (Ed.), *Restructuring caring labour: Discourse, state practice, and everyday life* (pp. 142–163). Toronto, Oxford University Press.

Ng, R. (1993). Sexism, racism, Canadian nationalism. In H. Bannerji (Ed.), *Returning the gaze: Essays on racism, feminism and politics* (pp. 182–196). Toronto: Sister Vision Press.

Ontario Public Service Employees Union. (1999a). *Developmental services sector questionnaire—preliminary results*. Toronto: OPSEU.

_____. (1999b). *Child welfare sector questionnaire—preliminary results*. Toronto: OPSEU.

Shragge, E. (1997). Introduction. In E. Shragge (Ed.), *Workfare: Ideology of a new underclass*. Toronto: Garamond Press.

Schwandt, T.A. (1997). *Qualitative inquiry: A dictionary of terms*. London: Sage Publications.

Strauss, A.L., & Corbin, J. (1990). *Basics of qualitative research: Grounded theory procedures and techniques.* Newbury Park: Sage Publications.

Swift, K. (1990). *Manufacturing "Bad Mothers"*. Toronto: University of Toronto Press.

Thomas, J. (1993). *Doing critical ethnography*. Newbury Park: Sage Publications.

Walker, G. (1990). *Family violence and the women's movement: The conceptual practices of power*. Toronto: University of Toronto Press.

Weeks, W. (1994). *Women working together: Lessons from feminist women's services*. Melbourne: Longman Cheshire.

Wineman, S. (1984). *The politics of human services*. Montreal: Black Rose.

Yuval-Davis, N., & Anthias, F.A. (1989). *Woman, nation and state*. Basingstoke: MacMillan Press.

Chapter 4

Structural Social Work as Seen from an Aboriginal Perspective

Cyndy Baskin
School of Social Work
Faculty of Community Services
Ryerson University

This chapter will explore both a structural social work perspective and an Aboriginal approach to helping. It will look at the strengths and challenges of structural social work as it applies to working with Aboriginal communities. Furthermore, it will briefly examine the area of research as connected to these two approaches. The identifying terms "Aboriginal," "First Nations," and "Indigenous" will be used interchangeably to refer to Canada's original peoples.

STRUCTURAL SOCIAL WORK

A definition of structural social work is as follows:

> Structural social work views social problems as arising from a specific societal context—liberal neo-conservative capitalism—rather than from the failings of individuals. The essence of socialist ideology, radical social work, critical theory, and the conflict perspective is that inequality: (1) is a natural, inherent (i.e., structural) part of capitalism; (2) falls along the lines of class, gender, race, sexual orientation, age, ability, and geographical region; (3) excludes these groups from opportunities, meaningful participation in society, and a satisfactory quality of life; and (4) is self-perpetuating. (Mullaly, 1997, p. 133)

Thus, structural social work's primary focus is the recognition that oppression is at the core of social problems. It emphasizes that social work is to be carried out with, or on the behalf of, oppressed people (Mullaly, 1997). This perspective peels away the mythical belief system that if a person works hard enough and is good enough, then he or she can overcome any obstacle in life. In other words, it is a myth that all social problems can be overcome and that all successes in life are achieved through individual merit alone. This is, of course, the myth of equality.

Structural social work is different from other social work models as it focuses on the structures in society (e.g., patriarchy, capitalism, racism) that oppress certain groups of people. Rather than blaming the victim for his or her situation, this approach examines the structures that create barriers to accessing resources, services, and social goods.

Another way in which structural social work is different from other social work models is through consciousness-raising. Mullaly (1997, p. 171) argues, "Much of consciousness-raising occurs in the form of political education whereby structural social workers, in the course of their daily work attempt to educate service users about their own oppression and how to combat it." Structural social workers advocate that educating oppressed people about their oppression helps to empower them. Most important, it stresses that social workers cannot empower people, they can only assist with the empowerment process (Mullaly, 1997). Structural social workers work collaboratively with those who are oppressed to help them have their own voices heard (Ibid.).

Moreover, structural social work does not endorse "power over" relationships when working with clients. Rather, it attempts to work from a "power with" or a shared power application. This is important when working with people who are of Aboriginal descent, a population that has been harmed enough by "power over" relationships. Empowerment, then, can involve structural social workers and Aboriginal peoples working collectively to end oppression through, for example, the support of culture-based agencies and services.

Structural social work includes a historical analysis. When it comes to oppressed groups of peoples, Mullaly (2002, p. 176) writes: "the loss of culture of these groups involved the erasure of subordinate groups from historical writings and records and/or distortions of their role and place in history." This understanding is critical when viewing the impact of the harmful experiences that oppressed groups have been forced to endure and how this applies to the present day. According to Mullaly (2002, p. 119), "of all the oppressed groups in Canada, First Nations people, by all indicators, suffer most from social inequalities and, therefore, experience the most structural violence." This analysis is directly connected to the destruction caused by the historical colonization of First Nations peoples in Canada. Thus, a structural approach acknowledges that history has an impact on groups of people and that a people's past (e.g., colonization) is linked to their present conditions of oppression.

This understanding of oppression linked to colonialism ties into an Aboriginal view. According to social work educator and activist Ben Carniol (2000, p. 13), "colonialism's bite has had a lasting, especially painful hold on First Nations people. It was official policy for the colonial authorities to systematically destroy the political, economic, and spiritual institutions of Aboriginal communities." The atrocities that were inflicted on Aboriginal peoples are outlined in the report of the 1996 Canadian Royal Commission on Aboriginal Peoples in the section titled, "The Ghosts of History." This report states that "the ghosts take the form of dishonoured treaties, theft of Aboriginal lands, suppression of Aboriginal cultures, abduction of Aboriginal children, impoverishment and disempowerment of Aboriginal peoples" (Government of Canada, Indian and Northern Affairs, 1996, p. 3).

There are many responses that people who belong to an oppressed group can have to oppression. A response that often happens for Aboriginal peoples, as with any oppressed group, is internalized oppression. Pharr (1997) explains internalized oppression as:

> When the victim of the oppression is led to believe the negative views of the oppressor, this phenomenon is called *internalized oppression*. It takes the form of self-hatred which can express itself in depression, despair and self-abuse. It is no surprise therefore, that the incidence of suicide is high … . [Oppressed people] are taught that the problem is with them, not society. Any difference from the norm is seen as a deficiency, as bad. (Pharr, 1997, p. 60)

Mullaly (1997) agrees with the above definition of internalized oppression and adds:

> This internalized oppression, in turn, will cause some oppressed people to act in ways that affirm the dominant group's view of them as inferior and, consequently, will lead to a process of inferiorized persons reproducing their own oppression. Through a process of cultural and ideological

hegemony many oppressed people believe that if they cannot make it in our society, if they are experiencing problems, then it is their own fault because they are unable to take advantage of the opportunities the dominant group says are available to everyone. (Mullaly, 1997, p. 151)

Aboriginal peoples are particularly vulnerable to internalized oppression in Canadian society. There is a constant negative presentation in society, through advertising and the media, lack of representation, and false and degrading images that inferiorize First Nations peoples. Furthermore, mainstream institutions leave no room or respect for the expression of authentic Aboriginal values or beliefs. This has a destructive and overwhelming impact on First Nations peoples since they are showered with negative beliefs, stereotypes, and images of themselves that arise from Eurocentric dominant culture.

This internalized oppression is articulated by Aboriginal educators Lauri Gilchrist and Kathy Absolon, who contend that the personal damage—specifically substance abuse, violence, sexual abuse, poverty, and unemployment that affects all First Nations communities—is a direct result of the colonization and racism that still exists for Aboriginal peoples today (Carniol, 2000). Such an analysis needs to emphasize an additional point, however—the lack of opportunities for members of oppressed groups. The reality is, of course, that opportunities are not available to everyone and are in fact reserved for the dominant group. This dominant group likes to live under the false belief that opportunities are for everyone. Therefore, if members of oppressed groups are not successful, there must be something wrong with them. Thus, the dominant group does not have to take any responsibility for their role in making and keeping the oppressed groups oppressed in order to retain their unearned privileges and power.

AN ABORIGINAL PERSPECTIVE

An Aboriginal perspective centres on two main areas: culture and historical context. Both refer to First Nations' distinct or unique place in Canada. The term "culture-based" incorporates an Aboriginal identity, holistic world view and values. Although there is great diversity among Aboriginal nations in how specific practices are carried out, the foundation is consistent in these three areas. Such a perspective is also about a connection to the land, family, and ancestors. It is about original languages and the power that comes from spirituality. It is about a shared oppression as well.

An Aboriginal perspective believes in and practises a holistic approach. It stresses that healing has to take place on all levels for an individual: emotional, psychological, physical, and spiritual. A holistic approach looks at the interconnectedness of people's lives, which include the individual, the family, and the community. Also, an integral aspect of a holistic approach is the concept of balance. Counselors Avalos, Arger, Levesque, and Pike (1997, p. 17) explain that, "Native cultural and traditional healing practices serve to restore balance to individuals by healing all aspects of the self." Healing is a prominent component of an Aboriginal perspective because it is through healing that First Nations are able to recover, regroup, and restrengthen from the long-standing wounds of colonization, assimilation, and current forms of oppression.

Another major aspect of an Aboriginal perspective is cultural values. These values clearly conflict with the values of mainstream dominant society. For example, First Nations culture is based on *co-operation*, rather than *competition*. First Nations peoples emphasize *giving*, which differs from mainstream culture where the emphasis is on *saving* and *acquiring*. Aboriginal culture focuses on the *group* and *clan*, whereas dominant society favours *individualism*. There is a great deal of respect given to *Elders and children* in First Nations culture, *but not so in mainstream society*.

First Nations peoples, as mentioned earlier, value the group and the clan. Marlene Echohawk (1997, p. 66), a First Nations counselor, writes about the importance of the clan. Using the example of the death of a loved one, she explains: "The profound grief related [to the] loss of a loved one is made somewhat easier because the entire community comes together to mourn the loss and support." The community is important in Aboriginal culture, particularly in times of pain. The group comes together and supports the grieving member. First Nations culture has recognized the importance of support systems for thousands of years, and it is only recently that non-Aboriginal people have begun to realize the great value of such systems in the helping professions.

An additional crucial element of an Aboriginal perspective is its relationship focus. It is important for a First Nations person to have a relationship with someone before he or she develops trust in that person and is able to confide in him or her. A First Nations person will not ask intrusive questions of others as so often happens within mainstream helping professions. They see that a relationship needs to be established before a dialogue can begin. There is an emphasis on taking the necessary time to develop relationships, which conflicts with the fast, task-oriented focus of dominant society.

As these teachings about traditional practices and cultural values become more widely known among Aboriginal service providers, this in turn shapes their practice. Communities determine their cultural models and how they will be integrated into community action. Community members must be able to examine and discuss how a cultural model works toward a process of decolonization. How does the model educate and help people out of their present condition? How does it validate and enable all the voices of the community to be heard? It is important to keep in mind, however, that culture is not static. It is constantly changing and Aboriginal communities require new information and education because revitalizing culture alone will not release us from the colonial masters.

All of these components are necessary for appropriate interventions with Aboriginal peoples and yet they conflict with the values of mainstream culture. Conventional social work, which is most widely practised with Aboriginal peoples and other oppressed groups, is a product of dominant society. It is limited by Eurocentric assumptions and values. Historically, the profession of social work has acted as an agent of social control and, therefore, of the oppression of Aboriginal peoples. A well-documented example of this is the child welfare system, which has removed thousands of First Nations children from their families and communities (Government of Canada, Indian and Northern Affairs, 1996). Despite its differences from conventional social work, structural social work too originates out of mainstream society.

An Aboriginal perspective challenges what non-Aboriginal people are taught about Aboriginal issues. It cannot support the forgetting of past injustices and their implications for the present. The continuing injustices and inequality that afflict Aboriginal peoples in this country are overwhelming. There is no way that the resistance of First Nations peoples alone can end the oppression. Non-Aboriginal people have a role as allies in accomplishing change. Recognizing the legacy of injustice and its implications for the present and the future is a crucial first step in this change process.

Because of the huge role it plays in the lives of Aboriginal peoples, the profession of social work must be a part of this change process. Schools of social work education are powerful institutions and play a particularly important role in reproducing values and knowledge. The choice of subject matter cannot be neutral. Whose history and perspective is taught and whose ignored? Which groups are included and which are left out of the reading list or text? From whose point of view is the past and present examined? Which theories are emphasized and which are not?

It is not enough to replace stereotyped representations of Aboriginal peoples with positive and diverse representations. If the goal is to change the power relations that support injustice, then instructors and students need to explore 500 years of oppression, unequal relations, and what sustains those unequal relations. If students are to understand the destruction caused by European colonization, then their investigation must extend to political and economic practices of Aboriginal peoples before contact. Aboriginal subject matter needs to be included in all areas of the curriculum. This includes pre- and post-contact periods and an examination of the relationship between Aboriginal peoples and other Canadians today.

If social work students learn that what happened to Aboriginal peoples a long time ago is, of course, wrong and sad, but today everyone is equal and should be treated the same in the name of equality, then Aboriginal history and culture vanish. So too does the need for change.

Although it is crucial to stress the uniqueness of oppression toward Aboriginal peoples because of the geography and history of Canada, it is also important to make linkages to other forms of oppression as well. Once again, a recognition of the schools of social work as agents of social change is needed and education must be relevant to students' interests and to diverse community needs. Students need to become aware of their own culture, identity, and values and to learn about and come to respect the culture, identity, and values of others. They must be taught to examine their own social locations, privileges, and oppression and how these will influence their work with First Nations peoples.

Anti-oppression education is meant to eliminate institutional and individual barriers to equity. It is intended to create a climate in the classroom where stereotypes and racist ideas can be exposed and argued out; where sources of information can be examined; where students can be equipped to look critically at the accuracy of the information they receive; where alternative and missing information can be provided and where the historical and current reasons for the continued unequal social status of different groupings can be explored (Fletcher, 2000). Therein lies the educational tie between an Aboriginal perspective and other anti-oppression areas.

An Aboriginal perspective and its connection to other forms of anti-oppression work contributes to the advancement of schools of social works' missions and values by inviting them to move forward in this area. It asks schools to make the curriculum more relevant and relational for Aboriginal students. It asks schools to make the curriculum more relevant for non-Aboriginal students so they can better understand and learn the skills necessary to work with Aboriginal families and communities.

In raising consciousness about the roots of Aboriginal peoples' oppression, which is colonization by Eurocentrism, schools of social work can provide leadership in the decolonization process, which targets students' ongoing mis-education about Aboriginal issues. This needs to be expressed through an Aboriginal perspective represented by Aboriginal voices, through curriculum content that includes Aboriginal writers, artists, and storytellers, and via the teaching about culturally appropriate assessment tools. It is also about the possibilities regarding what Aboriginal culture can contribute to social work knowledge. Some examples of such a contribution include the work that First Nations have accomplished in the areas of identity and the appropriate use of self-disclosure, restorative justice, holistic approaches, more equality in client-social worker relationships, the emphasis on the connection to family and community within child welfare, healing for everyone affected by family violence, circles or groups rather than a predominantly individual focus, and help for the helpers.

An Aboriginal perspective with an anti-oppression framework leads to collaborative initiatives with communities as well. It stresses how non-Aboriginal people cannot tell Aboriginal communities how to do social work. The decolonization process centres on initiatives with Aboriginal communities that are about first voice and empowerment; that are service-user led and community-needs driven; that have decision making based on consensus and an emphasis on process and relationship.

There are alternative and better ways of approaching social work with Aboriginal communities than what has occurred thus far. Communities must be asked what they need from schools of social work. What skills developed by students would be beneficial? How can more Aboriginal students be brought into the schools and supported to complete the programs? How can schools assist communities in their efforts in culture-based participatory research? How can structural social work approaches be integrated into student placements in Aboriginal agencies and communities?

COMPARISON OF STRUCTURAL SOCIAL WORK AND AN ABORIGINAL PERSPECTIVE

Although structural social work includes a historical perspective in its analysis of oppression (e.g., the explanation of the detrimental impact of colonization on Aboriginal peoples) in Canadian-First Nations relations, it lacks any discussion of culture, values, and spirituality. This is problematic from an Aboriginal perspective as all First Nations writers stress the significance of a cultural and spiritual foundation in working with communities. Aboriginal writer and counselor Diane Hill (1995, p. 32) reports on this important element in Aboriginal culture: "All Aboriginal cultures derive their understanding of life and how it is to be lived from a spiritual base. Thus, it follows that many of the teaching and learning activities which occur in Aboriginal societies are structured on a spiritual consciousness." Echohawk (1997, p. 66) adds, "Indigenous clients must be allowed to grieve and talk about their feelings of historical trauma, alienation, and poor sense of identity. Acceptance of their spiritual practices must be encouraged and viewed as high priority."

As Avalos et al. (1997) point out, traditional First Nations healing is different from most mainstream therapeutic practices:

> Mainstream society, in the past, has had a longstanding tradition of addressing the physical, emotional, mental, sexual and social aspects of the self in limited combinations or in isolation; very few attempts have been made to provide healing to the spiritual being and there is very little understanding of the individual's social and cultural experience. (Avalos et al., p. 17)

This important healing element in First Nations culture—spirituality—is omitted in mainstream models of helping. Few attempts have been made by the dominant culture to integrate spirituality into the helping professions. In fact, this is a component that often appears to be deliberately avoided in the area. With regard to spirituality, structural social work is no different from conventional social work. This is where it is challenging because it does not allow for this important cultural aspect that is so significant to First Nations communities. Structural social work is a Western perspective and Western culture strongly believes that spirituality should be contained within the realm of religious institutions (Hill, 1995). While structural social work is anti-oppressive, it is not a holistic approach and, therefore, is not an inclusive model for interventions with Aboriginal communities.

Another further question arises, however: would it be appropriate and acceptable for structural social work to incorporate elements of Aboriginal culture and spirituality or would this be considered appropriation (e.g., the taking of First Nations practices without permission), which is another form of oppression?

Another major component of anti-oppression work with First Nations communities is a decolonization process. Decolonization involves attempts to counter the effects of colonization and to reclaim a sense of positive identity. Reclaiming identity is about returning to traditional values and learning about First Nations culture. It involves First Nations peoples having control over their own health and social services.

Decolonization is also about education: the education of both Aboriginal and non-Aboriginal people about the authentic history of the original peoples from a First Nations perspective. This can happen in a classroom through, for example, an instructor who is of Aboriginal background teaching a course on First Nations issues to Aboriginal and non-Aboriginal students. This can also happen through the media, which is a powerful teaching tool, with Aboriginal peoples providing input into movies, television, and news coverage that involves them. Most significantly, decolonization is about First Nations self-government.

A decolonization process must, of course, uncover the roots of oppression and dismantle the institutions that continue to oppress First Nations peoples. Absolon and Herbert (1997) critically argue that:

> Structural analysis provides a way of examining how structures and institutions in Canadian society promote and perpetuate oppression. For example, rather than identifying individuals as unmotivated and lazy, a structural analysis of poverty in many First Nations communities reveals the lack of access to educational, social, and political opportunities for First Nations peoples and identifies the institutional omission in our culture. (Absolon & Herbert, 1997, p. 209)

Many Aboriginal leaders agree with this analysis. They reject the label of Aboriginal peoples as a "social problem." They contend that poverty is not responsible for Aboriginal marginalization in Canadian society. Rather, powerlessness as associated with colonization and the denial of Aboriginal rights is the source (Fleras & Elliott, 1999).

In terms of defining who is privileged in Western society, a structuralist social work perspective endorses that a social order is clearly set up and functions to benefit mainly White affluent males, while wielding power over people from other social groups. Such groups include women, visible minorities, gays and lesbians, the poor, and disabled people (Wachholz & Mullaly, 1997). Although this model clearly advocates for a change in power relationships, it makes no specific reference to a decolonization process.

Despite the interconnectedness, it must be emphasized that the oppression that has been experienced by First Nations peoples is different and unique from other oppressed groups. As community development worker and educator Anne Bishop (1994, p. 63) asserts, "the tendency of many people to throw the struggle of Aboriginal people in with all other human rights disregards the unique nature of Aboriginal rights … ." The struggles of First Nations peoples differ because much of the oppression is the result of colonization in Canada. All Canadians, but in particular the privileged sector of society, benefit from the stolen land, exploitation of resources, and violation of treaties.

Furthermore, the oppression of First Nations peoples exists to feed White privilege—material, political, social, and personal benefits are at the expense of those Aboriginal peoples living with little political, social, or personal power. White society—Westernism—did not rise to prominence because of its inherent superiority. Its success was built on the backs of Indigenous peoples (Graveline, 1998).

RESEARCH

When research focuses on First Nations peoples, it needs to be conducted from the perspective of First Nations peoples. As Henry, Tator, Mattis, and Rees (1995, p. 52) wrote, "Everyday racism must be studied from the perspective of the victims who experience it in looks, gestures, and forms of speech. Part of the problem may be that most researchers are White and have not themselves experienced these daily slights." This is, of course, accurate. However, the racism and oppression that First Nations peoples have endured and continue to endure goes far deeper than "daily slights."

In writing about the area of research, Aboriginal educator Lauri Gilchrist (1997) reports:

> The fact that much research does not confront ideologies of oppression prevents the application to research results of critical knowledge regarding traditional culture, colonial history and racist structure. This results in research, which does not use appropriate concepts as variables and defines one culture using the cultural beliefs of another. (Gilchrist, 1997, p. 76)

Gilchrist (1997) endorses that Aboriginal peoples need to be in control of Aboriginal research and points out that even though there is a wealth of research *on* Indigenous peoples in Canada, very little of it has been conducted *by* them. It seems as though both First Nations and non-Aboriginal people alike are so accustomed to accepting the opinions, studies, and research on Aboriginal peoples by non-Aboriginal people that not many question this practice. Usually the work of non-Aboriginal writers is seen as more valid somehow than the words of First Nations peoples. Why is it so acceptable to read about the lives of Indigenous peoples through the eyes of non-Aboriginal people?

In reviewing research conducted by non-Aboriginal researchers, it is blatantly evident that something is missing. The something missing is an Aboriginal perspective or any representation of Aboriginal voices. Note the following from non-Aboriginal researchers Frideres and Gadacz (2001, p. 17): "the strand that links Aboriginal peoples is the general sense of betrayal and injustice that they believe has been meted out over the past century." Although this is accurate, it covers only one area that ties First Nations peoples together. It makes no reference to the strong bonds of culture, spirituality, and identity that are at the basis of Aboriginal solidarity. Moreover, we do not merely believe that injustices have occurred—rather, centuries of history are evidence of such.

Even more problematic is this quote from Frideres and Gadacz (2001, p. 312): "today Aboriginal people are developing their sense of history and group identification. Ironically, it has been the White-educated Aboriginal intelligentsia that has been instrumental in discovering, packaging, and promoting this sense of history and unification." This statement is not only inaccurate, it is also offensive. First, "Aboriginal intelligentsia" have not "discovered" the history of First Nations peoples any more than Columbus "discovered" America. Aboriginal history is passed down from one generation to the next by the Elders of the communities. Second, the use of the writers' term "packaging and promoting" makes it sound as though some Aboriginal peoples are putting together and selling some idea of history. Certainly, Aboriginal peoples are coming together through their common history and identity. However, this is occurring due to the efforts of Aboriginal peoples reclaiming their culture.

At present, there are few Aboriginal researchers. The research that is being conducted differs from mainstream research because an Aboriginal perspective favours oral tradition over the written word as a way of transmitting knowledge (McCormick, 1995). Also, written accounts are not considered complete and accurate accounts by many First Nations peoples and scholars (McCormick, 1995). Métis/Cree writer Kim Anderson (2000) agrees with these statements. She writes:

> Indigenous stories are significant because they are anchors of resistance. They are also ways of preserving the language and the power and meaningfulness of the spoken word. Our stories are an unadulterated version of our history and creation. They are critical for Native people who seek a sense of identity founded within Native culture. (Anderson, 2000, p. 131)

Anderson (2000) views storytelling as an act of resistance on the part of First Nations peoples. She writes about it as strongly connected to identity formation in a four-step process involving:

- resisting negative definitions of being
- reclaiming Aboriginal tradition
- constructing a positive identity by translating tradition into the contemporary context
- acting on that identity in a way that nourishes the overall well-being of our communities (Anderson, 2000, p. 15)

The fact that the perceptions of valid research about Aboriginal peoples is decided upon by mainstream society (e.g., academia) is in itself problematic because it is oppressive. Decolonization means an acknowledgement and acceptance of Aboriginal oral tradition as a valid research methodology. Perhaps structural social work holds the possibility of endorsing these necessary changes to the perceptions of valid research.

At the core of the research issue is the lack of professionally trained Aboriginal researchers. However, this situation too is problematic. Having the "right credentials" to conduct research is once again determined by dominant culture. Forcing First Nations peoples to attend mainstream academic institutions to acquire the skills that are dictated by mainstream culture as necessary to conduct research in their own communities is another form of assimilation. It means that First Nations peoples have to conform to the ideology of the status quo, which is oppressive.

CONCLUSION

This chapter focused on an examination of a structural social work approach and an Aboriginal perspective. This comparison arrived at the conclusion that structural social work can be effective when working with First Nations peoples as long as it is applied in conjunction with an Aboriginal perspective. It cannot stand alone as it is not capable of addressing the cultural and spiritual needs of Aboriginal peoples. Perhaps further research could explore the possibility of combining the two approaches to arrive at a unique model of intervention and research methodology. Whether this were to occur or not, the priority must be one of focusing on an Aboriginal research agenda with Aboriginal methodologies. Aboriginal researchers do not need to be trained in mainstream approaches to conduct research in their communities. Rather, the worlds of academia and research in social work need to move over so that Aboriginal approaches can stand beside them. Then again, perhaps we need to Aboriginalize social work!

REFERENCES

Absolon, K., & Herbert, E. (1997). Community action as a practice of freedom: A First Nations perspective. In B. Wharf & M. Clague (Eds.), *Community organizing: Canadian experiences* (pp. 205–227). Toronto: Oxford University Press.

Anderson, K. (2000). *A recognition of being: Reconstructing Native womanhood.* Toronto: Second Story Press.

Avalos, C., Arger, L., Levesque, E., & Pike, R. (1997). Mooka'Am (a new dawn). *Native Social Work Journal 1*(1), 11–24.

Bishop, A. (1994). *Becoming an ally: Breaking the cycle of oppression.* Halifax: Fernwood Publishing.

Carniol, B. (2000). *Case critical: Challenging social services in Canada.* Toronto: Between the Lines.

Echohawk, M. (1997). Suicide: The scourge of Native American people. *Suicide & Life Threatening Behavior 27*(1), 60–67.

Fleras, A., & Elliott, J.L. (1999). *Unequal relations: An introduction to race, ethnic, and Aboriginal dynamics in Canada.* Scarborough: Prentice Hall Allyn & Bacon Canada.

Fletcher, S.D. (2000). Molded images: First Nations people, representation and the Ontario school curriculum. In T. Goldstein & D. Selby (Eds.), *Weaving connections: Educating for peace, social and environmental justice* (pp. 342–364). Toronto: Sumach Press.

Frideres, J.S., & Gadacz, R.R. (2001). *Aboriginal peoples in Canada: Contemporary conflicts.* Toronto: Pearson Education Canada Inc.

Gilchrist, L. (1997). Aboriginal communities and social science research: Voyeurism in transition. *Native Social Work Journal 1*(1), 69–85.

Government of Canada, Indian and Northern Affairs. (1996). Highlights from the report of the Royal Commission on Aboriginal People (people to people, nation to nation). Ottawa. <www.ainc-inac.gc.ca/ch/rcap/rpt/index_e.htm>

Graveline, F.J. (1998). *Circleworks: Transforming Eurocentric consciousness.* Halifax: Fernwood Publishing.

Henry, F., Tator, C., Mattis, W., & Rees, T. (1995). *The colour of democracy: Racism in Canadian society.* Toronto: Harcourt, Brace & Co.

Hill, D. (1995). *Aboriginal access to post secondary education: Prior learning assessment and its use within Aboriginal programs of learning.* Toronto: First Nations Technical Institute.

McCormick, R. (1995). The facilitation of healing for the First Nations people in British Columbia. *Canadian Journal of Native Education 21*(2), 251–319.

Mullaly, B. (1997). *Structural social work.* Toronto, Oxford University Press.

_____. (2002). *Challenging oppression: A critical social work approach.* Don Mills: Oxford University Press.

Pharr, S. (1997). *Homophobia, a weapon of sexism*. Berkeley, California: Chardon Press (pp. 41–46).

Wachholz, S., & Mullaly, B. (1997). Human caring: Toward a research model for structural social work. *Canadian Social Work Review 14*(1), 23–42.

Chapter 5

Cultural Diversity in Social Work Practice: Where Are We Now and What Are the Challenges in Addressing Issues of Justice and Oppression?

Connie H. Nelson and Dennis H. McPherson
Department of Social Work
Lakehead University

If a person falls freely, he won't feel his own weight.
—Albert Einstein, 1907

The unprecedented terrorist attack in New York on September 11, 2001, has left the world with an unmistakable message—there are serious repercussions for ignoring others' perceptions of injustice and oppression. This pattern of dominance and monolithic perspective seems to have been set centuries ago. According to Muldoon (2002), the confluence in the eleventh century of Christian ideals, Aristotelian notions of civilization, and law into a cohesive vision may have had a decided impact on patterns of globalization that sustain injustice and oppression. Lukacs (2002) adds insight by his analysis as to how, until about 500 years ago, "Christianity," "European," and "White" were synonymous terms. European imperialism expanded by globalizing its institutions, customs, industries, forms of expression, and laws across all continents. Likewise, Day (2000, p. 70) documents the persistent continuity of ideas of hierarchical differentiation based on gradations of human worthiness from just below the gods to barbarism and the assignment "to each people a set of timeless characteristics assumed to be representative of all who were 'part' of that people .... Through the early Christian and medieval theologians there was a clear line of descent from Herodotus to the fifteenth- and sixteenth-century Explorers, who, steeped in the European discourse on diversity, quite 'naturally' applied the Old definitions and methods in the New World."

Again, in more recent history, White and Jacoby (1946) provided this perspective on the consequences of the Western world, blithely misreading the meaning of events in World War II as it played out in Asia:

> This victory ... one achieved by an overwhelming weight of metal, guns, and superior technique. ... We had been threatened out of the darkness of the Orient; we had recognized the threat as something indescribably malevolent and had fashioned a steamroller that crushed it to extinction. But we had never stopped to inquire from what sources the threat had been generated. ... Throughout that continent men are still trying to free themselves from their past of hunger and suffering. (White & Jacoby, 1946, pp. xii–xv)

The nature and longevity of this ideology of hierarchical differentiation, categorization by representation, and objectivity in relationships means that hegemonic practices that perpetuate conditions of injustice and oppression that constrain, restrict, and assimilate identity are deep-rooted and well-established in the Western world to such an extent that they are viewed as the norm by which all other actions, institutions, and behaviours are judged. Since the scientific revolution of the seventeenth century, this ideology has been integrated into the positivist theoretical paradigm where reality is viewed as singular and absolute; is separate from any human-manipulated environmental influences; and is characterized by controlled predictability.

The argument put forward in this chapter is that social work practice primarily operates from a positivist paradigm that embraces differentiation, categorization, and objectivity; therefore, the current approach to cultural diversity in social work practice is oppressive and curtails efforts to address social injustice where one's identity would be allowed to flourish in a milieu of respect, openness, and honesty. This analysis is based on a sample of twelve textbooks purposively selected on the criteria of recent publication by mainstream publishing companies and thus easily accessible to post-secondary instructors of diversity courses.

DIFFERENCE

Is it understanding difference or similarity that facilitates social work practice? Research into culturally competent social work and textbooks encourage the idea that social work must understand cultural difference in order to practise (Weaver, 1999). Social work encourages compartmentalizing cultures into distinct differences that are presented as a knowledge base essential for a social worker to know in order to effectively communicate with a person from each identified culture. Furthermore, there is the assumption that not recognizing difference is actually problematic. "Racial difference of the worker and African American client can be problematic if not recognized" (Harper & Lantz, 1996, pp. 42–43). Difference appears to be given priority even though the next sentence encourages simultaneous recognition of differences and "genuine caring and respect for human sameness."

What is evident here is that culture is being viewed from within a framework of positivism. There must be a singular and absolute truth "out there" about culture that works in all cases if social work can just find it. In social work's persistent quest to find these cultural nuggets of truth, ideas have been constructed about universal characteristics of each recognized cultural group. The modernity concept of humanist universalism has merely been transferred into trying to capture universalism within diversity. And there is also the assumption of cultural stability through controlled predictability and "frozen identities" (Fine, 1994). Social work has created monolithic universalism within the hierarchical categories of culture and ethnicity. Viewing culture from a monolithic approach creates barriers and misunderstandings. For example, Devore and Schlesinger (1999, p. 24) have a table in their textbook that ranks ethnicity in this descending order: "English Origin People, Other White European People and some Latinos People, Jewish People, Asian People, African-American People, Native American People and Puerto Rican People and Mexican American People." Furthermore, hierarchical differentiation labels are placed on social work practice techniques when the following terms are explained (assumption of ascending from most devastating to most effective): cultural destructiveness, cultural incapacity, cultural blindness, cultural precompetence, cultural competence, and cultural proficiency (Appleby, Colon, & Hamilton, 2001). From this outlook, reinforced by diversity textbooks, a social worker can ascribe what is valued to what is seen. Broad assumptions, such as "Practice with Native Americans clearly falls within the social work mandate to serve vulnerable and oppressed clients," are stated (Weaver, 1999, p. 219).

Isajiw (1999) explains in detail how the emphasis on difference leads to reinforcing the boundaries, which results in increasing the distance between groups. The authors' teaching experiences substantiate this perspective in that many students enter courses on cultural diversity with the assumption that the outcome is a series of "Brownie badges" for each culture that they successfully study. They come with the assumption that if they do not study a particular culture, they should not take clients from that culture.

Thus, the students aspire to official endorsement of cultures in which they have received training. This model demonstrates that social work does indeed view itself as a profession that practises from the normalized White perspective.

Culture appears to have become the organizing principle for social workers to be ethnically sensitive and aware. Yet, "knowledge and the multiple truths of life are relational rather than representational" (Irving & Young, 2002, p. 24). Social work is missing the point when the emphasis is placed on knowing different cultures as an entry ticket to competent practice. Rather, it is in the interface of cultures where the practices of one group may prolong injustices and oppression for another. The emphasis on diversity and social work practice should reflect on how the dominant White, European-based culture suppresses and controls instead of focusing on learning the specifics of cultural differences. Yet, the profession of social work finds it difficult to focus on its role in the maintenance of social injustice and oppression. "It seems likely then that when white participants attempt to deflect discussion about their whiteness or refuse to make their own racial selves or identities explicit, they are attempting to hide their knowledge of their location and the ways in which they socially, culturally and politically produce relations of domination" (James, 1999, p. 44).

Day (2000) puts forth a strong argument that Canada created the state policy of multiculturalism in order to manage and control diversity. Something had to be done to solve the problem of the French, the immigrant, and the Indian, and this became multiculturalism. Through the Bilingual and Biculturalism Act, Canada disentangled language from culture and thus opened itself to official recognition of differences.[1] The authors argue that there is a parallel here with the approach that social work has taken to diversity. As Canada saw difference as threatening its national identity and addressed the issue through controlling the choices of who are recognized as "in" and who remain "problematic others," so social work has addressed threats to its professional identity by controlling the approach to diversity in such a way as to protect the essence of traditional social work practice. Gaining cultural knowledge allows for control. Thus, the impacts of managing cultural diversity for social work are predictability, stability, and continuity for the social worker within familiar patterns of social work practice.

However, Canada cannot address the "Indian Problem" in Canada within the framework of multiculturalism. Bannerji (2000, p. 96) puts it this way, "The issue of the First Nations—their land claims, languages and cultures—provides another dimension entirely, so violent and deep that the state of Canada dare not even name it in the placid language of multiculturalism." In a similar vein, the social work profession has dealt with Native issues by eliminating Native clientele from mainstream agencies through the promotion of culturally specific agencies. For example, the 1984 Ontario Child and Family Services Act provided an opportunity for Indian and Native communities to develop programs that would be based on Native customary care of children. The concept of neglect that was predominant in the pre-1984 child welfare legislation, which had allowed for the "sixties scoop" of Native children, where social workers removed children from their families and Indian reserve communities on the pretense of saving them from poverty, was removed. The 1984 act was heralded as a major breakthrough because of its strong emphasis on families and the removal of neglect as justification for the discretionary apprehensions carried out by well-meaning social workers. Within a decade, all of the First Nations programs that emerged as a result of the revised legislation, such as Dilico, Weechi-it-te-win, and Tikanagan, had succumbed to incorporation as Children Aid Societies (CAS) under the direction of the provincial minister and mandated to provide protective services under the Child and Family Services Act. In operation, their main interest appears to be access to funding using the auspices of child welfare to encourage economic development.

With the newly revised amendment of 2000 to the Child and Family Services Act of 1999, the concept of *neglect* emerges again in the name of children in need of protection. Thus, once again children can be "scooped" from their homes. For example "when the CAS is involved with a family because of concerns about the safety of the children, it will make a plan (either with or without the family's co-operation) detailing what must happen before it will end its involvement. For instance, if the CAS is concerned *because the family does not have proper housing, the plan of service will require that housing be found*" [emphasis added] (METRAC & OWJN, 2002). Such a plan is nearly impossible to achieve when applied in the setting of an Indian reserve where housing is at a premium and the waiting lists for any available housing are long. In addition, there are new statutes of limitations for permanent removal of a child from the family: "Once children under six have been in the care of the CAS for a total of 12 months—whether all at once or cumulatively—they will be made Crown Wards and placed for adoption" (METRAC & OWJN, 2002). Thus, a process that started out to provide cultural-specific services has ended up with only one thing changed—now Native workers scoop their own children. Day concludes a similar observation on Canada's multiculturalism policy: "I would suggest that integration within multiculturalism in a bilingual framework is best seen as a creative reproduction of the colonial method of strategic simulation of assimilation to the Other, and not as an overcoming or break with this past" (Day, 2000, p. 197).

CATEGORIZATION

The diversity textbooks typically use race to categorize culture even though it is stated that race is an arbitrary, socially constructed term that is problematic and deeply affects how people form their identity (Devore & Schlesinger, 1999; Green, 1982; Harper & Lantz, 1996; James, 1999). Cultural identity is primarily viewed through the lenses of race and ethnicity even though such characteristics as gender, age, ability, sexual orientation, education, citizenship, and political affiliation are deemed to have significant impacts on one's expression of identity. However, the comfort and security that can be had from placing the unknown "them" into categories prevails as the modus operandi when social work addresses diversity. This confounding categorization is explained well by Day (2000):

> Having moved through humanity and civilization, to race, culture, and ethnicity, differentiation within Canadian multiculturalism as state policy is accomplished with the help of yet another category: ethno cultural origin. ... A strange, frustrating, but definitely working circularity occurs here: ethnic origin is defined as dependent upon cultural, national, and racial origin, and race is said to depend upon ethnic origin! Of course, this "confusion" is very informative, as it provides evidence of the arbitrary nature of these categories. (Day, 2000, pp. 189–190)

The textbooks that were examined had a very similar structure of separate chapters to categorize culture. Fairly consistent was a chapter each on Natives, Asians, Latinos, and Blacks (Appleby et al., 2001; Harper & Lantz, 1996; Morales & Sheafor, 2002). A quick look at the following description of the cultural makeup of Afghanistan as one of many Asian cultures illustrates the superficiality of the attempt to give social workers a knowledge base through a single chapter labelled "Asians":

> Afghan society has always been deeply divided by tribal, linguistic, religious, and regional loyalties, and so it remains today. ... The Pathans are divided into many tribes of varying sizes, of which four predominate. ... The principal Pathan tribes

are again divided into far more important subtribes, and then subdivided into powerful clans, knows as khels. ... North of the snow-capped Hindu Kust are Afghanistan's other main ethnic groups: the elegant, fine-featured Tajiks ... the nomadic, Shia Muslim, Hazara ... Uzbeks of the Northwest. (Margolis, 1999, pp. 10–12)

This approach leads to a pan-view of cultures. Kelley (Postel, 2002) labels this a "zoological" approach to culture with Blacks, Latinos, and Asians in different cages. Furthermore, Appiah views pan-African and Black nationalists movements to identify qualities that are to be shared among all those of African descent as "just as fraudulent as the 19th century European notion of a racial hierarchy with whites at the top" (Postel, 2002, Multiple Worlds section, paragraph 9).

While race is a part of everyone's identity, there is total silence on a discussion of the White race. There are no chapters in any of the textbooks on either Western culture or White culture. White is not deemed to be a category. White is not recognized as a race, ethnicity, and/or culture. Through this omission, White is the invisible, unspoken, and implicit standard by which all the other categories are judged. For example, in the Canadian Association of Schools of Social Work (CASSW) *Board of Accreditation Manual*, Appendix E, race is defined as "an arbitrary classification of populations conceived in Europe, using actual or assumed biologically determined traits (i.e., skin color and other physical features) to place populations of the world into a hierarchical order, in terms of basic human qualities, with Europeans superior to all others." Is the White race thus too superior to be studied in textbooks?

OBJECTIVITY

The CASSW Code of Ethics states emphatically: "A social worker shall carry out her or his professional duties and obligations with integrity and objectivity." Objectivity is viewed as a key component of being a professional social worker. By upholding the value of objectivity, one is making the assumption of placing distance between the worker and the client. It is assumed that this distance between the worker and the client has an empty space, as if it were a vacuum or a place of nothingness. In fact, this vacuum, this space of nothingness has to do with communication—about who is in control, the nature of the relationship, and what values and norms are of importance and which can be disregarded as either inferior or pathological and therefore of no apparent consequence: "As Rahnema (1990, p. 218) observes: 'Relationship is the opposite of ... superficial relations. It is the mirror in which one can see oneself as one is. And one cannot see oneself that way if one approaches it with a conclusion, an ideology, or with condemnation or justification'" (Healy, 2001, p. 100).

By endorsing an approach to social work practice that encourages a categorized, generic, and objectified approach to diversity, social work remains in control of the impact of cultures on social work practice. Hence, social work continues to control and thus oppress identity. This universal objective approach to diversity causes people to lose touch with the richness of who they are. Differences become pathologies to be dealt with through treatment, and personal prejudice is normalized.

THREE APPROACHES

Presently, the efforts to provide social work with an ethnic-sensitive and culturally competent approach to addressing the needs of a more diverse clientele have created three major responses: the additive approach, the integrative approach, and the expansionary approach.

Additive Approach

Early efforts at including diversity within social work practice focused on activities that were to increase social workers' culture awareness. An agency or social work program identified themselves as addressing cultural diversity if they simply participated in or sponsored cultural festivities (Nelson & McPherson, 2000). Cultural knowledge gained in this manner was largely viewed as an ornamentation to be added on to existing ways of practice. A social worker's knapsack of knowledge simply got a little bigger. It did not require the social worker to modify his or her skills. Typically, these add-on cultural awareness activities were to be done in a milieu of empathy. Facing an ever-increasing diversity of clients, such as First Nations peoples moving to urban areas and the increasingly varied backgrounds of new immigrants to Canada, something had to be done to solve the problem of this diversity in the client base. The response by the profession of social work was to add on cultural awareness activities that focused on "food, fun, and frolic," and included multicultural events typically featuring customary dance and foods, traditional Indian pow-wows, Elder circles, and feasts. These types of activities may provide a safe haven. For example, "some Native people [who] have fled from the anguish of negative stereotypes, from double consciousness or outside-view predicates, by taking refuge in 'strange myths, pseudo-traditions, unusual spiritualism, ecstatic dances and festivals.' But these, of course, are just as much outside-view predicates as the negative stereotypes they were intended to replace" (McPherson & Rabb, 2001, p. 76). At the organizational level, the additive approach has resulted in human service organizations hiring "ethnic" social workers and endorsing the emergence of ethnic-based agencies even in times of severe fiscal restraint when the funding pie for the old and new agencies is the same (Tator, 1996).

All textbooks on cultural diversity include some information that attempts to expand the reader's understanding of the knowledge base for specific cultures. However, the knowledge provided on culture is cursory and lacks an understanding of the depth and complexity of culture. Cultural awareness focuses on more inconsequential mannerisms like the way one says hello or whether the client's eyes are focused on the social worker or the floor, rather than simply on human experiences such as love of child, siblings, and parent, anger or forgiveness, loss or happiness. For example, worker knowledge about behaviours such as children not making eye contact with an adult out of respect; confirmations of yes or no in Japanese and Korean meaning the opposite of these expressions in English; and expressions of politeness that may not be in agreement with worker expectations are deemed to be helpful toward a better therapeutic relationship with Asian clients (Appleby et al., p. 141). This type of information is provided about each of the identified cultures throughout the textbooks even though statements such as, "Stereotyping or reliance on culturally devoid psychological explanations is antithetical to cultural awareness" (Green, 1082, p. 47), are also woven throughout the texts.

Textbooks often place more emphasis on facts *about the culture* rather than *the cultures lived*, which is a dynamic, ongoing, and incomplete process: "Cultural patterns of behaviour are not necessarily learned as a complete and unchanging package. Rather, persons are taught cultural patterns selectively, and they are learned selectively" (Isajiw, 1999, p. 19).

Again, there is the assumption of a White, European-based cultural standard. Thus, in the descriptions of each culture, there are assumptions of dichotomies such as less or more of something, tighter or looser, and better or worse. "Such an imperialistic frame of mind can easily result in a practice focus of helping the minority client adjust to the status quo. Practice toward such adjustment can produce attempts by the social worker to 'help' the minority client to 'give up' those aspects of the client's cultural heritage that trigger anxiety in the worker" (Harper & Lantz, 1996, p. 3).

The additive approach of cultural awareness supports Canada's policy, ideology, and practice of multiculturalism; meets the CASSW accreditation standards on diversity in social work training; and binds cultures together as one so that they can be effectively managed and controlled. All of this is done without the social worker having to examine his or her role in the perpetuation of social injustice and oppression. Cultural awareness becomes a mechanism for knowing a culture in order to facilitate adaptation to the dominant society's way of doing things. Knowing facilitates integration and assimilation.

Integrative Approach
Under the integrative approach, attempts are made to fit cultural diversity into ecosystems, empowerment, and strengths practice perspectives. The assumption is made that these practice perspectives will all be more effective with clients from non-White cultures if cultural knowledge is squeezed into each practice perspective. New labelling arises, signifying that cultural knowledge is now going to be integrated into practice. Common terminology includes ethnic-sensitive practice and cultural competency. All of these initiatives are still based on differentiation, categorization, and objectivity within a positivist theoretical perspective.

The focus is on aspects of a culture that aid the social worker in continuing to practise social work as he or she has always done. The thinking goes like this: If the social worker becomes culturally competent, then he or she can build a positive relationship with the client that allows the worker to go past the perceived obstacle of diversity and continue on with the therapeutic relationship. A social worker practising from a culturally sensitive or competent approach begins with a defined knowledge based on the culture of the client. Beginning an assessment from a cultural perspective places a brake on listening. When the assumption is made that the worker is practising from a culturally competent perspective, then the worker has acquired previous knowledge about the client within culture. However, when the worker begins to build a relationship with the client in order to proceed with an assessment and intervention, the worker is processing information from the client through the knowledge that the worker has previously gained about the culture.

In these endorsed and advocated approaches of cultural sensitivity and cultural competency, the underlying assumption seems to be that the focus needs to be on bolstering the skill and knowledge level of the worker about cultures. There appears to be no discussion of the appropriateness of the assessment or intervention techniques themselves. The assumption is made that with cultural knowledge, the social worker can proceed: "With this knowledge, valid assessment and intervention can occur" (Harper & Lantz, 1996, p. xii). Thus, no matter how much a social worker learns about another culture, it can have no impact on enhancing practice with non-White clients if the normative values for family functioning, child rearing, psycho-social adjustments, and community well-being continue to be the framework for assessment and intervention—the trademark tools of the social worker. Social work standards thus continue to guide the ethnic encounter of the worker and the *person(s) seeking help.*[2] "Racial stereotyping often skews the initial assessment by the therapist, who may view a client's aggressive or passive behaviour as indicative of a personality disorder when it may in fact be an appropriate response to living in a racist society. There is a constant danger that majority-culture and class-bound values will be used to judge normality and abnormality in clients" (Tator, 1996, p. 163).

The ecological perspective is widely endorsed in social work practice. It is a favoured perspective for working with non-White clients because of its wide applicability and because of its focus on the environmental context. However, this perspective is likewise easily adaptable to managing "the fit" (Germain & Gitterman, 1980).

Similar to the ecological perspective and the empowerment perspective, the texts view the strengths perspective from within the context of first knowing the culture (Appleby et al., 2001; Harper & Lantz, 1996). The strengths-based practice focuses on a worker identifying the client's strengths in relation to the agreed-upon problem focus of the client-worker relationship and subsequently the strengths that can be beneficial toward the success of assessment and intervention. Such a strengths-based approach does nothing to contextually anchor the "*person(s) seeking help*" in an environment of ongoing support. Instead the "strengths-based perspective" floats in an artificial world of client-worker that can only embrace the perpetuation of the current modus operandi.

Expansionary Approach

In the expansionary approach, there are two predominant ways to address issues of diversity. The first is to extend the meaning of cultural diversity to include a wide range of cultures beyond ethnicity and race. These include age, gender, sexual orientation, religion, and disability. The second way is through bicultural techniques. Here the assumption is made that many diverse clients have, to varying degrees, been acculturated into the Western approach to helping, so the worker must be taught how to expand his or her practice to integrate the remnants of the client's culture into a Westernized approach.

A biculturalization of interventions model is proposed for both the assessment and intervention stages of the social work process. [Steps include] developing a framework and approach that integrates the values and techniques of the ethnic culture with the Western interventions; and applying the Western intervention, at the same time explaining to a family client how the techniques reinforce cultural values and support indigenous interventions. (Fong & Furuto, 2001, p. 105)

Again, under this approach there is evidence of the positivist perspective where "absolute truths" about cultures are sought. Social workers scrutinize from their predetermined understanding of the culture what significant alterations have been made by the clients as they are exposed to the White, Western culture. Such a transaction is full of assumptions based on a static knowledge of culture.

In Canada, the expansionary approach does not and cannot apply to Native peoples.

While it accepted the necessity of struggling with the Founding races and the Other ethnic groups, the B&B [Bilingual and Bicultural] Commission managed to lighten its load by shedding the Native peoples of Canada: "We should point out here that the Commission will not examine the question of the Indians and the Eskimos. Our terms of reference contain no allusion to Canada's native populations" (p. xxvi). This act of exclusion highlights a subtle, but important, difference between the status of the Native peoples and the Europeans within the regime of bilingualism and biculturalism. The Other Ethnic Groups were seen as potentially making "contributions" to the "cultural enrichment" of Canada, but the Native peoples were to enjoy their "preserved" cultures in solitude. For, while the Canadian state was able to consider the possibility of giving off more signs of the French race, and perhaps even displaying a touch of Ukrainian ethnicity, it could not imagine itself, under any circumstances, going Native. (Day, 2000, p. 181)

CONCLUSION

Social work cannot appropriately address diversity from the current practice methods and strategies such as cultural awareness and integration of diversity into ecological, strengths-based, and empowerment approaches to social work based on a positivist paradigm steeped in the techniques of differentiation, categorization, and objectivity. Continuing in the direction of further differentiation, increased fracturing of categories, and objectivity means that social work runs the risk of becoming less useful or even irrelevant. "If we insist that [complex things] must be reducible, all that we do is put ourselves into a box. ... And then, all we've reduced is ourselves" (Cole, 2001). Social work should abort its emphasis on cultural awareness, on culturally sensitive and culturally competent social work practice, and instead theorize diversity in practice by embracing practice that begins from the assumption of seeing people as people. Such an approach, while perhaps seeming simplistic in words and perhaps even thoughts, requires fundamental changes in the evolution of social work practice. Consequently, it is not enough to simply state that advocacy is an important aspect of the fight against social injustice and oppression, or that social work must re-examine its core values and practices to ascertain what is appropriate. There are fundamental issues that social work must address if the profession is to survive in the twenty-first century with any relevance. There is a need for a new paradigm. Cultures, ethnicity, and race are being categorized, managed, and controlled within the rubric of diversity. Either unknown or ignored by its policy-makers, social work is practising in an increasingly diverse milieu that contains a multiplicity of approaches to helping. To retain relevance, the profession of social work needs to change its stance. Instead of having the White, Western positivist approach as the unspoken standard by which all other approaches to helping are judged, approaches to helping need to be based on contextual fluidity within a given situation.

This new practice model of contextual fluidity would be embedded within the theoretical framework of postmodernism, adopting what has been called a polycentric perspective:

> Postmodernism celebrates multiplicity, diversity, contingency, fragmentation, and ruptures and accepts cheerfully that we live in perpetual incompleteness and permanent resolve. Postmodernism promotes the notion of radical pluralism, many ways of knowing and many truths (Irving & Young, 2002, pp. 19–20).
>
> This perspective, this polycentrism, recognizes that we finite human beings can never obtain a God's eye view, a non-perspectival view, of reality, of philosophical truth. Every view is a view from somewhere. Hence it follows that no one philosophical perspective can ever provide an entirely adequate metaphysical system. (McPherson & Rabb, 1993, p. 10)

This model squarely addresses the stated goal of the social work profession to be a helping profession; and helping demands sensitivity to the needs of others based on their personal feelings and understanding, not on object categories put forth by the professional social worker.

Contextual fluidity, as the proposed practice model, has the potential to be "the anti-oppressive" model that social work should be supporting in which people are simply viewed as people and there is mutual benefit in their relationships. *Mutuality is the cornerstone for how people relate to each other. ... Today I help you; tomorrow you may help me. Because I can help today does not give me any permanent right to feel superior or better. We all have things to contribute to the community* (Nelson, McPherson, & Kelley, 1987, p. 67). Helping would occur within the context of the situation. *A given social work method has distinct properties that are energized when used in a certain environmental context. The outcome is determined by the synergy of method and context* (Nelson, Kelley, & McPherson, 1985). Furthermore, interactions would flow between and among people, groups, and communities. Social meaning is fluid, not fixed, stable, and solid: "fluidity; to weave in and through horizontal, interdependent relationships that compose the local community" (Nelson et al., 1987, p. 81). Client identity would then be both fluid and complex and "rooted and particular" (Postel, 2002, p. 129).

Change is not easy and social workers operating within a contextual fluidity practice model would first have to modify their professional vocabulary because of the huge assumptions that are carried in their operational jargon. They would also have to discard all actions of assessment and intervention and instead engage in person-to-person dialogue within a helping relationship. Client(s) is replaced with *person(s) seeking help* and the worker(s) is the person(s) giving help. Workers would suspend objectivity, facilitate participant expertise, and spend time in both observation and participation within *the person(s) seeking help's* community (Green, 1982; Lum, 1999; Nelson et al., 1987). Practice would mean responding to *the person(s) seeking help* from within the context of the culture (Nelson & McPherson, 2000).

The contextual fluidity practice model emphasizes utilization of indigenous approaches to helping and the worth and importance of lay helping activities. And most challenging for the profession of social work— the contextual fluidity practice model—would include ways of helping "that are meaningful to clients and their community but which may on occasions be only incidentally meaningful in terms of agency accountability, agency managers, program evaluators, or professional service standards" (Green,

1982, p. 48). A tall order for a social worker who is increasingly pressed with issues of individual worker accountability, agency liabilities, more confining and overlapping legislation including fire codes, occupational health and safety codes, and legislatively driven service delivery mandates.

The contextual fluidity practice model is based on the following values: *Person(s) seeking help* are experts themselves; needs of all individuals vary according to their unique situation rather than societal-defined ethnicity or culture; facilitation is the only legitimate role for *person(s) giving help* in engaging the *person(s) seeking help* as the expert in perspectives on their culture; culture is not an "absolute truth" but a dynamic state of being that is individually lived; resources are more than the network of community agencies and referral services and include institutions, individuals, and customs embedded within the *person(s) seeking help's* own community (Nelson & McPherson, 2000).

The contextual fluidity practice model requires the social worker to engage in practice that blurs the accepted professional boundaries and focuses on the utilization of resources that are not likely to disappear with changes in government policies, legislated programs, or funding levels for program delivery.

The recent interest in social cohesion reflects government concern with destabilizing societal forces (Canadian Council on Social Development, 2000; Torjman, 2001). The dismantling of the social safety net, the rising economic inequities as a result of the implementation of neo-conservative policies, the lack of strong community networks, the failure of multiculturalism, and the inability to address Aboriginal issues has left the government concerned that there are strong forces in Canadian society attempting to disintegrate the Canadian fabric. The social service agencies' response largely has been to hunker down under low budgets and increased demands for accountability with social workers spending more of their time establishing paper trails than servicing clients. Moreover, the agencies appear to be more than ever occupied in practices that augment the adaptation of clients to existing conditions rather than addressing the structural issues of social injustice and oppression. Nevertheless, social cohesion, like multiculturalism, can never be attained until social work abandons such techniques as culturally competent social work practice in which all approaches—additive, integrative and expansionary—all lead to the same endpoint: the categorization of people served from the singular, dominant, White, Western world view in order to manage and control diversity.

The contextual fluidity practice model does offer the profession of social work an alternative, if only they would take it. Ultimately,

Is it that genius is really nothing more than a matter of seeing as simply as possible, that somewhere in this world the image already exists waiting for the camera, or the profound idea already exists waiting for the camera, or the profound idea already exists waiting for the mind to happen on it? After all, from a falling body Einstein pulled out relativity. (Paterniti, 2000, p. 126)

NOTES

1. Day states it this way: "The dissociation of language and culture enabled the claim that even though two languages were officially Canadian, this did not grant a superior position to the cultures associated with them. Dissociation also allowed the claim that even though a given language might not possess an official state connection, the culture associated with it could still be considered as one of many which were 'Canadian,' through its official recognition" (Day, 2000, p. 196).
2. The authors wish to distinguish between the traditional worker-client relationship based on power and control by using the term "person(s) who seek help." The person(s) include individuals, families, groups, communities, and nations. The term "client" is used in the text when the discussion is about the professional worker-client relationship. *Person(s) who seek help* is used to signal a new approach to social work founded on viewing all as people.

REFERENCES

Appleby, George A., Colon, Edgar, & Hamilton, Julia. (2001). *Diversity, oppression and social functioning: Person-in-environment assessment and intervention.* Toronto: Allyn & Bacon.

Bannerji, Himani. (2000). *The dark side of the nation: Essays on multiculturalism, nationalism and gender.* Toronto: Canadian Scholars' Press Inc.

Canadian Association of Schools of Social Work. (2000). *Board of Accreditation Manual.* Ottawa: Canadian Association of Schools of Social Work.

Canadian Association of Social Workers. (1994, January). *Code of Ethics.* Manitoba Association of Social Workers web site.

Canadian Council on Social Development (Andrew Jackson, Gail Fawcett, Anne Milan, Paul Roberts, Sylvain Schetagne, Katherine Scott, Spy Tsoukalas). (2000). *Social cohesion in Canada: Possible indicators: Highlights.* Reference: SRA-542, prepared for Social Cohesion Network, Department of Canadian Heritage, Department of Justice. <http://www.ccsd.ca/pubs/2001/si/sra-542.pdf>

Cole, K.C. (2001, October 1). If it's interesting, it's complex too. *Los Angeles Times.* Retrieved October 9, 2001 from <www.latimes.com/news/science>.

Day, Richard J.F. (2000). *Multiculturalism and the history of Canadian diversity.* Toronto: University of Toronto Press.

Devore, Wynetta, & Schlesinger, Elfriede G. (1999). *Ethnic-sensitive social work practice* (5th ed.). Toronto: Allyn & Bacon.

Fine, Michelle. (1994). Working the hyphens: Reinventing self and other in qualitative research. In Norman K. Denzin & Yvonna S. Lincoln (Eds.), *Handbook of qualitative research* (pp. 70–82). Thousand Oaks: Sage Publications.

Fong, Rowena, & Furuto, Sharlene. (Eds.). (2001). *Culturally competent practice: Skills, interventions and evaluations.* Toronto: Allyn & Bacon.

Germain, Carel B., & Gitterman, Alex. (1980). *The life model of social work practice.* New York: Columbia University Press.

Green, James W. (Ed.). (1982). *Cultural awareness in the human services.* Englewood Cliffs: Prentice-Hall, Inc.

Harper, Karen V., & Lantz, Jim. (1996). *Cross-cultural social work practice with diverse populations.* Chicago: Lyceum Books.

Healy, Karen. (2001). Participatory action research and social work: A critical appraisal. *International Social Work 44*(1), 93–105.

Hochschild, Adam. (2000, May 12). Leopold's Congo: A holocaust we have yet to comprehend. *The Chronicle of Higher Education*, B4–B6.

Irving, Allan, & Young, Tom. (2002). Paradigm for pluralism: Mikhail Bakhtin and social work practice. *Social Work 47*(1), 19–29.

Isajiw, Wsevolod W. (1999). *Understanding diversity: Ethnicity and race in the Canadian context.* Toronto: Thompson Educational Publishing Co.

James, Carl E. (1999). *Seeing ourselves: Exploring race, ethnicity and culture.* Toronto: Thompson Educational Publishing, Inc.

Lukacs, John. (2002, April 26). It's the end of the modern age. *The Chronicle of Higher Education*, <http://chronicle.com/weekly/v48/i33/33b00701.htm>. An excerpt from Lukacs, John, *At the End of an Age*, Yale University Press, 2002.

Lum, D. (1999). *Culturally competent practice.* Pacific Grove: Brooks/Cole.

Margolis, Eric S. (1999). *War at the top of the world.* Toronto: Key Porter Books Limited.

McPherson, Dennis H. (1998). A definition of culture: Canada and First Nations. In Jace Weaver (Ed.), *Native American religious identity: Unforgotten gods* (pp. 77–98). Maryknoll, NY: Orbis Books.

McPherson, Dennis H., & Rabb, J. Douglas. (1993). *Indian from the inside: A study in ethno-metaphysic.* Thunder Bay: Lakehead University, Centre for Northern Studies.

_____. (2001). Indigeneity in Canada: Spirituality, the sacred and survival. *International Journal of Canadian Studies 23*, 57–79.

METRAC (Metropolitan Action Committee on Violence against Women and Children) & OWJN (Ontario Women's Justice Network). (2002). Material on Legal Information Workshops for Women Experiencing Violence. (Family Law Glossary and Child Protection: Information on the Child & Family Services Act, The Children's Aid

Society and Parents' Rights and Responsibilities) <www.metrac.org> and <www.owjn.org>

Morales, Armando T., & Sheafor, Bradford W. (2002). *The many faces of social work clients*. Toronto: Allyn & Bacon.

Muldoon, James. (2002). The medieval church and the origins of globalization. *The Historical Society III*(3).

Nelson, C.H., & Kelley, M.L. (1985). Wiichiwewin: An insight into Indian helping. In *Ontario Collection* (pp. 175–189). Toronto: Ontario Centre for the Prevention of Child Abuse.

Nelson, C.H., Kelley, M.L., & McPherson, D.H. (1985) Rediscovering support in social work practice. *Canadian Social Work Review* 1985, 231–248.

_____. (1987). Contextual patterning: a key to human service effectiveness in the north. In Peter Adams & Doug Parker (Eds.), *Canada's subarctic universities* (pp. 309–330). Ottawa: ACUNS.

Nelson, C.H., & McPherson, D.H. (2000). Can a post-secondary social work training program appropriately educate professional social workers to be effective in native child welfare issues? *Canada's Children 7*(2), 16–21.

Neuman, Lawrence W. (2000). Social research methods: Qualitative and quantitative approaches (4th ed.). Needham Heights: Allyn & Bacon.

Paterniti, Michael. (2000). *Driving Mr. Albert: A trip across America with Einstein's brain*. New York: Random House, Inc.

Postel, Danny. (2002, April 5). Is race real? How does identity matter? *The Chronicle of Higher Education* <http://chronicle.com/free/v.48/i30/30a01001.htm>

Tator, Carol. (1996). Anti-Racism and the human service delivery system. In Carl E. James (Ed.), *Perspectives on racism and the human services sector: A case for change* (pp. 152–170). Toronto: University of Toronto Press.

Torjman, Sherri. (2001). *Reclaiming our humanity*. Caledon Institute of Social Policy in Partnership with Coalition of National Voluntary Organizations, Canadian Council on Social Development, and United Way of Canada, Centraide Canada. <http://caledonist.org/PDF/553820045.pdf>

Weaver, Hilary N. (1999). Indigenous people and the social work profession: Defining culturally competent services. *Social Work 44*(3), 217–225.

White, Theodore H., & Jacoby, Annalee. (1946). *Thunder out of China*. New York: William Sloane Associates, Inc.

Fields of Practice

Chapter 6

Child Welfare:
AOP's Nemesis?

Gary C. Dumbrill
School of Social Work
McMaster University

How can child protection workers address issues of child abuse and neglect with families in a way that is anti-oppressive? My struggles with this question, both as a practitioner and as an academic, have consistently led me to one conclusion—answers to working anti-oppressively do not lie in social work ideas but in the ideas of those receiving social work services. Acting on this conclusion, I have sought "client" ideas about how to work anti-oppressively. Before I present the results of this research, I will examine the challenge of working anti-oppressively within the context of child welfare. I begin by outlining the nature of anti-oppressive practice (AOP) and the ways it attempts to dismantle systemic inequalities that underlie social injustice. I then suggest that child welfare is a nemesis of such practice because modern child welfare's origins lie in the efforts of society's privileged to control those they perceive as a threat to their dominance. I will show that such control is not just historical—current child welfare practice continues to preserve systems of dominance. Child welfare, therefore, presents AOP with a poignant challenge: How can child welfare be transformed into an activity that challenges the dominant discourses that gave it birth while also protecting children? I contend that social work has no answer to this challenge because remedies formulated within social work simply perpetuate the discourses of domination in which child welfare is steeped. Instead, transformation lies in remedies formulated by service users—it lies in social work giving up speaking about what child welfare "clients" need and listening to what service users themselves say they need. I demonstrate the viability of listening to child welfare service users by presenting the findings of my research that examined parents' views of child protection services.

WHAT IS ANTI-OPPRESSIVE PRACTICE?

Anti-oppressive practice is concerned with eradicating social injustice perpetuated by societal structural inequalities, particularly along the lines of race, gender, sexual orientation and identity, ability, age, class, occupation, and social service usage. Young (1990) explains how such inequality is maintained, in part, by five forms of oppression: exploitation, marginalization, powerlessness, cultural imperialism, and violence. "Exploitation" results from fixed social relations between social classes and groups causing "a transfer of energies from one group to another that produce unequal distributions" (Young, 1990, p. 53). "Marginalization" pushes classes and groups of people to the edges of society where they are "expelled from useful participation in social life and thus potentially subjected to severe material deprivation" (Ibid.). "Powerlessness" leaves categories of people experiencing "inhibition in the development of [their] capacities, lack of decision making power in [their] life, and exposure to disrespectful treatment because of the status [they occupy]" (Young, 1990, p. 58). "Cultural imperialism" causes groups of people to find that "the dominant meanings of society render the particular perspective of [their] own group invisible at the same time as they stereo-type[sic] [that] group and mark it as the Other" (Young, 1990, pp. 58–59). "Violence" is systemically "directed at members of a group simply because they are members of that group" (Young, 1990, p. 62).

These five forms of oppression, and the social injustice they support, result from the domination and privilege held by select societal groups and classes. Figure 6.1 presents a spatial representation of the relationship between domination and oppression and shows how "mainstream" societal space is occupied by locations of privilege and "minority" locations are pushed to the social margins. The oppression shown in Figure 6.1 is accumulative with the more marginalized sites pushed further from the centre. For instance, a lesbian woman of colour living with a disability is likely to experience more marginality and other forms of oppression than a heterosexual White male with a disability. Just as sites of oppression interlock, so do sites of dominance and privilege with prime societal space monopolized by the dominant male, heterosexual, White, able, middle-class, professional/ managerial locations that situate themselves as epitomizing the Canadian social fabric (Yee & Dumbrill, 2003).

Figure 6.1: A SPATIAL ANALYSIS OF DOMINATION & OPPRESSION

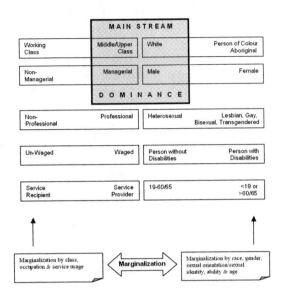

Although Figure 6.1 aids social analysis, it does not empirically represent society—it is abstracted from select characteristics of society. Figure 6.1 must not be taken literally because to do so would oversimplify and reduce the dynamics of oppression into a clash of binary opposites. Such reduction is problematic because although power is held within the locations shown in the centre of Figure 6.1, this is not universally so and the ways oppression operates are much more fluid and complex. Figure 6.1 is further complicated by its categories being social constructions. "Race," for instance, is a category that gains meaning only because of the oppression experienced as a result of racialization. Consequently, the significance of the locations shown in Figure 6.1 do not lie in an "essential" difference within the categories listed, but in the power held by the dominant groups to define specific locations as "different" and marginalize those so defined. Figure 6.1, therefore, does not provide a map of society that can be used to identify individuals who oppress and others who are oppressed, but it provides a broad topography of Canada's social landscape that reveals the socially constructed contours that shape oppression.

Social work was combating social injustice and dominance along the dimensions shown in Figure 6.1 long before the term "AOP" was coined;

feminists, anti-racists, and structuralists have addressed these forms of oppression for decades. Even interlocking oppression and the socially constructed nature of "difference" have been recognized for some time. In my own and others' anti-racist work in Britain in the 1980s, interlocking oppression was recognized and the term "Black" was used by those from oppressed groups as a term of resistance referring not only to race but also to others forced to society's margins (Gilroy, 1987; Hiro, 1971). More recently, the term "Whiteness" has been used to refer to the groups that dominate (Kincheloe, 1999; McIntosh, 1998; Yee & Dumbrill, 2003). AOP, therefore, does not bring a radically new perspective to social work; it brings a synthesis and refinement of earlier social justice perspectives. With the spatial analysis shown in Figure 6.1, AOP also brings attention to the social location of those who speak and are heard in social discourses. It is no longer sufficient for social work to speak of social justice without considering the location it speaks from, which is usually the dominant location at the centre of Figure 6.1. Indeed, laws governing social work, most Canadian social work institutions, and the theories that underpin social work intervention tend to be steeped in White European thought and ways of being. By speaking from a location of dominance, social work not only removes the opportunity for those on the margins to speak for themselves, it also perpetuates mainstream discourses that underpin injustice. Consequently, high on AOP's agenda is examining and dismantling the role that social work plays in maintaining oppression. This self-examination is not only required by the discipline as a whole, but by each of us within the discipline. For me, therefore, a White British male who appears to be located at the centre of Figure 6.1, I must not only ask how social work oppresses and how it might become anti-oppressive, I must also ask how I oppress and how I might become anti-oppressive. The question posed at the beginning of this chapter, therefore, is very personal for me: How can I address issues of child abuse and neglect with families while also being anti-oppressive? To understand the challenge of answering this question, one must first be aware of how child welfare systems protect dominance.

CHILD WELFARE: A SYSTEM OF DOMINANCE

Child welfare masks its propensity to oppress by presenting its efforts to protect children as the product of "civilized" society and contrasting its compassionate treatment of children with the barbaric treatment of children in past societies (Fraser, 1976; Radbill, 1974, 1980; Rycus, Hughes, & Garrison, 1995). Indeed, the protection of children from abuse is said to have begun in

1874 when the New York Society of Prevention of Cruelty to Animals discovered six-year-old Mary Ellen being beaten by her caregivers and "rescued" her after recognizing that children deserved at least the same rights as animals (Costin, Karger, & Stoesz, 1996; Lazoritz & Shelman, 1996; Litzelfelner & Petr, 1997; Mohr, Gelles, & Schwartz, 1999). Further advances occurred in 1962 when the medical team of Kempe, Silverman, Steele, Droegmueller, and Silver (1962) refocused society's attention on child abuse by discovering the "battered child syndrome." More progress was made in the 1970s when the extent of sexual abuse became evident (Committee on Sexual Offences against Children and Youth, 1984; Finkelhor, 1984; Kempe & Kempe, 1978; Russell, 1983). Now, children in the modern developed world are protected by social workers who police parenting with an array of risk-assessment instruments.

The above accounts misrepresent both the past and present. Life in ancient societies was often brutish for adults and children alike, yet efforts to protect children from physical abuse, sexual abuse, and also neglect can be traced back to the beginnings of recorded history (Corby, 2000; Dumbrill & Trocmé, 1999; Pollock, 1983). Historical accounts, therefore, contrasting ancient barbarism toward children with modern caring for children do not provide a basis for understanding the past but an oversimplified binary opposite against which modern child welfare characterizes itself as "advanced." Indeed, once the ancients are considered "barbaric," the moderns are more easily considered "civilized" and acts of modern child welfare that might be regarded as oppressive are more easily overlooked. For instance, portraying modern child welfare as "civilized" overlooks the fact that when Mary Ellen inspired the 1874 "advances" in child welfare, First Nations children were being removed from their families in a deliberate attempt to eradicate Aboriginal language and culture. Also overlooked is the fact that when Kempe and colleagues' 1962 "advances" occurred, the "sixties scoop" was underway in which, supported by a federal stipend for every Aboriginal child apprehended, provincial child welfare agencies "scooped" thousands of First Nations children from their parents and placed them with White families. Although the treatment of Aboriginal peoples is the clearest form of oppression by child welfare organizations, other marginalized groups have also been oppressed (Gordon, 1988; Pfhol, 1977; Swift, 1995a, 1995b). This oppression results from child welfare organizations not only being founded to protect children like Mary Ellen from harm, but also being designed to protect social order. Swift explains the motivation of those founding modern child welfare organizations:

They believed that in "saving" neglected children, they also could save themselves and their positions of privilege. They most certainly hoped to help neglected children, but they wanted to reduce threats to the existing social order that they believed these children might come to pose. Their scheme was ingenious, providing themselves and their representatives with the authority of the state to intervene in and alter the private lives of those they saw as dangerous to their own interests. ... This basic approach, with continual refinements, remains in place today. (Swift, 1995b, p. 74)

This approach remaining in place today is evidenced by the continued overrepresentation in care of children from groups that the founders of modern child welfare saw as a potential threat to their privilege. First Nations children are still removed from their parents in disproportionate numbers (Fournier & Crey, 1997a, 1997b) as are children of single parents (Callahan & Lumb, 1995). Child protection agencies' focus on marginalized groups is not just a Canadian phenomena; in the United States child removal is linked to poverty (Lindsey, 1994); gay, lesbian, bisexual, and transgendered parents consistently come "under fire" (Polikoff, 1999); and children of colour are overrepresented in care (Chand, 2000). Examining the impact of interlocking sites of oppression on involvement with child welfare services makes the scope of this problem apparent. Working with British statistics, Jones (1994) calculates the compound risk of child removal for a child aged five to nine from a single-parent family of mixed ethnic origin receiving social assistance with four or more children living in rented accommodation with one or more persons per room to be one in ten. In contrast, a similar child from a two-parent White family not receiving social assistance with three or fewer children living in a home they own with one or more persons per room faces a one in 7,000 chance of entering care. This 700:1 ratio does not result from the parenting of White middle-class families being 700 times better than single-parent mixed ethnicity families dependent on benefits; it results from prejudices and structural inequalities deeply embedded within child welfare and other social systems. Child welfare and AOP, therefore, are diametrically opposed: child welfare protects privilege by removing the children of those marginalized within society rather than examining the structural inequalities that disadvantage these families, while AOP demands that these structural factors be examined and dismantled—child welfare is AOP's nemesis.

TACKLING THE NEMESIS

To break its own cycle of abuse, child welfare must challenge and change the dominant discourses that gave it birth. Such challenge is not possible from within the child welfare system because remedies conceived from a site of dominance will simply reproduce the privilege-preserving activities initiated by those who founded the modern child welfare system. Indeed, the founders of modern child welfare did not meet and consciously plot ways to preserve their privilege, but attempting to prevent child abuse and neglect from their position of privilege caused their remedies to be steeped within the world view they operated within. Consequently, their ideal of a White, two-parent, heterosexual, able-bodied, hard-working Christian family became the solution they set for the children and families they helped—a solution that institutionalized the marginalization of families who did not match this ideal. Current child welfare remedies conceived from a location of dominance will do the same—although well intended, they will perpetuate a discourse in which the privileged conceptualize and determine what the marginalized need. Transforming child welfare, therefore, requires "privileging" voices from "the margins" and drawing solutions from outside dominant space.

AOP is already drawing on knowledge from the margins—a growing number of child welfare professionals speaking from personal experience of marginalization are challenging child welfare's dominance from the inside out. Literature from the margins is also being drawn into the centre of AOP social work education. Such work is crucial, yet efforts must go further—those outside social work who are directly affected by child welfare intervention must gain a voice in shaping the services they receive. Social work needs to listen to remedies rather than generate them—it needs to de-centre its own dominant knowledge and make space for service users' knowledge. Beresford explains that "there has always been service users' knowledge—from the earliest days of the secular religious charity and the beginnings of state intervention and the poor law." Such knowledge is based on the real lives, struggles, ways of being, and locations of those to whom services are directed. If the founders of modern child welfare services had drawn on knowledge from those in these locations rather than from their own positions of privilege, perhaps the systems they designed might have transformed the existence of those who received intervention rather than preserved the dominance of those who delivered it. If social work focused more on facilitating service users defining their own problems and remedies rather than establishing its right as a profession to speak for them, social work might have had more success in remedying rather than reinforcing social injustice. AOP, therefore, must facilitate and tap the development of service users' knowledge. Indeed, because "service users' knowledge grows out of their personal and *direct* collective experience of policy and provision from the *receiving end*" (Beresford, 2000, p. 493), such knowledge is crucial if AOP is to overcome the nemesis of child welfare.

UNDOING DOMINANCE: WHAT CHILD WELFARE SERVICE USERS SAY

Children have been gaining an increasing voice in Canadian child welfare (Strega, 2000) and this voice is crucial because ultimately it is children the system attempts to serve. My work, however, has focused on the voice of parents for two reasons. First, parents receiving child protection services are rarely heard in Canada. Second, my child protection practice usually placed me face-to-face with parents in attempting to bring change. It has been primarily in this face-to-face encounter with parents that I have struggled with the question of working anti-oppressively—what does AOP look like in this context? Answering this question requires me to hear what parents have to say. In previous work, reported elsewhere, I have explored parents designing and evaluating the services they received at mezzo levels (Dumbrill & Maiter, 1997; Dumbrill, Maiter, & Mason, 1995). My current work explores parental views at the micro level in an attempt to answer the question outlined at the beginning of this paper—how do I address issues of child abuse and neglect with families in a way that is anti-oppressive?

Previous Research
The few studies that examine the ways Canadian parents experience child protection intervention reveal that parents have a predominantly negative view of services. Anderson (1998) examined the views of six Native parents in Toronto who had been involved with child protection agencies and elicited themes of "anger, hate, fear, despair, isolation, frustration, pain, guilt, distrust, betrayal, and worry." Given the history of the residential school system and the "sixties scoop," such themes are not surprising. Yet not only First Nations parents held these views; McCullum (1995) examined the experiences of ten non-Aboriginal parents receiving child protection from an Ontario Children's Aid Society (CAS) and found that "parents were conscious, and frightened, of the extent of worker and agency power. Parents knew their children could be removed and feared they would never be returned" (McCullum, 1995, p. 55).

McCullum found that fear caused parents to feel angry, resentful, and frustrated with the agency. Parents in British Columbia felt similarly; Callahan,

Field, Hubberstey, and Wharf (1998) examined the views of thirty parents, twenty-one child protection workers, and five voluntary agency workers in an attempt to distil the elements of "best practice" within child protection. Parents not only feared workers, but saw one of their main parenting tasks as protecting their children from child welfare intervention. Also in British Columbia, Grams (1989) examined the views of thirty-five parents who were afraid of workers and felt that they had little control over the process or outcome of child protection intervention. Not all the findings of these studies were negative; variables mitigating against fear included workers and parents being open about their fears (Callahan et al., 1998); workers showing compassion, commitment, concern for the family's problems, and listening to what parents had to say (McCullum, 1995). When fears were not addressed, parents were unwilling to be honest with workers and began to "play the game," which involved "learning what workers expect and providing workers with the answers workers wanted to hear, even if this means lying," (McCullum, 1995, p. 119–120). One parent who took some time to learn the rules of this game reported that if she had known these rules earlier, "I would have been humbled a long time ago. ... I would have kissed their arses, bowed, whatever" (McCullum, 1995, p. 98). There is also evidence of parents fearing child protection workers in Britain and the United States (Cleaver & Freeman, 1995; Corby, Millar, & Young, 1996; Diorio, 1992) as well as evidence of parents "playing the game" (Corby et al., 1996; Howe, 1989). Whether the findings of these international studies can be transferred to Canada is unclear because of differences between British, American, and Canadian child protection systems. Even the transferability of Canadian study findings within Canada is problematic due to methodological limitations. More problematic is building anti-oppressive practice on these findings. Anderson, for instance, describes the feelings of First Nations parents toward child protection workers and contrasts these with qualities parents appreciated in workers through services they had received from outside the child protection system, but Anderson (1998) does not develop a viable means to utilize these qualities while delivering child protection intervention. McCullum (1995) attempted to develop a model of child protection intervention by using a grounded theory and recommended child protection workers intervene by building on parental strengths, but these recommendations are limited because her study examines only cases of sexual abuse. Grams (1989) also attempted to develop a model by using grounded theory, but his findings are limited by containing few recommendations for practice. Callahan and colleagues' (1998) study contains several implications for intervention and they provide workers with guidelines for "best practice." Central in their recommendations is that parents discuss with workers their fears of children being removed and that workers dialogue with parents about their fears of children being harmed. Callahan and colleagues, however, do not formulate "service users' knowledge" into theory that explains the process of intervention from a parental perspective. In fact, none of the above studies provide a theoretical model that explains the process of how parents experience and make sense of intervention. Such knowledge is crucial because if child welfare is to be transformed so that it does not oppress, it is essential to understand how those it oppresses consider it to oppress, and to understand the changes *they* believe are necessary for it to become anti-oppressive. Thus, to transform the child welfare intervention process into an anti-oppressive activity requires that the theories and ways of understanding of parents be used to develop appropriate interventions.

Research Design

I set out to discover how parents experienced and made sense of child protection intervention. A grounded theory design was used so that the research would map parental experience and also allow a model to be developed explaining intervention from a parental perspective. In-depth interviews lasting between forty to ninety minutes were undertaken with seventeen parents. Member checking interviews took place with four parents. A focus group of five child protection workers explored emerging themes and considered implications for their practice.

Sample Characteristics

Sampling took place primarily in Ontario with only one parent from outside Ontario (in British Columbia) being interviewed. Theoretical sampling was used, a process where as themes begin to emerge from data, cases are selected into the sample to allow the perimeters and characteristics of these themes to be tested and mapped. Although mapping of themes was possible, some limitations occurred as a result of workload pressures at the participating agencies, thus preventing them from providing an extensive sampling pool. Participants ranged in age from nineteen to over sixty with a mean age in the mid-thirties. Ten parents were men and seven were women. Most—seven fathers and three mothers—were single parents. Parents were primarily from lower socio-economic groups. Three of the fathers were employed in unskilled or semi-skilled work, one was a homemaker, one was unemployed, and one was on long-term disability. Three fathers did not specify their occupations, but lived in lower income, working-class neighbourhoods. One father was a successful businessperson and politician. Four mothers were homemakers living in working-class neighbourhoods and two—one a student and the other unemployed—were living in a women's shelter at the time of the interviews. One mother was a professional or semi-professional working in accounts for a large company and also owned her own home. Parents were predominantly White; two were women of colour and one father was Aboriginal.

Findings

Parents described the encounter with child protection services as being confronted with "absolute" power. Some parents connected this power with history and oppression on a political level. Mr. E., a First Nations parent, packed his bags and left home when child protection workers came to talk about concerns regarding his children—he had been taken from his mother in the "sixties scoop" and had no faith in talking with child protection workers. Mr. A. spoke of the physical and sexual abuse suffered by his family members two generations previously as orphans in state care, and was indignant that child welfare agents had now come back to criticize his parenting. Ms. O., a Black mother who had five children removed by White workers and placed with White foster mothers, found her baby developing an increasing inability to look into her "Black face" during access visits. Apologizing for talking about "discrimination," Ms. O. said she wonders "why they are having Black babies bonding with white women?" Mrs. B., a French-Canadian parent, was not only refused a French-speaking worker but was also prohibited from speaking French to her children in supervised access visits. Mrs. B resisted:

> I refused to speak to them in English, I have only spoken to
> my children in French since the day they were born. ... I was
> not about to give them, by an action of mine, the impression
> that authority means English. ... It is difficult enough to try
> and raise children in French in such an overwhelmingly English
> environment, without giving them the message that any time
> that there is anything serious going on we speak English.

Most parents did not connect child protection intervention to broader social or political issues, and with the exception of one parent, no difference existed in the ways parents experienced or dealt with intervention between those who recognized a political dimension to their experience and those who did not. All parents simply described child protection intervention as a force far more powerful than themselves and spoke of quickly learning that given the power differential between workers and themselves, they had to "play the game." This game was similar to that identified by earlier research where parents feigned co-operation to get child protection services out of their lives. Mr. J. was the exception to this rule: Mr. J., a single parent and full-time homemaker, learned legal skills in jail and devoted his full energies to challenging child protection and other social service departments. Mr. J. reported that his efforts gained him financial settlements and caused workers to be "fired," but said he was unable to change the system from exerting power over parents.

The ways power is wielded over parents by child protection services conforms to the three dimensions that Lukes (1974) claims social power is exercised through: coercion, controlling agendas, and controlling consciousness. In Lukes's first dimension, overt coercion is used to force a person to do something. The experience of Ms. F. typifies how such power was used. Ms. F. wanted her partner, Mr. E., to return home, but child protection services had concerns about his parenting abilities, Ms. F. describes the impact of intervention: "Every time she came here she made me cry, every single time she came here. Every time I said to her, 'You know what? You are scaring me.' She says, 'If we find Mr. E. here, your kids are gone!'"

In the second dimension, power is exercised through the control of agendas and by determining what is debated and what is not. The case of Mr. A. typifies how this power is used. Mr. A. became increasingly frustrated by decisions about his family being made by child protection services in closed meetings he had no access to; he described how this left him feeling powerless: "I cannot do anything because I am put against a wall. I am facing an enemy that is not a visible enemy—who do I fight? What do I do?"

In the third dimension, control is exerted through the power to shape or limit consciousness. When this type of power is wielded, there is an absence of observable conflict because power operates through establishing "taken-for-granted" practices. This power operates by parents accepting and not challenging how service is delivered. Mr. J. explains: "Most parent are so caught up in the struggle that they have with their children who are in need of services that they cannot perceive ways and means by which this service can be provided."

Although Lukes's framework reveals how parents are controlled by differing forms of power, the study's focus was on identifying how the theory of service users, rather than theory developed within the academy, explains parental experience. It is important to analyze power as defined by parents themselves because their definitions give access to the world of those receiving service rather than the world of those delivering it.

Parents articulated how workers had access to five specific power mechanisms: coercion, resources, knowledge, defining, and procedure. Parents not only articulated how workers gain "power over" them through these five mechanisms, they also described how these same mechanisms can be used in a constructive manner—as "power with" them. The concepts of "power over" and "power with" are well developed in social work literature (Miller, 1991). Simply stated, "power over" is a worker directing power at a client to cause him or her to conform, while "power with" is a worker joining his or her power with that of the client to achieve a jointly agreed objective.

How parents experienced "coercion" being used as "power over" them was described above—Ms. F. being reduced to tears for fear that her children would be removed. Such fear has enormous coercive power over parents. At the same time, however, parents recognized that coercive power could be used by workers on their behalf. Ms. P. explained: "If I ever had a problem, I would consult the CAS because I like to have some kind of power advice, advice from people who are very powerful." Ms. P. went on to describe how child protection services had sided with her and forced other agencies and landlords to co-operate with her. Similarly, Ms. C. recalled how her child protection worker came to her defence and demanded that she be released from a psychiatric ward when nurses were badgering her to remain.

The "resources" that child protection services have access to were also viewed by parents as providing workers with power. Ms. B. explained that because "they [child protection services] have this absolute power that corrupts absolutely, that it was best to ... consent to a supervision order for six months and get the children home instead of fighting them. Well I thought that really goes against the grain, but I did not have a couple of hundred thousand dollars to really argue about it." Unable to match the legal resources of child protection services, Ms. B. consented to a supervision order and proceeded to "play the game."

Child protection resources are not just financial; they include the ability to endure and maintain a long drawn-out struggle. Mr. J. explained that to contest child protection power, he needed to also learn to endure. As a result of his endurance and successful battles with child protection services, other parents now ask him for help with child protection services. Inevitably the parents who come to Mr. J. are overwhelmed; he describes the advice he gives them: "'You gotta stop crying and you gotta start acting.' But once I start telling them the process, then they can't because, uh, they're too caught up in the emotional issues that they cannot see the process behind it and they cannot detach themselves." According to Mr. J., therefore, parents are so involved in the struggle to manage their day-to-day affairs that they have difficulty finding the emotional resources to "fight" child protection services. Child protection workers can, however, use their resources to assist overwhelmed parents. Ms. K. describes her experience: "the CAS was very, very helpful. ... She [the worker] took us everywhere we needed to go and she was there for us, [had] different ideas about different things [regarding parenting] and so we had a really good rapport with the CAS."

Ms. K.'s experience of being supported by child protection resources changed when she was assigned a new worker and it quickly became evident to her that her "power with" experience was changing to a "power over" process. Ms. K. first became aware that the new worker was exercising power over her by the way he controlled "knowledge." She said "the biggest problem was the secretive part where he'd [the second worker] make decisions and then tell us and we had to go along with them whether we liked it or not, while she [first worker] never made a decision without our input."

The ability to "define" also afforded workers power. Ms. B. recalls a conversation with her worker: "When I heard her [worker] say to me that taking the TV away was 'too harsh a discipline,' I knew I had stepped into the twilight zone." Ms. B. elaborated that the "twilight zone" experience resulted not from the child protection worker defining an event in a way she disagreed with, but from the worker's "absolute" power to impose her definitions of an event upon her. No matter how absurd Ms. B. considered the worker's opinion, she felt unable to challenge it.

The combination of "absolute power" and worker opinion also provided a means to support parents. Ms. C., a teenage mother, describes how a worker used defining power to help her overcome the fears she experienced when first taking care of her newborn child:

> I didn't know what to do! I looked at this baby and was like, "Yeah, okay, what do I do? How do I know when to change her, how do I know when to feed her?" And she's [the worker] like, "You'll know—don't worry." She told me, "You can do it." ... Knowing somebody, especially a professional, believed in me helped me believe in myself.

Taken outside a power context, the above comment "You can do it" seems benign and almost insignificant. For this mother, however, who experienced her worker as having "absolute power," this comment defined the reality she existed within—the mother began to believe she really could be a good parent.

Child protection "procedure" is also experienced by parents as a form of worker power that can be used over them or with them. Ms. B. describes how procedure gave workers power over her: "I call it a song and dance. You know that in the mean time the period in which the children are away from home is going from one day, two days, to a month, while they [child protection services] are exercising their god-given right to do whatever they want." Ms. B. believed that the longer her children were in foster care while she was waiting for a court date, the weaker her case became for having them return home. Ms. K., on the other hand, experienced procedure as enabling: "For the first two years it took us that long to find out what was wrong with him [grandson], to get him on the right medication, to try and get the proper help for him. ... Our worker did a fantastic job, you know. She was right there to help us." For Ms. K., therefore, the careful methodical steps child protection services took to uncover the causes of her child management problems provided her with exactly the support she needed.

Parents' responses to intervention hinged on the way they experienced workers' use of power and they described three ways of responding: fighting child protection services, playing the game by feigning co-operation, and co-operatively working with services. Parents who described experiences of power being used over them tended to fight or "play the game." Parents who described power being used with them tended to speak of having co-operative relationships with their workers. There was, however, some overlap between "playing the game," "fighting," and "co-operative" working. Ms. K. explained that she co-operated with her first worker, who used "power with" her and fought her second worker, who used "power over" her, but in both situations she also "played the game" because, in her opinion, it was impossible to always fight or always co-operate.

Although parental experience and reaction hinged on their perception of a worker's use of power, the varying parental perceptions cannot be explained by worker style. It became evident in interviews that some parents shared the same workers and that the same worker could be experienced by one parent as exercising "power over" them and another as "power with" them. These differing perceptions cannot hinge on worker style unless workers change their styles with different parents. Similarly, perceptions cannot be explained solely by parental characteristics because some parents' experience of child protection power switched from "power with" to "power over" and vice versa with a change of worker. Neither do differences between "power over" and "power with" experiences hinge on workers and parents agreeing on issues—parents described disagreeing with workers in "power with" scenarios. More assistance from parents is needed, therefore, to identify the ways in which intervention can be shifted from "power over" to "power with" processes. Such identification is crucial because unless "power over" experiences can be transformed into "power with" experiences, parents resort to "playing the game" and child welfare workers will evoke no more than the appearance of co-operation from parents.

CONCLUSION

Parents in this study spoke of feeling afraid, powerless, intimidated, and silenced in the face of child protection intervention. Clearly, different ways of delivering child protection intervention must be identified and to be anti-oppressive, parents must be involved in identifying these different ways of delivering service. Such forms of practice are possible and parents can help identify such practice—parents described workers using the same powers that had been used to control them to help them with their problems. Parents described in detail the sources of power used by workers and gave coherent and detailed descriptions of the ways workers use that power either "over" them or "with" them. It should be possible, with the further assistance of parents, to gain more information about the ways to minimize the use of "power over" and maximize the use of "power with" in micro child protection casework. If additional research projects provide parents and families with further opportunities to evaluate and contribute to the redevelopment of child welfare practice on micro, mezzo, and macro levels, there is every reason to believe that new ways of working can be developed and that child welfare need not be AOP's nemesis.

REFERENCES

Anderson, K. (1998). A Canadian child welfare agency for urban natives: The clients speak. *Child Welfare 77*(4), 441–460.

Beresford, P. (2000). Service users' knowledges and social work theory: Conflict or collaboration? *British Journal of Social Work 30*(4), 489–503.

Callahan, M., Field, B., Hubberstey, C., & Wharf, B. (1998). *Best practice in child welfare: Perspectives from parents, social workers and community members.* Victoria: Child, Family and Community Research Program, University of Victoria School of Social Work.

Callahan, M., & Lumb, C. (1995). My cheque and my children: The long road to empowerment in child welfare. *Child Welfare 74*(3), 795–819.

Chand, A. (2000). The over-representation of Black children in the child protection system: Possible causes and solutions. *Child and Family Social Work 5*(1), 67–77.

Cleaver, H., & Freeman, P. (1995). *Parental perspectives in cases of child abuse.* London: HMSO.

Committee on Sexual Offences against Children and Youth. (1984). *Sexual offences against children* (Vol. 1). Ottawa: Canadian Government Publishing Center.

Corby, B. (2000). *Child abuse: Towards a knowledge base* (2nd ed.). Buckingham: Open University Press.

Corby, B., Millar, M., & Young, L. (1996). Parental participation in child protection work: Rethinking the rhetoric. *British Journal of Social Work 26*(4), 475–790.

Costin, L.B., Karger, H.J., & Stoesz, D. (1996). *The politics of child abuse in America.* New York: Oxford University Press.

Diorio, W.D. (1992). Parental perceptions of the authority of public child welfare caseworkers. *Families in Society 73*(4), 222–235.

Dumbrill, G.C., & Maiter, S. (1997). *Consumer centered child protection services.* Paper presented at the 74th Annual Orthopsychiatry Conference, Toronto, Canada.

Dumbrill, G.C., Maiter, S., & Mason, V. (1995). *Consumer empowerment: An out-of-home care example.* Paper presented at the Child Welfare League of America, Atlantic Region Training Conference, Boston, Massachusetts.

Dumbrill, G.C., & Trocmé, N. (1999). *The social construction of modern child welfare-learning about the present by researching the past.* Paper presented at the 1st International Interdisciplinary Conference on Advances in Qualitative Methods, Edmonton, Alberta.

Finkelhor, D. (Ed.). (1984). *Child sexual abuse: New theory and research.* New York: Free Press.

Fournier, S., & Crey, E. (1997a). *Stolen from our embrace: The abduction of First Nations children and the restoration of aboriginal communities.* Vancouver: Douglas & McIntyre.

_____. (1997b). Wolves in sheep's clothing. In *Stolen from our embrace: The abduction of First Nations children and the restoration of aboriginal communities* (pp. 81–114). Vancouver: Douglas & McIntyre.

Fraser, B.G. (1976). The child and his parents: A delicate balance of rights. In R.E. Helfer & C.H. Kempe (Eds.), *Child abuse and neglect: The family in the community* (pp. 315–333). Cambridge: Ballinger.

Gilroy, P. (1987). *There ain't no black in the union jack.* London: Hutchinson.

Gordon, L. (1988). *Heroes of their own lives: The politics and history of family violence.* New York: Penguin.

Grams, G.D. (1989). *Parents' perspective of their experience in the child protection service.* Unpublished doctoral thesis, University of Toronto, Toronto.

Hiro, D. (1971). *Black British, White British.* New York: Monthly Review Press.

Howe, D. (1989). *The consumers' view of family therapy.* Aldershot: Gower.

Jones, A., & Rutman, L. (1981). *In the children's aid: J.J. Kelso and child welfare in Ontario.* Toronto: University of Toronto Press.

Jones, J. (1994). Child protection and anti-oppressive practice: The dynamics of partnership with parents explored. *Early Child Development and Care 102*(2), 101–114.

Kempe, C.H., Silverman, F., Steele, B., Droegmueller, W., & Silver, H. (1962). The battered-child syndrome. *Journal of the American Medical Association 181*(1), 17–24.

Kempe, R.S., & Kempe, C.H. (Eds.). (1978). *Child abuse*. Cambridge: Harvard University Press.

Kincheloe, J.L. (1999). The struggle to define and reinvent whiteness: A pedagogical analysis. *College Literature 26*(3), 162–194.

Lazoritz, S., & Shelman, E.A. (1996). Before Mary Ellen. *Child Abuse and Neglect_20*(3), 235–237.

Lindsey, D. (1994). *The welfare of children*. New York: Oxford University Press.

Litzelfelner, P., & Petr, C.G. (1997). Case advocacy in child welfare. *Social Work 42*(4), 392–401.

Lukes, S. (1974). Power: A radical view. London: Macmillan.

McCullum, S.P. (1995). *Safe families: A model of child protection intervention based on parental voice and wisdom*. Unpublished doctoral thesis, Wilfrid Laurier, Guelph, Ontario.

McIntosh, P. (1998). White privilege: Unpacking the invisible knapsack. In P. Rothenberg (Ed.), *Race, class, and gender in the United States: An integrated study* (4th ed.), pp. 165–169. New York: St. Martin's Press.

Miller, J.B. (1991). Women and power. In J. Jordan, A.G. Kaplan, J.B. Miller, I.P. Silver, & J.L. Surrey (Eds.), *Women's growth in connection* (pp. 197–205). New York: Guilford.

Mohr, W., Gelles, R.J., & Schwartz, I.M. (1999). Shackled in the land of liberty: No rights for children. *Annals of the American Academy of Political and Social Science 564*, 37–55.

Pfhol, S.J. (1977). The "discovery" of child abuse. *Social Problems 24*(3), 310–323.

Polikoff, N. (1999). The limits of visibility: Queer parenting under fire: A history of legal battles. *Gay Community News 24*(3–4), 38–48.

Pollock, L. (1983). *Forgotten children: Parent-child relations from 1500–1900*. Cambridge: Cambridge University Press.

Radbill, S.X. (1968). A history of child abuse and infanticide. In R.E. Helfer & C.H. Kempe (Eds.), *The battered child* (pp. 3–17). Chicago: University of Chicago Press.

_____. (1974). A history of child abuse and infanticide. In R.E. Helfer & C.H. Kempe (Eds.), *The battered child* (2nd ed.) (pp. 3–21). Chicago: University of Chicago Press.

_____. (1980). Children in a world of violence: A history of child abuse. In C.H. Kempe & R.E. Helfer (Eds.), *The battered child* (3rd ed.) (pp. 3–20). Chicago: University of Chicago Press.

Russell, D.E.H. (1983). The incidence and prevalence of intrafamilial and extrafamilial sexual abuse of female children. *Child Abuse and Neglect 7*(1), 133–146.

Rycus, J.S., Hughes, R.C., & Garrison, J.K. (1995). *Child protective services: A training curriculum*. Columbus: Institute for Human Services, Child Welfare League of America.

Strega, S. (2000). Efforts at empowering youth: Youth-in-care and the youth-in-care networks in Ontario and Canada. In Marilyn Callahan, Steven Hessle with Susan

Strega (Eds.), *Valuing the field: Child welfare in an international context* (pp. 43–60). Aldershot: Ashgate.

Swift, K.J. (1995a). *Manufacturing "bad mother": A critical perspective on child neglect.* Toronto: University of Toronto Press.

_____. (1995b). An outrage to common decency: Historical perspectives on child neglect. *Child Welfare 74*(1), 71.

Yee, J.Y., & Dumbrill, G.C. (2003). Whiteout: Looking for race in Canadian social work practice. In A. Al-Krenawi & J.R. Graham (Eds.), *Multicultural social work in Canada: Working with diverse ethno-racial communities* (pp. 98–121). Toronto: Oxford University Press.

Young, I. (1990). *Justice and politics of difference.* Princeton: Princeton University Press.

Chapter 7

Services for Street Youth: Do They Reproduce, Contribute to, and Perpetuate Oppression?

Charis Romilly

Dusk to Dawn Street Youth Resource Centre
Family Services of Greater Vancouver

Street youth can be viewed as an oppressed population since most street youth experience one, if not all, of the five faces of oppression. Many street youth have common experiences of exploitation, powerlessness, marginalization, violence, and cultural imperialism. Some evidence of this is present in the literature, although street youth have rarely been described as an oppressed population. Using an anti-oppressive framework, an exploratory research study was done with a grassroots street youth advisory group in Vancouver to examine if the oppression of street youth is ever inadvertently contributed to, reproduced, or perpetuated by services that youth access voluntarily. A focus group methodology was used with eleven street youth members.

According to anti-oppressive theorists, many systems, institutions, and services, even when access to them is voluntary, can be perceived as having interrelated oppressive elements (such as racism) embedded within. The concept of voluntary services for street youth is itself often misleading as voluntary services are not always truly voluntary, and sometimes a choice (if it can even be called that) is really more related to taking the only available alternative. Many theorists within the anti-oppressive framework believe that there is value in deconstructing current practices and theories, as well as looking for various oppressive aspects embedded within them and the dominant society in order to to reconstruct more empowering practice that is committed to social justice, equality, and empowerment of oppressed populations. The anti-oppressive approach generally posits that people are socialized to reproduce the dominant culture and maintain the status quo.

Therefore, certain practices that support the dominant paradigm are often legitimized while the practices of challenging, questioning, or advocating to change current practices to be more empowering of oppressed groups is often at times repressed, discouraged, or discredited.

OPPRESSION IN SERVICES THAT STREET YOUTH ACCESS VOLUNTARILY

> All domination involves invasion—at times physical and overt, at times camouflaged, with the invader assuming the role of helping friend.
>
> —P. Freire (2000, p. 153)

Some of the literature states that either services contain oppressive practices, policies, expectations, and/or agendas or identifies elements in services that could be classified as oppressive (Dominelli, 1998; Runaway and Homeless Youth Study Committee, 1994). This chapter provides supporting evidence for the presence of the five faces of oppression in voluntary street youth services. It should be acknowledged that there is an inherent basic contradiction in social services in that "they 'deny, frustrate and undermine the possibilities of human liberation and a just society, at the same time that they work toward and, in part, achieve greater degrees of human well-being' (Galper, 1975, p. 45)" (Mullaly, 1997, p. 181). In fairness to current services, it should be stated that there are many existing conditions that make service delivery to street youth difficult such as: underfunding of current programs (Chand & Thompson, 1997); overburdened, overwhelmed, and/or burnt out staff (Canadian Paediatric Society, 1998); a large demand on existing services (Canadian Paediatric Society, 1998); and limited available funding that puts services in competition with each other (Bradshaw, 2000). Before exploring the ways that services inadvertently can contribute to oppression, we should acknowledge the amazing work that many services do with limited resources and within the current socio-political environment. While this chapter is aimed at helping service providers examine ways they might improve service delivery, there is an understanding that many services do not always have the resources, time, or freedom to do so. However, this does not absolve service providers from taking responsibility in whatever ways they can to address oppression in services.

Contributing to Exploitation in Services

Exploitation is a systemic and unreciprocated transfer of power between social groups where the privilege of one group depends on the exploitation of another (Young, 1990). In addition, exploitation can be sexual, physical, and economic, which is a serious risk for many street youth (Lesbian, Gay, and Bisexual Youth Project, 1995; McCreary Centre Society, 2001). For many street youth, the exploitation they experience on the street is a "carry over" from previous exploitation from adults they faced before becoming street involved (Demoskoff & Lauzer, 1994). According to some of the literature, often exploitation of street youth is either directly done by adults or is the negative consequence of adult actions (Demoskoff & Lauzer, 1994; Schissel, 1997).

Demoskoff & Lauzer (1994) highlight that exploitation of street youth sometimes occurs as "the result of well-meaning, but not well considered actions of government, caregivers and other adults" (Demoskoff & Lauzer, 1994, p. 34). Youth in the research for this chapter mentioned several ways in which they felt services often took unfair advantage of them. One way that services exploited youth was by using their images, often in photographs, for fundraising and public pamphlets without obtaining their consent:

> Frank[1]: ... I know I got a thing against [this medium-threshold[2] service]. A while back they were using other people in their pamphlets and stuff, and those youth were pretty choked about the stuff that was in the pamphlet and the fact that their pictures were plastered on something they give out at their fundraisers.

In addition, youth stated that sometimes programs would promote their services for fundraising with photographs of very young youth when their agency provided service only for older youth. Moreover, youth reported often feeling exploited when youth advisories were set up for public image, but the youth's input was not really considered or the youth had no power to influence the services they were being consulted about. This research highlights that it is very important that services do not consult youth if they do not plan to take their recommendations seriously and should not exploit youth by representing them without their consent.

Perpetuating Marginalization of Street Youth

According to Kinsley (1997, p. 41), "youth and children are marginalized long before they enter care or hit the streets." There are many ways that families, communities, and cultures contribute to the marginalization of these youth. Marginalization:

> is perhaps the most dangerous form of oppression. A whole category of people is expelled from useful participation in social

life and thus potentially subjected to severe material deprivation and even extermination. The material deprivation marginalization often causes is certainly unjust, especially in a society where others have plenty. (Young, 1990, p. 53)

At times the exclusion of street youth, in combination with the desperate material conditions that street youth live in, can contribute to a sense of despair and powerlessness. Inadvertently many youth can become further marginalized through voluntary street youth services.

One way that services at times contribute to the marginalization of street youth is by isolating or separating them from their cultures, peers, friends, families, and/or communities. Freire (2000) states that:

[i]t is in the interest of the oppressor to weaken the oppressed still further, to isolate them, to create and deepen rifts among them. This is done by varied means, from the repressive methods of government bureaucracy to the forms of cultural action with which they manipulate the people by giving them the impression that they are being helped. (Freire, 2000, p. 141)

Youth provided examples of the ways in which services contributed to their marginalization:

Researcher: Do you feel services ever contribute to the exclusion or separation of street youth from meaningful involvement in their culture or cultures, in society with their peers, friends, family and/or in their communities, and, if so, please give examples.

Frank: Almost word for word that is a [one of the medium-threshold services'] rule. ... No, it is straight up [meaning for real or seriously]. You are not allowed to associate or hang out with anyone on the streets or talk about anything you would talk about while you are on the streets whilst inside [this service]. You can't even mention panhandling, bumming cigarettes ... you can't mention none of that inside. You can't talk about squatting or like shared experiences if it involves street life—they're anti it!

June: Yeah, and it sucks because if you want to talk about it you want to talk about it. Some people want to get away from that and don't want to talk about it anymore, which is all right, but [light laugh] that's part of your life, you know.

Karen: That's just denial!

Youth specifically mentioned not being allowed to speak of anything related to their street culture or being allowed to acknowledge street involvement, activities, or their way of life. In addition, youth challenged whether they could really separate themselves from the identity of a street youth or from their street culture when entering a service. Other examples mentioned by youth included workers putting down their peers and services being structured so that youth are forced to separate from their family (which to them often includes significant others, friends, and pets) in order to access services. According to the United Youth Movement (1995), not being allowed to access services with pets or not having anyone to care for their pets if they wanted to access services was a significant barrier for many youth.

McCullagh and Greco (1990) state that relationships on the street "may be meaningful and fulfill many important functions" (cited in Demoskoff & Lauzer, 1994, p. 8), which can include: providing youth with companionship and their first sense of belonging after having been rejected by others; teaching each other how to survive; helping with feelings of despair, isolation, and loneliness; and providing protection and emotional support (Hagan & McCarthy, 1997). The sometimes deliberate as well as occasionally unintentional attempts to separate youth from their street "families" often result in youth just avoiding services. Thompson (1998, p. 16) points out that a dominant cultural paradigm can contribute to racism in that it "fails to recognize significant cultural differences and their importance for the people concerned." One does not have a chance of working well with these youth if at the same time one is devaluing their peers or their street family, and/or criticizing their street culture (Demoskoff & Lauzer, 1994; Plympton, 1997)! While often extremely difficult, there is a need to look at creative ways for services to acknowledge and facilitate existing support structures that youth bring with them (including pets and street families) in service delivery rather than reinforcing further isolation of these youth.

Many services do not provide the support necessary for a successful transition from childhood to independence and often abandon youth at the age of majority (Bradshaw, 2000). Anti-oppressive practice suggests relationship building and long-term consistent approaches (Dominelli, 1998) to working with street youth (Canadian Paediatric Society, 1998). Establishing a supportive relationship between workers and clients is important (Carniol,

2000). Workers can help street youth form positive relationships among peers or supportive peer networks (Plympton, 1997; Vorrath & Brendtro, 1985). Service providers can reduce marginalization of street youth and their own isolation by including and participating in positive community networks or alliances (Carniol, 2000; Leonard, 2001) where street youth can work *with* others (community members, allies, service providers, and stakeholders) collectively and in coordination (Freire, 2000; Leonard, 2001) to create solutions to problems or successful programs for street youth. Moreover, service providers should seek to become a positive part of the youth community rather than try to separate youth from it.

A second way that services sometimes perpetuate the marginalization of street youth is by offering services that street youth often cannot access due to many barriers (Bradshaw, 2000; Canadian Paediatric Society, 1998). A few of the common barriers to accessing services are: the structure of services (Chand & Thompson, 1997) such as "rigid organizational regulations that prohibit responsiveness to individual needs and circumstances" (Runaway and Homeless Youth Study Committee, 1994, p. 27); eligibility requirements to be able to access programs (Canadian Paediatric Society, 1998); and the expectations and demands placed on youth in programs, which are at times unrealistic or too strict (Webber, 1991), in order to continue using the services. Youth specifically challenged some policies and brought up examples of how certain policies might increase the risk of street youth or cause youth to remain on the streets. One example of problematic program policies brought up by the youth was a minimum age restriction, resulting in the turning away of younger youth from service. One of the youth confirmed that she was denied food because she was *too young*. While services have improved in the last few years, so that there is now a shelter for thirteen to sixteen year olds in Vancouver, youth below this age cannot access it. Because many of these younger youth have already been in care and had negative in-care experiences, most of them will not turn to the ministry for help, which leaves these youth with fewer options than some of the older youth in terms of accessing shelter and services. More questions need to be asked about the assumptions embedded in many of the rules of many different services whether certain policies created to *help* youth are *indeed* helpful. There is also a need for more flexibility in some rules or a greater ability to respond to the individual needs of youth in order to increase the accessibility of services. Some of the ways services can be more accessible might include: twenty-four-hour access to services (Chand & Thompson, 1997; United Youth Movement, 1995); programs that are extremely flexible (Chand & Thompson, 1997) in structure; eligibility requirements and procedures that are open-minded and that take into account extenuating circumstances; workers who are non-judgmental and work with youth "where they are at" (Canadian Paediatric Society, 1998; United Youth Movement, 1995); and programs that work with street youth in the mental state they are in and that do not have preconditions for service (Chand & Thompson, 1997).

A third way that the system contributes to the marginalization of street youth (or oppressed populations) that youth did not directly mention, but was evident in the literature, was material deprivation that occurs as a result of services failing to meet youth's basic needs and rights (Kingsley, 1997; Runaway and Homeless Youth Study Committee, 1994). One of the primary reasons why services are failing to adequately meet the needs of youth is that there are not enough services or resources (Canadian Paediatric Society, 1998; Chand & Thompson, 1997). In addition, "[r]ather than developing more successful responses in providing for street involved children, society sometimes withdraws services" (Demoskoff & Lauzer, 1994, p. 43). Furthermore, the services that are available for this population are often not designed to be able to work with the myriad of issues that this population presents.

Perpetuating Powerlessness in Services

The multiple oppressions that many street youth experience can often lead to a sense of powerlessness in youth (Bradshaw, 2000; Plympton, 1997). It is however, important to note that street youth, like other oppressed populations, are not merely passive victims; many youth resist these feelings of powerlessness and survive despite their harsh experiences. Unfortunately, there are also many youth who do not. Powerlessness can include being a member of a subordinate group that is often exposed to disrespectful treatment because of their status, as well as being subjected to orders from the dominant group (Young, 1990). Many traditional programs are criticized for perpetuating powerlessness in the populations with which they work or in street youth (Dominelli, 1998). Youth in the focus group provided their theories about why service providers might perpetuate powerlessness. Firstly, service providers' arrogance in assuming that they knew what was in the best interest of street youth was highlighted. Service providers' lack of understanding of street youth was a second reason cited. In addition, the fact that service providers are often working in larger oppressive systems was mentioned as another reason that service providers sometimes inadvertently perpetuate powerlessness. Lastly, youth stated that many service providers work in positions of power over street youth. Some of the literature states that services might perpetuate or maintain powerlessness in youth by maintaining hierarchical structures and/or trying to maximize or maintain client–worker power differences (Hartman, 1993). Several patterns in the research show how voluntary services can make youth feel powerless.

First, one pattern included the lack of service options, which often forces youth into making difficult choices (such as using services that conflicted with their value system or using services where they were inappropriately touched). Because a lack of service options often perpetuates oppressive situations for street youth, a comprehensive continuum of services is needed (Bradshaw, 2000; MacPherson, 1999). The literature states that there is "no single solution" or program that can work for the diversity of street youth and respond to their diverse needs (Runaway and Homeless Youth Study Committee, 1994).

Second, some street youth reported feeling powerless because they are often not consulted about the decisions being made about them that affect their lives (Hartman, 1993; Kingsley, 1997). This lack of decision-making power over their own lives has at times resulted in youth feeling revictimized by services and/or traditionally led to them to feel hostile toward some service providers. The literature also adds that services can make youth feel powerless by having workers act as experts and prescribe solutions for youth; services in which adults "monopolize" the helping (Vorrath & Brendtro, 1985); having services that are not accountable to youth (Dominelli, 1998).

To counteract the tendency of experts prescribing solutions *on* street youth, services should focus on empowering youth (Demoskoff & Lauzer, 1994; Kingsley, 1997). Empowerment strategies suggested by youth in the research included youth-run services; more positive meaningful opportunities for youth to access voluntarily; street youth being employed in services; workers showing unconditional respect for youth, which includes allowing youth to be angry, not judging youth, and talking to them to find out the cause of their anger; and encouraging and supporting youth's decisions no matter what they may be. Subsequently, youth stated that workers showing unconditional respect for youth made them feel empowered.

A few critical empowerment strategies mentioned in the literature included increasing street youth (or a populations') capacities, skills, and/or power, and/or recognizing their current capacities and strengths (Dominelli, 1998; Plympton, 1997); forming egalitarian and respectful relationships with youth (or clients) (Carniol, 2000; Dominelli, 1998); validating their experiential knowledge (Dominelli, 1998; Mullaly, 1997); and having caring rather than controlling relationships with youth (Kufeldt, 1991, cited in Runaway and Homeless Youth Study Committee, 1994; Webber, 1991). Mallon (1999) also highlights the importance of establishing effective alternatives before forcing people to give up crucial survival, adaptive, or coping strategies.

Third, youth expressed that they felt disempowered in services because they were often made to feel bad for who they were, how they talk, their strengths, and/or their opinions. Youth provided examples of being in conflict with staff at one medium-threshold service and even being punished by being "kicked out of a service" for the use of minor language such as "fuck" or "shit." According to a Marxist analysis, the youth's language can be seen as developing within a cultural and class context. Freire (2000, p. 138) states that "within an objective situation of oppression, anti-dialogue is necessary to the oppressor as a means of further oppression—not only economic, but cultural: the vanquished are dispossessed of their word, their expressiveness, their culture." Trying to completely restrict and restrain youth's expression can be seen as an oppressive tactic of silencing the youth altogether. The message, whether intentional or not, is often that if the youth cannot speak in the way of the dominant society, then they should not speak at all. Alinsky (1971, p. 75) highlights the importance and value of humour and states that "a sense of humor is incompatible with the complete acceptance of any dogma, any religious, political, or economic prescription for salvation. It synthesizes with curiosity, irreverence, and imagination." Many street youth have a good sense of humour (Canadian Street Children Project, 1993), and often use it as a way of coping with their daily difficult struggles. However, some workers viewed this sense of humour negatively rather than as a strength. Subsequently, youth also provided examples where they felt they were not allowed to voice their opinions or defend themselves and were even punished or restricted from using services for doing so.

Services for street youth should be relevant and socially and culturally appropriate to street youth (Canadian Paediatric Society, 1998; Chand & Thompson, 1997), which means having an understanding of the diverse street youth culture(s) and social structures. Mallon (1999, p. 32) asserts that "programs and practice interventions born outside of the appropriate cultural context pursue erroneous targets, squander scarce resources, and help few." The youth in the research specifically highlight diversity among staff and that workers be subculturally appropriate (subculture, according to the youth, refers to many alternative or non-mainstream cultures such as gay, lesbian, bisexual, trans, First Nations, punk, crusty, hip hop, skater, etc.). According to Plympton (1997, p. 83), "program models that target street youth must respect their cultural imperatives. Street institutions must be understood in their structural and functional perspectives. Misapplied social science interventions can do more harm than simple neglect can." One youth contributed the concept of *culture jamming*, which means having different workers from different subcultures in programs.

Reproducing Violence in Services

Violence includes assault (physical, sexual, and verbal), harassment, threats, and intimidation. Verbal assault can include discriminatory comments (such as homophobic slurs or racist jokes). It can also include fear of violence as defined above (Young, 1990). Young (1990) believes that:

> the oppression of violence consists not only in direct victimization, but in the daily knowledge shared by all members of oppressed groups that they are liable to violation, solely on account of their group identity. Just living under such a threat of attack on oneself or family or friends deprives the oppressed of freedom and dignity, and needlessly expends their energy. (Young, 1990, p. 62)

Sometimes helping professionals not only fail to provide safe services according to youth (Canadian Paediatric Society, 1998; Mallon, 1999), but revictimize or oppress youth (whether inadvertently or consciously) (Kingsley, 1997; Schmidt, 1997).

Youth in the research provided several examples where harassment and threats were used supposedly in their best interest:

> *Frank:* If you don't start behaving, then we're not going to help you. If you don't start conforming—that's a better word.

> *Jody:* If you don't start praying ... [lots of sarcasm]

In the above quote the youth makes the link that the worker telling him to behave is really telling him to conform. Other examples youth provided included outreach workers harassing youth into trying to access services; threatening to call the police on youth, and threatening to plant marijuana in a youth's room and then call the police for his own good.

Threatening youth to get a point across or in their supposed best interest is not acceptable practice. Threats, intimidation, harassment, discrimination, and abuse should not be tolerated. In addition, violence used to force street youth to follow their supposed best interests is an oppressive tactic that has been used throughout history to force oppressed groups into the dominant culture or to assimilate to a dominant way of life (such as in residential schools).

Service providers need to seriously challenge whose best interests they are representing, especially when youth often are not even consulted about what they think is in their own best interest. The youth highlighted the danger of best interest arguments, as these are sometimes used to perpetuate and justify cultural imperialism and violence. In addition, the youth identified how the status of professionals linked with power and the lack of accountability to anyone in how they treat youth seems to give workers the right to do whatever they want.

Violence is also reproduced in service delivery in various forms of discrimination (Canadian Paediatric Society, 1998) such as racism, ageism, homophobia (Mallon, 1999), or transphobia in all kinds of services. This discrimination is also reflective of the discrimination experienced by street youth from mainstream society. In this research youth also felt that workers at times blamed them for the discrimination they experienced. For example, youth repeated the following quotes that they had heard from workers: "If you got raped, it's your fault for dressing slutty" or "You wouldn't have gotten hit by the shovel in the head if you weren't panhandling." It would appear that the typical manner in which the dominant society blames street youth for their own discrimination is also at times reflected in social service workers' practice. In these examples provided by youth, violence and cultural imperialism are interconnected.

Contributing to Cultural Imperialism

Cultural imperialism is a complex phenomenon in which the dominant society tries to reproduce its way of life and repress, discourage, and eliminate other cultures or lifestyles through various mechanisms. It should be acknowledged that the dominant society has changed throughout time and continues to change, but always seems to have exclusionary tendencies toward oppressed populations. In Western society there is a history of a dominant group or ideology having power over another subordinate group or alternative ideologies such as, for example, men over women; heterosexual over homosexual; and capitalist over other political affiliations. Cultural imperialism often occurs when the dominant group strives to keep their power and privilege through a variety of tactics. Some tactics that affect the street youth population include various types of discrimination such as racism, homophobia, and ageism (McCreary Centre Society, 2001; Plympton, 1997); "contempt for the poor" (Plympton, 1997, p. viii); myths and stereotypes ("underclasses lack discipline") (Mallon, 1999; Plympton, 1997); and/or negative media portrayal of youth or certain populations that contribute to negative beliefs about them (Mallon, 1999; Schissel, 1997) such as anti-panhandling propaganda (Downtown South Youth Advisory, 2001).

Another mechanism of cultural imperialism is the dominant group defining what constitutes the norm and measuring every other group according to this norm, as well as sometimes negatively labelling or pathologizing those who do not meet this norm. Imposing the dominant values or norms on other groups (Young, 1990) is also a form of cultural imperialism. It is in the interest of the dominant society to support the ideology of personal abnormality, deviance, and or pathology of street youth as this is a way to avoid looking at broader societal problems and/or the dominant society's role in contributing to street youth's oppression. The literature reveals several ways in which the dominant way of life is validated, such as a trend in criminology that moves away from looking at people's desperate class circumstances that lead to crime in order to survive and toward a focus on individual background, motivations, characteristics, self-control, and morality (Hagan & McCarthy, 1997); a focus on youth's individual culpability instead of on the larger structural problems (Caputo & Ryan, 1991); and a tendency to attribute certain negative characteristics to a population when in fact they are common responses to the shared experience of oppression or the conditions in which they live rather than intrinsic personality traits (Appleby & Anastas, 1998).

Some of the literature reported that running from dangerous, intolerable, or unhealthy environments can be viewed as a healthy response or a positive adaptation (Radford et al., 1989, and Stefanidis et al., 1992, cited in Runaway and Homeless Youth Study Committee, 1994). To many youth, living on the streets is a better alternative than where they came from (Canadian Paediatric Society, 1998, Mallon, 1999). Street youth's breaking of mainstream societies' rules *to survive* is not deviance but adaptation. There are many dominant perceptions of how street youth should act that at times are more related to meeting societal expectations and reinforcing the dominant way of life rather than helping or alleviating street youth's struggles or oppression. For example, the culturally imperialist attitude, if carried to the extreme, suggests that youth should follow society's rules and values even if this means further exploitation, starvation, and/or oppression, and possibly even death because of a lack of viable ways to survive. Society also engages in cultural imperialism by using power to control the resources and opportunities to which other groups have access (Thompson, 1998); defining who is *valuable* or *deserving* in society and who is *disposable* and *undeserving*; trying to control other groups, usually stated as *for the good of the whole society* or *in the best interest of the individual* (which at times really means in the best interest of the dominant group); exploiting, marginalizing, and maintaining powerlessness in other groups; and blaming those they *oppress* for their own oppression (Young, 1990).

Cultural imperialism is present in many different ways throughout voluntary street youth services. According to Thompson (1998, p. 2), "traditional approaches that do not examine ideological assumptions run the risk of unwittingly contributing to oppressive inequalities." There was an abundance of examples and themes of cultural imperialism in services provided by youth, such as the common practice of controlling, restraining, and/or dominating street youth or oppressed populations in general (Dominelli, 1998; Mullaly, 1997), which is often cited as in their best interests; service providers' tendency to have an oppressive view of client resistance (Mallon, 1999; McMahon, 1998), which is sometimes clients reacting to culturally imperialist expectations or oppressive practices; the tendency to respond to resistance with punishment (Wolffersdorf, 1989 and Wooden, 1976, cited in Runaway and Homeless Youth Study Committee, 1994); services failing to meet the needs of youth largely as a result of emphasizing or focusing on meeting various agendas (social, political, religious) rather than on the needs of youth or the population (Dominelli, 1998; Mallon, 1999); and the pathologizing and/or blaming of populations (Carniol, 2000; Wachholz & Mullaly, 2000), often as a result of viewing problems or behaviours of youth in isolation from the broader contexts that often contribute to or cause them (Garbarino, 1992, cited in Runaway and Homeless Youth Study Committee, 1994; Mullaly, 1997).

One prevalent theme that emerged in the research was the common expectation of oppressed populations or street youth to conform, adapt, or assimilate to mainstream society (Carniol, 2000; Freire, 2000): "[T]he assimilationist's blindness to difference perpetuates cultural imperialism because the subordinate groups are the ones that must drop their culture and adopt the dominant culture, which is presented as a common, universal humanity" (Mullaly, 1997, p. 156). There are several oppressed groups that are overrepresented within the street youth population, including gay, lesbian, and bisexual populations, First Nations youth, and/or trans (includes transvestite, transgendered, and transsexual) populations (McCreary Centre Society, 2001). One youth states that service providers often have a common expectation of street youth: "You have to look a certain way in order to get off the streets and you know." The youth described one medium-threshold service where they felt there was significant pressure to conform to mainstream appearance and to not be oneself.

Some theorists have challenged dominant society for expecting oppressed groups to conform to mainstream values and ideals. According to

Pharr as cited by Appleby and Anastas (1998), lesbian, gay, and bisexual people are subjected to the following elements of oppression, which include: "the imposition of normative behavior supported by institutional and economic power; disincentives for nonconformity, including the threat of violence for those who do not conform; social definition as 'other'; distortion and stereotyping; blaming the victim; internalized oppression. ..."(p. 11). Throughout history some oppressed people have managed to obtain some of the privileges and benefits of the dominant society by *passing* or *identifying with the dominant society*. For example, some theorists have highlighted how gay or lesbian people who *pass* for heterosexual and/or *act or identify themselves as heterosexual* can experience less discrimination (Appleby & Anastas, 1998; Lesbian, Gay and Bisexual Youth Project, 1995). While *passing* or *identifying as one of mainstream society* or *learning to hide* in society is adaptive in the sense that it is a coping strategy (Hetrick & Martin, 1987, cited in Lesbian, Gay and Bisexual Youth Project, 1995) that reduces abuse and discrimination, it does not empower oppressed populations. Within oppressed populations there is often conflict between those who can pass or better hide their *other* status and those who cannot. This leads to a dynamic where those who are closer to the dominant norm sometimes are less discriminated against by mainstream society, but occasionally more discriminated against by the oppressed groups with which they might identify. In some cases these people face marginalization and rejection from their own communities based on their degree of assimilation. There are many examples of this. For instance, bisexual people often face discrimination in the gay and lesbian communities and the dominant heterosexual society. Trying to identify with mainstream society or pass has benefits, but also costs. In choosing to identify with the dominant society, oppressed groups are also being asked at times to give up their unique cultures, beliefs, and even, at times, to be willing to face rejection and/or hostility from their communities.

According to Kluckhom (1953, cited in Leonard, 1997, p. 62), culture is "the total way of life of a people." The anti-oppressive approach emphasizes embracing diversity. In the case of street youth, should they have to conform to the dominant society in order to live in society or be treated as equals? Many First Nations peoples have been struggling for decades to *legitimize* their culture(s) and way of life. It is oppressive that they even have to. If street youth wish to live in co-ops, pursue non-traditional occupations, or have alternative beliefs, then what right does the dominant society have to tell them that it is wrong? These things need to be considered and contemplated when one is inadvertently imposing one's cultural bias and morality on others.

A second way that service providers often contribute to cultural imperialism is in the perpetuation of many double standards, stereotypes, and myths about street youth that are present in the dominant society (Plympton, 1997; Schissel, 1997) and affect service delivery in many different ways: "The stereotypes applied to the culturally imperialized brand them as deviant and inferior, and are so pervasive in society that they are seldom questioned" (Mullaly, 1997, p. 150). Some programs have staff who have negative beliefs about street youth, such as that they are lazy, no good, or undeserving (Runaway and Homeless Youth Study Committee, 1994). The youth identified several stereotypes that affected service delivery, including the belief that all street youth are immoral or lacking in morality; are just going through a phase; believe in anarchy; are crazy because they want to live a different or non-mainstream lifestyle; and/or are addicts. In addition, youth commented on a double standard in how they are treated in services based on their gender, and are sometimes incorrectly diagnosed for physical conditions based on stereotypes (related to being dirty or a junkie, etc.). The youth challenged the universalization and characterization of street youth, as well as the stereotypes and the assumptions about the street youth population. Some theorists think that perpetuating stereotypes or myths about an oppressed population are how the dominant society maintains the status quo and keeps oppressed people in a lower status position (Freire, 2000; Mullaly, 1997).

Webber (1991) points out that the dominant society lacks will to help street youth because of their social position in society:

> Few people would question the moral rightness of demanding that our government make sure the basic needs of our youth, and indeed all Canadians, are met. A great gulf, however, separates agitating for what is right from understanding what is possible in a society that worships wealth and tolerates poverty ... widescale prevention, early intervention, and a serious rescue campaign, they [street youth and street workers] fear, will never happen. They fear it will never happen because of who the hard-core street kids—mostly, but not exclusively— are: from poor, or near-poor families, and therefore devalued and disposable. (Webber, 1991, p. 243)

Webber challenges the classist standards that suggest which people are valuable in our society and worthy of attention. In some of the literature professionalism has been challenged (Mullaly, 1997; Schissel, 1993). Mullaly

(1997) states that professionalism has created a distance between the workers and the populations that social workers aim to serve. In addition, the Runaway and Homeless Youth Study Committee (1994) and Mallon (1999) criticize some interventions for being at times inappropriate or irrelevant, and even professionals for being incompetent when it comes to working with certain populations within the street youth population or the street youth population in general.

Traditionally professional knowledge has been produced through dominant culture with the exclusion of minority voices. Mullaly (1997, p. 168) challenges "[w]hat could be more presumptuous and more disrespectful on the part of a social worker than to think that she or he knew exactly what the problem is and what the solutions are?" The exclusion of the knowledge and voices of oppressed populations in establishing knowledge about these populations has sometimes led oppressed groups to challenge professional knowledge:

Frank: The fact that they've never been on the street, half of them.

Mary: Most of the stuff they go by, they read from a book. ...

Researcher: Can you elaborate a little bit on that, Mary? Who do you think writes these books?

Mary: Some guy. [Lots of sarcasm indicating that whoever "this guy" is, he is not considered knowledgeable about street youth, according to Mary.]

According to Sarah, "They [professionals or service providers] think they know what we want, but they don't because they don't know where we are coming from." In the United Youth Movement (1995) questionnaire many youth also voiced similar sentiments. Service providers' lack of knowledge about street youth was also cited in the literature as problematic (Canadian Paediatric Society, 1998). Anti-oppressive practice with street youth could include having programs where workers have been street involved or that truly understand "where youth are coming from" (Canadian Paediatric Society, 1998; Plympton, 1997). Furthermore, to reduce inappropriate, irrelevant, and/or incompetent practice in working with certain groups within the street youth population or the street youth population in general (Mallon, 1999; Runaway and Homeless Youth Study Committee, 1994), there is a need for greater social work training and education on various issues (Mallon,

1999) including: how to work with or be sensitive to gay, lesbian, and bisexual populations (Mallon, 1999); understanding the dynamics of oppression (Freire, 2000); learning about the histories and current oppression of various oppressed populations (Mallon, 1999); and having an understanding of street youth subcultures. *The You Have Heard This Before* report (Chand & Thompson, 1997) recommends that workers receive training on how to work with street youth appropriately and that youth should be involved in designing and delivering this training.

In order to reduce the negative effects of the dominant social order on street youth, it is essential that services focus on decreasing the oppression of street youth (or certain groups within the street youth population)(Dominelli, 1998; Schissel, 1997). It is important to recognize and try to address the broader social issues that often contribute to their problems or circumstances (Dominelli, 1998; Schissel, 1997), and that negatively affect street youth and other oppressed groups. One way of doing this includes advocating, challenging, and/ or raising consciousness or critical awareness about various issues together *with* street youth or the oppressed (Carniol, 2000; Freire, 2000). In addition, workers need to more often consider a population's behaviour in the context of broader issues (Mullaly, 1997).

Service providers need to challenge structural oppression (Carniol, 2000) and injustices. Leonard (1994, p. 23) asserts that "critical social work education must renounce a commitment to privileged, objective knowledge, take a skeptical, questioning approach to all metanarratives, including its own, and explore alternative accounts, histories, and experiences of our social world." It is also critical that workers be aware of their social position and cultural biases, as well as their various privileges (such as being professional, heterosexual, male, Caucasian, upper middle class, etc.) (Mallon, 1999). Some of the literature also stated the need to work with street youth in a global or holistic way and not treat youth as a set of individual problems (Caputo & Ryan, 1991; Dominelli, 1998). Lastly there is a need for alternative programming (Carniol, 2000; Mullaly, 1997) that will create more egalitarian relationships and structures.

CONCLUSION

Somewhere in the struggle *to help* street youth, it appears that our mission has been lost. Many programs have standardized ways of responding to this population and have been socialized to meet the need of government or ministry mandates rather than those of the youth. The assumption that government and ministry mandates are *in the best interest* of the population are so ingrained within practice that many workers do not challenge them. In addition, service providers are often forced to work within institutions that have culturally imperialist agendas. The challenge for social work remains that of distancing oneself enough to challenge one's cultural biases in working with street youth and to take into consideration these street youth's unique histories (often including a history of oppression), their unique world view(s), and culture(s), and being able to work with these youth *where they are at* on the issues that they identify as important.

As this chapter has demonstrated, the oppression of street youth is at times reproduced, contributed to, or perpetuated in services. Practice with street youth instead needs to demonstrate a commitment to social justice, equality, and the struggle against oppression. In order for this to occur, there is a need to transform current social service delivery for this population into anti-oppressive programming that addresses social inequalities and injustices at the individual level, and challenges broader social issues, the status quo, and dominant ideologies that often sustain or create the inequalities and injustices in the first place. By working collectively with street youth in an egalitarian manner, we can develop new creative and unconventional solutions.

NOTES

1. All the names of the youth who participated in this research have been changed.
2. Services are described by their thresholds or "eligibility criteria for entrance into programs and the state of 'readiness' of individuals to participate and meet the demands of various programs" (MacPherson, 1999) and at times identified if they are faith-based. High-threshold programs (such as abstinence-based services) generally have many barriers to accessing them and low-threshold services (such as drop-in centres) often have minimal to no barriers. Describing services by their thresholds was done to encourage those reading this chapter to gain a greater understand of the dynamics of oppression in various services and systems and the implications for practice with this population, rather than becoming caught up in which service is the best or the worst. Many services have both empowering and oppressive elements within them.

REFERENCES

Alinsky, S.D. (1971). *Rules for radicals: a practical primer for realistic radicals*. New York: Random House Inc.

Appleby, G., & Anastas, J. (1998). *Not just a passing phase, social work with gay, lesbian, and bisexual people*. New York: Columbia University Press.

Bradshaw, C. (2000). *The challenges and obstacles faced by people who are homeless and the many community caregivers who help them every day: sampling of statements and reflections.* Government document.

Canadian Paediatric Society. (1998). *Getting street smart: re-imagining adolescent health care for street youth.* Unpublished document, report to Health Canada, Ottawa.

Canadian street children project: Phase one findings (Portage Foundation). (1993). Ottawa: Solicitor General Canada, Ministry Secretariat.

Caputo, T., & Ryan, C. (1991). *The police response to youth at risk.* Toronto: Ministry of the Solicitor General of Canada.

Carniol, B. (2000). *Case critical: challenging social work in Canada* (4th ed.). Toronto: Between the Lines.

Chand, M.K., & Thompson, L.B., (with Coralys Cuthbert, Social Planning, City of Vancouver). (1997). *You have heard this before: Street-involved youth and the service gaps.* Vancouver: Interministerial Street Children's Committee.

Demoskoff, L., & Lauzer, J. (1994). *Working with street youth: A resource manual* (for Health Canada, Health Promotion and Social Development Office, BC-Yukon Region). A.Chan, I. Thomson, & G. Wolfson (Eds.). Vancouver: Watari Research Association.

Dominelli, L. (1998). Anti-oppressive practice in context. In R. Adams, L. Dominelli, & M. Payne (Eds.), *Social work: Themes, issues and critical debates* (pp. 3–22). London: Macmillan Press.

Downtown South Youth Advisory (2001). *Report on DSYA Activities.* Unpublished document, Vancouver.

Freire, P. (2000). *Pedagogy of the oppressed* (30th anniversary ed.) M.B. Ramos (Trans.). New York: Continuum International Publishing Group Inc.

Hagan, J., & McCarthy, B. (1997). *Mean streets: Youth crime and homelessness.* New York: Cambridge University Press.

Hartman, A. (1993, July). The professional is political. *Social Work 38*(4), 365–366, 504.

Kingsley, C. (1997). *Finding our way: Report of the youth involvement project: Report to Ministry for Children and Families, Province of British Columbia.* Victoria: The Ministry.

Leonard, P. (1994). Knowledge, power and postmodernism. *Canadian Social Work Review 11*(1), 11–26.

_____. (1997). Culture. In P. Leonard, *Postmodern welfare: Re-constructing an emancipatory project* (pp. 59–76). London: Sage Publishing.

_____. (2001). The future of critical social work in uncertain conditions. *Critical Social Work 2*(1), <www.criticalsocialwork.com/01_1_future leonard.html>.

Lesbian, Gay and Bisexual Youth Project. (1995). *We are your children too: Accessible child welfare services for lesbian, gay and bisexual youth.* Toronto: Children's Aid Society of Metropolitan Toronto.

MacPherson, D. (1999). *Comprehensive systems of care for drug users in Switzerland and Frankfurt, Germany: A report from the 10th international conference of the* *reduction of drug related harm and a tour of harm reduction services in Frankfurt, Germany*. Vancouver: City of Vancouver, Social Planning Department.

Mallon, G.P. (1999). *Let's get this straight: A gay- and lesbian-affirming approach to child welfare*. New York: Columbia University Press.

McCreary Centre Society. (2001). *No place to call home: A profile of street youth in British Columbia*. Vancouver: McCreary Centre Society.

McMahon, A. (1998). Boilerplating. In A. McMahon, *Damned if you do, damned if you don't working in child welfare* (pp. 58–73). Brookfield: Ashgate.

Mullaly, R. (1997). *Structural Social Work: Ideology, Theory, and Practice* (2nd ed). Toronto: McClelland & Stewart Inc.

Plympton, T.J. (1997). *Homeless youth creating their own "street families."* Stuart Bruchey (Ed.). New York: Garland Publishing, Inc.

Runaway and Homeless Youth Study Committee. (1994). Issues affecting public policies and services for homeless youth. K. Kufeldt & B. Burrows (Eds.), *Report to National Welfare Grants*. Calgary and St. John's: University of Calgary and Memorial University of Newfoundland School of Social Work.

Schissel, B. (1997). *Blaming children: Youth crime, moral panic and the politics of hate*. Halifax: Fernwood Publishing.

Schmidt, Glen (1997). The Gove report and first nations child welfare. In, Pulkingham, J. & Ternowetsky G., (Eds.), *Child and family policies: struggles and options* (pp. 75–79). Halifax: Fernwood Publishing.

Thompson, N. (1998). *Promoting equality: Challenging discrimination and oppression in the human services*. London: Macmillan Press Ltd.

United Youth Movement. (1995). Street youth resource centre issues. In United Youth Movement, *Questionnaire on services for street youth for Vancouver action plan for sexually exploited youth* (pp. 8–9). Research conducted by the United Youth Movement; results compiled by Charis Romilly. Unpublished document, Vancouver.

Vorrath, H.H., & Brendtro, L.K. (1985). *Positive Peer Culture* (2nd ed.). New York: Aldine Publishing Company.

Wachholz, S., & Mullaly, B. (2000). The politics of the textbook. *Journal of Progressive Human Services 11*(2), 51–75.

Webber, M. (1991). *Street kids: The tragedy of Canada's runaways*. Toronto: University of Toronto Press.

Young, I.M. (1990). Five faces of oppression. In I.M. Young, *Justice and the Politics of Difference* (pp. 39–65). Princeton: Princeton University Press.

Chapter 8

"Meaningful" Participation and Governance: Lessons from Visible Minority Parents Using Child Care[1]

Evelyn Ferguson
Faculty of Social Work
University of Manitoba

INTRODUCTION AND THEORETICAL RATIONALE

In our current climate, the racial and cultural diversity of service users challenges us to closely examine the assumptions and beliefs underlying our practices, especially those we consider "progressive." As Carniol (2000, p. 130) argues: "Having developed a critical awareness, we sometimes become self-righteous and forget the importance of listening to, learning from, and sharing with the very groups we see as most oppressed."

It is from this perspective that this chapter explores the views, feelings, and preferences of a group of twenty-five visible-minority parents, mainly low-income mothers, including many recent immigrants and single parents, most with English as a second language, and a significant minority with severely disabled children. They all use child daycare centres in Metro Toronto or Winnipeg and therefore all have one or more preschool children. They are all employed, studying, or seeking employment. From a range of perspectives, including gender, race, and class, these individuals would be considered "oppressed" (Carniol, 2000; Mullaly, 2002).

The topics we explored with these parents are user participation and community governance in relation to their child care centres. These topics are of importance for several reasons.

Firstly, theoretical positions of welfare pluralists, progressive policy analysts, and academics argue strongly for the benefits of citizen participation in human service delivery. Community governance or participatory democracy

141

is seen as one important way "to enable those affected by issues to have a say in resolving them" (Wharf & McKenzie, 1998, p. 127). Also, community governance of the human services is seen as representing an essential addition to the limited range of opportunities for citizens to contribute to democratic self-governance (Reckart, 1993, p. 26; Wharf & McKenzie, 1998, p. 126). Mullaly (2002) argues that

> one way for anti-oppressive social workers to contribute to social transformation is to create, develop, and/or support alternative social service organizations that serve and are operated by members of particular oppressed groups. Attempts are made to institutionalize more egalitarian forms of social relationships by incorporating community control, mutual support and shared decision-making as key features. (Mullaly, 2002, p. 194)

Secondly, this topic is important because regulated group child care for preschool children is predominantly delivered in every Canadian province in non-profit voluntary organizations with extensive parental involvement or control (Ferguson & Prentice, 2001). While some provinces include varying amounts of commercial delivery, and two provinces include a small amount of public delivery, the trend has been for an emphasis on private, non-profit, community-based centres (Cleveland & Krashinsky, 2001).

The reasons for the popularity of this model include the opportunity for an accountable governance structure (probably a board with a parent majority); its flexibility to meet the needs of a local community; its potential to highlight the interests of immigrant families and First Nations peoples; and the potential for child care services to be community builders, helping to empower local populations (Prentice, 2001, pp. 207–210). In addition, there remains an assumption among many involved in child care policy that this model of delivery is preferable because it does not have the bureaucracy and inflexibility of the public sector, nor does it make money "on the backs of children" as in the commercial sector (Cleveland & Krashinsky, 2001, pp. 179–243).

Since the potential for user/consumer/parental involvement and control is a key issue within policy debates—specifically within the child care field and more generally in the human services literature—this study was designed to elicit data from the perspectives of users (in this case parents) themselves. Surprisingly, given the high profile of these issues in policy discussions, there was minimal data from the perspective of parents using licensed child care, and almost no data focusing on issues of gender, class, race, or culture.

In the spirit of Carniol's and Mullaly's commentary, this chapter reports how a group of "oppressed" human service users feel about involvement in and control of one of the most central human services in their lives—their child care centres. The interviews, which are qualitative, open-ended telephone conversations of one to two hours, allow us to explore their views and experiences. While the sample is not random or representative, what they tell us is instructive. On the whole, they are much less interested in governance or control of their centres than in a variety of other forms of "meaningful" input and participation. Why they feel this way is not surprising when we hear about the realities of their lives.

RESEARCH ON PARENTAL PARTICIPATION IN CHILD CARE

Discussion and research to date on parental involvement in child care includes several articles in the early 1990s (Doherty-Derkowski, 1994; Mayfield, 1990; Shimoni, 1992; Shimoni & Ferguson, 1992). These studies did not distinguish between mothers and fathers or focus on issues of class, race, or gender. Shimoni's (1992) review of the literature on parental involvement concluded that "The need for parental involvement in day care centers seems to be based on the beliefs, of many professionals that this is an important process rather than an empirical finding" (Shimoni, 1992, p. 91). This was echoed by Friendly (1994).

Since then Ferguson and Prentice have conducted several studies on the topic. One focused upon legislative control or influence on parent involvement in child care and found that provincial legislation regulating child daycare across Canada varied widely. Provinces fell into four categories ranging from those that were silent on the topic within the legislation and regulations to those that mandated full parental control in non-profit centres. This research established that in some provinces and territories, including Manitoba, legislation actually mandated parental involvement, being one of the few if any human services fields to legally mandate consumer involvement in delivery (Ferguson & Prentice, 2000, 2001).

Another study, strongly influenced by feminist perspectives (Baines, Evans, & Neysmith, 1998), involved interviewing forty-nine Winnipeg mothers who used group daycare centres (Ferguson, 1998). It found that mothers experience both internal and external pressures to participate in their centres. The internal pressure is strongly influenced by expectations of "good mothering" and is directed toward making their centres more caring places for their children, rather than wanting policy or management control. In addition, income level was found to be a critical variable, with subsidized mothers reporting more involvement than higher income mothers (Prentice & Ferguson, 1997, 2000). At the conclusion of this primarily quantitative study, the authors noted that more qualitative data was needed to more fully understand these findings and, in particular, the views of visible-minority parents needed to be examined to further explore the impact of culture and race.

SAMPLE AND METHOD

This chapter is based upon a third study by Prentice and Ferguson involving the analysis of seventy-seven qualitative interviews with parents in Ontario and Manitoba that investigated their views on volunteerism and parental involvement in their child care centres.

The thematic analysis of this subsample focused upon the views of visible minority parents.[2] This group comprised close to 33 per cent of our full sample (twenty-five of our seventy-seven parents). They included:

- twenty-one mothers and three fathers
- one great-grandmother raising her great-granddaughter after raising seven children and at least one of her twenty grandchildren
- fifteen single and ten partnered parents
- fifteen parents with English as a second language
- five parents with very high-needs children requiring special programming and support
- twenty-one low-income parents receiving subsidies and four non-subsidized parents
- twenty-three parents from Ontario and two from Manitoba
- seven parents using non-profit centres, four using commercial centres, and fourteen using municipally run centres
- parents from Canada, Africa, the Caribbean, eastern Europe, South Asia, and China

BROAD THEMES

In the following discussion of the themes that emerged from this data, a picture develops of a group of parents whose life experiences contextualize their values, beliefs, thoughts, and preferences in relation to their involvement in their child care centres. In the research process they revealed for us what has been most helpful and what forms of involvement or control appeal to them.

This discussion begins with their articulation of certain characteristics of their lives and families that have affected their involvement in their child care centres, and is followed by a discussion of the values that are most important to them in relation to their children's care. Finally the chapter discusses their views on volunteering, participation, and control.

Influential Characteristics of Parents

Mothers' and fathers' ability and motivation to volunteer in their daycare centres was strongly influenced by a number of factors, including low incomes, widespread parental underemployment, English as a second language, and the impact of having a special-needs child.

Low Incomes and Parental Underemployment

Low incomes and parental underemployment were two related issues. There were numerous examples of parents with professional or post-graduate training in their home countries whose credentials were not accepted in Canada. This meant trained and skilled individuals had to hold down one or more low-income jobs to support their families, which limited their time with their children, daycare centres, and communities. They had fewer resources to support their training and education needs and experienced a major shift in their class status from their own countries.

Examples include a thirty-five-year-old single mother from the Philippines with a university degree in chemistry, who resorted to doing computer upgrading in a free community centre program because she did not have the time or resources to pursue training elsewhere. She states: "Well, I have to work two jobs because my full-time job—the money that I'm making—is not enough" (#51). Other examples include a thirty-four–year-old partnered father, trained and licensed as a surgeon in China, who has an income of $1,300 month (#74); a single low-income thirty-three-year-old mother from Africa with three children under six years of age and a post-secondary education in her home country (#63); and a thirty-six-year-old single mother from Africa with two children (one with special needs), who is currently upgrading her nursing degree (#73).

English as a Second Language

Having English language difficulties was a common thread woven throughout many of these interviews. Not surprisingly, this affected their employability and ability to pursue training and education, contributing to their low incomes and underemployment. However, it also affected how they related to their daycare centres, providing both barriers and opportunities.

For some parents, poor English skills seriously limited their ability and confidence to be involved in their centres, including direct communication with the teachers about their own children. For instance, the Chinese surgeon (#74) stated: "Sometimes I talk to [the] teacher, but the teacher [in] the daycare, I don't understand sometimes. I can read, but sometimes when they talk, like I don't understand." This also affected his ability to talk to children and limited his involvement in the centre. Similarly, a thirty-two-year-old underemployed mother from China spoke about how language severely restricted both her husband's and her own abilities to participate in their daycare centre: "No, he [her husband] didn't do many thing[s], because he can't speak English well, so it's hard for him. ... Yes, because of his English. I think I don't know what to do exactly. You know, because I'm not very professional about how to communicate with not English-speaking children— talk with them, so it's a little hard for me, but if somebody [would] like to help me, I'd love to volunteer" (#61).

For other parents, their facility in their first language was translated into an opportunity to be helpful in the daycare. For example, a mother from Africa spoke about the role she could play in her centre: "And I used to go there sometime to help them. Because ... I think around four children ... [were] not speaking English. They [had a] very hard time to speak with the [other] children, to communicate with the children. And I was going sometimes there to help with them, supervise the kids, and just volunteer. ..." (#63).

Special-Needs Children

For the five parents who had a special-needs child, this factor tended to outweigh almost every other consideration in their discussion of their daycare centre, even if there were other challenges in their lives. Other research (Irwin & Lero, 1997) has documented the powerful impact that a special-needs child has on working parents. These interviews reinforce such findings and demonstrate how helpful a good daycare centre can be in these situations. For instance, one mother with a severely disabled child talked about the support she receives from her daycare: "They include me in everything and they offer new suggestions that I've never thought of before. That's what makes it such a wonderful centre. This care is number one. And there's the teaching she gets and the care and every teacher loves her—they hug her, they kiss her, and they do that with every child" (#50). The support she receives from this centre also means she "would do anything for the centre" and has a strong commitment to volunteer to the degree it is feasible for her.

But not all parents were as happy with their centres. Another mother with a seriously disabled child talked about her fears for her child and other special-needs children in the centre:

> Oh, you know what I [am] really concern[ed about] ... children with special needs need more attention. And I want [more] help for them. I know the staff is busy with the other kids [who are] normal. For example, [for] three kids inside the room, they can give one person for attention [to their] eating and playing with them because they don't speak. ... They eat very, very, slow[ly]. Yeah, ... one resource teacher is not enough. Just one and I think, one, two, three, four, I don't know how many kids got a problem in there. (#67)

Values of Importance
Significant values also dominated the thinking of these parents and influenced their perceptions and attitudes toward their centres and their children's care. These included the importance of collectivity and support for one another, learning and education for their children, fighting racism, and celebrating cultural diversity.

Importance of Collectivity
A significant number of parents articulated the importance of collectivity as a value and spoke about the daycare centre as a place for parents to support one another. This could be in relation to educating others about special-needs children, battling racism, sharing solutions for problem behaviour, adjusting to Canada's approach to discipline and child rearing, and many other topics. One of the few high-income mothers who came from eastern Europe articulated this clearly: "Especially [I like to] talk to other parents, like having once a month meetings about topics that are interesting for all of us. We talked [at] our last parents' meeting, but I don't know what will be [the] final decision. They said it is a good idea ... to work together and have some support for each other" (#75).

The mother of a severely disabled child, who was worried about the special-needs children in her centre, also talked about the centre as a place for parents with similar difficulties to help one another: "Oh, yeah, the other parents with the same problem—special needs—we [are] talking [about] the differences with the problems [with] our kids. Also [we] might share ... some news ... " (#67).

Importance of Education and Learning for Children

A common theme running throughout most of the interviews with these parents was the importance of learning and education for their children. This was articulated in relation to learning English, reading, numbers, learning to share and socialize with other children, and learning tolerance for differences. For example, when asked by our interviewer "So what kinds of things are most important for you that your children get at daycare, like trips, cuddles, learning to read?" a mother with three children on social assistance answered: "I mean, like the daycare is almost equal like school, like education. So I need them to be educated in a very good manner" (#66).

A twenty-four-year-old single African mother with three children under four years, who was referred to the daycare through a women's shelter, spoke about why she was satisfied with her children's care: "Yeah, they definitely [do] a good job with them. 'Cause when they are [at] home, they don't know how to speak, but when they go to daycare they [learn] how to talk, how to share. They [are] getting better" (#65).

Importance of Fighting Racism

A number of parents articulated very explicitly that it was important to them to have their children in an environment that challenged racism. One mother with a mixed-race child spoke about how she really liked the anti-racism committee in her child care centre, and commented that such committees were not found in many centres (#22). An East Indian mother with two children stated: "I did research on it. One of the most fantastic things is [that] they have an anti-racism committee that involves the parents and the families of the children who attend the daycare. ... And in this neighbourhood there's a great deal of parents who're on subsidy, a great deal of racial minorities" (#50).

Importance of Celebrating Culture and Diversity

Even more common were parents who spoke about the importance of celebrating diversity and the variety of cultures in their centres. They spoke about hosting social events with parents bringing food from various cultures, the appreciation that they had for multicultural staffing, and the importance of celebrating different religious and cultural holidays. A Black African mother with three children under five, who was parenting alone while awaiting her husband (who was still in Africa), spoke about such an occasion: "I decided to dress the African kids, you know. I told them we should do something a little bit cultural, seeing as there's a lot of cultures—we have all sorts, just name it. We have all sorts, so we decided, ... from Africa alone we have more than ten children from ten different African countries. ... It was so nice, it was fun, we all had fun. And we all prepared meals from our country" (#56).

Similarly, a twenty-three-year-old partnered Black mother with two children spoke about why she chose her centre: "The people looked more relaxed and they had a lot of different cultures in there and they had a lot of different things about different cultures, and that was important to me" (#72).

Views on Parent Volunteering, Participation, and Control

Mothers' and fathers' views on participating in their daycare centres were very much shaped by their life experiences and values. The parents interviewed used three different kinds of centres: commercial, private non-profit, and publicly delivered. All the non-profit centres had boards of directors with formal responsibility for the centre and extensive parental involvement, while most publicly delivered and commercial centres in this sample had a parent advisory committee. All had numerous other opportunities for parent participation, including field trips, volunteering in the centre, fundraising, parent support, educational groups, and social events.

Like other parents, their levels of involvement varied widely, depending on a function of varying family demands, opportunities, and desire (Prentice & Ferguson, 2000; Shimoni, 1992).[3] During the discussion of their centre participation (or lack thereof), a number of common themes emerged: volunteering and very busy lives; professionalism and skills of teachers; and input rather than control.

Volunteering and Very Busy Lives

The first theme, volunteering with very busy lives, has been found to some extent with every parent interviewed on this topic (Prentice & Ferguson, 2000; Shimoni, 1992). However, what was distinctive about this group of parents was the level of demand in their lives. Overall they had many children, lower levels of income combined with long working hours, many adjustment issues including language and cultural issues, and challenges associated with immigrant and visible-minority status. Many were single mothers raising children alone. Time to volunteer, therefore, was a major challenge and they spoke about it. For instance, it was not surprising when a single mother with an income of $10,000 a year, with three children under six years of age, and simultaneously using two child care centres, stated: "Right now I am busy with my work. Maybe later on I [would] like to volunteer again with my kids, you know, if I had more time. Right now I wouldn't mind money. [It's] hard to raise three kids" (#62). Nor was this mother's story that unusual within this sample of parents. While each family had at least one major challenge in their lives, most parents had multiple challenges. Time, therefore, was a very scarce commodity.

One South Asian single father, on a board of directors in a non-profit centre, spoke about the frustrations associated with this in relation to fundraising: "And you know more of the people, the parents, they were not able to commit and help in the fundraising activities, which is really difficult for them too [and] for us to get them behind these issues if both parents are working. They may not have [a] lot of time. ... To simply put it, in terms of the amount of time we put into those activities, and the amount of money we are able to raise, it is not worth doing year after year" (#47).

Such views were not universal, but fundraising expectations varied within the sample. Most municipally delivered centres had minimal fundraising expectations and they were disproportionately represented in this sample of parents. Some commercial centres do some fundraising, while most non-profit centres do some, and many do an extensive amount.

Professionalism and Skills of Teachers

A prominent theme in parents' interviews was the importance of professionalism and teachers' skills in the centres. As mentioned earlier, children's learning and education was important to these parents, so the teachers' skills were highly valued and respected.

Not surprisingly, this was clearly the case with the parents of children with special needs, many of whom needed skilled help to ensure that their children functioned on a daily basis. However, such views were not limited to those parents. A thirty-one-year-old single mother from the Caribbean with one son using a commercial centre stated this clearly when asked about parents' decision making in the centre:

> *Q.* Who do you think should make those decisions?
> *A.* Well, the teacher or whoever take[s] care of the kids.
> Because we are at work [all day], we [are] tired, you know. ...
> Well, it was important for me [that] he learn to talk, he learn
> to read. It was so nice because he learn[ed] to sing. (#45)

Another single mother, one of whose children was having some behaviour problems in the centre, appreciated the teachers' skills and help in dealing with this: "Yeah, I think they are very good teachers. ... They told me [that] now she's getting better" (#62).

A single African mother with three children under six spoke glowingly about the teachers in her daycare and what they had taught her child: "Everything she [has] now, when I see my daughter, I can see my daughter is a special girl. She speaks well, she talks well, she get[s] that from the daycare. Yeah, they help her very, very much and I'm very proud [of] the teachers [at] the daycare there" (#63).

Input Rather Than Control

Do these "oppressed parents" want management control of their child care centres? Almost unanimously, the answer is no. When asked directly whether they think parents should have control or input into the running of their centres, the vast majority answered that parents should have some kind of input, but not control. Some, like the single mother from the Caribbean (#45) quoted earlier, do not even value input from parents.

There are a variety of reasons articulated by parents for this position. Most are consistent with the perception that those who are on site running the centre need to make the decisions about what should happen there. For instance, a thirty-six-year-old single mother from Africa with two children (one with special needs) stated this explicitly: "Parents do not do it because, I don't know what to say, but I feel that they [are] just parents bring[ing] their child to the school, and then they leave. Okay, what the children do there they [the parents] don't see and they don't know, so whatever happens to the children should be [decided by] the daycare staff who are responsible [for] that" (#73).

Another mother, a recent immigrant from an east European country, had a particularly interesting view:

> I don't think they [parent] should have a lot of control, very much, especially in Canada where there are so many cultures, so many religions, so many ideas, and so much democracy. It would be very difficult to control everything, because you cannot be good for everybody. If something is good for one, it may be bad for somebody else. ... You know, [it's] not like the parents should go there and say you have to treat the kids this way. (#75)

One of the interviewers of the project summarized the position very nicely after she interviewed the great-grandmother who had raised her own seven children and was currently raising her grandson and her great-granddaughter (#78):

And something interesting from this interview that I've noticed with other interviews. When I ask about input or control in the daycare centre, she said that she thinks input is good, it's input that she thinks is important, that everybody should have a say, and other parents have said that too—that control isn't what's important in the daycare for parents, but input. (Interviewer #1)

CONCLUSIONS AND IMPLICATIONS

What lessons can we learn about "meaningful" participation from this group of busy, committed, resourceful, and highly challenged parents, whose lives reflect the profiles of "oppressed" individuals?

Firstly, it is clear that "meaningful" participation depends on respecting parents' involvement in the centres to the extent that is feasible for them given the multiple demands in their lives. This means recognizing and acknowledging each parent's strengths and skills that could be helpful for the child care centre when freely offered. Genuine participation should not be elicited by explicit or more subtle pressure to volunteer, expecting low-income busy individuals to sell chocolates or participate in other fundraising drives, or to sit on boards of directors and take responsibility for management when they do not understand or want those responsibilities.

At the same time, it also means providing concrete supports, creative opportunities, appropriately designed training, and encouragement for those who are hesitant or unable to participate due to shyness or more structural barriers such as language difficulties, low income, lack of transportation or child care, and limited time availability. Such respect, we see from these interviews, is dependent upon staff leadership and attitudes, not just formal mechanisms such as boards or advisory committees.

Meaningful participation for most of these parents is an opportunity for input to "have their say" in issues of importance to them, whether it be food, field trips, safety, racism, cultural diversity, or how to support special-needs children. It does not mean control or final authority in decision making. No parents interviewed from this sample wanted this authority. They were happy to leave management decisions to the staff of the centre. They felt parents were very busy people and their perspectives would differ from each other's. Also, no specific parents should control the centre, and staff caring for the children on a daily basis should have final decision-making authority.

These parents wanted to work with the staff as partners or helpers, providing a wide range of supports to staff. They helped on field trips, brought food for social occasions, volunteered when extra help was needed, and provided education on specific topics. Like mothers interviewed in other studies, their motivation was to enhance the quality and "caring" of their centres (Prentice & Ferguson, 1997, 2000).

We also learn from these parents that child care centres can be wonderful vehicles for celebrating cultural diversity, teaching tolerance and appreciation for difference, and for fighting racism. Those working in a multicultural environment providing care for young children can model respectful attitudes, provide support for parents experiencing racism, and give opportunities for parents to provide education and support for each other.

Child care centres can also be very important normative supports for families and parents experiencing very high demands at a particularly challenging time in their lives. As very busy people with little time for activities beyond work and children, child care centres can be natural community centres for parents with young children. They can provide a home for parent-support groups; special education seminars; toy, book, and clothes exchange programs; and social opportunities for parents and children. In that sense they can be important bulwarks for diminishing stress and preventing family breakdown. Many of these mothers and fathers spoke passionately about the benefits of their child care centres for themselves and their children. In so doing they make a strong case for expanding regulated child care so that it meets the needs of more than the 10–20 per cent of families who currently receive it.

This data raises important issues for those interested in policy and anti-oppressive practice. For child care centres it provides important ideas about how visible-minority parents want to be involved in their child care centres and what might facilitate such involvement. It also cautions centres and teachers to be cognizant of issues such as language, cultural differences, and racism.

For those developing provincial child care policy, this data raises concerns about the popularity of the private non-profit sector and parent boards in particular. While research indicates that some parents highly value parental control through parent boards, this finding is certainly not universal (Ferguson, 1992). Parents in this sample appear more interested in creative opportunities for input and collaboration with teachers than in policy control. In this sense the findings replicate the earlier findings of Prentice and Ferguson (1997, 2000).

The data also provides good evidence that municipal and commercial models of delivery can provide meaningful opportunities for parents. This does not mean this author equally prefers each of these delivery models.

The commercial sector, in particular, has some serious drawbacks, including lower wages and poorer working conditions (Doherty, Lero, Goelman, LaGrange, & Tougas, 2000; Prentice, 1997). However, the municipal delivery model has many benefits and bears further investigation.

For those interested in anti-oppressive social work practice, this data speaks to Carniol's warning that we professionals should not self-righteously decide for others what would be most empowering for them. While the idea of "community governance" is appealing to academics and activists looking for more opportunities for democratic self-governance, the idea is less appealing to those whose lives are preoccupied by financial survival and looking after small children. Given the realities of the lives of these mothers and few fathers in this sample, community governance appears to be a privileged luxury they have little time to consider.

However, those interested in anti-oppressive practice do have much to learn from these parents. They are remarkably courageous, determined, and resilient individuals who have experienced many challenges beyond the norm of most parents. Their stories are therefore moving, inspiring, and instructive. They reveal to us what is important to them in relation to their children, their own lives, and the delivery of human services. They also show us the very important role that their child care centres have played in their lives, in the process revealing how such centres can maximize the strengths of parents, while providing them support at a critical and challenging time in their lives.

They also throw us a challenge. Their desire to be involved in their community, in this case through their child care centres, was often voiced with passion and regret. Too often their wish to participate was impeded by structural barriers such as income, language, and sheer lack of time. Anti-oppressive practice can challenge those policies and practices that too often limit participation to the privileged. Given the creativity, ingenuity, and level of commitment voiced by these parents, we would have much to gain if we directed our energies in this direction.

NOTES

1. This chapter was originally presented at the 2002 Congress of the Social Sciences and Humanities: "Anti-Oppressive Practice and Global Transformation: Challenges for Social Work and Social Welfare," CASSW, University of Toronto, Toronto, Ontario, May 25–29, 2002. The author wishes to acknowledge the generous support of the SSHRC Women and Change Strategic Grant (#8197006). She wishes to express her thanks to Dr. Susan Prentice with whom the data was collected. Her influence on the

author's thinking on the topic of parent participation in child care was nurtured over a ten-year period and continues today. The author also wishes to thank research assistants and interviewers: Jodi Lee, Alex Marga-Haskiewicz, Windy Singleton, Cheryl Laurie, and especially Tracy Lavoie, whose interviewing skills made this chapter possible. Finally, many thanks to the very busy mothers and fathers who gave generously of their time.

2. Our recruitment strategy required contacting daycare centres that subsequently circulated letters to parents requesting their participation in the study. Parents contacted the researchers independently by letter or telephone. This process resulted in a sample that does not necessarily reflect the current composition of daycare provision in Ontario and Manitoba. Unfortunately this method, while ethical, resulted in very few Aboriginal parents volunteering. However, it did provide us with a rich sample of parents of other visible-minority backgrounds. In addition, this sample disproportionately represented parents using municipal daycare centres in Ontario.

3. As these parents did volunteer to participate in this study, we can also speculate that they would be more interested in participation than those parents who did not respond.

REFERENCES

Baines, C., Evans, P., & Neysmith, S. (1998). Women's caring: Work expanding, state contracting. In C. Baines, P. Evans, & S. Neysmith (Eds.), *Women's caring: Feminist perspectives on social welfare* (2nd ed.) (pp. 3–22). Toronto: Oxford University Press.

Carniol, B. (2000). *Case critical, challenging social services in Canada* (4th ed.). Toronto: Between the Lines.

Childcare Resource and Research Unit. (1997). *Child Care in Canada: Provinces and Territories.* Toronto: Childcare Resource and Research Unit.

Cleveland, G., & Krashinsky, M. (Eds.). (2001). *Our children's future: Child care policy in Canada.* Toronto: University of Toronto Press.

Doherty, G., Lero, D., Goelman, H., LaGrange, A., & Tougas, J. (2000). *You bet I care! A Canada-wide study on wages, working conditions, and practices in child care centres.* Guelph: Centre for Families, Work, and Well-being, University of Guelph.

Doherty-Derkowski, G. (1994) *Quality matters: Excellence in early childhood programs.* Don Mills: Addison-Wesley.

Ferguson, E. (1992). *Private or public? Profit or non-profit? Reasons for the auspice preferences of a sample of day care consumers in Ontario.* Unpublished doctoral dissertation, Faculty of Social Work, University of Toronto.

_____. (1998). The child care debate: Fading hopes and shifting sands. In C. Baines, P. Evans, & S. Neysmith (Eds.), *Women's caring: Feminist perspectives on social welfare* (2nd ed.) (pp. 191–217). Toronto: Oxford University Press.

Ferguson, E., & Prentice, S. (2000). Exploring parental involvement in Canada: An ideological maze. In J. Hayden (Ed.), *Landscapes in early childhood services: Cross national perspectives on empowerment and restraint* (pp. 219–237). Sydney: Peter Lang Publishing.

_____. (2001). Consumer involvement and control in child day care: A legislative analysis. *Canadian Review of Social Policy 47*, 25–44.

Friendly, M. (1994). *Child care policy in Canada: Putting the pieces together.* Toronto: Addison Wesley.

Irwin, S.H., & Lero, D. (1997). *In our way: Child care barriers to full workforce participation experienced by parents of children with special needs—and potential remedies.* Wreck Cove, Cape Breton: Breton Books.

Mayfield, M. (1990). Parent involvement in early childhood programs. In I. Dovey (Ed.), *Child care and education: Canadian dimensions* (pp. 240–254). Toronto: Nelson Canada.

Mullaly, B. (2002). *Challenging oppression: A critical social work approach.* Toronto: Oxford University Press.

Prentice, S. (1997). The deficiencies of commercial day care. *Policy Options 18*(1), 42–26.

_____. (2001). The case for community-governed childcare services. In G. Cleveland & M. Krashinsky (Eds.), *Our children's future: Child care policy in Canada* (pp. 201–217). Toronto: University of Toronto Press.

Prentice, S., & Ferguson, E. (1997). "My kids come first": The contradictions of mothers' involvement in childcare delivery. In J. Pulkingham & G. Ternowetsky (Eds.), *Child and family policies: Struggles, strategies and options* (pp. 188–202). Halifax: Fernwood.

_____. (2000). Volunteerism, gender, and the changing welfare state: A case-study in child daycare. In S. Neysmith (Ed.), *Restructuring caring labour: Discourse, state practice, and everyday life* (pp. 118–141) Toronto: Oxford University Press.

Rekart, J. (1993). *Public funds, private provision: The role of the voluntary sector.* Vancouver: UBC Press.

Shimoni, R. (1992). Parent involvement in early childhood education and day care. *Sociological Studies of Child Development 5*, 73–95.

Shimoni, R., & Ferguson, B. (1992). Rethinking parent involvement in child care programs. *Child and Youth Care Forum 21*, 105–118.

Wharf, B., & McKenzie, B. (1998). *Connecting policy to practice in the human services.* Toronto: Oxford University Press.

Chapter 9

Inclusion by Design:
The Challenge for Social Work in
Workplace Accommodation for
People with Disabilities

Donald R. Leslie
School of Social Work
University of Windsor
Kaye Leslie
Office of Diversity and Workplace Equity
Bank of Montreal
Michelle Murphy
Social Work Student
School of Social Work
University of Windsor

Since its inception, the mission of social work, as a profession, has included the concept of assisting each individual to meet his or her maximum potential. As well, a set of core values, including non-judgmental acceptance and positive regard for the dignity and worth of each individual, have framed social work practice efforts and approaches (Miley, O'Melia, & DuBois, 1998). Unfortunately, the reality has sometimes differed from the ideal. Ideally, everyone, regardless of his or her race, creed, sexual orientation, or physical attributes, would be free from oppression and discrimination, and would have access to equal opportunity.

The profession of social work and its practitioners have been diligent in identifying oppression and discrimination toward specific groups based on characteristics attributed to the members of these groups. In large part, the characteristics identifying these people as different have been shown to be social constructs based upon beliefs and attitudes of dominant culture groups (Hughes, 1999). As such, social work has fought to change these social constructs to emphasize the similarity and equality of all individuals and, therefore, the need to accept all identified groups and treat them no differently than the dominant cultural group. However, in the case of characteristics or attributes used to identify people with disabilities, there is acceptance of the idea that their abilities do differ from those of the able-bodied. While the values and goals remain the same, the process for combating oppression and discrimination for people with disabilities is quite different (Hughes & Paterson, 1997).

For social work as a profession, this process of combating oppression and discrimination against people with disabilities within its own ranks requires a proactive response. It is not sufficient to adjust our beliefs to insure that we do not treat people with disabilities differently from other groups in society; rather, it is crucial that we treat our clients, students, and colleagues with disabilities quite differently. This chapter argues that accommodation, particularly accommodation in the field of education and/or in the workplace, is an essential aspect of combating oppression and discrimination for this target population.

ISSUES IN ACCOMMODATION

The Legal Situation

Accommodation is a process to eliminate disadvantage, discrimination, and oppression. The duty to accommodate is a legal requirement of both the Canadian Human Rights and Employment Equity acts. Factors such as disability, sex, age, family status, ethnic origin, and religious belief are included as legitimate areas of focus for the duty to accommodate. In particular, the decision to employ, retain, or promote an individual with a disability must not be affected by the need to provide accommodation. In fact, accommodation must be provided short of creating an undue hardship. This means that unless the provision of accommodation will jeopardize the safety of others or create a severe and debilitating financial burden, the law requires accommodation. This process assumes that social work, as a profession, will insure that barriers do not exist for the inclusion of clients with disabilities in the service delivery system, for students with disabilities participating in social work education, and for employees with disabilities within the social service workforce.

The *Canadian Human Rights Act* (1977) prohibits discrimination in employment and the receipt of services in all federal jurisdictions, and specifically requires accommodation of individuals with disabilities in employment and the provision of goods and services. The *Employment Equity Act* (1986) requires federally regulated employers to achieve equality in the workplace and to correct conditions of disadvantage experienced by four designated groups: Aboriginal peoples, people with disabilities, visible minorities, and women (Canadian Human Rights Commission, 2001).

People have often assumed that the duty to accommodate was derived only as part of the employment equity legislation, when in fact it also has its roots in the *Canadian Human Rights Code* and the *Charter of Rights and Freedoms*. The duty to accommodate has been the law in Ontario for almost two decades. Despite this passage of time, accommodation is still interpreted by many as providing special treatment for these minority groups, as opposed to creating an atmosphere and reality of equal opportunity. It is often difficult to comprehend that in order to provide equal opportunity and remove barriers to meeting each individual's maximum potential, people with disabilities must not be treated equally but equitably. Equitable treatment requires that treatment of people with disabilities be different, not the same as treatment of the able-bodied.

Judge Rosalie Abella clarified, in her Royal Commission on Disability and Accommodation, the difference between equity and equality. She indicated that for many organizations, equity has been interpreted as the need to treat everyone the same. She further explained that by treating everyone alike, this in fact is discriminating against people with disabilities as it ignores their differences and their need for accommodation (Abella, 1984).

Myths and Misconceptions

In the past, employers were not concerned with the concept of accommodating employees in the workplace. Many of us will recall the concerns and anxiety expressed by employers when women began to enter the workforce. There was a prevalent notion that hiring women would prove to be a liability. Organizations were concerned that they would need to have separate washrooms and consider the implications of flexible time in order to accommodate child care responsibilities. Today, of course, over 50 per cent of the workforce is comprised of women, and the misconceptions regarding absenteeism and lower productivity have proven to be unsubstantiated. Organizations have come to recognize the importance of accommodating parents in the workplace, regardless of gender, in order to recruit and retain the best talent. Unfortunately, the attitude toward accommodating people with disabilities has not yet undergone the same positive transition.

Many employers perceive the hiring of employees with disabilities to be a risky business. They assume, regardless of candidates' skills and abilities, that their productivity will be lower and that they will be unable to keep up with the demanding pace and pressure of the workplace. These assumptions also include the notion that employees with disabilities will be emotionally vulnerable and will most likely have a higher accident and absenteeism rate (Gandz, 2001). Another myth that employers often hold is that the cost of accommodating people with disabilities will be excessive (Cantor, 1998).

Just as the fears and misconceptions about women in the workplace were unfounded, so too are the misconceptions regarding employees with disabilities. Vicky Winn, vice president of human resources at the Washington Mutual Bank, reported that hiring people with disabilities and accommodating them makes good business sense. Her reasons included the following:

- maintain a competitive edge by accessing an untapped, highly skilled labour pool
- employees with disabilities have already learned how to be flexible and adapt to change
- increased diversity leads to new and valuable perspectives, resulting in better customer service
- at Washington Mutual, the retention rate for people with disabilities is higher than that for the able-bodied workforce—a cost-saving reality
- a representative workforce that reflects all members of society motivates customers and employees, and the corporation is viewed as demonstrating principles of inclusion

According to a 1999 survey conducted by the Job Accommodation Network, a service of the President's Committee on Employment of People with Disabilities, 20 per cent of accommodations cost nothing, while 51 per cent of accommodations cost between U.S. $1 and U.S. $500 (Job Accommodation Network Web Site, 1999). Often accommodations require only creativity and the ability to think outside the box.

Accommodation that benefits people with disabilities is frequently viewed as special. In reality, accommodations can benefit everyone. For example, ramps that have been designed primarily to provide access for wheelchair users are also used by parents with strollers, seniors, individuals with carts, and people delivering heavy items. Speech-reading software for blind employees is also used by a range of sighted employees and customers on the Web. Large-print signs are much easier for seniors with decreased vision to read, which is a common need since the leading cause of visual impairment is age-related macular degeneration. Homes that are designed with wider doorways not only enable better wheelchair access, but also allow the homeowner to move appliances and furniture through more easily. Elevators, of course, are used by everyone, as are automatic doors. An employer does not often consider that the cost of providing lights, desks, and computers is an accommodation for able-bodied employees. However, if a large-print monitor or speech software is installed on a personal computer, it is regarded as special accommodation.

Despite attitudinal barriers, organizations have made progress in terms of accommodating employees in the workplace. For example, there are centralized accommodation funds so that individual departments are not negatively affected by the cost of accommodation. There are resources and specialists in place to manage accommodation. This may include human support, i.e., sign language interpreters, adaptive technology, adapted workstations, job modification, or changes to policies and systems in order to accommodate different needs.

There is an understanding of the legal duty to accommodate employees with disabilities in the public and private sectors. These sectors seem to have a common understanding about the need to provide appropriate accommodation in the workplace and the legal obligation to do so. There also appears to be an understanding that the duty to accommodate is a joint responsibility and that it should not fall only on the person with the disability. However, in the not-for-profit or voluntary sector, which includes a significant portion of organizations providing social work service, there is less evidence of such progress. Typically, organizations in this sector survive on limited resources that never seem to meet the service demands (Holosko & Leslie, 1998). Any consideration of increased costs to accommodate employees with disabilities seems out of the question. In addition, these organizations are often housed in older buildings, with cheaper rents, which are not accessible to the mobility-impaired without significant renovation costs. All of these factors conspire to perpetuate barriers that should be removed through appropriate accommodation. In spite of the legislation and enhanced understanding of the duty to accommodate, the employment situation for people with disabilities remains bleak and is evidence of our inability to provide sufficient accommodation and acceptance.

The Situation for People with Disabilities

In past work experience, it has been observed that many people with disabilities, regardless of levels of education and qualifications, continue to be underemployed. For example, the Health Activity Limitation Survey (Ministry of Supply and Services Canada, 1991, p. 32) stated that "Only 26.5% of the working age VIP (visually impaired population) is employed, compared to 69.9% of the working age NDP (non-disabled population)." In many cases, employers believe that different than means less than, and an able-ist mentality places a higher value on functionality. In other words, the more disabled the individual, the less valued she or he becomes. As women continue to battle against the glass ceiling, people with disabilities are fighting just to get in the door. This situation flies in the face of social work's commitment to the principle of social justice for all.

A widely shared argument for not accommodating people with disabilities and not considering access in the design and development of technology and other products has been the limited numbers of people with disabilities. In other words, there aren't really enough people to justify the cost of making goods and services accessible. While we recognize that the minority group status is not a viable excuse for lack of accommodation, it behooves us to realize that this is a rapidly growing segment of the population. For example, at the end of the 1990s there were 4.2 million Canadians who acknowledged having a disability, up from 3.3 million at the beginning of the same decade. It is estimated that this number will double in the next twenty-five years and that the current proportion of one in six Canadians having a disability will also increase (Human Resources Development Canada, 1999).

Rosa Parks started the civil rights movement fifty years ago when she, as a Black woman, refused to go to the back of the bus. Today, many people with disabilities cannot even board a public bus. Because society is beginning to recognize the value of diversity, an attitudinal shift is underway. As our population ages, increasing the number of people with disabilities, accommodation will become imperative for the successful functioning of society. We will not be able to afford to withhold accommodation. The needs of people with disabilities will one day be considered in the design stage of goods and services, with accommodations built right in. Then we will have achieved true equality and inclusiveness.

COMPARISON OF VALUES IN ACCOMMODATION AND SOCIAL WORK

There appears to be a very close similarity when comparing the values of generalist social work practice to those of accommodation approaches. An exploration of the underlying values espoused in support of workplace accommodation finds an almost perfect match with the core values of social work practice. These positive indicators should translate to a strong sense of identification with and attention to this important process. However, a review of the literature shows that social work has made little contribution in this area.

Social work, at the entry level, is referred to as generalist practice. A generalist practitioner is expected to have a foundation for the method, knowledge, values, sanctions, and purpose of social work practice. McMahon (1996) states the values of generalist social work practice as individualization, purposeful expression of feelings, controlled emotional involvement, acceptance, non-judgmental attitude, self-determination, and confidentiality. Although each value is viewed as imperative, this chapter speaks to the importance of individualization, acceptance, non-judgmental attitude, and self-determination in the process of workplace accommodation.

The process of workplace accommodation requires respect for one's dignity, provision of individualized accommodation, and allowance for integration and full participation of all employees with disabilities. "The right to accommodation is the right to equality: it's what allows people with disabilities to compete in the work force on a level playing field" (Falardeau-Ramsay, 1998, p. 35). Barak (2000) states that an inclusive workplace is one that: (a) values and uses individual and intergroup differences within its work force; (b) co-operates with and contributes to its surrounding community; (c) alleviates the need of disadvantaged groups in the wider environment; and (d) collaborates with individuals, groups, and organizations across national and cultural boundaries. An agency should provide accommodation within its organization and be active in advocating for it outside the workplace in the larger community. Agencies must embrace the unique perspectives and qualities that each individual brings, which incorporate a sharing of experiences and respect for each other regardless of differences.

As with generalist practice social work, workplace accommodation has a set of underpinning values. Individualization, acceptance, a non-judgmental attitude, and self-determination are identified as the core values. Individualization refers to the employer's responsibility to treat each employee as a separate person with individual strengths and weaknesses. We must begin by challenging our own attitudes and beliefs about those with disabilities and then learn to trust people with disabilities and allow them the opportunity to grow and expand within the agency (Marlett, Gall, & Wright-Felske, 1984). Demonstrating acceptance is another important aspect of workplace accommodation. In order to provide an effective means of workplace accommodation, individuals must accept co-workers with the differences they may have. The accommodating value of non-judgmental attitude involves eliminating inaccurate assumptions about and prejudice against those with disabilities. To successfully accommodate, agencies and organizations must remove physical barriers and assist their personnel in adjusting their attitudes (Forum, 2000). Misconceptions about individuals with disabilities continue to infect organizations worldwide and consequently, those individuals are discriminated against because of inaccuracies and misinformation. Finally, the value of self-determination must be explored. Employers and employees must continue to reinforce and focus on the strengths of the individual with the disability. They must allow the person the opportunity to grow and expand within the agency. The inclusion of individuals with disabilities recognizes their potential and ability to shift from dependence to independence and to be contributors rather than recipients (Forum, 2000).

Barak (2000) concludes that the profession of social work can and should play a key role in the conceptualization and implementation of workplace accommodation. The skills needed to implement programs and to increase workplace inclusion are consistent with the competencies of generalist practice social work. Social workers should begin evaluating their current practices, norms, values, policies, and programs to include individuals with special needs. Considerable time is spent in social work curricula focusing on the importance of accepting all individuals, yet students placed in human service agencies see a lack of representation of individuals with disabilities among their staff. Social workers should be masters at implementing the process of accommodation, yet they appear to have significant difficulty in doing so. It is not enough for social workers to empower their clients; they also must provide opportunities for those with disabilities to enter and fully participate in our profession and its institutions.

A review of the social work literature demonstrates social workers' general lack of awareness about promoting workplace accommodation. Although various articles discuss the importance of social work and diversity, there has been a modest amount published on the subject of the responsibility that social workers have in actively participating and aiding in the process of workplace accommodation. In particular, there is a dearth of models in the social work literature dealing with the process of accommodation. Social workers, in general, can and should be the driving force in helping organizations overcome the one-size-fits-all approach to accommodating people with disabilities. They can be instrumental in implementing programs to increase workplace inclusion by using their professional social work skills and competencies. Since social workers clearly possess the abilities to make a difference in this area, it is appropriate to question why there has been little evidence of impact in this regard.

THE DILEMMA FOR SOCIAL WORK

One of the major strengths of social work, as a helping profession, has been its ability to borrow knowledge from other disciplines and to incorporate this knowledge into practice approaches. However, in the case of taking an active role in workplace accommodation, social work, like other helping disciplines, has been hampered by the dominating influence of the bio-medical model. This model, when applied to working with and understanding people with disabilities, takes a predominately rehabilitative approach (Hanes, 2002). This focus upon rehabilitation results in a view that contemplates a process for either restoring function or overcoming limitation as its major goal (Phillips, 1985; Roulstone, 2000). While social work has been more successful than many other disciplines in broadening its change perspective to include changing the environment of the person with a disability, it has nonetheless remained preoccupied with the rehabilitation focus on individual abilities.

Historically, social work has made significant contributions through its role in deinstitutionalization and its support for mainstreaming. However, the major concerns, reflected in these activities, have revolved around people with disabilities as clients. As such, social workers have no difficulty in promoting and achieving change that results in people with disabilities living and being cared for in the least restrictive environment possible. They have also been quick to fight for the right of people with disabilities to be treated with maximum respect for their dignity and worth within these environments. While this has been of significant importance, it has also tended to maintain a perspective that simply broadens the bio-medical model interpretation rather than shift thinking to a new paradigm. It allows the person with a disability to be more successful in attaining the dominant (able-bodied) culture's vision of success, but does not allow for an actual redefinition of success (Phillips, 1985). Similarly, within our profession, it has allowed for the support and promotion of the changes in institutions and policies that will assist people with disabilities in overcoming their limitations and maximizing their success in society at large, without clearly embracing people with disabilities as colleagues in our profession and its human service organizations.

A Social Constructionist Approach

The paradigm shift to a social constructionist perspective on practice and people with disabilities shows great promise for truly including people with disabilities as equal participants in our profession, as well as in society in general (Hughes & Patterson, 1997; Mullaly, 2002). This perspective allows us to understand that disabilities are socially constructed understandings of difference rather than social realities. The social constructionist approach is, in some ways, an extension of labelling theory and, in other ways, a means for overcoming the negative effects of labelling. It posits that the functional limitation caused by some impairment is not the real issue; rather, it is the meaning that becomes attributed to being identified as having an impairment or disability that is the social reality. The approach would further postulate that there is a socially constructed ideal view of normalcy, and that people with disabilities deviate from this constructed ideal and are, therefore, not only different from but lesser than those who are not seen to differ (Hughes, 1999). The social constructionist approach therefore allows for the deconstruction of this meaning attributed to difference, and allows for the construction of a new non-pathological meaning to be established relative to the differences created by impairments. It is then a matter of simply accepting difference, and constructing different methods for achieving success and ways of defining success (Reindal, 1999).

This view of disability as difference is not only appealing to the profession but also to people with disabilities themselves, since it is ultimately a highly respectful perspective. On first blush, it appears to fit well with the social movement and human rights directions that have already been pursued for some time (Barnartt, 1996). However, whether we conceptualize disabilities as social constructs or as social realities, dominant culture attitudes and beliefs still prevail. The process for changing these constructs is as time consuming as the process for changing social attitudes. Simply changing how we conceptualize disabilities will not automatically bring about real change in the profession. Social work has always been a female-dominated profession and even though we have seen several decades of a feminist perspective, we still find senior management and education positions numerically dominated by males. Thus, there is no reason to believe that people with disabilities will be aided immediately through a change in perspective in our profession. Social work will continue to struggle with seeing people with disabilities as being lesser than or having limitations since the profession and its members often assimilate the prevailing views of the dominant culture (Leslie & Myers, 1996).

CONCLUSION

Implementation of this social constructionist perspective will pose difficulties since people with disabilities will still need their differences to be accommodated. The continuation of the human rights model of accommodation for and acceptance of people with disabilities will perpetuate the difficulty for social work in balancing competing or conflicting rights (Handley, 2000). For example, the social work administrator who has to decide whether or not to hire an individual with a disability will assess not only the individual's qualifications and skills but also the client population's ability and willingness to relate to the potential staff member with a disability. All too often the view that the client population will be disadvantaged in having to change their perspective about working with people with disabilities has been the deciding factor. Similar to the adage in business that the customer is always right, this view of the client's needs as being predominant has been a difficult stumbling block to the acceptance and accommodation of individuals with disabilities as colleagues and co-workers.

The process of facilitating this acceptance of people with disabilities as equal professional colleagues will require social work administrators, funders, and policy-makers to develop appropriate infrastructure to effectively accommodate these differences. For example, employing some social workers with disabilities will require the acquisition of up-to-date adaptive technologies to accommodate their differences. In other cases, renovations to existing facilities may be required. In either event, it is inappropriate for these accommodation costs to play a role in the hiring decision. Similarly, it is unacceptable for the newly hired social worker with a disability to work without appropriate accommodation while the funding resources for their accommodations are found. Efforts must be made to provide separate funding for accommodation costs that can be accessed quickly at any point during the fiscal year, and that do not alter existing budgets. Without such centralized and easily accessible resources, the individual with a disability will continue to be disadvantaged by this systemic barrier. This is particularly true since most social service agency budgets do not have sufficient leeway to absorb any degree of additional, unplanned costs without somehow affecting service delivery. Human rights legislation makes it clear that it is unacceptable not to hire a person with a disability because of feared costs for accommodation, but in order for this legality to be respected, decision makers must be relieved of the untenable process of weighing the hiring of a staff member with a disability against a reduction in client service.

In order to fully embrace workplace accommodation as a bona fide social work methodology for assisting people with disabilities in society at large, social work will first need to accept people with disabilities, along with their differences, as full members of its own profession. Social work will need to embrace an anti-oppression approach in order to view different ways of doing things as being equally acceptable ways of doing things. People with disabilities will need to be seen as people of difference, not as individuals with limitations. As indicated by Hughes (1999), the contention that the oppression of people with disabilities is reducible to social restrictions, which are the outcome of real physiological limitations, will need to be challenged. Social work practitioners will need to view people with disabilities as people with differences, but also as people absolutely equal to themselves.

REFERENCES

Abella, R. (1984). *Report of the Commission on Equality in Employment*. Ottawa: Supply and Services Canada.

Barak, M.E.M. (2000). The inclusive workplace: An ecosystems approach to diversity management. *Social Work 45*, 339–351.

Barnartt, S. (1996). Disability culture or disability consciousness? *Journal of Disability Policy Studies 7*(2), 2–19.

Canadian Human Rights Commission. (2001). *A place for all: A guide to creating an inclusive workplace*. Cat. no. HR21-55/2001. Ottawa: Minister of Public Works and Government Services.

Cantor, A. (1998). *Disability in the workplace: Effective and cost effective accommodation planning*. Paper presented at NATCON 1998, Ottawa, Ontario.

Falardeau-Ramsay, M. (1998). Duty to accommodate: The key to employment rights. *Abilities 36*, 35.

Forum (2000). Wellsizing the workplace: Towards inclusive employment. *Abilities 42*, 25.

Gandz, J. (2001). *A business case for diversity*. London: University of Western Ontario.

Handley, P. (2000). Trouble in paradise—a disabled person's right to the satisfaction of a self-defined need: Some conceptual and practical problems. *Disability & Society 16*(2), 313–325.

Hanes, R. (2002). Social work with persons with disabilities. In S. Hick (Ed.), *Social Work in Canada* (pp. 217–233). Toronto: Thompson Educational Publishing.

Holosko, M., & Leslie, D. (1998). Obstacles to conducting empirically based practice. In J. Wodarski & B. Thyer (Eds.), *The handbook of empirical social work practice* (2nd ed.) (pp. 433–453). New York: John Wiley & Sons.

Hughes, B. (1999). The constitution of impairment: Modernity and the aesthetic of oppression. *Disability & Society 14*(2), 155–172.

Hughes, B., & Paterson, K. (1997). The social model of disability and the disappearing body: Towards a sociology of impairment. *Disability and Society 12*(3), 325–340.

Human Resources Development Canada (1999). *Future directions to address disability issues for the government of Canada: Working together for full citizenship*. Cat. no. MP80-2/11-1999E. Hull: Government of Canada.

Job Accommodation Network Web Site, Accommodation Benefit/Cost Data Analysis tabulated through July 30, 1999. <www.jan.wvu.edu/mediat/Stats/BenCosts0799.htm>

Leslie, D.R., & Myers, L.L. (1996). Social work practice with persons with adult-onset disabilities. In D.F. Harrison, B.A. Thyer, & J.S. Wodarski (Eds.), *Cultural diversity and social work practice* (pp. 201–231). Springfield: Charles C. Thomas.

Marlett, N.J., Gall, R., & Wright-Felske, A. (Eds.) (1984). *Dialogue on disability: A Canadian perspective*. (pp. 127–160). Calgary: The University of Calgary Press.

McMahon, M.O. (1996). *The general method of social work practice: A generalist perspective* (3rd ed.). Needham Heights: Allyn & Bacon.

Miley, K.K., O'Melia, M., & DuBois, B. (Eds.). (1998). *Generalist social work practice* (2nd ed). Boston: Allyn & Bacon.

Ministry of Supply and Services Canada. (1990). *Health activity limitation survey.* Blindness and Visual Impairment in Canada special topic series. Cat. no. 82-615, vol. 3. Ottawa: Ministry of Supply and Services Canada.

Mullaly, B. (2002). *Challenging oppression: A critical social work approach.* Toronto: Oxford University Press.

Phillips, M. (1985). "Try harder": The experience of disability and the dilemma of normalization. *The Social Science Journal 22*(4), 45–57.

Reindal, S.M. (1999). Independence, dependence, interdependence: Some reflections on the subject and personal autonomy. *Disability & Society 14*(3), 353–367.

Roulstone, A. (2000). Disability, dependency and the new deal for disabled people. *Disability & Society 15*(3), 427–443.

Chapter 10

Communities That Foster Diverse Modes of Existence Versus Societies Based on Control: A Phenomonological Approach to Improving the Deinstitutionalization Process

Alain Beaulieu
Health and Prevention Social Research Group
GRASP/Centre-FCAR
Université de Montréal

If there is one virtue that can be demanded of a "professional intellectual," it is the obligation to remain objective in terms of one's personal authority with respect to all the ideals—even the most grandiose ones—that predominate in a given era, and if necessary, "to swim against the current."

—Max Weber

MENTAL HEALTH SERVICE DEINSTITUTIONALIZATION POLICIES

Mental health services were deinstitutionalized in a similar manner in Quebec and Ontario. In Quebec, in 1999–2000, the Ministry of Health and Social Services allocated $1.3 billion, or 8 per cent of its total budget of $16.7 billion, to various programs dedicated to mental health clients. The numbers for 1998–1999 were of the same order of magnitude. In 1989, the government of Quebec enacted its first official mental health policy (Ministère de la Santé Services Sociaux, 1989). It had five main objectives: (1) to ensure the primacy of the individual; (2) to enhance the quality of social services; (3) to promote fairness; (4) to seek solutions in the living environment; and (5) to strengthen partnerships. In 1998, the Quebec Ministry of Health and Social Services adopted an action plan (Ministère de la Santé Services Sociaux, 1998) stressing the importance of accommodation and work support and the quality of services to people whose fragility is heightened by mental health problems. One of the objectives of this reform is to reverse the ratio of in-hospital psychiatric care funding to money for integrating ex-psychiatric patients into the community from 60:40 to 40:60. The government instituted a five-year plan to deinstitutionalize 3,000 additional psychiatric hospital residents by the end of 2002 in order to lower the number of beds per 1,000 inhabitants from 1.00 to 0.40 (Ministère de la Santé Services Sociaux, 1997). But public, community, and social resources are still inadequate to accommodate these deinstitutionalized individuals. Occupancy rates are high and the waiting lists are long (Dorvil, Beaulieu, & Morin, 2001; Dorvil, Guttman, Ricard, & Villeneuve, 1997).

The situation is similar in Ontario. In 1983, the Ontario Ministry of Health published a document known as the Heseltine Report in which "a balanced and comprehensive mental health care system" and "separation of treatment and accommodation" are proposed (Ontario Ministry of Health, 1983). In 1988, the Graham Report announced a long-term plan aimed at orienting the mental health care system toward the community (Provincial Community Mental Health Committee, 1988). People with serious mental health problems were then identified as a priority for the mental health services. A widespread campaign was mounted to involve users and their families in the decision-making process. In 1993, the Ontario Ministry of Health (1993) evaluated the past decade of mental health service reform. Those elements that were working were reinforced, and a special program was added to divert resources from institutions toward the community, with the more specific goals of optimizing the number of beds reserved for psychiatric patients, the hospitalization rate, and service quality. The Ontario Ministry of Health plans to lower the ratio of psychiatric beds per 1,000 inhabitants to 0.30:0.35 by 2003, and wants to reduce the hospital-to-community expenditure ratio to 40:60, just as in Quebec. The recent document *Making It Happen* (Ontario Ministry of Health, 1999) describes the present state of the system and mental health services, and reports new priority challenges associated with deinstitutionalization: meeting the outpatient needs of former psychiatric patients, accepting the unforeseeable nature of some of their needs, and adequately managing the hospital-to-community-to-hospital "revolving-door syndrome" during periods of heightened instability. Lastly, Ontario community groups have had an annual budget of $4 million since the early 1990s (Blais, Mulligan-Roy, & Camirand, 1998). This is very little compared to the $1.4 billion that has been dedicated to mental health, on average, every year in Ontario since 1990. Once again, waiting lists for ex-psychiatric patient integration programs are long and the resources inadequate. This is why it is important to develop new integration paradigms and put them into practice (Nelson, Lord, & Ochocka, 2001).

It is now acknowledged that returning to community life is one of the most determining factors for the well-being of ex-psychiatric patients. This is affirmed by the World Health Organization (1998) in a report on world health: "Health is a state of complete physical, mental and social well-being and not merely the absence of disease or infirmity." Concretely, this view of recovery endorses the new policies on closing beds in psychiatric hospitals and returning patients to the community. But deinstitutionalizing psychiatric care services requires more than simply redefining the role of hospitals in treating people with mental health problems; it also requires a reassessment of the meaning of the word "community."

THE DANGER OF INSTITUTIONALIZING THE COMMUNITY

The natural reflex of institutional decision makers is to extend into the community the panoply of care given to people with psychiatric disorders who were previously treated in hospital. This form of deinstitutionalization is most often a pseudo deinstitutionalization that results in a new form of community institutionalization. Programs of assertive community treatment (PACTs) have been in place since the 1920s (Dorvil, 2001). Their aim is to develop alternatives to psychiatric treatments by training multidisciplinary teams responsible for assisting ex-psychiatric patients in their daily tasks (budgeting, job and accommodation searches, medication control, grocery shopping, etc.). The over-control exercised by the first PACT participants (checking mail, searching personal spaces, monitoring phone conversations, intruding into privacy, etc.) was so great that it discouraged some patients from leaving the hospital. Over time, the surveillance became somewhat relaxed so that PACT could coexist with a system of simple "personal life goal supports." Patients thus enjoyed greater liberty within the community. But even today, monitoring and community service practices place a heavy burden on mentally fragile people. Life in the community is still so oppressive that some people now living in psychiatric institutions (just like some prisoners), seeing what is in store for them on the outside, choose to remain in the institution. These obstacles to integration of ex-psychiatric patients are conditioned by, among other things, the obligation imposed upon them to visit a psychiatrist on a regular basis, to sign up for sharing and discussion days, to take part in a specific employment program, etc. All these obligations perpetuate a power model. We are closing hospitals and sounding the death knell of a disciplinary society, only to exercise even greater control over people. "We are entering controlled societies that function not by imprisoning, but through continuous control and instant communications" (Deleuze, 1990, p. 236).

With the new intersectorial paradigm (White, Jobin, McCann, & Morin, 2000), a trend seems to be developing toward a return to strengthening and intensifying in-community monitoring. The stated aim of the intersectorial shift is to promote integration of deinstitutionalized individuals into the community more effectively by giving them more direct access to resources, and to bring the various stakeholders (psychiatrists, social workers, psychologists, families, etc.) to the same table with the stated intent of promoting better communication between the various sectors of community life (education, hospitals, community agencies, job programs, accommodation resources, etc.). But beneath this goodwill lies the danger of rigidification and "bureaucratization," which could presage a return to the principles of the former programs of intensive in-community monitoring. This would lead us back to a positive control logic similar to the hospital model, in which the mesh of the net is woven so tightly that nothing can pass through. Furthermore, there is a risk that the pressure and oppression experienced by the individuals under surveillance in an intersectorial consultation system will affect their freedom to make personal choices.

One of the perverse effects of intersectoriality could therefore be the defining of new, subtler means of social control. This institution without walls would then result in a parallel world in which existence within the community would be standardized. In addition, one of the pressure groups around the intersectorial table would inevitably come to dominate since not all pressure groups are invested with the same powers, and agreements in principle can quickly shift to a specific sphere (e.g., the medical area). It is therefore essential to counter the danger of creating a kind of "Dictatorship of the Partnership" (Damon, 2002) inherent in the logic of intersectoriality, and under which the pretext of closer ties is very likely to result in legal imbroglios that would be harmful to the community integration of people who are vulnerable because of mental illness. One way to prevent such technocratic drift might be to encourage greater user participation at round tables. But we believe that the existing context (deinstitutionalization, the pressure applied by a performance-oriented society, the danger of decision maker rigidification, etc.) renders this new process inadequate. Instead, we believe that the danger inherent in developing controlling societies calls for a defence of the community against attempts to make society fairer by increasing the number and levels of controls and interventions. In other words, intersectoriality may be necessary, but it is equally essential to find ways to avoid the risks associated with this type of practice. And we believe that revisiting the meaning of community is one way to do so.

What type of community do we need? Certainly not the kind of community united by fraternal ties that Marx dreamed of. We no longer believe in a utopia of total obliteration of individual will in favour of a common, collective consciousness. We will therefore endeavour to define a new form of community that will protect and encourage a greater degree of lifestyle diversity. We believe this is the most urgent task to be accomplished in our era of massive deinstitutionalization and return to community life of ex-psychiatric patients.

THE COMMUNITY SPACE

According to Sivadon (1993), it appears that the great majority of people with mental illness are acutely sensitive to the space they call their own, even if they do not spontaneously express this and are unaware of it. For an autistic person, for example, going to a shopping centre is less of an outing in simple three-dimensional space than a confrontation with an environment filled with people who have feelings and generate effect. As such, the space is not merely geometric but eminently complex and comprised of an entire system of perceptions and sensations. Spatial sensitivity causes people to see a house not simply as a building enclosed and limited by its internal framework, but rather as a natural and permanent interaction with the reality of the outside universe. We could further extend these considerations on the subject of de-objectified spatiality and think of community space as a "network of possibilities" (Baudrillard, 1991) composed of differing areas of intensity, with an "existential geography" (Roux, 1999) whose purpose is to study variances and gradients. In this context, a person's well-being would be proportional to the degree of openness of his or her territory. The less defined a territory's limits, the greater the de-territorialization and re-territorialization movements (Deleuze & Guattari, 1980, 1991; Roux, 1999). In short, a multidimensional person is one for whom the borders themselves are changing (Pezeu-Massabuau, 1999).

Community space (which still needs to be opened up) has no borders. This type of space makes movement control pointless. Control of population location is a common practice in police states that literally sort populations by legislating spatial divisions. This is how urban zoning practices sometimes perpetuate exclusion policies and principles that result in the ghettoization of marginalized people. Some urbanistic practices thereby enable municipalities to exercise control over their populations through zoning (Morin, 1994). Isolated spaces are reserved for psychiatric hospitals, and construction by community mental health agencies is prohibited in some neighbourhoods inhabited by a high-income population. This is the case in Montreal, for example, where the Westmount and Pierrefonds districts have no community mental health resources. The "Not in my back yard" (NIMBY) syndrome (Piat, 2000) sometimes becomes "Not in my district" and soon, perhaps, "Not in my country." This goes against the fundamental principle of our new community in which managing to locate oneself freely within the environment enables one to enhance his or her interaction network, qualitatively and quantitatively (Malpas, 1997).

The new, authentically deinstitutionalized and deinstitutionalizing space is not meant to be a place for legislation but rather for experimentation. It is no longer a matter of trying to bring about a global revolution–something no one believes in any longer. Authentic community no longer implies utopia and is not ensconced in any closed, paradisiacal and homogeneous space. On the contrary, it becomes a place for and an expression of differences—a heterotopia disassociated from any messianic promises or quests for a new, ideal beginning or new era. In a text entitled *Des espaces autres* (*Alternative Spaces*), Foucault is clear on this point, saying: "We are living in a time of simultaneity, a time of juxtaposition, a time of the near and the far, of the dispersed" (Foucault, 1994). The heterotopic space of the authentically deinstitutionalized community is not a place where everyone comes together, either to share a universal brotherhood or (worse still) to encourage the unique lifestyle of *homo economicus*. Instead, it is what Foucault refers to as a space of the beyond, where different kinds of spaces juxtapose one another. This pleading in favour of alternative spaces is specifically intended to include all those (including ex-psychiatric patients) who seem to reside outside any place.

VARIOUS LIFESTYLES WITHIN THE COMMUNITY

The phenomenological approach has been adopted by many authors who have addressed the issue of rehabilitating ex-psychiatric patients living in the community. These specialists agree that people with mental illness need much more than mere relief from their identified symptoms. Well-being involves integration into the community in a more fundamental way to allow free fulfillment of one's existential, residential, vocational, and educational needs, etc.

One of the difficulties in this task, from the viewpoint of the host community, lies in what seems to be one of the particularities of the lifestyle of people in a fragile condition due to mental illness. This particularity may be what some people refer to as "positive withdrawal" (Corin, 1992, 1998; Corin & Lauzon, 1994). Positive and salutary withdrawal implies a specific need to live both within and outside of the community, detached from the community, yet not excluded from it. Investigations along these lines have shown how the special relationship that ex-psychiatric patients have with urban space sometimes induces them to transform public places into anonymous and solitary experiential centres for recovery (e.g., a chair and table away from others in a café or a low-priced or fast-food-style restaurant such as Dunkin Donuts, Starbucks, Second Cup, etc. (Knowles, 2000a, 2000b).

This resourcing practice of withdrawing temporarily from group activity in order to be able to return in a better state of mind is not entirely new; the ancients used to consider it a form of wisdom better known as anachoresis (etymologically, "being outside any place"). However, positive withdrawal takes on a new dimension within communities in our context of deinstitutionalization of psychiatric care. This desire to reconnect with ancient forms of wisdom can be explained by the heightened sensitivity to spiritual matters in those classified as mentally ill people returning to the community (Galanter, 1997). An approach centred on the meaning of the world and strategies developed for living in the community help promote better rehabilitation of individuals—rehabilitation appropriate to the complexity of the integration concept but which reserves a place for temporary withdrawal and respects the variety of meanings associated with this concept. Putting these integration dynamics into perspective gives new meaning to the term "community," now defined by inclusion of the margins (Corin, 1987, 1990), which now are regarded as propitious places for self-realization (Desjardins, 1994). Incorporating the more marginal lifestyles and people sensitive to the benefits of positive withdrawal also brings up new considerations with respect to the experience of continuity and interruption (Davidson, 1994). The "sense of self" process is complex and never fully realized. This makes it important to develop formal networks but, even more importantly, informal networks that encourage and facilitate the unending quest for self through all the complexity of the self-identify concept (Ricoeur, 1990). What is true for so-called normal people is even truer for people with heightened fragility due to mental illness (Davidson, 1992). These realities call for a redefinition of the traditional representation of disorder. Since disorder is part of community living, the model of pre-existing well-being, against which illness is judged to be deviant or deficient, is inadequate. Disorder and rehabilitation should therefore not be thought of as in strict opposition (Davidson & Strauss, 1995). Community space becomes not only heterogeneous but chaosmic (cosmos = order / chaos = disorder). It once again allows for the existence of a "village idiot" who finds a place, perhaps as a reporter, carrying news among the people (Dorvil, 1988).

COMMUNITY THAT PRODUCES A DIVERSITY OF LIFESTYLES

"Community" should no longer be considered completely fusional and self-transparent as a kind of romantic utopia but something that produces the (apparently) paradoxical effect of a "profoundly nonreciprocal mutuality" (Blanchot, 1983) by bringing together "disparate singularities" (Nancy, 1986; Nancy & Pontbriand, 2000) and "singularities with no pre-defined identity" (Agamben, 1990) who nevertheless remain united in their differences. The idea of a communal life that was respectful of individual differences was already assumed in Husserl's phenomenological concept of community. The authentic community envisaged by Husserl is therefore a fertile ground for responsible exploration of the new possibilities included in the concept of meaning (Buckley, 1992a, 1992b). The Husserlian definition of community as an ongoing and varied quest for meaning becomes, among other things, extremely anti-totalitarian, egalitarian, and participatory (Buckley, 1998). In this context, a community's value is proportional to the diversity of lifestyles that it produces and encourages. In other words, the "multi-" is an essential element of "being with" (Nancy & Pontbriand, 2000). Furthermore, it is the healthy person's relationship to abnormality—to what is strange or foreign—that reveals the meaning of being in the world (Bernet, 1994, p.108).

The theories of the German sociologist Ferdinand Tönnies can help us understand this concept of community more fully. In his classic book *Community and Society: Fundamental Categories of Pure Sociology* (1977), Tönnies differentiates between society—historically understood to be a contractual and artificial association or amalgamation whose methods of realization are decided upon by representatives designated by the citizenry—and community, which is generated by a set of intimate, organic, and emotional relationships among its members. It is this living together on which we base the phenomenological concept of community. We believe that it is useful to maintain the distinction between society and community in order to base interventions more effectively on a strengthening of the latter, which is also to say that the problems raised by deinstitutionalization (danger of institutionalizing the host community, risk of developing new and more subtle forms of control, etc.) can in no way be avoided by devising new policies and defining new standards of behaviour.

Collective interests are currently dominated by marketing and advertising imperatives. Very little effort is invested in enhancing communal life—not a life one seizes to keep for himself or herself, but a life that belongs to everyone and that is shared by many. Jean-Luc Nancy emphasizes the importance of redefining a non-exclusive community not dedicated to the finalization of a commercial or communicational and marketing effort. Openness and the capacity of inclusion make the new community an "inoperative community" inasmuch as its work cannot be completed and remains an ongoing production process in continuous relationship with the outside (Nancy, 1986; Nancy & Pontbriand, 2000). An exclusive community is totalitarian, while an inoperative community is decentralized. The novelty in this communistic requirement (Blanchot, 1983) lies in excluding fusional completion by refusing to make the community a completed and identity-based structure. The new community therefore does not come to be through an overthrow of existing authority (Marx, 1962) any more than communities exist today by requiring that their practices be protected by a state system of laws (Taylor, 1994, 1997). The new community is neither a Marxist utopia nor a communitarian ideal; it assumes no structure, existing or in progress.

In summary, the new community space is no longer homogeneous but includes a multiplicity of singularities with no a priori identities. This partially ordered, partially disordered assemblage comprises an "alternative space" or heterotopia not based initially on a system of laws—one that presents itself as an alternative to the old messianic utopia relative to the appearance of a new man and a new time. The new community that protects and encourages a large number of lifestyles remains independent of any legal or constitutional plan. Successful deinstitutionalization policies will be fully achieved only by promoting the production and self-production of a community that is itself of a deinstitutionalizing nature.

ACKNOWLEDGEMENTS

This study is part of a research program entitled "Housing and Work as Social Determinants of Health for Mental Health Service Users." This project was recommended by the CRSH/SSHRC in 2001 to provide a three-year grant under the Society, Culture and the Health of Canadians II program (file no. 839-2000-1065). I would sincerely like to thank Henri Dorvil and Stéphane Grenier for their judicious comments and many suggestions offered during the writing of this chapter.

REFERENCES

Agamben, G. (1990). *La communatué qui vient: Théorie de la singularité quelconque*. Paris: Seuil.
Baudrillard, J. (1991). *L'Amérique ou la pensée de l'espace: Citoyenneté et urbanité*. Paris: Esprit.

Bernet, R. (1994). *La vie du sujet: Recherche sur l'interprétation de Husserl dans la phénoménologie*. Paris: PUF.

Blais, L., Mulligan-Roy, L., & Camirand, C. (1998). Un chien dans un jeu de quilles. Le mouvement des psychiatrisés et la politique de santé mentale communautaire en Ontario. *Revue Canadienne de Politique Sociale 42*, 15–35.

Blanchot, M. (1983). *La communauté inavouable*. Paris: Minuit.

Buckley, P.R. (1992a). *Husserl, Heidegger and the crisis of philosophical responsibility*. Dordrecht: Kluwer Academic Publishers.

_____. (1992b). Husserl's notion of authentic community. *American Catholic Philosophical Quarterly, 46*, 213–227.

_____. (1998). Husserl's Göttingen years and the genesis of a theory of community. In L. Langsdorf (Ed.), *Reinterpreting the political* (pp. 39–49). New York: State University of New York.

Corin, E. (1987). Contraintes et stratégies: La pertinence de la notion de communauté dans le cas de patients schizophrènes. In E. Corin, S. Lamarre, P. Migneault, & M. Tousignant (Eds.), *Regards anthropologiques en psychiatrie* (pp. 179–194). Montreal: Girame.

_____. (1990). Fact and meanings in psychiatry: An anthropological approach to the lifeword of schizophrenics. *Culture, Medicine and Psychiatry 14*, 153–188.

_____. (1992). Positive withdrawal and the quest for meaning: The reconstruction of experience among schizophrenics. *Psychiatry 55*, 266–281.

_____. (1998). The thickness of being: Intentional worlds, strategies of identity, and experience among schizophrenics. *Psychiatry 61*, 133–146.

Corin, E., & Lauzon, G. (1994). From symptoms to phenomena: The articulation of experience in schizophrenia. *Journal of Phenomenological Psychology 25*(1), 3–50.

Damon, J. (2002). La dictature du partenariat. *Revue Futuribules 273*, 27–41.

Davidson, L. (1992). Developing an empirical-phenomenological approach to schizophrenia research. *Journal of Phenomenological Psychology 23*(3), 3–15.

_____. (1994). Phenomenological research in schizophrenia: From philosophical anthropology to empirical science. *Journal of Phenomenological Psychology 25*(1), 104–130.

Davidson, L., & Strauss, J.S. (1995). Beyond the biopsychosocial model: Integrating disorder, health and recovery. *Psychiatry 58*, 43–55.

Deleuze, G. (1990). *Pourparlers*. Paris: Minuit.

Deleuze, G., & Guattari, F. (1980). *Mille plateaux*. Paris: Minuit.

_____. (1991). *Qu'est-ce que la philosophie?* Paris: Minuit.

Desjardins, M. (1994). Les pouvoirs du signe: Histoire de l'anthropologie de la déficience intellectuelle, à travers l'oeuvre de Robert B. Edgerton. In *Élargir nos horizons: Perspectives scientifiques sur l'intégration sociale*. Paris: Ibis Press.

Dorvil, H. (1988). *Histoire de la folie dans la communauté 1962–1987. De l'Annonciation à Montréal*. Montréal: Émile-Nelligan.

_____. (2001). Réinsertion sociale et regards disciplinaires. In H. Dorvil & R. Mayer (Eds.), *Problèmes sociaux. Tome II: Études de cas et interventions sociales* (pp. 583–634). Quebec City: Presses de l'Université du Québec.

Dorvil, H., Beaulieu, A., & Morin, P. (2001). Les responsabilités de l'État à l'égard de la désinstitutionnalisation: le logement et le travail. *Éthique publique. Revue internationale d'éthique sociétale et gouvernementale 3*(1), 117–125.

Dorvil, H., Guttman, H.A., Ricard, N., & Villeneuve, A. (1997). *Défis de la reconfiguration des services de santé mentale—Pour une réponse efficace et efficiente aux besoins des personnes atteintes de troubles mentaux graves*. Quebec City: Government of Quebec.

Foucault, M. (1994). Des espaces autres. In M. Foucault, *Dits et écrits. Tome IV: 1980–1988* (pp. 752–762), Paris: Gallimard.

Galanter, M. (1997). Spiritual recovery movements and contemporary medical care. *Psychiatry 60*, 211–223.

Knowles, C. (2000a). *Bedlam on the streets*. London and New York: Routledge.

_____. (2000b). Burger King, Dunkin Donuts and Community Mental Health Care. *Health and Place 6*, 213–224.

Malpas, J. (1997). Space and sociality. *International Journal of Philosophical Studies 5*(1), 53–79.

Marx, K. (1962). *Manifeste du parti communiste* (1848). Paris: Éditions sociales.

Ministère de la Santé et des Services Sociaux. (1989). *Politique de santé mentale*. Quebec City: MSSS.

_____. (1997). *Orientations pour la transformation des services de santé mentale*, Quebec City: MSSS.

_____. (1998). *Plan d'action pour la transformation des services de santé mentale*. Quebec City: MSSS.

Morin, P. (1994). *Espace urbain montréalais et processus de ghéttoïsation de populations marginalisées*. Unpublished doctoral thesis, Université du Québec à Montréal.

Nancy, J.-L. (1986). *La communauté désoeuvrée*. Paris: Bourgois.

Nancy, J.-L., & Pontbriand, C. (2000). Entretiens (bilingual), *Parachute 100*, 14–31.

Nelson, G., Lord, J., & Ochocka, J. (2001). *Shifting the paradigm in community mental health towards empowerment and community*. Toronto: University of Toronto Press.

Ontario Ministry of Health. (1983). *Towards a Blue-print for Change: A Mental Health Policy and Program Perspective*. Discussion Paper (Heseltine Report). Toronto: Ontario Ministry of Health.

_____. (1993). *Putting people first: The reform of mental health services in Ontario*. Toronto: Ontario Ministry of Health.

_____. (1999). *Making it happen: Implementation plan for mental health reform*. Toronto: Ontario Ministry of Health.

Pezeu-Massabuau, J. (1999). *Demeure mémoire. Habitat: code, sagesse, liberation*. Marseille: Parenthèses.

Piat, M. (2000). The NIMBY phenomenon: Community residents' concerns about housing for deinstitutionalized people. *Health & Social Work 25*(2), 127–138.

Provincial Community Mental Health Committee. (1988). *Building community support for people: A plan for mental health in Ontario*. Toronto: PCMHC.

Ricoeur, P. (1990). *Soi-même comme un autre*. Paris: Seuil.

Roux, M. (1999). *Géographie et complexité: Les espaces de la nostalgie*. Paris: L'harmattan.

Sivadon, P.C. (1993). Proxémique et relations humaines. In P.C. Sivadon, *Psychiatrie et socialites* (pp. 129–155), Toulouse: Erès.

Taylor, C. (1994). *Multiculturalisme: Différence et démocratie*. Paris: Flammarion.

_____. (1997). *La liberté des modernes*. Paris: PUF.

Tönnies, F. (1977). *Communauté et société: catégories fondamentales de la sociologie pure* (1877). Paris: Retz.

White, D., Jobin, K., McCann, D., & Morin, P. (2002). *Pour sortir des sentiers battus: l'action intersectorielle en santé mentale*. Quebec City: Les publications du Québec.

World Health Organization. (1998). *World mental health: Problems and priorities in low-income countries*. London: Oxford University Press.

Chapter 11

Anti-Oppressive Practice with Older Adults: A Feminist Post-structural Perspective

Deborah O'Connor
School of Social Work and Family Studies
University of British Columbia

The ideas of post-structuralism are generating enthusiasm in the field of social work (Gorman, 1993; Leonard, 1994) and the need for a critical postmodern perspective in gerontology has been clearly advocated (Laws, 1995; Ray, 2000). To date, however, the relevance of these ideas for practice has not been well articulated. Rather, post-structural writings have tended to be conceptually dense and esoteric, making it very difficult to immediately grasp their practical applicability. This difficulty in transcending the intellectual, compounded by heavy grounding in the biomedical perspective, has made it particularly difficult to integrate critical post-structural ideas into practice in the field of gerontological social work despite the potential for these ideas to foster anti-oppressive social work practice.

The purpose of this chapter is to begin to explicate the practical relevance of feminist post-structuralist ideas for anti-oppressive practice in the field of aging. This will be done through the development of a framework for practice that draws upon these ideas.[1] The intent is to begin to articulate how these ideas have been used to ground each aspect of the framework in order to clearly make the link between practice and theory. I do not claim to be fully representing the complexities and nuances associated with post-structuralist ideas (an impossible task anyhow), but will only be highlighting those ideas that I perceive as particularly relevant for reconceptualizing gerontological social work practice.

I realize that this task could be perceived as fundamentally inconsistent with the ideas of post-structuralism, so I insert this cautionary note: The purpose of the emerging framework is *not* to provide a prescriptive approach to practice. Rather, it is to help practitioners think about how we are carrying out practice and to provide specific junctures for explicitly countering oppressive assumptions and challenging limiting perspectives.

The framework consists of six interrelated, overlapping dimensions. These include:

1. *Deconstructing:* Interrogating assumptions, personal values, and beliefs.
2. *Positioning:* Locating the knowledges of oneself and others.
3. *(Re)membering:* Realizing client expertise.
4. *Revisioning intervention:* Constructing a different story?
5. *Broadening the vision:* Beyond the personal.
6. Writing as resistance.

Each of these dimensions, which are overlapping, will be used to help develop an idea associated with feminist post-structuralisms. The intent will be to use each to explicate an idea associated with this approach, and then move beyond this theoretical lens to examine the practical relevance to gerontological social work.

DECONSTRUCTING: INTERROGATING ASSUMPTIONS, PERSONAL VALUES, AND BELIEFS

Poststructuralism, alternately referred to by some as postmodernism (Burman & Parker, 1993; Gavey, 1997), is used here to describe an intellectual and cultural movement that shifts the focus from a notion of pre-existing stable reality to the importance of language for constructing reality. Implicit in this shift is the recognized priority that discourses have in constructing experience. Discourses refer to interrelated systems of statements that cohere around common meanings and reflect sets of assumptions, values, and beliefs that are socially shared (Gavey, 1997; Ristock & Pennell, 1996). They provide the storylines on which individuals draw to make sense of the world and their own personal experiences.

At any given time, there are multiple discourses—or storylines— available through which one can make sense of the world. These storylines can complement one another or compete to create distinct and incompatible versions of reality (Davies & Harre, 1990). In practical terms, this means that one may potentially be simultaneously relying upon multiple, often incongruent, storylines to provide the framework for making sense of one's personal experiences. However, while there are different and competing storylines or discourses, not all are of equal importance. Rather, some have a privileged and dominant influence on language, thought, and action. These are the storylines that impress as "common sense" and can often be recognized by the implicit "should" that guides one's actions and decisions.

Unlike some post-structuralist approaches that have been accused of being overly abstract and apolitical, feminist or critical post-structuralists emphasize that it is through discourses that power relations are established and perpetuated (Gavey, 1997; Weedon, 1987). Specifically, power enables some to define what is or is not considered knowledge. Discourses are not neutral; rather, they represent political interests and are constantly vying for status and power (Weedon, 1987, p. 41). The goal of feminist post-structuralism is to disrupt and displace dominant, oppressive knowledges (Gavey, 1997); in part this is achieved by making visible the taken-for-granted assumptions underlying dominant discourses and by articulating the values supported by alternative conceptions of reality.

When the notion of discourse is applied to gerontological social work practice, the importance of beginning to deconstruct one's own systems of assumptions, values, and beliefs emerges as a critical starting point of practice with each client. When one deconstructs, ways of understanding the world are not accepted as givens but rather examined and interrogated in relation to their social, historical, and political contexts (Parton, 2002; Sands & Nuccio, 1992). This interrogation requires directing attention to the excluded and marginal because it is through this process that seemingly smooth social surfaces and accepted wisdom can be disrupted and the space created for alternative discourses (Opie, 2000, p. 23). This means, for example, asking who benefits from a particular storyline and who does not.

In gerontological social work, there are several dominant storylines that often provide the parameters for making sense of a situation and require deconstructing. One of these is the notion of family care.

> Mr. Green is a seventy-six-year-old husband who is identified as the primary caregiver for his wife, who has dementia. During an exploratory interview with him, he made it clear that he felt like a "prisoner" and would gladly relinquish the care of his wife except for the knowledge that he would "cease to have sons" should he not do his duty. He described himself as an impatient man with exacting standards for himself and others, and noted that these personal characteristics had served him well as a businessman, but were not conducive to effective

caregiving. He could not understand how people could expect him to change overnight and suddenly become a loving, patient man when this simply wasn't his nature. He identified his desire for a sexual relationship and expressed his bitterness that his wife's illness prevented him from attending to his own needs.

What a selfish, thoroughly dislikable man, I thought as I drove away. Later, surprised by the intensity and judgmental quality of my reaction, I began to reflect upon my response. I realized that I was offended by Mr. Green because his words had challenged the dominant notion of family care, a storyline that I obviously had bought into without even realizing it.

The underlying assumption used to construct this notion is that family care is better care—one "should" take care of one's frail, elderly relatives. This message is particularly strong for women who may simultaneously be relying upon the complementary, gendered storyline used to frame the ideal woman—one who is caring, compassionate, and who selflessly putting the needs of others before her own. This notion of family care is accepted as a given and rarely questioned. However, when scrutinized more critically, the implications of this storyline become clearer. For example, it implicitly places familial relationship above the personal qualities, skills, and capabilities required for providing good care and leaves family members feeling guilty and deficient when they are not able to provide care, even when the caring situation clearly exceeds their personal level of skill. By locating the family care storyline as preferred, other types of caring such as institutionalization, by definition, are positioned as inferior. This storyline works to the advantage of policy-makers, who save millions of dollars in health care through the efforts of family members. It is oppressive because it effectively removes choice from the decision on how to care. Social workers who buy unquestioningly into this dominant storyline may inadvertently be promoting a preferred reality that may not be in their client's best interest.

Feminist post-structuralist ideas, then, reposition practice as something that begins with the social worker. The importance of critically examining the storylines that one is using to make sense of a particular experience emerges as a critical starting point. Fook (1993) suggests that it is through this process that social workers begin to examine the ways that they contribute to social control by subtly holding clients in powerless positions and reinforcing identities ascribed to them by the dominant order. Some questions that can help guide this interrogation include the following:

- What are the "storylines" being used to make sense of this client's experience?
- What are the underlying assumptions, values, and beliefs being used to construct these storylines? Identify the "shoulds" in order to help illuminate the dominant discourse.
- Who defines this situation? Who has a voice? Who doesn't?
- What possibilities are being excluded when a particular storyline is taken up as the preferred reality?

POSITIONING: LOCATING THE KNOWLEDGES OF ONESELF AND OTHERS

The intent of examining systems of assumptions, values, and beliefs is not to develop a more sanitized, neutralized account that carries no values, beliefs, or assumptions—this is not seen as possible. Rather, the purpose is to open to scrutiny the unspoken and to recognize the limitations associated with all storylines. A second notion emerging from post-structuralist thinking challenges the belief that the world can be understood in terms of "grand theories" or "meta-narratives." Rather, knowledge is *always* seen as partial and incomplete.

For some, this notion is problematic, or at least unsettling, because it opens the world to uncertainty (Brotman & Pollack, 1997; Healy & Leonard, 2000; Parton, 2002). However, it can also be viewed as a positive move because one is never expected to know it all! Moreover, it means that there is never one "true" perspective but many ways of knowing and doing. One's theoretical perspective and world view—grounded as it is by a particular set of assumptions, values, and beliefs that reflect one's positioning in the world—are recognized as providing a particular way of looking at a situation that allows some things to be seen but renders other aspects invisible.

This has interesting implications for gerontological social work practice. In particular, it has tremendous potential for interdisciplinary teamwork. All professionals rely upon discipline-based discourses to conceptualize a client's situation. However, if knowledge is always partial and can never provide the full account, then no one team member can ever claim omniscience. Rather, the need for different perspectives is validated because it promotes a multifaceted, more holistic approach to client care. For example, this understanding challenges the privileging of the biomedical perspective, which has dominated gerontological social work, and explicitly begins to recognize it as offering only a partial, incomplete lens—*a* lens, not *the* lens.

However, for the potential associated with an interdisciplinary perspective to be realized, a different way of being part of the team is required.

Opie (2000) introduces the concept of "knowledge-based teamwork," which shifts the focus from how individual team members interact to how professionals on a team engage with the differently structured, differently powerful, discipline-based knowledges represented by various team members (p. 8)." She suggests that a key issue in knowledge-based teamwork is the production and management of "difference"; the work of an effective team is to identify and explore, rather than suppress or view as problematic the different accounts of the client circulating within it.

Pragmatically, this forces health care professionals, including social workers, to be more accountable for the lens each employs to understand the situation. Simultaneously a more humble approach is promoted because "actively engaging with uncertainty and difference requires us to relinquish the comforts of believing that our professional judgments (including those based on radical perspectives) *must* be right" (Healy & Leonard, 2000, p. 35).

(RE)MEMBERING: REALIZING CLIENT EXPERTISE

In dispelling the notion that the world can ever be completely known, or that there is one "true reality," not surprisingly, post-structuralism challenges the notion of an essential meaning (Sands & Nuccio, 1992). It also disrupts ideas about a fixed, coherent, and rational subject since each is drawing upon multiple, sometimes incongruent, storylines to provide the framework for making sense of personal experiences. Meaning, then, is viewed as multiple, unstable, and open to interpretation (Weeden, 1987), subjectively constructed within a particular social, political, and historical context.

At its most fundamental level, this notion positions the individual as expert over his or her reality. This challenges traditional power dynamics, which position the professional as undisputed authority. Pragmatically, this reinforces the importance of client-centred intervention—a central theme found in the literature on post-structural social work (Brotman & Pollack, 1997)—and highlights the importance of "beginning where the client is" as the first step in intervention. This is not a new thought; it simply provides a different rational for what has long been a social work axiom.

There are at least four implications associated with thinking about this dimension in gerontological social work. First, it begins to challenge the use of labels for understanding particular experiences. Even seemingly benign labels become problematic because they help construct artificial categories that prevent a nuanced understanding. Moreover, post-structuralists argue that when mutually exclusive categories are constructed, binary opposites are often created in which one of the terms gets its meaning from what it is not. In other words, one of the terms is privileged and the other is relegated to a negative state (Sands & Nuccio, 1992). For example, the caregiver/care-receiver dichotomy creates a vision of a one-way transaction that renders invisible what the "caregiver" might be obtaining from the "care-receiver" and positions the "care-receiver" as a passive recipient of care. Similarly, labels such as the "dementia sufferer" can shift the focus from the person with dementia to the dementia per se, effectively removing from sight all other aspects of the person. Even categories such as independent/dependent construct the person as either/or, but not both.

Second, the importance of contextualizing the client's experience emerges. There is an assumption that aging is lived and experienced differently according to cultural and historical life experiences. Developing a contextualized appreciation is critical for understanding how the client is making sense of an experience. For example:

> Mrs. Grey was brought into the hospital in a dishevelled, malnourished, neglected, and confused state. She was re-nourished and treated for a urinary tract infection, but was seen as too frail to return to independent living without some assistance. However, she was adamant that she would not accept home-support services, choosing instead to rely upon a daughter who was addicted to alcohol and heroin, and who in the past had become physically aggressive with Mrs. Grey. After some discussion, it was discovered that years earlier, two of Mrs. Grey's children had been apprehended by the local child protection services and her daughter was currently fighting to prevent the permanent removal of her son. Given this experience, she viewed support services as intrusive and threatening. Moreover, as a poor Black woman, she had experienced discrimination throughout her life—she didn't trust the all-White health care team who were trying to convince her that they knew best what she needed.

Third, recognizing that individuals make sense of their personal experiences using multiple, sometimes contradictory storylines, the social worker is forewarned to expect contradictions and inconsistencies. For example:

> Mr. Long was an eighty-two-year-old husband caring for his wife who suffered from dementia. He described himself as

totally exhausted and overwhelmed. He vehemently berated the government for providing such poor respite for family caregivers and was further enraged that there would be some expectation that family caregivers pay for what respite was available. This, he felt, punished family caregivers for requiring a break rather than recognizing the work that they were doing and the costs they were saving the government. However, despite his belief that caregivers deserved respite and his own fatigue, he was equally adamant in his refusal to use a local respite service, even if the user fees were waived. This seemed completely incomprehensible to me initially. Further discussions with Mr. Long revealed that he felt he was betraying his wife if he left her in the care of someone else. In other words, on an abstract level, he could legitimize generic rights to support for family caregivers, drawing on a storyline that recognized society's responsibility to care. However, at a more concrete and intimate level, this understanding competed with his assumptions about what it meant to be a caring husband.

Finally, insuring that the person's story is really heard is an imperative. At its most basic level, this requires allowing sufficient time for the person to "story" his or her experiences in his or her own words. It also turns attention to communication issues. For example, people with dementia, who may experience language deficits, will be left voiceless unless communication strategies are adapted that insure involvement (Purves, O'Connor, & Perry, 2001). Similarly, the need for effective translation that includes attending to who translates and insuring back-translation to confirm understanding becomes a much more complex issue to be addressed.

Feminist post-structuralism, then, explicitly draws attention to the client as expert and identifies the need to move beyond generalities and elicit particular understanding of individual circumstances and meanings associated with the situation. Questions that can help guide this exploration include:

- What difficulty is this person experiencing from her or his perspective?
- What cultural and historical storylines are influencing this person's understanding and interpretation of this situation?
- What can I learn from this person about his or her situation?

RE-VISIONING INTERVENTION: CONSTRUCTING A DIFFERENT STORY?

As previously noted, a key idea associated with post-structuralism is the importance of language for constructing reality. This notion directs attention to the use of language and the ways in which people tell their story as both a means of understanding and intervening. There is growing recognition that personal stories, or narratives, provide a very powerful means for understanding human experiences. People not only interpret but actually organize their experiences through storying and performing those stories (Bruner, 1987; Laird, 1994). One way to improve the quality of people's lives is to change the interpretations and stories that they tell about themselves. Since we write ourselves into being by reinterpreting and rewriting our life stories, we can *change* our way of being (Ray, 2000).

To some extent, the use of storying as a means of intervention has a long tradition in gerontological social work through the popularity of reminiscence or life review. Reminiscence or life review therapy is based on the premise that the recounting and assessment of one's life is a therapeutic and expected activity for older people; it is through this retelling that people are able to recognize and validate strengths and life successes, as well as come to terms with the past. However, there are important differences between this approach to interventions and narrative strategies that are grounded by the ideas of post-structuralism. Specifically, life review focuses on the story as a "true" representation of reality and typically ignores the ways that language and narrative are used as a "richly complex screen through which perceptions of self and reality are continually filtered (Ray, 2000, p. 26). The difference is that stories understood as objective realities demand passive acceptance, but stories understood as radically vulnerable can be challenged and re-authored (Rossiter, 2000, p. 27).

This latter development around narrative is gaining increasing prominence in the therapeutic literature through narrative therapy, but to date there have been few attempts to incorporate this understanding into practice with older people. However, some of the ideas associated with narrative therapy may be particularly appropriate in working with older adults and their families. For example, language can be consciously used to help develop an understanding of a problem that moves it outside of the person. Through a process known as externalizing, a problem is objectified and given a name. It can then be talked about as though it were an objective entity outside of the person. A common, albeit potentially risky, way of doing this in gerontological social work practice is to medicalize the problem.

Mrs. Cook spoke quietly of the shame she felt that her husband no longer recognized her. She felt that this lack of recognition must speak to the quality of her relationship with her husband. Surely if she had been a better wife he would not have forgotten who she was! Identifying the problem as an example of "the dementia" at work challenged this perception. She was able to begin to depersonalize the symptoms as somehow reflective of her own inadequacy and instead began to look for ways that she could minimize the power of the invading dementia.

The challenge associated with externalizing is to use the process as a means for constructing a new understanding that is empowering. This includes mapping the influence that the person has had on the problem and not just focusing on the power the problem has over the person. The intent is to reconstruct damaging stories about oneself by drawing on previously hidden ways of understanding and interpreting. Strategies for fostering this restorying are well developed in the narrative therapy literature and could usefully be integrated into practice with older adults and their families.

In addition to particular strategies, a post-structural understanding of narrative suggests a different way of conducting interviews. Specifically, it becomes imperative that through the interviewing process, the space be created for stories to emerge. This challenges the increasing focus on the use of checklists and screening tools, suggesting instead the importance of more open-ended interview structures for creating a conversational environment that encourages the client to tell his or her story.

BROADENING THE VISION: BEYOND THE PERSONAL

At first glance, the previous focus on personal narrative might seem to support a focus on individual subjectivity rather than a critical social analysis necessary for anti-oppressive practice. However, a post-structural understanding of narrative suggests that personal stories do not simply reflect individual experiences; they are organized according to culturally available but tacit "reasoning procedures" (Widdicombe, 1993). Culture, used broadly here to refer to societal values and beliefs, "speaks itself" through an individual's story (Rosenwald & Ochberg, 1992). This means that the personal story reflects the beliefs, ideas, and messages to which one has been exposed as one has interacted with one's familiar, social, political, economic, spiritual, and cultural milieus. Listening with a critical ear to personal narratives not only makes visible the individual's experience but also helps to contextualize that experience within a broader socio-political context. This understanding has enormous implications for anti-oppressive practice.

First, it provides an accessible avenue for identifying and better understanding the societal storylines that people rely upon to make sense of their personal experiences. In doing so, it offers a means for making oppressive storylines visible. More than this, however, exciting possibilities emerge in relation to change. Individuals are not simply passive recipients of a reality constructed by language but can also actively reconstruct this reality through their use of language. Identifying oppressive storylines and then challenging them by constructing alternative discourses and alternative forms of the "self" can change political relations (Foucault quoted in Fawcett & Featherstone, 2000).

Rossiter (2000) notes that social work has teetered between emphasis on the correction of internal landscapes of individuals or families and insistence on correcting social environments in which individuals are located. A post-structural understanding allows these two seemingly competing emphases to come together in practice by attacking the individual/social dichotomy that characterizes much practice. The individual is seen as both a by-product but also a co-constructor of social reality. It no longer makes sense to isolate personal change from broader societal change. Rather, the two become intertwined.

In gerontological social work, a focus on family caregiving demonstrates both the importance of, and some strategies for, moving between the personal and societal storylines. Prior to the 1970s, the work of caring for a frail, ill, or disabled family member was largely unremarkable. With its focus on family caregiving, researchers effectively began to construct a new way of understanding the caring that occurs in the family. During the process, they brought into reality an entity entitled "caregiver." While there are issues regarding the construction of this category (for example, it assumes a "care-receiver"), one of the benefits of developing this entity is that the work of family members taking responsibility for another, less able family member became visible as did the stress and negative responses that these caring activities could precipitate. In essence, we had a new language and way of understanding the private experience of caring for a family member.

Interestingly, while at a societal level this "caregiver" entity is assumed to exist, research suggests that it may be much more slowly integrated into the personal identity of individual members who frequently continue to ground their caring activities in the "should" of family caring (O'Connor, 1999). The problem here is twofold: First, if one does not see oneself as a caregiver, one certainly will not make the link between one's personal experiences and caregiver-support services. Second, when caring is grounded solely within the familial relationship, family members will feel deficient if they require support since one "should" be able to take care of one's relative. Here, then, is an example where an alternative storyline about taking care of one's family member is beginning to emerge at one level—the societal level—but at least for some people, continues to exert relatively limited influence at the personal level.

From this perspective, a focus of social work intervention might be on helping the individual incorporate this alternative storyline about caregiving into his or her own personal experience. Strategies for helping with this could include: naming the work of caring, defining what a caregiver is, and normalizing difficulties as situational rather than based in personal deficiencies. Once the problem is identified as situational rather than individual, a focus for change can shift from helping the individual cope with an unsatisfactory situation to changing the situation. A particularly viable avenue for helping family members construct and develop a more political consciousness and stronger coalition is through participation in family-support groups (O'Connor, in press).

WRITING AS RESISTANCE

Not only does the client story his or her experience; he or she is also storied by others. Sometimes this is done verbally, for example, in medical rounds or "case" discussions. However, the lasting construction of a client often occurs through the documents that form his or her chart. The contents and formats of these charts construct the person in a particular manner.

> Mrs. Jonas placed an emergency telephone call to the community mental health team where she had been receiving treatment for the past several months for depression and indicated that she "needed to talk to someone." She was in tears and stated she was feeling so hopeless that thoughts of taking all her medication so that she could "leave it all behind" had crossed her mind (although strong religious beliefs prevented her from acting on this impulse). A quick review of her chart identified her as a seventy-year-old widow living alone in her own home. It indicates she has a long-standing history of depression with the first episode occurring following the birth of her youngest child. Stable for the past several years, her most recent episode began several months ago

shortly after her husband died. There was mention of a strained relationship with a daughter, and information regarding how to contact this daughter is buried in the chart. From the detailed description of her medication treatment, located at the front of the chart, it was clear that Mrs. Jonas had been doing so well that a decrease in medication had taken place a week earlier.

With this information, Mrs. Jonas's problems are constructed primarily as a medical issue. The interpretation of her current crisis is that she is relapsing due to the medication changes. Given her despair and thoughts of suicide, a decision is made to admit her to the psychiatric unit in order to monitor and readjust her medication.

However, another story about Mrs. Jonas's experience could be written that is equally valid but largely absent in any documented form.

Mrs. Jonas's deceased husband was a violent man who abused both her and her two daughters physically and emotionally until his sudden heart attack nine months ago. Both daughters are bitter about their upbringing. Her eldest daughter, who left home very early because of the abuse, lives several hundred miles away; she rarely sees her mother, but does maintain periodic telephone contact and is available in times of crisis. The youngest daughter maintains a taut but involved relationship with Mrs. Jonas. However, she works full time, lives about thirty minutes away and, after trying for years, is pregnant for the first time and experiencing complications. Normally she spends Saturday with her mother, but because of her current health issues, she has not seen her mother for the past several weeks. This means that Mrs. Jonas is alone all weekend, a state she finds extremely distressing but about which she will not complain for fear of being perceived as a burden or endangering the baby. Mrs. Jonas's only other involvement outside her home is through her participation in a Senior's Day program. Initiated several months ago as part of her treatment plan, she attends the program on Mondays and Wednesdays and by all accounts is thriving in the program. Her call to the mental health team occurred on a Thursday morning of a long weekend; she was expecting to have no human contact until the following Wednesday. Finally, although the chart clearly documented all medication treatments, what it did not note was that Mrs. Jonas's regular worker had been calling her almost daily for several months. Although these calls were very brief, Mrs. Jonas had indicated many times that the calls made her feel as though someone cared. This worker had taken a brief leave and the replacement worker did not know about these calls, so no one from the team had been in contact with Mrs. Jonas for almost two weeks.

This construction of Mrs. Jonas's situation begins to move beyond the medical issues to encourage a different way of thinking about the situation and opens up alternative ways of responding.

Using the ideas of post-structuralism, paperwork is no longer viewed as a benign activity. Rather, it actively supports particular constructions. Questions begin to emerge regarding why some understandings get written, while others are noticeably absent. Moreover, opportunities are identified for resisting particular renditions by writing alternative stories into existence. Within gerontological social worker practice, this will typically require finding ways to transcend the medical perspective as the only reality. This entails examining written documentation to determine how oppressive or limiting storylines are being perpetrated. Some questions identified by Pare, Collings, and Gnanamuttu (2002) that can assist in this process include the following:

- What is the physical makeup of the document? For example, what sections are included? What is the sequence of sections and why?
- What is the purpose of the document? For example, why is it produced and for whom? How does it help with treatment decisions? How does it limit?
- What are the effects of the documentation? For example, what kinds of thinking does it encourage/discourage and what kinds of actions are encouraged or discouraged?
- Who reads the document? For example, is it used only by health professionals or do clients also read it? If not, why not?

Assessing the status of documentation can help make explicit the discourses that are guiding understandings. Once named, these practices can be challenged. This, for example, may mean finding ways to include content that draws on a different understanding. However, it also requires finding ways for this content to be read. For example, social work notes that are handwritten and segregated at the back of the document visually suggests the marginalization of this understanding. In contrast, intermingling these notes with those of other health professionals (including the physician) improves their visibility. Through their writing and documentation processes, social workers may quietly yet effectively subvert existing "realities."

CONCLUSION

To this point, ideas from post-structuralism have been used to frame the rationale for understanding and challenging practices that oppress older adults and their families. An implicit assumption guiding this discussion is that gerontological social work takes place in a context dominated by a biomedical discourse, and that practice grounded solely within this discourse is inadequate and oppressive because it limits what can be seen, heard, and acted upon. In particular, this discourse narrowly focuses on the individual removed from his or her culture. In this chapter I have articulated processes that could potentially support an alternative discourse about practice and promote a more holistic, contextualized account.

To conclude here would be both naïve and unjust. Social work does not occur in a vacuum; it occurs in historical, organizational, political, and economic contexts (Opie, 1995, p. 40) In the field of gerontology, the profession of social work has historically been marginalized and accorded lower status than other health professions. It is perhaps not surprising that an anti-oppressive or critical discourse about practice is largely absent in the field. Rather, despite the rhetoric regarding person-centred, holistic care, a biomedical discourse has not only dominated, it is gaining strength through a complementary "managerialist discourse" (Opie, 1995), which is driving organizational restructuring and fiscal cutbacks. Attempting to develop alternate discourses within this context can create cynicism, frustration, and anger as social workers try to balance the tension between organizational priorities and conflicting practice ideals.

To contend with this context, two conditions are identified. First, the need for social workers to articulate more clearly what they are doing and why has been clearly recognized (Globerman, 1999). The purpose of this chapter is to help provide a language for this articulation. Second, however, is the recognition that developing a critical social work practice in this area cannot occur in isolation. Rather, the need for individual social workers to develop supportive professional networks from which to examine their practice is clearly highlighted. Dominant discourses are powerful and can easily mute emerging voices when there is no external validation.

NOTE

1. I am indebted to the students who have participated in my graduate MSW aging course over the last three years. Through our discussions they have helped me develop and clarify the ideas presented in this chapter.

REFERENCES

Brotman, S., & Pollack, S. (1997). Loss of context: The problem of merging postmodernism with feminist social work. *Canadian Social Work Review 14*(1), 9–21.

Bruner, J. (1987). Life as narrative. *Social Research 54*(1), 11–32.

Burman E., & Parker, I. (1993). *Discourse analytic research.* New York: Routledge.

Davies, B., & Harre, R. (1990). Positioning: The discursive production of selves. *Journal for the Theory of Social Behaviour 20*(1), 43–63.

Fawcett, B., & Featherstone, B. (2000). Setting the scene: An appraisal of notions of postmodernism, postmodernity and postmodern feminism. In B. Fawcett, B. Featherstone, J.Fook, & A. Rossiter (Eds.), *Practice and research in social work: Postmodern feminist perspectives* (pp. 5–23). New York: Routledge.

Fook, J. (1993). *Radical casework.* St. Leonards: Allen and Unwin.

Gavey, N. (1997). Feminist poststructuralism and discourse analysis. In M.M. Gerber & S.N. Davis (Eds.), *Toward a new psychology of gender.* New York: Routledge.

Globerman, J. (1999). Hospital restructuring: Positioning social work to manage change. *Social Work in Health Care 28*(4),13–30.

Gorman, J. (1993). Postmodernism and the conduct of inquiry in social work. *Affilia 8*(3), 247–264.

Healy, K., & Leonard, P. (2000). Responding to uncertainty: Critical social work education in the postmodern habitat. *Journal of Progressive Human Services 11*(1), 23–48.

Laird, J. (1994). "Thick description" revisited: Family therapist as anthropologist constructivist. In E. Sherman & W.J. Reid (Eds.), *Qualitative research in social work* (pp. 175–189). New York: Columbia University Press.

Laws, G. (1995). Understanding ageism: Lessons from feminism and postmodernism. *Gerontologist 35*(1), 112–118.

Leonard, P (1994). Knowledge/power and postmodernism: Implications for the practice of critical social work education. *Canadian Social Work Review 11*(1), 11–26.

O'Connor, D.L. (1999). Constructing community care: (Re)Storying support. In S. Neysmith (Ed.), *Critical issues for future social work practice with aging persons* (pp. 71–96). New York: Columbia University Press.

_____. (in press). Toward empowerment: Revisioning family support groups. *Social Work with Groups.*

Opie, A. (1995). *Beyond good intentions: Support work with older people.* Wellington: Institute of Policy Studies.

_____. (2000). *Thinking teams/thinking clients.* New York: Columbia University Press.

Pare, A., Collings, S., & Gnanamuttu, M. (2002). Professional writing practices: A "critical" concern for social workers. Paper presented at the 2002 CASSW Conference, Toronto, May 26–29.

Parton, N. (2002). Postmodern and constructionist approaches to social work. In Adams, R., L. Dominelli, & M. Payne (Eds.), *Social work: Themes, issues and critical debates* (2nd ed.) (pp. 237–244). Great Britain: Palgrave.

Purves, B., O'Connor, D.L., & Perry, J. (2001). *From patient to person: Changing the lens in dementia care*. Interactive CD-ROM. Vancouver: University of British Columbia.

Ray, R. (2000). *Beyond nostalgia: Aging and life-story writing*. Charlottesville: University Press of Virginia.

Ristock, J., & Pennell, J. (1996). *Community research as empowerment: Feminist links, postmodern interruptions*. Toronto: Oxford University Press.

Rosenwald, G.C., & Ochberg, R.L. (Eds.). (1992). *Storied lives*. New Haven: Yale University Press.

Rossiter, A. (2000). The postmodern feminist condition: New conditions for social work. In B. Fawcett, B. Featherstone, J. Fook, & A. Rossiter (Eds.), *Practice and research in social work: Postmodern feminist perspectives* (pp. 24–38). New York: Routledge.

Sands, R., & Nuccio, K. (1992). Postmodern feminist theory and social work. *Social Work* 37(6), 489–494.

Weedon, C. (1987). *Feminist practice and poststructuralist theory*. New York: Basil Blackwell, Ltd.

Widdicombe, S. (1993). Autobiography and change: Rhetoric and authenticity of "gothic" style. In E. Burman and I. Parker (Eds.), *Discourse analytic research* (pp. 94–113). New York: Routledge.

Critical
Issues

Chapter 12

Social Work Identity and Purpose: Real or Imagined?

Ken Barter
School of Social Work
Memorial University of Newfoundland

Social work is predominantly practised within the structures of public laws, policies, regulations, and government bureaucracies or government-funded agencies (Schmidt, Westhuses, LaFrance, & Knowles, 2001). Public policy initiatives in Canada to reform and restructure health, education, and social welfare programs and services—concomitant with the shift from government to community-based systems of delivery—are affecting the profession. Concerns are expressed that the profession is being left "out in the cold" and is losing ground to nurses, health workers, occupational therapists, and others (Barter, 2000; Ife, 1998; Levin, Herbert, & Nutter, 1997).

Social work's identity, purpose, ethical obligations, and other distinctive features that give the profession its claim to legitimacy (Ife, 1998) are being challenged. What is happening in a profession that is "founded on humanitarian and egalitarian ideals" (Canadian Association of Social Workers, 1994) and is largely practised within structures mandated in children's protection, youth justice, mental health, education, public assistance, and personal social services to make it lose ground? Is the profession's claim to legitimacy more in professional discourse and activities to promote professionalism than it is in practice to promote social justice? Has the profession lost touch with its commitment to enhance human well-being and to address poverty and oppression (Schriver, 1998)? Should the profession embrace a new identity in community-based human service organizations (Jordan, 2000)?

This chapter not only explores these questions but also lays out some critical choices for social work and suggests some rethinking within the profession.

THE CONTEXT

Many significant challenges face contemporary society. They stem from the transition and changes that are taking place with respect to the global economy and competition, changing demographics, technological advancements, political upheaval and uncertainty, government reform and restructuring, and the reconfiguration of the Canadian welfare state. The events of September 11, 2001, and the world's response to combat terrorism are additional dimensions to these challenges. Public systems, policies, and structures in health, education, justice, and social services are either crumbling or being reconfigured, creating much controversy in virtually every social and economic sector.

All people, whether they seek or require services, provide services, or expect services to be available, are affected and bear varying degrees of disempowerment, inequalities, and social injustices. Millions of Canadians, who for reasons of abilities, age, gender, sexual orientation, culture, and colour, experience varying forms of discrimination that create struggles for them in terms of rights, basic needs, justice, and services (Campaign 2000, 1998); Canadian Council on Social Development, 1996; Carniol, 1995; Conway, 1997; Human Resources Development Canada, 1995; Murphy, 1999; Ross, Shillington, & Lochhead, 1994). There is concern that values associated with compassion, caring, and investments in people's developmental needs are being overruled by arrogance, dominance, power, and control. From this perspective, Murphy's (1999) book *The Ugly Canadian: The Rise and Fall of a Caring Society* makes for an appropriate title. Hurtig's (1999) book *Pay the Rent or Feed the Kids: The Tragedy and Disgrace of Poverty in Canada* reminds us of how much we fall short in investing in the developmental needs of people.

The capacity of hospitals, schools, child welfare agencies, social service agencies, and other helping organizations to respond is, at best, questionable. Social work is perhaps more concerned about this than any other profession. It has to be, in light of its Code of Ethics "in regard to the general welfare of society" (Hoffman & Sallee, 1994, p. 39); its "strong commitment to values and justice" (Hoffman & Sallee, 1994, p. 38); its being a "value driven profession" (Saleebey, 1994, p. 357) that is "founded on humanitarian and egalitarian ideals" (Canadian Association of Social Workers, 1994); and its primary purposes being "the enhancement of human well-being and the alleviation of poverty and oppression" (Schriver, 1998, p. 3).

Social work is philosophically and ethically positioned to be concerned about the questionable response of helping organizations in providing services, particularly to disadvantaged and marginalized groups. The distinctive features of the profession enhance its position to be concerned. The profession's responsibility and mandate to provide social services is one such feature (Zastrow, 1996). Social work is a profession that is largely practised within the structures of the welfare state and significantly practised under the auspices of legislated mandates in children's protection, youth justice, mental health, education, public assistance, and personal social services. Another distinctive feature is that, unlike medicine, law, and education—professions where clear lines can be drawn—social work is connected to many disciplines and other professions. This gives the profession a generic dimension and speaks to the importance of assuming both an ecological and social justice perspective in working with people and social problems. Where the ecological perspective alerts the profession to the principles of an holistic approach (the importance of sustainability, the value of diversity and difference, interdependence, and balanced relationships), the social justice perspective recognizes the significance of empowerment, rights, participation, and extending interventions into the political, social, and economic realms that affect people's lives (Ife, 1995).

The emphasis in the Code of Ethics of "not just on helping the client, but on working toward social justice in the larger community" (Rhodes, 1992, p. 44) reinforces this distinctive generic feature. Chapter 10 in the Code clearly delineates the ethical responsibilities with respect to society's conduct given the emphasis on social change, equal distribution, elimination of discrimination, and the promotion of social justice.

Social work's claim to legitimacy is grounded in its purpose, ethical obligations, and distinctive features (Ife, 1998). To suggest having this claim implies that the profession is true to its purpose and mission; that it is in a position to make a difference in the lives of disadvantaged and marginalized citizens; that a social justice perspective underpins interventions with people; and that the profession's identity fits with genuine commitment backed by action in terms of creating opportunities for people—individuals, families, groups, organizations, and communities—in order to bring about change. In other words, social work is an empowering profession and is in essence about empowerment of people, by people, and for people (Barter, 2001). These three categories of empowerment fit with social work's considered mission, that of community capacity building (Specht & Courtney, 1994).

HOW IS THE PROFESSION FARING?

How is the profession faring with respect to the empowerment paradigm, the empowerment of people, by people, and for people? Is the empowerment paradigm associated with the profession's identity? Is community capacity building seen as the profession's mission, hence the topic of this chapter: Social Work Identity and Purpose: Real or Imagined?

The literature on empowerment describes a process of change that occurs on the individual, interpersonal, and political levels (Gutiérrez, DeLois, & GlenMaye, 1995). This fits with empowerment of people, by people, and for people. *Of* people suggests enhancing, strengthening, and renewing people's capabilities, personal skills, self-knowledge, and self-awareness. This heightens capacity for self-determination in identifying needs and interests that are important based on personal experiences. *By* people suggests commitment, engagement, application of enhanced capabilities, skills and knowledge, participation, collaboration, self-governance, and ownership. *For* people implies mobilization of capacities to take action and work toward change, equal opportunities, and access to resources sustained in order to promote the collective good.

This empowerment framework, from a social work perspective, would suggest the significance of what Wharf (1990, p. 28) refers to as a "dual response: a personal trouble response of support, counselling, and membership in self-help groups; and a public-issue response that will change their environments at both the community and societal levels." This dual response integrates the ecological and social justice perspectives, social work cause and function, connecting personal troubles and public issues, and integration of individual and community practices. Unfortunately, the integration of these concepts has remained elusive in social work and the profession remains somewhat fragmented into the problem-solving micro camp (clinical) and the prevention macro camp (social change) (Morell, 1987; Norlin & Chess, 1997).

Evidence of this fragmentation can be found in social work literature and research. For example:

- the profession's ambivalence in its response to poverty (Parsloe, 1990; Riches & Ternowetsky, 1990; Rivera & Erlich, 1995)
- social workers' reluctance to work with poor families (Hagen, 1992; Wharf, 1993)
- the diminishing influence of social work in public welfare (Barter, 1992; Gibelman & Schervish, 1996; Keys & Capaiuolo, 1987)

- the diminishing role of advocacy in social work (Herbert & Mould, 1992; Walz & Groze, 1991)
- the emphasis on specialist practice versus generalist practice (Parsons, Hernandez, & Jorgensen, 1988)
- how social work has abandoned its mission in favour of psychotherapy (Specht, 1990; Specht & Courtney, 1994)
- how social workers are seen as being more in tune with being agents of social control as opposed to social change (Wharf, 1990)
- the crisis that exists for the social work profession given that social workers are in positions that deal with symptoms as opposed to root causes (Carniol, 1995)
- the profession's reluctance to undertake social action within a macro context; individual interventions, on their own, are inadequate and damaging in the long run because they put a bandage on social problems (McMahon & Allen-Meares, 1992)
- case, self-help, and class advocacy appear to be situational responses to unmet client needs rather than a regular social work activity directed at ongoing social structures and policies (Hardina, 1995)
- the history of the profession clearly reveals that its social change mission lost ground to the goal of adjustment; over the years, the commitment to cause and reform steadily gave way to preference for functional and technical proficiency (Abramovitz, 1992)
- research shows that social workers' formulations and perceptions of client problems tend to emphasize more of a personal focus as opposed to an interpersonal and environmental focus (Rosen & Livne, 1992)
- social work specialization has caused us to lose sight of more unified approaches to responding to human needs and social problems (Caragata, 1997)
- how the profession is losing ground in community health and social services systems as governments shift responsibilities to community-based systems of delivery (Barter, 2000)

These perceptions, criticisms, and opinions fly in the face of what social work is all about in terms of its history, theories, ethics, values, mission, its claim to legitimacy, and its commitment to promote social justice. This is indeed serious and raises fundamental concerns about social work identity and purpose in terms of what is being espoused in social work discourse and what is actually taking place in practice.

One may wish to question this literature, particularly for those who suggest that their experiences do not support what their professional colleagues say. In fact, further research inquiries would no doubt challenge many statements. This may be well and good, but it does not alter the fact that these are perceptions within the profession, within organizations that employ social workers, and within the community. These perceptions go a long way in influencing policy, management, political, and organizational decisions. They also go a long way in influencing professional identity. How much influence, for example, have these perceptions played in terms of social work losing ground in many health and community services jurisdictions? How much influence have these perceptions played in social worker burnout, turnover, dissatisfaction with the profession, low morale, and other critical difficulties for the profession? How much influence have these perceptions played in discouraging individuals to enter the social work profession or a particular field of practice, such as child protection services?

There is a need within the profession to address the above perceptions, criticisms, and opinions. The obvious incongruence between espoused theory and theory-in-use challenges a profession that is all about empowerment. It would suggest the profession coming together to discuss, to use Paulo Freire's words, "generative themes"—in other words, to discuss "what is close to people's hearts." What social work stands for is indeed "close to the heart"—a concern for vulnerable populations, poverty, discrimination, violence, and for people struggling to find purpose and hope in their lives. That it is close to the heart suggests that social work has a shared connection with the community and its citizens.

THE CHALLENGE

There is sufficient concern that social work discourse is not necessarily realized in action. It is much easier to talk than to do. Diminishing the distance between discourse and action is a move toward making social work's purpose and identity real and not imagined. This becomes a critical challenge for the profession. It means capacity building within the profession in order to connect public interest and the common good. It is critical for the profession to examine its roots; to reconnect case to cause and private troubles to public issues; to consider the needs of the future; to adapt social work interventions and education to community-based models; and to focus social work on its historical mission of working with people to improve the quality of their lives and to build community and social justice (Weil, 1996).

The profession's theoretical, philosophical, and ethical underpinnings—concomitant with its distinctive features—place it in an ideal position to take up this challenge and examination. It means creating opportunities to renegotiate relationships with client systems, professionals and their organizations, and citizens and their communities. Assumptions to support why this renegotiation should take place include the following:

- For too long the community has remained as an afterthought and was not necessarily integrated into services, programs, or human service organizations. The community role has to move beyond just funding systems and employing people to solve community problems. It is important for the community to be actively involved.
- Many public services are crisis-oriented and attempt to remedy or ameliorate events that have already transpired—that is, they are reactive in nature. Crises absorb most of the resources and there is little left to invest in primary prevention and early intervention strategies. Prevention is of fundamental importance.
- Many programs are categorical, divide problems into distinct entities, and have rigidly defined rules for service eligibility. It is important to reduce fragmentation as much as possible.
- To a large extent, public agencies have been negligent in communicating with each other in a timely and accurate manner. Agencies must collaborate if we are to have effective service systems.
- Existing services are insufficiently funded. As a result, public agencies are in a serious bind. They are expected to address and manage social problems on behalf of society, yet with reduced resources, they are forced to make critical decisions that affect quality and accessibility. Community and clients require opportunities to be involved in these decisions.
- For too long issues of poverty, discrimination, violence, and other injustices have remained hidden in the planning and implementation of interventions with disadvantaged and marginalized individuals, families, groups, and communities. Dealing with symptoms independent of the causes is no longer acceptable.

Social work, perhaps more than any other profession, understands the validity of these assumptions. There is an appreciation within the profession that "One of the most pervasive problems of modern society is the bureaucratization of work and relationships" (Schram & Mandell, 1997, p. 179). This problem must be faced head on. Relationships must be renegotiated on the premise and understanding that social issues of poverty, oppression, violence, and injustices elude hierarchical, bureaucratic, and expert-driven strategies. These issues equally elude any one profession or agency. It becomes necessary for professionals, organizations, clients, and citizens to understand that they share common barriers that affect them as a community. All require opportunities for empowerment personally, interpersonally, and politically (Gutiérrez, Parsons, & Cox, 1998; Lee, 1994; Miley, O'Melia, & DuBois, 1998; Robbins, Chatterjee, & Canda, 1998). Creating these opportunities presents a fundamental challenge—renegotiating relationships to move away from the professional/bureaucratic paradigm to the client/community paradigm.

The professional/bureaucratic environment is not necessarily the right environment for creating opportunities where caring, investment, and compassion take place. Instead it is an environment governed by rigid policies and procedures; where the power remains with high-level bureaucrats who are isolated from the grassroots; where the thinking is compartmentalized and often reactive in attempts to fix things; where there is unwarranted political involvement; where the system is closed and not necessarily user or family friendly; where professional autonomy is stifled; and where those who seek services or provide services are not seen as equal partners in the decisions.

Professional/bureaucratic environments create value conflicts and ethical dilemmas. Do professional ethics and values rise above organizational allegiance? Is the primary obligation to the client or to the organization? Are decisions made in the best interests of people or in adherence to policy? Labels of "do-gooder," "being idealistic," "naive," and "radical" are attached to social work in terms of dialogue about alleviating poverty and oppression and about social justice. Therapy, counselling, and treatment tend to take precedence over community capacity building and social action in these environments. Social justice, advocacy, client participation in decision making, individual empowerment, and professional autonomy are not necessarily embraced in bureaucracies. Social workers who remain true to these values and positions run the risk of being unfairly judged, not on their professional and creative competencies but on how well they uphold the norms and values of those in positions of power.

Many human services organizations are in crisis (Adams & Nelson, 1995). The ever-growing emphases on efficiency, effectiveness, and accountability have created organizational environments where management and policy practices often obstruct rather than facilitate social justice and empowerment of people. These organizational environments have not progressively moved to accommodate the ethical obligations of social work. As such, frustration, cynicism, blaming, hopelessness, powerlessness, hesitancy to challenge, and withdrawal are common experiences for many social workers.

A shift to the client/community paradigm suggests that public services and programs should be more community-based with communities assuming responsibility for governance based on the goals and priorities they see as important for the well-being of citizens. Such a significant shift in approach and responsibility for major public services and programs means abandoning many past practices and policies. Expectations associated with partnership, interprofessional teamwork, client participation and involvement, staff empowerment, user-friendly services, primary prevention and promotion, community development, seamless systems of delivery, integrated programs and services, and community decision making and governance dictate different practices and policies. Not only do these expectations fit with the client/community paradigm, they also fit with social work principles and values. Community-based systems, if true to the mission and principles underpinning them, are ideal environments for a profession with the commitment and interest to connect personal troubles and public issues.

Unlike the professional/bureaucratic paradigm, the client/community paradigm does not view the community as the perfect solution and as a programmatic tool to be harnessed and used (Schwartz, 1992). Instead, the community is being approached as a place where people, if given the opportunity to be empowered and to work together, can begin to renegotiate relationships as well as collaborate to not only redefine problems but to be innovative in attempts to do things differently. The client/community paradigm is about caring, respect, acceptance, and personal and social power. These are the results derived from relationships and respect for process as opposed to programs and services that are preoccupied with efficiency, effectiveness, and accountability.

The client/community paradigm replaces the traditional knowing-in-action approach with a reflection-in-action approach (Fabricant & Burghardt, 1992). A knowing-in-action approach identifies with the traditional top-down approach, which is spearheaded by the professional/bureaucratic paradigm. This approach, although well intentioned, is analogous to a group of players on an assumed chessboard, calculating moves within the constructs of the game itself (Schwartz, 1992). It is no longer appropriate to just throw money at problems that are only growing worse (Schorr, 1989). The thinking has to move beyond trying to "fix" things with a programmatic problem-solving approach. Experience has shown that despite efforts to introduce new policies, improve practice standards, increase professional accountability, and develop new practice approaches to working with individuals, families, groups, and communities—albeit worthwhile endeavours—minimal results are achieved in improving the lives of disadvantaged and marginalized citizens. Poverty is increasing, child abuse and neglect statistics are astounding, school and family violence is phenomenal, children and families relying on food banks are increasing in numbers, and there continue to be pervasive societal attitudes of contempt for poor people. As pointed out by Fabricant and Burghardt (1992), movements to develop more professional practice to improve both the quality of work life, as well as to meet the needs of clients, have not always been complementary goals. These authors suggest that "Too often, agendas advanced by professional associations have further insulated and isolated workers from community needs" (Fabricant & Burghardt, 1992, p. 195).

A reflection-in-action approach is a process of dialogue, analysis, and consciousness raising. This process creates the opportunity to pose problems and challenge the profession to revisit assumptions and values, and to consider innovative approaches to service delivery so that programs and services are responsive to the needs of communities and citizens. Reflective questions include:

- How can the profession make a difference?
- How can the community become more involved?
- How do workers address some of the root causes of the difficulties that client systems face?
- How can clients be more involved in organizations so they are partners in the decisions that affect them?
- How can social workers empower themselves and others to address social problems?
- How do workers share their knowledge and power with others?
- Are workers more preoccupied with looking after the needs of the organization than the needs of the clients and patients?
- Is the social work profession too much into power and control?

Reflective questions such as these attend more to the realization that social work practice, given its purpose and mission, must be connected to issues related to poverty, violence, diversity, health, justice, gender, and community. The profession's contemporary context, the perceptions and opinions on how the profession is faring, and the real or imagined question regarding the profession's identity and purpose suggest that reflective questioning and dialogue are fundamentally important.

A UNIFIED IDENTITY: INDIVIDUAL AND COMMUNITY INTEGRATION

It is time for the profession to seriously come to grips with establishing an identity that more fully integrates individual treatment and social reform. This means recognition, commitment, and support to think and work differently. For example:

- The profession must formally acknowledge that social work practices and training must be committed to and supportive of community capacity building—that is, creating opportunities for dialogue and reflection. Structures, systems, programs, policies, and services must all be equally committed and supportive.
- The profession must understand that individuals, families, and communities with whom the profession is involved are critical resources and partners. They must be welcomed in organizations in a way that focuses on their creative talents and strengths rather than just their difficulties.
- The profession must demonstrate a willingness to cross traditional professional and bureaucratic boundaries in order to provide a holistic approach in interventions. There must be flexibility so that professionals, systems, and the people they serve can work collaboratively on common issues of concern. This willingness means challenging traditional practices and assuming new roles and expectations, particularly in the area of community capacity building.
- The profession must be seen as credible and genuine in its efforts to work with individuals, families, and communities. This credibility needs to come not only from those working with the social workers but also from citizens seeing and experiencing behaviours that are indicative of commitment, caring, modelling, respect, trust, and sharing resources and power.
- The profession needs to be prepared to venture away from familiar practices and move toward non-traditional settings and hours of work. Activities outside of the bureaucracy are deemed essential. Professionals, in collaboration with all relevant stakeholders, need to redefine their roles and expectations in order to assume these activities.
- It is important for the profession to make a commitment to prevention and early intervention/outreach services. These services must complement and supplement interventions that are user friendly, accessible, coherent, flexible, and responsive to the needs of community as defined by its members.

These are "close to the heart" issues for the profession. They require not only innovation from a bureaucratic, procedural, and policy direction perspective but also a personal and professional commitment. Integrating individual and community practices (cause and function) acknowledges the significance of partnerships, collaboration, empowerment, and innovation— all of which recognize the importance of process and relationship building to increase personal, interpersonal, and political power with individuals, families, and communities so that innovation can take place and things can be done differently.

It is not a question of how social work can help individuals, families, and communities; it is more a question of how the social work profession partners with them so that there will be mutual help and learning. That is what empowerment, collaboration, innovation, and partnership are all about. An integrated approach suggests interventions and change not only for people requiring or needing services but for intervention and change at the professional, community, and organizational levels as well. Such an approach is not only empowerment-oriented practice but also reminds the social work profession that it is not "merely a tool of social control to enforce conformity to norms that may not be relevant or empowering to those who are in most need of liberation and justice" (Robbins et al., 1998, p. 114). It should also remind the profession that any initiative to enhance professionalism and its identity should be grounded in both the ecological and social justice perspectives as well as integrating cause and function.

Integrating cause and function supports social work's "insistence on a generalist rather than a specialist approach to practice" (Ife, 1998, p. 8). It requires the profession to grasp a broader domain in which social problems and solutions necessitate the investment of many institutions and professions, only a small portion of which will be social work (Parsons et al., 1988). If social work is to make this investment, it must be made on the recognition that going it alone with client systems no longer works, especially with the disenfranchised and economically and socially oppressed populations. "Social workers in the new era must be generalists prepared to design interventions for solving social problems, not in-depth specialists within a limited dimension of a particular social problem" (Parsons et al., 1988, p. 417). Fabricant and Burghardt (1992) likewise suggest that specialization must be minimized if practitioners are to more accurately understand and respond to citizen need. They state that: "Clearly, workers will preserve and develop specific areas of expertise, but this process must be balanced against the equally compelling need to develop a more holistic understanding of service situations" (Fabricant & Burghardt, 1992, p. 223).

A more holistic understanding, according to Robbins et al. (1998) is removing the professional "split" in the profession between clinical and community practice. According to these authors, "As we move into the twenty-first century, social work is in a unique position to renew its historical commitment to a holistic view of both people and their environments. This will entail looking outward at the social, economic, and political forces that shape behaviour as well as inward toward the spiritual realm of human existence" (Robbins et al., 1998, p. 414).

Associated with a more holistic understanding are the concepts of the common good and the public interest as discussed by Reamer (1993). The common good "refers to that which constitutes the well-being of the community—its safety, the integrity of its basic institutions and practices, the preservation of its core values" (Reamer, 1993, p. 35). The public interest, on the other hand, "is enhancing individuals' pursuit of their own interests. Professionals' contribution to the public interest can be carried out by the delivery of high-quality services to individual clients, strengthening the quality of the profession and its ranks, and so on" (Reamer, 1993, p. 35). Reamer suggests that the tension between the public interest and common good raises a critical question in social work: What is the public purpose of social work?

The challenge of this question for social work represents the same challenge as addressing whether or not social work's purpose and identity are indeed real or imagined. Of importance in picking up this challenge is the profession—concomitant to a more unified identity in terms of individual and community integration—assuming a more active political/advocacy role. Non-political social work is an impossibility (Gil, 1998; Ife, 1998). The profession's ethical and value commitments to social and economic justice imply challenging social injustices. Social workers cannot remain hidden by claims of neutrality and objectivity (Dworkin, 1990; Morell, 1987). Issues that are "close to the heart" cannot remain unspoken. To not speak out or be political is not a claim to being neutral. On the contrary, if neutrality is claimed, "a value is conveyed nonetheless—the value of accepting the status quo" (Rhodes, 1989, p. 99).

CONCLUSION

The status of social work vis-à-vis its purpose and identity and its status in health, community, and social services systems in Canada is of concern. The National Sector Study (Schmidt et al., 2001) provides evidence for this concern.

The profession, perhaps more than any other, is in a position to challenge itself and others given its philosophical and ethical underpinnings and its espoused capabilities and competencies with respect to:

- understanding and self-knowledge in the context of living circumstances and community
- establishing relationships where there is trust, respect, contribution, and caring
- increased awareness and sensitivity to diversity and difference
- abilities to collaborate and work together with others on common concerns and interests
- building social support networks and linkages
- skills and confidence to be comfortable with change and innovation
- creating opportunities to build a culture of support based on clear values and beliefs
- knowledge and understanding to work with significant others to challenge the status quo and gain power to influence and control their environment
- being challenged, to evaluate progress, to share experiences, and to be both accountable and responsible

Building relationships, social work's most fundamental underpinning in practice, facilitates processes for people to discover their power, strengths, talents, and skills to make a difference on an individual, family, group, organizational, professional, and community level.

Relationships involve trust, respect, responsibility, and acceptance. Relationships require action. If relationships are to be established within communities, organizations, within the profession itself, and with disadvantaged and marginalized people, it needs to be done with competence, knowledge, tolerance, education, and grounding in terms of beliefs and principles. If the profession is going to talk about things that are "close to the heart," it is important that it be done in a manner that is reflective, informed, inclusive, and that supports integrating individual and community practice, the ethical application of the Code of Ethics, and relationship building. Of significance in applying these concepts would be building relationships where:

- people develop awareness of the dynamics of power
- the voice of the professional is not substituted for the client

- there is a movement toward total inclusion—individuals and families, professionals and their organizations, and citizens and their communities are collaborative partners
- people's well-being is not treated as a commodity that can be rationed for the purposes of controlling people and their aspirations
- messages do not reinforce the idea that professionals and their organizations are the experts—they, like the clients, are a resource with strengths and capacities
- coordination and co-operation are replaced with collaboration—the willingness and commitment to mutually invest in common goals and doing things differently
- social justice principles are applied
- there is innovation—being innovative stresses opportunities rather than problems, uses collective intelligence, builds on strengths and diversity, and supports the emergence of new ways of doing things to facilitate change and growth

The challenges for social work are clear. It is important to approach these challenges with idealism. Idealism is a purposeful and powerful belief. The profession takes pride in being a values-driven profession. Like values, idealism is the belief that things should be better, how the world "ought" to be. It is important for social work to be creative, innovative, and collaborative in creating opportunities whereby society can benefit from the strengths and capacities of all citizens—the community, professionals, and people requiring or needing services. It is equally important for the profession to challenge itself, to discuss "close to the heart issues" and have that "professional spirit" that Abraham Flexner talked about in 1915. It is necessary for the profession to begin to truly integrate individual and community practices to insure that its identity and purpose are indeed real and are being realized and appreciated not only by those who belong to the profession but also by those who experience the profession at work.

REFERENCES

Abdullah, S.M. (1995). *The power of one: Authentic leadership in turbulent times*. Gabriolo Island: New Society Publishers.

Abramovitz, M. (1992). Should all social workers be educated for social change? *Journal of Social Work Education 28–29*, 6–18.

Adams, P., & Nelson, K. (Eds.). (1995). *Reinventing human services: Community- and family-centered practice*. New York: Aldine De Gruyter.

Barter, K. (1992). The social work profession and public welfare. *Perception 16*(2/3), 11–14.

_____. (2000). Reclaiming community: Shaping the social work agenda. *Canadian Social Work 2*(2), 6–18.

_____. (2001). *Capacity building as a core element of evaluation: A literature review.* Research paper prepared for Population and Public Health Branch, Atlantic Regional Office, Health Canada.

Campaign 2000. (1998). *Child poverty in Canada: Report card 1998.* Toronto: Child Poverty Action Group.

Canadian Association of Social Workers. (1994). *The code of ethics.* Ottawa: Canadian Association of Social Workers.

Canadian Council on Social Development. (1996). *The progress of Canada's children 1996.* Ottawa: Canadian Council on Social Development.

Caragata, L. (1997). How should social work respond? Deconstructing practice in mean times. *Canadian Social Work Review 14*(2), 139–154.

Carniol, B. (1995). *Case critical: Challenging social services in Canada.* Toronto: Between the Lines.

Conway, J.F. (1997). *The Canadian family in crisis.* Toronto: James Lorimer & Company Ltd., Publishers.

Dworkin, J. (1990). Political, economic, and social aspects of professional authority. *Families in Society: The Journal of Contemporary Services 71*, 534–541.

Fabricant, M.B., & Burghardt, S. (1992). *The welfare state crisis and the transformation of social service work.* New York: M.E. Sharpe, Inc.

Flexner, A. (1915). *Is social work a profession?* In *Proceedings of the National Conference of Charities and Correction* (pp. 576–590). Chicago: Hildmann Printing.

Freire, P. (1990). A critical understanding of social work. *Journal of Progressive Human Services 1*(1), 3–9.

Gibelman, M., & Schervish, P.H. (1996). Social work and public social services practice: A status report. *Families in Society: A Journal of Contemporary Human Services 77*, 117–124.

Gil, D. (1998). *Confronting injustice and oppression: Concepts and strategies for social workers.* New York: Columbia University Press.

Greenwood, E. (1957). Attributes of a profession. *Social Work 2*(3) 45–55.

Gutiérrez, L.M., DeLois, K.A., & GlenMaye, L. (1995). Understanding empowerment practice: Building on practitioner-based knowledge. *Families in Society: The Journal of Contemporary Human Services 76*(9), 534–542.

Gutiérrez, L.M., Parsons, R.J., & Cox, E.O. (1998). *Empowerment in social work practice.* Toronto: Brooks/Cole Publishing Company.

Hagen, J.L. (1992). Women, work, and welfare: Is there a role for social work? *Social Work 37*(1), 9–14.

Hardina, D. (1995). Do Canadian social workers practice advocacy? *Journal of Community Practice 2*(3), 97–121.

Herbert, M.D., & Mould, J.W. (1992). The advocacy role in public child welfare. *Child Welfare 71*(2), 114–130.

Hoffman, K.S., & Sallee, A.L. (1994). *Social work practice: Bridges to change.* Toronto: Allyn & Bacon.

Human Resources Development Canada. (1995). *Applied Research Bulletin 1*(2).

Hurtig, M. (1999). *Pay the rent or feed the kids: The tragedy and disgrace of poverty in Canada.* Toronto: McClelland & Stewart Inc.

Ife, J. (1995). *Community development: Creating community alternatives—vision, analysis and practice.* South Melbourne: Longman.

_____. (1998). *Rethinking social work: Towards critical practice.* South Melbourne: Longman.

Jordan, B. (2000). Conclusion: Tough love: Social work practice in UK society. In P. Stepney & D. Ford (Eds.), *Social work models, methods and theories* (pp. 139–146). Dorset: Russell House Publishing.

Keys, P., & Capaiuolo, A. (1987). Rebuilding the relationship between social work and public welfare administration. *Administration in Social Work 11*(1), 47–57.

Kreuger, L.W. (1997). The end of social work. *Journal of Social Work Education 33*(1), 19–27.

Lee, J.A.B. (1994). *The empowerment approach to social work practice.* New York: Columbia University Press.

Levin, R., Herbert, M., & Nutter, B. (1997). Preparing social work students for the new realities in health care practice: Implications for field education. *Canadian Social Work Review 14*(2), 167–183.

McMahon, A., & Allen-Meares, P. (1992). Is social work racist? A content analysis of recent literature. *Social Work 37*(6), 533–539.

Miley, K.K., O'Melia, M.O., & DuBois, B.L. (1998). *Generalist social work practice: An empowering approach.* Toronto: Allyn & Bacon.

Morell, C. (1987, March). Cause is function: Toward a feminist model of integration for social work. *Social Service Review 61*, 144–155.

Murphy, B. (1999). *The ugly Canadian: The rise and fall of a caring society.* Ottawa: J. Gordon Shillingford Publishing Inc.

Norlin, J.M., & Chess, W.A. (1997). *Human behaviour and the social environment: Social systems theory.* Toronto: Allyn & Bacon.

Parsloe, P. (1990). Social work education in the year 2000. *International Social Work 33*, 13–25.

Parsons, R.J., Hernandez, S.H., & Jorgensen, J.D. (1988). Integrated practice: A framework for problem-solving. *Social Work 66*, 417–421.

Reamer, F.G. (1993). *The philosophical foundations of social work.* New York: Columbia University Press.

Rhodes, M.L. (1989). *Ethical dilemmas in social work practice.* New York: Routledge, Chapman and Hall, Inc.

_____. (1992). Social work challenges: The boundaries of ethics. *Families in Society: The Journal of Contemporary Human Services 73*, 40–47.

Riches, G., & Ternowetsky, G. (1990). Unemployment and the work of social work. In G. Riches & G. Ternowetsky (Eds.), *Unemployment and welfare* (pp. 13–18). Toronto: Garamond Press.

Rivera, F.G., & Erlich, J.L. (1995). A time of fear; a time of hope. In F.G. Rivera & J.L. Erlich (Eds.), *Community organizing in a diverse society* (2ⁿᵈ ed.) (pp. 1–24). Toronto: Allyn & Bacon.

_____. (Eds.). (1998). *Community organizing in a diverse society* (3ʳᵈ ed.). Toronto: Allyn & Bacon.

Robbins, S.P., Chatterjee, P., & Canda, E.R. (1998). *Contemporary human behaviour theory: A critical perspective for social work*. Toronto: Allyn & Bacon.

Rosen, A., & Livne, S. (1992). Personal versus environmental emphasis in social workers' perceptions of client problems. *Social Service Review 66*, 85–96.

Ross, D.P., Shillington, R.E., & Lochhead, C. (1994). *The Canadian fact book on poverty*. Ottawa: Canadian Council on Social Development.

Saleeby, D. (1994). Culture, theory, and narrative: the intersection of meanings in practice. *Social Work, volume 39*, number 4, July 1994, 351–359.

Schmidt G., Westhuses, A., LaFrance, J., & Knowles, A. (2001). Social work in Canada: Results from the national sector study. *Canadian Social Work 3*(2), 83–92.

Schorr, L.B. 1989. *Within our reach: Breaking the cycle of disadvantage*. Toronto: Doubleday.

Schram, B., & Mandell, B.R. (1997). *Human services: Policy and practice* (3ʳᵈ ed.). Toronto: Allyn & Bacon.

Schriver, J. (1998). *Human behaviour and the social environment: Shifting paradigms in essential knowledge for social work practice*. Toronto: Allyn & Bacon.

Schwartz, D.B. (1992). *Crossing the river: Creating a conceptual revolution in community and disability*. Cambridge: Brookline Books.

Smale, G.G. (1995). Integrating community and individual practice: A new paradigm for practice. In P. Adams & K. Nelson (Eds.), *Reinventing human services: Community- and family-centred practice* (pp. 59–80). New York: Aldine De Gruyter.

_____. (1998). *Managing change through innovation*. London: National Institute for Social Work.

Specht, H. (1990). Social work and the popular psychotherapies. *Social Service Review 64*, 345–357.

Specht, H., & Courtney, M. (1994). *Unfaithful angels: How social work has abandoned its mission*. Toronto: Maxwell Macmillan Canada.

Stepney, P. (2000). Implications for social work in the new millennium. In P. Stepney & D. Ford (Eds.), *Social work models, methods and theories* (pp. 9–19). Dorset: Russell House Publishing.

Walz, T., & Groze, V. (1991). The mission of social work revisited: An agenda for the 1990s. *Social Work 36*(6), 500–504.

Weil, M.O. (1996). Community building: Building community practice. *Social Work 41*(5), 481–499.

Wharf, B. (1990). Introduction. In B. Wharf (Ed.), *Social work and social change in Canada* (pp. 1–30). Toronto: McClelland & Stewart Inc.

_____. (Ed.). (1993). *Rethinking child welfare in Canada*, Toronto: McClelland & Stewart Inc.

Zastrow, C. (1996). *Introduction to social work and social welfare.* Toronto: Brooks/Cole Publishing Company.

Chapter 13

Narrative Therapy: Reifying or Challenging Dominant Discourse

Catrina Brown
Maritime School of Social Work
Dalhousie University

Narrative therapy has emerged in recent years as an alluring and popular method of intervention for social workers. Situated within a constructionist frame and shaped by postmodernism, it nonetheless offers practical techniques toward deconstructing and reconstructing clients' stories. It has been described as "postmodernism in practice." Approaches to narrative therapy vary, however, and can result in significantly different practices. Indeed, I argue that narrative therapies may be differently located within modernist and postmodernist epistemologies. Some interpretations appear to have a blended grounding in modernist and postmodernist paradigms of knowledge, while others seem to be more thoroughly grounded in, for example, a postmodern frame. I will argue that a fractured foundationalism— blending the two paradigms—offers the strongest possibility for challenging dominant discourse.

Practice grounded in a blended epistemology may benefit from the strengths within these approaches while abandoning their respective weaknesses. Where modernism is critiqued for truth claims rooted in false universalization, its myth of objectivity, and the essentialism of the human subject, postmodernism is critiqued for its epistemological relativism—there is no one truth. A world view capable of producing social change typically requires overarching, unifying, or totalizing theories that a strict application of postmodernism forbids.[1] Therefore, within postmodernism there can be no substantial agenda for social change. Well-known Australian Michael

White adopts a blended epistemology in his work, one that I argue allows him to challenge dominant discourse.

Influenced by the French theorist Michel Foucault, White has been at the centre of narrative therapy development and differs from other proponents in his consistent theoretical connection between knowledge and power—that no story, no experience is neutral. No story is outside of power. The belief that neither dominant nor suppressed stories are neutral is woven throughout his narrative approach.

By comparing leading figures in this field, Harlene Anderson (1997) and Michael White (1989a, 1989b, 1989c, 1991, 1994, 2001; White and Epston, 1990), I investigate differences in their interpretation and thus treatment of clients' narratives. I will provide an overview of their approaches to narrative therapy, comparing their organizing constructs—experience, knowledge, and power—as well as how they position the therapist's knowledge, authority, and power in relation to the client. In doing so, I will explore the degree to which they are likely to reify or challenge dominant stories.

Anderson is grounded almost fully in postmodernism, while White blurs the edges of modernism and postmodernism. These theorists reflect both the strengths and weaknesses of both paradigms. Anderson reflects the weakness of postmodern relativism. Her view from everywhere becomes a view from nowhere (Bordo, 1990). For Anderson, therapy is about endless meanings and interpretation to be explored through mutual inquiry; however, seamless and endless multiplicity takes her unwittingly into the realm of neo-objectivity or neutrality while paradoxically claiming that there is no neutrality or objectivity.

Although both Anderson and White engage elements of postmodern theory, White's significant grounding assumptions reflect a modernist approach to politics. His politically positioned approach to clients' narratives is more likely to successfully challenge oppressive stories. His commitment to social justice, to an awareness of the relationship between power and knowledge, is modernist. His desire to deconstruct is postmodern, drawing on Foucault's nexus of knowledge/power. Further, as he does not simply invoke reified concepts or categories—central ingredients in the reification of dominant stories—he appears to largely escape the essentialism of modernism. Not only is he committed to challenging dominant stories, his practice is based on an emancipatory epistemology from which challenges to dominant discourses can emerge.

Emancipatory projects such as anti-oppressive practice must be grounded in emancipatory epistemology. Emancipatory epistemologies are reflexive, continually questioning whether foundational assumptions of knowledge foster fundamental challenges to oppressive social conditions rather than unknowingly reinforcing them. Thus, narrative therapy must be aware of the foundational constructs it uses if it is to achieve an empowerment-based/anti-oppressive approach to practice. Clearly, it will not be anti-oppressive if it simply reproduces dominant stories. An anti-oppressive approach must include a self-conscious deployment of foundational concepts such as experience, knowledge, expertise/authority, and power. In this chapter I argue that Anderson's narrative therapy risks reifying dominant discourse, while White is positioned to challenge it.

HARLENE ANDERSON

Postmodern Knowledge Base

Anderson (1997) is largely rooted in postmodern epistemology, which she views as an ideological critique of modernist premises of knowing as well as a philosophical stance toward interpreting life. She decisively rejects the idea of objectivity—that we can ever know social life objectively. Knowledge can only ever be partial; there are multiple ways of knowing, so there can be no universal truth. As such she eschews expert knowledge and suggests it is not only impossible to be neutral, it is undesirable. And while her philosophical stance includes her values and biases (Anderson, 1997, p. 94), she adopts a position of "multipartiality" (Anderson, 1997, p. 95), taking all sides simultaneously. This Anderson contrasts with neutrality, which she suggests means not taking any side at all.

Knowledge is constitutional, not representational; it is not "out there" in nature or reality to be discovered. What we claim to know does not then represent the world as it is. Instead, what we claim to know is actually constitutive of knowledge itself. We constitute ourselves, our experiences, and social life through what we assume to be knowledge. Anderson's rejection of objective knowledge leads her to believe there are multiple perspectives, many interpretations, and that meaning itself is endless. As a postmodernist she embraces multiplicity, contradiction, and uncertainty.

Anderson anticipates responses to her postmodern critiques of knowledge. She is quick to argue that she is not advocating neutrality but multipartiality, and is consequently able to escape the limitations of relativism. From her perspective, she isn't without position; she is taking a stance. She is taking all sides at once. This postmodern position has been strongly critiqued by feminist theorists, who believe that it empties theory and, by extension, practice of political content. Critics of postmodernism like Brotman and Pollack (1998, p. 11) argue that postmodernism is likely to "decontextualize and depoliticize our practice and help to retrench postmodern values that are antithetical to social change." There is no position from which to act, and thus no accountability for one's position. One can have it any way one wants. Most important, the pluralistic desire to engage multiple vantage points and interpretations is largely a fantasy.

Bordo offers this critique of postmodern relativism:

> [it] may slip into its own fantasy of escape from human locatedness—by supposing the critic can become wholly protean by adopting endlessly shifting seemingly inexhaustible vantage points; none of which are "owned" by either the critic or the author of the text under examination (1993, p. 142). Deconstructionist readings that enact this protean fantasy are continually "slip-slidin' away" through paradox, inversion, self-subversion ... they often present themselves as having it any way they want. They refuse to assume a shape for which they must take responsibility. (Bordo, 1993, p. 144)

Supporting Bordo, Haraway suggests that relativism like objectivism is a "god trick" that promises a view from everywhere and nowhere simultaneously:

> Relativism is a way of being nowhere while claiming to be everywhere equally. The "equality" of positioning is a denial of responsibility and critical inquiry. Relativism is the perfect mirror twin of totalization in the ideologies of objectivity; both deny the stakes in location, embodiment and partial perspective; both make it impossible to see well. Relativism and totalization are both "god tricks" promising vision from everywhere and nowhere equally and fully. (Haraway, 1988, p. 584)

Ironically, the posture of multiplicity begins to resemble that of good old-fashioned neutrality or objectivity. What is the difference, ultimately, between taking all sides simultaneously and taking no side at all? Endless pluralism reflects the desire to seem unbiased and inclusive, but denies that it is impossible to actually be everywhere. Arguably, Anderson's postmodern relativism reflects a new form of objectivity—neo-objectivism.

For Anderson, therapy should not aim to discover truth. We should not be detectives whose goal is to uncover truth. Anderson is adamant that the narrative therapist's role is to encourage the telling and retelling of clients' stories. In the telling and retelling, multiple meanings and interpretations will emerge. Pivotal to her approach is the belief that we may not, under any condition, think of ourselves as superior masters of the story. Indeed, the client is the expert, the teacher. She states:

> In my view, such attempts at modifying a client's narrative take the form of narrative editing-revising, correcting, or polishing. A therapist's task is not to deconstruct, reproduce, or reconstruct a client's story but to facilitate and participate in its telling and retelling.

Narrative editing is a slippery slope. A narrative editor position requires the technical expertise to edit. This entails certain risks: it implies the assumption that a therapist has more credibility as a master of human stories than a client. It assumes that a therapist can read a client like a text. It makes a therapist an archaeological narrativist who believes there is *a* story, with an imagined significance, that needs to be uncovered or retold (Anderson, 1997, p. 96).

The Narrative

The narrative is "more than a storytelling metaphor" (Anderson, 1997, p. 212). The "[n]arrative is a dynamic process that constitutes both the way that we organize the events and experiences of our lives to make sense of them and the way we participate in creating the things we make sense of, including ourselves" (Ibid.). According to Anderson, "we live storied lives with one another… . Our stories form, inform, and re-form our sources of knowledge, our views of reality" (Ibid.). The stories we tell are then a "source of transformation," which is critical to narrative therapy. Anderson's work centres on the idea of the "dialogical conversation," which "facilitates the unsaid and the yet-to-be-said" (Anderson, 1997, p. 118). This is a mutually constructed generative process in therapy conversation. New meanings and different understandings of experiences are then able to emerge and this may lead to both self-agency and resolving the problem.

Conceptualizing Experience and "The Self"

As a postmodernist therapist, Anderson is careful to consider how we talk about the "self," and as such she attempts to avoid simple reification of the human subject and problematic essentialism. She argues that there is no autonomous, given, essential, fixed, stable, unified, or discoverable self. The self, like our stories, is forever emerging, forever multiple. The self, experience, and the stories told are multiple; they are not static. At the same time, Anderson emphasizes the client as the expert, and stresses the first voice as the focus of therapy. Therapists are not permitted to deconstruct and reconstruct stories with their clients in Anderson's dialogical conversation, only to facilitate telling and retelling.[2] When clients tell stories about themselves that reflect dominant discourse and that perpetuate their own oppression, we might want to ask what the limitations are in so fully authorizing the clients' knowledge/expertise. In Anderson's schema, the narrative therapist is not permitted an agenda and, therefore, should not have an agenda to challenge the dominant story or to reconstruct a more positive alternative.

Yet clients do tell stories about themselves and their lives that are deeply problematic and that need to be unpacked. What this means, if we are honest with ourselves, is that we do systematically and necessarily privilege our own narratives within anti-oppressive work. According to Anderson, "[e]ven therapists who purport to fight certain dominant social discourses inadvertently and paradoxically marginalize a client when they assume their counternarrative (for example, social injustice, gender inequality, institutional colonization) is better for a client" (Anderson, 1997, p. 97).[3] If Anderson's narrative conversation is truly dialogical, both therapist and client (as active subjects shaping emerging narratives) should be "content experts," or, put differently, actively and critically engaged with the content of therapy. Anderson positions the client's narrative as authorative, dictating legitimation and validation regardless, it seems, of the story told. Similar to well-ensconced empowerment models of therapy, she fears marginalization of the first voice if we don't validate the client's account. And relatedly, she presumes that challenging the client's narrative unequivocally reflects a "hierarchical and dualistic position in relation to the client" (Anderson, 1997, p. 97). The assumption that challenging a narrative reflects a hierarchical approach to therapy or an act of oppressive domination needs to be critically interrogated. I suggest that underneath this belief are a number of serious flaws, including overly simplified dualistic notions of knowledge and power, and essentialist notions of experience. How can our work be anti-oppressive if we merely reify the dominant stories that clients tell?

Anderson's reliance on the authority of the clients' stories or their content expertise decontextualizes and depoliticizes the social processes by which these stories are put together. Although Anderson does not theorize power explicitly—the word doesn't appear in her book—power is present.

Insofar as it is acknowledged, it is through her construction of the client/ therapist relationship, which she characterizes as non-hierarchical, egalitarian, collaborative, and mutual. Her failure to theorize power is evident in the implicit way she conceptualizes power in this relationship and is, moreover, not consistent with the level of rigorous interrogation and theoretical sophistication typical of her work. As a starting point to her dualistic interpretation of power, she seems to suffer from the mistake of granting too much inherent power to the therapist and too little to the client. From this miscalculated degree of inequality, she chooses to remove all power or authority about content from the therapist and grants carte blanche authorization of content power to the client. In this manoeuvre, experience is problematically glorified, elevated, and essentialized in a decidedly non-postmodern manner. Here she departs from her postmodern premises.

She is unable to stay consistently within its parameters, and if she did, one might wonder how she could practise at all. Nothing could ever have any truth value, for even a second, for as soon as it emerged, it would become something else. Therapy would simply be a nonsensical indulgence in infinite questions and momentary infinite responses with no discernible beginning or end. This particular fissure in her epistemological foundation— the expert client—allows truth value to exist, however individual, local, and temporary. There is, however, a place from which to step off. And while Anderson is unquestionably postmodern, modernist remnants such as these may well make conducting therapy possible. That said, a stronger modernist thread within postmodern therapy practice is arguably one that preserves the modernist commitment to politics, to being politically positioned, rather than the modernist conceptual limitation of essentialism reflected in Anderson's uninterrogated authorization of experience and first voice.

There is no agenda to historicize or contextualize experience or self. She is clear that we must avoid generalizing about population or problems, instead emphasizing that each individual has a unique experience. Consistent with postmodernism, the focus is on the local, the particular, not the extra-local or generalizable. From here we must then unfortunately assume that we can't make generalizations about the social impact of racism, sexism, or heterosexism, for example. Significant clinical experience working with specific populations, such as those engaged with harmful substance use or eating problems, must be bracketed in order to focus on the individual as though she or he were somehow fully unique and separate from other clients' experiences.

There can be no social analysis without generalization. "Social" implies group life, that we move past the individual. Sociology, is of course, distinguished from psychology because it recognizes that individuals do not live in a vacuum, and that they can make meaning only within the context of social interaction. There must be a minimum of shared knowledge and shared experience or intersubjectivity within societies in order for normative, typified, taken-for-granted everyday reality to exist (Berger & Luckman, 1966; Durkheim, 1966; Mead, 1977). The social construction of knowledge depends on the processes of this intersubjectivity (Schutz, 1967). This doesn't mean there is consensus, agreement, inclusion of all experiences, or equal benefit. The objectification of social life allows it to appear as though it were independent of human creation (Berger & Luckman, 1966).

According to Anderson, we can get close to another's experience, but we can never fully understand it because there is no "transparent intersubjectivity." This belief rationalizes the individual and local therapeutic focus and risks producing not only a dehistoricized and decontextualized approach but a subjectivist or individualist approach as well. The notion of the "personal is political" was coined by feminists in the 1970s and is central to, for example, feminist therapy practice. Anderson's therapy is the personal is personal. She is advocating a focus on the decontextualized, depoliticized, individual story.

Narrative Therapy: Knowledge, Power, and Authority

Postmodern narrative therapy is non-interventionist, a "joint performance" in which the client and the therapist are "conversational partners" in a mutual inquiry. They share responsibility and accountability for the therapy and co-influence each other. The therapist should not occupy a meta-position and is, therefore, encouraged to ask curious questions from a position of "not-knowing." Drawing on Derrida, not-knowing "does not mean that we know nothing but that we are beyond absolute knowledge ..." (Anderson, 1997, p. 137). According to Anderson, "not-knowing does not mean withholding, pretending dumbness, being deceitful, or maintaining neutrality" (Ibid.). As it is inevitable that the therapist's knowledge enters therapy, I suggest we should be deliberately positioned and thereby accountable for its presence without actually presuming we hold absolute knowledge.

She wishes to see both the therapist and the client as active, embodied subjects in therapy. Her desire is to "[b]ring the person of both therapist and client back in the room" (Anderson, 1997, p. 94). Locating herself in the conversation, she is openly authentic and reveals herself. She is not a keeper of secrets. Anderson refers to this as "being public," echoing the feminist therapy principle of self-disclosure, which reduces the we/they distinction in therapy.

Anderson, however, makes a clear we/they distinction in her construction of "the expert" by assigning one the role of the content expert and the other that of the process expert. The therapist is the process expert, the inquiring other, only a temporary guest in the client's life. In contrast, the client is the content expert or the teacher. This artificial split between content and process erases the likelihood that both the therapist and client contribute content and process.[4] Anderson suggests that:

> [A] client brings expertise in the area of content: a client is the expert on his or her life experiences and what has brought that client into the therapy relationship. When clients are narrators of their stories, they are able to experience and recognize their own voices, power, and authority. A therapist brings expertise in the area of process: a therapist is the expert in engaging and participating with a client in a dialogical process of first-person story-telling. It is as if the roles of therapist and client were reversed. *The client becomes the teacher.* (Anderson, 1997, p. 95)

Her view reflects a naive authorization of experience, as though experience were somehow outside discursive formulation, somehow outside culture, power, and knowledge construction. According to Joan Scott, new ways of thinking about change can come about when we interrogate the creation of experience: "Experience is at once always already an interpretation and in need of interpretation" (Scott, 1992, p. 37). To not deconstruct the discursive construction of experience as an interpretation is to treat it as a privileged voice presumed to speak authorative, unquestionable truth.

She does not problematize subjugated knowledge; instead, her focus is on the expert first voice. While she wishes to avoid marginalizing the first voice and even recognizes that clients' stories can be self-limiting (Scott, 1992, p. 233), she treats it as though it were outside power. Her acknowledgement that "we are always embedded in the local and universal historical pasts and the cultural, social and political contexts of our narrative making" (Scott, 1992, p. 215) is undermined by her skepticism of intersubjective understanding or shared meaning and she is subsequently left with a subjectivist focus. Thus, the therapeutic conversation remains individualized and depoliticized.

Rooted in a solid postmodern foundation and influenced by impressive theorists such as Derrida, Gadamer, Heidigger, Wittengstein, and Brumer, Anderson's work is epistemologically rich, yet within her schema she leaves very little room for social or political analysis. While the endless interpretation, multiple meanings, and possibilities of socially constructed stories, the nonlinearity and embrace of complexity and contradictions are all strengths of Anderson's work, there is an agnostic abandonment of the modernist commitment to political goals and agendas that emphasize social justice and anti-oppressive practice.

MICHAEL WHITE

Epistemology: The Power/Knowledge Nexus

White's post-positivist epistemology blends modernism and postmodernism. His conceptualization of experience, knowledge, and power are located within a postmodern paradigm of knowledge. Yet for White, therapy is a political activity and his commitment to social justice reflects the modernist possibility of being politically positioned. His work is a creative application of Foucault's conception of knowledge/power to therapy practice whereby techniques of power are woven through everyday discourse, including therapy.[5]

As we can't have direct knowledge of the world, we can only know what we know through lived experience (White, 1989a, p. 1). White (Ibid.) claims, "We make sense of our lives, and the lives of others, by interpreting or attributing meaning to our experiences." Hence, all meaning is interpretative. Dominant discourses, however, produce the myth of a knowable and observable universal knowledge. Subjugated knowledges are hidden or obscured, yet when exposed, they reveal ruptures in universality. White terms such knowledge "disqualified knowledge." Disqualified knowledges include marginalized knowledge—knowledge at the fringe— and erudite knowledge "written out of history."

It isn't possible to "deny knowledge, that is to act apart from and experience the world from outside of the mediating effects of knowledge and discursive practices" (White & Epston, 1990, p. 7). When one form of knowledge prevails over another form, it often disqualifies it. As there can be no universal challenge to dominant knowledge, resurrecting subjugated knowledge—making visible conflict and struggle—is a form of political action. To uncover alternative stories flaunts their possibility, which not only exposes the fantasy of universal truth claims but reveals how knowledge discourses are practices of power—how knowledge and power are intertwined. For Foucault, and thus White, techniques of power are not separate from the production of dominant knowledge. Our lived experience exists within a field or web of power/knowledge. Power is everywhere; it is insidious, and we can't escape it. As we are always inside power, we can't act apart from it. Power is constitutive largely through normalizing truths. "Thus it can be seen that a domain of knowledge is a domain of power, and a domain of power is a domain of knowledge" (White & Espton, 1990, p. 22). We can see White's origins in Foucault, who describes power and knowledge in this way:

> There can be no possible exercise of power without a certain economy of discourses of truth which operates through and on the basis of this association. We are subjected to the production of truth through power and we cannot exercise power except through the production of truth. (Foucault, 1980b, p. 83)

Again reflecting Foucault's approach to power, White argues that it is not dualistic; both the therapist and client have power. Therapy practices cannot be benign or outside power regardless of self-awareness or motive. Power is organized and reified through discourse, including therapeutic discourse. And because we are "always participating simultaneously in domains of power and knowledge" (White & Epston, 1990, p. 29), we must remain critical of our own work.

On power, Foucault states:

> Power is not something that is acquired, seized or shared, something that one holds onto or allows to slip away; power is exercised from innumerable points, in the interplay of nonegalitarian and mobile relations. ... Power comes from below. ... Power relations are both intentional and nonsubjective. ... Where there is power, there is resistance, and yet, or rather consequently, this resistance is never in a position of exteriority in relation to power. Should it be said that one is always "inside" power, there is no "escaping" it, there is no absolute outside where it is concerned. ... (Foucault, 1980a, pp. 94–95)

White rejects the postmodern view that power is constructed only in language—that it doesn't really exist. But he also rejects the argument of "the left" that power is real, wielded by some over others in order to oppress them (White & Epston, 1990, p. 1).

Experience

For White (1989c, pp. 3–4), knowledge and social reality are socially constructed, therefore, all experiences are socially constructed or organized.

To make sense of life, people must develop "coherent accounts of themselves" and their world. People "organize and give meaning to their experience through the storying of experience" (White & Epston, 1990, p. 12). "These stories are constitutive-shaping lives and relationships" (Ibid.). Narratives are constructed and this is a selective process in which information is filtered. The performance of these stories expresses selected aspects of lived experience. No story can encompass the richness of experience, the gaps, and contradiction of lived experience (White & Epson, 1990, p. 13).

He adopts a constructionist approach to experience; experience is discursive. For White, "persons organize their lives around specific meanings and how, in so doing, they inadvertently contribute to the 'survival' of, as well as the 'career' of, the problem" (White & Epston, 1990, p. 3). People seek therapy when stories about experiences—theirs or others—do not represent their lived experiences and they subsequently desire new meaning or possibilities. At such times people may feel stuck in their lives, as though nothing were changing, and uncertain how to begin looking for new meanings or possibilities (White & Epston, p. 36).

White does not privilege or idealize experience. He does not equate it with truth as it is not outside the power/knowledge nexus. It is socially constructed and historicized, thus not authoritative or essential. Experience can be contested. White's process of externalization challenges and contests experience, and in so doing reveals unique outcomes that enable the re-storying of people's lives.

The Narrative

White elicits a "text analogy"—meaning is derived through structuring experience into stories (White & Epston, 1990, p. 27). As we "ascribe meaning and constitute our lives and relationships through language," storying is dependent on language (Ibid.). However, we can construct stories only through culturally available discourses. Like Anderson, White argues that our stories don't just represent us, they constitute us. Stories don't then simply reflect life, they are constitutive of life (White, 1989c, p. 4). Perhaps the most significant difference between Anderson and White is that for White, no story is outside power. Consequently, there are no neutral stories and no neutral hearing of stories. According to White, all stories need to be told, deconstructed, and reconstructed, not simply heard. Clients' narratives reflect both dominant and subjugated knowledges and they are contextualized in terms of power.

White's (1989c) conceptualization of the narrative is encapsulated here:

The personal story or self-narrative is not radically invented inside our heads. Rather, it is something that is negotiated and disrupted within various communities of persons and in the institutions of our culture. ... Our lives are multi-storied. No single story of life can be free of ambiguity and contradiction. No sole personal story or narrative can handle all of the contingencies of life. ... The personal story or self-narrative is not neutral in its effects. ... Different personal stories or self-narratives are anything but equal in their real effects. ... The narrative metaphor is associated with a tradition of thought that rules out the possibility of "anything goes" moral relativism. ... This tradition of thought encourages therapists to assume responsibility for the real effects or consequences of his/her interaction with persons who seek help. (White 1989c, pp. 3–4)

Narrative Therapy
New narratives are co-authored in the therapy process. This approach recognizes that both the therapist and the client bring knowledge to therapy; both are active embodied subjects. In this construction, one is not the content expert and the other the process expert. Because White's narrative therapy places the power/knowledge nexus at the centre of story construction, deconstruction, and reconstruction, he is able to move past dichotomous notions of "the expert," instead emphasizing that all experiences and stories are inside power. And while he recognizes the subjugated knowledge in experience, the suppressed voice, he explores how stories both reify and challenge dominant discourse. His narrative therapy deconstructs how stories are constructed from available discourses (i.e., experience, empowerment, disease, identity, or addiction).

The idea that the person is not the problem—the "problem is the problem"—shifts therapy away from "problem-saturation" and is attractive to many social workers who take up narrative therapy as a new form of empowerment-based practice.[6] For White, the problem is constructed as the "performance of [the] oppressive, dominant story or knowledge" (White & Espton, 1990, p. 6). The process of externalization helps people to separate from "truth" discourses or unitary knowledge. The history of effects of these "so-called" truths can be explored and facilitate the development of a more reflexive perspective on one's life. Ideas, feelings, interactions, and social practices can all be externalized. Ideas such as "men aren't supposed to cry" or social practices such as "mother blaming" or racism can be contested. Externalization is then at the heart of deconstructing "the problem" or the unhelpful story, whereby new options may become available in challenging the dominant "truths." Taking apart clients' narratives will often involve challenging the normalizing truths that constitute people's lives and hence the techniques of power, which, he argues, subjugate people to a dominant ideology (White, 1989c, p. 3; 1994).

The desired outcome in the process of externalization is the generation of alternative stories that include aspects of lived experience left out, which will permit the creation and performance of new narratives. "[A]spects of experience that fall outside the dominant story provide a rich and fertile source for the generation or re-generation, of alternative stories" (White & Epston, 1990, p. 15). Those aspects outside the dominant story are called unique outcomes. Unique outcomes illustrate that other stories exist, that dominant discourse does not always prevail, and offers rich alternatives that can begin to form reconstructed stories. Identification of unique outcomes is facilitated by externalizing the problem. Externalization helps interrupt the dominant story and its ongoing performance. "Thicker description" can emerge from externalizing conversations and allow for greater possibilities in the re-authoring of one's life (White, 2001, p. 33). Clients are invited to impute meaning to the unique outcomes identified as they begin to develop an alternative story to re-author their lives.

Augusta-Scott's (2001a) work with men who batter illustrates the importance of not simply reproducing the dominant stories about their identity. Inviting men to explore, for example, ways they can be gentle and kind in their relationships, or the shame they feel as batterers challenges dominant scripts that construct and naturalize their identities as "bad." Such ruptures to the dominant story of identity are pivotal to effective therapy (Augusta-Scott, 2001b). The emergence of alternative claims enable the reconstructed story to replace the problem-saturated story into which the person has been recruited (White, 2001).

Critical to White's narrative therapy as a form of political action is the "[i]nsurrection of the subjugated knowledges" (White & Epston, 1990, p. 29). Identifying and incorporating the subjugated into new narratives challenges unifying dominant and often oppressive truths. This contrasts sharply with Anderson, who does not challenge techniques of power. Following Foucault, White suggests that:

> techniques of power that "incite" persons to constitute their lives through "truth" are developed and perfected at the local level and are then taken up at the broader levels, then, in

joining with persons to challenge these practices, we also accept that we are inevitably engaged in a political activity. (We would also acknowledge that, if we do not join with persons to challenge these techniques of power, then we are also engaged in political activity.) This is not a political activity that involves the proposal of an alternative ideology, but one that challenges the techniques that subjugate persons to a dominant ideology. (White & Epston, 1990, p. 29)

He does not advocate that the therapist seek objectivity or neutrality because therapy is political activity. In his article "The politics of therapy: Putting to rest the illusion of neutrality," White (1994) states that:

It is never a matter of whether or not we bring politics into the therapy room, but it is a matter of whether or not we are prepared to acknowledge the existence of these politics, and it is a matter of the degree to which we are prepared to be complicit in the reproduction of these politics. (White 1994, p. 1)

White is joined by other narrative theorists who underscore the importance of unpacking dominant stories (Adams-Westcot, Dafforn, & Sterne, 1993; Hare-Mustin, 1994). For example, the dominant social stories of single parents, the unemployed, the Black family, the battered woman, or the Native alcoholic all cast viciously pathologizing, blaming, and decontextualized accounts that reify dominant social reality and maintain social oppression. Identifying subjugated knowledge and the suppressed voice in therapy is not a neutral act, nor can it be. It involves both the client's and the therapist's expert content. White cautions the narrative therapist, however, from taking up the suppressed story at face value as though it were more true, genuine, or authentic. Because the resurrection of the suppressed story is central to re-authoring conversations in therapy, it is often seen as "liberatory" (White, 2001, p. 36). The re-authored story may then be viewed as the "freeing of people to live a life that is more accurately a reflection of their 'true nature' or their 'essential humanness,' and of their 'authenticity'" (White, 2001, p. 36). This humanist and modernist interpretation of the suppressed story separates the re-authored story from power, from its social construction, and, in so doing, potentially and inadvertently reproduces oppressive and dominant stories of power. At the heart of this interpretation of life and identity is the belief that:

the problems that people experience are the outcomes of forces that are oppressive of, repressive of, or distorting of the essences of elements of human nature. The solution to people's problems that is proposed by these naturalistic notions is to identify, to challenge, and to throw off these oppressive, repressive and distorting forces so that people might have the opportunity to become more truly who they really are, so that they may live a life that is a more accurate reflection of their human nature. (White, 2001, p. 37)

White's conviction that clients do not and cannot tell an objective story about themselves or their experience anymore than anyone else suggests that we cannot take up any story at face value—that is, we cannot idealize, authorize, or privilege the subjugated voice. If we accept these stories at face value without deconstruction, we naively accept the discursive constitution of the story. We cannot assume that the re-authored story discovers innate human nature or the suppressed identity, or that it allows the "true" self to emerge. It is clear that how we approach the suppressed voice is critical to producing new non-oppressive stories. The therapeutic search for the "real self," or to reconstruct one's "own story" reveals slippage into essentialist notions of self and, furthermore, moves outside a constitutionalist narrative framework. There is no real fixed self, and thus no real story to discover outside social discourse.

CHALLENGING DOMINANT DISCOURSE: COMPARING ANDERSON AND WHITE

Harlene Anderson and Michael White represent two approaches to experience, knowledge, and power in narrative therapy. White's politically positioned approach reflects a blended modernist/postmodernist epistemology and is thus more able to challenge oppressive stories. White maintains that the social worker/therapist must be politically positioned and work from this vision. For White no story is neutral, and thus all stories need to be unpacked. Moreover, no telling or hearing of a story is neutral. He urges us to see the clients' stories as inside social practices of power. This means we need to explore the practices of power within the clients' stories rather than simply reify them by telling and retelling the stories. Clients' dominant stories often shape or structure their lives, and these dominant stories reflect culturally dominant stories. Together we co-author new stories that work better for clients in living their lives. New or reconstructed stories emerge through processes of understanding the social construction of the existing stories and their subsequent deconstruction.

In contrast, Anderson's postmodern foundation is reflected in her belief that practitioners should help only in the telling and retelling of stories. For Anderson there is no power, there are only stories. Because she does not theorize power, clients' narratives are presumed to be outside power. When interrogating both of these approaches, it becomes clear that Anderson's view risks reifying dominant stories and, therefore, does not enhance an empowerment based anti-oppressive practice. Alternatively, White's focus on the social construction of narratives addresses the contradictions, gaps, and uncertainty of clients' stories in an effort to create more empowering life stories and experiences. He addresses the complexities of clients' stories, so they can both reify and challenge dominant discourse. They can be subjugated and dominant simultaneously. Compared to Anderson, White's approach to narrative therapy is more able to challenge dominant discourse, which is necessary for both empowerment and anti-oppressive practice.

Anderson and White also adopt different stances on how practitioners should position themselves—their knowledge and power—in narrative therapy. Anderson's postmodern multipartiality or "view from nowhere" is one of "moral relativism," according to White (1989c, p. 4). If as social workers we have a world view and are politically positioned, we will reject moral relativism (Ibid.). We interpret clients' stories from within our world view and political position whether we know it or not. From here we will decide in our own minds the "real effects" of the self-narrative on the clients' lives. Although Anderson clearly states that the therapist is not a *tabula rasa* or blank screen, it is very difficult to see where and how the therapist's knowledge will shape therapy, except through the therapeutic questions themselves. I can only assume that she interprets stories as equally valid—one story is as good as another in her stance of multipartiality. As a result, "there can be no 'solid' basis for making decisions about different actions" (Ibid.). In attempting to not invoke a privileged narrative, to not adopt one positioned stance—to simply tell and retell stories—or to mimic neutrality, she unwittingly encourages reified storytelling.

Her position of multipartiality or neutrality is antithetical to challenging dominant discourse. Narrative therapy on the side of social justice is necessarily politically positioned. A socially constructed view of the world, one that sees stories as constitutionalist rather than representationalist, are more likely to facilitate a process of unpacking dominant stories because representational approaches are more inclined to take up stories at face value. Within a constitutionalist approach, socially constructed narratives reflect both dominant and subjugated knowledges. White's approach to knowledge and power is helpful in deconstructing both subjugated and dominant knowledge and in the process of reconstructing alternative stories that work better for clients.

A postmodern approach suggests that we not reinforce false dualisms. Postmodern approaches to narrative therapy that contribute to challenging dominant discourse need to recognize that power is not dualistic; both the therapist and client have power and both are active embodied subjects in therapy. Similarly, knowledge is not in the hands of either the therapist or the client; both contribute knowledge. New narratives are, therefore, co-authored in therapy. When we recognize that both the therapist and client are active embodied subjects in therapy, therapists are better able to responsibly situate their own knowledge, power, and authority. They need not deny either their knowledge or power in order to participate in an empowerment-based approach to narrative therapy—one that can challenge dominant discourse.

While both Anderson and White argue that the therapist and the client should be active, embodied subjects in therapy, in Anderson's schema the therapist and client are ascribed dichotomous expert roles in relation to content and process. Anderson fails to expose the client as "content expert" to the same level of scrutiny that the expert knowledge of the practitioner undergoes. Moreover, this conceptualization appears to contradict her claim that all narratives are constitutive. She states: "We live our narratives and our narratives become our living; our realities become our stories and our stories become our realities" (Anderson, 1997, p. 216). Although the narratives that clients construct are fully social and hence not outside dominant and oppressive discourse, the therapist may not invoke a meta-narrative or a privileged narrative such as engaging in processes of reframing, revising, or editing a client's story. We can only listen and facilitate the client's storytelling through the process of curious questions. Clients as content experts presume they are their own best experts, that they are always immediately able to see the impact of the dominant discourses that shape their lives. Where feminist therapists and politically situated narrative therapists such as White would reframe the battered woman's self-blame, for example, Anderson's model prohibits this as unwelcome privileging of the therapist's narrative, the invoking of a master storyteller role. We must do more than encourage the telling and retelling of stories in the belief that they are valid, legitimate, and authoritative as Anderson's postmodern narrative work suggests. We cannot, as White's argues, simply encourage reified storytelling.

As social workers we need to determine how to interpret the story of the suppressed voice. For Anderson, there is a paradoxical desire to the take up the suppressed story at face value as though it were more true. Our commitment as social workers to working in a way that facilitates our clients' empowerment has arguably led to a naive and fear-based authorization of clients' stories.[7] This subjectivist interpretation separates the client's story from power, from its social construction and, in so doing, may inadvertently reproduce oppressive and dominant stories of power. There is often a fear that exercising our knowledge and power is necessarily oppressive and pernicious. These dualistic conceptualizations of knowledge, expertise, and power in narrative practices are likely to contribute to the reification of oppressive stories. Narrative therapy requires further reflection on the positioning of the suppressed voice if we wish to avoid reproducing clients' oppressive narratives in our work.

According to White, power is organized and reified through discourse, including therapeutic discourse, so therapists need to be vigilant about their own practices of power. Within White's politically positioned approach we invoke our own privileged narratives when we reframe or reconstruct our clients' stories because *we believe* they are oppressive or damaging. However, we need to ask ourselves: When do we accept, legitimate, and validate our clients' stories within a narrative approach, and when do we challenge them through reframing and reconstruction?

If we wish to challenge dominant discourse, we cannot simply take up socially constructed categories and discourses as they are presently constituted. The social constitution of social categories and discourses means that they will often reflect "dominant truth claims," and dominant relations of power. Postmodernism offers a lens from which to examine our conceptual foundations in order to avoid reproducing dominant discourse. Foundational concepts in social work like experience, knowledge, power, and self or identity require critical deconstruction. We see then that experiences are socially organized and, hence, do not in themselves represent truth. The stories people tell about their experiences are contextualized in terms of power, and they are always incomplete. All stories, therefore, need to be told, deconstructed, and reconstructed, not simply heard.

CONCLUSION

Narrative therapy that is to be useful as an emancipatory practice committed to social justice is necessarily rooted in emancipatory epistemology. An approach to narrative therapy that avoids reifying dominant and oppressive stories will involve holding onto the combined strengths of modernist and postmodernist frameworks while abandoning their limitations. This blended epistemology or fractured foundationalism will avoid the relativism of postmodernism and its subsequent inability to take a stance from which one can take action, while emphasizing its self-reflexive capacity for deconstruction. We can then unpack foundational concepts such as experience, knowledge, and power previously constituted within a modernist paradigm. However, within modernism we may be politically positioned, which may enable us to challenge oppressive stories.

I have focused on two significantly different approaches to narrative therapy. The first, Anderson's postmodernist narrative therapy, is at risk of reifying socially dominant stories and thus dominant social relations. The second, White's blended modernist/postmodern narrative approach to therapy, is grounded in an emancipatory epistemology and is thus positioned to offer significant challenges to dominant stories that both organize and are organized by social relations of power. While this discussion has centred upon Anderson and White—significant contributors to the field of narrative therapy—those identified features that challenge dominant discourse are transferable to our understanding of narrative therapy in general.

NOTES

1. Postmodernism is anti-foundationalism, which suggests that it can't be held to or advocate a particular foundation of knowledge. As postmodernism has discernible epistemological features, it clearly has a knowledge foundation. To assert that there is no knowable unified truth is an epistemological position, although it has been cleverly pointed out by many that if there is no knowable and unified truth, how can one say there is no knowable unified truth?

2. Curiously, despite her emphasis that the clients are the experts about their lives, she argues that self-stories are not "necessarily truer than other stories." This begs the question is it not necessarily truer, but *possibly* truer? How would one know? How does one ascertain truth? Every story is then just one more among many.

3. From this standpoint she does raise critically important issues about the dilemma of reframing and restructuring clients' narratives. And while reframing or privileging the therapist's narrative continues to be an unresolved paradox of empowerment-based work, a commitment to anti-oppressive practice requires a corresponding commitment to systematically challenging oppressive stories. Yet this practice contradicts the empowerment principle that one must validate and legitimate clients' stories as they are considered the experts about their own lives. However, if we do unequivocally validate and legitimate clients' stories, we are likely to inadvertently reify dominant stories. An alternative would be to emphasize a dialogue between therapist and client in which both bring knowledge to the creation of new stories.

4. Therapists have still not resolved how to be most effective as co-authors in collaborative approaches to working with clients in the process of re-storying their

lives—how we should best situate our own knowledge/"expertise" and power? However, Anderson constructs a problematic and curious dualism especially for a postmodernist. How does she distinguish content and process? Isn't therapy precisely the weaving together of these by both the client and the therapist?

5. Techniques of power include science, normalizing judgments, observation/surveillance, research, apparatuses of control, registration, classification, normalization, exclusion, and institutionalized isolation such as in prisons or psychiatric confinement (White & Epston, 1990, p. 25).

6. White's narrative therapy, however, transcends the simple story metaphor and the related emphasis on the wisdom/expertise of experience or first voice. He doesn't represent a reconstituted modernist-based empowerment therapy. Empowerment theory/therapy is grounded in modernism and White is, I argue, grounded in a more complex epistemology that combines modernism and postmodernism.

7. Other narrative therapists such as Parry and Doan (1994, p. 27) echo Anderson in their belief that no "narrative has greater legitimacy than the person's own." Each person's story becomes "self-legitimizing in a world that lacks a legitimizing yardstick against which to measure one's own and other's lives" (Parry & Doan, 1994, p. 26). This belief is central to practising therapy and in shaping the role that the client's knowledge and the therapist's knowledge have vis-à-vis each other. At the extreme end of the discursive "client is expert" argument, Parry and Doan (1994, p. 27) state: "Therefore, attempts by others to question the validity of such a story are themselves illegitimate. They are coercive, and to the extent that such methods are used to silence or discredit a person's stories, they represent a form of terrorism."

REFERENCES

Adams-Westcot, J., Dafforn, T., & Sterne, P. (1993). Escaping victim life stories and co-constructing personal agency. In S. Gilligan & R. Price (Eds.), *Therapeutic conversations* (pp. 258–276). New York: W.W. Norton.

Anderson, H. (1997). A philosophical stance: Therapists' position, expertise, and responsibility. In H. Anderson, *Conversation, language and possibilities: A postmodern approach to therapy* (pp. 93–107). New York: Basic Books.

Augusta-Scott, T. (2001a). Dichotomies in the power and control story: Exploring multiple stories about men who choose abuse in intimate relationships. *Gecko: A Journal of Deconstruction and Narrative Ideas in Therapeutic Practice 2*, 31–54.

_____. (2001b). A response to the responses. *Gecko: A Journal of Deconstruction and Narrative Ideas in Therapeutic Practice 2*, 67–68.

Berger, P., & Luckmann, T. (1966). *The social construction of reality: A treatise in the sociology of knowledge.* New York: Anchor Books.

Bordo, S. (1990). Feminism, postmodernism, and gender skepticism. In L. Nicholson (Ed.), *Feminism/Postmodernism* (pp. 133–156). New York: Routledge.

Brotman, S., & Pollack, S. (1998). Loss of context: The problem of merging postmodernism with feminist social work. *Canadian Social Work Review 14*(Winter), 9–21.

Brown, C. (1994). Feminist postmodernism and the challenge of diversity. In A. Chambon & A. Irving (Eds.), *Essays on postmodernism and social work* (pp. 35–48). Toronto: Canadian Scholars' Press.

_____. (2001a). Postmodernism and feminist therapy. Unpublished paper.

_____. (2001b). *Talking body talk: An analysis of feminist therapy epistemology.* Unpublished Ph.D. dissertation, University of Toronto, Toronto.

Carey, M. (2001). Acknowledging complexity. *Gecko: A Journal of Deconstruction and Narrative Ideas in Therapeutic Practice 2,* 64–66.

Durkheim, E. (1966). *The rules of sociological method.* New York: The Free Press.

Elliot, H. (1998). En-gendering distinctions: Postmodernism, feminism, and narrative therapy. In S. Madigan & I. Law (Eds.), *Praxis: Situating Discourse, Feminism and politics in narrative therapies* (pp. 35–64). Vancouver: Cardigan Press.

Foucault, M. (1980a). *The history of sexuality, Volume 1: An introduction.* New York: Vintage.

_____. (1980b). *Power/knowledge: Selected interviews and other writings 1972–1977.* New York: Pantheon.

Gormond, J. (1993). Postmodernism and the conduct of inquiry in social work. *Affilia 8*(3), 247–264.

Griffith, J., & Griffith, M. (1992). Owning one's epistemological stance in therapy. *Dulwich Centre Newsletter 1,* 5–11.

Haraway, D. (1988). Situated knowledges: The science question in feminism and the privilege of partial perspective. *Feminist Studies 14*(3), 575–599.

Hare-Mustin, R. (1994). Discourses in the mirrored room: A postmodern analysis of therapy. *Family Processes 33*(March), 19–35.

Jenkins, A. (1991). Intervention with violence and abuse in families: The inadvertent perpetuation of irresponsible behaviour. *A.N.Z. Family Therapy 12*(4), 186–195.

_____. (1994). Therapy for abuse or therapy as abuse. *Dulwich Centre Newsletter 1,* 11–19.

Madigan, S. (1998). Practice interpretations of Michel Foucault: Situating problem externalizing discourse. In S. Madigan & I. Law (Eds.), *Praxis: Situating discourse, feminism and politics in narrative therapies* (pp. 15–34). Vancouver: Cardigan Press.

Margolin, L. (1997). The rhetoric of empowerment. In L. Margolin, *Under the cover of kindness: The invention of Social Work* (pp. 117–150). Charlottesville: University Press of Virginia.

McLean, C. (2001). A response. *Gecko: A Journal of Deconstruction and Narrative Ideas in Therapeutic Practice 2,* 61–63.

Mead, G. (1977). *On social psychology.* Chicago: University of Chicago Press.

Parry, A., & Doan, R. (1994). *Story re-visions.* New York: Guilford Press.

Rondeau, G. (2000). Empowerment and social practice, or the issue of power in social work. *Social Work 45,* 216–222.

Saleebey, D. (1997). Introduction: Power in the people. In D. Saleebey (Ed.), *The strengths perspective in social work practice* (pp. 3–17). New York: Longman.

Sands, R., & Nuccio, R. (1992). Postmodern feminist theory and social work. *Social Work 37*(6), 489–494.

Schutz, A. (1967). *The problem of social reality: Collected papers*. The Hague: Martin Nijhoff.

Scott, J. (1992). Experience. In J. Butler & J. Scott (Eds.), *Feminists theorize the political* (pp. 22–40). New York: Routledge.

Verco, J. (2001). Reflecting on working with men on issues of violence. *Gecko: A Journal of Deconstruction and Narrative Ideas in Therapeutic Practice 2*, 55–60.

White, M. (1989a, October). The world of experience and meaning. *Dulwich Centre Newsletter*, 1–2.

_____. (1989b, October). Therapy in the world of experience. *Dulwich Centre Newsletter*, 4–6.

_____. (1989c). Narrative therapy: What sort of internalizing conversations? *Dulwich Centre Newsletter*, 1–5.

_____. (1991). Deconstruction and therapy. *Dulwich Centre Newsletter 3*, 21–40.

_____. (1994). The politics of therapy: Putting to rest the illusion of neutrality. *Dulwich Centre Newsletter. No 1*, 1–4.

_____. (2001). Narrative practice and the unpacking of identity conclusions. *Gecko: A Journal of Deconstruction and Narrative Ideas in Therapeutic Practice 1*, 28–55.

White, M., & Epston, D. (1990). *Narrative means to therapeutic ends*. W.W. Norton: New York.

Chapter 14

Reconceptualizing Empathy for Anti-Oppressive, Culturally Competent Practice

Janet L. Clarke
Doctoral Candidate
Faculty of Social Work
University of Toronto

A commitment to anti-oppressive practice requires far more than adherence to a fundamental value stance. It requires radical rethinking of historic, time-honoured theories and concepts and critical re-examination of taken-for-granted assumptions about the helping process.

Among the core concepts in need of renewed theoretical attention and interrogation is the venerable concept of *empathy*. Although most classic and contemporary social work texts identify empathy as a *sine qua non* of the helping relationship (e.g., Biesteck, 1957; Compton & Gallaway, 1999; Fisher, 1978; Goldstein, 1973; Hepworth, Rooney, & Larsen, 1997; Kadushin, 1990; Perlman, 1979; Strode & Strode, 1942), the idea that practitioners can put themselves into the shoes of the other or see the world through the other's eyes is increasingly seen as presumptuous—and even oppressive.

Some of the most vigorous challenges to the concept of empathy have come from the burgeoning multicultural practice literature that has arisen in response to repeated calls for anti-oppressive, culturally competent models of practice. The Eurocentric, hegemonic perspectives and assumptions embedded in traditional practice theories and concepts have been strenuously critiqued (e.g., Green, 1995; Locke, 1992; McGoldrick, 1998; Pinderhuges, 1989; Ridley, 1995; Sue, Ivey, & Pedersen, 1996; Sue & Sue, 1990) and the underlying "myth of sameness" (Kadushin, 1990) has been widely discredited as a variant of the folk belief that "deep down we are all the same" (Pinderhuges, 1989, p. 24).

Although empathy has long been considered a primary means of facilitating interpersonal understanding across difference, multicultural practice writers such as Devore and Schlesinger (1996) question the degree to which practitioners can empathically identify with clients whose life experiences may be vastly different from their own. Ibrahim (1991) questions whether traditional means of establishing and conveying empathy are appropriate with all cultural groups. The focus in empathy theory on tuning in to feelings rather than cultural meanings has been challenged (Green, 1995), and the failure to situate self-experience in the socio-political context of power and oppression has been identified as a glaring gap (Keefe, 1980; Pinderhuges, 1979).

Further challenges to the concept of empathy have been raised on epistemological grounds. Intense insider/outsider debates (Headland, Pike, & Harris, 1990) and the postmodern emphasis on the "otherness" of people's experiences of themselves and the world (Gellner, 1992) have further contributed to widespread questioning of the adequacy and usefulness of empathy in the contemporary context of vast social and cultural diversity.

Paradoxically, while empathy is facing serious challenges on conceptual grounds, a large body of clinical outcome research offers substantial evidence that relationship factors, including empathy, are more predictive of successful clinical outcome than treatment method or technique (e.g., Duncan & Moynihan, 1994; Hubble, Duncan, & Miller, 1998; Lambert & Bergin, 1994; Patterson, 1984). Further support for the clinical importance of empathy is found in the therapeutic alliance literature where empathy is identified as a key aspect in securing the bond in the alliance (Bordin, 1979; Horvath & Greenberg, 1994; Meissner, 1996; Patton & Meara, 1992). Despite empathy's near axiomatic status—or perhaps because of it—there has been surprisingly little research or theoretical development in this area in recent years.

The time is overdue for a fresh re-examination of fundamental questions lying at the heart of anti-oppressive practice, including the following:

- Is empathy still a useful concept for understanding the other's frame of reference?
- Are there other conceptual tools that can enlarge our understanding of how to create space for shared understanding and meaning across difference?
- Can empathy be reconceptualized in ways that reduce the risk of oppression by more fully attending to the multiple, intersecting diversities of participants in social work encounters?

These questions form the focus of the following discussion.

Throughout this exploration, the term "culture"—with a small *c*—will be used in a broad sense to include ethnographic variables (e.g., ethnicity, nationality, language, religion), demographic variables (e.g., age, sex, place of residence), status variables (e.g., social, educational, economic), and affiliations (formal, informal) (Pedersen, 1997).

PROBLEMATIZING EMPATHY

The following limitations and contestable assumptions constrain the usefulness of traditional conceptualizations of empathy from an anti-oppressive perspective.

Epistemological Assumptions

The expansive empathy literature spans several decades and contains numerous definitions and conceptualizations, almost all of which are rooted in a clinical/medical paradigm. Examples include: listening with the third ear (Reik, 1948); vicarious introspection (Kohut, 1959); emotional knowing (Greenson, 1960); sensing and relating to the feelings underlying another's words and actions (Perlman, 1979); attempting to see and experience things from another's perspective (Beck, Rush, Shaw, & Emery, 1979); entering into the feelings and experiences of another (Compton & Galaway, 1999); and taking on the perspective of another (Sheafor, Horejsi, & Horejsi, 1994).

Carl Rogers (1957, 1966, 1975), arguably the most influential empathy theorist, described empathy as the accurate perception of the clients' private world as if it were one's own, but without ever losing the "as if" quality (Rogers, 1957, p. 409). Accuracy was seen as desirable and attainable. The "as if" condition was viewed as an essential element in stepping back and acquiring objective understanding.

A proliferation of empathy research followed Roger's formulations (e.g., Cabush & Edwards, 1976; Kolb, Beutler, Davis, Crago, & Shanfield, 1985; Lafferty, Beutler, & Crago, 1989; Luborsky, Chandler, Auerbach, Cohen, & Bachrach, 1971; Truax & Carkhuff, 1967; Truax & Mitchell, 1971), almost all of which utilized paradigmatic models and correlational designs that reduced empathy to scientifically quantifiable measurements, observable behaviours, and techniques.

This argument of this chapter is that traditional empathy theory and research have been severely constrained by these modernist/empiricist preoccupations with objectivity, accuracy, subject-object dualism, quantifiable measurement, and technique. A shift to an interpretive/

constructionist epistemological perspective (e.g., Bateson, 1979; Bruner, 1990; Geertz, 1983; Rodwell, 1987, Scott, 1989; Sherman, 1987) is proposed as a way of opening an enlarged space for re-examining empathy and exploring alternative ways of knowing and understanding another person's phenomenological experience. With its focus on accessing "lived experience," interpretive epistemologies (such as phenomenological, ethnographic, and narrative perspectives) offer a different way of knowing that is inductive, reflexive, dialogical, meaning-focused, and contextualized. Re-examining empathy from an interpretive lens thus constitutes a key aim of this chapter.

Focusing on Feelings Rather Than Meanings

Another limitation of traditional empathy theory is the underlying universalist assumption that empathy is a transcultural phenomenon that draws on "kindred feelings" (Paul, 1967) shared by all human beings. Green (1995) forcefully argues, in contrast, that one cannot presume to enter into the "sensibilities" of another without first learning the context from which those sensibilities arise. He contends that empathy is inadequate unless it is recast from tuning in to "feelings" to rigorous attention to the "cultural meanings" that clients and practitioners attach to behaviour, events, people, and words. This is not to say that feelings are unimportant, but rather that they have a particular social and ethnographic context that needs to be explored. Overestimating one's capacity to empathically understand feelings without apprehending idiographic cultural meanings can be a particularly insidious form of oppression.

Inattention to Socio-political Context

The emphasis in empathy theory on tuning in to the client's self-experience has not been accompanied by a corresponding emphasis on tuning in to the socio-political context of power and oppression that shapes lived experience as well as the meanings and interpretations ascribed to experience. Largely missing in traditional empathy theory is any recognition that the helping relationship itself takes place in the context of racism, classism, sexism, heterosexism, ageism, ableism, and so on. Without critical consciousness of the social locations and the associated power distributions of participants in the social work encounter, the adequacy and usefulness of empathy is severely constrained (Keefe, 1980).

The Practitioner as Expert Knower

Influenced by its roots in a medical model, traditional conceptualizations of empathy position practitioners as expert knowers who supposedly understand their clients' lives better than the clients themselves. Empathy is typically framed as a "practitioner-offered" condition (Rogers, 1957, 1975)— that is, as something offered by the practitioner to the client in a unidirectional fashion as opposed to something that is created together. This lack of a reciprocal or dialogical dimension in traditional conceptualizations of empathy is another conceptual weakness that needs to be addressed in developing clearer understandings of anti-oppressive practice encounters.

CONCEPTUAL INSIGHTS FROM OTHER THEORETICAL PERSPECTIVES

Rather than discard the concept of empathy altogether, it is argued that alternative theoretical frameworks can provide new ideas, insights, metaphors, vocabulary, and conceptual tools for illuminating the process of creating shared understanding and meaning in practice encounters. By shifting to an interpretive epistemological framework, the traditional concept of empathy can be expanded and reformulated by incorporating conceptual insights from multicultural, ethnographic, and narrative theoretical perspectives. Each of these three theoretical perspectives will be examined in turn, weaving together compatible concepts and building a proposed reconceptualization of empathy that is offered as a fundamental component of anti-oppressive, culturally competent practice.

Contributions from Multicultural Practice Theory

Unlike most traditional practice theories, including empathy theory, the multicultural practice literature places culture at the centre of its conceptual framework. A proliferation of literature in recent years has been directed toward conceptualizing culturally competent practice (e.g., Cross, Bazron, Dennis, & Isaacs, 1989; Green, 1995; LaFromboise & Foster, 1992; Sue, Ivey, & Pedersen, 1996; Sue & Sue, 1990) and formulating practice guidelines and recommendations for working with diverse populations (e.g., Devore & Schlesinger, 1996; McGoldrick, Giordano, & Pearce, 1996; Nakanishi & Rittner, 1992; Pinderhuges, 1989).

A common theme in almost all conceptualizations of culturally competent practice is the need for practitioners to gain a deep and profound understanding of the client's world view or cultural frame of reference. A review of this literature, however, reveals two very distinct approaches to acquiring this kind of understanding.

In what has been called a "modernist" (Dean, 2001) or "cultural literacy" approach (Dyche & Zayas, 1995), practitioners are urged to study the history, background, and characteristic traits of diverse client groups as a requisite pathway to understanding the life world of the other person. The weakness in this cognitively oriented model is that it positions the practitioner as expert knower, fails to account for intersecting diversities, ignores within-group heterogeneity, and sets an unattainable goal of becoming conversant with a staggering multiplicity of culture-specific approaches (Dyche & Zayas, 1995; Ho, 1995; Saleebey, 1994). Furthermore, normative nomothetic cultural information may inadvertently elicit oppressive stereotypes and practices in the very attempt to avoid it.

A second approach to understanding the other's frame of reference— one that is rooted in an interpretive epistemological stance—has been called an "experiential-phenomenological" approach (Dyche & Zayas, 1995) and finds resonance in the writings of Green (1995), Ho (1995), Laird (1998), Leigh (1998), and Saleebey (1994). In this approach, the practitioner is positioned not as an expert but as a learner who seeks to explore and understand idiographic cultural meanings by attending to client narratives with an attitude of deliberate naiveté and respectful curiosity. The focus is on a process of open exploration and negotiated understandings rather than the acquisition of specific expert knowledge.

The fundamental distinction between cultural literacy models and experiential-phenomenological models is a difference in epistemology, not only methodology. Dyche and Zayas (1995) describe cultural literacy models as exemplifying a cognitive approach to understanding that emphasizes abstract and categorical thinking, whereas the experiential-phenomenological perspective is a process-oriented approach in which the practitioner seeks understanding of the client's lived experience through phenomenological inquiry. This latter approach favours dialogue and exploration over explanatory epistemologies as the preferred "way of knowing" the other.

Saleebey (1994) expands on these ideas, emphasizing that the initiatory act of understanding is the "suspension of canon or theory" in favour of attending to the "context and meaning systems wherein the client dwells" (Saleebey, 1994, p. 355). He underscores how extraordinarily difficult it is for practitioners to hear and respect clients' understandings, particularly if they are in a socially subordinate position. Such listening requires a radical shift in stance whereby practitioners position themselves as "collaborators" and "co-facilitators" in a dialogical approach to creating and understanding meaning.

This experiential-phenomenological approach to cross-cultural understanding makes an important contribution to a reconceptualization of empathy by offering a rich source of interpretive concepts, perspectives, and inquiry processes for exploring and attending to the cultural and contextual meanings that shape lived experience.

Contributions from Interpretive Ethnography

While the multicultural literature draws attention to cultural dynamics that are neglected in traditional empathy theory, the field of ethnography takes the discussion one step further by providing cross-disciplinary conceptual insights and highly developed processes for understanding lived experience. Though once associated with the anthropological study of cultures in faraway places, ethnography is increasingly recognized by a growing number of disciplines as offering a unique approach to understanding human and social phenomena.

Clifford Geertz's (1973, 1983) interpretive ethnography is particularly illuminating in terms of the current discussion. Geertz is widely credited for revolutionizing ethnography by advocating an interpretive analysis of culture "in search of meaning" rather than a scientific analysis "in search of laws" (Geertz, 1973, p. 5). Geertz challenged the historic epistemological base of ethnography with its Cartesian assumptions of value-free inquiry and its claims to objective truth. Instead, he advocated for an emic or *verstehen* approach to understanding local knowledge and pluralist standpoints (Geertz, 1983). To commit oneself to an interpretive approach to the study of culture, he said, was to commit oneself to a view of ethnographic assertions as "essentially contestable" (Geertz, 1973, p. 29). The practitioner can no longer presume to be able to present an objective, non-contested account of the other's experience (Denzin, 1997).

The ethnographic concepts of contextual meaning, local knowledge, pluralist standpoints, emic inquiry, contestable accounts, and interpretive understandings hold great promise for expanding and enriching conceptualizations of empathy in the context of diversity. The following ethnographic principles and processes are particularly salient.

The Learner's Stance

The starting stance in interpretive ethnography is the explicit positioning of the professional as an inquirer who seeks to learn. Ethnographers are trained to ask "What do the informants know that I can discover?" as opposed to "What expert knowledge do I possess that will help me explain this?" (Spradley, 1979). This depiction of the learner stance is strikingly similar to the stance of naiveté and curiosity advocated in the multicultural practice literature (Dyche & Zayas, 1995). What ethnographers add to the discussion is an emphasis on reducing power differentials by inviting respondents to participate as collaborators in the exploration of a given phenomenon (Sells, Smith, & Newfield, 1997). Ethnography's explicit focus on eliciting and documenting silenced and subjugated voices reflects its epistemological emphasis on a collaborative approach to understanding in which no one's perspectives are privileged (Denzin, 1997).

Listening for Meaning

Another contribution is the concept of "ethnographic listening," which focuses less on attending to feelings and more on underlying cultural meanings (Green, 1995). While multicultural practice theorists also emphasize attentiveness to cultural meanings, what ethnography adds to the discussion is its particular focus on language as a pathway to the discovery of meaning. According to Spradley (1979, p. 17), "language is more than a means of communicating about reality: it is a tool for constructing reality." In practice, this means that instead of directly asking respondents "What do you mean?" ethnographers seek to discover tacit meanings by attending to how phrases and terms are used as interviewees tell their stories "in their own words" (Sells, Smith, & Newfield, 1997). Ethnographers use strategies such as *restating* and *incorporating* the respondent's words, terms, and phrases into the dialogue so that professional language does not override and distort client meanings (Spradley, 1979). These techniques stand in contrast to the traditional empathic technique of *rephrasing* and *reframing*.

Dialogical Understanding

Yet another contribution from interpretive ethnography is the illumination of the process of dialogical understanding. Unlike traditional conceptualizations of empathy where understanding depends largely on the expertise of the practitioner, ethnographers are trained to hold theoretical preconceptions in abeyance in order to hear the client's story openly without attempting to make sense of it on the basis of pre-existing frameworks. Emerging understandings are framed as tentative hypotheses that are supported, disconfirmed, or modified by respondents themselves in a reciprocal, iterative exchange. Only at the end of the process do ethnographers look at how inductively derived understandings fit with relevant theoretical materials (Sells, Smith, & Newfield, 1997).

Although multicultural writers also emphasize collaborative processes, an important contribution of ethnography is the use of the "conversation" metaphor to underscore the mutual, dialogical nature of ethnographic knowing. Lambek (1993, p. 27) describes ethnographic inquiry as seeking access to the conceptual world of respondents in order to create "a mutually comprehensible dialogue" and "a ground for further conversation." The gap or clash between various kinds of meanings is seen not as problematic but rather as opening up conversational space for mutual learning. This idea that the conversation depends not on shared meanings but on shared *exploration* of meanings is markedly different from traditional conceptualizations of empathic understanding and needs to be claimed as a key insight.

Reflexivity

A final contribution from interpretive ethnography is its emphasis on vigilant self-reflexivity in order to interrogate the ways in which the autobiographies, cultures, and historical contexts of inquirers determine what is seen and not seen, heard and not heard (Hamersley & Atkinson, 1989). In ethnographic inquiry the control or elimination of bias is not assumed possible or even desirable. Subjectivity is not controlled but *incorporated* into the inquiry by making biases explicit and acknowledging how biases dictate questions and category construction (Sells, Smith, & Newfield, 1997). Ethnographers practise reflexivity by writing reflexive journals that contain the introspective record of ideas, fears, mistakes, confusion, breakthroughs, and problems that arise in the course of inquiry (Spradley, 1979; Wax, 1971).

In sum, interpretive ethnography contributes important epistemological and conceptual insights to a re-examination of empathic processes, including an emphasis on a learner's stance, collaborative exploration, attentiveness to meaning, dialogically created understanding, and vigilant reflexivity.

Contributions from Narrative Practice Theory

While ethnography provides a rich source of interpretive concepts and processes for expanding our understanding of empathy, narrative practice theory adds a further dimension by demonstrating how interpretive processes can be applied in clinical practice. Narrative therapy is best described as an evolving approach to practice rather than a tightly defined model, the common thread being an interpretive philosophical perspective that views narrative as a "way of knowing" (Hoffman, 1992; White & Epston, 1990). What distinguishes narrative therapies from other therapeutic approaches is that the key microprocess is "listening for stories" (McLeod, 1997; Hoffman, 1992, p. 117). Stories are viewed as the basic means by which people organize, interpret, and communicate to other people the meaning of lived experiences. Therapy is conceptualized as a conversation in which problematic stories are deconstructed, preferred directions are identified, and alternative stories are developed that support these preferred directions (Freedman & Combs, 1996, p. 118).

Several key concepts in narrative practice theory resonate with multicultural and ethnographic perspectives as well as contributing unique insights to the current discussion

Epistemological Premises

What distinguishes narrative practice theory from most traditional therapeutic models is the attempt to move beyond modernism through the incorporation of social constructionist and hermeneutic perspectives into clinical practice (Anderson & Goolishian, 1988; Doan, 1998; Gergen, 1985; Weingarten, 1998; White & Epston, 1990). The modernist view of the practitioner as the expert, objective, and individual knower is repudiated in favour of an alternative epistemological position that sees meaning and understanding as neither objective nor subjective but as "intersubjectively constructed" (Anderson & Goolishian, 1988, p. 372). People are seen as making sense of their lives through the cultural narratives they are born into and the personal narratives they construct in relation to cultural narratives (Freedmen & Combs, 1996). This epistemological perspective provides an alternative conceptual centre for a reformulation of empathy from an interpretive standpoint.

The Not-Knowing Position

A second distinguishing feature of narrative practice is its particular stance, frequently called the "not-knowing" position (Anderson & Goolishian, 1988). This position maintains that understanding is always interpretive and that there is no privileged standpoint for understanding (Anderson & Goolishian, 1992). The not-knowing position aims to diminish the hierarchical relationship that typically exists between client and practitioner and to create conversational spaces that do not perpetuate the myth of therapist expertise and client inadequacy.

While similar to the "learner stance" in multicultural and ethnographic literature, a clear distinction is made between a "not-knowing" position and an "I don't know anything" position (Freedman & Combs, 1996, p. 44). In narrative therapy, the practitioner is seen as having particular knowledge about the process of therapy, but not about the content and meaning of people's lives. The practitioner's understandings are not controlled, dismissed, or kept secret from the client, but instead are offered to the client as an alternative perspective in a dialogical process of negotiating understanding and meaning. The modernist preoccupation with obtaining accurate understanding is de-emphasized in favour of viewing the practitioner as always "on the road to understanding" but never fully arriving (Anderson

& Goolishian, 1992, p. 32). This alternative starting stance points to new ways of conceptualizing the empathic stance.

Situating Personal Stories within Structural Stories

Yet another important contribution of narrative practice theory is the conceptualization of "story" as a powerful means of contextualizing self-experience within a broader socio-cultural framework of meaning. A person is seen as existing within a culture that comprises a stock of stories and is continually engaged in negotiating the fit between his or her personal experience and the story lines that are available (McLeod, 1997; White & Epston, 1990).

While the ethnographic perspective also emphasizes the interrelatedness of personal, cultural, and structural dimensions of human experience, narrative practice theory differs in that it takes an overtly "critical" stance toward the ways in which subjugating and dominating societal narratives shape personal stories (Freedman & Combs, 1996). Following a Foucaultian analysis, White and Epston (1990) emphasize the need to understand how people tend to internalize the dominant narratives in society, easily believing that they speak the truth of their experience and being blind to the possibilities that other subjugated or local narratives might offer.

These ideas point to ways of addressing Keefe's (1980) concern that empathy be reconceptualized to include a critical consciousness of the ways in which personal experience is situated within historical and socio-political contexts of power and oppression.

Mutually Negotiated Understanding

A further contribution from narrative practice theory is the conceptualization of the therapeutic conversation as involving "a mutual search for understanding and exploration through dialogue" (Anderson & Goolishian, 1992, p. 29). Meaning and understanding are seen as a matter of negotiation between participants, a two-way exchange, a criss-crossing of ideas—not a practitioner-offered condition such as in traditional conceptualizations of empathy. The process of understanding shifts from the sphere of individuals to the shared space of interaction between them (Lax, 1992). The "struggle to understand" in therapy is viewed as collaborative (Anderson & Goolishian, 1992, p. 30). Since there are no fixed meanings to be discerned, understanding is seen as inherently negotiable and tentative.

Critical Self-Reflexivity

Along with interpretive ethnographers, narrative theorists emphasize that unflinching, critical reflexivity is essential to the process of understanding and interpreting the meanings underlying lived experience. In the words of Anderson and Goolishian (1988, p. 383), "the therapist maintains a dialogical conversation with himself or herself." Particular attention is paid to interrogating the context of ideas in which the therapist's own practices are situated and acknowledging the effects, dangers, and limitations of these interpretations and practices (White & Epston, 1990).

Taken together, narrative therapy's epistemological perspectives and interpretive processes offer a rich source of insights for reconceptualizing empathy for anti-oppressive practice.

A PROPOSED RECONCEPTUALIZATION OF EMPATHY

From the foregoing cross-theoretical analysis, salient concepts and insights can be culled and interwoven into an enlarged conceptualization of empathy that more fully attends to the cultural and contextual dimensions of human experience. A considerable convergence of concepts in these perspectives allows for the formation of an integrative conceptual framework that views empathy not as a practitioner-offered condition but as a collaborative process of creating space for the mutual exploration of meaning and the negotiation of shared understandings.

The distinguishing features of this reconceptualization of empathy are summarized in Table 14.1. Note that the contrasting points do not necessarily represent dichotomous, either/or polarities but rather different frames for conceptualizing the process of empathic understanding.

Table 14.1: FEATURES OF TRADITIONAL AND RECONCEPTUALIZED EMPATHY

Traditional Empathy	Reconceptualized Empathy
• expert stance	• learner stance
• attunement to feelings	• attunement to meanings
• reality seen as objective and knowable	• reality seen as socially constructed
• deductively derived understanding	• inductive, dialogical understanding
• practitioner-offered	• co-created
• focus on empathic responding	• focus on empathic inquiry
• a precondition for dialogue	• a hoped-for outcome of dialogue
• attention to psychodynamics	• attention to dynamics of power and oppression
• requires self-awareness	• requires self-reflexivity

Implications for Practice

This reconceptualization of empathy carries with it profound implications for anti-oppressive practice. It means first and foremost that the empathic stance be understood as a learner's stance, characterized by openness, deep respect, curiosity, tentativeness, and a profound awareness of the partiality of one's own knowledge and perspectives. Adopting this stance may appear deceptively simple, but it requires a profound epistemological shift to a position that honours and legitimates many ways of knowing. Epistemological humility regarding the tentative nature of professional theories and interpretations is viewed as a requisite for empathic knowing.

The proposed model also recasts the role of practitioner from that of independent, objective, and expert knower to that of a collaborative participant who joins with the other in a reciprocal process of dialogical exploration and inductive discovery. Empathic understanding is conceptualized as being co-created in the dialogue, not offered by the practitioner. Empathy is seen as a two-way street: both client and practitioner make a contribution and both are changed in the process.

A further implication of the model is the recasting of empathic practices from techniques for reflecting feelings to conversational processes for advancing dialogical understanding. Empathic conversational processes are manifested in a pattern of interaction that moves the dialogue toward mutual understanding. Acknowledging differences between dialogue partners and communicating one's inability to fully understand another's experience are viewed as facilitative rather than problematic. Empathy, in this reconceptualization, is not dependent on shared meanings but on shared exploration of meanings.

A final implication of the proposed model is that empathic listening takes precedence over empathic responding. Empathic listening is conceptualized as acute attentiveness to the *meanings* implicit in personal and cultural narratives. The practitioner's focus is on guiding conversations that elicit rich, detailed narratives that make visible the meanings and the source of meanings that shape lived experience. Empathic listening is expanded to include critical attentiveness to how dominant and subjugating societal narratives shape the meanings ascribed to self-narratives. Critical consciousness of socio-political dynamics of power and oppression, and critical self-reflexivity regarding one's own social location, thus become primary empathic capacities.

This proposed reconceptualization of empathy represents a step forward in the formulation of anti-oppressive conceptual frameworks by explicating collaborative processes of inquiry, dialogue, and critical reflection that facilitate shared understanding and meaning. Reconceptualized empathy has profound relevance to practice at all levels, including international work, because the capacity to empathize with other people and perspectives is fundamental to all our undertakings in social work. A commitment to anti-oppressive practice, pedagogy, and research entails a corresponding commitment to co-creating shared, anti-oppressive spaces for mutual exploration of meaning and collaborative understanding. In our increasingly diverse and globalized society, the capacity for reflexive, collaborative, empathic understanding of other people and perspectives may well become one of the most important aspects of anti-oppressive practice.

REFERENCES

Anderson, H., & Goolishian, H.A. (1988). Human systems as linguistic systems: Preliminary and evolving ideas about the implications for clinical theory. *Family Process 27*(4), 371–393.

_____. (1992). The client is the expert: A not-knowing approach to therapy. In S. McNamee & K.J. Gergen (Eds.), *Therapy as social construction* (pp. 25–39). Newbury Park: Sage.

Bateson, G. (1979). *Mind and nature: A necessary unity.* New York: Ballantine Books.

Beck, A.T., Rush, A.G., Shaw, B.F., & Emery, G. (1979). *Cognitive therapy of depression.* New York: Guilford.

Biesteck, F.P. (1957). *The casework relationship.* Chicago: Loyola.

Bordin, E.S. (1979). The generalizability of the psychoanalytic concept of the working alliance. *Psychotherapy: Theory, Research, and Practice 16*, 252–260.

Bruner, J. (1990). *Acts of meaning.* Cambridge: Harvard University Press.

Cabush, D.W., & Edwards, K.J. (1976). Training clients to help themselves: Outcome effects of training college student clients in facilitative self-responding. *Journal of Counseling Psychology 23*, 34–39.

Compton, B.R., & Galaway, B. (1999). *Social work processes.* Pacific Grove: Brooks/ Cole.

Cross, T., Bazron, B.J., Dennis, K.K., & Isaacs, M.R. (1989). *Towards a culturally competent system of care.* Washington: Howard University Press.

Dean, R.G. (2001). The myth of cross-cultural competence. *Families in Society: The Journal of Contemporary Human Services 82*(6), 623–630.

Denzin, N. (1997). *Interpretive ethnography: Ethnographic practices for the 21ˢᵗ century.* Thousand Oaks: Sage.

Devore, W., & Schlesinger, E.G. (1996). *Ethnic-sensitive social work practice.* Toronto: Allyn & Bacon.

Doan, R.E. (1998). The king is dead; long live the king: Narrative therapy and practicing what we preach. *Family Process 37*(3), 379–385.

Duncan, B.L., & Moynihan, D.W. (1994). Applying outcome research: Intentional utilization of the client's frame of reference. *Psychotherapy 31*, 294–301.

Dyche, L., & Zayas, L.H. (1995). The value of curiosity and naiveté for the cross-cultural psychotherapist. *Family Process 34*, 389–399.

Fisher, J. (1978). *Effective casework practice.* New York: McGraw-Hill.

Freedman, J., & Combs, G. (1996). *Narrative therapy: The social construction of preferred realities.* New York: W.W. Norton.

Geertz, C. (1973). *The interpretation of cultures.* New York: Basic Books.

_____. (1983). *Local knowledge: Further essays in interpretive anthropology.* New York: Basic Books.

Gellner, E. (1992). *Postmodernism, reason and religion.* New York: Routledge.

Gergen, K.J. (1985). The social constructionist movement in modern psychology. *American Psychologist 40*, 266–275.

Goldstein, H. (1973). *Social work practice: A unitary approach.* Columbia: University of South Carolina Press.

Green, J.W. (1995). *Cultural awareness in the human services* (2nd ed.). Toronto: Allyn & Bacon.

Greenson, R.R. (1960). Empathy and its vicissitudes. *International Journal of Psychoanalysis 41*, 418–424.

Hamersley, M., & Atkinson, P. (1989). *Ethnographic principles in practice.* Cambridge: Cambridge University Press.

Headland, T.N., Pike, R.L., & Harris, M. (Eds.). (1990). *Emics and etics: The insider/ outsider debate.* Newbury Park: Sage.

Hepworth, D.H., Rooney, R.H., & Larsen, J. (1997). *Direct social work practice: Theory and skills.* Pacific Grove: Brooks/Cole.

Ho, D. (1995). Internalized culture, culturocentrism, and transcendence. *The Counseling Psychologist 23*(1), 4–24.

Hoffman, L. (1992). A reflexive stance for family therapy. In S. McNamee & K.J. Gergen (Eds.), *Therapy as social construction* (pp. 7–24). Newbury Park: Sage.

Horvath, A.O., & Greenberg, L.S. (Eds.). (1994). *The working alliance: Theory, research and practice.* New York: Wiley.

Hubble, M.A., Duncan, B.L., & Miller, S.D. (1998). *The heart and soul of change: What works in therapy.* Washington: American Psychological Association.

Ibrahim, F.A. (1991). Contribution of cultural worldview to generic counseling and development. *Journal of Counseling and Development 70*, 13–19.

Kadushin, A. (1990). *The social work interview: A guide for human service professionals.* (Original work published 1972) New York: Columbia University Press.

Keefe, T. (1980). Empathy skill and critical consciousness. *Social Casework,* 387–393.

Kohut, H. (1959). Introspection, empathy, and psychoanalysis: An examination of the relationship between mode of observation and theory. *Journal of the American Psychoanalytic Association 7*, 459–483.

Kolb, D.L., Beutler, L.E., Davis, C.S., Crago, M., & Shanfield, S. (1985). Patient and therapy process variables relating to dropout and change in psychotherapy. *Psychotherapy 22*, 702–710.

Lafferty, P., Beutler, L.E., & Crago, M. (1989). Differences between more and less effective psychotherapists: A study of select therapist variables. *Journal of Consulting and Clinical Psychology 57*, 76–80.

LaFromboise, T.D., & Foster, S.L. (1992). Cross-cultural training: Scientist-practitioner model and methods. *Counseling Psychologist 20*(3), 472–489.

Laird, J. (1998). Theorizing culture: Narrative ideas and practice principles. In M. McGoldrick (Ed.), *Re-visioning family therapy: Race, culture, and gender in clinical practice* (pp. 20–36). New York: Guilford.

Lambek, M. (1993). *Knowledge and practice in Mayotte: Local discourses of Islam, sorcery, and spirit possession.* Toronto: University of Toronto Press.

Lambert, M.J., & Bergin, A.E. (1994). The effectiveness of psychotherapy. In A.E. Bergin & S.L. Garfield (Eds.), *Handbook of psychotherapy and behavior change* (4th ed.) (pp. 157–212). New York: Wiley.

Lax, W.D. (1992). Postmodern thinking in clinical practice. In S. McNamee & K.J. Gergen (Eds.), *Therapy as social construction* (pp. 69–85). Newbury Park: Sage.

Leigh, J.W. (1998). *Communicating for cultural competence.* Toronto: Allyn & Bacon.

Locke, D.C. (1992). *Increasing multicultural understanding: A comprehensive model.* Newbury Park: Sage.

Luborsky, L., Chandler, M., Auerbach, A.H., Cohen, J., & Bachrach, H.M. (1971). Factors influencing the outcome of psychotherapy: A review of quantitative research. *Psychological Bulletin 75,* 145–185.

McGoldrick, M. (Ed.). (1998). *Re-visioning family therapy: Race, culture, and gender in clinical practice.* New York: Guilford.

McGoldrick, M., Giordano, J., & Pearce, J.K. (Eds.). (1996). *Ethnicity and family therapy* (2nd ed.). New York: Guilford.

Meissner, W.W. (1996). *The therapeutic alliance.* New Haven: Yale University Press.

Nakanishi, M., & Rittner, B. (1992). The inclusionary cultural model. *Journal of Social Work Education 28,* 27–35.

McLeod, J. (1997). *Narrative and psychotherapy.* Thousand Oaks, CA: Sage.

Patterson, C.H. (1984). Empathy, warmth, and genuineness: A review of reviews. *Psychotherapy 21*, 431–438.

Patton, M.J., & Meara, N. (1992). *Psychoanalytic counseling.* Chichester: Wiley.

Paul, N.L. (1967). The use of empathy in the resolution of grief. *Perspectives in Biology and Medicine 11*, 153–170.

Pedersen, P.B. (1997). *Culture-centered counseling interventions: Striving for accuracy.* Thousand Oaks: Sage.

Perlman, H.H. (1979). *Relationship: The heart of helping people.* Chicago: University of Chicago Press.

Pinderhuges, E. (1979). Teaching empathy in cross-cultural social work. *Social Work 14*, 312–316.

Pinderhuges, E. (1989). *Understanding race, ethnicity and power: The key to efficacy in clinical practice.* New York: The Free Press.

Reik, T. (1948). *Listening with the third ear.* New York: Farrar, Straus.

Ridley, C.R. (1995). *Overcoming unintentional racism in counseling and therapy.* Thousands Oaks: Sage.

Rodwell, M.K. (1987). Naturalistic inquiry: An alternative model for social work assessment. *Social Service Review 61*(2), 231–246.

Rogers, C.R. (1951). *Client-centered therapy: Its current practice, implications, and theory.* Boston: Houghton Mifflin.

_____. (1957). The necessary and sufficient conditions of therapeutic personality change. *Journal of Consulting Psychology 21*, 95–103.

_____. (1975). Empathic: an unappreciated way of being. *The Counseling Psychologist 5*, 2–10.

Saleebey, D. (1994). Culture, theory, and narrative: The intersection of meanings in practice. *Social Work 39*(4), 351–359.

Scott, D. (1989). Meaning construction and social work practice. *Social Service Review 63*, 39–51.

Sells, S.P., Smith, T.E., & Newfield, N. (1997). Teaching ethnographic research methods in social work: A course model. *Journal of Social Work Education 33*(19), 167–184.

Sheafor, B.W., Horejsi, C.R., & Horejsi, G.A. (1994). *Techniques and guidelines for social work practice* (3rd ed.). Toronto: Allyn & Bacon.

Sherman, E. (1987). Hermeneutics, human science, and social work. *Social Thought*, 34–41.

Spradley, J.P. (1979). *The ethnographic interview.* Toronto: Harcourt Brace Jovanovich.

Strode, J., & Strode, P. (1942). *Social skills in casework.* New York: Harper.

Sue, D.W., Ivey, A.E., & Pedersen, P.B. (1996). *A theory of multicultural counseling and therapy.* Pacific Grove: Sage.

Sue, D.W., & Sue, D. (1990). *Counseling the culturally different.* Toronto: Wiley.

Truax, C.B., & Carkhuff, R.R. (1967). *Toward effective counseling and psychotherapy.* Chicago: Aldine.

Truax, C.B., & Mitchell, K.M. (1971). Research on certain therapist interpersonal skills in relation to process and outcome. In A.E. Bergin & L.L. Garfield (Eds.), *Handbook of psychotherapy and behavior change* (1st ed.) (pp. 299–344). New York: Wiley.

Wax, R. (1971). *Doing field work: Warnings and advice.* Chicago: University of Chicago Press.

Weingarten, K. (1998). The small and the ordinary: The daily practice of a postmodern narrative therapy. *Family Process 37*, 3–15.

White, M., & Epston, D. (1990). *Narrative means to therapeutic ends.* New York: W.W. Norton.

Chapter 15

Seeking Cultural Competence: What Is It, How Do You Develop It, and How Do You Know When You've Got It?

Charmaine C. Williams
Faculty of Social Work
University of Toronto

The question of how to address culture in clinical practice was previously addressed on an "as needed" basis. Social workers became concerned with cultural variations when situations arose that forced us to confront the special needs of a so-called special population. We are now at a point, however, where we recognize that most social workers are practising in the context of cultural difference all the time. Across the world, social workers are realizing that conventional methods of practice are not adequate to meet the needs of a diverse population (Beiser, Gill, & Edwards, 1993; Giordano, 1994; Husband, 2000). Cross's (1988) designation of cultural competence as a goal for systems, agencies, and professionals working in a multicultural environment was an attempt to create a framework within which we could provide effective service across the cultural spectrum. Yet our understanding of what cultural competence is, how it is developed, and how it should be evaluated is still quite limited.

This chapter addresses these questions by drawing on the author's experience of developing, delivering, and evaluating a cultural competence training program for practising social workers in an addiction and mental health care setting. Excerpts from learner narratives are used to explore these very important issues related to cultural competence in social work. An important lesson learned in that process is that cultural competence in social work involves more than the accumulation of skills or knowledge to add to the professional repertoire. Social workers view cultural competence as a specifically anti-oppressive enterprise, designed to dislodge and replace existing practices that marginalize certain communities and maintain privilege for others. This belief has implications for how we should discuss cultural competence, how we should teach it, and the criteria by which we should assess our progress in making it part of social work practice. As this training experience revealed, social workers in practice are quite aware of these implications.

CULTURAL COMPETENCE: WHAT IS IT?

There are several sources for information about specific practices understood to be indicative of cultural competence (e.g., see Dana, Behn, & Gonwa, 1992; Devore & Schlesinger, 1999; Foster, 1998; Manoleas, 1994; Weaver, 1999). To address the specific issue of how anti-oppressive practice intersects with cultural competence, the following discussion of its definition focuses on its emergence as a framework for cross-cultural practice.

The idea of social difference has been explored using a wide variety of terms in the social sciences and social work. In the past, theorizing about culture usually referred to the comparison of various racial groups against the positioned norm of White European or American functioning (Berry & Laponce, 1994; Williams, 2001). The emergence of a remedial discourse centred on "diversity" has stimulated some progress in integrating an expanded idea of culture into practice. Diversity encompasses a broad range of identity groups, including those defined by race, gender, age, religion, sexual orientation, class, disability, and other social markers. There are, however, important limitations in the application of a diversity perspective to social work.

The diversity framework is usually silent with regard to power relations and social justice issues. Although it draws attention to heterogeneity, it shapes the dialogue to suggest that differences are value-free and power-neutral (Bannerji, 2000). As social work is a discipline grounded in concerns of social justice and equity, the failure to address this component of intergroup relations is a serious deficit. This ideological vacuum creates a specific problem. There is no value base in place to prevent the language of diversity from being used to reinforce divisions between empowered and disempowered groups. This is evident in social work practice literature that provides specialized guidelines for working with clients and colleagues who are now identified as "diverse" (for example, see Bond, 1999; Dana et al., 1992; Panos & Panos, 2000). A diversity perspective must be used with great diligence to insure that social justice issues are addressed and inequities are not reinforced. This sophisticated understanding of diversity content cannot be assumed to be the norm in social work. Many in the field are just beginning to grapple with integrating cultural difference into their professional practices.

Social work has consistently held the perspective that individuals are linked to an environmental context that must be seen as an equally important target of intervention (DeHoyos, 1989; Haynes & White, 1999; Mizio, 1998; Shank, 2001). This multilevel focus has been integrated into social work literature addressing cultural competence (see Cross, Bazron, Dennis, & Isaacs, 1989; Dana et al., 1992; Dyche & Zayas, 2001; Tsang & George, 1998). Yet there is still some evidence that clinical issues are addressed under the heading of cultural competence, while organization and community-level interventions are addressed separately (Davis & Gelsomino, 1994; Ridley, Mendoza, & Kanitz, 1994). Although cultural competence may be defined as applying to multiple levels of practice, there is a popular conception that organization, community, and system-level activities are part of the more macro-focused world of anti-oppressive social work (e.g., see Dominelli, 1997; Thompson, 1997). Theoretically, it seems that it is difficult to merge these agendas. In practice, however, social workers make the connection.

In the needs assessment conducted for the educational program discussed in this chapter, potential participants were asked to indicate their reasons for seeking cultural competence education. Individuals expressed concerns and learning goals that were consistent with the conventional understanding of cultural competence as a combination of knowledge, skills, attitudes, and self-awareness. However, it was also striking that they made connections between the micro, mezzo, and macro issues that enhanced and impeded the cultural competence of the health care system. For example, one learner noted that:

> I'm amazed at how few ethnic minority clinicians are providing services to clients within the system. In an agency where I was a manager, all clinicians were White, and within any given month I received approximately twenty to thirty complaint calls from clients saying the workers don't understand their needs, or they cannot connect with them. This sparked my interest in not only insuring that the staff are culturally competent but to begin to hire a more diverse staffing complement to meet the needs of all people/clients. (R41)

Other comments about goals within cultural competence were similarly focused on multilevel concerns. Desires for learning included:

Gaining insight and awareness of the barriers that prevent clients with diverse backgrounds from accessing services and how to break down these barriers. (R4)

Would like more persons of various cultures using the services of our program. There are many barriers in the communities of minority populations on all sides. (R39)

These comments and others also clearly pointed to an understanding of cultural competence as involving anti-oppressive practices. Typical learning goals included:

To improve my skill in working with clients of different cultures than my own; to examine and learn about my biases and attitudes and increase my awareness of these; to learn to make my clinical work more sensitive in working with diversity, especially adapting assessment and treatment modalities. (R8)

Strengthen group norms re: anti-oppression; finding ways to make anti-oppression more understood and valued (clinically); looking at countertransference (what happens to me when a client is racist, etc.); I guess my life experience generally. I see that societal oppression is so very linked to people's health. (R12)

Therefore, social work literature and practising social workers offer a consistent answer to the question of what is involved in cultural competence. It is apparent that goals for cultural competence in social work include challenging personal and organizational bias and discrimination, redressing inequities that contribute to barriers to care, and transforming "mainstream" approaches that are currently privileged.

CULTURAL COMPETENCE: HOW DO YOU DEVELOP IT?

One of the limitations of the literature regarding cultural competence is that it is largely theoretical. Little empirical work has been published that can answer specific questions about what strategies are best used to develop cultural competence. Despite this, there are many recommendations available in the existing literature. Specific instructional techniques advocated by theorists include:

- exposure to biographies, readings, and presentations about the psychosocial effects of oppression and marginalization (Chau, 1992; Jackson, 1980; Morrison Van Vooris, 1998; Ronnau, 1994)
- reflective writing assignments (Coleman, 1997; Edwards, 1997; Garcia, Wright, & Corey, 1991)
- structured and unstructured contact with individuals from marginalized communities (Carlson, Brack, Laygo, Cohen, & Kirkscey, 1998)
- role plays and case study analysis (Cashwell, Looby, & Housley, 1997; Leong & Kim, 1991; Montalvo, Lasater, & Valdez, 1982; Ridley et al., 1994)
- practice paired with opportunities for constructive feedback and supervision (Brown, 1992; Constantine, 1997; D'Andrea & Daniels, 1997; Garland & Escobar, 1988; Marshack, Hendricks, & Gladstein, 1994; Norton, 2000; Peterson, 1991; Shergill, 1998; Williams & Halgin, 1995)

Although the empirical cultural competence training literature requires further development, the strategies advocated are consistent with the evidence base available for general clinical training. Yet there is an important component of instructional strategy for developing cultural competence that is not addressed extensively in general clinical training—cultivating a safe learning atmosphere. Unfortunately, learning about diversity, racism, cultural competence, and related topics is known to create unsettling, divisive, and even traumatic experiences (Garcia & Van Soest, 2000; Poole, 1998). Srivastava (1993) speaks of the specific potential for oppressive dynamics that exist outside the classroom to be amplified in the context of this type of learning experience. Memories and anticipations of these types of negative experiences enter the classroom before a single word has been spoken. Specific thought needs to be given to the potential for the learning experience to perpetuate oppression or to disengage learners from challenging oppression in their practice. Learning about cultural competence is an uncomfortable experience. This is particularly true if cultural competence is defined as an intervention against oppressive practices that are exercised by individuals, organizations, and systems. Accepting this tension as part of the learning process can be essential to learning about cultural competence as it is an opportunity to learn strategies for addressing similar tensions in practice. In addition, well-managed tension can promote a deeper level of learning than is possible from an uninvolved distance. It is necessary, however, for the learning experience to be structured so that learners are prepared for the tensions and engaged in the process of working through them together.

One of the strategies used to address safety in this educational experience was building the program around facilitated group learning. The learners were asked to think of themselves as continually developing their ideas about cultural competence and aiding others in the same process. Time and activity were set aside to prepare the group for the inevitable experience of tensions developing around different perspectives on the complex issues to be discussed. The experience demonstrated that education for cultural competence and diversity issues benefits from explicit strategies to establish peer support in learning. The effectiveness of this strategy was reflected in learners' comments after the program ended:

> Facilitator style was important—[it] felt comfortable, which I believe helped to open up discussion. (R4)

> Best: reflection, group discussion in safe, pleasant atmosphere ... difficult aspects. She made it easy for people to speak and to speak from different perspectives. (R9)

> Biggest impression: the openness of discussion the level of tolerance, acceptance, and openness of my social work colleagues. (R11)

> I really enjoyed this course. I was afraid of what I would think and feel at first because of the content and due to my past experiences in classes where I have been chastised for asking questions. There was a lot of support for discussion and questions here. (R26)

These narratives reinforce that there is a special need for attention to process in a cultural competence training experience. Learning in an atmosphere in which it is possible to speak openly and be challenged respectfully is clearly valued. This is evidently an aspect of training that depends on contributions from both the learners and the facilitator. If learning takes place in an alienating environment, it is very difficult to foster the collective investment and mutual support necessary for cultural competence at the agency and system level. Peer support established during training experiences can be the foundation of peer support in a practice environment. One of the outcomes reported by participants after the training experience was that they had identified colleagues with whom they were providing peer consultation on cultural competence issues. Through these activities, individuals become part of a collective effort to transform oppressive practices and policies.

CULTURAL COMPETENCE: HOW DO YOU KNOW IF YOU'VE GOT IT?

Finally, the question of how to evaluate cultural competence is a dilemma for both researchers and practitioners. There are several self-report scales of cultural competence, including the commonly cited Multicultural Awareness Knowledge and Skills Survey (D'Andrea, Daniels, & Heck, 1991), the Multicultural Counseling Inventory (Sodowsky, Taffe, Gutkin, & Wise, 1994), the Multicultural Counseling Awareness Scale (Ponterotto, Rieger, Barrett, Sparks, Sanchez, & Magidis, 1996), and the Cross-Cultural Counseling Inventory (Revised) (LaFromboise, Coleman, & Hernandez, 1991). These measures are based on the conceptualization of "multicultural competence" defined by Sue and his colleagues (Sue, Bernier, Durran, Feinberg, Pedersen, Smith, & Vasquez-Nuttall, 1982b). They have been extensively tested by their creators to assess psychometric properties, reliability, and validity. These instruments, however, have been criticized for assessing anticipated rather than actual professional behaviours, and for being vulnerable to social desirability expectations (Constantine, Juby, & Liang, 2001; Constantine & Ladany, 2000). They pose an additional problem for social workers. There is a tendency for these scales to focus on cultural competence as something executed within a counselling relationship. This assumption overlooks the range of social work practice, which includes addressing organizational and systemic practices that necessitate cultural competence as an intervention. Evaluations for cultural competence in social work need to include these dimensions.

Self-report measures tell us something important about an individual's ability to respond appropriately to questions about cultural competence. In the context of practice, however, we are ultimately more interested in a practitioner's ability to demonstrate culturally competent practice. Dixon's (1978) classic article on educational evaluation set an important standard for health and helping professions. She asserted that evaluations focused on the declaration of knowledge, and that values relevant to practice were insufficient to judge professional competency. Her taxonomy of learning outcomes (see Table 15.1) was used to choose the tools that would evaluate the outcomes from this educational program.

The methods of evaluation used to assess outcomes and their respective contributions are illustrated in Table 15.1. The Multicultural Counselling Inventory (MCI) (Sodowsky et al., 1994), a self-report measure, was used to

**Table 15.1: DIXON'S LEARNING TAXONOMY AND EVALUATIONS OF
CULTURAL COMPETENCE**

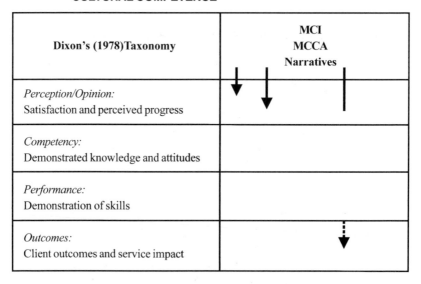

Dixon's (1978)Taxonomy	MCI MCCA Narratives
Perception/Opinion: Satisfaction and perceived progress	
Competency: Demonstrated knowledge and attitudes	
Performance: Demonstration of skills	
Outcomes: Client outcomes and service impact	

gather information about knowledge, awareness, skills, and relationship capability relevant to cultural competence. The forty-item scale elicited declarations relevant to cultural competence that corresponded to the "competency" level described in Dixon's taxonomy. The Multicultural Case Conceptualization Ability task (MCCA) (Ladany, Inman, Constantine, & Hofheinz, 1997) presented vignettes that asked respondents to identify and integrate issues relevant to culture into ideas about etiology and intervention. The MCCA task elicited a performance relevant to cultural competence, corresponding to the "performance" level of Dixon's taxonomy. Finally, written evaluations during and after the intervention, in addition to follow-up interviews with a subset of participants (six to eight weeks after the training), explored the extent to which individuals had been able to transfer any learning to practice. These semi-structured opportunities for gathering people's reflections and stories elicited narratives relevant to cultural competence. The narratives that were gathered after the learning experience were the best opportunity to evaluate the transfer of learning to practice and, therefore, approached Dixon's final level of evaluation, "outcomes." In addition, without the constraint of responding to an imposed idea of what constituted cultural competence in practice, participants were free to describe the range of practices they believed were relevant. The findings reinforced that these social workers saw cultural competence as having implications for individual practitioners, the agency, and the care system. They reported new, specific activities in each of these areas:

I'm working with ethnically/racially and culturally diverse clients and I find I explore the context more. (R8)

I am much more aware of checking out assumptions and offering culturally appropriate referrals or interpreters. I have gotten involved on a mezzo/macro level with making changes in agency and community by partnering to meet client needs. (R10)

I tend to reflect more about where each client is at in terms of cross-cultural issues, [and] also reflect on my own position. (R45)

It wasn't just about patients; it also applied to our colleagues that may have some issues of their own, and that in itself was also very valuable and something that I brought back to my team and suggested inviting (the facilitator) or someone else to come talk to our team in terms of these issues. (R15)

We have revised our intake form to be a bit more sensitive, conscious of diversity issues, right down to gender. ... Also, you know, I sit on a committee—we're doing a screen form. The course was ... I was sort of mindful of diversity issues in developing that form as well. So, you know, you can carry these issues and concepts wherever you go. (R2)

The narratives seem most able to reveal how individuals conceptualize cultural competence and act on it. Yet different methods of evaluation contribute to understanding different aspects of working across cultural difference. In this experience, the declarative, performance, and narrative aspects of cultural competence contributed to a multidimensional understanding of its development. At some point, standardized assessment scales may be available that assess cultural competence in ways that are more relevant to social work. For example, Soto (2001) has developed a self-assessment scale based on Cross's (1988) definition of cultural competence, which includes assessments of practice at multiple levels. Similarly, emerging definitions of generalist and advanced cultural competency in social work integrate a multilevel perspective (Lu, Lum, & Chen, 2001). These discussions emphasize expectations for practice that includes advocacy in organizations and systems. It is reassuring to know that social work practitioners are already practising with awareness of the necessity of this perspective.

CONCLUSION: WHAT DOES CULTURAL COMPETENCE MEAN IN SOCIAL WORK?

Cultural competence is an issue that is being addressed by all of the helping professions. Social work can benefit from assessing the applicability of developing guidelines that are emerging in fields like psychology (Sue et al., 1982a), nursing (Leininger, 1992), and medicine (Carrillo, Green, & Betancourt, 1999). However, the experience of developing, delivering, and evaluating this program reinforced that definitions based in other fields that do not share social work's explicit social justice agenda may not be appropriate for our use. Boyle and Springer (2001) have raised this concern, noting that there is a need for social work to move forward using discipline-specific definitions of cultural competence. Such definitions should integrate the anti-oppressive agenda that social work brings to the issues that arise from working across cultural difference. Cultural competence is necessary because of at least two oppressive practices in the human services. First, cultural competence is the remedy to the inflexibility of systems and theories that have been developed from the narrow perspective of dominant groups that have traditionally privileged Western, White, heterosexual, middle-class-focused knowledge and values. Second, cultural competence is a remedy for the marginalization of populations who have been part of North American and European contexts for hundreds of years but have been rendered invisible by those who control the recognition of voice, expertise, and status. Social work education needs to include training for individual social workers to effect changes in these areas. Practitioners have a crucial role to play as the interface between marginalized people and a system that can be alienating (Seck, Finch, Mor-Barak, & Poverny, 1993). Specific avenues for change include advocating for resources to be devoted to culturally competent practice (Mizio, 1998), building capacity via community networks (Johnson & Babiola, 1996), and confronting exploitative and discriminatory practices in the workplace (Casimir & Morrison, 1993; Mercer, 1984). Effective, evidence-based cultural competence training and education will be an important component of making such interventions possible.

REFERENCES

Bannerji, H. (2000). The paradox of diversity: The construction of a multicultural Canada and "Women of Color." *Women's Studies International Forum 23*(5), 537–560.

Beiser, M., Gill, K., & Edwards, R.G. (1993). Mental health care in Canada: Is it accessible and equal? *Canada's Mental Health 41*(2), 2–7.

Berry, J.W., & Laponce, J.A. (1994). *Ethnicity and culture in Canada: The research landscape.* Toronto: University of Toronto Press.

Bond, M.A. (1999). Gender, race, and class in organizational contexts. *American Journal of Community Psychology 27*(3), 327–355.

Boyle, D.P., & Springer, A. (2001). Toward a cultural competence measure for social work with specific populations. *Journal of Ethnic & Cultural Diversity in Social Work 9*(3/4), 53–71.

Brown, P. (1992). Using a group process in the teaching of cultural awareness for students in a multicultural society. *Australian Social Work 45*(4), 3–8.

Carlson, M.H., Brack, C.J., Laygo, R., Cohen, R., & Kirkscey, M. (1998). An exploratory study of multicultural competence of counselors in training: Support for experiential skills building. *Clinical Supervisor 17*(2), 75–87.

Carrillo, J.E., Green, A.R., & Betancourt, J.R. (1999). Cross-cultural primary care: A patient-based approach. *Annals of Internal Medicine 130*, 829–834.

Cashwell, C.S., Looby, E.J., & Housley, W.F. (1997). Appreciating cultural diversity through clinical supervision. *The Clinical Supervisor 15*(1), 75–85.

Casimir, G.J., & Morrison, B.J. (1993). Rethinking work with "multicultural populations." *Community Mental Health Journal 29*(6), 547–559.

Chau, K.L. (1992). Educating for effective group work practice in multicultural environments. *Journal of Multicultural Social Work 1*(4), pp. 1–15.

Coleman, H.L.K. (1997). Portfolio assessment of multicultural counseling competence. In D.B. Pope Davis & H.L.K. Coleman (Eds.), *Multicultural counseling competencies: Assessment, education and training, and supervision* (Vol. 7) (pp. 43–59). Thousand Oaks: Sage.

Constantine, M.G. (1997). Facilitating multicultural competency in counseling supervision: Operationalizing a practical framework. In D.B. Pope Davis & H.L.K. Coleman (Eds.), *Multicultural counseling competencies: Assessment, education and training, and supervision* (Vol. 7) (pp. 310–324). Thousand Oaks: Sage.

Constantine, M.G., Juby, H.L., & Liang, J.J.-C. (2001). Examining multicultural counseling competence and race-related attitudes among White marital and family therapists. *Journal of Marital and Family Therapy 27*(3), 353–362.

Constantine, M.G., & Ladany, N. (2000). Self-report multicultural counseling competence scales: Their relation to social desirability attitudes and multicultural case conceptualization ability. *Journal of Counseling Psychology 47*(2), 155–164.

Cross, T.L. (1988). Service to minority populations: Cultural competence continuum. *Focal Point 3*(1), 1–4.

Cross, T., Bazron, B.J., Dennis, K.K., & Isaacs, M.R. (1989). *Towards a culturally competent system of care*. Washington: Howard University Press.

Dana, R.H., Behn, J.D., & Gonwa, T. (1992). A checklist for the examination of cultural competence in social service agencies. *Research on Social Work Practice 2*(2), 220–233.

D'Andrea, M., & Daniels, J. (1997). Multicultural counseling supervision: Central issues, theoretical considerations, and practical strategies. In D.B. Pope Davis & H.L.K. Coleman (Eds.), *Multicultural counseling competencies: Assessment, education and training, and supervision* (Vol. 7) (pp. 290–309). Thousand Oaks: Sage.

D'Andrea, M., Daniels, J., & Heck, R. (1991). Evaluating the impact of multicultural counseling training. *Journal of Counseling and Development 70*, 143–150.

Davis, L.E., & Gelsomino, J. (1994). An assessment of practitioner cross-racial treatment experiences. *Social Work 39*(1), 116–123.

DeHoyos, G. (1989). Person-in-environment: A tri-level practice model. *Social Casework 70*, 131–138.

Devore, W., & Schlesinger, E.G. (1999). *Ethnic-sensitive social work practice* (5th ed.). Boston: Allyn & Bacon.

Dixon, J. (1978). Evaluation criteria in studies of continuing education in the health professions: A critical review and a suggested strategy. *Evaluation and the Health Professions 1*(2), 47–65.

Dominelli, L. (1997). *Anti-racist social work* (2nd ed.). London: MacMillan Press Ltd.

Dyche, L., & Zayas, L.H. (2001). Cross-cultural empathy and training the contemporary psychotherapist. *Clinical Social Work Journal 29*(3), 245–258.

Edwards, S.L. (1997). *Teaching strategies for multicultural competence*. Unpublished doctoral dissertation, University of South Carolina.

Foster, R.P. (1998). The clinician's cultural countertransference: The psychodynamics of culturally competent practice. *Clinical Social Work Journal 26*(3), 253–270.

Garcia, B., & Van Soest, D. (2000). Facilitating learning on diversity: Challenges to the professor. *Journal of Ethnic & Cultural Diversity in Social Work 9*(1/2), 21–39.

Garcia, M.H., Wright, J.W., & Corey, G. (1991). A multicultural perspective in a undergraduate human services program. *Journal of Counseling and Development 70*(1), 86–90.

Garland, D.R., & Escobar, D. (1988). Education for cross-cultural social work practice. *Journal of Social Work Education 24*(3), 229–241.

Giordano, J. (1994). Mental health and the melting pot: An introduction. *American Journal of Orthopsychiatry 64*(3), 342–345.

Haynes, D.T., & White, B.W. (1999). Will the "real" social work please stand up? A call to stand for professional unity. *Social Work 44*(4), 385–391.

Husband, C. (2000). Recognising diversity and developing skills: The proper role of transcultural communication. *European Journal of Social Work 3*(3), 225–234.

Jackson, A. (1980). Social work education for multi-racial practice: A British example. *Contemporary Social Work Education 3*(2), 158–168.

Johnson, A.E., & Babiola, G.V. (1996). Integrating culture and healing: Meeting health care needs of a multicultural community. *Minnesota Medicine 79*, 41–45.

Ladany, N., Inman, A.G., Constantine, M.G., & Hofheinz, E.W. (1997). Supervisee multicultural case conceptualization ability and self-reported multicultural competence as functions of supervisee racial identity and supervisor focus. *Journal of Counseling Psychology 44*(3), 284–293.

LaFromboise, T.D., Coleman, H.L.K., & Hernandez, A. (1991). Development and factor structure of the Cross-Cultural Counseling Inventory (Revised). *Professional Psychology: Research and Practice 22*, 380–388.

Leininger, M.M. (1992). *Cultural care diversity and universality: A theory of nursing.* Publication no. 15-2401. New York: National League for Nursing Press.

Leong, F.T.L., & Kim, H.H.W. (1991). Going beyond cultural sensitivity on the road to multiculturalism: Using the intercultural sensitizer as a counselor training tool. *Journal of Counseling and Development 70*, 112–118.

Lu, Y.E., Lum, D., & Chen, S. (2001). Cultural competency and achieving styles in clinical social work: A conceptual and empirical exploration. *Journal of Ethnic & Cultural Diversity in Social Work 9*(3/4), 1–32.

Manoleas, P. (1994). An outcome approach to assessing the cultural competence of MSW students. *Journal of Multicultural Social Work 3*(1), 43–57.

Marshack, E.F., Hendricks, C.O., & Gladstein, M. (1994). The commonality of difference: Teaching about diversity in field instruction. *Journal of Multicultural Social Work 3*(1), 77–89.

Mercer, K. (1984). Black communities' experience of psychiatric services. *International Journal of Social Psychiatry 40*, 22–27.

Mizio, E. (1998). Staff development: An ethical imperative. *Journal of Gerontological Social Work 30*(1/2), 17–32.

Montalvo, F.F., Lasater, T.T., & Valdez, N.G. (1982). Training child welfare workers for cultural awareness: The culture simulator technique. *Child Welfare 61*(6), 341–352.

Morrison Van Vooris, R. (1998). Culturally relevant practice: A framework for teaching the psychosocial dynamics of oppression. *Journal of Social Work Education 34*(1), 121–133.

Norton, R.A. (2000, August 5). *A model of cross-cultural supervision.* Paper presented at the 108th Annual Meeting of the American Psychological Association, Washington.

Panos, P.T., & Panos, A.J. (2000). A model for a culture-sensitive assessment of patients in health care settings. *Social Work in Health Care 31*(1), 49–62.

Peterson, F.K. (1991). Issues of race and ethnicity in supervision: Emphasizing who you are, not what you know. *The Clinical Supervisor 9*(1), 15–31.

Ponterotto, J.G., Rieger, B.P., Barrett, A., Sparks, R., Sanchez, C.M., & Magidis, D.M. (1996). Development and initial validation of the Multicultural Counseling Awareness Scale. In G.R. Sodowsky & J.C. Impara (Eds.), *Multicultural assessment in counseling and clinical psychology* (pp. 247–282). Lincoln: Buros Institute of Mental Measurements.

Poole, D.L. (1998). Politically correct or culturally competent? *Health and Social Work* *23*(3), 163–166.

Ridley, C.R., Mendoza, D.W., & Kanitz, B.E. (1994). Multicultural training: Reexamination, operationalization, and integration. *The Counseling Psychologist 22*(2), 227–289.

Ronnau, J.P. (1994). Teaching cultural competence: Practical ideas for social work educators. *Journal of Multicultural Social Work 3*(1), 29–42.

Seck, E.T., Finch, W.A., Mor-Barak, M.E., & Poverny, L.M. (1993). Managing a diverse workforce. *Administration in Social Work 17*(2), 67–79.

Shank, B.W. (2001, June 19–23). *Social justice: The link between clinical social work practice and social development.* Paper presented at the 12th International Symposium Inter-University Consortium on International Social Development, Istanbul, Turkey.

Shergill, A.S. (1998). *An evaluation of the social cultural competency for success training program for the acquisition of intercultural interpersonal competency skills among health care trainees.* Unpublished doctoral dissertation. University of British Columbia.

Sodowsky, G.R., Taffe, R.C., Gutkin, T.B., & Wise, S.L. (1994). Development of the Multicultural Counseling Inventory: A self-report measure of multicultural competencies. *Journal of Counseling Psychology 41*(2), 137–148.

Soto, J.J. (2001, April 22). *21 cultural competencies for the 21st century: A self-assessment.* <www.inmotionmagazine.com/soto6.html>.

Srivastava, S. (1993). Voyeurism and vulnerability: Critiquing the power relations of anti-racist workshops. *Canadian Woman Studies/Les Cahiers de la Femme 14*(2), 105–109.

Sue, D.W., Bernier, J.E., Durran, A., Feinberg, L., Pedersen, P., Smith, E., & Vasquez-Nuttall, E. (1982a). Position paper. *Cross-cultural Counseling Competencies 10*, 45–52.

_____. (1982b). *Multicultural counseling competencies: Individual and organizational development.* Thousand Oaks: Sage Publications.

Thompson, N. (1997). *Anti-discriminatory practice* (2nd ed.). London: MacMillan Press Ltd.

Tsang, A.K.T., & George, U. (1998). Towards an integrated framework for cross-cultural social work practice. *Canadian Social Work Review 15*(1), 73–93.

Weaver, H.N. (1999). Indigenous people and the social work profession: Defining culturally competent services. *Social Work 44*(3), 217–225.

Williams, C.C. (2001). Confronting the racism in research on race and mental health services. *Canadian Social Work Review 18*(2), 231–248.

Williams, S., & Halgin, R.P. (1995). Issues in psychotherapy supervision between the White supervisor and the Black supervisee. *The Clinical Supervisor 13*(1), 39–61.

Chapter 16

Listening to the Voices of Service Participants in Child Protective Services, Children's Mental Health, and Psychotherapy

Marshall Fine
Faculty of Social Work
Wilfrid Laurier University
Sally Palmer
Faculty of Social Work
McMaster University
Nick Coady
Faculty of Social Work
Wilfrid Laurier University

All I can ask is to be treated like a human being and not a number.

—Service participant quoted in
Wilford & Hetherington (1997, p. 62)

This chapter resulted from a community-university research alliance (CURA) project[1] established to explore in depth and from multiple perspectives the social service arenas of child protective services (CPS) and children's mental health. One of our purposes was to understand and highlight the experiences of service participants[2] as they engaged in and travelled through these systems. We hold that an understanding and appreciation of service participants' experiences is essential to the development of respectful and helpful delivery systems. As a backdrop for our research in service participants' experiences, we reviewed the literature with respect to service participants' voice. We define voice in this chapter as *documented feedback from service participants who are given formal opportunity to express their opinions regarding the services in which they participated.* This chapter gives the results of our review and is an adaptation of a larger, more detailed report (Fine, Palmer, & Coady, 2001).

The active pursuit of service participants' voice is a relatively new phenomenon. In the early history of service delivery, an assumption was made and accepted broadly that service participants did not know best what was helpful for them (Gergen & Kaye, 1992; Illich, 1977; Payne, 2000; Wilson & Beresford, 2000). It is interesting and ironic that the very people for whom service was developed and provided, and upon whom it was sometimes imposed, were often not thought competent to judge the nature of their problems or what might be most helpful for them (Gergen & Kaye, 1992). These attitudes took firm purchase in modernity, where the power of the professional service provider[3] and the professional "gaze" was deemed unquestionable (Foucault, 1979).

Postmodernity brought with it a questioning of the foundational knowledge laid down in the helping professions (Atkinson & Heath, 1990; Hartman & Laird, 1998). Given that service providers had developed and embraced ideas and approaches for working with service participants that were almost completely devoid of feedback from service participants (Bowman & Fine, 2000), this questioning was indeed warranted. In addition, these theories and approaches often depicted service participants and their concerns in particularly narrow ways, in that they were often acontextual and did not take into account the diversity of human experience (Chave Herberg, 1993; McGoldrick, 1998; Waldegrave, 1998). Consequently, some service participants suffered at the hands of ill-informed and oblivious service providers. Discrimination against women in service delivery leading to such a practice phenomenon as mother-blaming is one example of this type of blindness (Kravetz, 2002; McCollum & Russell, 1992; Wedenoja, 1991). Recent critiques and analyses (Hare-Mustin, 1994; Hines Moore, Preto Garcia, McGoldrick, Almeida, & Weltman, 1999; Van Den Bergh, 1995a) have helped professionals extend their vision, yet the road is long and the potential for harm still looms large.

Given our concern for service providers' potential oppression of service participants, we think it is essential for service providers to question regularly their understandings and approaches to working with service participants. Blind acceptance of any theory or approach can erase or marginalize the service participant. Like Maturana's frog (Simon, 1985)—who cannot see a fly unless it is moving in a particular direction and who will starve to death surrounded by motionless food—we can see only what we are structured to see, and when we are enchanted with a particular way of seeing, we tend to see little else. This narrowed vision not only limits us as service providers, but more importantly and more tragically, it can condemn service participants to become the objects of our desires, not the authors of their own. The potential for oppression works particularly well given the power invested in us through our credentials and our social institutions. Our words and actions, therefore, can have enormous effects, both positive and negative, on the lives of service participants. As such, in a world where power and social construction reign, it is imperative that service participants have a significant voice in shaping the ideas and helping approaches that are developed to "change" them.

We recognize that much beneficial work has been done with service participants. Indeed, our review suggests that service participants are able to identify very positive aspects of service delivery. We also recognize that service providers have the best of intentions in their work with service participants. However, good intentions are not enough (Margolin, 1997). As Kimelman (1985, p. 276) stated when referring to the problematic way many child protective agencies have dealt with Aboriginal peoples: "The road to hell was paved with good intentions and child welfare agencies were the paving contractors." Let us not become the paving contractors on the road to hell for our service participants.

OVERVIEW OF THE LITERATURE REVIEWED

We reviewed the literature that examined service participants' voice in three service sectors: child protective services, children's mental health, and psychotherapy. The choice of the first two service sectors was dictated by the research project from which this literature review stemmed. The third service sector, psychotherapy, was included in order to tap into the broader research on service participants' experiences of counselling in general. Each body of literature tended to capture voice somewhat differently. A number of studies in child protective services used in-depth qualitative interview approaches with participants as a way of bringing voice forward. The studies in children's mental health tended to be more quantitative in nature. They focused largely on gathering information regarding service participants' satisfaction with, and the outcome of, services; however, many of these studies included findings based on service participants' responses to open- and closed-ended questions. The psychotherapy literature produced research that was somewhat mixed in methodology, though the majority of studies used some form of qualitative design that was aimed largely at understanding the service participants' views of the process and outcome of therapy.

To afford the reader some grasp of the literature studied, we summarize below the studies we reviewed in each of the three service sectors. In order to meet space requirements, we do not reference the specific studies in each sector; however, the reader may refer to the references for each service sector at the end of the chapter.

The literature review of parents' voices in child protective services showed a scarcity of research examining their perceptions. Eight studies were found, all published since 1990: four in Canada, two in the United Kingdom, and one each in the United States and Australia. In terms of methodology, six of the studies were conducted through personal interviews, with one of these using structured questionnaires as well. The remaining two studies used focus groups of parents and child protective services workers; one of these combined discussion with collaborative work on a task.

The literature review of service participants' voices in the field of children's mental health services was construed broadly to include in- and out-patient treatment of the emotional, behavioural, and psychiatric problems of children and adolescents. The literature search identified twenty-one studies, fifteen of which were published since 1990. Many (thirteen of twenty-one) studies relied on mailed questionnaires or telephone interviews, some involved interviewer- or self-administered questionnaires (often allowing for open-ended comments), and only a few involved in-depth interviewing. Most studies (fourteen of twenty-one) relied exclusively on parental feedback, and many (thirteen of twenty-one) included some form of participant satisfaction rating. The studies were conducted primarily in the United States; however, there were some Canadian and British studies.

The studies found in the psychotherapy sector covered a vast array of psychotherapy-type settings. Overall there were twenty-two studies. Ten of the studies were from family and couple therapy, eleven studies were focused on individual therapy, and one study elicited the voices of group therapy participants. The concerns that brought people to therapy ranged from psychiatric issues regarding depression and survivorship, to addictions, and to problems of the troubled. Settings included university counselling centres, psychiatric hospitals, homeless shelters, and individual and family counselling agencies. Study participants were primarily Caucasian.

First we report on the findings that were common across the three service sectors. Following this we discuss findings that were specific to each service sector. We close with suggestions for practice and future research.

OVERALL FINDINGS

Findings from the three service sectors were analyzed in order to assess and assemble categories and themes of similar content across the areas. A total of five categories, with two themes in each, emerged from these analyses and are reported below.

Category 1: Relationship-Enhancing Aspects of the Service Provider
The themes under this category describe characteristics of the service provider that were important to service participants and that enhanced their experience and willingness to work with the provider.

Theme: Caring Ways-of-Being
Many of the ideas expressed about the characteristics of service providers echoed similar sentiments: courteousness, friendliness, warmth, compassion, understanding, showing interest, listening well, dedication, kindness, empathy, sympathy, being dependable, and showing concern.

Theme: Service Provider as Human
Participants identified service provider characteristics that suggested the importance of participants feeling that the service provider was a "real" and humane person who was similar to them in some way. Participants described "good" service providers as authentic and personal, easygoing, patient, enthusiastic, open, flexible, fun, interactive with children, and low-keyed and streetwise with youth. In addition, service participants commented on the importance of self-disclosure by the service provider and having some similarity in values and experiences (e.g., age, family status, gender).

Category 2: Helpful and Change-Enhancing Actions of the Service Provider
Themes under this category address aspects of service provider interventions or actions that service participants regarded as positive and helpful.

Theme: Helpful Actions
Participants found the following actions by service providers to be helpful: facilitating self-exploration; validating changes; providing new viewpoints; offering opinions and perspectives; teaching; giving pragmatic suggestions and specific advice; offering social skills training for youth; and advocating for the service participant.

Theme: Validating Actions
This theme represents service providers' actions that helped the participants feel validated and respected as human beings: fairness; sharing power; being an ally; not imposing provider views; including participants in the planning of their service; accepting service participants for who they

are; involving service participants in decision making; sharing knowledge; talking at their level; being supportive; showing loyalty; being responsive; and facilitating self-acceptance and self-exploration. In addition, providers were appreciated for helping participants to see the small changes that they were making, and believing that the parents were doing the best they could for their children.

Category 3: Unhelpful and Change-Discouraging Aspects of the Service Provider
Themes under this category address aspects of service provider ways-of-being, interventions, and actions that were seen as discouraging and unhelpful to service participants.

Theme: Unhelpful or Negative Ways-of-Being
Participants viewed some service providers as conducting themselves in ways that felt unhelpful, negative, or invalidated them as people: provocative, inactive, critical, judgmental, uncaring, patronizing, condescending, controlling and overtly directing, disapproving, unsupportive, authoritarian, and rigid in their approach to service. Other unhelpful ways-of-being involved showing no interest in participants' opinions; showing a superior attitude; not including participants in decision making; and conveying an attitude that the service provider was "just doing the job."

Theme: Unhelpful or Negative Actions
Participants identified a number of service provider behaviours as being unhelpful and having negative effects on them. These actions were: talking about irrelevant things; being too quick to interpret service participants' behaviour; competing with service participants for talk time; misinterpreting what the service participant is saying; not guiding the direction of service; and lacking clarity and preparation. Other actions were: asking redundant and irrelevant questions; giving orders; not being able to find timely solutions to problems; underestimating difficulty for participants in implementing suggestions consistently; lacking preparation for and agreement about termination; not linking sessions with real life; and indicating discouragement with lack of service participants' progress.

Category 4: Professionalism
There were findings across areas that spoke to what we term "professionalism." These are personal characteristics or actions that indicate

competence or incompetence with regard to the expectations of professional associations for professional behaviour.

Theme: Professional Competence

Certain issues identified by service participants spoke to the competence of the service provider. Participants described competence with words such as well informed, helpful, knowledgeable, organized, decisive, open to the limits of his or her power, and ethical regarding issues of confidentiality.

Theme: Professional Incompetence

Some participants noted service provider characteristics and actions that were clearly unprofessional. These included the service provider being hurtful, uninformed about resources and the service provider's role, and not being up-to-date on ethical standards.

Category 5: Organization Features

These themes relate specifically to issues experienced by service participants regarding the larger agency or organization from which they sought help.

Theme: Organization-Friendly Features

Some participants talked about characteristics of organizations that made them seem more friendly and welcoming. Participants noted such features as quick appointments, availability of service providers, easy accessibility to the clinic, program clarity, well-developed organization, and income-based fees.

Theme: Organization-Unfriendly Features

Participants identified a number of features that made certain organizations quite unwelcoming. These features were: a generally negative environment; long waits for first appointments; inconvenient appointment times; too few and too infrequent sessions or services; difficultly with transportation to the agency; stigma associated with being involved with the organization; the high cost of counselling sessions; difficulty in switching service providers; and being exposed by sharing a waiting room.

RESULTS SPECIFIC TO EACH SECTOR

Having outlined the overall themes across all three service sectors, we now look at findings that were unique to each service sector.

Child Protective Services

Involvement with CPS may be a very stressful experience for parents. For most, their involvement is involuntary, resulting from an outside concern that they are not caring adequately for their children; they may view themselves as being ostracized by the community. Often they are also contending with poverty and social marginalization, so this stress may be added to an existing sense of despair. Fear is another common experience of parents receiving CPS because the agency, with court support, has the power to take away their children.

Non-responsiveness of Agencies

Some parents found CPS agencies to be non-responsive when they asked for help. First Nations caregivers recalled that traditional CPS agencies had been very supportive of their children, but not of them as parents: "I would be crying out for help [with addictions], and there would be no one listening to me" (Anderson, 1998, p. 446). Parents in a comparative England–Germany study complained of "having to ask again and again" for help in managing their children (Wilford & Hetherington, 1997, p. 65).

Experiences of Conflict, Oppression, and Intrusion by Agencies

Some parents experienced conflict between their agendas and those of the social worker, e.g., a mother said her worker wanted her to participate in parent training, whereas the mother wanted daycare so she could spend time on her studies (Baistow, Hetherington, Spriggs, & Yelloly, 1996). Many of the English parents, who had troubled backgrounds themselves, felt overwhelmed by the task of child care, and experienced the CPS agencies as oppressive: "The last thing you want when you are on the edge of a nervous breakdown is to be expected to be even more responsible than you have been in the past" (Wilford & Hetherington, 1997, p. 64).

Parents who had their children taken into care spoke about agency intrusiveness and their own sense of loss. A German mother experienced her children's time in care as "theft" of their lives in terms of living with her and living in normal surroundings (Wilford & Hetherington, 1997). Two Aboriginal caregivers expressed their feelings of loss: "When the child is gone away from home ... that bond is taken away from you—it's like you're losing that child" (Anderson, 1998, p. 448).

Relationships with Workers

Parents appreciated workers whom they could trust, and who reached out to them. The importance of trust in the worker-parent relationship was mentioned by several parents in McCallum's (1995, p. 77) study. One parent noted the paramount importance of "a person they can count on, even if they are a bad parent, somebody who they can trust is going to do the right thing for themselves and their children." The importance of relationship was expressed by a group of young, single, low-income mothers who were assessed as being at high risk for abusing; they appreciated service providers who had been kind and who had gone "the extra mile" for them (McCurdy & Jones, 2000). The researchers concluded that these mothers valued the social contact that reduced their extreme isolation more than the parent training they received.

On the negative side, parents who were being investigated or charged with child abuse sometimes felt they were being negatively labelled. A father who was convicted of child sexual abuse felt the service provider had labelled and rejected him (McCallum, 1995). In child welfare, the sense of a worker being uncaring was interpreted by some parents as an indication that the worker did not value the child: "he [service provider] was just very cold, to me, uncaring ... I guess it was just the way he said it ... the tone of his voice ... like my kid didn't matter" (McCallum, 1995, p. 65). Concern about being helpless with respect to agency power was elevated for parents dealing with CPS agencies. Many of them expressed great fear about the possibility that they might lose their children. McCallum (1995, p. 56) found that "all 10 respondents ... said they felt alienated, intimidated, threatened, and/or controlled for at least part of their time with the agency." Some parents in the Wilford and Hetherington (1997, p. 65) study echoed this, feeling they had been "coerced into collaborating" with CPS in making plans for their children to be cared for elsewhere.

Problems with Child Placement Interventions

First Nations parents and grandparents wanted more information and preparation for the placement of their children: "Talk to the parents. Let them know what is going to happen to their child ... and let the child know that they're going to be leaving the home ..." (Anderson, 1998, p. 451). These caregivers also wanted involvement in choosing a placement: "I would want myself or someone that I knew ... to interview these people [with whom my child would be placed]" (Anderson, 1998, p. 452). Another First Nations caregiver simply wanted the worker to take more time: "At that time [of apprehension], if she [CAS worker] would have actually just sat down and talked with me, instead of just running off" (Anderson, 1998, p. 448).

Children's Mental Health

Although the overall, across service sector findings presented earlier capture most of the insights derived from the review of the children's mental health literature, there were two sets of findings. First, a few studies provided some information about the expectations that service participants had of what service would be like, prior to their actual involvement with the program under study. Stallard, Hudson, and Davis (1992) found that, for a number of families, the uncertainty of what to expect of service involvement was problematic. These families indicated a desire for more preparatory information regarding what the first appointment would be like and what the role of the service provider would be. Similarly, Carr, McDonnell, and Owen (1994) found that only 22 per cent of families knew what to expect when they attended a mental health clinic for the first time. Two other studies documented service participants' negative expectations. Garland and Besinger (1996) found that 39 per cent of adolescents expected counselling to be "frightening or intimidating." Coady and Hayward (1998) found that a majority of their small sample of families had negative expectations of service based on prior experiences with helping professionals. These negative expectations included professionals' lack of understanding and insensitivity to cultural issues, and the ineffectiveness of services.

A second set of findings specific to children's mental health concerned service participants' satisfaction with services. As mentioned earlier, thirteen of the twenty-one studies reviewed used a measure of service participants' satisfaction, which was usually a four- or five-point standardized scale. Overall, the high satisfaction ratings of service participants in these studies are quite striking. The percentage of service participants who reported they were either satisfied or very satisfied with services ranged between 65 per cent and 90 per cent, with an across study mean of 80 per cent. Studies that included the satisfaction ratings of youth (Garland & Besinger, 1996; Godley, Fiedler, & Funk, 1998; Shapiro, Welker, & Jacobsen, 1997; Stuntzner-Gibson, Koren, & DeChillo, 1995) also indicated relatively high levels of satisfaction, although they were always somewhat lower than parental ratings. This finding is consistent with the consensus in the broader literature that agreement between youth and parental ratings can vary significantly and that both have a place in comprehensive evaluation (Godley et al., 1998; Shapiro et al., 1997; Stuntzner-Gibson et al., 1995).

A number of studies (Carscadden, George, & Wells, 1990; Godley et al., 1998; Plante, Couchman, & Hoffman, 1998; Shapiro et al., 1997) investigated the association between service participants' satisfaction and service participants' improvement or level of distress. Overall, as one might expect, there were significant, positive associations between participants' satisfaction and good outcomes. One interesting finding in a number of studies was that service participants' satisfaction was more closely associated with emotional than with behavioural outcomes. Shapiro et al.'s (1997, p. 96) findings suggested that "client satisfaction measures may place less weight on improvement in public, behavioural aspects of adjustment." For example, Plante et al.'s (1998) study of service participants' satisfaction and outcome in children's mental health services demonstrated that parents' satisfaction with services remained high over a period of time even though ratings of problematic behaviours and symptoms did not improve. The authors conclude that "stable reports of symptoms, combined with high satisfaction, may indicate that important 'care' (as compared with 'cure') is occurring" (Plante et al., 1998, p. 54).

Two studies (Garland & Besinger, 1996; Shapiro, et al., 1997) that explored determining factors of service participants' satisfaction suggested that the two main factors in service participants' satisfaction are the perceived benefits of the interventions and the quality of relationship with the service provider. This lends further support to two ideas endorsed broadly by clinical research: (a) that service participants' satisfaction and outcome are intertwined, and (b) that the quality of the helping relationship is the most important factor in service participants' satisfaction and outcome.

It should be noted that the findings of high levels of service participants' satisfaction with children's mental health services are in keeping with those in the broader literature on service participants' satisfaction (Stallard et al., 1992) and that these results must be viewed cautiously due to numerous methodological issues. First, studies that rely on mailed or telephone questionnaires have significant numbers of service participants who do not respond, which likely skews the results in a positive direction (Stallard, 1995). Second, most studies do not include dropouts, which probably has the effect of underrepresenting dissatisfied service participants and skewing the results in the direction of higher satisfaction ratings (Shapiro et al., 1997). Third, social desirability is a factor that could inflate satisfaction ratings. Fourth, it is clear that high ratings of global service participants' satisfaction do not preclude specific service participants' dissatisfactions, which are best elicited by open-ended questions and qualitative interviewing (Godley et al., 1998; Stallard et al., 1992). Still, the overall high levels of service participants' satisfaction with children's mental health services cannot be dismissed.

Psychotherapy

Much of what emerged from the psychotherapy literature is covered in the overall findings section. However, some findings are specific to psychotherapy and are highlighted here.

An area that was investigated in a number of studies related to service participants' prior expectations of psychotherapy. Some of the families who sought help with their adolescent children's drug misuse expected family therapy to be sombre, with lots of interrogation, particularly directed at the adolescents' drug use. These parents expected quick answers to their problems because they were working with "experts" in the area of drug misuse (Newfield, Joanning, Kuehl, & Quinn, 1991). Another study (Stith, Rosen, McCollum, Coleman, & Herman, 1996) noted that children did not often understand why they were coming to therapy. In addition, Mayer and Timms (1970) and Kuehl, Newfield, and Joanning (1990) remarked that many service participants simply did not know what to expect. Maluccio (1979) reported that a number of service participants expected treatment to solve their problems quickly. They also thought that service providers would be active in helping them by expressing opinions, giving advice, and offering suggestions. Mayer and Timms (1970) found that some service participants thought that service providers would listen to their stories and decide who was right or wrong. They reasoned that, after the service provider made this decision, she or he would offer them advice regarding what to do about the problem.

There were also findings with regard to aspects of service provider action and ways-of-being that were specific to the psychotherapy literature. Newfield et al. (1991) found that parents tended to want service providers to be more direct—to question more intently their adolescents who were misusing drugs and to give them advice. In addition, some service participants wanted more action and advice, but were hesitant to challenge the "expert." These service participants tended to drop out of counselling (Mayer & Timms, 1970).

Wark (1994) found that service participants were upset when the service provider did not find an immediate solution or did not give them what they wanted from therapy. Maluccio (1979) observed that service participants who left therapy prematurely did so for reasons such as not making an emotional connection with the service provider or feeling at the end of the first session that they had only a vague idea of what the future plans of therapy would be.

A number of studies looked at issues that were specific to couple therapy. Bowman and Fine (2000) found that some participants thought rules regarding a partner's verbal abuse were important to the general safety in the therapy room. They also found that service participants liked sessions to end on a positive note, and appreciated being able to talk about what was important to them rather than what was important to the service provider. Some felt unacknowledged because the service providers seemed preoccupied with their partners. Similarly, Wark (1994) noted that couples valued service providers who were able to give both partners equal time.

Certain issues also arose from studies looking at family therapy, particularly with respect to adolescents and children. Newfield et al. (1991) found that some adolescents thought counselling was unnecessary, embarrassing, and an invasion of privacy. In the Stith et al. (1996) study, some children didn't like one-way mirrors and videotape recorders. Moreover, they did not like sitting in the waiting room for parts of a family session. McConnell and Sim (2000) reported that some mothers in their study felt that the service provider did not communicate enough with them about the job the providers were doing with their children, which had a negative effect on their relationship with the providers. Regarding family therapy, Kuehl et al. (1990) found that families would have liked individual as well as family sessions.

Many couple and family therapists use reflecting team practices as part of service delivery (Andersen, 1987; Smith, Sells, & Clevenger, 1994). A number of studies focused on the voices of service participants involved in this practice. Participants in Sells, Smith, Coe, Yoshioka, and Robbins (1994) study found reflecting teams useful as the team acted as a buffer when anger or fear was played out in the couple session. Couples appreciated being able to sit back and listen to the team—this removed the pressure and allowed them to digest information. Service participants in the study by Sells et al. (1994) noted other benefits of the reflecting team process, such as offering participants alternatives so that they could think differently about their issues. Smith, Yoshioka, and Winton (1993) noted that the single most important aspect of reflecting teams mentioned by service participants in their study was the opportunity to have multiple perspectives on their issues. The team discussion regarding the different perspectives helped them clarify which was the best fit for them. On the other hand, some couples in the study by Sells et al. (1994) thought that introduction of the reflecting team too early in therapy was intimidating and not effective.

CONCLUSION

This chapter has explored the voices of service participants in three service sectors: child protective services, children's mental health, and psychotherapy.[4] The emphasis has been on service participants' voices, even when studies included the perceptions of service providers, in order to highlight and privilege the ideas and opinions of the participants—voices that have not typically been heard or welcomed.

Not surprisingly, there is strong support across the three service sectors for the importance of a good relationship between service provider and service participant. Important contributions by the service providers to the relationship were: warmth, compassion, self-disclosure, empathy, authenticity, and concern. There are also preferences for particular service provider interventions. These include: advocating; facilitating self-exploration; sharing power and knowledge; being an ally; giving pragmatic suggestions; and validating changes. Service participants are also aware of what they think should constitute professionalism, such as maintaining confidentiality; being organized and well informed; and being transparent about the limits of power.

On the negative side, service participants identified service provider attitudes and behaviours that damage the therapeutic alliance, such as being critical, judgmental, controlling and patronizing, and not being able to find solutions. These aspects, in addition to issues identified as demonstrating professional incompetence, should be examined in more detail by researchers and service providers as they lead ultimately to the demise of relationship and, as such, they are the very antithesis of the service provider's charge and concern.

Service participants identified concerns about service organizations. Problematic organizational issues included: inaccessibility to services; long waits for first appointments; and difficulty in changing service providers. Although some identified agency problems such as stigma and intrusiveness may be difficult to alter, especially in child protective services, other organizational factors can be altered. For example, potentially important changes include making services more accessible to service participants (e.g., developing local satellite services) and providing some supportive services to service participants who are on long waiting lists. In addition, more thought can be given to the issue of privacy in the waiting room, which is certainly of ethical relevance.

The specific issues raised in each of the three areas warrant further study. Child protective service issues are indeed complex. Given that it is a sphere in which there is a great possibility for intrusiveness and misuse of power, service participants' voice must be a priority. The children's mental health literature reminds us of the important and intertwined nature of service satisfaction, outcome, and the provider-participant relationship. The psychotherapy area points out specific issues particularly in couple and family therapy that speak to the importance of addressing all service participants in sensitive and equitable ways.

The voices that formed the essence of this chapter add greatly to our understanding of the service provision relationship. Many of our findings speak to the importance that service participants place on core therapeutic conditions and issues of respect and validation. Service providers are trained to see these fundamental relationship skills as essential. We wonder if it is possible that such core relationship conditions appear so basic that some providers tend to overlook them in favour of loftier interventions, or if they fade in light of heavy demands on their time. With regard to the latter point, there is no doubt that increasing agency demands and cutbacks can limit the time devoted to the development of working alliances. From an anti-oppressive, structural perspective, it is important that service providers work together to challenge these structural impediments to effective service delivery (Shera & Page, 1995).

We strongly urge service providers to seek constantly and incorporate earnestly service participants' voices and ideas into the service delivery process. A partnership model (as opposed to a dominator model) (Van Den Bergh, 1995b), is one respectful and equitable approach in which the spirit of co-creation and mutual endeavour is sought in a common space that is not blind to the inevitable power differences between the service participant and the service provider.

We have attempted in this chapter to privilege the voices of service participants. Let us listen, learn, and join with service participants in the pursuit of respectful and effective service provision. We leave the last word to a service participant in couple therapy: "I felt that she was legitimately concerned about the two of us and our relationship. It wasn't just a job to her" (Bowman & Fine, 2000, p. 299).

NOTES

1. Funding for the project came from the Social Science and Humanities Research Council, Community-University Research Alliance Grant #833-1999-1026.
2. We use "service participant" throughout this chapter rather than "client," "patient," or "consumer."
3. "Service provider" stands for helping professionals such as social workers, psychotherapists, psychologists, and so on.
4. There are a number of important methodological issues that were not identified in the discussion of the research reported in this chapter. We refer the reader to Fine, Palmer, and Coady (2001) for an explicit examination of these issues.

REFERENCES

Andersen, T. (1987). The reflecting team: Dialogue and meta-dialogue in clinical work. *Family Process 26*, 415–428.

Atkinson, B.J., & Heath, A.W. (1990). Further thoughts on second-order family therapy: This time it's personal. *Family Process 29*, 145–155.

Bowman, L., & Fine, M. (2000). Client perceptions of couples' therapy: Helpful and unhelpful aspects. *American Journal of Family Therapy 28*, 295–310.

Chave Herberg, D. (1993). *Frameworks for cultural and racial diversity: Teaching and learning for practitioners.* Toronto: Canadian Scholars' Press.

Fine, M., Palmer, S., & Coady, N. (2001). *Service participant voices in child welfare, children's mental health, and psychotherapy.* Wilfrid Laurier University, Partnerships for Children and Families. <www.wlu.ca/fsw/cura/index_cura.html>

Foucault, M. (1979). *Discipline and punishment: The birth of the prison.* New York: Springer-Verlag.

Gergen, K.J., & Kaye, J. (1992). Beyond narrative in the negotiation of therapeutic meaning. In S. McNamee & K.J. Gergen (Eds.), *Therapy as a social construction* (pp. 166–185). Newbury Park: Sage.

Hare-Mustin, R.T. (1994). Discourses in the mirrored room: A postmodern analysis of therapy. *Family Process 33*, 19–35.

Hartman, A., & Laird, J. (1998). Moral and ethical issues in working with lesbians and gay men. *Families in Society 79*, 263–276.

Hines Moore, P., Preto Garcia, N., McGoldrick, M., Almeida, R., & Weltman, S. (1999). Culture and the family life cycle. In B. Carter & M. McGoldrick (Eds.), *The expanded family life cycle: Individual, family, and social perspectives* (3rd ed.) (pp. 69–87). Boston: Allyn & Bacon.

Illich, I. (1977). Disabling professions. In I. Illich (Ed.), *Disabling professions* (pp. 11–39). London: Marion Boyars.

Kimelman, E.C. (1985). *No quiet place: Review committee on Indian and Metis adoptions and placements.* Winnipeg: Manitoba Department of Community Services.

Kravetz, D. (2002). Social work practice with women. In A.T. Morales & B.W. Sheafor (Eds.), *The many faces of social work clients* (pp. 17–41). Boston: Allyn & Bacon.

Margolin, L. (1997). *Under the cover of kindness: The invention of social work.* Charlottesville: University Press of Virginia.

McCollum, E.E., & Russell, C.S. (1992). Mother-blaming in family therapy: An empirical investigation. *American Journal of Family Therapy 20*, 71–77.

McGoldrick, M. (Ed.). (1998). *Re-visioning family therapy: Race, culture, and gender in clinical practice.* New York: Guilford.

Payne, H. (2000). Introduction. In H. Payne & B.G. Littlechild (Eds.), *Ethical practice and the abuse of power in social responsibility: Leave no stone unturned* (pp. 7–15). London: Jessica Kingsley.

Shera, W., & Page, J. (1995). Creating more effective human service organizations through strategies of empowerment. *Administration and Social Work 19*, 1–15.

Simon, R. (1985). A frog's eye view of the world. *The Family Therapy Networker 9*(3), 32–37, 41–43.

Van Den Bergh, N. (1995a). *Feminist practice in the 21ˢᵗ century.* Washington: NASW Press.

    _____. (1995b). Feminist social work practice: Where have we been … where are we going? In N. Van Den Bergh (Ed.), *Feminist practice in the 21ˢᵗ century* (pp. xi–xxxix). Washington: NASW Press.

Waldegrave, C. (1998). The challenges of culture to psychology and postmodern thinking. In M. McGoldrick (Ed.), *Re-visioning family therapy: Race, culture, and gender in clinical practice* (pp. 404–413). New York: Guilford.

Wedenoja, M. (1991). Mothers are not to blame: Confronting cultural bias in the area of serious mental illness. In M. Bricker-Jenkins, N. Hooyman, & N. Gottlieb (Eds.), *Feminist practice in social work settings* (pp. 179–196). Newbury Park: Sage.

Wilford, G., & Hetherington, R. (1997). *Families ask for help: Parental perceptions of child welfare and child protection services in an Anglo-German study.* Unpublished report, Centre for Comparative Social Work Studies, Brunel University, London.

Wilson, A., & Beresford, P. (2000). Surviving an abusive system. In H. Payne & B.G. Littlechild (Eds.), *Ethical practice and the abuse of power in social responsibility: Leave no stone unturned* (pp. 145–174). London: Jessica Kingsley.

Child Protective Services

Anderson, K. (1998). A Canadian child welfare agency for urban Natives: The clients speak. *Child Welfare 77*, 441–460.

Baistow, K., Hetherington, R., Spriggs, A., & Yelloly, M. (1996). *Parents speaking: Anglo–French perceptions of child welfare interventions: A preliminary report.* Unpublished report, Centre for Comparative Social Work Studies, Brunel University, London.

Callahan, M., & Lumb, C. (1994). My cheque and my children: The long road to empowerment in child welfare. *Child Welfare 74*, 795–819.

Drake, B. (1994). Relationship competencies in child welfare services. *Social Work 39*, 595–601.

McCallum, S. (1995). *Safe families: A model of child protection intervention based on parental voice and wisdom.* DSW dissertation, Wilfrid Laurier University, Waterloo.

McCurdy, K., & Jones, E. (2000). *Supporting families: Lessons from the field.* Thousand Oaks: Sage Publications.

Wilford , G., & Hetherington, R. (1997). *Families ask for help: Parental perceptions of child welfare and child protection services in an Anglo-German study.* Unpublished report, Centre for Comparative Social Work Studies, Brunel University, London.

Winefield, H.R., & Barlow, J.A. (1995). Child and worker satisfaction in a child protection agency. *Child Abuse & Neglect 19*, 897–905.

Children's Mental Health

Brannan, A.M., Sonnichsen, S.E., & Helfinger, C.A. (1996). Measuring satisfaction with children's mental health services: Validity and reliability of the satisfaction scales. *Evaluation and Program Planning 19*, 131–141.

Byalin, K. (1993). Assessing parental satisfaction with children's mental health services: A pilot study. *Evaluation and Program Planning 16*, 69–72.

Carr, A., McDonnell, D., & Owen, P. (1994). Audit and family systems consultation: Evaluation of practice at a child and family centre. *Journal of Family Therapy 16*, 143–157.

Carscaddon, D.M., George, M., & Wells, G. (1990). Rural community mental health consumer satisfaction and psychiatric symptoms. *Community Mental Health Journal 26*, 309–318.

Charlop, M.H., Parrish, J.M., Fenton, L.R., & Cataldo, M.F. (1987). Evaluation of hospital-based outpatient pediatric psychology services. *Journal of Pediatric Psychology 12*, 485–503.

Coady, N., & Hayward, K. (1998). *A study of the Reconnecting Youth Project: Documenting a collaborative inter-agency process of program development and client views of the process and outcome of service.* Waterloo: Faculty of Social Work, Wilfrid Laurier University.

DeChillo, N. (1993). Collaboration between social workers and families of patients with mental illness. *Families in Society 74*, 104–115.

Eppel, A.B., Fuyarchuk, C., Phelps, D., & Tersigni-Phelan, A. (1991). A comprehensive and practical quality assurance program for community mental health services. *Canadian Journal of Psychiatry 36*, 102–106.

Fairchild, H.H., & Wright, C. (1984). A social-ecological assessment and feedback intervention of an adolescent treatment agency. *Adolescence XIX*, 263–275.

Fiester, A.R. (1978). The access system: A procedure for evaluating children's services at community mental health center. *Community Mental Health Journal 14*, 224–232.

Garland, A.E., & Besinger, B.A. (1996). Adolescents' perceptions of outpatient mental health services. *Journal of Child and Family Studies 5*, 355–375.

Godley, S.H., Fiedler, E.M., & Funk, R.R. (1998). Consumer satisfaction of parents and their children with child/adolescent mental health services. *Evaluation and Program Planning 21*, 31–45.

Johnson, H.C., Cournoyer, D.E., & Bond, B.M. (1995). Professional ethics and parents as consumers: How well are we doing? *Families in Society 76*, 408–420.

Kirchner, J.H. (1981). Patient feedback on satisfaction with direct services received at a community mental health center: A two-year study. *Psychotherapy: Theory, Research and Practice 18*, 359–364.

Kotsopoulos, S., Elwood, S., & Oke, L. (1989). Parent satisfaction in a child psychiatric service. *Canadian Journal of Psychiatry 34*, 530–533.

Lishman, J. (1978). A clash in perspective? A study of worker and client perceptions of social work. *British Journal of Social Work 8*, 301–311.

Plante, T.G., Couchman, C.E., & Hoffman, C.A. (1998). Measuring treatment outcome and client satisfaction among children and families: A case report. *Professional Psychology: Research and Practice 29*, 52–55.

Shapiro, J.P., Welker, C.J., & Jacobson, B.J. (1997). The Youth Client Satisfaction Questionnaire: Development, construct validation, and factor structure. *Journal of Clinical Child Psychology 26*, 87–98.

Stallard, P. (1995). Parental satisfaction with intervention: Differences between respondents to a postal questionnaire. *British Journal of Clinical Psychology 34*, 397–405.

Stallard, P., Hudson, J., & Davis, B. (1992). Consumer evaluation in practice. *Journal of Community and Applied Social Psychology 2*, 291–295.

Stuntzner-Gibson, D., Koren, P.E., & DeChillo, N. (1995). The Youth Satisfaction Questionnaire: What kids think of services. *Families in Society 76*, 616–624.

Psychotherapy

Bachelor, A. (1995). Clients' perception of the therapeutic alliance: A qualitative analysis. *Journal of Counseling Psychology 42*, 323–337.

Bennun, I., Hahlweg, K., Schindler, L., & Langlotz, M. (1986). Therapist's and client's perceptions in behaviour therapy: The development and cross-cultural analysis of an assessment instrument. *British Journal of Medical Psychology 59*, 275–283.

Bischoff, R.J., & McBride, A. (1996). Client perceptions of couples and family therapy. *American Journal of Family Therapy 24*, 117–128.

Bowman, L., & Fine, M. (2000). Client perceptions of couples' therapy: Helpful and unhelpful aspects. *American Journal of Family Therapy 28*, 295–310.

Cohen, M.B. (1998). Perceptions of power in client/worker relationships. *Families in Society 79*, 433–442.

Elliott, R., & Shapiro, D.A. (1992). Client and therapist as analysts of significant events. In S.G. Toukmanian & D.L. Rennie (Eds.), *Psychotherapy process research: Paradigmatic and narrative approaches* (pp. 163–186). London: Sage Publications.

Johnson, H.C., Cournoyer, D.E., & Bond, B.M. (1995). Professional ethics and parents as consumers: How well are we doing? *Families in Society 76*, 408–420.

Kuehl, B., Newfield, N.A., & Joanning, H. (1990). A client-based description of family therapy. *Journal of Family Psychology 3*, 310–321.

Lietaer, G. (1992). Helping and hindering processes in client-centered/experiential psychotherapy. In S.G. Toukmanian & D.L. Rennie (Eds.), *Psychotherapy process research: Paradigmatic and narrative approaches* (pp. 134–162). London: Sage Publications.

Llewelyn, S.P., Elliott, R., Shapiro, D.A., Hardy, G., & Firth-Cozens, J. (1988). Client perceptions of significant events in prescriptive and exploratory periods of individual therapy. *British Journal of Clinical Psychology 27*, 105–114.

Maluccio, A.N. (1979). *Interpersonal helping as viewed by clients and social workers.* New York: The Free Press.

Mayer, J.E., & Timms, N. (1970). *The client speaks: Working class impressions of casework.* New York: Atherton.

McConnell, R., & Sim, A.J. (2000). Evaluating an innovative counselling service for children of divorce. *British Journal of Guidance and Counselling 28*, 75–86.

Newfield, N.A., Joanning, H.P., Kuehl, B.P., & Quinn, W.H. (1991). We can tell you about "Psychos" and "Shrinks": An ethnography of the family therapy or adolescent drug abuse. In T.C. Todd & M.D. Selekman (Eds.), *Family therapy approaches with adolescent substance abusers* (pp. 277–310). Boston: Allyn & Bacon.

Rennie, D.L. (1994). Clients' accounts of resistance in counselling: A qualitative analysis. *Canadian Journal of Counselling 28*, 43–57.

Sells, S.P., Smith, T.E., Coe, M.J., Yoshioka, M., & Robbins, J. (1994). An ethnography of couple and therapist experiences in reflecting team practice. *Journal of Marital and Family Therapy 20*, 247–266.

Shilts, L., & Knapik-Esposito, M. (1993). Playback of the therapeutic process: He said, she said, they said. *Journal of Systemic Therapy 12*, 41–54.

Smith, T.E., Sells, S.P., & Clevenger, T. (1994). Ethnographic content analysis of couple and therapist perceptions in a reflecting team setting. *Journal of Marital and Family Therapy 20*, 267–286.

Smith, T.E., Yoshioka, M., & Winton, M. (1993). A qualitative understanding of reflecting teams I: Client perspectives. *Journal of Systemic Therapies 12*, 28–43.

Stith, S.M., Rosen, K.H., McCollum, E.E., Coleman, J.U., & Herman, S.A. (1996). The voices of children: Preadolescent children's experiences in family therapy. *Journal of Marital and Family Therapy 22*, 69–86.

Telfair, J., & Gardner, M.M. (2000). Adolescents with sickle cell disease: Determinants of support group attendance and satisfaction. *Health and Social Work 25*, 43–50.

van Ryn, E., & Fine, M. (1997). Client perceptions of collaborative meaning-making in couples' therapy. *Journal of Collaborative Therapies 5*, 22–29.

Wark, L. (1994). Client voice: A study of client couples' and their therapists' perspectives on therapeutic change. *Journal of Feminist Family Therapy 6*, 21–39.

Chapter 17

A Community Approach to Combating Racism

Roopchand Seebaran
School of Social work and Family Studies
University of British Columbia

Over the last few years, the United Nations has recognized Canada as one of the best countries in the world in which to live. This has been due to a number factors, including the size and richness of our physical environment, the potential of our natural resources, the quality of life that our citizens enjoy, the nature of our social and economic policies, and the multicultural profile of our population.

Despite these many attributes, widespread racism still exists at a variety of levels in our society. Across the country, the news media regularly report incidents of racism in schools, at the workplace, and in the community. To be sure, the existence of racist attitudes and behaviours in our society is one of the most critical issues confronting us today. It is imperative, therefore, that all levels of our government, the institutions in our society, local communities, and individual citizens convey a clear message and take appropriate action to indicate that racism is unacceptable.

To some extent, this is already being done. We do have existing legislation, such as the Canadian constitution and the *Canadian Charter of Rights and Freedoms*, which prohibit discrimination on the basis of race. Some of our institutions, agencies, and organizations are taking action to become more inclusive. Local communities do, from time to time, take a stand and bring to public attention people who are promoting hate activity. Funding bodies, including government, allocate resources to combat racism in schools or in specific communities. As well, many citizens make individual efforts against the racist incidents that they encounter.

While these efforts are to be applauded and encouraged, racism is not being dealt with in the consistent, systematic, and vigorous manner that the problem requires. It is argued here that the elimination of racism is primarily the responsibility of government and our various societal institutions, and this chapter will focus on the presentation of a community-based approach through which this responsibility could be effectively carried out. It should be noted that the conceptual model being presented draws from the findings of a recent study co-conducted by this author and Susan Johnston (Seebaran & Johnston, 2001). That study focused on an examination of the impacts of initiatives by organizations that had received government grants to combat racism in their local communities.

The content of this chapter includes a rationale for initiatives to combat racism; the components of a community-based model of intervention; identification of some barriers and obstacles in implementing the model; some suggested outcome measures for determining the impact of anti-racism programs; and implications for social work in terms of professional education and training of students for anti-oppressive practice.

RATIONALE FOR INITIATIVES TO COMBAT RACISM

A strategic approach to the elimination of racism in Canada must acknowledge and be responsive to at least the following:

- Given our projected domestic population and demographic trends, it is obvious that Canada will require an open door policy to many new immigrants from around the world for a considerable period. This will lead to greater diversity in our population in terms of race, ethnicity, and culture. We know from current and past experience that greater cultural and ethnic diversity in the population has the potential to increase racism.
- Racism toward a person, group, or community is an illegal act and a violation of an individual's human rights. While the existence of legislation to prohibit discrimination is a necessary measure in our society, it is not sufficient. To be effective, there must also be mechanisms for monitoring and enforcement.
- Racism is abuse. Whether its impact is physical, emotional, or psychological, there is often enormous damage to an individual's self-identity and self-worth.
- Racism leads to various forms of exclusion, which can have very serious negative consequences for the targeted person or group.

For example, social exclusion can lead to a lack of participation in community activities and in society at large, political marginalization, denial of a variety of entitlements and services, basic physical insecurity, and emotional disorders.

- Racism undermines the social, economic, political, cultural, and spiritual fabric of our society. It causes the targeted person to feel inferior and diminishes his or her participation and productivity in society. Thus, racism is a blight on our national well-being.
- Racism will not disappear if we simply deny its existence or avoid addressing it.
- The wide diversity in Canadian society provides us with an opportunity to demonstrate that it can be successfully embraced in the drive toward social inclusion. We have an opportunity to be a global leader in the area of diversity and nation building.
- Over the last few decades, governments and community organizations have made many initiatives to combat racism. However, it still exists in both overt and subtle forms at the individual, institutional, and systemic levels. This, indeed, can be discouraging. But even if it is impossible to eliminate racism entirely, governments and our societal institutions need to constantly convey, in both public policy and visible actions, that racism is not acceptable in our society. We need to create a culture in our communities that sends a clear message that racism will not be tolerated.
- As some communities have already demonstrated, action at the local geographic level can be very effective. Consider, for example, the role played by citizens of Kelowna, British Columbia, in addressing racism (B.C. Ministry Responsible for Multiculturalism and Immigration, 1998b). Charles Scott, a minister in the anti-Semitic Church of the Aryan Nations, moved into the community in 1995 and began promoting hate through letter writing, street preaching, and Internet messages. When citizens complained to the police, they were advised that very little could be done until Scott actually broke the law. Determined not to ignore the issue, local citizens and organizations formed a community coalition and took up the challenge to fight racism and to rid their community of Scott. In the beginning, most of the community were silent on the issue. The community coalition persisted, however, and soon they were able to attract the involvement of the wider community. A local businessman who owned a printing establishment printed material against racism free of charge; the mayor and the local MLA became involved; and the media began

to focus on the issue. Gradually, more concerned citizens became involved. Teens in the community organized a dance, "Rock against Racism." Within months of his arrival in Kelowna, Charles Scott left. Observers concluded that it was the concerned people of the community who ran him out.

A COMMUNITY-BASED MODEL FOR ADDRESSING RACISM

The following model is premised on the assumption that the task of addressing racism in our society is the responsibility of each of its citizens every day, every year, year after year. And, further, it is the government's responsibility to facilitate this process and to provide the necessary resources to do so, not on an ad hoc or project basis but as an ongoing and continuing role.

The principles inherent in this model are congruent with the philosophy and practice approaches offered by other authors on a variety of related themes. See, for example, Kretzman and McKnight (1993) on asset-based community mobilization; Mattessich and Monsey (1997, pp. 83–89), Nyden (1997), and Jason (1997) on community building; Ife (1995), Berlin (1997), and Nozick (1992) on community development; and Roseland (1997, 1998) on building sustainable communities.

The model assumes that attempts to effectively address racism must occur simultaneously at the individual, institutional, and systemic levels. To focus on one level and ignore the others will, at best, achieve change that is temporary and fragile. The model consists of the following principles and components:

- declared acknowledgement and commitment by government that it has a continuing responsibility for addressing racism
- focus on local geographic communities
- collaboration between government and the local community
- continuity of focus and funding
- comprehensiveness of the approach
- use of a community development strategy
- placing value on the utility and impact of ceremonies and celebrations

Government's Declared Acknowledgement of and Commitment to the Responsibility

Implementation of the above model requires the government's clear acknowledgement of and commitment to its responsibility to address racism in society. This commitment must be expressed both in policy and practice.

The commitment must be reflected in resource allocation to communities and in the role of government staff in serving communities. Government and its agencies must be seen not only as a funding source but also as partners with a joint responsibility for addressing racism and building healthy local communities. In this model, the responsibility is not placed on community agencies and organizations to develop proposals for funding to combat racism. Rather, the government sees itself as having responsibility to engage the local community, not individual agencies, to develop plans and processes to address racism.

Focus on the Local Geographic Community

The usual current practice and procedure sees community agencies developing proposals for funding to address racism in their local communities. In the recommended model, funding would not be granted to local agencies but to the local community. Funding would be allocated in order to encourage and facilitate structures to address racism that are community-based and community-directed. These structures would have broad representation from the community, including local community organizations, diverse cultural groups, and service-providing agencies. A key objective would be the establishment of a local community-wide committee that would be responsible for the following: providing community leadership and taking initiatives to promote positive intergroup relations; planning events to value and celebrate the existing diversity in their community; developing structures, such as a community response team, to deal with incidents or potential incidents of racism; and monitoring the impact of anti-racist programs.

Collaboration between Government and the Local Community

Neither government nor local communities can deal effectively with racism by themselves. This is at once an individual, institutional, community, societal, and government responsibility. Therefore, addressing racism in a given community should be a partnership between government, community agencies and institutions, and the local community.

It should not be up to communities alone to identify issues relating to racism that need addressing. There is an equal onus on governments to monitor geographic areas in their jurisdictions that need to be targeted for action, and to engage the local communities in the task of combating racism.

Continuity of Focus and Funding

The model advocated here suggests that in order to effectively address racism, there must be sustained funding and allocation of adequate resources.

Short-term or "one-off" funding that may have only a temporary positive impact often results in despair and frustration at the local community level. This is particularly tragic when positive momentum developed in a local community cannot be sustained because funding is discontinued. Adequate resources over an extended period are critical for positive impact in addressing racism. Governments should see it as their ongoing responsibility to build the capacities of local communities to deal with racism. This cannot be done with time-limited funding on an ad-hoc or project basis.

Comprehensiveness of the Approach

Efforts and initiatives aimed at addressing racism should be comprehensive. They should be focused on bringing about change in several areas in the local community, such as curricula in public schools, policies in the workplace, hiring practices, reporting by the media, the justice system, the health system, arts and culture, recreation and sports, and official community events.

As far as possible, there should be an emphasis on planning and implementing a combination of programs and initiatives that are interrelated and grounded in a community vision rather than initiatives that are reactive, separate, isolated, and fragmented.

Use of a Community Development Strategy

The successful implementation of this model requires the knowledge and skills to facilitate a community development strategy and process in local communities. Community development relies on local initiative in partnership with government to solve problems and build community. Community development assumes that the local community is its greatest resource in its own development.

Local communities cannot address the issue of racism by relying solely on volunteers; staff assistance is critical for success. Some communities may already have the personnel with the knowledge and skills to perform the community development role, and may require only the funding resources to initiate or sustain the process. Other communities may have staff who are keen to carry out this role, but they may need initial and ongoing training in community development. In either case, this type of staff support is essential, especially in communities where the volunteers are actually staff in local community agencies who are already heavily occupied with their other agency duties. In implementing this approach, there would be added value in providing community development training, not only for staff but also for community volunteers.

Placing Value on the Utility and Impact of Ceremonies and Celebrations

Ceremonies and celebrations have enormous power to build community. These events provide opportunities for citizens to get to know one another. They have the potential to raise awareness and increase understanding about the different cultures in the community. What might appear on the surface to be just food, song, and dance is indeed much more. These are opportunities that citizens use to develop relationships that have undeniable value in celebrating diversity and building community. One effective way to address racism is to continuously provide opportunities to celebrate our diversity and to help in building a community culture where racism is not acceptable.

OBSTACLES AND BARRIERS TO IMPLEMENTATION

It is important to note that the implementation of the recommended approach described earlier will face a number of barriers and obstacles. In the study referred to earlier (Seebaran & Johnston, 2001), study participants identified several factors as barriers to achieving the fullest possible impact from programs or projects to address racism. The following obstacles were most frequently mentioned:

- Negative attitudes by members of the dominant cultural groups toward minority and visible minority groups, including Aboriginal and First Nations
- Lack of local community acknowledgement that racism is an issue in their community, and a corresponding low level of community commitment to address it
- The existence of systemic and institutionalized racism in the community as observed, for example, in the education system, health care, law enforcement, justice system, employment, and the media
- The government's flawed conceptualization in how it views racism and how it organizes itself to deal with the problem; the practice of racism is a violation of this country's existing legislation such as the Canadian constitution and the Canadian Charter of Rights, so it should be addressed by the ministry responsible for upholding the laws of the land, the ministry responsible for justice and the safety of citizens. This responsibility is appropriately in the Ministry of the Attorney General at the provincial and territorial levels. To assign this responsibility to a ministry or division of multiculturalism is to send a message that racism is not a violation of existing laws but a

multicultural issue. The practice of racism should be addressed in the same way that we deal with people who contravene the laws of the land. This is a continuing and ongoing government responsibility in partnership with the community, and should not be dealt with on a project basis.

- Lack of competency in knowledge and skills on the part of staff whose designated roles include responsibilities related to combating racism in local communities
- The existence of internalized racism; one needs to be aware that many visible-minority communities and members of these communities feel negative toward themselves
- Fragmentation, separation, and lack of communication between different cultural groups in the local community. There is distancing and disengagement between groups. In several communities, there is conspicuous hostility between minority groups.
- Funding and resource allocation patterns and policies. There is a distinct view that government funding policies and practices maintain the status quo. Funding is a function of government's priorities and is often cut just when communities are developing a momentum that will have an impact on addressing racism.
- Potential negative impact of an irresponsible media. Clearly, the media can fuel racism depending on how they portray minority groups and their members. Misrepresentation of facts and an inappropriate focus on ethnicity or cultural background instead of on the issue at hand can reinforce racist attitudes and behaviours.
- Lack of appropriate government action on a range of public policy issues, for example, matters relating to Aboriginal self-government, taxation policies, employment equity policies, immigration and refugee policies, and so on. These issues in the wider societal context are inextricably connected to negative attitudes and behaviours that citizens have toward people of a different ethnocultural background.
- Lack of awareness among citizens at large about the range of diverse cultural groups in the population, and the contributions they have made and are making to the social, economic, and cultural development of the country. A key factor in the degree of ignorance about different groups in the population is the exclusion of this type of information in curricula in our public schools. The most tragic example of this deficiency is the dearth of information in our public education system about Aboriginal peoples, their history, and their special rights.

SOME MEASURES FOR ASSESSING THE IMPACT OF ANTI-RACISM PROGRAMS IN LOCAL COMMUNITIES

This section is included because of the author's view that local communities could find it useful to know the type of data they might collect and the analyses they might undertake. The following list of items could serve as some measures for determining outcomes of anti-racism programs in local communities.

Understanding and Awareness
- residents' increased knowledge and understanding about other cultures and the diversity in their community
- increased awareness of and sensitivity toward people from a different culture

Attitude and Behaviour
- improved positive attitudes, beliefs, and views about people of a different culture
- improved positive behaviour toward people of a different culture
- improved positive behaviour against discrimination and incidents of racism

Participation
- increase in the number of people from different cultural groups participating in multicultural activities and events
- increase in the number of different cultural groups involved in the planning and implementation of multicultural activities and events
- increase in the number of members of different cultural groups who attend social, recreational, cultural, and political activities in the community
- increase in the number of informal social groups—for example, in schools—comprising members of different ethnocultural groups
- increase in the number of members of the wider community who participate in the celebrations and festivals of cultural groups that are different from their own

Institutional Change
- increase in the number of institutions and organizations in the community that have policy or mission statements that value diversity

- increase in the number of institutions and organizations in the community that reflect the diversity of the community at all levels in the organization, including governance structure, staff profile, programs, and services
- increase in the number of institutions and organizations in the community that include the range of diversity in their community in the planning, implementation, and evaluation of their policies, procedures, and services
- increase in the number of people from different cultural groups who are employed by local businesses in the community
- increase in the number of businesses that employ people from different ethnocultural backgrounds

Incidents of Discrimination and Racism
- reduction in the number of incidents of discrimination and racism as indicated by statistical records or self-reports
- reduction in number of incidents of discrimination and racism either experienced or observed by members of different ethnocultural minority groups in the community

Media
- more balanced and less biased reporting in articles and stories on minority cultural groups
- more reporting of the positive contributions made by different cultural groups in the community
- more letters to the editor that value diversity and condemn racism
- more balanced portrayal and coverage of different cultural events and celebrations
- more editorials that reflect the value and benefits of diversity

Public Displays and Promotional Materials
- more murals, artwork, posters, and community signs and symbols that reflect and celebrate diversity
- increase in the number of public and private agencies that have promotional material, signs, and symbols that reflect and welcome diversity

Formal Community Leaders
- civic and community leaders of different cultural groups acknowledge and make commitments to address racism

- leaders of different cultural groups are invited to public/official functions
- leaders of different cultural groups attend official functions
- civic and public officials are invited to and attend events and functions of different cultural groups

Public Community-wide Facilities and Amenities
- are available for people from different cultural groups
- are accessible to everyone
- are utilized by people from different cultural groups in the community
- provide opportunities for the participation of all cultural groups

Local Public Schools
- increase in the number of students of different cultural backgrounds who mix and mingle with each other
- fewer numbers of students who, for safety reasons, stay in cliques that are based on a common ethnicity or culture
- decrease in the number of incidents of bullying that are perpetrated as a consequence of racist attitudes
- decrease in the number of students who feel vulnerable to bullying or harassment because of their ethnicity or cultural backgrounds
- increase in the extent to which diversity is reflected in the operation and administration of the school, such as staff composition, student projects, artwork, cafeteria menu, and school events and celebrations
- increase in the extent to which the formal and informal school curricula reflect the diversity in community, for example, teaching assistants from Aboriginal and other cultural communities
- the membership of parent advisory committees (PAC) reflects an increase in number of members from diverse cultural groups
- increase in the participation rate of members of visible minorities in PAC events and other school activities

Multicultural and Intercultural Events and Celebrations
- increase in the number of members of different cultural groups that are involved in planning and organizing multicultural and intercultural events and celebrations at different locations such as schools, art galleries, civic centres, community parks, and so on
- increase in the number of community-wide events and activities aimed at providing opportunities for citizens to celebrate the diversity in their community, or aimed at healing wounds and hurts caused by racism

- increase in the number of community awareness and training events and activities that provide opportunities for community members to increase their understanding and awareness of the different cultural groups in their community

Community Building and Response Team
- the community has a body that takes responsibility for community building and for responding to incidents, or potential incidents, of racism
- the community has structures and mechanisms for monitoring issues related to racial conflict and takes action to mediate or alleviate such conflict

Research at the Community Level
Research is carried out in the community to determine:

- the level of acceptance of different cultural groups in the community
- the extent to which community service organizations are inclusive
- the level of consumer satisfaction regarding culturally responsive services

Level of Safety
- fewer citizens feel vulnerable to discrimination and racism
- members of ethnocultural minority groups feel a greater sense of safety from verbal, physical, or emotional abuse resulting from racist attitudes and behaviour on the part of other members of the community
- decrease in the number of citizens who feel unsafe in their workplaces, or in public places, as a result of their ethnicity or cultural background

IMPLICATIONS FOR SOCIAL WORK EDUCATION

It is this author's position that schools of social work have a responsibility to prepare their graduates for anti-oppressive practice. Clearly, this includes preparation for anti-racist practice that focuses on working with communities to achieve greater social justice and to eradicate oppression. This is consistent with the social work education task of providing opportunities for students to acquire the requisite knowledge and skills for working toward social change.

There are a variety of ways in which schools might prepare students for this type of practice (George, Shera, & Tsang, 1998), and some are offered here as examples of what could be done.

Identifying the School Community as a Target of Intervention and Learning
To practise what they preach, schools could focus on the school community itself as a laboratory for action and learning regarding anti-racism practice. This would require an assessment of the administration component of the school. The school's policies, procedures, and practices could be examined to determine the extent to which they reflect and acknowledge cultural diversity. Analysis would focus on the extent to which, and in what areas, the school is practising institutional or systemic racism. Areas for analysis could include student recruitment and application procedures, admission criteria, faculty recruitment and criteria for appointment, the range of field practicum agencies and criteria for their selection, curriculum content, pedagogical approaches, practices and criteria for grading students' assignments, and so on.

Of critical significance here is the demonstration of the school's commitment to its values about diversity, the building of its credibility about its stated mission, and its accountability to the community it serves. Thus, it would be important for the school to establish structures and processes, such as committees or working groups, that involve the various components of the school community, including students, field agencies, and other constituencies to which the school relates. These structures would be used to develop and implement objectives in the area of diversity. Moreover, this type of activity would be ongoing rather than opportunistic, such as when the school is seeking accreditation.

Addressing Incidents of Racism at the School and at Field Agencies
The school must recognize that the subtle and overt racism in the wider society will be reflected in the school and the university. Incidents of racism will occur in the classroom and at the field agencies where students carry out their practica. Although individual faculty members and field supervisors have a responsibility to deal with such incidents, many of them do not feel sufficiently competent to do so. It is important to recognize that the school has an institutional responsibility to insure that individual faculty members and field supervisors develop the relevant knowledge and skills to deal effectively with racism in the classroom and the school community. In doing so, the school will be providing opportunities for its students to learn about how they themselves could deal with racism in their field agencies, in the school itself, and in their future practice.

Engaging in Research with Local Communities
In keeping with one of the primary roles of the university, the school could carry out research, including action research, in collaboration with local

communities to assist in the development of knowledge and models of intervention for combating racism. It could consider the collection of relevant data about what communities have done and are doing to address racism. This could include tools and instruments for measuring impact and outcomes of anti-racism programs and initiatives.

Developing Curriculum and Teaching Materials

A core responsibility of any school is the development of curriculum. Focusing on the school as a community for anti-racist practice, and engaging in research on this issue with local communities could provide a wealth of data that could enhance the school's ability to continually develop and update curriculum and teaching materials in the area of anti-racist practice.

Focusing on Experiential Learning

One way to adequately prepare students for anti-oppressive practice is to provide them with an experience of how this can be done. An ideal time and location for this experience is during their education and training at the school of social work itself. By engaging in the above activities, students at the school could actually have an experience of how anti-racism practice could be carried out at the community level.

CONCLUSION

This chapter has presented a conceptual model for a community-based approach to combating racism. It is argued that government must take ultimate responsibility for the task of addressing racism, and that it can effectively do so by using a community development strategy in collaboration with local communities. To have sustained impact on racism, government must see its role as ongoing, and local communities must be provided with adequate funding and other appropriate resources on a continuous rather than an ad hoc basis. Barriers to implementation of the model have been presented, along with some measures for assessing the impact and outcomes of anti-racism programs in local communities.

Whether or not the various levels of government commit themselves to the responsibility described earlier, social work as a profession has a significant role to play in working toward the elimination of racism and the various forms of oppression that exist in our society. The profession of social work encompasses this role because of its stated mission, which, variously described, is concerned with the elimination of oppression, the promotion of social justice, and the building of inclusive communities.

Locally, nationally, and globally, communities everywhere bear witness to the fact that racism and oppression are alive and well. Social work, as a profession that is committed to social change, must be conspicuously visible in its efforts to address these problems at the individual and the broader societal level. If social work is to survive as a credible profession, it must demonstrate by its actions and achievements that it is equal to its stated mission. For far too long, its mission has been ambitious and its achievements, by comparison, scant.

It is suggested that schools of social work have a critical role to play in preparing their graduates for anti-oppressive practice. Preparation for such practice requires that schools provide opportunities for their graduates to acquire the pertinent attitudes, knowledge, and skills to progressively advocate for social change, and to work effectively with communities in addressing social issues. Some ideas as to how this preparation for practice might be accomplished include: a focus on the school community as a target of intervention and learning about anti-racism; dealing with incidents of racism in the school and the field agencies; collaboration with local communities in joint research initiatives; the development of curriculum and teaching materials related to anti-racism practice; and a focus on experiential learning.

Providing students with opportunities to use the community-based approach to address racism presented in this chapter can be of enormous value not only in the education of students for anti-oppressive practice but also for social work practice in general.

REFERENCES

B.C. Ministry Responsible for Multiculturalism and Immigration. (1998a). *The many faces of Mission Hill Elementary.* Video, 10:35 minutes, English. Vernon: Kla How Ya Communications.

_____. (1998b). *The courage to stand.* Video, 27:30 minutes, English. Kelowna: CFMT Television.

Berlin, S. (1997). *Ways we live: Exploring community.* Gabriola Island: New Society Publishers.

Fleras, A., & Elliott, J.L. (2002). *Engaging diversity: Multiculturalism in Canada.* Toronto: Nelson Thomson Learning.

George, U., Shera, W., & Tsang, A.K.T. (1998). Responding to diversity in organizational life: The case of a faculty of social work. *International Journal of Inclusive Education* 2(1), 147–161.

Government of Canada. (1981a). The Canadian constitution.

_____. (1981b). The Canadian Charter of Rights and Freedoms.

Graveline, F.J. (1998). *Circle works: Transforming Eurocentric consciousness*. Halifax: Fernwood.

Green, J.W. (1999). *Cultural awareness in the human services: A multi-ethnic approach* (3rd ed.). Needham Heights: Allyn & Bacon.

Henry, F. (2000). *The colour of democracy: Racism in Canadian society* (2nd ed.). Toronto: Harcourt Brace.

Ife, J. (1995). *Community development: Creating community alternatives—vision, analysis, and practice*. Melbourne: Longman.

Jason, L.A. (1997). *Community building: Values for a sustainable future*. Westport: Pine Forge Press.

Kalbach, M.A., & Kalbach, W.E. (Eds.). (2000). *Perspectives on ethnicity in Canada*. Toronto: Harcourt Canada Ltd.

Klein, E. (1997). Sustainable community indicators: How to measure progress. In M. Roseland (Ed.), *Eco-city dimensions: Healthy communities, healthy planet* (pp. 152–166). Gabriola Island: New Society Publishers.

Kretzman, J.P., & McKnight, J.L. (1993). *Building communities from the inside out*. Chicago: ACTA Publications.

Li, P.S. (Ed.). (1999). *Race and ethnic relations in Canada* (2nd ed.). Don Mills: Oxford University Press Canada.

Mattessich, P., & Monsey, B. (1997). *Community building: What makes it work*. St. Paul: Amherst H. Wilder Foundation.

Nancoo, S.E. (Ed.). (2000). *21st Century Canadian diversity*. Mississauga: Canadian Educators' Press.

Nozick, M. (1992). *No place like home: Building sustainable communities*. Ottawa: Canadian Council on Social Development.

Nyden, P. (1997). *Community building: Social science in action*. Thousand Oaks: Pine Forge Press.

Ratansi-Rodriques, J. (1998). "Multicultural/anti-racism organizational change." United Way of Greater Toronto. Presentation to the Canadian Council for International Cooperation, Diversity in the International Cooperation Sector Workshop, June 1988.

Rivera, F.G., & Erlich, J.L. (1998). *Community organizing in a diverse society* (3rd ed.). Boston: Allyn & Bacon.

Roseland, M. (Ed.). (1997). *Eco-city dimensions: Healthy communities, healthy planet*. Gabriola Island: New Society Publishers.

_____. (Ed.). (1998). *Toward sustainable communities: Resources for citizens and their governments*. Gabriola Island: New Society Publishers.

Saloojee, Anver. (2003). *Social Inclusion, Anti-Racism, and Democratic Citzenship*. Toronto: Laidlaw Foundation.

Seebaran, R.B. (2000). Social policy and ethno-cultural diversity. In S.E. Nancoo (Ed.), *21st century Canadian diversity* (pp. 207–237). Mississauga: Canadian Educators' Press.

Seebaran, R.B., & Johnston, S.P. (1998). *Anti-racism theatre projects for youth*. Vancouver: Community Liaison Division, Ministry Responsible for Multiculturalism and Immigration.

_____. (2001). *Impact of anti-racism programs: A study of three selected communities in B.C.* Vancouver: Ministry of Multiculturalism and Immigration.

Seebaran, R., et al. (1991). Special issue on multiculturalism and social work. *Canadian Social Work Review 8*(2), (entire issue).

Stevens, S.B. (1993). *Community-based programs for a multicultural society.* Winnipeg: Planned Parenthood Manitoba.

Thomas, B. (1984). Principles of anti-racist education. *Currents 2*(3), 21–25.

Wharf, B., & Clague, M. (Eds.). (1997). *Community organizing: Canadian experiences.* Toronto: Oxford University Press.

Other

"Racism No Way" Web site, Conference of Education Systems Chief Executive Officers 2000, <www.racismnoway.com>

Chapter 18

Community Practice in the Internet Age

Steven F. Hick
School of Social Work
Carleton University

The Internet and emerging information and communication technology (ICT)[1] in general has important ramifications for activism and community practice. As a rapidly emerging technology, it is facilitating acceleration in economic globalization and the concentration of power, but at the same time, it is becoming a key tool for community practice that is challenging this concentration of power. In this regard the Internet can be viewed as a double-edged sword.

Who is using the Internet for community practice and activism and how is it being used? What is the impact on anti-oppressive practice and activism, both globally and locally? What dangers does the Internet pose for practitioners and society in terms of the digital divide, isolation, and community building? Does the Internet confer a new potent force that will encourage democracy and empower communities? These are just a few of the questions that researchers and practitioners will need to study and analyze. This chapter will begin to unravel a few of the key issues and build on the existing literature in this area.

This chapter explores what the author sees as the three most important technology-related issues facing community practice today.[2] These were chosen, not because they relate neatly to each other, but because they are today's vital issues. The discussion draws on background research for two recent books entitled *Advocacy and Activism on the Internet* (Hick & McNutt, 2002) and *Human Rights and the Internet* (Hick, Halpin, & Hoskins, 2001) and interviews with Noam Chomsky.

317

The three crucial issues concerning the Internet and community practice are:

1. What is the impact of ICT on conventional social activist and community organizing methods? How does new technology alter or improve traditional community practice?
2. Can you truly have a sense of community on-line? What roles do virtual communities fulfill?
3. How will corporate structures that are increasingly controlling the Internet attempt to suppress its usefulness as a tool for community practice and social activism?[3]

In answering these questions, we must first recognize that communities do not just organize themselves—with or without new technology, it requires people. In all cases, communities need strong leadership and someone on board with the appropriate organizing skills and knowledge. Second, we must consider the nature of group participation on-line, known as "virtual communities." Do they fulfill the same needs as real life communities? Is the Internet a valid "third space" for us to grow a healthy public sphere to support real community, activism, and advocacy? Is it possible to have real community on the Net? Finally, even if the answers to the above questions lead us to accept that there are concrete and useful benefits to using the Internet for community practice, we must analyze and be prepared for corporate structures that are increasingly controlling the Internet and attempting to suppress its capacity for social change.

ON-LINE ORGANIZING: PRACTICE PLUS TECHNOLOGY

Community work represents a central method of traditional social work practice (Lee, 1999; Wharf, 1979; Wharf & Clague, 1997). In this era of globalization, community practice is a key component of anti-oppressive practice. Under this label falls a variety of sub-methods that range from community development and consensus organizing through social planning to social action. Use of the term "community practice" intends to capture a range of strategies and activities undertaken under the rubrics of community organizing, social work advocacy, and social activism—a range wider than that usually intended by the term "community work."

Community practice covers many methodologies and addresses many issues. Rothman (2001) divided community work into three models: locality development, social planning, and social action. Locality development involves developing the capacity of community to meet needs. Social planning is a more research and rationale problem solving approach to community decision making. Social action deals more with empowerment of oppressed communities. Hick has added a fourth model—participatory action research or PAR (Hick, 2002, p. 83). PAR is research directed toward changing structures that promote inequality by the direct participation in knowledge creation by people living in the circumstances (Hick, 1997). Community practice includes these four different models, and extends to any community/ network-oriented change or development strategy rooted in an ethos of solidarity and participation. It includes strategies that may normally be categorized under the work of social movements or as social activism, advocacy, or network organizing.

Community practice using the Internet is referenced by several labels: electronic organizing (Wittig & Schmitz, 1996), netactivism (Schwartz, 1996), e-advocacy (Bennett & Fielding, 1999), cyberactivism (Friess, 1999; Price, 2000), virtual activism (Krause, Stein, & Clark, 1998), and electronic advocacy (Boland, 1998; Fitzgerald & McNutt, 1999; McNutt, 2000). Three themes are common to all these labels: (1) the use of Internet-based technologies; (2) a move away from traditional media approaches, including mass media (television and radio), and toward "new media"; and (3) practices that complement long-established approaches to community work.

A variety of methods that rely on new technology are used in community practice.[4] These technology-based methods are combined with traditional techniques or, at times, used independently. The techniques include:

Table 18.1: TECHNOLOGY-BASED TECHNIQUES

E-mail	On-line petitions
Newsgroups	On-line surveys
Discussion groups or "listservs"	Video conferencing
Web pages	Graphical worlds
Chat rooms	On-line petitions
On-line fundraising	Banner ads
Virtual communities	Targeting and mapping software
Alternative news and information services	Virtual civil disobedience (hacktivism)

Community practice on the Internet is not a radical departure from conventional community practice activities. The same skills and knowledge are required. The Internet introduces new possibilities using technology-based techniques. Nevertheless, these new activities do not fundamentally alter the foundations of community practice. Whether we are on-line or face-to-face, the skill and knowledge of community work is required. The emergence of Internet options has not negated the need for traditional skills and the building of strong communities and relationships.

Extensive use of the Internet for community practice is a recent development, but has already gone through several shifts. Within social work, community organizers were probably the first to extensively use the Internet (some may argue that social policy analysts were also at the forefront). In its early stages of development, the Internet was seen as an appropriate and useful tool for community organizers. In the early period some social workers thought that the Internet would revolutionize their community work, replacing much of what had traditionally taken place in meeting halls and church basements. Over time, social workers using the Internet for community practice found that on-line and traditional organizing needed to merge and operate together, each reinforcing the other. They found that all community organizing efforts have a similar value base and share many processes and techniques. They found that on-line methods added new possibilities, but did not usurp the need for time-honoured methods. All place substantial weight on coordination, communication, information sharing, and education.

The need for community practice on a global scale has never been more important. At this point in history, characterized by the rapid growth of powerful global corporations that are altering relations between people and nations, the need to organize and form global communities of people is essential. Economic globalizing must be met with social, political, and cultural globalizing. The Internet is enabling communities to link together, allowing individuals to join struggles at a distance and forging new global movements, even given the inequities in computing resources, Internet access, and technical knowledge. The same technologies that have helped large corporations organize globally can also assist people to organize globally and insure that people's issues and human rights are part of the global agenda.

The Internet is different from past incorporation of new technology into community practice. The capabilities of the Internet extend beyond that of a communications device, such as the fax or telephone, and beyond broadcast technology such as the television or radio. The Internet is a comprehensive and integrated communications, information, and broadcast network with a global reach. As we reposition our practice toward the technology-based approaches, the differences become more apparent. The link to the local community becomes less of an issue or the community becomes defined differently. We have always discussed non-place communities in the community literature (Lyons, 1987), but organizing within them was rarely mentioned. With the communications capabilities of the Internet, organizers are increasingly finding that organizing people separated by space and time is readily enabled.

The advent of the Internet has spawned the emergence of two developments. First, people are working at a distance and occasionally (or in some cases more frequently) joining in face-to-face meetings or events. The organizing of local committees for the protest against the Free Trade Agreement of the Americas (FTAA) in Quebec City used the Internet to coordinate the coming together of people and groups. In Ottawa, poverty activists use a listserv, called pub-par (short for public participation) to educate and mobilize the public on poverty issues. In other cases, citizens send e-mail letters of protest and support for political prisoners. The second phenomenon is the organization of virtual communities and networked organizations.[5] People, usually disconnected by distance and with limited resources, connect on-line and undertake on-line protest and advocacy actions. For example, a variety of people, groups, and organizations formed a virtual coalition called Jubilee 2000 to fight Third World debt (Hick & McNutt, 2002, p. 129).

At local, national, and international levels, self-help groups, social action groups, coalitions of organizations, and social service user-based advocacy groups are effectively leveraging the Internet to improve services and change policy. For example, the Ontario Coalition against Poverty (<www.ocap.ca>) has successfully used the Internet to communicate their message, influence public opinion, organize demonstrations and petitions, and influence local and provincial government policy. At an international level, the Association for Progressive Communications (<www.apc.org>) has created a global network of civil society organizations committed to enhancing their work for peace, human rights, development, and protection of the environment through effective use of electronic communications. SelfAdvocateNet.com, a provincial-oriented Web site in British Columbia with national and international linkages, (<www.selfadvocatenet.com>) provides a voice for people with intellectual disabilities. They enable people to "speak up and stand up for their rights." On the Web site they share positive experiences through other people's stories and let people know about important upcoming issues. These sample Internet-based organizations illustrate how people, communities, groups, and organizations are networking in new ways at different levels and across different types of oppression.

The virtual space in which these people meet is generally seen as neutral ground where people can participate regardless of class, gender, race, age, (dis)ability, or sexuality. Theoretically, everyone starts off on an equal footing. Proponents argue that this has enabled powerful social action groups to be formed on-line. In many instances, virtual communities come together to connect leaders of existing community organizations to form a kind of supraorganization—one with more power to influence policy and debate. This is true of poverty, anti-racism, environmental anti-globalization, feminist, and human rights groups (Hick & NcNutt, 2002).

Even with these new capabilities, the tie between traditional community practice and on-line community practice remains important. Those efforts that are conducted largely in cyberspace still need a connection in the physical world. Prior organization is needed for any communications medium to work. This means that in order to do any meaningful organization, we will need to do the work of traditional methods. It is, of course, possible to do some or all of that work via the Internet, but much of the work is still within the traditional arena.

The various oppressions in Canadian society organize and perpetuate the social relations of a digital divide. For anti-oppression social workers, the digital divide is an important issue that needs to be addressed. Access to cyberspace is an important concern. There are economic (getting on-line takes money and time), educational (communication here is all done with reading and writing), and cultural (communication is primarily in English) barriers one must overcome to participate. What is often referred to as the digital divide—this clustering of connectivity in the wealthy nations and, in terms of home access, in the more wealthy communities—would seem to severely limit its usefulness as a technique of empowerment or anti-oppressive practice. The digital divide issue is beyond the scope of this chapter, but in order for Internet-dependent community practice methods to advance, the issue must continually be addressed. There are indications that, at least in industrialized countries, access is being developed—Internet cafés, library access, and other public access points are critical to facilitate the participation of those who are least able to participate.

CAN WE HAVE COMMUNITY ON THE INTERNET?

A central aspect of community practice is the development of community relations. People coming together and acting in some manner to improve their situation, and perhaps the situation of others, is key to community practice. Clearly, the majority of communities are of a place-based, face-to-face nature, but increasingly they are existing in virtual space. Known as virtual communities, these non-place-based groupings of people are emerging from all spheres of society and countries. Often they are involved in social action community practice rather than PAR, social planning, or capacity building, but without a doubt a new and at times powerful virtual "public sphere" is emerging. But is it really a community?

The ability to develop a sense of community through the medium of the Internet is necessary for virtual communities to be truly effective. The capabilities of the Internet have proven to be extremely valuable to community practitioners. But if virtual communities are going to succeed, if communities of people are going to come together with shared concerns to act for social change, then it must be possible to develop a sense of community on the Internet.

Identifying what we mean by "a sense of community" is difficult. It is a vague and amorphous term, and we understand little about it in its traditional form. Understanding it in its virtual form is even more complex. Community practitioners will agree that in either its real or virtual form, it does signify a familiar social environment where a sense of belonging develops. Therefore, a group coming together with a sense of community will have strong interpersonal connections and a social environment that builds a feeling of belonging. Given this, what is the effect of being virtual in this social environment?

We should ask two questions: whether technological advances have caused individuals to become more interconnected, and whether these forms of communication have made interpersonal relations superficial and homogenized or provided strong interpersonal connections. Put in another way, are our interactions over the Internet the building blocks of communities? Discussions of the Internet as a form of community and as an area for political and social involvement are split. Proponents argue that the interactivity of on-line participation is different, but it does create a social environment, while critics argue that we are just continuing the trend of more artificial interaction and further the risk of a declining involvement in the real world.

Virtual communities may be providing alternatives for the lost causal meeting places of the past and involvement in civic organizations. The effect of losing the local public "third spaces" has a tremendous effect on our commitment to our community and its affairs. Oldenberg (1989) discusses the great decline in public life over the century: "Available information suggests that we've probably lost half of the casual gathering places that existed at mid-century—places that hosted the easy and the informal, yet socially binding, association that is the bedrock of community life." He also finds that "The average citizen's interest in public or community affairs [has] been aptly described as 'diluted' and 'superficial.' The individual's present relationship to the collective is as empty as it is equitable: community does nothing for them and they do nothing for community" (Oldenberg, 1989, p. 285). For Oldenberg (1989), these third places were vital to the formation of community, and their loss makes the discussion of on-line meeting places all the more important.

Can virtual communities replace these lost "third spaces"? The evidence is not clear. Studies on the social implications of the Internet are few and the results contradictory. Some point toward a decrease in civic participation. Putnam (1995) argues that civic life is collapsing—that Americans aren't joining, as they once did, the groups and clubs that promote trust and co-operation. We are "bowling alone," according to Putman—since 1980, league bowling has dropped 40 per cent. Similarly, using longitudinal data from seventy-three households, Kraut and Lundmark (1998) found that greater use of the Internet is associated with declines in communication with family members and declines in the size of their social circle. Differing evidence in an interesting study of the National Capital FreeNet in Ottawa, which provides free Internet access, found that of the 1,073 users surveyed, people spent less time watching television and more time socializing (outside NCF) (Patrick, 1997 p. 1).

Several conclusions can be drawn from this contradictory evidence. The proliferation of virtual communities may be a reaction to the loss of our physical gathering places and the decline of participation in civic organizations. If "third place" settings are really no more than a physical manifestation of people's desire to associate with those in an area once they get to know them, then there is really no reason why the computer conferencing sites can't be considered third spaces as well, even if the physical manifestation is in a very different form. Or is our involvement in technologically contrived communities furthering or even causing this decline in the real world, continuing a trend begun by other forms of mass media and commercialization? These are a few of the key questions that need to be answered to clearly understand the role of Internet communication in forming social bonds and community relationships.

Community involvement, whether it be on-line or off-line, seems to be an essential part of community practice. Organizations and social movements need roots in communities and, at least to some extent, this connection can be fulfilled through virtual communities. It remains to be seen just how effective these communities will be in the social and political realm. It will be interesting to see whether involvement in on-line activism takes the place of, or inspires more real world involvement.

Clearly, there are significant differences between off-line and on-line communities and each has its strengths and weaknesses. While virtual communities may provide a way to recapture some of the bonds between people that some critics fear we are losing in our society, those connections are still not as valued as those made face-to-face. Clearly, more research is needed in this emerging field.

ACTIVISTS BEWARE: THE CORPORATE AGENDA FOR THE INTERNET

Is there a corporate agenda for the Internet? Will the Internet be a democratizing force with public participation, or will it end up being only a mechanism for corporate propaganda, creating artificial wants, and enabling us to buy things more quickly? These are just a few of the issues that community workers must confront. If individuals and communities do not act quickly to counter the corporate push to control the Internet's future, it will likely take the latter path, due to the balance of forces (Chomsky, 2002, p. viii).

The Internet was a public creation. The Pentagon, the National Science Foundation, universities, and private corporations (usually under government contract) developed the Internet. The World Wide Web was created in an international laboratory, the IAUG Physics laboratory in Geneva. In the early days, the Internet and the World Wide Web were the monopoly of relatively privileged sectors of people with access to computers in universities, government, and research centres. In the academic world it became a useful means of sharing scientific results. In 1995, these largely public creations were then handed over to private corporations—but no one seems to know how this was done (Chomsky, 2001).

The corporate structures that are increasingly controlling the Internet will undoubtedly attempt to control its use for community practice and activist virtual communities. They want the Internet to contribute to profits by focusing our attention on e-commerce or on-line shopping and as a medium for advertising. Virtual shopping malls, banner ads, product information, and on-line ordering are the priorities of commercial firms, not building communities advancing social justice. To the contrary, if social justice-oriented community practice includes challenging economic globalization and the power of large corporations, then commercial interests would likely structure the Internet (if they control it) to limit its use for community work. It is likely that attempts will be made to insure that people are funnelled into commercial pursuits and activities within "public spheres" hampered or made impossible.

Although the future of technology is unpredictable, it is likely that there will be a further corporate takeover (Chomsky, 1995). Heather Menzies (1996, p. 53), in *Whose Brave New World?: The Information Highway and the New Economy*, maintains that government funding directed at furthering the Internet is predominantly directed at commercialization or the "communications-as-commodity model dominating the corporate agenda." To consolidate the model, the business world needs to cut large parts of the Internet out of the public domain altogether, turning it into *Intranets* that are fenced off with firewalls and used exclusively for internal corporate operations. They would also need to control access to the Internet to insure that users are guided to the commercial areas, trapped in e-commerce, advertising, and other profit-making activities. Alternative sites would continue to exist, but finding and accessing them would become progressively more difficult.

Corporations will surely undertake to make it difficult for people to use the Internet in ways that are subversive of concentrated power. Even today, access is largely controlled through a small number of portals or entry points, and major corporations such as AOL TimeWarner control those. Such control will not make it easy for those who want to use the Internet for social activism. Although corporations probably can't make it impossible—the nature of the system is such that it is technologically impossible to block all such use—they can create the conditions whereby it is difficult to escape e-commerce and to use the Internet for other purposes by distributing fast and slow channels, by leading users through particular paths, and so forth. Numerous techniques can make it extremely difficult to use the free resources of the Internet in ways other than those intended by the corporate owners. In fact, one could say the same about the print media. It is not illegal in the United States and Canada to publish a newspaper to compete with the corporate media; anyone is legally entitled to do so, but the organization and structure of the system are such that it is impossible. Media corporations will make every effort to move the Internet in this direction as well. Whether they are successful depends on the reaction of citizens.

The Internet need not become a tool for corporate control and propaganda. It can instead be a significant instrument for promoting human rights and social justice. The future of the Internet is something that people ought to fight about—it does not have to turn out to be mostly negative. Internet access is a new freedom that will require the same nurturing and protection that our other freedoms required. Through active struggle, society can create a public entity under public control, but that will mean a lot of hard work at every level, from the federal government down to local organizations, unions, and other citizens' groups that will struggle in all the usual ways. The Internet itself will be an important component of this struggle.

Clearly, the Internet has liberating potential. It has the capacity for community practice, activism, and social change, and there are numerous positive consequences of this new technology for grassroots organizing. One indication of the success of Internet-mediated social activism is the rapid increase in government funding for security-oriented investigations into what they are calling "netwar." Beginning with the Zapatista experience in Mexico and culminating with the World Trade Organization (WTO) protests in Seattle, the U.S. government is spending large sums to find a way to counter Internet-mediated activism. According to Arguilla and Ronfeldt (1996), two prominent "netwar" researchers, the Internet provides advantages over traditional hierarchical forms of organizing, especially given that conflicts increasingly involve knowledge and information.[6]

CONCLUSION

The three prominent and vital issues discussed here emphasize the extent of uncertainty in the field of ICTs and community practice. ICTs, with the Internet being primary, present numerous opportunities and challenges for community and anti-oppressive practitioners. They present a powerful infrastructure for economic globalization and concentration of corporate economic power and control. This infrastructure, if successfully controlled by commercial interests, will obstruct anti-oppressive practice, community practice, and activism.

At the same time, the Internet is being used effectively for anti-oppressive and community practice in numerous ways. But for this trend to continue, large parts of the Internet must remain in the public domain and other digital divide issues must be confronted. The struggle over who controls the Internet and who can access it is critical for anti-oppressive practitioners. Opportunities to advance these struggles are often overlooked. It is difficult to get excited about practice directed at Internet control and access, especially with so many other pressing issues, but this is perhaps one of the most vital issues of our era for practice.

There is a need for further research in the areas explored here. Community practice is a critical component of anti-oppressive practice, but the implications of the Internet on such practice and on communities and social participation are largely unknown. The nature of virtual communities and their potential for anti-oppressive practice and social change have not been adequately documented. And, finally, we do not really know what works best in the realm of virtual community practice.

Even with these uncertainties, social workers practising from an anti-oppressive perspective need to leverage the benefits of Internet-mediated community practice. The Internet is connecting people who experience a similar oppression across geographic locations. It is bringing people together to advocate for their own rights. It facilitates the forging of alliances across oppressive categories (gender, race, class, sexual orientation). By linking into, or becoming part of, such connections and alliances, anti-oppression social workers can strengthen their practice.

NOTES

1. ICTs include a wide range of technologies including the Internet, computer systems, databases, software applications, wireless devices, etc. The Internet is the major component of the ICT field today. The Internet is a global pool of information and services accessible through individual computers, each of which is part of interconnected computer networks.

2. Based on over twenty-five years of practice using ICTs for community practice and extensive research and writing in the area.

3. Discussion relating to the third question is based primarily on an interview with Noam Chomsky.

4. An excellent description of many of the community practice techniques can be found in *Communities in Cyberspace* by Marc Smith and Peter Kollock (New York: Routledge, 1999), pp. 4–9.

5. The network form of community practice is a new phenomenon resulting from innovations made possible by information technology. This topic is beyond the scope of this chapter, but remains a vital area for further discussion and analysis.

6. One disturbing aspect of this research is the mixing of crime, warring groups, White supremist groups, and social change communities in the same discussion.

REFERENCES

Arquilla, J., & Ronfeldt, D. (1996). *The advent of netwar*. Santa Monica: RAND, MR-789-OSD.

Bennett, D., & Fielding, P.P. (1999). *The net effect: How cyber-advocacy is changing the political landscape*. Merrifield: E-Advocates Press.

Boland, K.M. (1998). *Electronic advocacy: An introduction to the use of electronic techniques for social change*. Boxboro: New England Network for Child, Youth and Family Services. Retrieved May 6, 2002, from <www.nenetwork.org/info-policy/ElecAdvo/index.html>

Brainard, L.A., & Siplon, P.P.D. (2000). *Cyberspace challenges to mainstream advocacy groups: The case of healthcare activism*. Paper presented at the 2000 Annual Meeting of the American Political Science Association, Washington, August 31–September 2.

Chomsky, N. (1995). Interview by RosieX and Chris Mountford. Retrieved May 1, 2002, from <www.zmag.org/chomsky/>

_____. (2001). Interview by Steven Hick, MIT, Cambridge, MA.

_____. (2002). The Internet, Society and Activism. In S. Hick & J.G. McNutt (Eds.), *Advocacy, activism and the Internet* (pp. vi–xi). Chicago: Lyceum Press.

Drost, K., & Jorna, M. (2000). Empowering women through the Internet: Dutch women unite. *First Monday*. Retrieved February 2, 2002, from <www.firstmonday.dk/issues/isssue5_10/drost/index.html>

Fitzgerald, E., & McNutt, J.G. (1999). Electronic advocacy in policy practice: A framework for teaching technologically based practice. *Journal of Social Work Education 35*(3), 331–341.

Friess, S. (1999, March 2). Cyberactivism. *The Advocate 35*.

Hick, S. (1997). Participatory research: An approach for structural social workers. *Journal of Progressive Human Services 8*(2), 63–78.

_____. (2002). *Social work in Canada: An introduction.* Toronto: Thompson Educational Publishers.

Hick, S., & Halpin, E. (Eds.). (2001, May). Children's rights and the Internet. *The Annals of the American Academy of Political and Social Science 575*, pp. 56–70.

Hick, S., Halpin, E., & Hoskins, E. (Eds.). (2001). *Human rights and the Internet.* London: Macmillan Press Ltd.

Hick, S., & McNutt, J. (Eds.). (2002). *Advocacy and activism on the Internet: Community organization and social policy.* Chicago: Lyceum Press.

Krause, A., Stein, M., & Clark, J. (1998). *The virtual activist: A training course.* NetAction. Retrieved May 2, 2002, from <www.netaction.org/training/>

Kraut, R., & Lundmark, V. (1998). Internet paradox. *American Psychologist 53*(9), 1017–1031.

Lee, B. (1999). *Pragmatics of community organizing.* Mississauga: Common Act Press.

Lyons, L. (1987). *The community in urban society.* Philadelphia: Temple University Press.

McNutt, J.G. (2000). Coming perspectives in the development of electronic advocacy for social policy practice. *Critical Social Work 1*(1). Retrieved May 7, 2002, from <www.criticalsocialwork.com/00_1_coming_mcn.html>

Menzies, H. (1996). W*hose brave new world?: The information highway and the new economy.* Toronto: Between the Lines.

Oldenberg, R. (1989). *The great good place.* New York: Paragon House.

Patrick, A.S. (1997). *Personal and social impacts of going on-line: Lesson from the National Capital FreeNet.* Ottawa: Government of Canada.

Price, T. (2000). *Cyberactivism: Advocacy groups and the Internet.* Washington: Foundation for Public Affairs.

Putman, R.D. (1995). Bowling alone: America's declining social capital. *Journal of Democracy 6*(1), 65–78.

Rothman, J. (2001). Approaches to community intervention. In J. Rothman, J.L. Erlich, & J.E. Tropman (Eds.), *Strategies of community intervention* (pp. 27–64). Itasca: F.E. Peacock.

Schwartz, E. (1996). *NetActivism: How citizens use the Internet*. Sebastopol: O'Reilly.

Wharf, B. (Ed.) (1979). *Community work in Canada*. Toronto: McClelland & Stewart.

Wharf, B., & M. Clague (Eds.). (1997). *Community organizing: Canadian experiences*. Toronto: Oxford University Press.

Wittig, M.A., & Schmitz, J. (1996). Electronic grassroots organizing. *Journal of Social Issues 52*(1), 53–69.

Chapter 19

The Right to Food:
An Essential Element in a
Successful War against Terrorism[1]

William H. Simpson Whitaker
Boise State University School of Social Work

September 11, 2001, will be remembered as a day that changed the way many North Americans perceive the world. It is no longer possible to view world issues with detachment, to assume that whatever happens, residents of Canada and the United States will be safely beyond the fray. Above all, September 11 underscores the interdependence of the nations of the industrialized North with those of the developing South.

There can be no justification for the terrorist acts of September 11, nor can there be justification for the continuing social and economic injustices that provide a fertile breeding ground for terrorism. The war against terrorism that is being conducted by George W. Bush, Tony Blair, and others fall short of what will be required for success. Although military interventions may succeed in routing one or many terrorist networks, as long as the conditions that breed terrorism persist, new generations of terrorists will emerge. Addressing the social and economic needs of humankind is essential to a successful war against terrorism.

This chapter traces the development of food security as a basic human right and argues that an internationally guaranteed *right to food* must be affirmed by the United Nations and implemented globally as an essential element in a successful war against terrorism.

MARGINALIZATION, POVERTY, AND HUNGER

Nearly 800 million people—one-sixth of the world's developing nations' populations—are malnourished. In these countries 6 million children die needlessly each year, mostly from hunger-related causes. In developing nations one child in ten dies before the age of five (Bread for the World, 2001), compared with one in 125 in the United States, one in 167 in Canada and the United Kingdom, and one in 250 in Sweden (*World Guide, 2001– 2002*, 2001). Approximately 880 million people in the developing world lack access to adequate health services, and 2.6 billion are without access to basic sanitation. The richest fifth of the world's population consume 86 per cent of the earth's goods and services, while the poorest fifth consume 1 per cent. Thirty-two per cent of the population in developing countries subsist on less than U.S. $1 per day (Bread for the World, 2001). These are conditions under which terrorism flourishes.

WORLD FOOD SUPPLIES AND FOOD SECURITY

Throughout the world there is enough food to provide at least a basic vegetarian diet to every human being now alive.[2] Given the global abundance of food, the right to food should be the most fundamental of universal human rights. Marginalization, poverty, and hunger, however, persist as consequences of political and economic choices resulting in entitlement failures that undermine food security at the household level. Hunger and malnutrition persist because of a lack of political will to foster the policies necessary to insure universal food security.

Food security involves *access to culturally acceptable nutrients, through normal channels, in quantities sufficient for daily life and work* (Whitaker, 2000). Food security means access to enough food, without relying on emergency food sources such as food aid, breadlines, pantries, or soup kitchens. Food security means access to enough food without necessity for extraordinary coping mechanisms such as begging, stealing, or prostitution.

Food security depends upon a stable supply of culturally acceptable, uncontaminated, good quality food—providing necessary energy, nutrients, and micronutrients such as vitamins and iron—available to every household. Food security implies environmental, economic, and social sustainability. Economic and social sustainability involves access to food through a combination of just income distribution and effective markets, together with various forms of public and private, formal and informal supports and safety nets (Eide, 1995b).

Having enough to eat depends on access to at least a minimal level of subsistence. Kates and Millman (1990) suggest that human history itself may be understood as a process of guaranteeing access to subsistence to ever-larger circles of people, from household to clan and beyond. Beginning about 200 years ago, they contend, entitlement to subsistence was extended to most Europeans. The challenge today is to extend that entitlement throughout the globe.

Although the global proportion of hungry people is diminishing, the total number of hungry people continues to increase. The number of hungry people is, however, projected to peak in the near future and then gradually decline to equal 3 per cent of the world's population by 2050. "In the meantime," as Kates and Millman (1990, p. 405) put it poignantly, "half of the world's women who carry the seeds of our future may be anemic, a third of the world's children may be wasted or stunted in body or mind, and perhaps a fifth of the world's people can never be sure of their daily bread, chapati, rice, tortilla or ugali."

HUMAN RIGHTS

Human rights are "enforceable claims on the delivery of goods, services, or protection by others," meaning that people in need can insist upon the delivery of assistance, with recourse, if necessary, to legal or moral enforcement of their demand (Eide, Oshaug, & Eide, 1995, p. 426). Human rights are based on social obligations that are accepted by all people without distinction of race, gender, nationality, language, religion, or socio-economic class. Human rights may be promulgated globally, but must be implemented locally within nationally determined limits (Barker, 1991; Eide, Oshaug, & Eide, 1995).

Human rights may be separated into civil/political rights and social/economic/cultural rights. Civil and political rights are basic "rights recognized in democratic constitutions, such as life, liberty and personal security; freedom from arbitrary arrest, detention, or exile; the right to fair and impartial hearings by impartial tribunals; freedom of thought, conscience, and religion; and freedom of peaceful association" (Barker, 1991, p. 105). Economic, social, and cultural rights include the right to eat as well as "the right to work, education and social security; to participate in the cultural life of the community; and to share in the benefits of scientific advancement and the arts" (Barker, 1991, p. 105).

Economic/social/cultural rights emphasize protection of vulnerable groups such as the poor, people with disabilities, and First Nations and other Indigenous peoples. In doing so these groups make a claim on the state for protection and assistance and their rights are realizable only at substantial monetary costs to government (Eide, 1995a; Eide & Rosas, 1995). Such rights are sometimes referred to as entitlements, societal obligations to provide support as a right when people have insufficient resources to live under conditions of health and decency (Melnick, 1994).

The right to food is an essential and, in light of Maslow's hierarchy of common human needs (1970), arguably the most important building block in the foundation of an adequate social compact.

TYPES OF HUNGER SITUATIONS

Lucile Newman and her colleagues at Brown University (1990) described three types of hunger situations: regional food shortage, household food poverty, and individual food deprivation.

Regional food shortages occur when food available within a geographical area is insufficient to meet the needs of the region's population. Regional food shortages are often but not always a direct consequence of natural disaster, war, and societal disruption. Household food poverty occurs when a household cannot access enough food to meet the needs of its members. Household food poverty is often but not always a result of resource poverty, excessive taxes and rents, and entitlement failure. Individual food deprivation occurs when an individual is unable to consume the nutrients that he or she needs. Individual food deprivation may be a consequence of disease, unmet special needs such as those of pregnant women or nursing mothers, neglect, abuse, and discrimination (Newman, Crossgrove, Kates, Matthews, & Millman, 1990, cited in DeRose, Messer, & Millman, 1998).

For a right to food to have meaning, it must be implemented where food is actually consumed—by individuals at the household level. The presence of food supplies in a nation or region of a nation is no guarantee of food security if households lack access to them. Household food security requires "access to a basket of food which is nutritionally adequate, safe, and culturally acceptable, procured in a manner consistent also with the satisfaction of other basic human needs, and obtained from supplies, and in ways, which are sustainable over time" (Eide, Oshaug, & Eide, 1995, p. 455).

Even if a household has access to a supply of food that, if equitably shared, could meet the needs of all its members, that food may or may not be distributed according to individual needs. In some societies, for example, women and girls are fed only after adult men and boys have eaten their fill.

CAUSES OF HUNGER

When one thinks about the causes of hunger, the first things that come to mind are likely to be drought and other forms of natural disaster, population increases that outstrip the capacity of the land to produce food, and human conflicts. While these are important contributing causes, they fail to explain why it is that when there is an abundance or a shortage food, some people thrive while others do not. To understand the political economy of hunger, it is important to ask why, regardless of the extent of the food supply, some people have enough to eat while others go hungry. The concept of entitlement failure (Drèze & Sen, 1990a, 1990b, 1990c, 1991; Sen, 1981) by Nobel laureate economist Amartya Sen is a powerful analytical tool for understanding and intervening in the political economy of hunger.

Entitlement failure is the inability to acquire food through the various forms of exchange relationships to which one has access (Sen, 1981). For Sen, entitlement failure is the central cause of hunger, starvation, and famine. People suffer malnutrition and die of starvation, he says, because of their inability to claim sufficient food resources to meet their nutritional needs. According to Sen, food entitlement may be achieved in any of three basic ways. People must either have access to resources to gather or to produce food; or they must be able to exchange property, money, or work for food; or they must receive gifts of food or have resources to acquire food (Drèze & Sen, 1990a, 1990b, 1990c, 1991).

These three basic forms of entitlement have not changed over time. However, the mix has changed historically "from a primary emphasis on household self-provision to slave, servant or serf status where labor is appropriated in return for minimal entitlement, to market exchange of labor and production, and most recently to the development of extensive safety-nets of food security" (Kates & Millman, 1990, p. 398).

An entitlement approach to food security "requires a shift in thinking from what exists? to who can command what?" (Eide, 1995b, p. 95) and helps avoid the pitfall of assuming that per capita food supplies that seem adequate, on average, necessarily result in universal food security for hungry people. Experience demonstrates clearly that food insecurity frequently occurs in nation-states, regions, and even households in which there is a seemingly sufficient average food supply. Focusing on the question "Who can command what?" enables one to understand hunger as a consequence of human choices made at international, national, regional, community, and household levels.

HISTORICAL MILESTONES TOWARD A RIGHT TO FOOD

The human rights from which the right to food is derived are grounded in the philosophy of Locke and Rousseau, in the 1690–1691 British *Bill of Rights*, the 1776 United States *Declaration of Independence*, and the 1779 French *Declaration on the Rights of Man and the Citizen*. Growing contemporary support for a right to food is the culmination of several hundred years of struggle to affirm and extend basic human rights to wider arenas and constituencies (Dobbert, 1978).

The modern journey toward a universal right to food has now lasted more than half a century. It is the story of the interwoven dreams, leadership, and hard work of many people acting primarily through non-governmental and intergovernmental organizations.

Attitudes toward human rights were fundamentally changed by the events surrounding World War II. Before the war, the right to food could be claimed only for members of the armed forces, who were entitled to food in exchange for their willingness to fight and for inmates of penitentiaries, almshouses, and similar public institutions who were prevented from self-provision. International law provided no basis for a universal right to food. Acute food shortages experienced in wartorn Europe and elsewhere contributed to the emergence of the concept of a universal right to food (Dobbert, 1978).

In 1941, in his "Four Freedoms" State of the Union address, U.S. President Franklin Delano Roosevelt introduced the concept of "freedom from want" into modern political discourse. Later that year the Atlantic Charter, adopted by Roosevelt and British Prime Minister Winston Churchill, called for international collaboration to secure "improved labor standards, economic advancement and social security" for all. Finally, in his 1944 State of the Union message, Roosevelt proposed an international "Economic Bill of Rights," recognizing that "true individual freedom cannot exist without economic security and independence." "People," Roosevelt said, "who are hungry and out of jobs are the stuff of which dictatorships are made" (cited in Dobbert, 1978).

In 1945, before the conclusion of World War II, the Food and Agriculture Organization (FAO) was founded "with a mandate to raise levels of nutrition and standards of living, to improve agricultural productivity, and to better the condition of rural populations." Today FAO functions as an intergovernmental organization whose 184 members constitute one of the largest specialized agencies of the United Nations (Food and Agriculture Organization, 2002).

Following the war, on December 10, 1948, the United Nations adopted the Universal Declaration of Human Rights (UDHR), the key document from which contemporary attempts to secure a universal right to food are derived.

The UDHR envisions worldwide rights—to be implemented nationally and monitored internationally—for all people. Article 25(1) anticipates the right to food. "Everyone," it states, "has the right to a standard of living adequate for the health and well-being of himself and his family, including food, clothing, housing and medical care and necessary human services" (cited in Dobbert, 1978).

The UN Commission on Human Rights, which drafted the Declaration, could not get agreement to include civil/political and social/economic/cultural rights in a single legally binding convention. Twenty-two years passed. Finally, in 1966, the UN General Assembly adopted separate international covenants on civil/political rights and social/economic/cultural rights (Eide & Rosas, 1995).

The International Covenant on Civil and Political Rights (CCPR)[3] has generated less controversy than has the International Covenant on Economic, Social and Cultural Rights (CESCR).[4] In 1964, following impassioned advocacy by Dr. B.R. Sen, FAO director-general, strengthening language was adopted, thus providing for a right to an adequate standard of living based on universal subsistence rights to adequate food and nutrition, clothing, housing, and necessary conditions of care (Dobbert, 1978).

FAO's efforts to alleviate poverty and hunger have been constrained by the self-interests of its dominant members. Its role in promoting the right to food has varied from virtual inactivity to strong support. While FAO was instrumental in founding, in 1961, the World Food Programme (WFP), which has emphasized the right to food as a fundamental human right and necessary precondition to development, it was not until 1965 that the Preamble to the FAO constitution was amended to insure "humanity's freedom from hunger" (Eide, Oshaug & Eide, 1995, pp. 442–443; Whitaker, 2002, p. 1589).

In 1974, FAO played a major role in organizing the UN World Food Conference in Rome, which focused global attention on hunger and malnutrition as solvable problems. The conference recommended the adoption of an International Undertaking on World Food Security recognizing (paragraph I.1) "that the assurance of world food security is a common responsibility of the entire international community." World Food Conference participants adopted a goal of ending hunger worldwide in ten years (Tomasevski, 1987).

Subsequently, three major agencies—the World Food Council (WFC), the International Fund for Agricultural Development (IFAD), and the United Nations Administrative Committee on Co-ordination, Sub-Committee on Nutrition (ACC/SSC)—were established to help achieve World Food Conference goals.

CITIZEN MOBILIZATION AGAINST HUNGER

The period leading up to and following the World Food Conference was a time of increasing anti-hunger mobilization in many countries. In the United States, for example, Oxfam America, Food for the Hungry, the Food Research and Action Center, and the Campaign for Human Development were founded in 1970; Bread for the World in 1974; Food First and World Hunger Year in 1975; the World Hunger Education Service in 1976; the Hunger Project in 1977; and Results in 1980. Each of these non-governmental organizations (NGOs) has made important contributions to the struggle to establish a universal right to food.

For example, the first major campaign of Bread for the World (BFW), an interdenominational Christian organization that lobbies the United States Congress on behalf of poor and hungry people throughout the world, was conducted in 1974 in response to the recommendations of the UN World Food Conference. BFW mobilized its newly recruited members in support of a congressional Right to Food Resolution, affirming the sense of the U.S. Congress that:

1) the United States reaffirms the right of every person at home and abroad to food and a nutritionally adequate diet;
2) the need to combat hunger shall be a fundamental point of reference in the formulation and implementation of United States policy in all areas that bear on hunger;
3) the United States should seek to improve domestic food assistance programs for Americans in need, to insure that all eligible recipients have the chance to obtain a nutritionally adequate diet; and
4) the United States should increase substantially its assistance for self-help development among the poorest people of the world with particular emphasis on increasing food production and encouraging improved food distribution and more equitable patterns of economic growth; this assistance should be coordinated with expanded efforts by international organizations, donor nations, and recipient countries to provide a nutritionally adequate diet for all. (U.S. House of Representatives, 1976)

The Right to Food Resolution (H. Con. Res. 393) was passed in the U.S. House of Representatives by a vote of 340 to 61. The companion resolution (S. Con. Res. 138) was passed in the U.S. Senate by voice vote.

Intergovernmental organizations also have made key contributions to the concept of food security. In 1977, the World Food Council adopted the Manila Communique, intended as an action program to eliminate hunger and malnutrition, and in 1979 framed the Mexico Declaration, urging international consideration of "practical ways and means to achieve a more equitable distribution of income and economic resources" so that "food production increases result in a more equitable pattern of food consumption" (Tomasevski, 1987, pp. 39–40, 346–347). As has been the case with FAO, however, the WFC has been prevented, by its practice of operating on consensus, from adopting the analyses of root causes of hunger proposed by some of its members. Its Secretariat has shown only moderate commitment to advancing the right to food through legal strategies (Eide, Oshaug, & Eide, 1995).

Since its creation in 1978, the International Fund for Agricultural Development (IFAD) has "focused exclusively on rural poverty reduction, working with poor rural populations in developing countries to eliminate poverty, hunger and malnutrition; raise productivity and incomes; and improve the quality of their lives." IFAD's mission is to "enable the rural poor to overcome their poverty." Consistent with key values of social work and community development, IFAD asserts "Poverty reduction is not something that governments, development institutions or NGOs can do for the poor." These organizations, IFAD contends, can assist best by forging partnerships and helping to promote "the conditions in which the poor can use their own skills and talents to work their way out of poverty" (IFAD, 2002). Food security is a major focus of IFAD's work.

In 1981, FAO organized the first World Food Day, an event observed on October 16 by participants in more than 150 nations (Food and Agriculture Organization, 2002). That same month the United Nations University organized a meeting in Gran, Norway, which resulted in the 1984 publication of *Food as a Human Right.* The report emphasized that human food supplies are "filtered through socio-economic processes which deny an adequate supply of food to many while delivering a large over-dose to a 'lucky' few" and concluded that solutions to hunger "will probably require deep structural changes" (Eide, Eide, Goonatilake, Gussow, & Omawale, 1984, p. ix).

In June 1984, the Netherlands Institute for Human Rights Right to Food Project and the Norwegian Human Rights Project co-sponsored an international conference, The Right to Food: From Soft to Hard Law, in the Woudschoten conference facility near Utrecht, Netherlands. The forty-two participating lawyers, nutritionists, and development experts from governmental and non-governmental organizations from countries throughout the world criticized discussions of world hunger as frequently oversimplified. Rather than defining hunger in terms of calorie/protein deficiencies, they proposed analysis of the "economic, social, political, cultural and structural factors, which deprive some people of access to land, work and food" (Alston & Tomasevski, 1984, pp. 7, 217).

The Woudschoten conferees proposed translating "soft law" norms of human rights into "hard law" capable of adjudication, monitoring implementation of the right to food through co-operation among UN agencies, redesigning the CESCR reporting system and creating an NGO network using a "mobilization of shame" strategy modelled on Amnesty International. Conference proceedings were published in a book, *The Right to Food*, that attempted "for the first time . . . to put the right to food on the agenda of national and international human rights agencies" (Alston & Tomasevski, 1984, p. 220).

In 1985, the World Institute for Development Economics (WIDER), established by the United Nations the previous year, initiated its program Hunger and Poverty: The Poorest Billion. In 1986, WIDER sponsored the Helsinki Food Strategies Conference to identify "feasible opportunities" for reducing world hunger. The Helsinki conference emphasized the entitlement failure approach embraced the previous year in Woudschoten and articulated by Amartya Sen and others. In response, participants urged public intervention in low-income nations to improve literacy rates, life expectancy, and infant mortality (Eide et al., 1984).

In 1986, human rights activists founded the Foodfirst Information and Action Network (FIAN) to work to implement and realize the right to adequate food. FIAN understands the right to food as "the right to feed oneself" through either adequately remunerated work or through tilling the land. A grassroots organization based in Heidelberg, Germany, with members in 2002 in "some 60 countries and sections and coordinations in 19 countries on three continents," FIAN works both for implementation of the right to food in individual countries and for procedures at the international level that help implement the right to food nationally. It is attempting to foster "a human rights culture in which social, economic and cultural rights are on an equal footing with political and civil human rights" (FIAN, 2002).

In 1989, the World Hunger Program at Brown University assembled, at the Rockefeller Foundation Study and Conference Center in Bellagio, Italy, a group of twenty-four "planners, practitioners, opinion leaders, and scientists" from national and international agencies, advocacy and grassroots organizations, and universities and research institutes in fourteen industrialized and developing nations. Participants endorsed the Bellagio Declaration, crafted by MacArthur Fellow Robert Kates. The declaration sought a "common middle ground" between the incremental approaches advocated by defenders of the status quo in Rome and Helsinki and the more structural approaches to the elimination of hunger advocated in Gran, Norway and in Woudschoten. By utilizing the "better and the best" of current programs, Bellagio participants believed it would be feasible to reduce world hunger by half in a decade. Strategies included eliminating deaths by famine, ending hunger in half of the world's poorest households, cutting malnutrition in half for mothers and small children, and eradicating iodine and vitamin A deficiencies (Kates & Millman, 1990).

That same year, in November 1989, the UN General Assembly adopted the Convention on the Rights of the Child (CRC), including several provisions that support the right to food. Article 24 addresses the right to health, Article 25 the right to social security, and Article 27 "the right of every child to a standard of living adequate for the child's physical, mental, spiritual, moral and social development" (cited in Eide, Oshaug & Eide, 1995). In 1990, promotion of the CRC was the focus of the World Summit for Children, sponsored by the United Nations Children Fund (UNICEF) and attended by more than seventy heads of state. By February 2002, the CRC had been ratified by 191 nations. The convention was signed by the United States in 1995 as a memorial to UNICEF Executive Director James Grant, a U.S. citizen. In 2002, the United States and Somalia were the only members of the United Nations that had not yet ratified the CRC (United Nations High Commission on Human Rights, 2002).

Also in 1990, Drèze and Sen (1990a, 1990b, 1990c) published their groundbreaking three-volume work, *The Political Economy of Hunger*.

In 1992, in preparation for the International Conference on Nutrition in Rome, the World Alliance on Nutrition and Human Rights established a Task Force on Children's Nutrition Rights. The task force encouraged national workshops as a base for launching locally based, long-term campaigns focused on articulating and implementing laws to strengthen children's rights to nutrition. Workshops were held in Guatemala and Mexico in 1993 and planned in additional countries (Kent, 1993a).

The Task Force on Children's Nutrition Rights collaborated with FIAN, which, at the June 1993 World Conference on Human Rights in Vienna, took the lead in advocating for an optional protocol for the CESCR that would empower individuals to bring human rights complaints to the UN Committee on Economic, Social and Cultural Rights (Kent, 1993b). By 2002, the protocol had not yet been adopted.

In November 1996, FAO hosted 186 heads of state at the World Food Summit in Rome to discuss and consider strategies for combating world hunger (Food and Agriculture Organization, 2002). Summit participants adopted a Declaration on Food Security and Plan of Action that reaffirmed "the right of everyone to have access to safe and nutritious food consistent with the right to adequate food and to be free from hunger" and pledged to reduce the number of hungry people by half by 2015, a goal criticized by many activists as too slow. Participating NGOs, contending that the final outcome of the summit was too contradictory and its recommendations too weak to achieve its goals, called for developing a Code of Conduct of the right to adequate food and a food security convention to make trade policies "supportive to those suffering hunger and malnutrition" (FoodFirst Information & Action Network, 2002).

In 1997, the FAO campaign initiative, "Telefood," reached a global audience of 500 million (Food and Agriculture Organization, 2002). By November 2001, however, when the World Food Summit—Five Years Later meeting was held in Rome, it was clear that progress in many countries was insufficient to meet the 2015 goal for reducing world hunger by half (FoodFirst Information & Action Network, 2002).

The aphorism "there is many a slip between cup and lip" is aptly applied to issues of food security. Realization of the theoretically universal principles of the International Covenant on Economic, Social and Cultural Rights still eludes many people in countries that have ratified the treaty. The retreat from the goal of the 1974 World Food Conference of ending hunger in ten years to the goal of the 1996 World Food Summit of reducing hunger by half in twenty years reflects both improved understanding of the complexities of entitlement failure and reduced commitment on the part of the wealthy nations to a legal right to food.

NGOs such as FIAN contend that the right to food, as an integral part of international human rights law, provides a basis for legal claims, enforceable in national and international courts, requiring the community of states to insure universal access to adequate food. The normative standard to the right to food, from this perspective, is set forth in the United Nations' "1999 General Comment No.12 paragraph 6 as physical and economic access to adequate food or means for its procurement." Subsequent paragraphs of the comment clarify that access to adequate food must be possible through purchase or other means of procurement, must be sustainable, and must be possible with dignity (Künnemann, 2002).

The political climate in the United States Congress has changed dramatically from its overwhelming support for the 1974 Right to Food

Resolution to the concerns expressed repeatedly during the two years of negotiations that shaped the 1996 World Food Summit's Declaration on Food Security—that a legally enforceable right to food could expose rich countries to lawsuits and trade complaints from the developing world.[5]

It seems likely, then, that the United States' unwillingness to ratify[6] the CESCR, the Convention on the Elimination of All Forms of Discrimination against Women (CEDAW), the Convention on the Rights of the Child (CRC), various related optional protocols, and the treaty establishing an International Criminal Court stems from concern that advocates such as FIAN might prevail in court. As one of the world's wealthiest nations, should it ratify these treaties, the United States might be found liable to help pay for the redress of global poverty-related conditions.

In 2002, the United States government is at best a reluctant advocate of global food security. It remains to be seen if the U.S. perspective may change in response to the tragic events of September 11. Increasingly, advocates from non-governmental and intergovernmental organizations contend that a hungry world is a breeding ground for terrorism.[7]

It is not so much that terrorists are themselves hungry. Although this may be so, more importantly, marginalization, poverty, and hunger contribute to a sea of people without hope among whom terrorists may find support. A successful war against terrorism will need to foster hope that undermines terrorists' appeals.

IFAD contends correctly that "Poverty reduction—and indeed peace, stability and sustainable economic growth—can only be achieved by modifying the unequal power relations[8] that contribute to generating poverty, and by making a conscious effort to enable historically excluded people to exercise their full potential" (International Fund for Agricultural Development, 2002).

Three levels of obligation are involved when governments attempt to maximize people's capability to provide food for themselves and their households through their own resources and efforts. First, governments must respect individual freedoms and resources. For example, government actions to insure the land rights of Indigenous peoples and to clarify smallholders' title to their land enable people to maximize self-reliance and their ability to earn an adequate living. Second, governments need to protect the rights of the less powerful against more powerful interests that may exploit them and reduce their ability to be self-reliant. Third, when no other possibilities exist, governments are obliged to fulfill rights through actions such as providing for basic needs through programs of food or social security (Eide, 1995a).

The most important next step to be taken today to promote food security is for members of the United Nations to ratify an International Code of Conduct on the Human Right to Adequate Food along the lines being promoted by FIAN International (FoodFirst Information & Action Network, 2002). Promulgation of the right to feed oneself is required by basic justice. It is also an essential ingredient in a successful war against terrorism.

NOTES

1. Portions of an earlier version of this paper appeared as Whitaker, W.H. (2000). Food entitlements. In K.F. Kiple and K.C. Ornealas (Eds.), *The Cambridge World History of Food*. Cambridge: Cambridge University Press.

2. Peter Uvin, cited in DeRose, Messer, and Millman (1998), reports that the 1993 world food supply potentially could support 112 per cent of the world population with a near-vegetarian diet, 74 per cent of the world population with a diet in which 15 per cent of calories was derived from animal foods, and 56 per cent of the world's population with a diet in which 25 per cent of calories was derived from animal foods.

3. By February 2002, 148 nations had ratified the International Covenant on Civil and Political Rights (CCPR). Canada ratified the treaty in 1976 and the United States finally did so in 1992. Seven more nations have signed but not yet ratified the treaty (United Nations High Commission on Human Rights, 2002).

4. By February 2002, 145 nations had ratified the CESCR. Canada ratified the treaty in 1976. The United States signed the agreement in 1977, but—together with Belize, the Lao People's Democratic Republic, Liberia, Sao Tome and Principe, South Africa, and Turkey—had not yet ratified the treaty (United Nations High Commission on Human Rights, 2002).

5. The U.S. delegation took a particularly disturbing position in opposition to the Declaration on Food Security, contending that the right to food is only an "aspiration" that creates no international obligation for governments.

6. As of February 2002, the United States had signed but not ratified the CESCR, the CEDAW, and the CRC. President Clinton signed the treaty establishing an International Criminal Court, but President Bush rescinded that signature. The United States had signed but not ratified two optional protocols to the CRC. It had neither signed nor ratified two optional protocols to the CCPR, the optional protocol to the CEDAW, and the International Convention on the Protection of the Rights of All Migrant Workers and Members of Their Families (MCW) (Sengupta, 2002; UNHCR, 2002).

7. Not everyone agrees with this perspective. Daniel Pipes (2002), for example, after citing many people who link the development of militant Islam to poverty, argues that militants—aka terrorists—tend to be educated and relatively well off economically and that residents of the poorest Muslim countries are not the most likely to be militant Islamists.

8. Global institutions such as the World Bank, International Monetary Fund, World Trade Organization, and "free trade"-related treaties, such as NAFTA and GATT, contribute to power imbalances affecting sustainable development, poverty reduction, and the replacement of global hunger and malnutrition with food security. Issues of hunger and poverty—and ultimately terrorism—cannot be addressed successfully without tackling these mechanisms. The recent worldwide mobilization of concern about these power imbalances is cause for hope.

REFERENCES

Alston, P., & Tomasevski, K. (1984). *The right to food.* The Hague: Martinus Nijhoff.

Barker, R.L. (1991). *The social work dictionary* (2nd ed.). Washington: NASW Press.

Bread for the World. (2001). *Hunger basics: International facts on hunger and poverty.* Retrieved November 30, 2001 from <www.bread.org/hungerbasics/international>

DeRose, L., Messer, E., & Millman, S. (1998). *Who's hungry? How do we Know? Food shortage, poverty and deprivation.* New York: United Nations University Press.

Dobbert, J.P. (1978). Right to food. In R.-J. Dupuy (Ed.), *The right to health as a human right* (pp. 184–213). The Hague: Sijthoff & Noordhoff.

Drèze, J., & Sen, A. (1990a). *The political economy of hunger, Vol. 1: Entitlement and well-being.* Oxford: Clarendon Press.

_____. (1990b). *The political economy of hunger, Vol. 2: Famine prevention.* Oxford: Clarendon Press.

_____. (1990c). *The political economy of hunger, Vol. 3: Endemic hunger.* Oxford: Clarendon Press.

_____. (1991). Public action for social security: Foundations and strategies. In E. Ahmad, J. Drèze, J. Hills, & A. Sen (Eds.), *Social security in developing countries* (pp. 1–40). Oxford: Clarendon Press.

Eide, A. (1995a). Economic, social and cultural rights as human rights. In A. Eide, C. Krause, & A. Rosas (Eds.), *Economic, social, and cultural rights: A textbook* (pp. 21–40). Boston: Martinus Nijhoff.

_____. (1995b). The right to an adequate standard of living including the right to food. In A. Eide, C. Krause, & A. Rosas (Eds.), *Economic, social, and cultural rights: A textbook* (pp. 89–105). Boston: Martinus Nijhoff.

Eide, A., Eide, W.B., Goonatilake, S., Gussow, J., & Omawale (Eds.). (1984). *Food as a human right.* Tokyo: United Nations University.

Eide, A., Oshaug, A., & Eide, W.B. (1995). Food security and the right to food in international law and development. *Transnational Law and Contemporary Problems 1*, 415–467.

Eide, A., & Rosas, A. (1995). Economic, social and cultural rights: A universal challenge. In A. Eide, C. Krause, & A. Rosas (Eds.), *Economic, social, and cultural rights: A textbook* (pp. 15–19). Boston: Martinus Nijhoff.

Food and Agriculture Organization. (2002). FAO: What it is—what it does. Retrieved May 18, 2002, from <www.fao.org/UNFAO/e/whist-e.htm>

FoodFirst Information & Action Network. (2002). FIAN for the human right to feed oneself: About FIAN. Retrieved May 18, 2002, from <www.fian.org/english version/ fian presentation.htm>

International Fund for Agricultural Development. (2002). Strategic framework for IFAD 2002–2006. Retrieved May 18, 2002, from <www.ifad.org/sf/index.htm>

Kates, R.W., & Millman, S. (1990). On ending hunger: The lessons of history. In L.F. Newman (Ed.), *Hunger in history: Food shortage, poverty, and deprivation* (pp. 389–407). Cambridge: Basil Blackwell.

Kent, George. (1993a). Children's right to adequate nutrition. *International Journal of Children's Rights 1*, 133–154.

_____. (1993b). Nutrition and human rights. *SCN News 10*, 9–12. United Nations, ACC/ SCN.

Künnemann, Rolf. (2002). Food security: Evading the human right to food? Retrieved May 18, 2002, from <www.Fian.org/English-version/wfs2.htm>

Maslow, Abraham. (1970). *Motivation and personality.* New York: Harper & Row.

Melnick, R.S. (1994). *Between the lines: Interpreting welfare rights.* Washington: Brookings Institution.

Newman, L.F., Crossgrove, W., Kates, R.W., Matthews, R., & Millman, S. (Eds.). (1990). *Hunger in history: Food shortage, poverty and deprivation.* Cambridge: Basil Blackwell.

Pipes, Daniel. (2002). Does poverty cause militant Islam? Retrieved January 19, 2002, from <http://capitalismmagazine.com>

Sen, A. (1981). *Poverty and famines: An essay on entitlement and deprivation.* Oxford: Clarendon Press.

Sengupta, S. (2002). U.S. fails in UN to exempt peacekeepers from new court. Retrieved May 18, 2002, from <www.nytimes.com/2002/05/18/international/18NATI.hmtl>

Tomasevski, K. (Ed.). (1987). *The right to food: A guide through applicable international law.* Boston: Martinus Nijhoff.

United Nations High Commission on Human Rights. (2002). Status of ratifications of the principal international human rights treaties as of February 8, 2002. Retrieved February 8, 2002, from <www.unhchr.ch/pdf/report.pdf>

U.S. House of Representatives, Committee on International Relations, Subcommittee on International Resources, Food and Energy. (1976). *Hearings on H. Cong. Res. 393, The right to food resolution.* Publication no. 74-782. Washington: Government Printing Office.

Whitaker, W.H. (2000). Food entitlements. In K.F. Kiple and K.C. Ornealas (Eds.), *The Cambridge world history of food.* Cambridge: Cambridge University Press.

The World Guide, 2001–2002. (2001). Oxford: New Internationalist Publications.

Social Work Education

Controversies, Tensions, and Contradictions: Anti-Oppression and Social Justice in the Social Work Curriculum

Judy Hughes
Shirley Chau
Pamela James
Steven Sherman
Doctoral Candidates
Faculty of Social Work
University of Toronto

The idea for writing this chapter has come directly from our combined experiences as teaching assistants for various Master of Social Work courses at the University of Toronto. In putting together course materials, preparing lectures, and leading classroom discussions, we continually found ourselves struggling to come up with readings that clearly described and explained concepts such as oppression, social justice, exploitation, domination, and diversity while retaining the inherent complexity and inevitable tensions within each of these broader concepts. We also struggled continually with creating and maintaining safe yet effective learning environments that would challenge students and ourselves to really engage with difficult and contentious issues about social justice and oppression.

Our intent in teaching these courses and discussing these issues with students was to make anti-oppressive practice and social justice come alive for them. That is, we wanted to encourage students to explore issues of oppression and social justice through their own personal experience, in their own lives, by examining the practice theories and techniques taught in other courses, and, more important, in their future practice with clients. What we discovered in the practice of teaching is that students were interested in these issues and were able to grapple with difficult, complex, and often contentious theories of oppression. Yet we also encountered tense moments of student pain, anger, frustration, and the adoption of hardened positions that in themselves were oppressive to other students and even ourselves. As instructors in these courses, we also encountered our own struggles, concerns, and fears when our values conflicted with students' values as reflected in classroom discussions and assignments and in attempts to evaluate and mark very personal and private information in students' journals.

These struggles and concerns led us to examine the social work education literature to discover how others were teaching similar courses. We found that professors and instructors who were writing about their approaches to teaching courses on culture, ethnicity, diversity, oppression, and social justice were also struggling with issues and challenges similar to our own (Lee & Greene, 1999; Nagda, Spearmon, Holley, Harding, Balassone, Moise-Swanson, et al., 1999; Plionis & Lewis, 1995; Razack, 1999; Van Soest, Canon, & Grant, 2000; Van Voorhis, 1998). Overall and with only one exception (see Van Voorhis, 1998), these social work educators reject an approach to teaching these issues that simply provides students with information and theory *about* the sources and consequences of oppression and injustice. Instead, these educators are opting for critical or transformative pedagogical approaches in which students are encouraged to explore their personal experiences of oppression, difference, and injustice and to challenge their values, beliefs, knowledge(s), and attitudes about oppression and injustice through dialogue, discussion, and interaction with other students in the classroom. These methods and approaches are offered as providing the greatest opportunity to fully explore and understand the dynamics and complexity of issues related to oppression and injustice and the greatest possibility of encouraging students to develop a firm commitment toward overcoming oppression and injustice in their future practice with clients (Lee & Greene, 1999; Nagda et al., 1999; Plionis & Lewis, 1995; Razack, 1999; Van Soest et al., 2000). Yet these same teaching methods and approaches that offer such opportunity and possibility are also being described as engendering the greatest risk and harm to both students and instructors (Campbell, 1999; Ellsworth, 1989; Lee & Greene, 1999; Nagda et al., 1999; Plionis & Lewis, 1995; Razack, 1999; Van Soest et al., 2000).

In this chapter, we explore a variety of pedagogical models for teaching and learning about social injustice and oppression. Then we examine the assumptions and contradictions inherent in these approaches. Our intent is not to offer firm resolutions for overcoming the difficulties of teaching and learning about oppression and injustice but to highlight the tensions, controversies, and contradictions of presenting and discussing these issues in the classroom. Lastly, we suggest that situating anti-oppression and social justice in the social work curriculum requires an examination of broader curricular issues that go beyond course design and the nature and quality of interaction among students in the classroom.

SEARCHING THE SOCIAL WORK LITERATURE

In developing courses to teach social work students about oppression, social injustice, and discrimination, social work educators are proposing and using teaching methods that combine a didactic format with experiential-affective classroom processes and exercises (Nagda et al., 1999; Plionis & Lewis, 1995; Razack, 1999; Van Soest et al., 2000). In using these methods, the focus is on students' subjective understandings and experiences of oppression and the relation of these personal experiences to dominant social relations of privilege and oppression. Through in-class discussion and exercises, students are encouraged to connect their subjective experiences to their membership(s) in social and cultural groups; to develop an awareness of the complexity and overlapping nature of their social identities and group memberships; and to recognize the system of domination and subordination that produces complex patterns of privilege for some and penalty for others based on group membership (Nagda et al., 1999; Razack, 1999; Van Soest et al., 2000; see Nagda et al., 1999 and Razack, 1999 for a review of earlier approaches).

For example, Nagda et al. (1999, p. 437) describes a developmental approach to teaching a course on cultural diversity and social justice appropriately named "Difference-Dominance-Transformation." In the initial component of the course, students explore differences among various social and cultural groups; the next component conceptualizes these group differences as occurring within social relations of domination and exploitation; and the final component presents models of working across difference, including in-class exercises of coalition and alliance building. Students are encouraged to connect the "difference-dominance-transformation" theory to their own personal experiences through intergroup dialogues. In these peer-facilitated groups, students from different racial/ethnic groups meet to "share personal experiences, exchange information about each other's cultures, and examine both personal and cultural narratives in the context of systems of oppression and privilege" (Nagda et al., 1999, pp. 437–438). Similarly, Razack (1999) proposes a framework for teaching a course on anti-discriminatory practice that combines theory with affective-experiential exercises. Working in dyads, students map their own multiple identities in relation to ethnicity, culture, immigration, sexual orientation, level of ability/ disability, race, and so on and recognize their simultaneous locations in oppressed and oppressor groups. Student coalition-building groups are designed to allow students to gain an in-depth understanding of a particular "ism" and to recognize how power is shared among various members of the coalition group as they work together on a common social justice issue.

What is clear from the above descriptions is that social work educators are not presenting knowledge of oppression to students as objective, knowable facts, but instead are opting for teaching approaches that combine theories of oppression with students' own experiences and understandings. In fact, the sharing of personal experiences and interaction and discussion among students in the classroom are central components of these courses both as a basis for learning about oppression as well as understanding the oppressive experiences of others. In the description of these models, interaction and discussion among students is deemed to be necessary, despite repeated reports of student pain, fear, anger, frustration, and feelings of guilt and isolation resulting directly from the use of these teaching methods in the classroom (Campbell, 1999; Nagda et al., 1999; Plionis & Lewis, 1995; Razack, 1999). Writers describing these courses repeatedly clearly recommend against returning to purely didactic and objective methods for teaching these courses.

In part, this necessity for sharing personal information and for interaction and dialogue among students stems from current knowledge and thinking about oppression as socially constructed and subjectively experienced. This understanding of the dynamics of oppression suggests that students need to engage in affective-experiential exercises rather than just be provided with objective, neutral descriptions of the lives and experiences of members of marginalized social and cultural groups (Fook & Pease, 1999; Stainton & Swift, 1996). Providing students with objective, neutral descriptions collapses the experiences of whole groups of people and reduces the complexity of oppression and oppressive experiences to static and easily knowable packages, rather than fully describing the complexity and contradictions of oppression and identity, and the subjective experience of identity formation (Fook & Pease, 1999; Stainton & Swift, 1996; Williams, 1999). Neutral descriptions of the lives and experiences of members of marginalized social and cultural groups can lead to a focus only on the differences among groups and the problems encountered by these groups. This allow students and even instructors of these courses to voyeuristically view the lives and experiences of members of these groups. Neutral descriptions also reinforce stereotypes of minority groups, and produce disempowering and demoralizing accounts of the lives of members of these social and cultural groups (Akerlund & Cheung, 2000; Gilson & DePoy, 2000; Fook & Pease, 1999). Thus, beginning with personal experiences of oppression and injustice seems to provide a means to avoid these traps offered by static, neutral, and objective approaches to teaching and learning about oppression and injustice.

In part, this reliance on personal sharing, student discussion, and interaction also comes directly from critical, transformative, and empowerment-based pedagogical approaches, which are the teaching methods and models used in these courses (see Ellsworth, 1989; also see Campbell, 1999; Pennell & Ristock, 1999; Rossiter, 1993; Zapf, 1997 for discussion of these approaches in social work). Rossiter (1993) describes critical pedagogy as an educational practice that makes clear the connections between education, power, and knowledge. In these approaches, students are encouraged to share personal experiences and knowledge in collaboration and dialogue with other students and the instructor/professor in order to reflect critically on the ways in which dominant cultural understandings and knowledge have shaped and regulated these personal experiences and knowledge.

Through this process of engagement and reflection, it is assumed that students are empowered when their personal experience is taken as valid knowledge and their "authentic voice" or "subjugated knowledge" is liberated from imprisoning and dominant social relations. Ellsworth (1989, p. 309) describes how this process is supposed to occur for students "from disadvantaged and subordinated social class, racial, ethnic, and gender groups—or alienated middle-class students without access to skills of critical analysis, whose voices have been silenced or distorted by oppressive cultural and educational formations. By speaking, in their 'authentic voices,' students are seen to make themselves visible and define themselves as authors of their own world." The outcome for courses using these critical or empowerment approaches is not students' absorption of specific course content or theory, but students' personal growth and change (Campbell, 1999; Ellsworth, 1989; Rossiter, 1993; Zapf, 1997).

At first glance, there seems to be a good fit between the tenets of critical and transformative pedagogy and current knowledge and understanding of oppression as a subjectively experienced, socially constructed, and complex phenomenon. Social work educators' assumption in this literature is that learning about oppression and injustice needs to begin with students' own understanding of their personal experiences of oppression and their own bias, beliefs, and attitudes toward members of other marginalized social and cultural groups. This understanding of oppression and injustice as subjective and relational experience, rather than objective and fixed, requires students to engage in contentious and difficult dialogue with one another in order to comprehend the dynamics of oppression and injustice. Paradoxically, it is also because oppression is relational, because it does occur and is created out of our interactions with one another, and because power, privilege, and oppression are played out among students and instructors in the classroom context that difficulties and tensions occur in classroom discussions.

We now explore these controversies, tensions, and contradictions in the remainder of this chapter. In this exploration, we were guided by the following questions. Can dialogue about difference be safe, open, honest, respectful, and free of conflict? What are the risks of engaging in discussion and interaction regarding issues related to oppression and social justice for members of minority and dominant groups? Why are the goals of these courses largely focused on growth and change in student attitudes and values? Can student growth and change in relation to experiences and understanding of oppression be evaluated using traditional methods of academic evaluation? Why is the focus largely on student learning and the nature and quality of discussion and interaction among students in the classroom? What else needs to be changed in our combined understanding about the profession of social work, in the diversity of students and professors/instructors in our schools of social work, and the social work curriculum?

CONTROVERSIES, TENSIONS, AND CONTRADICTIONS

Rational, Productive Dialogue and the Voices of Privilege and Oppression

The common concern shared by social work educators in the literature is the need to create and maintain open, safe, and respectful classroom environments to facilitate discussion, interaction, and sharing among students. With one exception (Razack, 1999), these educators assume that discussions of racism, classism, colonialism, heterosexism, and so on can take place in a forum where all student voices are treated as equal and, further, that these discussions can be both rational and "productive" (Van Soest et al., 2000, p. 464). The following quote provides an example of this assumption: "all participants need to have a voice, the right to express differing perspectives, and the assurance that they will be listened to and challenged respectfully. The expression of conflicting ideas, when handled productively, can be an integral part of the learning process necessary for growth and change" (Van Soest et al., 2000 p. 464). Embedded within the description of these courses in the social work literature is the premise that rational and unemotional interaction and discussion among students is both possible and desirable and, further, that this interaction and discussion can lead to "utopian moments" of shared understanding about oppression (Ellsworth, 1989, p. 308).

However, as professors/instructors and students, we enter classrooms with various personal investments in privilege and struggle that are carried into discussions in the classroom (Ellsworth, 1989). When these discussions are about our lives, our identities, and how we live our lives, then we cannot be expected to engage easily in unemotional and rational discussions that examine the truth or validity of our various knowledge claims and experiences. This complication of competing knowledge claims in an arena of oppression and privilege among students makes calls for egalitarian, democratic, safe, and productive dialogue highly problematic.

Safety in the Classroom and the Need for Diversity and Difference in Dialogue

Concerns in these courses centre on safety in the classroom and the need to create safe classroom environments to insure equal and respectful dialogue among students. Strategies to provide for these safe environments range from establishing guidelines or ground rules for dialogue among students (Razack, 1999), using an anonymous interactive Web site (Van Soest et al., 2000), and using a team management model to manage diversity that discourages and minimizes acrimony and conflict among students (Plionis & Lewis, 1995). Yet these attempts to provide equal and safe dialogue are difficult as power, voice, and legitimacy are not equally or safely shared among students from different social and cultural groups outside of the classroom, and consequently it cannot be assumed that these are shared equally and safely within the classroom (Ellsworth, 1989; Razack, 1999). Guidelines for dialogue and interaction should reflect the understanding that all voices in the class are not equal and that each member of the class is implicated in the oppression of others through a complex system of privilege and oppression. Most important, the notion of safety in the classroom cannot be conceptualized as neutral; rather, safety has to be problematized and reconceived to reflect differences in what "safety" means for students from both dominant and minority groups.

Conceived as a neutral concept, safety in the classroom becomes about opening up space for minority students to be called upon repeatedly to relate their experiences of oppression and/or to act as "spokespersons" or representatives of particular oppressions or oppressive experiences (Nagda et al., 1999; Razack, 1999). This type of interaction among students breeds the notion that students from minority groups (socially and historically) should educate students from dominant groups about their experiences of oppression. Interactions of this type in social work classrooms leads to extra "work" and even additional discomfort as painful experiences have to be retold and re-experienced. Bruyere (1998) describes how, as an Aboriginal student in a Canadian school of social work, he had to experience and re-experience the pain of hearing descriptions and experiences of colonialism and residential schools and was repeatedly asked by instructors and other students to share his life, his experiences, and even his culture. Focusing in this manner on the experiences of members of oppressed groups and even exoticizing these experiences creates not only additional pain and work for minority students but simultaneously allows students with dominant subjectivities to remain silent about their own implication in relations of domination and exploitation and to leave unexplored their own privileged status in these social relations.

As a neutral concept, safety in the classroom for students with dominant subjectivities becomes confused with comfort (Srivastava, 1997). Safety as comfort for dominant students does not translate into understanding and speaking about unearned privilege but rather safety as comfort becomes the use of power and privilege to speak from a dominant privilege about so-called experiences of reverse discrimination, defensiveness (especially White defensiveness), and guilt. For example, Van Soest et al. (2000) designed an interactive Web site as an anonymous forum for students to engage in further dialogue and discussion about issues raised in their cultural diversity and societal oppression class. This forum did become a place for students to express fears and anxieties about course content as predicted, but the Web site also became a forum for students to reveal sexist and homophobic attitudes and statements and to engage in White defensiveness in relation to course content on race and racism.

Safety, comfort, privilege, and oppression need to be discussed as these processes occur among students in the classroom. When, as individuals, we choose to speak or remain silent about our experiences of oppression or injustice, we do so based on a variety of complex decisions, as described by Ellsworth (1989, p. 313): "what they/we say, to whom, in what context, depending on the energy they/we have for the struggle on a particular day, is the result of conscious and unconscious assessments of the power relations and safety of the situation." If we choose to stay silent about areas of our identities/social locations in which we are privileged, this decision is also about safety as we may not want to risk saying oppressive, racist, homophobic, and so on statements or we may not want to reveal how little we know or understand of the experiences and lives of those different from ourselves. We should not, however, stay silent about privilege in our lives. We often feel immune from the consequences of particular oppressions and, by extension, immune from needing to discuss and engage in dialogue not only about the consequences for others but how we ourselves are implicated in the oppression of these others. As Robinson (1999) points out, we have no choice in being privileged, but we do have choice in what we do about this privilege. For example, the focus in anti-oppressive/anti-discriminatory classes should not be on what heterosexuals need to know about the lives and experiences of gay, lesbian, bisexual, and transgendered people. Rather, the focus should be on what all of us who are heterosexual need to know about ourselves as heterosexuals in a homophobic society. Without discussion of this understanding of both safety and silence in the classroom, safety remains comfort for everyone, which is actually safety only for those students with dominant subjectivities.

Efforts to Evaluate Student Growth and Change
In the description of these courses, social work educators reveal two assumptions they share concerning the goals or outcomes for these courses. One assumption is the belief that all students will experience growth in their understanding of the diverse and different experiences of others, and consequently change their values, beliefs, and attitudes to reflect the values and beliefs of anti-oppressive or anti-discriminatory approaches to social work practice. Educators' second assumption is that student growth and change can be detected and then evaluated by the course instructor. Instructors are using various methods to evaluate students, ranging from personal journals to standard papers (Razack, 1999; Van Soest et al., 2000). Whatever the particular assignment, marking and evaluation are always focused on student personal growth and change.

These efforts and methods to evaluate students are problematic in the context of justice-orientated, anti-oppressive, and anti-discriminatory courses. Evaluation of student personal growth and change implies, first, that there is an anticipated end product—that is, that we can transcend our own racist, homophobic, sexist, and so on ideas and behaviours and, second, that we, as instructors of these courses, will be able to recognize and judge these changes in students. Here, the traditional authority of the instructor is replaced by the notion of "emancipatory authority" in which students are urged to adopt the justice-oriented approach and values determined by the instructor of the course (Ellsworth, 1989, p. 308). Evaluation and marking of students is carried out by judging students' work based on their adherence to the values of anti-discriminatory practice.

We can reject this idea that all students should adopt our own views or notions of anti-oppressive or anti-discriminatory practice in favour of an approach to evaluation that focuses on the individual growth of each student

(Zapf, 1997). The distinction here is that we are not searching students' assignments for evidence of particular ways of thinking or articulating social justice concerns, but we are searching for evidence of each student's personal growth and change across assignments from the beginning to the end of the course. But ethically, is this how we want to evaluate students—that is, by focusing solely on students' intimate experiences? Do we or can we even evaluate students' articulation of privilege? Even where this may seem possible, do we want to then mark minority students' recognition, understanding, and retelling of their painful experiences of oppression and injustice? If we do mark these personal transformations, how do we decide if a particular piece of work deserves an A or B grade? If the course is a required course, then this marking of changes in self-awareness becomes even more problematic. Students have no option but to take these courses as required, despite the potential for personal pain (Plionis & Lewis, 1995).

Totally abandoning the idea of evaluation and marking can also be problematic. In the current context of post-secondary education, course assignments and students' grades may be required by a university. Students themselves may demand to have clearly articulated assignments and assigned grades that are consistent with and reflective of their performance/work during the class. In the competitive, hierarchical context of some post-secondary institutions, high marks or good grades—that is, grades higher than one's colleagues—can mean access to scholarships and competitive master's and doctoral programs.

Perhaps then our focus should not be on the students themselves but on the practice of social work, especially anti-oppressive/anti-discriminatory social work practice. Thus, we still begin with personal experience, but we ask students to articulate how this personal experience fits or does not fit with anti-oppressive/anti-discriminatory theory and practice. We can then ask students to examine their own identities and the impact they think their identities will have on their practices and clients' perceptions of them as social workers. There are many possibilities that allow us to evaluate students' work based on their own understanding of themselves in relation to anti-oppression and anti-discrimination practice theory, rather than just focusing on personal growth and change.

Students' Feelings of Pain, Isolation, and Anger

All accounts from these courses suggest that students will experience feelings of pain, anger, frustration, and even guilt. Dialogue about such issues as racism, colonialism, sexism, and ableism will be fraught with difficulty as these discussions occur in a societal context that ignores or denies both the existence of oppressive experiences and knowledge derived from these experiences and maintains silence about privilege. If students experience shame and pain in these difficult classroom discussions, they may leave these classrooms feeling guilty and uncertain. Once we have problematized and demonstrated the complexity of oppression and even the idea of social justice and communicated to students that there are no easy understandings, answers, or strategies to offer, where have we left them? Can we still convince students that they can in practice understand and know different others and that they can act on behalf of oppressed "others" or participate in social movements for change from positions of partial knowing and /or privileged social positions?

Often, students enter schools of social work wanting to know prescriptively how to practise social work. That is, students enter schools of social work feeling anxious and uncertain about the many and different others they will encounter and are eager to learn theory about human behaviour and the strategies and skills needed to deal with this human behaviour. Rather than simply handing these students theory and practice skills through which they can control this anxiety or simply suggesting that the inevitable tension of engaging in social justice/anti-oppressive practice can be overcome through dialogue, Meihls and Moffat (2000) suggest we communicate to students that uncertainty and anxiety are inevitable as they encounter different others and their experiences. Following this approach, anxiety and uncertainty cease being weaknesses and become strengths in insuring that we reject easy, objective knowing about others and that we do not impose our own understandings, theories, or frameworks on the lives and experiences of others. This requires us to embrace uncertainty and partial knowing, and we begin the process of understanding ourselves, our identities, and our subjectivities in relation to others (Razack, 1999).

After all, the practice of social work, especially anti-oppressive and social justice-orientated practice, should be about learning and understanding one's own perceptions of power and privilege in relation to others and maintaining a position of uncertainty and partial knowing about the lives and experiences of others, especially clients. In teaching students this approach, we do indeed offer students a means to at least begin to understand the diverse and different experiences of others, as well as a means to work within and for social movements for change.

Why Is the Focus Only on Students?

Most of the discussion in the social work education literature focuses on what to teach students about the dynamics of oppression (Stainton & Swift,

1996) as well as efforts to engage students in meaningful dialogue about these issues with an accompanying discussion of the difficulties and tensions encountered in this dialogue. Situating issues of oppression and social justice in the social work curriculum can not simply be focused on efforts to design the right course with the right kinds of anti-oppressive readings (Razack, 1999) or optimal methods to improve the nature and quality of student interaction or discussion in the classroom. Efforts to integrate issues of oppression and injustice in the social work curriculum require us to critically examine the knowledge base of our profession. Further, we need to look at ourselves and our schools of social work in terms of who gets admitted or accepted as students and professors/instructors in a program, and the overall social work curriculum.

This issue of who is on faculty and which students are admitted is larger than just insuring that minority faculty and students become a part of social work departments. This is what Pennell and Ristock (1999, p. 463) refer to as "revolving door access," where students/faculty from minority groups are brought into university classrooms, but the more fundamental institutional, organizational, and curricular changes to accommodate these diverse students and instructors are never attempted. This kind of access results in situations where increasing numbers of diverse students find themselves in universities, but also find themselves forced to conform to expectations and norms that are different from their own in an environment that does not accept difference (Bruyere, 1998).

All of us, but particularly those of us with dominant subjectivities, need to be prepared to do work in both understanding and recognizing privilege. We need to recognize the ways in which our knowledge, our universities, our faculties, and classrooms are welcoming and comfortable and, most important, we need to recognize the ways in which classrooms and institutions are not welcoming and comfortable for others. We need to examine the knowledge base of the profession of social work, what we are teaching to students, and how we are teaching this knowledge. Whose knowledge(s) are reflected in the social work knowledge base and whose knowledge(s) are excluded? What account or stories are being told about the lives and experiences of minority social and cultural groups? What ways of knowing are privileged in our knowledge production and research endeavours? In this questioning, we will have to submit ourselves to the same painful and emotionally charged moments currently experienced by students in our anti-oppression and social justice-orientated courses.

CONCLUSION

We began this chapter out of our struggles, concerns, and fears about what and how to teach oppression and social justice to social work students. This led us to a search of the social work education literature and a critical examination of the tenets of critical, transformative, and empowerment-based pedagogy that informs the design of many of the courses in this literature. Our intent has not been to criticize and then call for an end to the use of these methods and approaches in teaching courses about oppression and social justice. Rather, we wanted to examine and highlight some of the assumptions and contradictions in the use of these pedagogical models. Our aims have also been to open up the discussion of how to situate anti-oppression and social justice in the social work curriculum beyond just discussion of how to design individual courses. As instructors/professors convinced of the importance of anti-oppressive practice and social justice for the profession and practice of social work, we need to begin the painful and difficult process of determining whether our professional knowledge base, our curriculum, and the practices of the institutions in which we work reflect our commitments to anti-oppressive practice and social justice.

REFERENCES

Akerlund, M., & Cheung, M. (2000). Teaching beyond the deficit model: Gay and lesbian issues among African Americans, Latinos, and Asian Americans. *Journal of Social Work Education 36*, 270–292.

Bruyere, G. (1998). Living in another man's house: Supporting Aboriginal learners in social work education. *Canadian Social Work Review 15*, 169–176.

Campbell, C. (1999). Empowerment pedagogy: Experiential education in the social work classroom. *Canadian Social Work Review 16*, 35–48.

Ellsworth, E. (1989). Why doesn't this feel empowering? Working through the repressive myths of critical pedagogy. *Harvard Educational Review 59*, 297–324.

Fook, J., & Pease, B. (1999). Postmodern critical theory and emancipatory social work practice. In B. Pease and J. Fook (Eds.), *Transforming social work practice: Postmodern critical perspectives* (pp. 224–229). New York: Routledge.

Gil, D.G. (1998). *Confronting injustice and oppression*. New York: Columbia University Press.

Gilson, S.F., & DePoy, E. (2002). Theoretical approaches to disability content in social work education. *Journal of Social Work Education 38*, 153–165.

Lee, M., & Greene, G.J. (1999). A social constructivist framework for integrating cross-cultural issues in teaching clinical social work. *Journal of Social Work Education 35*, 21–37.

Miehls, D., & Moffat, K. (2000). Constructing social work identity based on the reflexive self. *British Journal of Social Work 30*, 339–348.

Nagda, B.A., Spearmon, M.L., Holley, L.C., Harding, S., Balassone, M., Moise-Swanson, D., et al. (1999). Intergroup dialogues: An innovative approach to teaching about diversity and justice in social work programs. *Journal of Social Work Education 35*, 433–449.

Pennell, J., & Ristock, J.L. (1999). Feminist links, postmodern interruptions: Critical pedagogy and social work. *Affilia 14*, 460–481.

Plionis, E.M., & Lewis, H.J. (1995). Teaching cultural diversity and oppression: Preparation for risk—The Coverdale model. *Journal of Teaching in Social Work 12* (1/2), 175–192.

Razack, N. (1999). Anti-discriminatory practice: Pedagogical struggles and challenges. *British Journal of Social Work 29,* 231–250.

Robinson, T.L. (1999). The intersections of dominant discourses across race, gender, and other identities. *Journal of Counseling & Development 77*, 73–79.

Rossiter, A.B. (1993). Teaching from a critical perspective: Towards empowerment in social work education. *Canadian Social Work Review 10*, 76–90.

Scheurich, J. (1997). *Research method in the postmodern.* Qualitative studies series, Vol. 3. Washington: The Falmer Press.

Srivastava, A. (1997). Anti-racism inside an outside the classroom. In L.G. Roman & L. Eyre (Eds.), *Dangerous territories: Struggles for difference and equality in education* (pp. 113–126). New York: Routledge.

Stainton, T., & Swift, K. (1996). "Difference" and social work curriculum. *Canadian Social Work Review 13*, 75–87.

Van Soest, D., Canon, R., & Grant, D. (2000). Using an interactive website to educate about cultural diversity and societal oppression. *Journal of Social Work Education 36*, 463–479.

Van Voorhis, R.M. (1998). Culturally relevant practice: A framework for teaching the psychosocial dynamics of oppression. *Journal of Social Work Education 34*, 121–133.

Williams, C. (1999). Connecting anti-racist and anti-oppressive theory and practice: Retrenchment or reappraisal? *British Journal of Social Work 29*, 211–230.

Zapf, M.K. (1997). Voice and social work education: Learning to teach from my own story. *Canadian Social Work Review 14*, 83–97.

Chapter 21

Beyond the Role Play: Alternative Teaching Methods in an Anti-Oppression Classroom

Samantha Wehbi
School of Social Work
McGill University

THE IVORY TOWER BETWEEN SHADOWS AND LIGHT: AN INTRODUCTION

> I learned to be more sensitive to oppression in whatever form
> it may exist. I learned what to look for. I became aware of the
> shadows!
>
> —Student

I came to university teaching from an activist background in a diversity of social issues—rape, poverty, racism, and homophobia. An anti-oppression approach had come to define and shape my social work practice and research interests. I was thrilled when the director of the McGill School of Social Work offered me the required "Anti-Oppression Practice" course (Course 344B) to teach in my first year as an assistant professor. As a community organizer I had developed several workshops on anti-oppressive practice for other community professionals, but I had somehow convinced myself that none of this experience would be helpful in my new career. After all, teaching at a university must be radically different from teaching in the community, or so I thought. Even as I write this, I hear the voice of the establishment telling me that university teaching is a serious endeavour that involves the teacher filling students' brains with countless theoretical concepts that they then miraculously find a way to translate into practice. Certainly, Paulo Freire, the Brazilian educator, has already enlightened us on this subject, challenging such a rigid conception of teaching and learning, yet this conception was a constant companion for me in my first year of teaching the anti-oppression course. It was this same conception that led me to dread Friday mornings in the winter of 2001.

Every Friday I entered the classroom after a night of tossing, turning, and endless worrying about the impending three hours of "teaching" a mostly involuntary group of future social workers about the pleasures of anti-oppressive practice. Everything about me gave the impression that I would rather be elsewhere. I found the course tedious, uninteresting, and certainly non-challenging. There was no excuse for this, considering that I was solely responsible for course design! It was only during the summer, after the course had ended, that I began to reflect critically on this experience. I realized that I had placed myself between the proverbial rock and hard place. *The rock*: Lurking in my mind was the belief that lecturing, and perhaps some role-playing, was the only way to pass on a message in a university classroom. Karl Smith (2001), the American university educator, points to this belief as an ingrained limitation that prevents professors from exploring other possible ways of teaching. *The hard place*: How do I teach about anti-oppression without being "preachy"? My practice experience had instilled in me a sense of humility about the complexities of oppression. I knew that I couldn't stand at the top of the tower teaching certainties and rigid principles about the much more fluid and subtle reality of everyday oppression. Certainly, I had had my share of preachy professors in supposedly anti-oppression courses where dissent was seen at best as proof of the student's internalized oppression and at worst as an example of intellectual inferiority.

Fortunately for myself and my students, I issued a challenge to extract myself from between this rock and hard place. The result was a much more enjoyable teaching and learning experience in the winter of 2002. My personal journey from anxiety to empowerment is the guiding thread of this chapter, where I argue that alternative teaching methods are not only a legitimate way of achieving academic goals, they are also personally empowering for students and professors. In substantiating this argument, I will rely on the example of the anti-oppression course, including empirical data from an exploratory study that I conducted with students in that course.

THE JOURNEY FROM ANXIETY TO CREATIVITY: COURSE 344B AS AN EXERCISE IN EMPOWERMENT

The anti-oppression course is required of all students completing a Bachelor of Social Work (BSW) degree. For students in the regular stream, the course is offered in the second term of the second year,[1] after students have had some experience in the field that they could reflect upon. For students in the Special BSW[2] stream, the course is offered in the third term of a four-term intensive program. The course is offered in two sections, one for students in each stream. The section I taught was the one designated for Special BSW students. The class consisted of approximately seventy students ranging in age from their mid-twenties to late fifties. All of the students already had a bachelor's degree in another discipline. The instructor of the other section and I share a similar understanding of anti-oppression. Both sections of the course focus on a critical examination of social work theory, research, policy, and practice from an anti-oppression theoretical framework.

In my first year of teaching, I had relied on small group discussions of the articles as well as some role-playing. Year-end evaluations were positive, but not overwhelmingly exciting; I knew I could do better. Driven by a genuine desire to instill in future social workers the importance of an anti-oppression approach, I challenged myself to revamp the course. In doing so, I attended an energizing workshop by Karl Smith on making large classrooms interactive. (As an aside, the workshop was offered through the Faculty of Engineering and I was the only faculty member from the social sciences.) The workshop affirmed my desire to teach in an interactive manner and challenged me beyond the rigid conception that this could be done only in small seminar-style courses. Indeed, whereas I had been able to teach in a manner that I was more accustomed to in my other courses with smaller enrolments (thirty to forty students), I had found it quite difficult to do so in a course with seventy students.

More important, beyond technical teaching skills, the workshop filled me with elation that perhaps I was on the right track. In my first year of teaching, I had begun to introduce alternative teaching methods into the classroom, but not on a consistent basis for all of the reasons I detailed in the introduction and also because of the size of the class. Moreover, I was constantly filled with an insecurity that what I was doing was not "university teaching." In the summer following my first attempt at teaching the anti-oppression course, I resolved to experiment with teaching in an alternative manner in a more consistent and systematic way. Some of the teaching methods I introduced into the classroom are presented below, followed with a discussion of student reactions to learning in an alternative way. The literature on alternative teaching methods will be interwoven throughout this discussion.

Alternative Teaching Methods
"Alternative" is a catch-all term that I use in this chapter to refer to methods that diverge from the lecture style and discussion format. Other terms used

in the literature are "innovative" (Maynard, 1996), "non-traditional" (Race & Powell, 2000), "co-operative" (Walker, 1996), "collaborative," or "participatory" (Heuser, 1995). The term "alternative" is used in this chapter to denote a teaching approach that favours three principles highlighted to varying degrees in the literature: participation, interaction, and application.

Participation can range from student involvement in course design (Heuser, 1995) to involvement in classroom activities (Magel, 1996). Student participation in my course was mostly the latter—for example, students participated in the construction of an anti-oppression puzzle that I had created to introduce them to the main concepts included in an anti-oppression framework. There were thirteen main points that I wanted to highlight; however, I did not want to engage in a linear and simplistic discussion of what I know to be the complex phenomenon of oppression. Therefore, I developed three interlinked sessions that would expose students to the various aspects of the puzzle of oppression; examples of these aspects were intersectionality, contextuality, resistance, compliance, etc. I literally constructed a puzzle (35 × 45 inches) that consisted of thirteen pieces, one piece for each concept. In addition to one term denoting the concept, each piece had a card attached to it that explained the concept. Over three sessions, I began each class with a distribution of the pieces to small groups, with each group receiving a different piece each session. The groups were given a few moments to familiarize themselves with the concept, after which I showed a film that touched on aspects of oppression.[3] Following each film, students were asked to discuss the concept on their piece of the puzzle; their specific task was to render the theoretical concept more concrete by reflecting on their assigned reading for the week as well as the film that they had seen. At the end of the third session, we constructed the puzzle together piece by piece on the blackboard. As each piece was pasted on the board, each group shared with the rest of the class their own thoughts and analysis of the concepts that they had worked with over the past few sessions. Throughout the remainder of the term students referred to the characters in the films and to the various pieces of the puzzle in their discussions of oppression.

Interaction is also an important principle characterizing alternative teaching methods. Walker (1996) relied on this principle in teaching a feminist course on gender and family relations in which students worked together on a research project. Interaction was also favoured in my course, where students were encouraged to interact with each other and not simply with the professor. Two examples of this principle come to mind, the first of which is an exercise on developing anti-oppression practice principles. During one session, students were encouraged to reflect on our previous work together to make a list of anti-oppression principles that they would like to carry with them into their practice. Once each small group had created a list, I asked them to exchange it with another group; I gave the groups time to discuss their fellow classmates' principles. The exchange was done twice so that each student group had the chance to become familiar with three sets of principles. Large group discussion revolved around developing a common list of principles based on the individual lists generated in small groups.

A second example of interaction derives from one of the course assignments, which consisted of creating posters that analyzed a specific example of oppression in social work practice, research, theory, or policy. In the last hour of every session, six or seven teams of two students each would present their posters and would stand next to their work in order to answer any questions as other students circulated among the posters. Not surprisingly, this poster exercise provided students with a rich experience that many referred to as being helpful in their learning process because it provided them with the valuable opportunity of learning from each other.

A final principle to be discussed here is that of application. One of social work's distinguishing features is its applied nature. As educators, we attempt to bridge the gap between theory and practice while emphasizing the importance of both. Yet as the existence of an overabundant literature on the topic illustrates, this is not always a straightforward endeavour. Not only do many students have an aversion to "theory," which they feel is removed from their real interest—that of "helping people"—many also have difficulty seeing how their course work is relevant to their practice experience. At the McGill School of Social Work, as well as at several others, students are offered an "integration seminar" (currently optional at McGill) that aims to bridge the gap between theory (course work) and practice (fieldwork). Yet, hoping that students will become less averse to theory and more able to find those links to practice only through fieldwork is inadequate. Course work itself must begin to introduce students to the necessity of understanding the role of theory in practice; this task should not be left for field supervisors or coordinators alone. Moreover, it is not enough to *lecture* students about the applicability of theory to practice; this assertion must be demonstrated. One way of doing so is by creating classroom environments where students are actively engaged in applying course material to their chosen area of practice. While role plays are often used in social work courses to bridge the gap between theory and practice, I would argue that other teaching methods could be used to introduce a variety of ways of learning and thinking into the classroom. The anti-oppression course aimed to do so through several classroom activities and also in the assignments, an example of which came to be referred to as Option B.

The final assignment for the course consisted of a choice between two options, the first of which was a reflection paper that asked students to select an incident of oppression that they had witnessed and to analyze it by relying on course material as well as the broader scholarship. The aim of the assignment was to assist students in theorizing a personal experience. This first option favours the principle of application, even if in a more subtle way than Option B, which was a team assignment that consisted of designing an anti-oppression tool. This tool could be a workshop, a play, a video, etc., but had to be accompanied by a written document explaining its theoretical underpinnings. The main idea underlying this assignment is that teaching is one way of learning. The challenge for students was to take the theoretical concepts they had learned in class and to pass them on to others in an accessible way. A total of ten students (five projects) selected this option, and their assignments were presented briefly to the other students during the last session of the course.

Two teams created workshops accompanied by manuals for facilitators. One workshop, created by a team of two students, tackled the issue of racism in rape crisis centres. This workshop was to be implemented by both students in a rape crisis centre where one of them is involved. I also encouraged the students to approach other centres to gauge their interest in receiving this workshop. The other workshop was created by a team of three students who wanted to address the issue of ageism through an intergenerational approach. The team created a workshop and implemented it in a Montreal college classroom for future social service workers. They then created a video of the workshop, accompanied by a study guide, to assist others interested in implementing this workshop elsewhere. Even though the course is finished, the team indicated an interest in developing three other workshops (and videos) that would tackle different aspects of ageism.

Another team of three students created a reflection document addressing mostly future social workers. This tool consists of four interrelated workshops that focus on motivation for entering the profession, with an emphasis on empowerment and disempowerment. I have invited these students to conduct one of their workshops in the introductory course that I teach for incoming BSW students.

Two other teams created games, one dealing with the issue of funding and the other with social housing. In both cases, the game boards are accompanied by instruction manuals that also explain the theoretical underpinnings of the game. The first game, targeting community workers struggling with issues of funding and the impact of funding choices on organizational mandate and mission, focuses on the consequent oppressive situations for service recipients. The second game targeting social work professionals and students, "Metropoly," is modelled after Monopoly with a focus on the impact of poverty on housing choices and homelessness.

As apparent from the above discussion, there are three levels at which I introduced alternative teaching methods: the entire session, parts of a session, and assignments, such as the poster presentation and Option B, discussed above. At a much simpler level than assignments, I introduced classroom activities that favoured interaction, participation, and application, such as those described previously. These activities were often combined with large group discussions as well as some lecturing. For example, the anti-oppression practice principles exercise was followed by a lecture on practice principles selected from the literature on the topic.

I also designed entire sessions in an alternative manner. For example, the first two sessions of the course introduced students to Iris Young's (1990) five faces of oppression without any formal lecturing on my part. In the first session, students were asked to divide themselves into groups of five students and then asked to select a sheet of paper with exercise instructions that I had developed. Each sheet described one of the five faces of oppression (marginalization, exploitation, powerlessness, violence, and cultural imperialism) and asked students to think of an example either from their own experiences or from something that they had witnessed. This exercise was intended to render the concept more concrete. Five groups of students (twenty-five students) were given the additional task of creating a five-minute skit that would teach others about the meaning of one of the faces of oppression. I have to admit that I was somewhat worried that students may not come up with relevant examples considering that for many, the concept of oppression was not a familiar one. Much to everybody's delight, the skits were amazing—I still regret not having had the foresight to videotape them. The skits were performed in front of the other students and generated much hilarity, indignation, and feelings of frustration at the presence of oppression. One example is a skit in which students chose to portray exploitation by showing migrant workers in a sweatshop. Within the span of five minutes, the students had managed to portray sexual harassment, racism, lack of social and health protection, poor working conditions, and fear of authority. This particular skit drew many jeers and much frustration from the audience. More important, the skit provided a tangible example of the theoretical concept of exploitation.

The second session explored responses to oppression and was my way of insuring that students experienced empowerment and the real possibility of responding to oppression; I did not want them to stay with the frustration and indignation that the first session had generated. I wanted them to appreciate the many stories of resistance and resilience that oppressed social groups and their allies have created throughout history. During this session, students were asked to go back into the small groups that they had formed the week before. Once more, they were provided with instruction sheets; this time, the sheets also included information about responses to oppression drawn from the literature. While most of the classroom engaged in small group discussions, the five acting groups were asked to rehearse their skits once more. Following a brief period of discussion, each group was provided with a horn and instructed to assign one person to blow the horn whenever any member of the group felt the urge to respond to the oppression that the actors in the skits were experiencing or perpetrating. The skits were then performed and instead of jeering as they had done the week before, students blew their horns to stop the actors and direct them into responding differently to the oppression that they were experiencing. To go back to the example of exploitation, suggestions for alternative responses to oppression ranged from personal forms of resistance to collective ones such as union organizing. Also discussed was the role of social work in responding to exploitation as exemplified in the skit.

I have previously mentioned that I did not lecture in any formal way during these two sessions. However, this does not mean that I did not share with students my own ideas about the five faces of and responses to oppression. Clearly, the instruction sheets as well as my active facilitation of classroom discussions provided me with the opportunity to pass on much of the same information that I would have had I been lecturing. However, unlike a lecture, the process was dynamic, engaging, and thoroughly enjoyable for both myself and the students. Furthermore, the process rendered the material concrete for students who may not have had any self-aware[4] experience of oppression. In addition, the information that I presented was enriched by students' own thoughts about the subject matter discussed in those two sessions. Moreover, I would argue that the process was empowering for students because they had a chance to educate other students about a specific aspect of oppression. They were also provided with a chance in the second session to respond to oppression, albeit within a simulated environment. Furthermore, for students with previous experience in responding to oppression, this was their chance to share with others their accumulated personal wisdom, yet these two sessions and the others in the course left me uneasy. Despite the fact that students appeared to be enjoying the course and despite their constant verbal feedback that they were actually learning something, I was filled with doubts. Ever present in the back of my mind was the nagging question: "Sure they're having a good time, but are they learning anything?" I decided it was time to put my doubts to rest.

An Exploratory Study: Student Reactions to Alternative Teaching Methods
At the end of the course, I decided to conduct a small-scale exploratory study to answer my nagging question about student learning. I created a three-question survey[5] that I distributed to students while course evaluations were being conducted. I explained that as with course evaluations, filling out the survey was optional. I also insured that students knew not to include their names on the survey. The course was attended by approximately fifty-five to sixty students on a regular basis even though I did not make attendance mandatory; the course had a total of seventy enrolled students. However, the survey was conducted close to the end of the term (before the last class) when many students were too busy working on papers and studying for exams to come to an 8:30 a.m. Friday winter class! This meant that only the thirty-four students present completed surveys. It is important to note that there are no student mailboxes at the School of Social Work, which limited the possibility of contacting the students who were not present.

The results of this study are in no way meant to be generalized. They are simply intended to begin to gauge the impact of teaching methods on student learning in a specific course. Whereas course evaluations focus on an evaluation of the instructor and course material, the survey I distributed focused on the learning experience of the students. I deliberately left the questions as open-ended as possible. Instead of asking students if the teaching methods were helpful in their learning, I asked them in general what they found to be helpful. I anticipated that some might mention teaching methods. Two main conclusions can be drawn from the results of the survey: the academic learning goals that I initially enunciated in the course syllabus were achieved; and the teaching methods that I had introduced were helpful in achieving these learning goals.[6] Only one student pointed to teaching methods as being detrimental to the learning process—I will return to this point later in this chapter.

What Did Students Learn?
The initial learning goals listed in the syllabus were the following: assist students in understanding the interconnections between various forms of oppression and how these affect social work practice, policy, theory, and

research; increase students' knowledge of alternative models of intervention in social work; and encourage students to critically examine their own social work experience in view of a better understanding of the operation of power and privilege. The answers to the first question in the survey—about what students felt they learned in the course—demonstrate that these goals were achieved, as the following typical responses illustrate:

> It isn't enough to recognize oppression—we can be effective as "insiders" in making changes. Oppression is not simple or obvious—we have to check ourselves, own biases, values, etc.

> There is a lot more oppression occurring in the field of social work than I previously thought. It is vital that social workers think critically about the five faces of oppression and who is benefiting from their interventions.

> Anti-oppression practice is limited by my own awareness of the implicit issues. Addressing these issues has now become a professional imperative.

> I now analyze every aspect of social work on the lookout for [the] possibility of oppression. This will hopefully make me into the social worker I want to be.

> I learned how to think about oppression in terms of distinct categories and clear principles for practice.

> I learned how to be critical of my own social work practice as well as the system I work in. Same about society in general.

> [I learned] that not being anti-oppressive is oppressive in its own way.

> I learned how important it is to position myself in order to be as anti-oppressive as I can be. I learned to develop critical thinking. Now when I hear, read, or discuss things, I am aware of the different ways oppression is present.

The eye opener is realizing my own tendencies to oppress people under my care and also to constructively use my privilege to enhance human life.

I see oppression through different eyes now. I look for it, I identify it, and I try to empower and enable rather than continue in the same past venue set by others. I may not make the ultimate change, but I know I will try to adhere to the principles of anti-oppression practice.

Not only do these excerpts demonstrate that the learning goals of the course had been achieved, I would argue that they also convey a sense of empowerment and hopefulness. The clear sense that arises from these student responses is that they feel they will be able to address oppression should they encounter it in their practice. Far from being wound up in passive feelings of guilt about privilege, they see an active role for themselves in challenging oppression.

What Was Helpful in Their Learning?

As anticipated, students mentioned teaching methods as being helpful in their learning. As these excerpts will illustrate, several students mentioned specific methods as having had a positive impact not only on their enjoyment of the course but also on concrete acquisition of knowledge. In answer to the question about what was most helpful to their learning process, students mentioned the following:

Interactive presentations, creative ways of introducing topics, i.e., puzzle, movies. Really personalizing and giving "faces" to the issues.

Small group discussions: as I'm not comfortable talking to the whole class, this was often where I was able to develop my own opinions.

Group discussions were excellent in gaining perspective.

When people would bring real life examples (or when teacher brought her own examples). The videos were interesting to watch as well.

The interactive learning with the fun activities. The group discussions and learning from each other rather than an "expert." The movies were absolutely great.

Creative approach of instructor and open learning environment. I felt we got to talk about real issues of concern in our practice in a way that wasn't available in other courses.

I enjoyed the group activities. They really helped to integrate what we discussed in the course.

Applying theory to real life scenarios.

The creative way in which the topics were presented. The puzzle was great. It was also really helpful to watch the films because it's something concrete to talk about.

Poster presentations were great. I learned a great deal from the other posters and felt I learned a lot through my own. It was a nice change to be able to demonstrate my knowledge and ideas in such an open and creative format.

As these excerpts illustrate, students felt that the learning process was helped by the aforementioned principles of participation, interaction, and application. Classroom activities as well as assignments were empowering as they provided students with a place to develop their own thoughts on the issues under discussion. Students also had the opportunity to "demonstrate their knowledge" and to learn from each other. Authors such as Slavin and Cooper (1999) and Solomon, Watson, and Battistich (1996) argue that this type of learning environment in which students are encouraged to learn from each other fosters more harmonious group relations as well as a sense of community among students. In addition to such potential short-term benefits, I hope that the example set by this course will be used by students in their future work as educators, should they choose to undertake that role in their careers.

What Was Least Helpful?

While the responses were overwhelmingly positive, not all students enjoyed my introduction of alternative teaching methods into the classroom. Most found it refreshing, whereas a very small number (three) preferred to see more lecturing:

While I felt the discussions were great on one level, I would have liked more of a balance between class discussions and information from the instructor regarding the articles, etc.

[I] love the group work, but sometimes I think that a fifteen- to thirty-minute lecture would be helpful for some class members who have dealt with these issues in undergrad degrees/ personal experience.

I would have liked to have more theory presented in lecture form.

It is worthwhile noting, however, that only one student expressed a total discomfort with teaching methods:

I would have preferred to see more lecturing. It is silly to be playing games and talking all the time. This is not serious enough for us as future social work professionals.

The data from this study is not sufficient to support clear claims about the reasons why these students preferred to see more lecturing. It could simply be that students have varying learning styles. It could also be that some students had more knowledge than others and felt that more lecture material would have pushed their thinking further. And perhaps more balance would be a useful strategy for addressing the diverse levels of knowledge in the classroom. But more interestingly, it could be that when introducing alternative teaching methods, the instructor is going against an unnamed norm that posits lecturing as *the* serious academic method of passing information. This area remains to be addressed in future studies, as do the limitations of this present study.

There are at least three main limitations to this small-scale exploratory study. First, only half (49 per cent) of the students enrolled in the course provided feedback. It could be argued that only those students who are actively involved in the learning process and who may favour alternative methods would attend the last sessions in a term. This certainly could bias the results of the study. It is worth noting that in the International Social Work course where I conducted the same survey and had a much higher rate of return (twenty-eight out of forty, or 70 per cent), the results were similar to those obtained from the survey in the anti-oppression course. Nonetheless, future studies could conduct the survey at the midpoint of the course when student attendance might be higher. Another option would be to make student attendance during the last class mandatory in order to obtain a more accurate evaluation picture. A final suggestion would be to integrate the evaluation of teaching methods into the course so that students are required to reflect on their learning process. For example, in one of my courses in Fall 2002 the final assignment requires students to reflect on their learning process in the course and to examine how the teaching methods and course structure may have affected their learning.

A second limitation concerns the nature of learning. The survey attempts to discern student learning at a specific point in time even though learning is an ongoing process. As Myron Frankman (1999), a Canadian university professor, points out, learning is an ongoing process that cannot be confined into the time span of a course. In fact, one student remarked in responding to the first survey question:

> It is difficult to briefly describe this [learning]. Much of the material, knowledge, theories, ideas, suggestions, guidelines, etc., are still sinking in. I guess I learned that anti-oppression is not easy to discuss, perhaps because of its newness as a framework. I'm interested for the future, what the discourse becomes.

It would be useful to conduct a longitudinal study to assess student learning, especially after students have begun their professional careers in social work.

Finally, the study does not differentiate among students. Students are presented as a homogeneous group whereas they differ in terms of social location (age, race, class, gender, sexual orientation, etc.) as well as academic trajectory (previous degree before enrolling in the Special BSW program, previous exposure to subject matter, etc.). These factors may or may not have an impact on learning experiences, but the study does not provide the possibility of ascertaining this. Future studies would need to take these factors into account in order to produce more reliable results.

EMERGING FROM THE SHADOWS: A FEW CONCLUDING THOUGHTS

"People like working at happy places so they're more likely to stick around and do a better job," or so thinks Strand (cited in Murphy, 2002, p. E1), one of the authors of a best-selling book on improving the quality of the working experience. Walker (1996) makes a similar argument that introducing alternative teaching methods into the classroom could prevent teacher burnout. So why is it that professors aren't more encouraged or at least supported by their departments to explore new ways of teaching? In fact, a year ago I could not have envisioned writing this chapter. I was still hiding my work from my colleagues, convinced that if the establishment found out how I was teaching, my "licence would be revoked." And then two events coincided in an auspicious way. I attended Karl Smith's workshop and at the end of the same week, my friend Mark came from Toronto to accept an award for his research on head injuries. Mark is a psychiatrist trained at the medical school at McMaster University where the problem-solving teaching approach is interactive, participatory, and applied. Over dinner I told him about some of my work and, as only a close, long-term friend could do, he gently chided me for being so insecure about the value of my work. On the contrary, he said, "you should be sharing your passion for teaching with others." Here I am doing so, hoping that my own process and some of the information I have presented in this chapter will be encouraging or affirming for others.

But it's not all gardenias. While I found the process of introducing my own vision of education into the classroom to be empowering and thoroughly enjoyable, I had to learn to be comfortable with a central contradiction noted by Briskin (1990, p. 9), a Canadian university educator: "An overemphasis on the principles of sharing power and validating student knowledge can take female teachers full circle: to a place where they again abdicate both expertise and authority, which is, in fact, an abdication of the role as teacher." Because the learning environment reflects and perpetuates societal power relations, relinquishing the role of "expert" in the sexist context of university teaching can potentially be disempowering. Teaching in an alternative manner meant finding the balance between sharing power in the classroom and not abdicating my responsibility as a teacher. It would be dishonest and naive to say that I have achieved this balance. It would be more honest and more realistic to say that the attempt to find balance is a significant part of the teaching/learning process and that any difficulty this may present is well worth the energy.

Teaching in an alternative manner also meant learning to be comfortable with a great deal of uncertainty. I was never sure what would come out of students' mouths. Creating an open and creative learning environment means not always being able to predict the results. Teaching becomes a shared activity where many partners are engaged in the process of creating a common learning experience, even if only for the limited time span of the course. In the case of Course 344B, seventy-one main actors played a part to varying degrees in determining the specific content and process of each session. I did come into the classroom with a general structure, but this provided a guideline, no more and no less. While not abdicating my responsibility as a teacher, I learned that teaching in an alternative manner means relinquishing the belief that education is the unidirectional flow of information from teacher to students. It also means learning to become more authentic.

One of my biggest lessons over the past two years has been to express my own personal reactions as one way of navigating the uncharted seas of student contributions. Kohler Reissman (1994) speaks of the "positioned investigator" in discussing the researcher as an active participant in the research process. Similarly, I would argue that an important stance to adopt in learning to teach in an alternative manner is one of the "positioned teacher-learner." Throughout the process of teaching, I learned to respond to students' reactions in ways that were non-scripted: I expressed joy, frustration, discomfort, and shock when the occasion called for them. And the more human I became in my students' eyes, the more they allowed themselves to learn about the ways that they themselves may be oppressive. This created an opening in the classroom that no amount of preaching could have generated. On the contrary, assuming a position of detached observer with expert knowledge to impart would have done no more than alienate the seventy involuntary students, many of whom were already resentful about having to take yet another required course.

In a sense, my own learning process mirrored the students' own: together we became aware of our shadows, saw our misconceptions and limitations, and confronted them. As students became aware of the shadows where oppression lingers, I was able to become aware of the disempowering conceptions about teaching that lingered in the shadowy recesses of my mind. Teaching my students about the need to break free from the "prisons in our minds" became my very own act of self-liberation.

NOTES

1. For students from the CEGEP system in Quebec, an Arts Bachelor degree consists of ninety credits usually taken on a full-time basis over three years.
2. The Special BSW is a forty-eight-credit program offered over one calendar year and designed for students who already have a bachelor's degree in another discipline.
3. The two films I showed were: *Bread and Roses* about labour activism and *If These Walls Could Talk* (parts I and II) about reproductive choice and lesbianism. In the third session, students were shown a documentary film co-produced by a Two-Spirited Montreal activist and social worker. She was also present to speak about the film.

4. One of the problematic aspects of oppression is that we are not always aware of the role we play in its perpetration. For many students, this course was revelatory.
5. The wording of the survey was the following: "I would appreciate getting your comments about your learning process in this course. Your comments will be helpful to me in improving on this course and on my teaching methods." This paragraph was followed by three questions:
    1. Please briefly describe what you feel you learned in this course.
    2. What did you find was most helpful to your learning process?
    3. What do you find was least helpful?
6. I also distributed the survey in the other course that I taught during the winter 2002 term, International Social Work. I also teach this course based on an anti-oppression framework, and I did so by relying heavily on alternative teaching methods. Perhaps not surprisingly, the results of both surveys are similar.

REFERENCES

Briskin, L. (1990). *Feminist pedagogy: Learning and teaching liberation*. Ottawa: Canadian Research Institute for the Advancement of Women.

Frankman, M. (1999). *Tennis, anyone?* Retrieved May 15, 2002, from McGill University Web site: <http://vm1.mcgill.ca/~inmf/http/mf/tennis.html>

Heuser, L. (1995). Death education: A model of student-participatory learning. *Death Studies 19*, 583–590.

Kohler Reissman, C. (1994). Subjectivity matters: The positioned investigator. In C. Kohler Reissman (Ed.), *Qualitative studies in social work practice* (pp. 133–138). Thousand Oaks: Sage Publications.

Magel, R.C. (1996). Increasing student participation in large introductory statistics classes. *American Statistician 50*, 51–56.

Maynard, P. (1996). Teaching family therapy theory: Do something different. *American Journal of Family Therapy 24*, 195–205.

Murphy, D. (2002, April 29). Hooking workers with fish tales. *The Gazette*, E1.

Race, K.E., & Powell, K.R. (2000). Assessing student perceptions of classroom methods and activities in the context of outcomes-based evaluation. *Evaluation Review 26*, 635–646.

Slavin, R.E., & Cooper, R. (1999). Improving intergroup relations: Lessons learned from cooperative learning programs. *Journal of Social Issues 55* (4), 647–663.

Smith, K. (2001, November). *Enhancing large lecture classes with active and cooperative learning*. Workshop presented at McGill University, Montreal.

Solomon, D., Watson, M., & Battistich, V. (1996). Creating classrooms that students experience as communities. *American Journal of Community Psychology 24*, 719–748.

Walker, A.J. (1996). Cooperative learning in the college classroom. *Family Relations 45*, 327–335.

Young, I.M. (1990). *Justice and the politics of difference*. Princeton: Princeton University Press.

Chapter 22

Understanding Multiple Oppressions and How They Impact the Helping Process for the Person Requesting Assistance

Gilles Tremblay
School of Social Work
University of Laval

CONCEPTUAL FRAMEWORK

At nineteen or twenty, students come to the university to learn the social service profession with all the buoyant enthusiasm and energy of youth. They are focused on the future and on the interventions they will be called upon to carry out, and do not think much about themselves, seeking only to learn "how to." They want to learn to become "experts," capable of using the authority conferred on them by their knowledge to define the problem and choose the appropriate type of intervention program (Goldstein, in Pozzuto, 2000). This is somewhat similar to what Schon (1983, in Pozzuto, 2000) calls the "technical rationality model," i.e., one that posits professional activity as an instrumental and rigorous application of a scientific theory and its resulting techniques. It is a search for "What to do" and "How to do it" without examining "For whom?" and "Why?" This perspective assumes that science is neutral, and omits any critical socio-political analysis. This is, to a certain extent, the modernist perspective, which tends to base interventions on scientific knowledge perceived as being *the* absolute truth, and excludes all personal and subjective dimensions (Neuman & Blundo, 2000; Ungar, 2002). Science-based modernism, with its focus on organization and structure, has led to significant technological developments, among other things. But on the human level, by attempting to force complexity into hermetic categories, modernism represents a significant source of alienation for a number of groups. In concrete terms, the modernist vision of social work tries, in a way, to induce marginalized people to conform to social standards—standards that are perceived as progress (Ungar, 2002). This perspective denies the political nature underlying any social action and leaves little room for diversity. Teaching anti-oppressive practices thus represents a necessary break with modernism.

Beyond the percentages and numbers, some groups—referred to as "minorities" (Denis, Descent, Fournier, & Millette, 2001)—find themselves in a position of inequality on a variety of levels, including power, because of physical, cultural, or other traits that distinguish them from the dominant group, which is perceived as the majority. Such traits, whether real or imaginary, become stigmata (Goffman, 1973) that characterize social exclusion and marginalization. Greene, Watkins, McNutt, and Lopez (1998) identify those minority groups most often cited in writings as potential targets for anti-oppressive practices. We would expand this list and add the more specific forms of oppression associated with each minority:

Table 22.1: OPPRESSION ASSOCIATED WITH MINORITIES MINORITY SPECIFIC FORM OF OPPRESSION AND DISCRIMINATION

Ethnic groups	Racism, ethnocentrism, Eurocentrism, Americanocentrism
Aboriginals	Colonialism, racism
Women	Sexism, genderism, misogyny
Men[1]	Sexism, genderism, misandry[2]
Elderly	Agism
Youth[3]	Adultism
Gays, lesbians, bisexuals, transsexuals, transgenders, two-spriteds, queers	Heterosexism, homophobia, genderism
Disabled people, people living with mental health problems	Ableism[4]
Socio-economically deprived people, poor, or less advantaged social classes, bottom of the ladder	Classism
Religious or spiritual groups	
Jewish community	Anti-Semitism
Palestinians and Arab communities contiguous to Israel	Zionism on the part of the Israeli government
Other marginalized groups: sex workers, drug addicts, homeless, etc.	
Etc.	Etc.

In fact, this vision of minority groups fits with the postmodern vision of Bourdieu (1972) and leaves room for a multiplicity of groups living under different forms of oppression. This includes any person marked by a diversity that does not conform to the standard framework, subject to hegemony in one manner or another.

Gramsci (1971) has developed the concept of alienation, the ideological dimensions of which were first described by Marx and Engels. Alienation, in all its forms, is an expression of the psycho-emotional injuries associated with oppression (Van Voorhis, 1998). According to Gramsci, alienation is possible only because of the dominant classes' ability to promote their values and have them tacitly adopted by the majority—what he calls "hegemony." In fact, these dominant values are conveyed by existing institutions, for the most part—the family, schools, churches, political parties—but also the media and all cultural channels (movies, television, etc.). Hegemony is the ideological vehicle that drives the marginalization process. "Being marginalized means being part of the whole, but outside the main group" (hook, 1984 in Van Voorhis, 1998).

Needless to say, neither students nor professors are immune from such influences. What is more, most professors and students are part of the dominant majority, having internalized sometimes discriminatory ways of doing things without even realizing it. Keep in mind that for Gramsci (1971), intellectuals play a social function by their affiliation. Their activity is not neutral. Gramsci stipulates that they can become potential allies of the oppressed masses and, for this reason, emphasizes the attention that should be paid to intellectuals.

Adopting an anti-oppressive vision is a commitment—a social choice—but also a commitment to intellectual and affective learning that helps enhance interpersonal and rights-defending skills as well as one's understanding of self (Garcia & Van Soest, 1999). Schon (1983, in Pozzuto, 2000) believes that this type of teaching requires a place and a space for students to develop, redefine, and modify their pre-existing knowledge, attitudes, and concepts through a process of critical thinking about society and self.

The postmodernist perspective considers social work not only as knowledge-based but as an art as well—an art that requires mastery of basic values and the ability to perceive reality in all its complexity. This requires calling into question one's learned conceptual patterns (Neuman & Blundo, 2000). From a postmodern perspective, reality is perceived as dynamic, multi-determinate, socially constructed, and diversified (Thorne-Beckerman, 1999; Ungar, 2002). From this perspective, being sensitive to anti-oppressive dimensions implies being aware of socialization processes and the diversity of experience, and adapting one's intervention accordingly. It also means paying particular attention to one's power relationship with the client, the language one uses, and the client's own experience (Ungar, 2002). According to Van Voorhis (1998), any anti-oppressive practice reference framework should incorporate four aspects:

1. Listening to the client's stories
2. Evaluating the psychosocial impacts of oppression experienced by the client
3. Intervening in order to develop the client's identity and change the oppressive social conditions
4. Assessing our intervention practices

The Canadian Association of Schools of Social Work has manifested the importance it attaches to this dimension by integrating the teaching of anti-oppressive practices into its standards. Unlike other disciplines, social work inherently involves not only acquisition of theoretical knowledge and clinical know-how but also internalization of "professional values." In fact, only a combination of these three dimensions (knowledge, practice, and values) is identified as comprising the basis of quality disciplinary knowledge.

Acquiring professional values is undoubtedly the most complex element to teach. Social justice is the first of these values. It is part of a socio-political vision and a personal analysis of the social reality in which the people, groups, and communities with whom social workers work must live. It keeps the relationship between the individual and his or her environment constantly in the forefront. It puts the individual at the focus of his or her social relationships with his or her environment, and recognizes how that environment can, to a certain extent, produce a specific form of oppression. On the professional level, it assumes that the practitioner has the ability to recognize this oppression in its specific aspects, or at least to try to understand, together with the individual, the meaning of his or her experience and actions, in order to help him or her more effectively. It also demands a self-introspection capacity—the ability to examine one's own processes that are themselves influenced by society. Attaining the level at which one can think critically about the society in which the intervention experience is taking place, and criticize oneself as the subject engaging in and influencing the practice, remains a significant but necessary challenge.

Developing an anti-oppressive practice also involves revisiting classical clinical models based on empathy and the expression of emotions. Traditionally, empathy has been defined as the ability to put oneself in the other person's shoes (Rogers, in Clark, 2000), a notion that should be central to establishing a therapeutic relationship. It is fundamentally centred on the person doing the consulting, in a perspective that avoids judging. Clark (2000) pointed out that this technique carried with it implications that could, in fact, be prejudicial. For example, by focusing on the person, the empathic approach ignores the socio-political context. Moreover, it positions the intervenor as expert—a person capable of understanding the "other"—even though the other's burdens are sometimes poles apart from the intervenor's knowledge, experience, values, etc. Furthermore, it is an intrinsically one-way process that reinforces the inequality between the two protagonists. The technique of expressing emotions is also more associated with a Western, Eurocentric (or North-Americanocentric) perspective, one that is most often feminine and much more difficult to use with more traditional men (Tremblay, 1996; Tremblay & L'Heureux, 2002) or people from certain cultures, for example.

We must therefore induce students to see things from a more postmodern perspective that emphasizes diversity, a perspective that puts social work practice in a context of intersubjectivity (Berzoff & de Lourdes Mattei, 1999). The "other" is no longer the object of an intervention but instead becomes a subject, just like the therapist—two subjects interacting—not just for the wellness of the person concerned, but also for society as a whole.

In short, learning to intervene from an anti-oppressive perspective involves a comprehensive consciousness-raising process (Freire, 1970) that should place the students in a positive intellectual conflict situation (Cyr, 2002), questioning society and themselves on both intellectual and emotional levels. Dean (1993 in Neuman & Blundo, 2000) believes that we need to train reflective practitioners whose practice combines intuitive, artistic processes with logical thinking and rigorous evaluation. Greene et al. (1998) identify three categories of skills to be developed: (1) knowledge skills; (2) emotional skills; and (3) technical skills.

According to these authors, there should be special emphasis on self-awareness. To accomplish this, they propose a whole series of self-evaluation exercises focusing primarily on attitudes. For Doll (1993, in Neuman & Blundo, 2000), anti-oppressive practices can be taught only through a constant iterative and interactive process of action and criticism, criticism and action.

THE COURSE: SOCIO-POLITICAL BASICS FOR SOCIAL SERVICE

We are teaching a basic course that is required in the first trimester of the bachelor's degree program. This course is also mandatory for people registered in the preparatory year for the Master of Social Services program, the curriculum of which does not include any general sociology course. The goal of this course is to familiarize the student with the basic theoretical elements of sociology and political science that have the most influence on social service. The course is approached from the angle of social justice and social change values and the tradition of the anti-oppressive social service perspective. More specifically, this course is designed to enable the student to:

- incorporate basic socio-political concepts into the social intervention context: social structures, system, culture, values, norms, ideologies, roles, status, socialization, historicity, etc.
- understand the impacts of the major sociological paradigms in the way we apprehend social reality and define current social service practice models.
- develop a critical social vision in analyzing social phenomena, particularly from the viewpoint of social justice and social change.
- begin to understand the anti-oppressive dimensions of social service associated with social class, gender, ethnic group, sexual orientation, age, state of health, spirituality, and political choices.

The course is designed with a participative approach. Formal lectures are interspersed with class exercises and discussions to promote assimilation of theoretical concepts and better understanding of the potential applications of these theoretical elements in social service. The exercises also encourage critical thinking about oneself as a learning role player, and help affirm, supplement, or correct knowledge acquired in the course as a whole. Naturally, questions are welcomed in the class. Students are encouraged to keep a log throughout the trimester. Students can also verify their assimilation of the subject matter by completing self-evaluations at the end of each module. The course is divided into three major modules:

1. Social service as social science, its clientele, values, and basic model.
2. Social service: The influence of the major sociological paradigms. We use the grouping of paradigms made by Lallement (2000):
   - System-based schools (Functionalism, Marxism, Culturalism, Structuralism)
   - Actor-based schools (Interactionism, Actionism)
   And we add a third group of paradigms:
   - System- and actor-based schools (Eco-systemic Perspective, Constructivism, and Postmodernism)

3. Current issues:
   - In praise of diversity (sex and gender, identity and sexual orientation, race and ethnicity, etc.)
   - Social change at the dawn of the twenty-first century

Ideally, we would like to structure learning methods so that the class or course becomes an educational and reflective environment (Neuman & Blundo, 2000), not just a place of academic studies. We want to provide as many opportunities to promote a "community of learning" (Tinto & Love, 1995; Tinto & Riemer, 1998). To do so, we integrate discussions by the Internet and other facilities. The following exercise, used last year, is another example.

THE CONSCIOUSNESS-RAISING EXERCISE

In the first module, we use an exercise in class adapted from the work of Maurice Moreau. When combined with the logbook, this exercise has proven to be a powerful lever to motivate students to reflect upon their own counter-transference reactions. The exercise helps students become more aware of social work values. It also helps them achieve a fuller understanding of the sometimes complex and difficult process of clients asking for assistance. It highlights the full significance of non-judgmentalism and the importance of distinguishing between the person and his or her behaviour—two underlying basics of intervention. Finally, it helps inculcate the anti-oppressive perspective toward social work with its openness to diversity in a more personal, more internalized way, so that it is not just so much university rhetoric.

The exercise is relatively simple. The class is divided into subgroups of about twenty participants each, with each subgroup led by someone familiar with group facilitation—ideally, someone with a working knowledge of adult education. Allow at least one and a half to two hours for the exercise. Each of the steps should be followed carefully, and the group leader should provide enough time for discussions so that the entire reflective process inherent in the exercise can play out.

The basic material required for the exercise is an envelope for each student, containing nine cards. To facilitate the work, we used different colours, with each envelope containing one card of each colour. The choice of colour is unrelated to the dimension it is associated with. The cards correspond to characteristics pertaining to nine personal dimensions:

Table 22.2: DIMENSIONS AND CHARACTERISTICS ON CONSCIOUSNESS-RAISING EXERCISE CARDS

Card Colour	Dimension	Examples of Characteristics Listed on the Cards
Brown	Occupation	Works full time, part time, studies, is unemployed or on social assistance
Grey	Schooling	From primary school to the highest university level, illiterate
Green	Sexual preference	Homosexual, bisexual, heterosexual, paraphilia (pedophilia, voyeurism, exhibitionism, etc.)
Beige	Race and ethnic origin	Multiple choice: Serbia, Rwanda, Russia, etc.
Yellow	Religion and spirituality	Atheist, Buddhist, Jehovah's Witness, Mormon, Evangelist, Muslim, etc.
Turquoise	Civil status	Celibate, married, common law, separated or divorced, with or without children, blended family (first number: own children; second number: other person's children)
Lilac	Age	From adolescent to elderly, any age
Pink	Health status and disability	AIDS, spina bifida, severe language problems, aphasia, deafness, enuresis, encopresis, etc.
Blue	Sex and gender	Male, female, transsexual, transvestite

It is important to ask everyone to respect the periods of silence so that the exercise can be internalized more effectively.

The four steps are as follows:

1. Hand out the envelopes. Maintain silence. Ask that they be opened at the same time. Each person then opens his or her envelope and examines the personal characteristics on the cards. First, ascertain that the characteristics presented are understood and provide brief and concise explanations, if required, to insure a basic understanding. This is an important time to help the students become aware of the diversity of situations and to provide a minimum of information to expand their horizons in the face of situations that are often unknown.

2. In the second step, the students keep six of the characteristics and discard three others that seem of less or no interest to themselves; i.e., if applied to themselves rather than to a client or a potential client. This should all be done in silence. Next, go around the table to allow everyone to express his or her choices and the motivation behind the choices. During the facilitation, it is appropriate to take note that what seems difficult for some is not for others, and vice versa. Make sure that all participants express themselves.

3. In the third step, each student places the six retained characteristics in the envelope and takes back the three discarded characteristics. A few minutes of silence are then given during which the students are asked to imagine being someone with these characteristics. Everyone then takes the time to identify the emotions and feelings that he or she experienced in doing so. Sometimes it is not possible to juxtapose all three characteristics in a single individual; in this case, the students concerned are asked to try different scenarios. If someone claims to be incapable of putting himself or herself into the shoes of someone with the characteristics in question, the facilitator then asks the student to make an effort, but does not put too much pressure on him or her. Another turn is then made around the table to discuss each person's reactions. It is important that the students always be encouraged to express themselves in the first person in order to avoid lapsing into generalities and to keep their thinking on an emotional level instead. If necessary, the facilitator should help out by saying "I'd like you to try again, but this time saying 'I.'" You can also focus attention on the person's thinking process—how his or her reactions changed between the second and third steps. Make sure all participants have an opportunity to express themselves.

4. The last step consists of identifying what might induce this person to seek assistance, on one hand, and on the other, the attitudes, behaviours, etc., that this person would like to find in the one providing the assistance—the one he or she was consulting. As in the previous steps, give personal reflection time followed by a turn around the table. Elicit the identified expectations, which are, in fact, the attitudes and qualities that need to be developed as a social worker. Note also how the assistance process is sometimes complex and often requires an immense effort on the part of the person doing the consulting, and the concomitant importance of assigning value to the process being undertaken.

Once the steps are completed, everyone returns to the main group to share their thoughts on the exercise itself and to identify the basic values of social work and the process of asking for help.

CONCLUSION

We have proposed a relatively simple but powerful consciousness-raising exercise that can be used in a variety of anti-oppressive practice education courses. It allows the re-examination of various assumptions that interfere with the assistance process, both from the point of view of the individual being helped as well as that of the social worker. It helps put in perspective ideas relating to gender, ethnic origin, sexual orientation, health condition, age, spiritual or religious affiliation, social class, etc. Finally, it is based on the principle that there are thousands of ways to live one's reality as a human being, and that one of the fundamental attitudes in intervention should be to recognize the innate value of each person in a non-judgmental manner.

NOTES

1. We also include men, contrary to most writings on anti-oppressive practices that identify men in general as oppressors. From a postmodern perspective, we believe that masculinity remains a social construct, a product of culture and history. It is, to use an expression of Weeks (1991), an "ongoing fiction." Rather than perceiving a universal masculinity, we profoundly believe in a multiplicity of masculinities. Not all men are identical. Individuals are actively involved in constructing their gender identity (West & Zimmerman, 1987). There is therefore a multiplicity of masculinities and we should also consider this "fluidity of representations" (Connell, 1995) by

highlighting the complexity of the masculine experience (Wilcox & Forrest, 1992). Increasingly, working with men has brought out the negative impacts on many men of what Connell (1995) calls "hegemonic masculinity," and some significant shifts in the application of the feminist analysis that confuses person and behaviour (Tremblay, 2000).

2. There is a relatively new reality, brought to light by Nathanson and Young (2000) among others, that ridicules men, especially through advertising.

3. Greene makes no mention of youth. However, work with adolescents in particular leads one to reflect on the various forms of adultism, in the school setting in particular, in relations with parents, etc.

4. There does not seem to be any French word for the English neologism "ableism." We propose the expression *capacitisme*.

REFERENCES

Berzoff, J., & de Lourdes Mattei, M. (1999). Teaching intersubjectivity: Paradox and possibility. *Smith College Studies in Social Work 69*(2) 373–387.

Bourdieu, P. (1972). *Esquisse d'une théorie de la pratique.* Paris and Geneva: Droz.

Clark, J. (2000). *Beyond empathy: An ethnographic approach to cross-cultural social work practice.* Paper presented at the Joint Conference of the FITS and IASSW, Montreal.

Connell, R.W. (1995). *Masculinities.* St. Leonards: Allen & Unwin.

Cyr, G. (2002). *Les dynamiques des theories et pratiques anti-oppressives et critiques: Conflits intellectuels positifs.* Paper presented at the RUFUTS (ASFAS) Seminar, Quebec City.

Denis, C., Descent, D., Fournier, J., & Millette, G. (2001). *Individu et société.* Montreal: Chenelière/McGraw-Hill.

Freire, P. (1974). *Pédagogie des opprimés: suivi de Conscientisation et révolution.* Paris: Maspero.

Garcia, B., & Van Soest, D. (1999). Teaching about diversity and oppression: Learning from the analysis of critical classroom events. *Journal of Teaching in Social Work 18*(1/2), 149–167.

Goffman, E. (1956/1973). *La mise en scène de la vie quotidienne.* Paris: Minuit.

Gramsci, A. (1971). *Selections from the prison notebooks of Antonio Gramsci.* New York: International Publishers.

Greene, R.R., Watkins, M., McNutt, J., & Lopez, L. (1998). Diversity defined. In R.R. Greene and M. Watkins (Eds.), *Serving diverse constituencies: Applying the ecological perspective* (pp. 29–58). New York: Aldine De Gruyter.

Lallement, M. (2000). *Histoire des idées sociologiques de Parsons aux contemporains.* Paris: Nathan (CIRCA).

Nathanson, P., & Young, K. (2001). *Spreading misandry: The teaching of contempt for men in popular culture.* Montreal: McGill-Queen's University Press.

Neuman, K., & Blundo, R. (2000). Curricular philosophy and social work education: A constructivist perspective. *Journal of Teaching in Social Work 20*(1/2), 19–38.

Pozzuto, R. (2000). *Power & knowledge in social work.* Paper presented at the Joint Conference of the FITS and IASSW, Montreal.

Thorne-Beckerman, A. (1999). Postmodern organizational analysis: An alternative framework for social worker schools. *Social Work in Education 21*(4) 177–188.

Tinto, V., & Love, A.G. (1995). *A longitudinal study of learning communities and the reconstruction of communities at La Guardia Community College.*

Tinto, V., & Riemer, S. (1998). *Remedial education in higher education: Learning communities and the reconstruction of identity.* Available on request from vtinto@syr.edu.

Tremblay, G. (1996). L'intervention sociale auprès des hommes—Vers un modèle s'adressant à des hommes plus traditionnels. *Service Social 45*(2), 21–30.

_____. (2000). *"Les femmes et les enfants d'abord," ou quelle place reste-t-il poru les homme s dans l'intervention familiale?* Paper presented at the Joint Conference of the FITS and the IASSW, Montreal.

Tremblay, G., & L'Heureux, F. (2002). L'intervention psychosociale auprès des hommes: Un modèle émergeant d'intervention clinique. *Intervention* 116, 13-25.

Ungar, M. (2002). *Surviving as a postmodern social worker in direct practice: Now you see me ... now you don't.* Paper presented at the Canadian Association of Schools of Social Work Annual Conference, Toronto.

Van Voorhis, R. (1998). Culturally relevant practice: Addressing the psychosocial dynamics of oppression. In R.R. Greene and M. Watkins (Eds.), *Applying the ecological perspective* (pp. 97–112). New York: Aldine De Gruyter.

Weeks, J. (1991). *Against nature: Essays on history, sexuality and identity.* London: Rivers Oram Press.

West, C., & Zimmerman, D. (1987). Doing gender. *Gender and Society 1*, 125–151.

Wilcox, D.W., & Forrest, L. (1992). The problems of men and counseling: Gender bias or gender truth? Special issue: Mental health counseling for men. *Journal of Mental Health Counselling 14*(3), 291–304.

Chapter 23

Principles and Practices of Anti-Oppressive Pedagogy as Represented by Dr. Terri Swice

Carolyn Campbell
Maritime School of Social Work
Dalhousie University

INTRODUCTORY NOTE

Lusted (1986, p. 10) states: "Critical theory often carries a contradiction in its address, calling for change in its content while reproducing the existing relations in its form." Many social work educators committed to preparing students for anti-oppressive practice are attempting to address this contradiction by developing pedagogical practices that support and enhance anti-oppressive curricular content. As a contribution to this initiative, this chapter presents the partial results of a research project that asked the question "How do educators strive for congruency between the content and process of education for anti-oppressive social work practice?" (Campbell, 2002). Using a collective case study methodology (Stake, 2000; Yin, 1989), I explored the joys, struggles, principles, and practices of a selected group of Canadian social work educators teaching curricular content directed toward preparing graduates for anti-oppressive practice. For a number of ethical and methodological reasons I used an analytical technique known as "the ideal type" to represent the findings of the study. Devised by Max Weber, an ideal type is

> A construct that serves as a heuristic device developed for methodological purposes in the analysis of social phenomena. An ideal type is constructed from elements and characteristics of the phenomena under investigation but it is not intended to

correspond to all of the characteristics of any one case. An ideal type is a sort of composite picture that all the cases of a particular phenomenon will be compared with. (Iverson Software, undated)

The ideal type does not refer to normative or moral ideals, nor is it meant to describe an existing reality. Rather, it serves as an abstraction that assists in understanding and representing particular phenomena, in this case the educational principles and practices of selected social work educators. The ideal construct employed here is Dr. Terri Swice (*S*ocial *W*ork *I*deal *C*ongruent *E*ducator), a social work educator who is applying for a position at a social work school working within an anti-oppressive framework. By following Dr. Swice through selected aspects of this application process, the reader is introduced to many central concepts of the research enquiry—social identity, professional education, power, and barriers to educational congruency—in an engaging and informative fashion. This ideal type is not used as a means of presenting the perfect congruent educator that all should ascribe to, but as a technique for illuminating the noteworthy degree of consensus among research participants. (Other sections of the original research report explore the diversity that was evident among participants.)

Please accompany Dr. Swice as she presents her statement of pedagogical principles and practices, takes part in question-and-answer sessions with members of the school community and students of the school, and is interviewed by the school search committee. As a partial representation of the work of a number of dedicated Canadian social work educators, this information advances our pedagogical practice, enhances students' understanding of anti-oppressive practice, and ultimately improves service to clients.

STATEMENT OF PEDAGOGICAL PRINCIPLES AND PRACTICES PRESENTED BY DR. TERRI SWICE

My overall responsibility as an educator is to facilitate a process that establishes an environment that promotes learning. Within the context of teaching anti-oppressive social work content, a variety of interconnected principles and practices inform my educational endeavours, including:

1. *A comprehensive conception of the role and responsibility of educators.*
   I strongly believe that teaching should be grounded in solid pedagogical theory that accounts for elements of both teaching and learning. I have been

significantly influenced by educators such as M. Knowles, P. Freire, b. hooks, and P. Lather, learning that nurturing a collaborative, enabling, and mutually illuminating process of teaching and learning is essential. I see the content and process of teaching and learning as inexorably linked, in that the process is frequently the content and the content is the process.

As an educator in a university I have accepted the privileges and responsibilities that come with the position. I attend to issues of authority in the classroom, acknowledging my privileged position in the presence of students. It is my responsibility to be adequately prepared for classes; to present course material in a clear and organized fashion; to be clear and forthcoming about my expectations; to be accessible to students; to accommodate unique learning needs; to use multiple methods of instruction; to present different perspectives, bodies of knowledge, and concepts; to foster critical thinking and self awareness; to foster integration of the course content and process; and to facilitate a learning process that is both creative and fun.

To reflect this principle in my practice, I take note of who speaks in the classroom and monitor my use of institutional and professional authority. I develop very detailed course outlines and clearly describe participation requirements and assignments and the criteria that will be used for evaluation. My office door is generally open and I sometimes give out my home phone number. I encourage students, both verbally and in writing, to inform me if they have accommodation needs in relation to (dis)ability. I use a variety of educational methods such as experiential exercises, co-operative learning activities, presentations by community resource people, critical questioning, directed study groups, debates, large and small group discussions, case analyses, skill practice, and talking or healing circles. It has been my experience that most social work students learn inductively—that is, they build theory from practice, and I structure my teaching processes accordingly. I also use a number of creative techniques such as role-playing, collages, and puppetry.

2. *Promoting critical analysis.*

The promotion of critical analysis is central to anti-oppressive pedagogy. Critical analysis implies the deconstruction of knowledge, concepts, and professional practices by asking questions: What does the information mean? Why might one say what one said? Where do beliefs and practices come from? What might other people think about this topic? How would this idea affect social work practice? What contradictions are evident? What are the implications for people on the margins? How does the language used influence how we think about the issue? Does your thinking shift as you consider this topic? Integral to the promotion of critical analysis is an overt rejection of my position as an "expert, all-knowing" instructor who can provide the answers to all questions and concerns.

There is no list of specific practices that reflect this principle in my practice. Rather, this principle would be evident in my course descriptions and designs; in my choice of assigned reading (many first-voice readings); in the way I use critical questioning during classroom activities and interactions; in the validation of students' opinions and the use of multiple sources of knowledge (such as students' experiences, guest speakers, audiovisual material); in encouraging students to resist the desire to find recipes for practice; in the use of multiple teaching methods; and in analysis of the impact of constructs such as race, class, gender, ability, age, and sexual orientation.

3. *Supporting student engagement in learning.*

Learning theory has clearly shown us that people learn better if they are actively engaged in their learning. I attempt to facilitate student engagement in a number of ways, especially by asking them to engage in a participatory learning process that may be very different from processes they have experienced before. Many come to us having experienced what Freire calls the "banking" method of education, where they have been fairly passive recipients of instructors' information and knowledge. In contrast, I ask students to actively engage in defining their own learning needs and interests, to contribute to the development of a classroom community that fosters mutual learning, and to understand why such pedagogical processes are important to social work education and practice.

I do this by overtly explaining my pedagogical philosophy and by collaboratively determining course design, timing, content, processes, and evaluation schemes. The multiple methods of instruction referred to above engage a broad range of students. I seek out both formative and summative feedback from students and use this to modify course content and process. I also rely on a variety of techniques to encourage the participation of all students. For example, focused rounds and talking circles give everyone, even those unwilling or unable to speak in a large group context, an opportunity to express themselves. I make concerted efforts to validate any participation by students and class participation is frequently an aspect of the evaluation process that contributes to students' final grades.

I also acknowledge that students have lives outside of school and each student will have a different constellation of supports and barriers to their learning. While I am clear about not engaging in a counselling role with students, I do try to remain empathic and sensitive to the joys and fears that accompany learning, and to help them reduce the material, social, and psychological barriers that thwart learning. Similarly, I recognize that previous educational experiences may differentially influence students' responses to classroom pedagogical processes. Finally, trusting in students' capacity to engage in the learning process and actively explore the questions and answers of interest to them, I encourage inquisitiveness, engagement, self-direction, collaboration, responsibility, and active participation in all aspects of the course.

4. *Nurturing relationships and establishing community.*

Relationships are central to effective teaching and learning. Two categories of relationships are important: relationships between myself and the students, and relationships among the students. I work to establish respectful and dialogical relationships with students by being accessible, listening to their concerns, mentoring when appropriate, and engaging in joint projects such as writing or presentations.

While I assume primary responsibility for classroom processes, I use the participatory learning process to encourage students to invest in the classroom as a learning community, and to make their own individual and collective contributions to the creation of a respectful, trustful, and honourable learning environment. In such an environment people are able to take risks, to make mistakes, to compassionately challenge themselves and each other, and to explore deeper parts of themselves. I try to help students understand that if we are to develop our awareness of oppression and domination, some personal risks will be necessary and a trusting community will enable such risk taking. Developing such a community takes hard work, compassion, consideration of students as complex individuals, and extensive attention to classroom processes, including the provision of ongoing and supportive feedback.

Practices that contribute to the development of such a learning environment include specifically articulating its importance in course outlines and other documents; collaboratively developing classroom guidelines; check-ins or writing stems at the beginning of each class to help students identify what they bring to class and then leave behind; community times that give students time to talk about "non-academic" community concerns; and encouraging and modelling respectful listening, critique, challenge, and change.

Related to the establishment of a respectful learning community is the concept of classroom safety. For some, "safety" means never feeling uncomfortable, never being challenged or disagreed with, or never being asked to examine and change behaviour. In my experience, allegations of not feeling "safe" arise when dominance or privilege is being challenged. "Safety" is a nebulous concept—the world is not safe for a lot of people and, depending upon our social location, we experience safety quite differently. While I vehemently support the notion of a respectful classroom community or environment, I do not find the construct of classroom safety to be a useful one.

5. *Using experience as a pedagogical base.*

Students have a rich experiential base that can contribute to their own and others' development as a social worker. Courses are structured to build on this experience and to help students bring it to the process of working with others. I frequently rely on student participants to help me construct a worthwhile pedagogical experience. When inviting students to have an active role in class design, content, and process, I encourage them to speak from their subjective experiences and to learn from the experiences of classmates. Often, at the beginning of a course, I will do a circle round in which students identify their social work experience. From this I prepare a list of collective experience, demonstrating the rich experiential base of the classroom community. Similarly, I try to teach analyses and skills that are relevant to their lives.

However, experience is not taken as an unexamined given. Self-reflective and reflexive thinking are essential within anti-oppressive practice, and we need opportunities to explore the various ways we have learned to make meaning of the world. Such self-awareness and self-reflection about personal values, beliefs, social location, and experience are necessary for students to decide on the kinds of social workers they want to be.

I facilitate such reflection in a variety of ways. Students are encouraged to verbalize their thoughts and feelings about how the course content relates to them. First-voice readings, critical questioning concerning the application of theory to their experiences, small group discussions, role plays, and a wide range of assignments are all used to promote self-awareness and personal reflection.

Just as I ask students to bring their own experiences and reflections to their learning, I ask the same of myself. I understand that my pedagogical principles and practices are an outgrowth of my political and personal beliefs and values and my vision of life and education. I make it clear to students that I am speaking my truth, which arises from my experience and my teachings, as a woman with a particular background and social location.

When it will contribute to learning, or to the development of the classroom community, I share this background and identity. I also draw upon instances from my practice background to illustrate particular points and to model the analyses and deconstruction of experience. I strive for congruency between my beliefs and my actions and reflect on this struggle, alone and with colleagues or friends.

As part of this self-reflection I monitor my thoughts, feelings, and behaviours in relation to students: Do I hear some students more than others? How do I respond to feedback? How am I using my power in student-instructor relationships? Have I contributed to inequity based on race, class, gender, ability, age, or sexual orientation?

6. *Facilitating classroom and practice connections.*

We are educating future practitioners and, upon graduation, students will need to be able to do something with the knowledge and skills they have gained. I assist students in learning a range of skills, including analysis, which they will need in professional practice and in their daily lives. I hope I am encouraging students to grow, to understand that learning is lifelong, and to know that they must continue their learning upon graduation. I hope I am also teaching them in a way that enhances their ability to transfer their learning to practice settings, be that during practicum or upon graduation. Moving their educational experience beyond the bounds of the classroom by inviting community and professional "voices" into the classroom and establishing links with the practice community is central to these aims. These voices are especially crucial when I am teaching content that diverges from my own social identity and/or experience. Most assignments have a community action piece and I encourage students to do systematic inquiry within the community.

7. *Working with affect in the classroom.*

Critical analysis, active engagement in the learning process, and self-reflection and transformation, coupled with the content of anti-oppressive curricula, present considerable challenges for students. We are not only asking students to learn new values, knowledge, and skills, we are also asking them to critique and perhaps transform long-standing patterns of thinking, feeling, and behaving. This involves being self-reflective, engaging in critique, being open to challenge from others, considering the classroom a community, and moving their learning into family, community, and professional contexts. Such learning and "unlearning" can be both painful and exciting, and the ramifications extend far beyond the walls of the classroom. Personal and professional relationships are often affected, and this creates distress and turmoil for students. The educational process is an affair of the heart and soul as well as the hand and the head (personal communication, Clews, 2001), and instructors need to be cognizant of the potential toll on students and support and encourage them in their affective struggles and growth.

Numerous classroom processes can assist: exercises such as check-ins, checkouts, writing stems, and unstructured circle rounds all give students an opportunity to focus themselves on the task at hand. It is helpful to alert students in advance, via both written and verbal communications, to the fact that they might experience emotional reactions to course content and process. This is particularly true when we know through experience that specific topics may serve as "triggers" for some students. They can then be given permission to participate at a level that is appropriate for them and to identify when it may be too difficult to engage with specific content. Debriefings that include a discussion of feelings are extremely important.

It is not surprising that resistance, conflict, and distress, as well as excitement and joy, become evident. Working with these feelings in an educational context demands inordinate attention to classroom content and processes and effective group facilitation skills. In an effort to minimize the potential of difficult situations that inhibit learning, I scrutinize the course content to insure it does not marginalize particular categories of students. Within the classroom I pay close attention to who is speaking and who is not, and look for patterns of participation. I note unspoken issues and conflicts and raise them when I consider that it might be helpful to the learning process. I try to be cognizant of the ways in which social relations of inequality are reproduced within the classroom and to intervene in ways that mitigate such relations. I return to the classroom guidelines at regular intervals, especially when difficult interpersonal situations do arise. If necessary I ask for third party assistance in mediating conflicts, usually from other colleagues. Finally, I consistently strive to improve my skills at responding to and negotiating critical incidents within the classroom.

EXCERPT FROM QUESTION-AND-ANSWER SESSION WITH DR. TERRI SWICE AND MEMBERS OF THE SCHOOL COMMUNITY

Question from the audience: As a social worker and an activist member of the local Black community, I have a vested interest in seeing more non-White social workers within professional practice? Could you comment on how you work with the question of identity in your educational practice?

Dr. Swice: Of course, the whole question of social identity politics is a contested one and one that gets us in trouble sometimes. I think we have to be really cautious about making assumptions about people from so-called marginalized communities. We try and establish neat and clear boundaries, but students or professors don't always fit those boxes and such classification negates the reality that we all have multiple identities. We also need to respect people's self-definition of their social location while recognizing that this may change as they become exposed to more theory and analysis.

Having said all that, I fully embrace the importance of having a diverse faculty and in surfacing and analyzing issues of power and privilege. Identity clearly makes a difference in student-instructor relationships and one cannot overstate the impact of, for example, a Black student having a Black instructor for perhaps the first time in his or her educational career. Because of the lack of a critical mass of faculty from "marginalized communities" (the language is still a challenge for us), this identification results in excessive workload for those faculty.

Question from the audience: Do you feel your identity affects how you teach and do you disclose your identity to students?

Dr. Swice: Certainly it affects who I am, and therefore how I teach. As a lesbian woman, I probably give more attention to lesbian, gay, bisexual, and two-spirited issues than a non-lesbian woman might. I might "come out" to students, but generally I will just talk about my experiences and some people read into them and some don't. I firmly believe that disclosure is useful only if it promotes learning as opposed to meeting any of my needs. When my sexual orientation is known to students, it really makes a difference—they come in and speak about their sexuality, asking if I have something they can read or if I know of other resources. Disclosure may leave those who do not share your identity feeling isolated from you, but I hope it models the importance of claiming an identity and working in that context.

Similarly as a White, able-bodied woman, I clearly label my privilege and explain to students why I am interested in anti-oppressive work. For example, if I am teaching about race, it is important for me to articulate the experiences that have left me committed to doing anti-racist work. If I don't, people could easily accuse me of arrogance—who is this White woman who presumes to talk about anti-racist work, especially to Aboriginal or African Canadian students? Again, though, I think we have to be careful about putting too much emphasis on connections based on social identity—it may set students up for disappointment.

While my political perspective, practice experiences, and social identity can't be conflated, they are quite connected. This means that I am more likely to engage with issues like critical consciousness and consciousness raising than issues of professionalism, for example.

Question from the audience: Could you explain that a bit more? What do you mean by disappointment?

Dr. Swice: For example, there was a lesbian student in one of my classes, but her understanding of lesbian identity did not match mine. She found this very difficult and it felt like a betrayal to her. She wanted to avoid writing her self-location paper for me and I think the resistance was because she would have been more comfortable writing for a straight person because she could evoke the dynamic of insider/outsider. Political or value orientation of a given instructor, as opposed to his or her social identity, may be more significant.

Question from the audience: How do you encourage students to engage with issues of social identity?

Dr. Swice: In a number of ways. I demonstrate that I don't know everything about every culture by bringing in guest speakers, using other resources, and working in partnerships with other faculty, especially faculty who represent social identities that differ from my own. I ask students to look at the elements of their identity that give them power.

I try to be skilful in handling classroom dynamics. A lot of critical and difficult incidents arise around issues of identity, especially when people are asked to look at privilege. This is when working with other faculty is especially helpful. Sometimes it is easier to engage students in self-examination of their identity if we share some similar characteristics, but there is no surety in this.

I select my readings with care and rely on a lot of first-voice writing to sensitize students to experiences different from their own. I use journals and other reflective assignments such as the self-location paper I referred to before. One assignment encourages students to take on an aspect of identity different from their own and to look at things like the media and their day-to-day experiences from that identity lens. It is a bit of a constructed experience, but a sensitizing experience nonetheless.

Question from the audience: I am a social work practitioner and a member of the Provincial Association of Social Workers. As such, I am invested in insuring that students are ready to be competent practitioners upon graduation. What do you see as the unique features of education preparing students for professional practice?

Dr. Swice: I think there are many unique features, but would highlight two. Initially, social work is a normative, value-based profession, and this sometimes poses challenges for social work education. Not everything goes. We make judgments about what are appropriate and inappropriate values and opinions for practice, maintaining that there are some value systems that are fundamentally incompatible with social work. The fact that we are educating students for a professional practice demands that we consider responsibility as an essential construct.

However, there is always a struggle with being too rigid or ideological and inadvertently shutting out other voices. While I don't subscribe to a moral relativism, we need to be sure we do not shut out dissent. We need to be more vigilant about insuring that we subject our positions (for example, anti-oppressive theory and practice) to ongoing critical analysis as well.

Secondly, while some educators and writers have commented that the existence of a mandated curricula (as established by educational policy documents and accreditation standards) is an impediment to critical analysis and the deconstruction of foundational knowledge, I have not found this to be the case. I think mandated curricula provides us a framework from which we can engage in critical analysis, asking how our foundational knowledge has affected people on the margins, and what we need to do to shift to make that impact better. There is still room to teach in one's own way and to deal with classroom processes while covering the required content.

Of more concern to me is the debate between education and training, education being seen as more critical analysis and training as more skill based. While this is an oversimplification, there is a tension. Students want to be taught what to do, and are sometimes looking for recipes for practice that are transferable from one practice situation to another. The tension is also evident in the profession's move toward defining practice in terms of competencies, which some educators see as making practice more technical and less critical. The market model of education and practice is becoming more influential. But educators also understand that we have to link education to the real world of work and insure that what students learn can be applied in human service agencies. This balancing act can generate conflict between school and community.

Dr. Search: I think it is about time we broke for lunch and would like to thank everyone for coming and Dr. Swice for the presentation. I remind faculty of this afternoon's meeting and students of the breakfast meeting tomorrow.

EXCERPT FROM QUESTION-AND-ANSWER SESSION WITH DR. TERRI SWICE AND STUDENTS

Student: Within an anti-oppressive curriculum we are taught to think of power as a process and to examine how power is expressed in different contexts. How you think power is expressed in the classroom?

Dr. Swice: That is a huge question. There are all sorts of power expressed in the classroom—power of the institution, of the instructor, of students. Some of the manifestations of power are very elusive. I find Starhawk's notion of power very helpful—she distinguishes between "power over," "power to," and "power with." Working within these distinctions helps people understand that power can be used constructively, resistantly, or destructively.

Institutional power is evident in the very notion that the professor is expected to come in and provide the knowledge and teachings and the students are to take it in. There is the power of the dominant thinking expressed within a classroom. For example, the majority of students are White, so there is a majority "racial" knowledge that makes sense in the classroom. That is an expression of power.

Instructors carry both institutional and positional power and authority. They have the power to politicize the curriculum and to determine what students read. They have the power to directly ask students questions or to tell students to be quiet, which is what usually happens when the instructor speaks. Then, of course, they have the power to grade.

Students can exercise power as well. If students collectively agree to go after something, they can be pretty powerful and an anti-oppressive curriculum teaches them collective methods. This can be really positive in that students can influence what is going on in the class and the program. They can become involved in joint projects with faculty. However, this collective power can be used in oppressive ways—they have the ability to hurt each other, they can manipulate group dynamics, they can engage in exclusionary practices with someone who has a different perspective or identity, and they can form cliques. Students can use identity politics, or victim politics, to move ahead. Within the classroom, students get bored, they tune out, they rustle papers, they talk, they get up and go outside, they read another paper. They also have the opportunity to grade instructors; the end-of-term evaluations influence how an instructor grows in an institution. One angry student can really pull down averages.

Student: Could you explain what you mean by politicizing the curriculum?

Dr. Swice: Perhaps an example would help. Sometimes students don't do the readings. What, for example, does it mean if the majority of students do not complete the readings on anti-racist social work? As a White instructor I cannot collude with this and let them leave the class without talking about racism. I either need to give a lecture about it or insure the material is covered somehow. In this way I am putting the curriculum in a political context, and insisting that students discuss anti-racism is an absolute assertion of my power.

Student: How do you as an instructor work with power in the classroom?

Dr. Swice: In a number of ways. I try to facilitate the development of a community and a climate that attends to process, is challenging and caring, allows for mistakes, meets diverse needs, and allows people to participate at their own level. I hope this lowers the power parameters. I share parts of myself; if I am asking students to share with me, to explore personal connections and I don't disclose my struggles in these areas, then it tips the power balance. I call attention to the dominant knowledge that exists, and try to counteract that dominance. I try to avoid the expert role. Most important, I think, I try to reflect on how I use power—to step back and step forward in my use of power—to be attentive to myself and my pedagogical practice.

Student: Can we talk about grading and evaluation for awhile?

Dr. Swice: Of course. There is no question that the whole grading and evaluation process really affects the nature of the relationship between students and instructors. I sometimes think students are relating to me in a particular way because they are afraid that I might not like them or that they might fail, and I definitely experience a shift in relationships after the first grades are distributed. No matter how much we try and practise from an inclusive, non-hierarchical place, the reality of grades is always going to overshadow interactions. I do experience significant contradictions—I want to encourage students to do whatever they need in order to learn and to take some risks, but at the same time I know they are trying to do what I want them to do in order to get a good grade.

I would like to do away with grades, but the bottom line is that they are my responsibility and it would take a major institutional reorganization to be able to change that. I always acknowledge the power that lies behind grading and the privilege I have as a teacher in the position of grading students' work and thoughts. I try to be fair and to use my position as a stepping stone to be creative in grading. Grades and transcripts are important for students and we need to continue to struggle with ways to do it well.

Student: How do you structure and mark assignments?

Dr. Swice: Assignments should maximize students' learning, get them to think, and to learn something they did not know before the assignment. I rarely use exams as I don't believe they help people learn. I try to provide a range of assignment options, sometimes using alternate methods such as non-graded videos, oral presentations, collages, and video presentations.

I have experimented with different ways of grading: co-negotiating the criteria for an excellent, good, or fair assignment; getting students to assign their own grade, with a rationale, and comparing that with the grade I have assigned—if there is a big difference, we meet to discuss it, doing pass/fail in some courses.

I try to be really clear in my expectations for assignments and in the criteria I will use to evaluate them. I am willing to spend a lot of time discussing and answering questions about assignments, either in the class or individually with students. I have redeveloped assignments if they have not been clear to students. The criteria I use in evaluating assignments are always clearly spelled out and include critical thinking (does the assignment move beyond description), use of the readings, presentation of a cogent argument, self-critique, and implications for practice.

If one sees the purpose of assignments as maximizing learning, then giving detailed feedback is really important. I am very specific in comments, in summarizing feedback, in pointing out positives and areas that students need to strengthen. Sometimes I use a multiple-stage process where I return assignments with my feedback but no grade, ask the student(s) to respond to the feedback and suggest a grade, and then I look at all that and decide on a final grade. I do this because when students see a grade, they sometimes use the grade as the lens for interpretation of any of the feedback and they don't really absorb or get the benefit of the feedback.

Student: Do you think it is fair for instructors to grade us on our own thoughts and feelings? They ask us to express ourselves and disclose who we are, then that is evaluated. Sometimes it feels like our worth as a person is being graded.

Dr. Swice: The establishment of clear criteria is especially important in self-reflective or personal awareness assignments. While I have some discomfort grading a personal self-disclosure or opinions, I stress that it is not the feelings or opinions I am grading, but how they have pulled it together, how they reflect upon themselves and their thoughts, how in-depth they go with that reflection, as well as the other criteria I mentioned. Sometimes I don't grade subjective or reflective assignments or I give full marks for just completing the assignment. This encourages a more unguarded reflection and self-critique.

Student: Are you willing to discuss grades with students?

Dr. Swice: I try to be accessible to students in relation to grades. I want to be fair and am willing to talk over the specifics of my feedback and grades. I encourage them to come and see me about grades—even if I appear upset, I ask them to try and get beyond me looking upset because I may just be busy. While I am open to talking, I do expect students to clearly point out what they think I have missed or how I have not been fair. I am not very sympathetic to unsupported complaints, or to the argument that they need a higher grade to get into grad school. I will also consult with colleagues.

Student: Do you permit rewrites?

Dr. Swice: The question of pre-submitting drafts and rewrites is a difficult one. Depending upon the number of students I have in a term, time is a factor—there just is not enough time. I wonder about the fairness of looking at written drafts. Does that give some students an advantage over others? I tend to discuss assignments with students and try and give them some verbal direction as opposed to written commentary. Sometimes students expect an "A" after they have submitted a draft, so that is awkward.

I have tried different things with rewrites and permit them most often in pass/fail courses. Sometimes I will accept rewrites with the caveat that the grade will be raised only to a particular level. I have tried different things in different classes, but have not really found a satisfactory solution.

EXCERPT FROM AN INTERVIEW WITH DR. TERRI SWICE AND THE SEARCH COMMITTEE

Search Committee Member: You have spoken at length about your commitment to anti-oppressive pedagogy and the principles and practices that support that commitment. Have you encountered barriers to doing this work and, if so, what shape and form have those barriers assumed?

Dr. Swice: Most certainly, but it is difficult to organize an answer to that question. The barriers are so varied and wide-ranging. I have found it helpful to think of external and internal barriers—external being those that are outside of social work programs or curricula and internal those that we generate ourselves.

Externally, there is the institution of academia itself. Many conventions and practices of the university mitigate against pedagogical congruency. For example, the notion of grades and the investment that students must have in their grades; the expert role we are expected to assume; course evaluation processes, tenure, and promotion criteria; and the multiple demands on faculty.

Search Committee Member: How do you see the course evaluations as a barrier?

Dr. Swice: Well, they are valuable in that they give students an officially recognized voice in promotion decisions, and I certainly support that. However, learning is a cumulative process and students may not integrate their learning until long after the course is over. Course evaluations are not able to reflect this learning process. Also, anti-oppressive pedagogy often involves confronting and challenging students, which can be uncomfortable, no matter how hard one works to create a supportive environment. Student resistance to this discomfort can be expressed in instructor evaluations.

Search Committee Member: And the tenure and promotion criteria?

Dr. Swice: Faculty hired in designated positions assume that the special requirements that come with such designation will be considered. However, the criteria for tenure and promotion are "one size fits all" and there is no reflection of unique needs or demands in the criteria. As well, anti-oppressive work lends itself to collaboration and co-operative work—writing, publishing, working with students, etc.—and the extra time that such work takes is also not recognized in the criteria.

Search Committee Member: Are there other external barriers?

Dr. Swice: In my more despairing moments I sometimes wonder if we are just training foot soldiers for the state or handmaidens for the patriarchy (personal communication, Hersing, 2001). We are often seen as, and see ourselves as, training grounds for employment, and the influence of corporate and market ideologies is increasing daily. How do our students wrestle with the theory we give them in sometimes very oppressive workplaces?

Search Committee Member: You also mentioned internal barriers. Could you expand upon that please?

Dr. Swice: I am not sure we have really refined our curricula to insure that we are giving students the foundational concepts of anti-oppressive theory in a way that facilitates a deep and complex understanding of them. Do they really understand concepts like oppression, domination, power, language, or difference? Or are they just leaving with very superficial notions of these concepts that will translate into ineffective practice?

There is a lack of theoretical clarity within the body of knowledge that is broadly defined as anti-oppressive. We use the term loosely, thinking we are all talking about the same thing, but there are meaningful differences among structural, radical, critical, post-structural, and postmodern theory, all of which seemed to get thrown in the same basket. What are the assumptions of each of these perspectives? How are they similar or different? We sometimes don't apply the same measure of critical analysis and deconstruction to anti-oppressive theory that we do to other theories and students pick up on this discrepancy. I think this lack of clarity and critique is one of the reasons why students may leave with only a surface understanding of some of the concepts. We need to clarify our framework.

Member of the Search Committee: Can you give us a specific illustration of this lack of theoretical clarity?

Dr. Swice: One of my frustrations with anti-oppressive theory is what I see to be the inordinate attention given to oppressed groups. Why does the focus not shift more to dominant groups, or away from groups completely? The problem with a structural analysis focusing solely on politically or socially identified groups is that it assumes that everyone from the same group will have the same consciousness and the same location and relations. Perhaps we should pay more attention to language or discourse. I think these debates are rooted in a theoretical uncertainty. Perhaps we are in the midst of a move from structural theory to something else, but it is all quite cloudy at the moment.

We are also not building our own knowledge sufficiently, especially with regard to practice. How do our graduates do out there? How does the classroom relate to practice? I think we really have to look onward and address these deficiencies or contradictions if we are going to advance the project of anti-oppressive social work.

Member of the Search Committee: Many of us have spoken about the personal risks and challenges of doing this work—at times feeling tired, vulnerable, etc. I wonder if you have experienced these reactions or feelings.

Dr. Swice: Most definitely. There is the despair I referred to earlier, and I sometimes have felt real isolation and fear that I am not going to be supported in my work or in difficult interpersonal situations, especially conflicts with students. Sometimes I don't have the strength to face the conflicts or processes that need attention. I lose my confidence and courage. There is also a personal vulnerability that comes with self-disclosure: if we believe in modelling by sharing our social location, that modelling may leave you vulnerable and sometimes, to put it bluntly, it is taken advantage of. Students often see us as invulnerable, not recognizing that we can be hurt too. This is particularly difficult for faculty "from the margins" as they are judged more harshly and students criticize in a nasty way that is not as likely to happen with "mainstream" professors. Such criticism—often implicitly or explicitly— is criticism of one's life, family, community, and heritage and it is very painful.

Member of the Search Committee: In the midst of these barriers and risks, what keeps you at this work? What joys or satisfactions do you find?

Dr. Swice: Oh, there are many and, in spite of all we have spoken of, the work is worth it. It is an absolute thrill to create places of movement with students, to watch them grow and develop, to see their thinking shift, to watch them struggle with integrating all they have learned, to see them connect theory with their own experiences and say "Oh, that makes sense now." All of this is very rewarding. I find it a positive challenge to use the skills I have developed over the years to try and create a learning environment for us all.

When the process is working well, there is an amazing mutuality about it, which is incredibly satisfying.

For me, the classroom is a space where I feel a great sense of independence and where subversion can take place. Most of us committed to this work have a vision of a healthy society and our work within the classroom is planting the seeds of that vision. In a similar vein, if we want our profession to change, then working within an educational context can also contribute to that change.

More personally, I feel a real need to pursue a sense of what could be and to enter into a sense of possibility. I never do the same thing twice. I'm not stagnant but always on the edge of my learning curve. I enjoy bringing in another lens to look at practice and to share my truth with students and colleagues. I like meeting new people, learning from others, and doing collaborative work with students and colleagues, both in my own school and nationally or internationally. Ultimately, I believe it will change social work practice and thereby improve the lives of the individuals, families, and communities with which we work.

REFERENCES

Campbell, C. (2002). *Struggling for congruency: Principles and practices of anti-oppressive social work pedagogy.* Unpublished doctoral dissertation, Memorial University of Newfoundland.

Iverson Software. (undated). *Glossary/Dictionary of terms & terminology of sociology.* Available from: <www.iversonsoftware.com/sociology/ideal_type.htm>

Lusted, D. (1986). Why pedagogy? *Screen 27*(5), 2–14.

Stake, R. (2000). Case studies. In N. Denzin & Y. Lincoln (Eds.), *Handbook of qualitative research* (2nd ed.) (pp. 435–454). Thousand Oaks: Sage Publications.

Yin, R. (1989). *Case study research: Design and methods.* Newbury Park: Sage Publications.

Chapter 24

Are We Ready to Take a Stand?
Education about Heterosexism—
Fostering Anti-Oppressive Practice

Mike Woodward
Doctoral Candidate
Faculty of Social Work
University of Toronto
Leslie Bella
School of Social Work
Memorial University of Newfoundland

Oppression, including that associated with heterosexism, occurs in many forms and at many levels. Social work, committed to social justice, aims to be anti-oppressive in its work with individuals, families, groups, communities, and organizations. But are social work practitioners prepared for anti-oppressive practice? Specifically, are they prepared to work toward empowerment and social justice with lesbian, gay, bisexual, transgendered, two-spirited, and queer/questioning (LGBTTQ) people? Such preparation is a priority for social work education in Canada, according to the accreditation standards of the Canadian Association of Schools of Social Work (CASSW) (2000). While, the literature offers educational strategies in some areas of oppression, such as racial and ethnic diversity and anti-oppression as outlined on the CASSW Web site (<www.mun.ca/cassw-ar/>), educational models concerning heterosexism and anti-oppression have received minimal attention.

To advance anti-oppressive practice with LGBTTQ people, we created an educational model to help social work practitioners and students understand heterosexism and adopt an anti-heterosexist approach to intervention. This chapter defines oppression, anti-oppression, and heterosexism; presents various educational strategies concerning homophobia and heterosexism from the literature; and describes the development, implementation, and evaluation of our educational model. We conclude with implications for social work education.

OPPRESSION, ANTI-OPPRESSIVE PRACTICE, AND HETEROSEXISM

Oppression still affects the lives of social work clients everywhere (Rose, Peabody, & Stratigeas, 1991). Some are denied human rights and privileges because of their sex, race, ethnicity, age, ability, sexuality, or class, for example. Structural inequalities and injustices result in oppression and marginalization. Power imbalances are at the heart of oppression: "the power to enforce a particular worldview; the power to deny equal access to housing, employment, and health care; the power alternately to define and/or efface difference; the power to maim, physically, mentally, and emotionally; and most importantly, the power to set the very terms of power" (Pellegrini, 1992, p. 54). The social organization of sexuality also reflects a system of power (Eichstedt, 1996). Social workers have a responsibility to engage in anti-oppressive and emancipatory practice that challenges forces that perpetuate oppression (Pinderhughes, 1995). Dominelli conceives anti-oppressive practice as:

> A form of social work practice which addresses social divisions and structural inequalities in the work that is done with "clients" (users) or workers. Anti-oppressive practice aims to provide more appropriate and sensitive services by responding to people's needs regardless of their social status. Anti-oppressive practice embodies a person-centered philosophy, an egalitarian value system concerned with reducing the deleterious effects of structural inequalities upon people's lives; a methodology focusing on both process and outcome; and a way of structuring relationships between individuals that aims to empower users by reducing the negative effects of hierarchy in their immediate interaction and the work they do together. (Dominelli, 1993, p. 24, as cited in Dominelli, 1998)

This definition applies equally to micro, meso, and macro practice, for anti-oppressive practice challenges current social relations that perpetuate inequality (Dominelli, 1998; Pinderhughes, 1995). Education for anti-oppressive practice involves empowering students to work toward transforming "unjust and oppressive social, economic, and political institutions into just and nonoppressive alternatives" (Gil, 1998, p. 1).

Homophobia, biphobia, and heterosexism are complex phenomena that oppress LGBTTQ people. Homophobia involves a dislike, fear, or hatred of homosexuals, leading to prejudice, discrimination, and even violence toward homosexuals or people thought to be homosexual (Mallon, 1998). Biphobia, a related concept, refers to the irrational fear, dislike, or hatred of bisexuals

(Van Wormer, Wells, & Boes, 2000). Throughout this chapter, homophobia is assumed to include biphobia. Heterosexism, the root cause of homophobia, is more pervasive and often more subtle. Heterosexism is "an ideological system that denies, denigrates, and stigmatizes any nonheterosexual [*sic*] form of behavior [*sic*], identity, relationship, or community" (Herek, 1992, p. 89), which holds heterosexuality as the norm and privileges it in relation to all other sexualities (Eichstedt, 1996; Logan & Kershaw, 1994; Sears, 1997). Heterosexuality becomes the standard against which LGBTTQ people are judged and seen as abnormal (Wise, 2000), pathological (Rudolph, 1988), deviant, and intrinsically less desirable (Berkman & Zinberg, 1997). Heterosexism, in essence, is concerned with social and institutional power (DiAngelo, 1997) and assigns superiority to heterosexuality that leads to control over LGBTTQ individuals by neglect, omission, and/or distortion. This assigned superiority is manifested in societal customs and institutions, individual attitudes and behaviours (Herek, 1992), and in laws, media, and language, "which either actively discriminate against non-heterosexuals or else render them invisible through silence" (Wise, 2000, p. 154). "Homophobia and heterosexism together form a system of institutionalized domination" (Appleby & Anastas, 1998, p. 11). Heterosexism "permeates the culture in which social institutions and social work practice are built" (Berkman & Zinberg, 1997, p. 320).

The Heterosexism Enquirer (*THE*) (Bella, n.d.) and the Challenging Heterosexism project (Bella & Yetman, 2000) explored the ways that non-heterosexuals are either assumed to be heterosexual, or are treated differently from heterosexuals. For instance, a physician assumed that a pregnancy might be the cause of a woman's health condition, even though she denied this possibility (she is lesbian, but did not feel comfortable disclosing this). Homosexual couples applying for income support in Newfoundland and Labrador have to submit separate applications because homosexual relationships are not recognized in policy regulations (Bella & Yetman, 2000). LBGTTQ individuals who feel extremely anxious about accessing services from an agency because of its heterosexist bias go without help. Employees in homosexual relationships often do not include their partners in health benefits because applying for such benefits requires them to "come out" or such benefits are not applicable to same-sex partners. The established literature confirms that heterosexist views are problematic in social work with lesbian, gay, bisexual, or transgendered clients; some are denied services, and others subjected to judgmental responses when they "come out" to a worker (Cramer, 1997). Counsellors' heterosexist bias also jeopardized mental health treatment for gay and lesbian clients (Rudolph, 1988).

EDUCATING ABOUT HETEROSEXISM

Recent literature has put forward educational strategies to prepare learners for anti-oppressive practice (e.g., Canadian Association of Schools of Social Work, n.d.; Morrison Van Voorhis, 1998; Razack, 1999). Articles suggesting various ways to educate helping professionals and students about homophobia focus primarily on clinical intervention, giving little attention to subtle and pervasive heterosexism. The presence of heterosexism in social work and other helping professions is well documented (see Berkman & Zinberg, 1997; Glenn & Russell, 1986; Logan & Kershaw, 1994; Morin, 1977; Rudolph, 1989), but has received less attention than other forms of oppression (Logan & Kershaw, 1994). As a result, this chapter explores a model for educating social work students and practitioners about heterosexism and its implications for anti-oppressive practice at all intervention levels.

While social work education is a cognitive process for gaining new knowledge, this alone is insufficient preparation for practice with people from oppressed groups (Congress, 1993). Education for anti-oppressive practice also involves exploring one's "assumptions and values, and the structure of the world around them" (Cain, 1996, p. 65). Education concerning heterosexism must deal with values, attitudes, and beliefs (Cain, 1996; DiAngelo, 1997). Because social work professionals and students come with a range of values, experiences, and prejudices, the impact of such education can be challenging on many levels. Learners not only respond out of unexamined values but also out of the defensiveness born of guilt and shame (I'm a social worker and I am supposed to be unbiased, but I have these beliefs). The educator must therefore lead learners through multiple emotions into a place where biases, including heterosexist ones, can be confronted and change can begin. The educational process involves shared exploration of students' (and the instructor's) values and practices, analyzing consistency between personal and professional values, and between those principles and the actual practices engaged in by social workers. The experience of dissonance between personal and professional values, or between values and practices, is experienced as a "challenge" that must be resolved.

Homophobia can be addressed by providing information, addressing self-awareness, and exposure to lesbians and gay men (Ben-Ari, 2001; Herek, 1990). Cramer (1997), for instance, employed educational units, course assignments, instructor self-disclosure, and speakers' panels. She found that "ethnographic research and combined experiential-didactic assignments can reduce social work students' homophobia. Instructor self-disclosure as lesbian/gay, within the context of an ongoing relationship of trust and respect, has also reduced homophobia" (Cramer, 1997, p. 295). Cain (1996) agreed on the value of instructor self-disclosure. Cramer (1997) found that speakers' panels and information alone had mixed effects. Serdahely and Ziemba (1984) found that a multifaceted module on homophobia (consisting of assigned readings, dyadic role-playing, and small group discussion) with college students was most effective with those with an initially high level of homophobia.

In contrast, DiAngelo (1997) offers a unique pedagogical approach for specific education about heterosexism. She emphasizes both micro and macro aspects of oppression, with heterosexism seen as a "heterosexual problem." The workshop aims to expose "the subtle ways in which heterosexuals maintain, benefit, and are complicit in the oppression of gays and lesbians, regardless of intentions" (DiAngelo, 1997, p. 5). In particular, heterosexuals are led through a process of uncovering "the deeply embedded messages and dynamics of sexual stratification they have received and participate in" (DiAngelo, 1997, p. 7). From this position, learners can select a course of action that "actively contributes to equity rather than contributes to the maintenance of the status quo" (Ibid.). This model, though, has not been evaluated.

Eichstedt (1996), teaching within sociology, also offers educational strategies concerning heterosexism that were positively reviewed by learners. In dyadic exercises students discuss and analyze "their own location in a gender/sexuality system, and the system itself" (Eichstedt, 1996, p. 385). A field project challenges students who have a problem with non-heterosexuals "flaunting" their sexuality in public. For other classroom exercises concerning LGBTTQ issues, see Blumenfeld (1992). These are also summarized in Appendix 2 of *Not Just a Passing Phase: Social Work with Gay, Lesbian, and Bisexual People* (Appleby & Anastas, 1998).

In summary, students and practitioners should be helped to understand the impact of heterosexism and to value an anti-oppressive stance. Both didactic and experiential learning, encouraging both intellectual and emotional responses, are needed. A multi-method educational approach appears most relevant and effective when educating about homophobia (Cramer, 1997; Herek, 1990) and heterosexism. A combination of "cognitive, affective, and behavioral [sic] content" supported by "a multimethod [sic] teaching style including experiential exercises, speakers' panels (or instructor disclosure), case studies, discussion, and small groups activities" are most effective in reducing homophobia (Cramer, 1997, p. 296, brackets in original) and addressing heterosexism. Moreover, a safe and supportive atmosphere that promotes collegiality is fundamental. Eichstedt (1996), Cramer (1997), and Cain (1996) all acknowledge that exploring deeply held values and attitudes requires a degree of emotional safety in the classroom, and this is consistent with our experience. Ground rules, attention to process, instructor modelling, and use of self all help with this.

OUR APPROACH TO EDUCATION ABOUT HETEROSEXISM

We both place the discussion of heterosexism within a critical framework "that questions the categorizations of people and the accompanying constructions of power and privilege" (Eichstedt, 1996, p. 384). Critical theory is used to consider issues of oppression for all marginalized groups. Thus, content on heterosexism is integrated into the overall pedagogical framework. Further, we must be upfront about our treatment of non-heterosexuality. We avoid problematizing LGBTTQ people; rather, we problematize society's treatment of sexual minorities, which is clearly grounded in heterosexism.

We developed a multifaceted educational model concerning heterosexism, rooted in the principles of experiential learning and adult education. The model consists of (a) presenting factual information about heterosexism, including its impact on clients and staff of human service organizations (many examples were drawn from *The Heterosexism Enquirer*); (b) sharing personal experiences with heterosexism and its impact (as instructors we "came out" during this process); (c) inviting learners to share personal experiences and/or observations about heterosexism and its impact; and (d) exploring ways to start addressing heterosexism in social service agencies and policies, including the invitation to form an alliance to continue to discuss the issues and to advocate for change. While all of these elements are necessary, the latter component is crucial because "to only explore the dynamics of oppression without exploring positive action would contribute to immobilization and continued externalization" (DiAngelo, 1997, p. 15). The innovative facet of our approach is our invitation to learners, regardless of sexual orientation, to publicly "come out" and take an anti-oppressive stand alongside LBGTTQ people through a gay-straight alliance. Deciding to publicly advocate against heterosexism can challenge comfort levels and facilitate advanced insight into the dilemmas and challenges that LGBTTQ individuals face. Learners can understand what "coming out" really means for sexual minorities, where we must negotiate daily a world in which we must decide where and when to risk rejection by telling people who we really are. Throughout this educational process, participants are encouraged to utilize critical thinking and reflection skills in examining their own heterosexist beliefs. In doing so, they explore the dissonance between an anti-heterosexist stance and their deeply held heterosexual values.

This approach was used with three different groups: practising social workers in Newfoundland and Labrador, undergraduate students participating in the Women and Social Welfare course at Memorial University of Newfoundland, and graduate students enrolled in the Organizational Behaviour and Change course offered at the University of Toronto. This model was used as the guiding framework for all sessions, with course-specific variations.

MODEL DEVELOPMENT: THE ORIGINS OF THIS PEDAGOGICAL APPROACH

Our educational model developed out of an exploration of the impact of heterosexism on the health and income security of lesbians living in rural Newfoundland and Labrador. The Challenging Heterosexism project (Bella & Yetman, 2000), funded by the Maritime Centre for Excellence in Women's Health, was supported by local women's organizations, the Provincial Women's Policy Office, and the Newfoundland Gays and Lesbians for Equality. The project developed a Web site and associated on-line discussion forum within which lesbians (and those from other sexual minorities) could identify issues arising from heterosexism in health and social agencies. The project also developed educational tools for assessing one's personal heterosexism and for assessing heterosexism in one's workplace (both used in the subsequent educational model), together with a page of answers to politically incorrect questions. Discussions on-line and with participating organizations led to the identification of two strategies for change: gay-straight alliances for use among student, union, and professional groups, and positive space campaigns for use in institutions, such as hospitals and universities, and in personal spaces, for example, offices. The project Web site, *The Heterosexism Enquirer* <www.mun.ca/the>, has "morphed" over the last two years into a resource providing thought-provoking educational materials.

Inspired by our experience with *THE*, we delivered a workshop on heterosexism at the 2001 biennial conference of the Newfoundland and Labrador Association of Social Workers (NLASW). "Making Our Agencies Safe for Gay and Lesbian Clients and Workers" was crowded with over twenty participants. We presented results from the Challenging Heterosexism project (Bella & Yetman, 2000), added some personal experiences, and outlined the change strategies. Given the nature of the audience, we assumed they would support gay-straight alliances and positive space campaigns. Therefore, we suggested that the NLASW have its own gay-straight alliance, and that since those in this room were clearly supportive, the alliance could begin with those present. The creation of an alliance would be announced in the association's next newsletter, with a list of members. The room immediately became tense and quiet. In response, we suggested that those who felt uncomfortable with such an initiative might leave, and those remaining could continue. Several brave souls admitted that they hesitated because they might be thought to be gay, and feared the reaction from colleagues, bosses, or even spouses and children. Others shared this concern, trying to persuade us that while such an alliance was a good idea, it was premature. At our invitation, several present admitted feeling their stomachs were tied in knots over the issue. Others nodded in agreement.

This very teachable moment helped those present understand what "coming out" really means for sexual minorities. They finally understood the emotional burden of being non-heterosexual in a heterosexist world. This was confirmed by the workshop exit slips, which described the experience as "powerful" and "revealing." For instance: "open [sic] my eyes to the challenges for gays and lesbians to come out," "the implications of coming out became very clear," "seeing social workers moving toward talking about our own views/values/bias instead of the outward look of all workers [being] totally open-minded," "the idea of alliance—interesting reaction—very interesting." Although the possibility of an NLASW gay-straight alliance will have to wait for a safer time, we were delighted at the success of such a simple strategy, and hoped it could be replicated with other groups, such as social work students. Thus, the workshop was replicated (more or less), with social work students in St. John's and Toronto, and formally evaluated.

MODEL EVALUATION WITH SOCIAL WORK STUDENTS

An evaluation tool was developed and implemented consisting of a self-assessment questionnaire, which asked respondents to indicate their overall perceptions of the effectiveness of this model in terms of knowledge building and self-awareness (before and after questions were included to evaluate the impact of the session). Respondents were also asked to assess the contribution of this educational experience to anti-oppressive practice and the effectiveness of each teaching strategy used, and to identify ways in which the model could be improved. The questionnaire used a combination of closed-ended statements, each with a five-point Likert scale (1 being the lowest ranking and 5 the highest), coupled with space for comments, and opened-ended questions asking about improvements and other comments.

This type of evaluation has obvious limitations, such as not assessing skill acquisition (Cramer, 1997). Further, the instrument was untested.

Evaluation of the model for research purposes required ethical approval from our universities' research ethics committees. Given the nature of the session, its previous implementation with practising social workers in Newfoundland and Labrador, its relationship to course objectives, the age and interests of participants, and the anonymous evaluation process (i.e., voluntary completion and forms submitted unsigned), ethical approval was expected to be straightforward. However, the ethics committee at Memorial University was concerned about the nature of the challenge proposed and the risks it presented to students. Their concerns reflected the committee's lack of understanding of experiential education and the processes involved. The committee also wanted to know more about the course and the educational strategies employed. The committee actually asked difficult questions about the nature of social work and social work education. In response to these concerns, Leslie drafted a seven-page, single-spaced letter contextualizing the concept of challenge within social work and social work education, normalizing discomfort within social work educational processes, and detailing her course structure and process. Approval to continue the project was received approximately ten days before the session and its evaluation was to take place. At the University of Toronto, Mike requested and obtained an expedited review. Unlike Leslie's experience, the review committee sought no additional information.

THE MEMORIAL UNIVERSITY OF NEWFOUNDLAND IMPLEMENTATION

Heterosexism was included in a fifth-year undergraduate elective, Women and Social Welfare, taught from an explicitly feminist perspective. Leslie introduced feminist social work theories in the first half of the semester, and implemented a series of specific policy and practice application workshops in the second half. Because of overlap with fifth-year field practicum, only third- and fourth-year students registered in the course. Third-year students had not yet completed a field placement, and thus found assignments asking for practice applications to be problematic. As a result, the class enrolment decreased from twenty to eleven. Consequently, those remaining in the class, and completing the content on heterosexism, were probably those students most predisposed to feminism.

Content on heterosexism was introduced in two places. First, in the context of lesbian feminism (see Saulnier, 1996), Leslie used a standard presentation developed to disseminate research findings from Challenging

Heterosexism (Bella & Yetman, 2000) about the nature and impact of heterosexism, and the idea of gay-straight alliances and positive space campaigns. This class was one of a series that reviewed various forms of feminism, and their implications for practice, which were the basis for a mid-term examination. On the exam, most students selected an essay question on caring theory, suggesting that this had more relevance for them at that point than other content, such as that on heterosexism.

Second, the latter half of the course focused on specific practice applications, including a group assignment on gender-based analysis of social policy, using a Newfoundland-produced guide that extended such analysis to include concerns with other bases of oppression (e.g., age, race, sexual orientation). All groups focused on gender in their analysis. A second project looked at feminist practice with long-term mental health patients and was led by a community practitioner. Another community practitioner described the impact of the Provincial Strategy against Violence with its community development approach and its implicit feminist framework. In this context, Leslie developed a workshop for one three-hour class that would help students understand heterosexism emotionally as well as cognitively.

The experiential session with NLASW had explored the possibility of a gay-straight alliance, and Leslie originally intended to replicate this discussion with social work students. However, during the semester a "real life" issue arose involving the campus's LGBTTQ group, LGBT-MUN (Lesbian, Bi, Gay, and Transgendered at Memorial University of Newfoundland), and the undergraduate student council. The student council was considering creating council positions for marginalized groups, such as Aboriginal, differently abled, and sexual minority students. Several weeks before the scheduled class on heterosexism, the student council hosted a forum to explore the issues, and those present expressed support. At the subsequent council meeting, a vote to create an Aboriginal seat on council was passed. Thereafter, the addition of other seats for marginalized students was voted on as a group and defeated after heavy debate. The council then voted to have a referendum on the issue, with the campaign officially beginning the same day as Leslie's second class on heterosexism. The referendum vote was held ten days later.

This context offered the possibility of introducing realism to class discussion. As a result, Leslie invited her student assistant (working as an on-line reporter for *THE*) to join her as a guest. Leslie began the class by revisiting the concept of heterosexism and discussing how heterosexism affected her directly. Her student assistant also described incidents involving the destruction of LGBT-MUN posters, and her doctor's assumption that she needed birth control advice. Leslie then revisited the two strategies introduced in the first class on heterosexism. In a discussion of positive space, the student assistant described how nothing in the school, except for Leslie's office, indicated positive space. Leslie described positive space campaigns at other Canadian universities, and her assistant described the Canadian Federation of Students' upcoming initiative to fund positive space campaigns on other campuses, including Memorial, starting in the fall of 2002. Leslie noted her class's immediate enthusiasm for the project, describing it as a "good idea."

Then Leslie returned to the idea of gay-straight alliances, and suggested this might be an appropriate strategy for dealing with the upcoming referendum. Leslie asked her student assistant to describe the development of the issue and the purpose of the referendum, and its significance for marginalized groups. Would the students in the social work class support such a referendum campaign? Unanimously they said yes. Then the student assistant described various opportunities to support the campaign, and Leslie offered students the option of focusing their practice papers on this experience if they wished. A number of students offered to help, and none seemed reluctant or embarrassed by the possibility of doing so. Leslie asked explicitly if participation in the campaign would present problems with friends, partners, or children. Several students described their family support for such issues. Leslie warned that some people might think them lesbian as a result of their involvement, and their "gut" reaction to that assumption would give them an idea about their own residual homophobia or heterosexism. Leslie said she did not need to know about this, but that they could address it in papers and she hoped they would use it in practice. At the close of the class, students wrote notes to the student assistant indicating what they could do to support the campaign (she felt very supported as a result), and completed the evaluation forms provided by Leslie.

THE UNIVERSITY OF TORONTO IMPLEMENTATION

The heterosexism workshop was implemented with policy, organization, and community (POC) students enrolled in the first-year master's course Organizational Behaviour and Organizational Change at the University of Toronto. The students lacked an undergraduate degree in social work, but had completed one semester of the Master of Social Work program and were in their first field placement. A Master of Nursing student and a second-year Master of Social Work student were also enrolled. This required course for

POC students without a Bachelor of Social Work provides a conceptual understanding of human service organizations and how they can be changed to become more effective. Even though traditional theories of organizations are also covered, empowerment theory is the guiding framework for analysis and change. A critical lens (see Mills & Simmons, 1995) is used to explore issues of oppression within and by organizations. For example, learners actively explore the impact of organizations on women, different racial groups, ethnic minorities, and sexual minorities. From this position, heterosexism was explored.

Consistent with Mike's educational philosophy, empowerment theory guided the overall teaching and learning process. In the empowerment context, mutual respect, trust, and shared responsibility for the success of the teaching and learning endeavour are promoted (Parsons & Woodford, 1998). Creating a safe environment for adult learning is an extension of these characteristics of empowerment. From the outset, Mike aimed to facilitate student empowerment by leading the group through an exploration of empowerment in teaching and learning. This resulted in a definition, indicators, and value statements that guided student-instructor and student-student interaction. A mid-term evaluation confirmed student experience of empowerment.

The week before scheduled implementation, the heterosexism workshop, including the planned evaluation, was briefly discussed with the group. At the beginning of the workshop, an information sheet and evaluation form were distributed. Mike intended to conduct the session in one class, but two were required because of a late start to the first class and extensive ensuing participation. Group membership changed between classes and necessitated a review at the beginning of the second class.

Like Leslie, Mike presented information about heterosexism and its impact, drawn from *The Heterosexism Enquirer*. Mike then discussed the effect of heterosexism in his life, and then invited the group to talk about their observations and/or experiences with heterosexism. This discussion was dynamic, with many personal and practice examples. Some students challenged others' heterosexist assumptions. Action planning followed in the second class, specifically, exploring the potential for gay-straight alliances and positive space campaigns. Mike also shared with the group the NLASW conference participants' reaction to the idea of a gay-straight alliance.

The Toronto participants, similar to the Memorial students, had a different reaction from the NLASW members to the possibility of a gay-straight alliance, in that they did not have an overt reaction to the idea. Consistent with the course's focus, however, they critiqued the university's

Positive Space campaign, questioning its effectiveness. Many students observed that many supposedly positive spaces in campus were heterosexist. While Mike has no empirical evidence to support this, some sexual-minority students at the University of Toronto have made similar remarks.

Even though students did not have an overt response to the idea of forming a gay-straight alliance, not all students contributed to the discussion. When Mike raised the possibility of alliance members being assumed to be LGBTTQ, no one commented. Nevertheless, qualitative comments on the evaluation, such as "there is a need to further investigate what it means when people don't want to run the risk of mistakenly being identified as gay or lesbian," suggest otherwise. The faculty's emphasis on anti-oppressive practice and the diverse nature of Toronto may mean that participation in a gay-straight alliance is not an issue. Additional probing was possible, but Mike concluded it important to respect students' boundaries. Similar to Leslie, though, he encouraged students to reflect further on this.

DATA ANALYSIS AND RESULTS

Eight Memorial University students and twelve University of Toronto students completed the evaluation form. While some differences between the two groups were observed for all variables, these differences were not statistically significant using a Mann-Whitney rank-sum test. For analysis purposes, ordinal measures were treated as continuous. Given the narrow range of the scores (i.e., 1 to 5), differences are small. The descriptive statistics showed that the knowledge levels of Memorial students were slightly greater than that of the University of Toronto students before the workshop (means of 3.00 at MUN and 2.83 at U of T), as were the self-awareness levels (means of 3.13 at MUN and 3.00 at U of T). This may reflect the presence of *The Heterosexism Enquirer* within Memorial's School of Social Work, or the course being an elective and attracting students who identify with feminism and an anti-oppressive stance. For all other variables, the University of Toronto scores were slightly higher, albeit, differences were not statistically significant.

Based on the samples combined, the majority of students (sixteen) indicated a moderate to high level of knowledge and self-awareness regarding heterosexism before the workshop (mean scores of 2.90 and 3.05 respectively). Following the session, *all* students reported at least a moderate level of knowledge and self-awareness (mean scores of 4.25 and 4.35 respectively). To determine the impact of the workshop on student knowledge and self-awareness, both samples were combined and Wilcoxon matched-pairs signed-ranks test was performed using the items "knowledge before" and "knowledge after," and "self-awareness before" and "self-awareness after" as the respective matched pairs. There was found to be a statistically significant difference for both knowledge and self-awareness. Therefore, the workshop, based on student self-reporting, had a positive impact on knowledge ($Z = -3.710$, $p = .000$) and self-awareness ($Z = -3.589$, $p = .000$). All but one respondent indicated that the workshop would have a moderate or higher contribution to the effectiveness of their social work practice from an anti-oppressive stance.

In terms of teaching strategies, fifteen respondents ranked the instructor's sharing of personal experiences with heterosexism to be highly effective (5 on the five-point scale). This strategy was seen as the most effective among the four teaching activities employed (mean = 4.65). The qualitative comments reinforced this: "The disclosure of the instructor made the material more personal, relevant, and human and made me more comfortable to disclose personal information about myself," "it's good for understanding how heterosexism is present in our life [*sic*] and how it can hurt people," and "the instructor's discussions of his personal experiences of 'coming out' at work and in his family were the most memorable part of the session." Having a Memorial student (i.e., Leslie's student assistant) share her personal experiences with heterosexism was also seen as positive: "it was *powerful* having a student come in and make the issue more concrete by applying it to a real life situation." Several students suggested more personal stories would be helpful.

Informational content was also well received (mean = 4.37), although some respondents wanted more advanced material, possibly through another session. Group discussion was also seen as effective based on both quantitative data (mean = 4.37) and in comments such as "this part was really interesting and helped remind me how heterosexist our society still is." One student found the group discussion "scary in that I observed that some have an excellent ability to centre the gaze on issues of personal offence (i.e., I can't believe 'she' [lesbian woman] was offended by 'us') and away from the lived experiences and observations of heterosexism." This observation speaks to the deep-rooted nature of heterosexism and oppression.

In contrast to our experience using this model with a professional group, the effectiveness of the action planning was positive, but ranked lowest among the various strategies (mean = 4.32). However, one student commented, "I started thinking about some of the issues, but I would have liked to go into more depth and use more concrete examples of ways institutions have combated heterosexism."

Respondents generally reported that the workshop, if repeated, should be longer and with more time for an in-depth exploration. One student suggested the use of an interactive activity. Another observed "a need to challenge discourse about feeling bad about the issue and translate it into concrete action that moves beyond the notion of 'care taking' people in an identified group." This clearly reinforces the need for an anti-oppressive stance.

IMPLICATIONS FOR SOCIAL WORK EDUCATION

Social workers pursuing social justice require an anti-oppressive approach (Dominelli, 1998), but appropriate educational models are not readily available. Some social work educators are creating their own approaches and frameworks, while others are left bewildered. Although additional empirical testing would be worthwhile, our experiences with this educational model on heterosexism have reinforced the contention that factual information is insufficient. Internalization of heterosexist views "is deep and pervasive and cannot be addressed from an intellectual place; it must be [an] experiential, long-term process" (DiAngelo, 1997, p. 10). Learners need an environment and process that allow them to explore deep-rooted values and assumptions. Our model was effective in this regard and increased participant knowledge and self-awareness. Consistent with other studies, this evaluation also showed that the opportunity to learn about the instructor's first-hand experiences with heterosexism was the most significant educational strategy. Therefore, heterosexual instructors may wish to invite non-heterosexual guests to address this issue, despite the mixed results associated with this strategy (Cramer, 1997). Furthermore, our experience with a workshop for professional social workers implies that for practising social workers who have not been exposed to anti-oppressive content as part of their education, the opportunity to experience a process similar to that of "coming out" can provide personal insight into the dynamics of oppression and heterosexism.

Our experience also reinforces the significance of a safe, supportive, non-judgmental environment when educating students and practitioners about heterosexism. This context is essential in promoting critical reflection and personal sharing. Faculty comfort and teaching competence are crucial in such teaching. Safety for an instructor "coming out" to students must also be a concern for schools. Assured that such a choice is understood and valued by colleagues, instructors can safely model dialogue and reflexivity about difficult issues, thus creating a classroom climate that facilitates student exploration and learning about heterosexism and promotes change.

Finally, even though we delivered a specific session on heterosexism in our courses and at a professional conference, we believe that content on heterosexism, like other forms of oppression, needs to be integrated throughout the curriculum. Addressing deep-rooted heterosexual biases is a long-term process; therefore, it is advisable to provide students and practising social workers with multiple opportunities to do so.

REFERENCES

Appleby, G.A., & Anastas, J.W. (1998). Homophobia and heterosexism: Understanding the context of gay, lesbian, and bisexual lives. In G.A. Appleby & J.W. Anastas, *Not just a passing phase: Social work with gay, lesbian, and bisexual people* (pp. 3–43). New York: Columbia University Press.

Bella, L. (Ed.). (n.d.). *THE: The Heterosexism Enquirer* (on-line newsmagazine), <www.mun.ca/the/>

Bella, L., & Yetman, L. (2000). *Challenging heterosexism. Final report: Towards non-heterosexist policy and regulations in health and social security agencies*. St. John's: Memorial University of Newfoundland.

Ben-Ari, A. (1998). An experiential attitude change: Social work students and homosexuality. *Journal of Homosexuality 36*(2), 59–71.

_____. (2001). Homosexuality and hetrosexism: Views from academics in the helping professions. *The British Journal of Social Work, 31*(1), 119–131.

Berkman, C.S., & Zinberg, G. (1997). Homophobia and heterosexism in social workers. *Social Work 42*(4), 319–332.

Blumenfeld, W.J. (Ed.). (1992). *Homophobia: How we all pay the price*. Boston: Beacon Press.

Bruess, C.E., & Greenberg, J.S. (1981). *Sex education: Theory and practice*. Belmont: Wadsworth.

Cain, R. (1996). Heterosexism and self-disclosure in the social work classroom. *Journal of Social Work Education 32*(1), 65–76.

Canadian Association of Schools of Social Work. (2000). *Accreditation manual*, <www.cassw-acess.ca/xACCR/ac1x2.htm>, including the planned evaluation. Ottawa: Canadian Association of Schools of Social Work.

Canadian Association of Schools of Social Work. (n.d.). *Canadian Schools of Social Work: Anti-racist training and materials project*, <www.mun.ca/cassw-ar/>. St. John's: Canadian Association of Schools of Social Work.

Congress, E.P. (1993). Teaching ethical decision-making to a diverse community of students: Bringing practice into the classroom. *Journal of Teaching in Social Work 7*(2), 23–36.

Cramer, E.P. (1997). Strategies for reducing social work students' homophobia. In J.T. Sears & W.L. Williams (Eds.), *Overcoming heterosexism and homophobia: Strategies that work* (pp. 287–298). New York: Columbia University Press.

DiAngelo, R. (1997). Heterosexism: Addressing internalized dominance. *Journal of Progressive Human Services 8*(1), 5–21.

Dominelli, L. (1998). Anti-oppressive practice in context. In R. Adams, L. Dominelli, & M. Payne (Eds.), *Social work: Themes, issues and critical debates* (pp. 3–22). London: Macmillan Press Ltd.

Eichstedt, J.L. (1996). Heterosexism and gay/lesbian bisexual experiences: Teaching strategies and exercises. *Teaching Sociology 24*(4), 384–388.

Gil, D. (1998). Confronting injustice and oppression: Concepts and strategies for social workers. New York: Columbia University Press.

Glenn, A.A., & Russell, R.K. (1986). Heterosexual bias among counselor trainees. *Counselor Education and Supervision 25*(3), 222–229.

Herek, G.M. (1990). Homophobia. In W.R. Dynes (Ed.), *Encyclopedia of homosexuality* (pp. 552–555). New York: Garland.

_____. (1992). The social context of hate crimes: Notes on cultural heterosexism. In G. Herek & K.T. Berrill (Eds.), *Hate Crimes* (pp. 89–104). Newbury Park: Sage.

Logan, J., & Kershaw, S. (1994). Heterosexism and social work education: The invisible challenge. *Social Work Education 13*(3), 61–72.

Mallon, G.P. (1998). Appendix: Definitions of key terms. In G.P. Mallon (Ed.), *Foundations of social work practice with lesbian and gay persons* (pp. 271–278). New York: The Haworth Press, Inc.

Mills, A., & Simmons, T. (1995). *Reading organization theory.* Toronto: Garamond Press.

Morin, S.F. (1977). Heterosexual bias in psychological research on lesbianism and male homosexuality. *American Psychologist 32*(8), 629–637.

Morrison Van Voorhis, R. (1998). Culturally relevant practice: A framework for teaching the psychosocial dynamics of oppression. *Journal of Social Work Education 34*(1), 121–133.

Parsons, J.E., & Woodford, M. (1998). *Revisioning social work education: A collaborative teaching and learning model.* Paper presented at the Annual Conference of the Canadian Association of Schools of Social Work Annual Conference, Universite d' Ottawa.

Pellegrini, A. (1992). S(h)ifting the terms of hetero/sexism. In W. Blumenfeld (Ed.), *Homophobia: How we all pay the price* (pp. 39–56). Boston: Beacon Press.

Pinderhughes, E. (1995). Empowering diverse populations: Family practice in the 21st century. *Families in Society 76*(3), 131–140.

Razack, N. (1999). Anti-discriminatory practice: Pedagogical struggles and challenges. *British Journal of Social Work 29*(2), 231–250.

Rose, S.M., Peabody, C.G., & Stratigeas, B. (1991). Responding to hidden abuse: A role for social reforming mental health systems. *Social Work 36*(5), 408–413.

Rudolph, J. (1988). Effects of a workshop on mental health practitioners' attitudes toward homosexuality and counseling effectiveness. *Journal of Counseling and Development 67*(3), 165–168.

Rudolph, J. (1989). Effects of a workshop on mental health practitioners' attitudes toward homosexuality and counseling effectiveness. *Journal of Counseling and Development 68*(1), 81–85.

Saulnier, C.F. (1996). *Feminist theories and social work: Approaches and applications*. New York: Haworth.

Sears, J.T. (1997). Thinking critically/intervening effectively about heterosexism and homophobia: A twenty-five year research retrospective. In J.T. Sears & W.L. Williams (Eds.), *Overcoming heterosexism and homophobia: Strategies that work* (pp. 13–48). New York: Columbia University Press.

Serdahely, W.T., & Ziemba, G.J. (1984). Changing homophobic attitudes through college sexuality education. *Journal of Homosexuality 10*(1/2), 109–116.

Van Wormer, K., Wells, J., & Boes, M. (2000). *Social work with lesbians, gays, and bisexuals: A strengths perspective*. Needham Heights: Allyn & Bacon.

Wise, S. (2000). Heterosexism. In Martin Davies (Ed.), *The Blackwell encyclopaedia of social work* (p. 154). Oxford: Blackwell Publishers Ltd.

Chapter 25

Critical Issues in Field Instruction: Empowerment Principles and Issues of Power and Control

Jeanne Bertrand Finch
Jean Bacon
Donna Klassen
Betty-Jean Wrase
School of Social Welfare
Stony Brook University

The mission of social work is to create a more just society based on equality, human dignity, and social justice. Respect for the dignity of individuals and recognition of each person's strengths and inherent worth, regardless of existing problems, are prime values of social work practice. Our mission, our values, and our purpose as social work educators are woven together by a commitment to affirm individual and group strengths as a means to effect social change. To meet this end, the profession has been actively engaged in defining strengths-based approaches to guide our work. A body of theoretical constructs and practice guidelines to match this ideology has emerged utilizing empowerment principles (DuBois & Miley, 2002; Saleebey, 1992; Simon, 1994). These models also provide guidance for the issues of power and control within student supervisory relationships.

The ways in which the power differential become manifest are often related to structural and institutionally based inequalities such as those related to age, gender, sexual orientation, (dis)ability, and culture (Brown & Bourne, 1996; Nelson & Holloway, 1990). As field instruction takes place within the context of agency-based training, and students must negotiate their way around the organizational structures within these sites, a critical factor for consideration is the ethnic reality of the student and how that reality intersects with the socio-economic and cultural environment of the host organization (Timberlake, Farber, & Sabatino, 2002). An individual's struggle for parity and search for access to resources are often parallel experiences. A student's experiences of political power, authority, and access to resources affect the student's ability to respond with empathy to the client system's problems and dilemmas, and shape the dynamics of the supervisory relationship. Therefore, the field instructor's task is to tailor the student's training to promote self-realization and to enhance the professional use of the personal self. This task must include an open dialogue regarding the dynamic role of ethnic identity, experiences and perceptions of devaluation in society, and cultural beliefs.

However, problems experienced between the student and field instructor are not often addressed as related to the imbalance of power within this relationship. This is due both to the social taboo of talking about such matters and to the recognized phenomenon that those who are devalued, oppressed, or discriminated against are afraid to raise the issue for fear of further negative consequences and retribution (Jacobs, 1996; Pinderhughes, 1989). An often chosen student method of dealing with the conflict is to keep a low profile, buckle down to survive the year, and "don't rock the boat more than it already has been." Frequently the field instructor notices that the student is not engaged in the educational endeavour, or is hostile, or won't submit requested process recordings and other materials from which the field instructor may concretely assess the student's work. Additional power is then exerted by the field instructor through a negative assessment of the student's performance. This serves to further alienate the student and may prolong the student's withholding behaviour. The withholding behaviour, for a short time, provides the student with some respite and seems to place the student paradoxically in a power position. The student achieves, for that time, control over the pace of the learning. The resulting hostility and frustration build into a crescendo that may negatively affect the working relationship before the field instructor or student explore the underlying factors and power dynamics. Such a complex phenomenon becomes more complicated when the student and field instructor have opposing world views, when these issues are not openly addressed, and when the dynamics parallel the work between student and the client system. Our understanding of the reality of parallel process in supervision gives special warning to the expectation that even the most caring and well-meaning field instructor may be likely "under such pressures, to behave in persecuting or collusive ways" (Hughes & Pengelly, 1997, p. 172; Mattinson, 1975; Williams, 1997).

Rules and guidelines regarding ethical transactions between client systems and workers explicate boundaries needed to protect dependent client systems from the abuses of power that workers have over them. In a similar manner, the current National Association of Social Workers' Code of Ethics includes guidelines covering education and training. These ethical guidelines specify that field instructors provide training within their area of expertise, evaluate students in a fair and respectful manner, and insure that students inform clients of their student status. Dual or multiple relationships with students in which there is a risk of exploitation or potential harm to the student are prohibited. Finally, the Code specifies that field instructors are responsible for setting clear, appropriate, and culturally sensitive boundaries (National Association of Social Workers, 2002).

These guidelines set the basic and essential criteria to prevent anti-discriminatory and anti-oppressive supervisory practice. Anti-oppressive supervisory practice implies a basic conviction in the latent capabilities of each student. Further, it

> recognizes and tries to understand the obstacles to growth that may have developed for that person [student] in the face of their past oppression and discrimination, and works actively to enable them to increase their personal confidence and professional competence. To achieve this aim an empowering interpersonal relationship will often not be enough. The evidence of the supervisor's serious intent needs to be demonstrated in actively challenging those structural inequalities in the organisation that are oppressive and impeding the supervisee's development. However, anti-oppressive supervision does not mean colluding with the supervisee if their work is not satisfactory. Holding to professional standards and meeting agency requirements will sometimes mean confronting difficult issues, whilst valuing the person being confronted and acknowledging extrinsic discriminatory factors. (Brown & Bourne, 1996, p. 37)

Hartman (1992) challenges the social work profession to examine the field instructor's relationship with students from this perspective and warns against the danger of disempowering students when the field instructor assumes the role of expert. In her terms, the task involves "power sharing" and "power shedding." The tenets of the strengths perspective from an empowerment tradition offer guidance in meeting this challenge. Bertrand Finch, Lurie, and Wrase (1997) utilize the empowerment model to guide the education of social work students. Here we extend their work by examining how this model informs our understanding of the inherent power differential in the relationship between student and field instructor, and how we might begin to recognize its presence in the struggles that emerge in this relationship. The manner in which the field instructor handles power and control in supervision models ways for the student to approach the power differential with client systems.

Bertrand Finch et al. (1997) utilize Saleebey's (1992) work and delineate seven principles of the strengths perspective as applied to student supervision, which are summarized below.

- *Students and field instructors share a common dignity and mutual respect.* Students and field instructors work together to define and determine educational goals. They join the relationship from their different perspectives, each possessing valid viewpoints.
- *Students are adult learners who are responsible, self-directing, autonomous, and who have accumulated life experiences that are resources to be tapped and that enhance learning.* Students possess the inherent capacity to know, learn, and change. The theoretical constructs of adult learning theory (Knowles, 1972, 1975) delineate ways that adults learn best and outline characteristics of conducive learning environments. Kadushin and Harkness (2002) emphasize that positive feedback, providing access to successful experiences, active involvement in the learning process, and freedom to question and doubt are particularly important in the empowerment of adult learners.
- *The nature and quality of the relationship between field instructor and student is an essential factor in the supervisory process.* Collaboration, trust, and the sharing of power are critical to the helping relationship in empowering practice and, by parallel, to the supervisory relationship (Dodd & Gutierrez, 1990).
- *The educational process focuses on the strengths, interests, and aspirations of the student.* The identification of a student's areas of competence provides a foundation to the educational assessment that enhances the opportunity to extend the student's skill base and knowledge into previously unexplored areas.
- *Learner-driven concepts engage the student toward the realization of educational goals.* Individualization of the student's learning provides direct experience of the problem-solving and partialization skills often required in the specification of the learning tasks undertaken. The individuation also heightens the student's involvement and commitment to the challenges of learning. Introduction to, and direct experience of, these critical processes will more likely involve the student in incorporating these skills into work with client systems.

- *Students are encouraged to choose from among options defined and provided by the field instructor.* Time pressures often result in giving into the temptation to teach a specific action or technique rather than providing a range of options from which the student is helped to choose and to analyze applicability in one situation to the next. The field instructor's task is to teach how to be a critical thinker as well as specific skills and techniques.
- *The community is a potential source of collaboration in the learning process.* This involves a two-pronged approach—that is, helping students understand the power of groups and communities for their client systems, and helping students identify their own community of peers for support and sustenance. Group supervision and seminars for students that help integrate their experience are crucial resources.

These principles yield consensus among educators and practitioners, yet continued problems exist in the delivery of field instruction. Students continue to experience the abuses of power, and field instructors express confusion and bewilderment when confronted by their students' definitions of the struggles experienced in these terms. Our conceptual understanding of the power imbalance needs more practical help and increased awareness of the ways the inherent power present in this relationship get expressed and experienced. We are not proposing that the aim is to erase power and conflict from the supervisory relationship, or that power and control should always be seen as negative forces. On the contrary, power and control are inherent dynamics and a natural offspring of the very nature of the relationship, and can provide essential structure and safety. However, the potential for conflict arising from the power differential should be expected in order to minimize its potential negative outcome on the educational endeavour. Burke, Goodyear, and Guzzard (1998) go so far as to recognize the work toward resolution of these inherent power struggles as opportunities to repair and strengthen the working alliance between field instructor and student. Whether conflict arises or not, the manner in which the power differential is negotiated in this relationship ultimately serves as a model for the student's working relationships with client systems.

An analysis of the ways in which power differentials play out within the student/field instructor relationship provides insight to these challenges. Ultimately, guidelines for addressing the potential negative influences of power and control in the student/field instructor relationship may emerge. The following examples are provided to heighten our awareness of the unspoken power differential so that we may recognize it in the day-to-day scenarios between field instructor and student and learn how the strengths perspective can aid in steps toward resolution.

DISCUSSION OF PRACTICE CONCERNS

Authority and Expertise

The fact that the field instructor has something to teach and the student has something to learn may get translated by the field instructor into "I am the expert, you must listen," or by the student into "You are the expert and I know nothing." This stance requires reframing to include an understanding that the student brings much to the table and that the process of learning will be enhanced if the field instructor is able to find ways to build upon the student's experience and knowledge rather than replacing the student's ways of knowing with that of the field instructor's. The social work principle of "starting where the client is" is usefully applied to the student's field instruction experience. The field instructor starts where the student is and builds from there. The task is not to start where the student is not, or to teach the student what is not known. This is not a semantic difference. It represents a major shift in approach and attitude to the task. Depending upon the approach taken, the student may experience a sense of overwhelming hopelessness in the face of all there is to learn or a sense of helplessness in the search for perfection. Questions of competence and ability to make the grade automatically emerge. If these emotions are allowed to build and ferment, the student may harbour feelings of resentment and frustration, and feel powerless as learning tasks are undertaken. What is required is acceptance that there is much to learn and that the field instructor can be an instrumental force toward that aim while also giving acknowledgement to the reality that each student brings many positive qualities from which this joint effort can progress and succeed. The assessment is not of what the student does not know but rather what is understood and known as the basis from where to grow and build—a subtle, but important difference.

Occasionally a student will report being assigned a task for which the student feels unprepared. This may be expressed as "It's as if I am being tested to see whether I can do it as well as my field instructor." The power differential is experienced as who is in the know and who is not. In this situation, the student does not have adequate understanding of the reasons for the assignment or does not understand how to begin, feels cut off from useful information that would facilitate the achievement of the task, and fears failure. Help comes to the student in framing questions that clarify the next steps in the task and in enabling the student to articulate the felt uncertainty about what is realistic to achieve in this situation.

Feedback

Often the student fears asking for direct feedback and expresses this in terms of self-expressed doubts of progress made, or in expressing uncertainty as to whether it is all right to ask for such feedback. There is an equal fear of finding out the worst. The student wants to know, but at the same time is afraid of what the field instructor will say. The field instructor's task is validating that sharing perceptions of the student's progress is essential. Ongoing feedback from the field instructor is crucial to measure progress and to confirm abilities. However, feedback is a two-way street. Inviting response and input from the student forms the basis of a mutual relationship. By helping the student understand that this type of feedback is part of the evaluative process, the student is empowered to voice unspoken questions. This promotes ownership for progress and achievement.

A situation sometimes difficult to address is when a student is confronted with an aspect of practice or performance that requires honing or change, and the student feels criticized. This student finds the negative evaluation intolerable, but does not question the authority of the field instructor's perception and experiences shame. Simon (1994, p. 13) refers to this process as one that confirms "mythical and degraded self portraits" that become internalized by the powerless. The student's shame remains debilitating or turns into blame and outrage against the field instructor. This, in turn, threatens the student's ability to trust the field instructor, and supervision may become an unsafe place. As noted earlier, reaching for student input is crucial to furthering the field instructor's task of identifying areas that require additional growth and skill enhancement. Including the student's understanding illustrates, for the student, that his/her feedback is important in the supervisory process. It allows for supplementary discussion and enables the partnership to counteract previously perceived or experienced negative critical analysis. The task is to incorporate mutuality within the feedback process and to provide an ongoing evaluation of both positive and negative aspects of the student's performance. This encourages the development of the student's self-assessment skills and models a relationship based on mutual interaction.

The Use of Time

Another way that power influences the supervisory relationship is through the use of time. Time is a precious resource and serves as a vehicle to exert power. Sometimes the field instructor does not give adequate or consistent time for supervision. This is both an insult to the normal expectations of field instruction and a withholding of the field instructor's key resource of information and guidance. Obviously, emergencies arise, and supervision may need to be interrupted. However, this should be the exception rather than the rule. The student needs to feel that the field instructor values supervisory time. The willingness to protect supervision is easily demonstrated by doing everything possible to prevent interruptions or cancellations. Otherwise the message is sent that supervision is not as important as these other demands and that other tasks take priority over the student's learning. This is a particular challenge for today's practice given the challenges of crisis management and the many work demands placed on field instructors.

Sometimes the student is not consistent with supervision. However, this needs to be looked at in the context of the power imbalance. When a student is inconsistent in attending supervision, it may be a symptom of a greater problem. The field instructor needs to consider what the student is attempting to communicate by this behaviour. Not coming to supervision, or not preparing for supervision may be the student's only way of exerting power, achieving a shift in the balance of power, or setting a different pace to the learning. Sharing power requires accepting reciprocal responsibility. Open discussion about these issues becomes an opportunity for readjustment in the supervisory alliance (Burke et al. 1998).

Decision making

The field instructor's role requires him or her to make decisions for the student throughout the entire year. A couple of examples include client assignments and determining required attendance at agency meetings. If the field instructor makes these decisions without any input from or discussion with the student, the student is less likely to take ownership of the resulting responsibilities. Mutuality is diminished, the student's felt lack of power is verified, and the lack of involvement confirms the student's marginal position. For example, a director of a placement site moved a student's room mid-year to a much smaller office without a phone. The move occurred suddenly without explanation to the field instructor or the student. The student felt unimportant and powerless. In this case, the field instructor recognized the possible learning for the student. The field instructor helped the student extract the organizational implications regarding the room change and facilitated the student's ability to discuss the manner in which it was handled with the director. This seemingly ordinary part of organizational life was incorporated into the student's educational experience and modelled how communication can occur with those in authority. The aim was not to achieve reassignment to the larger room but to facilitate the student's ability to explain the impact of the director's decision and to advocate for how room assignments for students could be handled in the future. The field instructor assisted the student in exerting power in the organization and in gaining insight into the institution's decision-making processes. Unfortunately, the field instructor's own lack of power in the organization or existing political undercurrents often prevent this from occurring. More frequently such incidents pass without comment, or the student is told to accept the difficulties associated with institutional life and, by implication, to accept the powerless position of student status. In this manner, opportunities to facilitate learning regarding agency structure and negotiating within hierarchical decision-making processes are often lost.

Many of the decisions made on behalf of students take place at the beginning of the year and affect the remainder of the year. These decisions may be political in nature. Because the student has no input in them, this confirms the felt lack of power in the organization. An example of this involves an agency that handled students in the same way each year with much success. The agency typically accepted four students each fall, and the protocol was for the staff to meet with the students on their first day to provide an agency orientation. All of the field instructors met with the students. At the end of the day, staff met to decide which students were placed with each field instructor and at which part of the agency. One year a Hispanic student spoke to some staff members to request a specific location and field instructor. The staff had reasons of their own to decide differently. This was the way it had always been done, and no thought was given for the need to respond another way in this situation. The reasons were not explained to the student, and the student was assigned to the site chosen by staff. Subsequently, this student was hostile and guarded. It was noticed that he would sit far away from the rest of staff during staff meetings and that he did not participate. The entire staff, including the field instructor, became increasingly frustrated and angry with the student as this behaviour continued for many weeks. The staff, not understanding that the initial decision affected his behaviour, simply felt that the student did not want to be there and began to question whether he was suited for social work. However, the staff decided to examine their own actions and asked themselves whether they had done anything to contribute to his behaviour. By involving the student in the discussion, answers emerged. The staff engaged in a long and difficult discussion regarding race and power, and the student's acting out behaviour stopped. Ultimately, the student was able to express how the decision to place him at this particular program, against his expressed desire, made him feel powerless and angry. The student perceived the agency as racist and hostile to the needs of students of colour. In response, he distanced himself from the administrators and field instructor. It was only when the agency personnel and field instructors took notice of the possible realities of being a member of a devalued ethnic minority, combined with the experience of being a powerless student, that not receiving the placement site requested could be understood from the student's perspective and not interpreted from a power position that further oppressed and devalued the student.

TOWARD A SOLUTION

Open Dialogue

The field instructor is in a prime position to empower students and to engender quality service. As social work supervision parallels the helping relationship in which the field instructor imparts empathy, acceptance, freedom, and openness, the power differential is lessened when students are treated with dignity, provided with the resources to learn, and valued for their input (Fox, 1989). Inevitably, inequalities occur in these transactions. Therefore, field instructors must assume that the power differential exists, matters, and needs to be addressed if it is to be resolved (Dublin, 1989). Making the power differential explicit and creating an open dialogue about the inherent potential for conflict related to the imbalance in power give both parties the opportunity to examine anticipated difficulties and possible individual responses. When conflict does arise, these previous discussions set the scene for additional clarification and renegotiation. In this manner, the field instructor makes it possible to receive feedback from the student and to learn how the student experiences the field instructor. As students are given the validation of their rights to become partners in the educational endeavour, they will achieve the ability to ask to be heard and to be given explanations about decisions made on their behalf.

Finding Common Ground

Nelson and Friedlander (2001) emphasize the concepts of role conflict and role ambiguity as integral components of the interpersonal conflicts in supervision. In this framework, what is important is the way in which the field instructor and student complement each other in their respective roles, or the manner in which incongruence emerges in the fulfillment of these respective roles. Differences in status between the field instructor and student are also sources of disparity and potential abuses of power (Nelson & Holloway, 1990). Utilizing the skills of conflict resolution is helpful when conflict occurs. Understanding that reaching a conclusion that satisfactorily addresses the interests of those involved is crucial. These concerns centre on psychological, substantive, and procedural areas of interest. Psychological interests involve concerns regarding personal treatment and interrelatedness. Substantive interests involve resources, goods, services, and tangible outcomes. Procedural interests are related to a student's needs, input, participation, or information sharing (Mayer, 1995). Therefore, a prime tool of conflict resolution is the identification of common ground from which to build consensus. In the field instructor/student relationship the primary common ground is the process of education—that is, the desire to educate and the desire to be educated and to learn. By emphasizing this fact, the field instructor and student are facilitated in rejoining together toward the achievement of this mutual goal. The field instructor is helped to reaffirm the aim to instruct while incorporating the role of mentor and the student is helped to understand that learning involves dialogue. The examples provided above are related to psychological, substantive, and/or procedural interests. To reach resolution, both the field instructor and student must be able to provide a clear and honest assessment and discussion about what each expects from the educative process.

Building Community and Support

Building a community for field instructors and for students is an important aspect for both the student and the field instructor. Schools of social work possess the resources to provide community for students through contact with other students and faculty. Agencies that offer field placements to a number of students have the opportunity to provide a community for students via peer supervisory groups. These groups provide mutual support for students through discussions of field and agency issues. The validation and normalization of concerns is a powerful tool that may empower students to conquer their isolation and to raise their ideas, strategies, and questions to their field instructors and faculty.

Similarly, building a community for field instructors is important for the development of creativity and instructional improvement. Too often, assuming the role of field instructor is an additional responsibility for which agencies do not make adjustments in the field instructor's other responsibilities and assignments. Support for the assumption of these extra tasks and responsibilities may not exist within the normal framework of agency practice. "Identifying the calculus of opportunities and constraints at work with a peer group of fellow workers [and field instructors] is an important first step in assessing the degree to which one is losing, retaining, or gaining control over the conceptualization and enactment of one's responsibilities"

(Simon, 1994, p. 191). Schools of social work are potential resources to field instructors and carry special responsibility for the creation of community for their field instructors. Equally, agencies carry a similar responsibility to staff that fulfills this role. Field instructors themselves may identify other field instructors within the field placement agency and institute periodic meetings for discussion about field instruction issues. Mutual aid and sharing of teaching methods provide support in maintaining the professional boundaries needed to provide quality student education. Increasingly, schools of social work are instituting regular seminars for field instructors. Although this is a much-needed development, more needs to be done in creating professional supports for those fulfilling this crucial role.

Awareness of Power

Providing opportunities for students to gain insight into institutional decision-making processes should be a primary concern to field instructors. As students create their role within the agency structure and negotiate systems to assist their client systems in reaching goals, there are many opportunities for this exposure (Appleton, 1991). In this way students are on both sides of the application of power. They are guided by their field instructors to enact agency preferences, which are the norms regarding how treatment and/or services should be provided. Yet students are also in the position to negotiate for resources and to wield power in their assistance to clients. Introducing students to the power of their position and modelling ways for them to exercise this power is crucial.

CONCLUSIONS

We have been examining the management of power and control as field instructors carry out the heavy responsibility of educating students. Issues of power and control are inherent to the supervisory relationship, so the field instructor must work with this awareness to successfully impart social work values.

Students generally feel powerless or somewhat diminished in their student role. They see their field instructor as holding power over their futures. They fear that the evaluative nature of the relationship will reveal them as lacking, and that they may fail the practicum. This fear may rule their judgment regarding their performance of duties. The student's voice becomes hampered. The power differential may evoke issues of subordination to a parent, sibling, or unjust society in which they are judged by the nature of their minority status. Their actions are influenced by this transference, and they are rendered feeling powerless and ineffectual to advocate for social justice for themselves or others.

The evaluative and gate-keeping function of field instruction reinforce the power differential between field instructor and student and are at the heart of the inherent pressures that pull for and against the use of power and control. Student evaluations are utilized to mark student competence and identify growth points, but students can also perceive evaluations as a yardstick with which to confirm their incompetence (Itzhaky, 2000). The manner in which the field instructor views the task of evaluation is a source of potential conflict. The field instructor's choice and style of management of the anxiety associated with new learning, if mistimed or mismatched with the student's needs, can be experienced as the field instructor being overcontrolling, overprotective, paternalizing, or the opposite— unsupportive, uncaring, or expecting too much too soon. This aspect introduces the element of an individual's personalized attitude toward authority and how this inevitably affects any relationship that involves accountability, development, and assessment (Hughes & Pengelly, 1997; Pearson, 2000). The field instructor and the student each have his or her own respective experiences of being supervised and being taught. Each imports these experiences into the current supervisory relationship.

The field instructor has power over the student in relation to assignments chosen, access to information and resources, and to the evaluative nature of the field instructor's task. How issues of power are handled within supervision is at the core of the formation of the supervisory relationship, both in terms of the working relationship formed between the student and field instructor and in terms of the working relationship achieved with the client systems assigned to the student. Yet, social work has narrowly focused on the dependency engendered by the supervisory relationship, leaving the mutuality of the relationship overlooked (Dublin, 1989). Strategies chosen to instruct students have been presented utilizing empowerment principles from a strengths perspective, which support the shift in our conception of the relationship between field instructors and students to one that involves a consideration of learners as active constructors rather than passive receptors (Boyer Commission, 1998; Knowles, 1972). Making explicit what the field instructor is looking for in the student's progress; whether, when, and over what issues the field instructor asks for input from the student; how the field instructor gives directions; whether culture and its impact on the style of supervision provided is addressed; and whether reasons for actions taken or responses made are explained are all aspects of the supervisory style proposed here.

As our understanding regarding the power sharing required to confront oppression increases, the ways that power remains locked and embedded in some relationships are highlighted. The examination of power inequalities must include a look at the larger systems involved and ways that decision making, coalitions, negotiation, and compromise are institutionalized (Moore, 2000). Keenan (2001) examines the instruments of our profession that perpetuate the inequalities of power through the lens of Foucault's conception of disciplinary power. Supervision is cited as an example of "hierarchical observation" through which the profession performs its function of normalizing judgment and examination. Keenan explains that Foucault's concern is less with "*why* someone dominates another and more ... in *how* subjects are constituted [to continue] to operate in such a way" (Keenan, 2001, p. 212). Although Keenan's analysis is focused on an interaction with a client, the import of her point remains equally applicable here.

[L]ocal analysis increases understanding of global power relations while also understanding how such local interactions are inextricably connected to them. ... The potential for this [implementing disciplinary power] is ripe in social work, since social work agencies frequently serve persons with little or no income who are often persons of color, while social workers continue to be disproportionately middle class and white, creating a multi-leveled power differential by virtue of race, class, and employment. In addition, clients may or may not believe that social service agencies will be helpful for them due to prior experiences. (Keenan, 2001, pp. 214–215)

Conflicts in student supervision arise when people have differences in expectations or outcomes. Sorting out the emotions and realistic issues concerning the problems, interests, and needs of the individuals involved provides opportunities for resolution. This resolution provides a model for working toward solutions of broader structural and institutionally based inequalities. Providing the opportunity for mutuality within the student/field instructor relationship is a step toward the development of professional skills and the achievement of anti-oppressive practice.

REFERENCES

Appleton, J.R. (1991). The context. In P.L. Moore (Ed.), *Managing the political dimension of student affairs: New directions for student services 55* (pp. 5–15). San Francisco: Jossey-Bass.

Bertrand Finch, J., Lurie, A., & Wrase, B.J. (1997). Student and staff training: Empowerment principles and parallels. *The Clinical Supervisor 15*(1), 129–144.

Boyer Commission on Educating Undergraduates in the Research University. (1998). *Reinventing undergraduate education: A blueprint for America's research universities.* Stony Brook, NY: Carnegie Foundation.

Brown, A., & Bourne, I. (1996). *The social work supervisor: Supervision in community, day care and residential settings.* Buckingham, Philadelphia: Open University Press.

Burke, W.R., Goodyear, R.K., & Guzzard, C.R. (1998). Weakenings and repairs in supervisory alliances: A multiple case study. *American Journal of Psychotherapy 52*(4), 450–462.

Dodd, P., & Gutierrez, L. (1990). Preparing students for the future: A power perspective on community practice. *Administration in Social Work 14*(2), 63–78.

Dublin, R. (1989). Supervision and leadership styles. *Social Casework: The Journal of Contemporary Social Work 70*(December), 617–621.

DuBois, B., & Miley, K.K. (2002). *Social work: An empowering profession* (4th ed.). Boston: Allyn & Bacon.

Fox, R. (1989). Relationship: The cornerstone of clinical supervision. *Social Casework: The Journal of Contemporary Social Work 70*(3), 146–152.

Hartman, A. (1992). Editorial: In search of subjugated knowledge. *Social Work 37*(6), 483–484.

Hughes, L, & Pengelly, P. (1997). *Staff supervision in a turbulent environment: Managing process and task in front-line services.* London: J. Kingsley Pub.

Itzhaky, H. (2000). Secret in supervision: An integral part of the social worker's professional development. *Families in Society: The Journal of Contemporary Human Services 81*(5), 529–537.

Jacobs, C. (1991). Violations of the supervisory relationship: An ethical and educational blind spot. *Social Work 36*(2), 130–135.

Kadushin, A., & Harkness, D. (2002). *Supervision in social work* (4th ed.). New York: Columbia University Press.

Keenan E.K. (2001). Using Foucault's "disciplinary power" and "resistance" in cross-cultural psychotherapy. *Clinical Social Work Journal 29*(3), 211–227.

Knowles, M.S. (1972). Innovations in teaching styles and approaches upon adult learning. *Journal of Education for Social Work 8*(2), 32–39.

_____. (1975). *Self-directed learning: A guide for learners and teachers.* Englewood Cliffs: Prentice Hall/Cambridge.

Mattinson, J. (1975). *The reflection process in casework supervision.* London: Institute of Marital Studies, Tavistock Centre for Human Relations.

Mayer, B.S. (1995). Conflict resolution. In R.L. Edwards (Ed.), *Encyclopedia of social work* (19th ed.) (pp. 613–622). Washington: National Association of Social Work Press.

Moore, P.L. (2000). The political dimension of decision-making. In M.J. Barr & M.K. Desler (Eds.), *The handbook of student affairs administration* (2nd ed.) (pp. 152–170). San Francisco: Jossey Bass.

National Association of Social Workers. (2002). Code of Ethics. <www.socialworkers.org>

Nelson, M.L., & Friedlander, M.L. (2001). A close look at conflictual supervisory relationships: The trainee's perspective. *Journal of Counseling Psychology 48*(4), 384–395.

Nelson, M.L., & Holloway E.L. (1990). Relation of gender to power and involvement in supervision. *Journal of Counseling Psychology 37*(4), 473–481.

Pearson, Q.M. (2000). Opportunities and challenges in the supervisory relationship: Implications for counselor supervision. *Journal of Mental Health Counseling 22*(4), 283–294.

Pinderhughes, E.B. (1989). *Understanding race, ethnicity and power: The key to efficacy in clinical practice*. New York: The Free Press.

Saleeby, D. (1992). *The strengths perspective in social work practice* (2nd ed.). New York: Longman.

Simon, B.L. (1994). *The empowerment tradition in American social work: A history*. New York: Columbia University Press.

Timberlake, E.M., Farber, M.Z., & Sabatino, C.A. (2002). The general method of social work practice: McMahon's generalist perspective (4th ed.). Boston: Allyn & Bacon.

Williams, A.B. (1997). On parallel process in social work supervision. *Clinical Social Work Journal 25*(4), 425–435.

Chapter 26

Promoting Anti-Oppressive Social Work Education: The University of Calgary's Access Learning Circle Model

Michael Kim Zapf
William Pelech
Betty Bastien
Ralph Bodoy
Jeannine Carriere
Gail Zuk
BSW Access Division
Faculty of Social Work
University of Calgary

While there is evidence in the recent literature of a vision of anti-oppressive social work developing as a welcome and necessary challenge to the profession's dominant generalist approach, most accounts deal only with anti-oppressive practice. Little attention has been paid to the process of education for anti-oppressive social work. One can find conceptual frameworks for understanding various dynamics and forms of oppression, as well as principles for anti-oppressive practice at the micro and macro levels. But what about the related issues facing social work education? Can an anti-oppressive social work perspective be advanced within a hierarchical education system grounded in dominant-subordinate relationships, a Eurocentric world view, objective assessments of product, unequal opportunities, and potentially oppressive rules and procedures?

In his book *Challenging Oppression: A Critical Social Work Approach*, Mullaly (2002) argues that anti-oppressive practice must strive "to expose the Eurocentric biases" of mainstream social work practice and move the profession in the direction of:

(1) changing the personal attitudes and behaviours that portray a negative image of marginalized groups;

(2) combatting those cultural stereotypes, values, and thought patterns that endorse superior/inferior group relationships; and

(3) eliminating institutional patterns, practices, and procedures that discriminate against subordinate groups. (Mullaly, 2002, Preface, p. X)

Following from this argument, an anti-oppressive approach in social work education might be expected to focus on attitudes and behaviours at the personal level that perpetuate negative stereotypes; cultural mindsets and values that perpetuate oppressive relationships; and oppressive rules and practices within educational institutions themselves.

This chapter examines the BSW Access learning circle approach at the University of Calgary's Faculty of Social Work as an attempt to tackle these issues through anti-oppressive design and delivery of undergraduate social work education in Alberta's rural, remote, and Aboriginal communities.

DIRECTIONS FROM THE LITERATURE

Populations and healing practices in non-urban settings have generally been marginalized in the mainstream social work literature with its urban assumptions. Following early work from the 1930s (Brown, 1933), the profession confirmed a specialization of rural social work with a flurry of activity in the 1970s. That decade saw formation of the Canadian Rural Social Work Forum, establishment of a Council on Social Work Education Task Force on Rural Practice, launch of the journal *Human Services in the Rural Environment*, and initiation of an annual Institute on Social Work in Rural Areas (Zapf, 2002). From this rural base, the Canadian social work literature went further to make an argument for the recognition of remote practice to account for unique features of isolated northern regions with a different world view (Arges & Delaney, 1996; Collier, 1993; Delaney, 1995; Schmidt, 2000; Zapf, 1992, 1999, 2001). Recent contributions point to a developing knowledge base in print for Aboriginal social work (Borg, Delaney, & Sellick, 1997; Bruyere, 1999; Hart, 2001; Meawasige, 1995; Proulx & Perrault, 2000; Stevenson, 1999).

Published accounts of social work education outreach programs for non-urban populations offer potential guidelines and cautions for such endeavours. There is general agreement that courses must be developed around themes and frameworks that have meaning in the rural context. Such material needs to be core rather than optional or peripheral, and must be connected to community life and current needs in specific locations (Charleston, 1994; Cheers, 2001; Cooke-Dallin, Rosborough, & Underwood,

2000; Green, 2000; Haas & Nachtigal, 1998; Sturmey, 1992). Flexibility and accessibility must be features of any delivery model designed for isolated regions. Zapf (1998) pointed out how rigidly sequenced courses and prerequisites can impose a barrier for students in rural and remote regions; in the words of Martinez-Brawley (1986, p. 60), it may be necessary "to subordinate sequencing to accessibility." How material is taught will be just as important as what is taught, with an emphasis on flexibility and cultural relevance (Puckett & Fook, 1993; Senkpiel, 1997).

A large-scale Australian survey of education for rural social work concluded that the emphasis must be on training local people for social work careers if there is to be any change in the oppressive recruitment and retention patterns characteristic of isolated hinterland regions (Sturmey, 1992). BSW rural outreach efforts from the University of Victoria (Callahan & Wharf, 1989) and the University of Regina (Martinez-Brawley, 1986) found that rural students tended to be mature individuals already employed in the human services field. As a response to the needs of this group, courses are offered on a part-time basis "not as a second class alternative but as the main programmatic thrust" (Martinez-Brawley, 1986, p. 56). In their study of increasing retention rates of Aboriginal social work students, Tate and Schwartz (1993) also stressed the importance of evening and weekend classes to overcome barriers experienced by older Aboriginal students under family and financial pressure. Without flexible offerings for local students/workers, the educational institutions perpetuate the familiar pattern of urban-trained graduates moving to outlying regions to gain experience before returning to the city while local workers are relegated to low-status paraprofessional positions.

Based on a distance model of independent study, the University of Victoria developed and delivered a distance BSW program with rural emphasis using a model of independent study (Callahan & Wharf, 1989; Cossom, 1991). Students in their home communities worked on self-contained course modules that included unit objectives, assigned readings, and written assignments often geared to their own learning needs in the local context. Although practice courses featured face-to-face classes in regional centres, much of the program was delivered using print-based material and telephone contact with instructors located on campus in Victoria. Apart from the practicum experience, local instructors and facilities were not involved with course delivery.

One regional university in Australia (Ballarat) developed a BA in Rural Social Welfare in the early 1990s. Rather than seeing rural content consigned to the margins as one of many practice contexts, they attempted to put rural practice at the centre of their mission, curriculum design, instructor recruitment, and teaching strategies. They report some success in their efforts to integrate rural material with required core content: "Students are encouraged to learn the theories, knowledge and skills of generic welfare practice, and then explore how these might be affected by a rural context, and how strategies might need to be modified" (Green, 2000, p. 282). A similar integration of core content and local focus is reported from the Northern Human Service Worker/BSW Program offered jointly by the University of Regina and Yukon College. This program "encouraged—explicitly and centrally—the study of the region and validated, even embraced, First Nation culture and values while developing the modes of professional thought and practice characteristic of the well-trained professional" (Senkpiel, 1997, p. 31). Pelech (1993) participated in a similar process through the Aboriginal Social Work Program from Grant MacEwan Community College in northern Alberta. He observed that the task of integrating local content with core material "did not entail the dilution or deletion of core course concepts, but rather the enhancement of existing course materials and the application of course concepts to the students' communities and lives" (Pelech, 1993, p. 152). If the rural context and regional issues are not central in the curriculum, students are left with learning only urban models from mainstream textbooks that are of questionable relevance in their home communities.

A New Zealand report critical of social service delivery to rural communities (Rangihau, 1986) led to government initiatives to increase the number of Maori social work graduates. The School of Social Work at Victoria University of Wellington found that taking on this task required much more than simply boosting student numbers. Meaningful reform "involved establishing a new curriculum structure, new teaching material, and adult learning methods, plus recruitment of appropriate staff" (Cairns, Fulcher, Kereopa, Nia Nia, & Tait-Rolleston, 1998, p. 161). Working in collaboration with regional social service agencies and tribal groups, the university developed a program that could be "portable" through the use of a "modular teaching format" focused on specific themes and "taught in partnership with Maori people" (Cairns et al., 1998, pp. 158–159). Particularly in cross-cultural situations, it is not enough simply to recruit local students and incorporate local content as add-ons to core curriculum. Local ways of knowing, healing, and teaching must be foundations of both curriculum and delivery. Charleston (1994, p. 27) warned that sincere attempts to make curriculum culturally relevant can result in a destructive "quasi-Native education" if they teach only about Aboriginal topics rather than teaching through an Aboriginal perspective. De Montigny (1992, p. 73) similarly cautioned that the very programs "developed to redress colonialism [can] operate as another apparatus of colonial power" if they are more focused on meeting the needs of the institution rather than the communities.

The literature also offers insights into the experiences of social work students, particularly Aboriginal students (Beaulieu, 1993; Grieves, 1992; Lalonde, 1993; Peacock, 1993). For the most part, these accounts document the overwhelming pressures of family, parenting, finances, personal healing, fears of returning to school after many years away, and confirmation of the tremendous importance of staying in the home community. Considering the alternative of moving to a non-Aboriginal academic setting, German (1997, p. 34) described such a move as a "spiritual challenge" where the student has to deal with transition needs related not only to the education itself but also to the social, physical, emotional, and spiritual transition as well. Using stronger terms such as "spiritual dislocation" and "emotional desolation" to describe a move to the urban centre for educational purposes, Griffin-Pierce (1997, p. 5) explained that "far from mere homesickness, such feelings are based on an unconscious sense of having violated the natural and moral order in a culture which reifies order. Such stress is profound and unrelenting."

The Native Human Services Project at Laurentian University featured an extensive process of community consultation, the establishment of regional working groups, and eventually a program committee (with community and university representation) "to ensure the ongoing effectiveness of the program" (Alcoze & Mawhiney, 1988, p. 47). The Northern BSW Program in Thompson, Manitoba, established a similar policy advisory committee. With representatives from government, the university, students and faculty, northern social agencies, and regional Aboriginal groups, this committee met twice a year to keep the program "connected with remote communities on a senior administrative level" (Paziuk, 1992, p. 70). Formal mechanisms for ongoing collaboration between the educational institution and the regions are important to insure continuing voice for the community as well as relevance and accountability of the program.

A COLLABORATIVE VISION FOR BSW ACCESS

The Faculty of Social Work at the University of Calgary has been graduating students for more than thirty years. For most of this time, however, the accredited BSW degree program was available only at three urban campus locations in Alberta: Calgary, Edmonton, and Lethbridge. Recognizing the importance of access to a BSW education for people living in rural, remote, and Aboriginal communities throughout the province, a consortium of interest groups came together in 1998 to develop a proposal for Access funding from the Alberta provincial government. As articulated in this proposal, the vision of BSW Access represented the collaborative work of many stakeholder groups, including the University of Calgary Faculty of Social Work; the Northern BSW Stakeholders' Council (representatives from Children's Services regions, Métis settlements, Métis zones, First Nations and tribal organizations, northern regions of Family and Social Services, private northern service agencies, post-secondary institutions under the Alberta North umbrella); the First Nations Adult and Higher Education Consortium, with member colleges and education boards from the Treaty 6 and Treaty 7 areas, plus the North Peace Tribal Council; and the Alberta College of Social Workers.

Several principles for a redesigned BSW curriculum were declared in the funded BSW Access Proposal (Rogers, 1998). Overall, the proposal was dedicated to "increasing accessibility, responsiveness, and affordability of University of Calgary accredited social work degrees" (Rogers, 1998, p. 1). Recognizing the unique needs of potential students in rural, remote, and Aboriginal communities, "changes in traditional BSW delivery methods" were declared to be "a central component of the proposed program expansion" (Rogers, 1998, p. 3). Specific guidelines then called for "innovative course content" that would be "culturally and geographically relevant" (Rogers, 1998, pp. 6, 9). BSW curriculum content and delivery modes were to be "adapted" and "re-designed" to be "sensitive to First Nations and Metis peoples" and "aligned with traditional philosophies and knowledge systems" (Rogers, 1998, pp. 6–11). Course delivery methods were to be "flexible in time, place, and mode," with course scheduling "based on a flexible entry model and home community placements" (Rogers, 1998, pp. 5, 11). This new model was to feature a "mutually designed infrastructure" to integrate "the best of distance education technology with face-to-face professor/student and student/student educational opportunities" (Rogers, 1998, p. 2). These components of the BSW Access vision fit well with the direction of anti-oppressive social work education outlined earlier. It was also made very clear at the outset that the new model had to be "of the same quality as the programs currently delivered on-site by the Faculty," leading to the "University of Calgary accredited social work degree," which "adheres to national accreditation standards" (Rogers, 1998, p. 1).

RECRUITMENT

Once funding for the BSW Access Proposal was announced in the spring of 1999, recruitment commenced for the new Access faculty positions. For the first time in the university's history, an academic selection committee included Aboriginal people from community stakeholder groups as full voting members. An Elder from Grande Prairie and an education counsellor from Old Sun College participated in the selection committee, along with representatives from the Faculty of Social Work and an Aboriginal faculty member from Sociology. The original team recruited for the new BSW Access Division included women and men of diverse cultural backgrounds: First Nations, Métis, and non-Native. Given the nature of the university environment, a decision was made to create a new division, roughly parallel in structure and reporting relationships to the existing Edmonton or Lethbridge divisions, to support the proposed BSW Access activities. A senior faculty member with relevant experience was assigned as head of this new BSW Access Division.

Real diversity within the BSW Access Division has meant that curriculum design work has been passionate and intense, requiring a great deal of trust, respect, and shared commitment to the overall Access vision. Access Division members must work constantly to be open and accepting of each other's cultural perspective, at the same time acknowledging the constraints imposed by core curriculum requirements. The team faces a constant challenge to pursue a workable balance among three authoritative guiding frameworks that do not always fit well together: Canadian Association of Schools of Social Work Accreditation Standards, the faculty's on-campus BSW model, and the principles declared in the funded BSW Access Proposal. The BSW Access Division functions as a cross-cultural team that attempts to model for their students such anti-oppressive values as inclusiveness, mutual respect, and collaborative decision making. Conflict is often experienced within the Access team arising from differing world views and perspectives on issues. Wherever possible, these differences are incorporated into the curriculum to expose students to alternative methods and ways of knowing.

CURRICULUM AND DELIVERY: THE LEARNING CIRCLE

Access Division faculty members began with the vision from the BSW Access Proposal and the content from the existing accredited on-campus BSW program in their work to develop a variation of the Calgary BSW curriculum with geographic and cultural relevance for students outside urban centres. Following the faculty's accredited undergraduate generalist practice curriculum, core BSW academic content was grouped into four major theme areas considered crucial for social work in rural, remote, and Aboriginal communities: Generalist Practice in Context; Communication and Information; Diversity and Oppression; and Social Work Methods. In collaboration with community stakeholder groups, general theme areas were transformed into theme courses with core curriculum material specifically adapted for application in rural, remote, and Aboriginal contexts.

Through a community consultation process in the summer and fall of 1999, it became clear that any new BSW Access model could not require full-time study because most students in rural areas would be employed throughout their Access course experience. In fact, Access students actually form the backbone of the local service network in many of the communities where BSW Access courses are delivered. Local agencies and the community could not afford to have all these people leave their jobs to attend school full-time, even with local classes. The basic BSW Access delivery pattern of nine-hour modules every two weeks was in direct response to needs expressed by both potential students and community agencies. Typically, this pattern involves three hours one evening, followed by six hours the following day (Friday night and Saturday in some communities; Thursday night and Friday in others).

Following an extensive round of community meetings for feedback and revisions, the Access Division brought forward formal course numbers, syllabus statements, and admission processes that were subsequently approved by Faculty Assembly and Faculty Council prior to the offering of the first BSW Access courses in six communities in January 2000. Within each of the four theme areas, students take a theme course consisting of eight nine-hour modules. At least one module in each theme course is devoted to "local applications," allowing local healers, Elders, agency workers, and community resource people to present information and lead discussion with students in an attempt to connect course content with the history, current practices, and policy issues in the local region. Accompanying each theme course is a related portfolio project course that challenges the student to integrate his or her professional and lived experience (including learning from the theme course) into a reflective project involving supported independent study.

The basic format of this BSW curriculum variation can be represented in circular form based on a medicine wheel framework that was affirmed in Aboriginal communities during the collaborative developmental work. This non-sequential and non-hierarchical model for curriculum and delivery has come to be known as the learning circle:

Figure 26.1: THE LEARNING CIRCLE

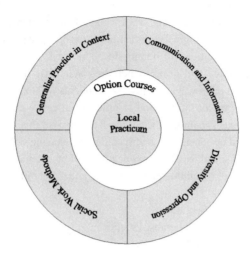

Content of the theme courses can be summarized with the calendar statements and brief overview of the modules comprising each of the following.

SWKA 300: Generalist Practice in Context Theme Course
This course provides a broad conceptual framework for the practice of generalist social work utilizing problem-solving methods with a range of client systems, including individuals, families, groups, and communities. Students will be encouraged to challenge the history, philosophy, and cultural values underlying the mainstream generalist practice model with particular attention to implications for practice in non-urban settings. Ethical issues, adaptations, and alternative approaches will be considered for effective practice in rural, remote, and Aboriginal communities.

- Orientation/Seminar
- Generalist Social Work Practice (History, Assumptions, Components)
- Rural Context Considerations
- Northern Context Considerations
- Aboriginal Context Considerations
- Values and Ethics Considerations
- Local Applications
- Integration/Summary

SWKA 302: Communications and Information Theme Course

This course examines effective communication and information management practices for professional social work with particular emphasis on practice in rural, remote, and Aboriginal communities. Concepts and processes of various research methodologies will be introduced as ways of building knowledge to inform practice and policy (including scientific method, traditional knowledge, and other ways of knowing). Students will explore the best ways to gather and present information in order to influence decision making in the local context. The importance of interviewing within a generalist practice framework will be considered, and specific interviewing skills will be taught. The context of social work communication will be examined with particular attention to issues of culture, power, gender, and differential use of language.

- Orientation/Seminar
- Research and Generalist Practice
- Knowledge Building in Context
- Program Evaluation
- Interviewing in Generalist Practice
- Interviewing in Context
- Local Applications
- Integration/Summary

SWKA 304: Diversity and Oppression Theme Course

This course examines issues of diversity, colonization, and intergroup relations associated with the practice of professional social work with particular emphasis on practice in rural, remote, and Aboriginal communities. Frameworks will be introduced for understanding the importance of diversity within generalist social work practice. Processes such as colonization, human development, social policy, and program evaluation will be examined and analyzed critically for their cultural foundations and impact on history and current social service delivery patterns.

- Orientation/Seminar
- Diversity and Generalist Practice
- Colonization and Decolonization
- Canadian Social Policy
- Human Development and Environments
- Local Applications
- Integration/Summary

SWKA 306: Social Work Methods Theme Course

This course examines assessment and intervention approaches for the practice of generalist social work, with particular emphasis on practice in rural, remote, and Aboriginal communities. Theoretically diverse practice methods will be examined for their relevance and applicability with a range of populations, settings, and levels of practice (micro, mezzo, macro). Students will also be challenged to explore a common methods dilemma encountered in the field when the generalist approach with a broad social justice perspective suggests macro interventions, but employers have assigned caseloads of individuals or families to be "fixed."

- Methods within Generalist Practice
- Approaches and Contexts with Individuals
- Approaches and Contexts with Groups and Families
- Approaches and Contexts with Communities and Organizations
- Integration/Summary

BSW Access theme courses and portfolio projects have different course numbers than on-campus courses, and cannot be taken by students at the main campus locations. Elective courses within the Learning Circle curriculum, however, are numbered the same as the on-campus option courses. An Access student then has the option to take spring/summer electives at any Access location or on campus. This arrangement also means that on-campus BSW students can travel to Access sites to take spring/summer electives (which are generally offered in six-day block format in Access sites). Some students have already started travelling to take elective courses in other locations, and there has been a stimulating mix of urban and rural students at some sites.

Once the theme course areas and related portfolio projects are completed, BSW Access students can take a practicum placement in their own region with a flexible schedule negotiated between student, agency, and faculty. In response to the often limited number of agencies and qualified supervisors available in many rural, remote, and Aboriginal communities, the Access Division allows students the option of one practicum placement (rather than the conventional two) during their program of studies. Of course, that one placement must meet the requirements specified by the faculty and the accreditation standards including the total prescribed number of hours. Accompanying the practicum is an integrative practice seminar that promotes the integration of theory and practice within the local region practicum.

Consistent with the on-campus BSW program, an Access student must complete the equivalent of twenty social work half-courses to meet the degree requirement. Within each theme area, an Access student can complete one full course, plus one half-course portfolio project, for a total of three half-course credits per theme area. Once all of the four theme areas are complete, a student will have twelve half-course credits. Another three can be achieved through completion of social work elective courses offered in block format during spring/summer sessions. The remaining five half-course credits for the degree are earned through the practicum placement (four for the field placement itself and one for the integrative seminar).

BSW ACCESS STUDENTS AND SERVICES

In January 2000, seventy-three students began taking learning circle courses through the faculty's new BSW Access Division in six sites across the province: Standoff, Hobbema, Slave Lake, Grande Prairie, Peace River, and High Level. Formal contracts were negotiated between the university and host institutions (community colleges) in the various Access delivery sites. In this way, local resources are made available to the BSW Access students while they are taking courses (classroom space, audiovisual equipment, library privileges, computing services, etc.). The university pays the colleges a lump sum per academic term, plus a per student amount for each Access student who registers in a course that term in that location.

Through increased enrolment at these original delivery locations and the addition of new sites, BSW Access student numbers have grown steadily. There were 109 students in September 2000 with the addition of a site in Red Deer; 128 students in January 2001; 137 students in September 2001; and 202 students in January 2002 with the addition of sites in Medicine Hat and St. Paul/Lac La Biche. In other words, there are now 202 more students in rural, remote, and Aboriginal communities across Alberta with access to a BSW program than there were two years ago. Other communities in Alberta are preparing for Access delivery in the future by arranging the necessary prerequisite general education courses for their students now.

Another initiative is currently underway for a pilot project to respond directly to a strong need expressed from the Métis community in Alberta. Although Métis world view, traditions, and healing practices are often assumed under the general label "Aboriginal," there are distinct features that have a direct bearing on the provision of effective services within that community. Following the faculty's Access model, active collaborative planning is proceeding with the Faculty of Social Work, the Métis Nation of Alberta, the Métis Settlements General Council, Métis Child and Family Services, and related departments of the Alberta Government (Métis Bursary

Program, Aboriginal Recruitment and Retention, Aboriginal Adult Services). The shared vision is one of a funded cohort of Métis BSW students with Métis instruction and materials relevant to Métis history and healing practices following the learning circle curriculum and delivery model.

The BSW Access Division has a student services operation with 2.5 staff. Much time is spent on the telephone with students and potential students advising them on program requirements and details, and helping them to assess their own situations relative to Access requirements. Many Access students and potential students have a history of negative experiences dealing with large bureaucracies. For many, English is not a first language. A great deal of support is necessary. Access student services staff also travel to Access delivery sites when required for information workshops and direct assistance with forms, etc., at crucial times of the year for application and registration deadlines.

Most BSW Access students are employed full-time while taking their courses in nine-hour evening and weekend blocks every second week. Their identification is with the job, the community, and the family, not with the student life. There is great interaction among students at particular Access sites where a real cohort spirit emerges, but there is little time or energy for the larger connections and identification with on-campus student issues. This is not surprising since Access students come together on weekends when the on-campus students are not in class. Access student social events tend to be location specific because of cost, time, and local identification. They tend to participate in local activities related to governance and evaluation of the BSW Access experience (such as the Northern Distance BSW Planning Circle or community meetings with the Access Division head or faculty administration), rather than Calgary-based student government opportunities.

Approximately half of the BSW Access students identify themselves as Aboriginal. This means that the learning circle approach has provided the opportunity for more than 100 new Aboriginal social work students so far to work toward their BSW degrees with a relevant curriculum in their home communities. The learning circle itself is based on a medicine wheel framework. Through the theme courses and portfolio assignments, Aboriginal students are encouraged to explore healing traditions within their own communities. Elders and healers are invited into the classroom for the local applications modules to connect course content to local history, vision, issues, and practices. Readings from Aboriginal social workers are included with each theme course. Meaningful inclusion of an Aboriginal world view and healing practices in the BSW Access curriculum has also been well received by non-

Aboriginal students who regularly encounter Aboriginal clients, colleagues, and resources during their practice in rural and remote regions of the province.

ACCESS TEACHING

Teaching assignments in the BSW Access Division differ from the on-campus situation where the basic units of the teaching economy are the individual instructor and distinct half-courses. BSW Access course outlines are developed collaboratively and are common across delivery sites (although there can be considerable variation in the local applications modules). One Access faculty member assigned to a site generally serves as instructor-of-record for the theme course and is responsible for delivery of the first module (introduction) and the final module (summary/integration). For the rest of the course, the assigned Access faculty member serves more as a coordinator or homeroom teacher, arranging for community resource people and other faculty members to deliver modules. A student taking a course at an Access delivery site then has exposure to a combination of community and university-based instructors offering specific modules in their area of interest and expertise. Rather than being tied into conventional course assignment assumptions, Access faculty members have the opportunity to teach from their areas of interest and passion. (For example, consider the Generalist Practice in Context theme course. An Aboriginal faculty member may deliver the nine-hour Aboriginal Context Considerations module in four or five different sites. Similarly, an Access faculty member with northern practice experience, or a qualified northern practitioner, can deliver the Northern Context Considerations module across a number of sites.)

ONGOING COMMUNITY COLLABORATION

The original BSW Access Proposal declared that "a Distance Planning Circle will be created, consisting of representatives from all participating and stakeholder groups" (Rogers, 1998, p. 3). The CASSW Standards similarly call for schools to provide opportunities for participation in planning and evaluation of programs by "stakeholders" (2.12), "Aboriginal communities" (2.13), and "professionals and professional associations" (2.14). Terms of reference were drafted and approved by the Northern BSW Stakeholders Council in June 2000 for a Northern BSW Distance Planning Circle to serve an ongoing advisory function and provide a forum for identification of critical issues facing social workers and communities in northern Alberta. Meeting at least once each academic term, they review BSW Access Division activities and make recommendations to the faculty regarding curriculum, delivery, and connections with the community. A parallel Southern BSW Distance Planning Circle is under development now that additional delivery sites are offering BSW Access courses in southern Alberta.

Membership of the Northern BSW Distance Planning Circle includes:

- Two representatives of northern social work employers (one public, one private)
- Three representatives from First Nations/Tribal Councils
- One representative from the Métis Nation of Alberta
- One representative from the northern Métis settlements
- One representative from a northern client advocacy group
- Two representatives from the northern colleges
- One representative from the Alberta College of Social Workers (formerly AARSW)
- One representative from the Northern BSW Stakeholders Council (Chair or delegate)
- Two northern student representatives from the BSW Access Division
- One representative from the BSW Access Division (division head)
- Ex-officio members will include the dean of the Faculty of Social Work (or delegate) and the faculty members of the BSW Access Division

One good example of the collaboration process can be found in a recent meeting of the Northern BSW Distance Planning Circle for which the northern social work employers developed a profile of the attitudes and skills they wanted to see in a northern BSW graduate. These qualities were then matched against the learning circle course outlines to assess relevance, determine gaps, and identify resources.

BSW ACCESS AS ANTI-OPPRESSIVE SOCIAL WORK EDUCATION

Developed in consultation with stakeholder groups in the community and the profession, the University of Calgary Faculty of Social Work's new BSW Access learning circle model features many curriculum and delivery innovations to insure cultural and geographic relevance for rural, remote, and Aboriginal communities across Alberta. The learning circle has made the University of Calgary BSW degree accessible for many students who might otherwise have practised in outlying areas without the benefit of professional education in social work at the degree level. Much of this work has involved active expression of the principles of anti-oppressive social work education. Personal attitudes and behaviours of BSW Access students and instructors are challenged through class discussion, curriculum development, portfolio work, and group assignments. Students and instructors are encouraged to express their developing models of practice and the world views on which they are based. Cultural assumptions underlying practice models and approaches to building knowledge are identified and assessed for local relevance within each theme area of the curriculum. Some institutional patterns have successfully been modified and adapted (recruitment, admissions, teaching assignments, course scheduling), but there is still a long way to go in other areas. For example, the whole area of grading (a foundation of the institution) presents a real challenge for the BSW Access Division. How can local oral traditions and personal expression be honoured in a system that requires graded output? A story shared or built between two people does not exist as the objective product of one to be assessed by the other.

As a closing comment on the development and implementation of the BSW Access vision, consider these observations by an Elder from Grande Prairie who was involved in the original community consultation process:

> An institution where people go to become more knowledgeable and gain wisdom should be sharing the knowledge of the world. The place of learning should never be restricted to "western/eastern" or any other specific identifiable area. Knowledge should be attainable through our learning institutions without the biases of where the knowledge comes from. This concept, it is my belief, has not existed in Canada since colonization. With open minds and open hearts perhaps we, as Canadians, can welcome and respect the values and beliefs of all people and continue to introduce the world's collective knowledge to students and the public at large. It is with this thought in mind that I equate your introduction of the rural, remote, and Aboriginal BSW with the discovery that the world is not flat. (D. Lajeunesse, personal communication, November 1999)

REFERENCES

Alcoze, T., & Mawhiney, A. (1988). *Returning home: A report on a community-based Native human services project.* Sudbury: Laurentian University Press.

Arges, S., & Delaney, R. (1996). Challenging the southern metaphor: From oppression to empowerment. In R. Delaney, K. Brownlee, & M.K. Zapf (Eds.), *Issues in northern social work practice* (pp. 1–22). Thunder Bay: Lakehead University Centre for Northern Studies.

Beaulieu, B. (1993). A new vision. In K. Feehan & D. Hannis (Eds.), *From strength to strength: Social work education and Aboriginal people* (pp. 195–196). Edmonton: Grant MacEwan Community College.

Borg, D., Delaney, R., & Sellick, M. (1997). Traditional healing practices: Contextual patterning strategies for northern social work practice with First Nation communities. In K. Brownlee, R. Delaney, & J.R. Graham (Eds.), *Strategies for northern social work practice* (pp. 129–141). Thunder Bay: Lakehead University Centre for Northern Studies.

Brown, J.C. (Ed.). (1933). *The rural community in social casework.* New York: Family Welfare Association of America.

Bruyere, G. (1999). The decolonization wheel: An Aboriginal perspective on social work practice with Aboriginal peoples. In R. Delaney, K. Brownlee, & M. Sellick (Eds.), *Social work in rural and northern communities* (pp. 170–181). Thunder Bay: Lakehead University Centre for Northern Studies.

Cairns, T., Fulcher, L., Kereopa, H., Nia Nia, P., & Tait-Rolleston, W. (1998). Nga pari karangaranga o puao-te-ata-tu: Toward a culturally responsive education and training for social workers in New Zealand. *Canadian Social Work Review 15*(2), 145–167.

Callahan, M., & Wharf, B. (1989). Distance education in social work in Canada. *Journal of Distance Education, 4*(2), 63–80.

Charleston, G.M. (1994). Toward true Native education: A treaty of 1992. Final report of the Indian nations at risk task force, draft 3. *Journal of American Indian Education 33*(2), entire issue.

Cheers, B. (2001). Globalization and rural communities. *Rural Social Work* (special Australian/Canadian issue) *6*(3), 28–40.

Collier, K. (1993). *Social work with rural peoples* (2nd ed.). Vancouver: New Star.

Cooke-Dallin, B., Rosborough, T., & Underwood, L. (2000). The role of Elders and Elder teachings: A core aspect of child and youth care education in First Nations communities. In J.C. Montgomery & A.D. Kitchenham (Eds.), *Issues affecting rural communities (II)* (pp. 172–176). Nanaimo: Rural Communities Research and Development Centre, Malaspina University-College.

Cossom, J. (1991). Commentary on chapter 3. *The Northern Review* (Summer), 53–57.

Delaney, R. (1995). Northern social work practice: An ecological perspective. In R. Delaney & K. Brownlee (Eds.), *Northern social work practice* (pp. 1–34). Thunder Bay: Lakehead University Centre for Northern Studies.

De Montigny, G. (1992). Compassionate colonialism: Sowing the branch plant. In M. Tobin & C. Walmsley (Eds.), *Northern perspectives: Practice and education in social work* (pp. 73–82). Winnipeg: University of Manitoba.

German, N.R. (1997). Northern student education initiative. *Native Social Work Journal* *1*(1), 33–41.

Green, R. (2000). Rural social welfare: Preparing students to work effectively in rural communities: An Australian experience. In J.C. Montgomery & A.D. Kitchenham (Eds.), *Issues affecting rural communities (II)* (pp. 280–283). Nanaimo: Rural Communities Research and Development Centre, Malaspina University-College.

Grieves, F. (1992). My first year. In M. Tobin & C. Walmsley (Eds.), *Northern perspectives: Practice and education in social work* (pp. 67–68). Winnipeg: University of Manitoba.

Griffin-Pierce, T. (1997). When I am lonely the mountains call me: The impact of sacred geography on Navajo psychological well being. *American Indian and Alaska Native Mental Health Research 7*(3), 1–10.

Haas, T., & Nachtigal, P. (1998). *Place value.* Charleston: Appalachia Educational Laboratory.

Hart, M.A. (2001). An Aboriginal approach to social work practice. In T. Heinonen & L. Spearman (Eds.), *Social work practice: Problem solving and beyond* (pp. 231–256). Toronto: Irwin.

Lalonde, P. (1993). In retrospect. In K. Feehan & D. Hannis (Eds.), *From strength to strength: Social work education and Aboriginal people* (pp. 197–200). Edmonton: Grant MacEwan Community College.

Martinez-Brawley, E.E. (1986). Issues in alternative social work education: Observations from a Canadian program with a rural mandate. *Arete 11*(1), 54–64.

Meawasige, I. (1995). The healing circle. In R. Delaney & K. Brownlee (Eds.), *Northern social work practice* (pp. 136–146). Thunder Bay: Lakehead University Centre for Northern Studies.

Mullaly, B. (2002). *Challenging oppression: A critical social work approach.* Don Mills: Oxford University Press.

Paziuk, L. (1992). The northern BSW program: Maintaining community connections. In M. Tobin & C. Walmsley (Eds.), *Northern perspectives: Practice and education in social work* (pp. 69–72). Winnipeg: University of Manitoba.

Peacock, C. (1993). Growing together and finding the balance. In K. Feehan & D. Hannis (Eds.), *From strength to strength: Social work education and Aboriginal people* (pp. 188–194). Edmonton: Grant MacEwan Community College.

Pelech, W. (1993). A return to the circle. In K. Feehan & D. Hannis (Eds.), *From strength to strength: Social work education and Aboriginal people* (pp. 147–162). Edmonton: Grant MacEwan Community College.

Proulx, J., & Perrault, S. (2000). *No place for violence: Canadian Aboriginal alternatives.* Halifax: Fernwood.

Puckett, T.C., & Fook, J. (1993). Educating for rural social work: Models for delivering professional education. *Rural Social Work 1*, 51–56.

Rangihau, J. (1986). *Puao-te-Ata-tu (daybreak): Report of the ministerial advisory committee on a Maori perspective for the department of social welfare.* Wellington: Department of Social Welfare, Government of New Zealand Printing Office.

Rogers, G. (1998). *Alberta social work degree accessibility plan—virtual learning circles: A BSW for rural, remote, and Aboriginal communities.* Unpublished report, University of Calgary Faculty of Social Work.

Schmidt, G. (2000). Remote northern communities. *International Social Work 43*(3), 337–349.

Senkpiel, A. (1997). Side by side in the Yukon: The development of the northern human service worker/BSW program. In K. Brownlee, R. Delaney, & J.R. Graham (Eds.), *Strategies for northern social work practice* (pp. 29–44). Thunder Bay: Lakehead University Centre for Northern Studies.

Stevenson, J. (1999). The circle of healing. *Native Social Work Journal 2*(1), 8–21.

Sturmey, R. (1992). *Educating social welfare and community workers for rural/remote areas.* Armadale: The Rural Development Centre.

Tate, D.S., & Schwartz, C.L. (1993). Increasing the retention of American Indian students in professional programs in higher education. *Journal of American Indian Education 33*(1), 21–31.

Zapf, M.K. (1992). Educating social workers for the north: A challenge for conventional models and structures. *The Northern Review 7*, 35–52.

_____. (1998). Crossing cultural and social boundaries: Teaching social work courses in Aboriginal outreach programs. In L. Ginsberg (Ed.), *Social work in rural communities* (3rd ed.), (pp. 233–246). Alexandria: CSWE.

_____. (1999). Barriers to the acceptance of Indigenous knowledge: Lessons from social work in Canada's north. *Rural Social Work 5*, 4–12.

_____. (2001). The geographic base of Canadian social welfare. In J.C. Turner & F.J. Turner (Eds.), *Canadian social welfare* (4th ed.) (pp. 67–79). Toronto: Pearson Education Canada.

_____. (2002). Geography and Canadian social work practice. In F.J. Turner (Ed.), *Social work practice: A Canadian perspective* (2nd ed.). Toronto: Prentice Hall.

Chapter 27

Managing Institutional Practices to Promote and Strengthen Diversity: One School's Journey

Nancy MacDonald
Wanda Thomas-Bernard
Carolyn Campbell
Jeanne Fay
Judy MacDonald
Brenda Richard
Maritime School of Social Work
Dalhousie University

The Maritime School of Social Work (MSSW) has been working to institutionalize diversity since the early 1970s. In the course of that journey we have tried various strategies; some have succeeded, some have failed. What we have learned along the way has been invaluable to the evolution and revision of these strategies. The positive response we have received from other schools of social work and colleagues to a workshop presentation led us to write this chapter.

"The term diversity has become a buzzword with a variety of connotations and synonyms" (Goodman, 2001, p. 4). The word "difference" is one of these synonyms.

> "difference" is increasingly used in academic and common discourse, [but] its meaning is not at all clear. Difference is generally understood to refer to a broad and ever expanding set of particular groups or categories such as race, gender, age, sexual orientation, class, and physical or mental ability. The defining features of "difference," as a general concept, however, remain ambiguous.
>
> (Stainton & Swift 1996, p. 76)

While we appreciate the ambiguity of these terms, we are accepting Stainton and Swift's conceptualization as a working definition. Thus, in this chapter, we identify and explore institutional practices that may either include or exclude, within higher education, the meaningful participation of individuals from particular groups or social categories.

We also assert, as have many others (Adams, Bell, & Griffin, 1997; Goodman, 2001; Newton, Ginsburg, Rehner, Rogers, Shrizzi, & Spencer, 2001; Roman & Eyre, 1997), that such meaningful participation demands moving beyond institutional practices that encourage "people to challenge stereotypes, overcome prejudices, and develop relationships with different kinds of people" (Goodman, 2001, p. 4) to practices that address "issues of equity, power relations, and institutionalized oppression" and seek "to establish a more equitable distribution of power and resources so that all people can live with dignity, self-determination and physical and psychological safety" (Ibid.) within institutions of higher education.

We have identified nine components of institutional practice that must be changed in order to promote and strengthen diversity. For each, we have raised key questions and necessary changes. Next, we provide illustrations and examples from the experience of the MSSW together with the barriers, supports, and future directions we have identified. In the conclusion we tease out key themes and fundamental principles essential to making institutional change.

COMPONENTS OF INSTITUTIONAL PRACTICE

Program Design and Objectives

Is a commitment to diversity clearly stated within program descriptions or objectives? If not, what strategies could get such a statement included? Departmental self-studies? Accreditation processes? Curricular reviews? If such a commitment is clearly stated, does the institution consistently draw attention to the statement and use it whenever possible?

1. Town and Gown

Equitable and effective relationships with groups and individuals from diverse communities are essential to promoting and strengthening diversity within an academic institution. What strategies develop and sustain these relations? Community membership on academic committees? Participation in educational activities? Involvement in program reviews?

2. Governance

Organizational structures, whether formalized in governance documents or traditionally established, must reflect a commitment to diversity. How can these structures include and privilege those groups whose voice and experience has been excluded?

3. Student Recruitment, Admission, and Retention

Another key component of institutional change is developing and sustaining a student body reflective of groups historically absent and marginalized from the mainstream. What groups have been historically excluded from higher education in the province or region? Does the school have affirmative action admission policies to address this? What outreach recruitment initiatives to these groups are in place? Does the school have relevant and culturally accessible support services? Clear and public procedures for responding to conflict and complaints? What strategies are in place to create and sustain supportive environments? Are they maintained with diligence?

4. Faculty Recruitment and Retention Is Equally Essential

Strategies to make faculty membership more diverse would include outreach recruitment initiatives, designating positions for historically excluded groups, support provisions that recognize historic exclusion and move beyond tokenism to concrete measures and sensitized collegial relationships.

5. Curriculum Changes: Beyond Tokenism

Curricula changes must move beyond a token inclusion of content about diverse groups to a fundamental integration of different ways of knowing. Such integration presents significant challenges to foundational curricula. How are the experiences of diverse groups included in the curricula? What strategies and resources are used to make curricula inclusive? Whose voice is privileged? What elements are necessary to insure the curricula has moved beyond tokenism?

6. Pedagogy

What we teach, how we teach it, and how students learn are all elements of pedagogical practice. All these elements must be scrutinized to insure they are not bound by unitary conceptions of teaching and learning.

7. Field Program

Placements must support and encourage diverse practices among all students, not just those of historically excluded groups. What kind of supervision is appropriate to the organizational culture and practices of placement agencies serving marginalized communities and individuals? What supports do students need to grapple with privilege and oppression in field placements? What procedures and practices are essential for positive relations between a school of social work and field agencies?

8. Institutional Privilege

Institutional privilege includes the unearned benefits of belonging to the dominant groups in an institution and the ways that institution reinforces those benefits. How can it be used to promote and strengthen diversity? What institutional changes in attitude and behaviour are essential to acknowledge the privilege and take responsibility for using it in positive, anti-oppressive ways?

This chapter is part of a larger work in progress. Two of the practices—academic program design and objectives and field programs—will not be covered here.

TOWN AND GOWN

Town and gown refers to the relationship between community and academy. The Canadian Association of Schools of Social Work (1991) recognizes the invaluable contributions that diverse communities can make to the educational process, be it through program administration, curriculum development, pedagogical applications, and/or field instruction. Community linkages need to be formalized by schools of social work in order to respect the contributions that communities make and to avoid exploitation of their resources. In the past, marginalized groups, individuals, and communities have been used as resource people in classes and/or as subjects of research, with little regard to communities' needs. This limited participation is reflective of tokenism and embedded in institutional discrimination.

We believe that substantive community interface is essential to promoting diversity initiatives. As well, we recognize the complicated nature of establishing such relationships. We present the relationship with the Association of Black Social Workers (ABSW) as an illustration of this commitment.

The ABSW was established in Nova Scotia in 1979, affiliated with its American counterpart originating in San Francisco in 1968. The ABSW's concerns centre on the quality of human services provided to African Nova Scotians (a historically excluded group in the province) and the lack of Black representation in the profession of social work. The goals of the ABSW are to provide a forum for Black social workers and to work co-operatively with community projects to serve the interests of the Black community and the community at large.

One of the ABSW's many activities was the creation of an anti-racism workshop to train social workers, students, and human service workers to examine critically their own power and privilege. Facilitated by members of ABSW, this workshop became a regular component of the introductory social work course at the undergraduate level and the colloquium series at the graduate level. A key part of the workshop exposed participants to the first-hand experience of racist oppression. Movement was initiated to construct a formal partnership between ABSW and the MSSW to recognize this valuable work and to create a venue for dialogue about student concerns arising from participation in the workshop. The faculty member who taught the introductory course wrote a letter to the ABSW in the spring of 1997 to request a meeting with the ABSW and the MSSW's Committee on Racial and Ethnic Affairs (COREA). During the course of this meeting, a key question arose concerning the division of roles and responsibilities between the instructor and the workshop facilitators regarding students' needs.

The ABSW responded in the fall by outlining recommendations for the workshops. A number of letters were exchanged raising questions about the roles and responsibilities of both parties in relation to the workshops and in evaluating students' competencies in anti-oppressive practice. In January 1998, a meeting was scheduled to explore the possibility of a formal partnership. Due to busy agendas and complicated scheduling, progress was stalled. At the beginning of the 1998 fall semester, the ABSW resumed the initiative by writing a letter of support. Toward the end of the term, the MSSW faculty agreed to the principle of a partnership. In February 1999, a meeting was held between ABSW and the MSSW in which objectives of the partnership were identified and arrangements specified. A subcommittee was formed to draft the contract. The next meeting, however, never took place and the process remains incomplete.

While supported ideologically, the MSSW's commitment to formal community interface needs more practical applications. The barriers resulting from this example serve as an indication of the complexity of this work. Potential barriers include scheduling difficulties, communication breakdown, increasing demands on community workers in a milieu of taxed resources, historical relationships of groups, feelings of uncertainty and vulnerability, and the risk of being misunderstood. The length of time required to create institutional change is exacerbated by structural rearrangements; for example, the chair of faculty changed, which shifted priorities. As well, curriculum restructuring redesigned the introductory course into two distinct courses, thus creating a dilemma about the best location for the workshop.

An institutional commitment to diversity is needed in order to make lasting changes: this begins with the dedication of a few faculty members and it takes time and persistence to foster and grow. We are conscious of progressing toward this initiative and have made substantive efforts toward this end. The MSSW has historically been connected with various communities—women's groups, anti-poverty advocacy, (dis)ability, gay, lesbian, bi-sexual, transgendered rights, youth initiatives, and Aboriginal health research. Faculty members have served on a number of community boards, delivered guest lectures at community functions, conducted joint research initiatives, reflecting the value they place on relationships between academy and community. The Canadian Association of Schools of Social Work Accreditation Standards (2000) specify that:

> The school shall show that it has formed links with agencies and networks responding to the needs of various ethnic, cultural, racial and other diverse populations which are presently under-represented and/or under-served and that the school is involving these agencies and networks in its program review and developmental processes. (Canadian Association of Schools of Social Work, 2000, p. 16)

Community liaisons currently initiated by the MSSW include consultations through the affirmative action review, a (dis)ability community connection at the local and national level, revisiting partnership with ABSW, and the hiring of faculty from historically excluded groups. Given the MSSW's history and long-standing relationships with community groups, directives from our national organization (CASSW), and our current initiatives, we hope that new energy will emerge to strengthen the interrelationship between town and gown.

GOVERNANCE

Governance describes the act or manner of conducting the affairs of any given organization or entity. Organizational structures (committees, councils, caucuses) and decision-making processes (both formal and informal) that privilege the groups and structures that speak for previously disenfranchised groups or perspectives are essential in the promotion of equity and diversity.

The MSSW has tried a variety of governance structures and process. Most notable among these is the Committee on Racial and Ethic Affairs. Established in 1983, COREA was preceded by an Internal Minorities Task Force (the task force), which consisted of a few committed volunteer faculty and students who attempted to move the school forward in relation to issues of affirmative action admissions, student retention, and support. The task force had no formal institutional recognition, no place in official decision-making bodies, was supported though voluntary work, and engendered no wide sense of responsibility among faculty.

In contrast, COREA was officially formed as a standing committee in 1983 and received official recognition from the Human Rights Commission as sponsoring an affirmative action program. The mandate of COREA is broad, addressing issues such as recruitment of applicants from designated groups, overseeing and promoting the affirmative action policy, nurturing community links, and supporting students. Status as a standing committee entails formal recognition within the governance document; designated representation on all decision-making committees; workload recognition for faculty participation; involvement in a myriad of school processes such as recruitment, admissions, orientation, curricular review, program development, and organizing and sponsoring conferences; and representation on university-wide committees.

The Gay Lesbian Bisexual Transgender (GLBT) Caucus represents, by contrast, one of the organizational structures that has no formal recognition within the governance document. It does not receive the explicit institutional support accorded a formalized entity. The GLBT Caucus began as a student/faculty-initiated group in 1988. That year several students approached a faculty member with concerns about the MSSW's library collection. At that time the MSSW had its own library maintained by a staff librarian. The texts specifically related to gay and lesbian people uniformly pathologized "homosexuality." The faculty member agreed to attempt to rectify the situation by suggesting better texts and removing the extremely homophobic material. In volunteering to do this at a subsequent faculty meeting, the faculty member implicitly came out to her colleagues as the only gay or lesbian member of faculty.

Revising the composition of the library collection, from the librarian's point of view, was problematic. The conundrum emerged of "no funds available" for new texts with a refusal to remove the offensive material because "that's all we have." The request for a separate section for gay and lesbian issues designated in the library (a small structure) was considered "inappropriate." Wishing to make visible the invisible gay and lesbian material in our social work institution would necessitate, we were informed, "creating a separate section for every social work topic, which was hardly feasible." Intending neither offence nor implying malevolence, the request was treated simply as insignificant. To gay and lesbian students and faculty, however, this denial was a strongly perceived symbol of heterosexist privilege. It maintained rather than redressed the harm that such texts perpetuated.

Institutions manifest privilege, but individuals experience its encoded marginalization (O'Neill, 1995). Gay, lesbian, bisexual, and transgendered people historically have been subject to enforced invisibility and exclusion. Social work education and social work practice are no exceptions to this (Berkman & Zinberg, 1997). The year before the library episode, 1987, a graduate student at the MSSW surveyed his classmates for a master's project on gay men's identities. Students reported a high comfort level with concepts related to gay and lesbian issues. They also indicated a low comfort level related to contact with a supervisor or anyone with whom they worked closely who was perceived as gay. This discomfort and its concomitant repercussions for gay and lesbian colleagues had institutional precedence.

The students who had earlier determined that the MSSW library must be held accountable formed a group. Eventually this group, along with a faculty member, became the GLBT Caucus. The caucus provides support for gay, lesbian, bisexual, and transgendered students while also identifying areas within the MSSW that are homophobic or heterosexist in design or practice. A few years ago a GLBT Caucus-initiated revision of the graduate curriculum was done. A faculty member has acted as chair of the caucus to provide continuity and viability in a necessarily changing student body. This is a volunteer collaboration, which is not recognized in deployment calculations. The GLBT Caucus itself, however, is recognized in the MSSW as an important voice for gay, lesbian, bisexual, and/or transgendered students. Its most important provision, however, continues to be the unique support that the faculty and students are able to give each other. This undoubtedly strengthens the possibilities for gay, lesbian, bisexual, and transgendered students to navigate the educational system successfully.

The GLBT Caucus at the MSSW has in some ways mirrored the significant social changes in relation to gay, lesbian, bisexual, and transgendered people that have transpired in Canada over the past decade. In 1991, the province of Nova Scotia, after intense and sustained lobbying by Lesbian Gay Rights Nova Scotia for several years, passed an amendment to the Human Rights Act to include sexual orientation as a prohibited ground for discrimination. A member of the MSSW faculty was involved in that effort. As a non-tenured member of the faculty, she became vulnerable by taking this public stand. In 1992, when the Gay and Lesbian Caucus of the Canadian Association of Social Workers was established, a MSSW faculty member was a founding member. In 1993, the Gay and Lesbian Youth Project was founded in Nova Scotia. It emerged from a BSW field placement and continues today. In 2000, the Nova Scotia Association of Social Workers developed the Ken Belanger Memorial Award to recognize a social worker whose work benefits gay, lesbian, bisexual, and transgendered people. This may be the only award of its kind in Canadian social work. A MSSW faculty member was the inaugural recipient.

Safety is still an issue for gay, lesbian, bisexual, and transgendered students. A couple of years ago, a notice went into every MSSW student's mailbox announcing the GLBT Caucus's first meeting of the year. A couple of students telephoned the MSSW administrative officer to say that they did not want such "offensive" material placed in their mail folders again. GLBT Caucus meetings are held at a time and place designed to maintain confidentiality. Many gay, lesbian, bisexual, and transgendered students in schools of social work across Canada feel isolated in their programs. This highlights the critical role that an institutional body such as the GLBT Caucus plays in protecting and promoting the well-being and rights of its members.

Informal bodies such as the GBLT have limitations because they are not entrenched in the governance process. At the same time, however, institutionalized structures can be defining and limiting. For example, our affirmative action program was expanded in 1995 to encompass students with a (dis)ability, but, as COREA was originally established to deal with issues of race and ethnicity, there is no structure for addressing (dis)ability within our governance document. In addition, although community involvement was integral to the initial design of COREA, this was voluntary on the part of community members who are now less able to offer their time, given increasing practice demands. Similarly, student involvement has decreased due to many other responsibilities.

At this time in our development, we are discussing what sort of organizational structure would allow us to maintain the strengths of COREA but also move us toward a more encompassing structure that would reflect an understanding of the intersecting nature of diversity issues. We briefly experimented with an anti-oppressive alliance, but, for a number of political and structural reasons, this was not feasible. We are, however, committed to developing a new structure that will be an institutionalized component of all governance activities.

STUDENT RECRUITMENT, ADMISSION, AND RETENTION

Student recruitment is an essential part of community/academy interface. In the late 1960s and early 1970s, human and civil rights became a key issue for communities historically marginalized in Nova Scotia. Two MSSW faculty members responded in 1973 by forming a task force (see Governance above) to initiate recruitment and admission policy changes. This work has changed as demands and reflection on experience have made us wiser and more responsive.

The task force linked with an officer of the newly developed Nova Scotia Human Rights Commission, which had identified three groups for special assistance and affirmative action programs: Aboriginal peoples, Acadians, and African Nova Scotians. The task force began a consultation process with organizations and students from these groups. A heightened awareness of the issues and barriers resulted and five areas of difficulty were identified: admissions, financial problems, program supports, minority group faculty, and curriculum content. In response, an outreach policy was publicized in relevant community newspapers. As well, brochures were sent to community organizations each year. Internal governance changes were also made: at least one member of the task force was represented on the admissions committee. A rating scale was developed that allowed candidates to rank below average in one area and above in another. Admissions policy was changed to recognize factors other than academic requirements such as personal suitability, potential for relevant employment, and community experience (Moore, 1991).

Limited financial assistance was available since university scholarships were based on merit and often excluded the application of minority group students. In a similar context, very little could be done to increase program supports and minority group faculty due to lack of funding and resources.

Modest progress was made during the 1970s. One change in curriculum content occurred with the offering of Canadian Minority Group Issues as a half credit elective course and later as a core course. Diploma programs were eliminated. Part-time study was introduced, as well as a distance education program on sites in Prince Edward Island, Cape Breton, Nova Scotia, and New Brunswick.

Major changes to program occurred in the early 1980s: a two-year BSW program and a one-year specialized MSW program replaced the two-year generic program in 1980. In 1982, the MSSW formally developed an affirmative action agreement, which was recognized by the Nova Scotia Human Rights Commission as equivalent to such an agreement under Nova Scotia legislation (Moore, 1991, p. 203). The development of the agreement was directly linked to student recruitment and admissions from the three underrepresented groups in the Atlantic region. Rating scores were abolished. However, mature students could test their competency for two full credits with the implementation of competency credits. Modest progress was again made in the 1980s with the Affirmative Action Agreement extending to the MSW program. The result of these efforts was an increase in graduates from each of the three identified groups: thirty-two Acadian, twenty-four African Nova Scotian, and eight Aboriginal students were graduated between 1981 and 1990 (Moore, 1991, p. 203).

A case example of the MSSW linking its Affirmative Action Agreement to community experience was the development of the Mi'kmaq BSW program in 1985, which graduated twenty-one students in 1989. This program was considered similar to the regular BSW program, but had modified culturally relevant curriculum content. The program rotated on-site and off-site in response to the needs of students.

Many students in the Mi'kmaq program expressed concerns about the negative attitudes they encountered on campus as well as in the wider community. Often difference was denied outright, implying that no special knowledge or skill is necessary when working with one's own group. Examples of how social work practice and education are perceived and experienced by underrepresented populations include the stigma attached to affirmative action programs with respect to recruitment and admissions: students experienced backlash from the mainstream students for alleged preferential treatment. Students stressed that recruitment issues should be understood in relation to the problems encountered by students in classroom and field situations. While noting that faculty members could be sensitive and fair, students mentioned inaccurate or biased course content and conflicts with individual professors and field supervisors. Above all, they spoke of their resentment that they had to be the ones responsible for raising issues of race and prejudice in classroom situations.

In 1995, the Affirmative Action Policy was revised to include people with (dis)abilities. Currently, another revision is underway. We are focusing on a more inclusive approach to recruitment and admission and looking for ways to be more responsive to the national population. To frame the question as "Who should be included?" ultimately sets up an exclusionary process. The community consultation process to revise the policy has not yet been completed. It will be publicized in the upcoming months. The commitment to inclusion has been demonstrated time and again by working with the Nova Scotia Human Rights Commission and the community at large to address these challenges.

FACULTY RECRUITMENT, HIRING, AND RETENTION

In discussing faculty recruitment, we emphasize the need to engage in outreach recruitment initiatives, to establish designated positions, and to actively recruit faculty members from designated equity groups. Equally important, though, is retention of faculty from these groups. Retention requires concrete support that recognizes historic exclusion and that moves beyond tokenism and the institutional comfort zone to develop sensitized collegial relationships.

Since the inception of the affirmative action students' admission policy in the mid-1970s, the MSSW had talked about increasing diversity among its faculty, especially from the designated groups. Despite numerous attempts at recruitment through normal academic processes, the MSSW was not successful in recruiting and retaining diverse faculty until it established a designated position following a retirement in 1989. The first African Canadian faculty member was hired in that position in January 1990, with a master's level qualification and the expectation that she would complete course work toward doctoral studies during the first seven years of the appointment. This equity hiring broke through one of the most significant barriers in this work: *qualifications*. This was made possible though mentorship and support from within the institution, as well as a recognition of the impact of historic exclusion.

In 1993, a First Nations woman was recruited through an equity hiring. Unfortunately, this was not a successful initiative for a variety of reasons that cannot be elaborated on here. The MSSW has learned from some critical reflection and introspection about that very challenging experience. An internal review of issues relating to First Nations and African Canadian students made a report to faculty in 1996. One of the work group's recommendations was that two of the next five faculty vacancies be designated to these groups. In 1999, we were successful in recruiting and hiring a person with a (dis)ability who is now able to provide leadership in this area. In 2000, we hired a First Nations faculty member. Both are being mentored and supported through doctoral studies and are in continuing appointments that allow for such training.

A significant barrier raised earlier was qualifications. Universities and professional schools, in particular, are moving toward hiring new faculty who are educated at the doctoral level with established research and publication portfolios. People with a history of marginalization do not tend to have such academic opportunities. Diversity initiatives must take this into account and, if serious about hiring and retention, will put support mechanisms in place to assist faculty in undertaking doctoral studies.

The culture of the academy is another barrier. It is not enough to invite people in. The academy must be willing to look at those institutional barriers that make it difficult for people to stay (see institutional privilege below for examples). Negative student evaluations, for example, must be reviewed in context. It is also a challenge to move beyond tokenism and so-called designated expertise. Assigned teaching should not be only in the designated area. Mentorship should be provided for teaching, research, and writing.

At the MSSW we do provide supports for doctoral study. Initially we provided unpaid leave; however, we have successfully argued that faculty recruited under employment equity should be given some paid leave. Faculty at the MSSW who are untenured have a reduced workload and are not normally expected to take on management roles. We have also formalized our mentorship program and now match new faculty with a senior faculty member. This can be challenging in a number of ways, especially for smaller schools where the numbers of faculty from designated groups might be quite small. There are also a number of supports available through the Faculty of Health Professions (FHP) (of which the MSSW is a part) for new faculty, such as funding for research and a reduced workload for one term prior to tenure. Opportunities for mentorship in research development are also available through the FHP and more through the MSSW as senior faculty are engaged in more research.

The most significant support is the willingness among faculty to discuss and deal with issues as they arise. Providing sensitivity training for all faculty members is essential to the retention of faculty from diverse communities. Recognition of the dual role and multiple responsibility of faculty from designated groups is also important. There will be extra demands from students, other faculty, the wider university, and the community. These demands need to be balanced against the demands of the academy itself and recognized in the formal and informal structures of the academy.

Given where we are at the MSSW, where do we need to go with this initiative? First, we must always be vigilant about the issues, especially retention. A critical mass of diverse faculty within the university itself is a modest goal. This will require university-wide supports and a commitment to change the *face* of faculty and staff at Dalhousie. Secondly, designated hiring needs to be continued. The MSSW model of designated hiring is now being used by some other departments at Dalhousie and other schools of social work in Canada. Finally, it is important to have a specific plan that is part of a larger institutional strategic plan to address the issues from a holistic perspective. There needs to be a commitment to more equity hiring beyond tokenism, and opportunities for advancement for those faculty members.

Faculty and administrators need to develop better understandings of systemic discrimination and its reality and impact on students and faculty. We would like to see a diversity lens as a central component of all research conducted. In addition, our future work on systemic discrimination and diversity issues needs to be firmly rooted in our research and scholarly productivity on these issues.

CURRICULA

Introducing diversity content into social work curricula demands that attention be given to both the specifics of curricular content and to the methods of integrating such content. Students must be given information concerning the variety of groups or categories referred to in the Stainton and Swift quote. They must be introduced to concepts such as oppression, domination, difference, power, a structural understanding of human behaviour, the social construction of knowledge, and practise actions and interventions consistent with a critical analysis of diversity (Adams et al., 1997; Canadian Association of Schools of Social Work, 1996; DeMaria, 1992; Garcia & Melendez, (1997); Harlow & Hearn, 1996; Laird, 1994; Stainton & Swift, 1996).

There are a variety of methods for integrating diversity content. Enrichment activities such as workshops, speakers, and student projects can be used. Elective courses related to particular groups or social categories may be offered, or such courses may be required courses for all students. Diversity content may be included in certain courses or it may be expected content in all courses within a given program of study (Center for Teaching and Learning, 1997).

Since 1973–1974, the Maritime School of Social Work has employed all of these methods. The earliest elective offered was Minority Group Issues, followed by Feminist Social Work in the late 1970s. The Minority Group Issues course was renamed Cross-cultural Issues when it became required in 1990. In 1993–1994, it was added to the MSW curriculum as a required course. The focus on cross-cultural issues was changed to anti-oppressive theory and practice in 1995 as a required course at the master's level. An elective in Africentrism is offered at both the BSW and MSW level as of 1999. Aboriginal Issues was added as an elective at both levels in 2000. Disability: Policy and Practice is an elective in the BSW program and has been offered since 1997–1998.

As well as these required courses and electives, integration of content on all diverse groups has been underway since the mid-1990s. Feminist theory and practice, and the impact of various social policies on women were integrated through the 1980s. African Canadian, Aboriginal, immigrant community and gay, lesbian, and transgendered issues have been slower in coming. Faculty unfamiliarity and discomfort with the subject material, and, in some cases, resistance to the addition of diverse course content, pose a barrier to the further integration of diversity in the curriculum. Something as basic as lack of teaching space can mean that electives, such as the Disability course, can be offered only once every three years. Supports for faculty would include training and in-services, and the development of research projects about working with diversity. There can be no doubt, however, that the greatest single support to instituting curricula change is the presence of faculty from diverse groups and their willingness to challenge and encourage the school to move forward.

PEDAGOGY

Institutional changes to enhance diversity must also encompass reform of pedagogical processes. National accreditation policies mandate attention to pedagogy: "The process and experience of social work education shall be consistent with the curriculum content" (Canadian Association of Schools of Social Work, 2002, section 3.2). Educators working with anti-oppressive or diversity-based curricular content are struggling to develop pedagogical practices that are congruent with their curriculum. Such congruency supports learning and enhances students' ability to transfer their learning to their future practice.

Many students are initially disoriented by the teaching practices employed at the school. Instructors incorporate collaborative learning, group work, active student participation, and self-directed learning into their classrooms and students are often not familiar with these pedagogical practices. Also, effectively addressing content related to diversity and difference implies self-examination and self-awareness. Such learning can be emotionally and personally challenging: dealing with the affective as well as the cognitive components of learning is a key aspect of pedagogical practice within the MSSW.

Many conventions and practices of the larger university context mitigate against pedagogical congruency: grading, the need to have course outlines prepared in advance, the lack of understanding of the emotional nature of learning about diversity content, the individualized nature of university teaching, and class size. Similarly, students may express resistance to such learning, which also creates challenges for instructors. On the other hand, those of us interested in developing new pedagogical practices draw support from each other, try and engage in team teaching, and discuss various teaching strategies.

We need to strengthen our collective attention to pedagogy by incorporating relevant questions into program reviews, by structuring formal and informal times to analyze critically our pedagogical practices, and by involving students in more effective formative evaluations of pedagogy.

INSTITUTIONAL PRIVILEGE

Institutional privilege is the normalized, taken-for-granted benefits of being part of the intellectual, spiritual, social, and physiological mainstream in a formally organized set of power relations. It also includes the ways those power relations reinforce the benefits organizationally, administratively, pedagogically, and ideologically. In the struggle to promote diversity and anti-oppressive theory and practice, there is often an incongruence between the experience of those who enjoy institutional privilege and those who are marginalized. Sincere attempts to address the incongruence by people with power and privilege do not always have the desired effect.

The problem is the depth and extent of oppression and the failure to recognize the manifestations of that oppression that are hidden from the mainstream view of the world. Narayan (1989, p. 319) says "goodwill is not enough to overcome assumptions and attitudes born out of centuries of power and privilege" when people with privilege address oppression, even when that goodwill is in the context of concrete, positive, anti-oppressive measures. Intentional or not—prior, current, and subsequent anti-oppressive measures notwithstanding—oppression hurts. The question is how can institutional privilege be used to respond reflexively in an anti-oppressive manner when someone says "ouch."

Strategies to use institutional privilege to promote diversity consist of three parts. First, the "invisible knapsack" (McIntosh, 1990) of privilege has to be unpacked. Individuals who are privileged by being in some dominant positions in our society (White, straight, male, able-bodied, English-speaking, of Christian descent) need to recognize that

- curricula and course content reflects them
- literature and research materials on topics about them are readily available
- most colleagues and students share most of these attributes
- students will not doubt their ability to teach because of their race, sexual orientation, gender, ability, fluency in English, or religious background

- their way of knowing is privileged
- they are not personally assaulted daily with trivial and/or major manifestations of oppression
- their efforts at anti-oppressive pedagogy and practice will be praised by most of their colleagues
- they can choose whether to become involved in the struggle against oppression, which does not affect them directly (olsson, 1996–1997)
- when they speak in public, their race, sexual orientation, gender, ability, fluency in English, or religion is not on trial (McIntosh, 1990)
- when they fail or make a mistake, it will not be attributed to their race, sexual orientation, gender, ability, fluency in English, or religion (McIntosh, 1990)

For each of these dominant positions, there are specific privileges that individuals can count on—that is, if they are straight, they can bring their partners to social functions without experiencing discomfort based on sexual orientation; if they are of Christian descent, they can be sure that university holidays and vacations will reflect their heritage.

The second part of strategies to use institutional privilege to promote diversity requires that those with privilege take responsibility for and use the benefits and power derived. Other sections of this chapter document the MSSW's strategic actions in the areas of curriculum and course content; hiring and retaining faculty through affirmative action; designated group status for student entrance, administration, and governance. In each of these areas, there are macro-, mezzo-, and micro-level actions where faculty and administration must act. For example, in curriculum and course content, actions include, at the macro-level:

- designing all course content to be inclusive
- encouraging the library to carry material relevant to all perspectives
- investing in materials that promote diversity
- promoting and doing anti-oppressive research

At the mezzo-level:

- actively supporting anti-oppressive pedagogical training for all faculty
- learning about the experiences and perspectives of groups with whom most of the faculty are not familiar rather than waiting for the minority to educate the majority

- taking on teaching about diversity and not expecting colleagues who are from oppressed groups to do all of it

At the micro-level:

- modelling anti-oppressive behaviour in the classroom and teaching students how to do it

In the area of affirmative action, concrete action requires supporting and defending colleagues when they complain of harassment or discrimination. Minimizing or denying their experience perpetuates injustice.

Finally, those with institutional privilege need to learn to act and react with methodological humility and caution (Narayan, 1989). Examples of this methodology include

- understanding that the desire for congratulation for anti-oppressive work may be resented by those who experience the oppression directly (Narayan, 1989, p. 327)
- accepting that those who have institutional privilege will make mistakes and be held to account by colleagues and students who belong to oppressed groups
- accepting that those who experience oppression first-hand have a right to complain and a right to redress—even against those who are actively working toward change
- reacting humbly and cautiously to criticism and complaints by colleagues and students who belong to oppressed groups
- accepting the restraints this imposes on spontaneity and ease of reaction (Narayan, 1989, p. 327)

The goodwill trap poses a significant barrier to using institutional privilege to promote diversity. Those with institutional privilege feel good about themselves and their institution when concrete, positive steps are being taken toward anti-oppressive action. From that vantage point sometimes comes resentment about criticism—what could be called the "We're-so-good-therefore-we-can't-be-bad" syndrome. This syndrome gives rise to counterproductive behaviours and attitudes such as defensiveness (the critique is unfounded); minimization (the critique is petty); and transferal (the person making the critique is held responsible for making the change). Methodological humility and caution dictate different responses, including recognition of the experience with no minimization or denial; an

acknowledgement of culpability; and an undertaking toward specific action. Developing a consistent practice of methodological humility in all aspects of diversity promotion is a key support to faculty and students from diverse backgrounds.

Anti-oppressive theory and practice does not prosper without faculty, staff, and administration support and acknowledgement that the struggle and the learning never end. This support and learning cannot be genuine without transforming institutional relations of power and privilege. As with all social change movements, this one must include the grassroots—the communities, the clients, and students we serve—as key stakeholders. Making inclusivity more than window dressing means practising epistemic privilege and methodological humility (Narayan, 1989) in our relations with the grassroots.

CONCLUSION

In the course of developing the materials for the workshop and this chapter, we have identified key actions and actors in the process to promote and strengthen diversity.

1. Faculty Commitment and Student Resolve

Managing institutional practices to promote and strengthen diversity cannot happen without faculty commitment. As our journey demonstrates, faculty members who have been willing to raise the issues, challenge the status quo, and work to make changes are crucial. Both mainstream faculty members and faculty from oppressed groups make essential contributions to keep the process unfolding within all the components of the institutional practices we have identified. So, too, the resolve of students from oppressed groups to challenge the MSSW to address their needs and concerns has kept the need for ongoing change near or at the top of the institutional agenda.

2. Planning and Strategy

Any initiative to promote diversity within an institution must be planned strategically. Departments and universities must consider issues of timing and those other factors that influence the pace of change. What is the focus of the diversity initiative being considered, and why? Consider what internal and external support mechanisms are needed, and identify those that are already in place. What policies actually support systemic discrimination? What policies will need to be changed to support the diversity initiative?

How will conflicts be resolved? How will this initiative change the culture of the organization? This work takes a lot of time and, as our history has shown, a few committed individuals to facilitate it in their institutions. The current climate in academia demands, however, that the work of promoting diversity be shared among a wider group of faculty and administrators. Diversity work must be reflected in workload policies. Good planning also requires periodic reviews and evaluation.

3. Understanding Power and Resistance

Creating diversity is often perceived as challenging traditional power structures within the institution. Resistance will come (directly or indirectly) as not everyone will support institutional changes in student composition and faculty, in curricula and programming. As we have learned, resistance comes not only from faculty, staff, and administration but also from students. Strategies to address resistance from each of these groups are essential, as are actions to promote a more equitable balance of power.

4. Research and Writing

Research and writing are part of the political economy of the academy. Resistance to diversity initiatives has sometimes come in the form of questioning the current expectation in universities to do more research and scholarly writing while also paying more attention to diversity issues. We believe that our work on diversity is researchable. Moreover, we have a responsibility to share our knowledge with others in the academy and the community. The MSSW has been working on these issues for the past thirty years, yet we have done little research and writing on our work. Our future vision includes an emphasis on making research and publication a central component of our diversity initiatives.

5. Community and Academic Interface Is Essential to Promoting Diversity Initiatives

The academy must not work in isolation but rather ground change efforts in local, national, and international groups that strategically support the promotion of diversity. The academy is often criticized for operating from an ivory tower. If change is to continue, community stakeholders must be involved at the beginning stages by incorporating their voices and knowledge.

REFERENCES

Adams, Maurianne, Bell, Lee Anne, & Griffin, Pat. (Eds.). (1997). *Teaching for diversity and social justice: A sourcebook.* London: Routledge.

Berkman, C.S., & Zinberg, G. (1997). Homophobic and heterosexism in social workers. *Social Work 42*(4), 319–332.

Canadian Association of Schools of Social Work. (1991). *Social work education at the crossroads: The challenge of diversity.* Report of the Task Force on Multicultural and Multiracial Issues in Social Work Education, Ottawa, Ontario.

Canadian Association of Schools of Social Work. (2000). *Accreditation manual* (Rev. ed.). Ottawa: Canadian Association of Schools of Social Work.

DeMaria, William. (1992). On the trail of a radical pedagogy for social work education. *British Journal of Social Work 22*(3), 231–252.

Garcia, Betty, & Melendez, Michael. (1997). Concepts and methods in teaching oppression courses. *Journal of Progressive Human Services 8*(1), 23–40.

Goodman, Diane. (2001). *Promoting diversity and social Justice: Educating privileged groups.* Thousand Oaks: Age Publications

Harlow, Elizabeth, & Hearn, Jeff. (1996). Educating for anti-oppressive and anti-discriminatory social work practice. *Social Work Education 5*(1), 5–17.

Laird, Joan. (1994). Family-centered practice: Cultural and constructionist reflections. In J. Laird (Ed.), *Revisioning social work education: A social constructionist approach* (pp. 77–109). New York: Haworth Press.

McIntosh, Peggy. (1990). White privilege: Unpacking the invisible knapsack. *Independent School* (Winter), 31–36.

Moore, Dorothy. (1991). Recruitment and admission of minority students to schools of social work. *Canadian Social Work Review 8*(2). 190–210.

Narayan, Uma. (1989). Working together across differences. In B. Compton & B. Galaway (Eds.), *Social work processes* (pp. 317–328). Belmont: Wadsworth.

Newton, Janice, Ginsburg, Jerry, Rehner, Jan, Rogers, Pat, Shrizzi, Susan, & Spencer, John. (2001). *Voices from the classroom: Reflections on teaching and learning in higher education.* Aurora: Garamond Press.

olsson, jona. (1996–97). For white anti-racists: Avoiding the detours in the journey toward justice. *Women's Education des Femmes 12*(4), 16–20.

O'Neill, B.J. (1995). Canadian social work education and same-sex sexual orientation. *Canadian Social Work Review 12*(2), 159–174.

Roman, Leslie, & Eyre, Linda. (Eds.). (1997). *Dangerous territories: Struggles for difference and equality in education.* New York: Routledge.

Stainton, Tim, & Swift, Karen. (1996). "Difference" and social work curriculum. *Canadian Social Work Review 13*(1), 75–87.